A Lost History of the Baha'i Faith

A Lost History of the Baha'i Faith

The Progressive Tradition of Baha'u'llah's Forgotten Family

Shua Ullah Behai
Eric Stetson, Editor

Vox Humri Media
Newark, Delaware

Copyright © 2014 by Eric Stetson
All rights reserved

Layout and cover design by Eric Stetson

ISBN: 978-0-692-33135-4

Vox Humri Media
Newark, Delaware, USA
www.voxhumri.com

Standing (L to R): The grandsons of Baha'u'llah: Amin Ullah Bahai, Shua Ullah Behai, Mousa Bahai, Salah Bahai.
Seated (L to R): Mohammed Ali Bahai and Badi Ullah Bahai, sons of Baha'u'llah and his second wife Mahd-i-'Ulya.

"Say: all things are of God." This exalted utterance is like unto water for quenching the fire of hate and enmity which smouldereth within the hearts and breasts of men. By this single utterance contending peoples and kindreds will attain the light of true unity.

—Baha'u'llah, *The Book of My Covenant*

Contents

——☼——

A Note on Middle Eastern and Baha'i Terminology	xiii
Foreword by Maliha and Negar Bahai	xvii
Preface by Eric Stetson	xxxiii
1. The Origin of the Baha'i Movement—by Kamar Bahai	1
2. The Cultural and Religious Precursors of Baha'ism by Shua Ullah Behai	7
3. A Brief Biography of Baha'u'llah—by Mohammed Ali Bahai	27
4. Baha'i Principles—by Shua Ullah Behai	37
5. Stories of Baha'i Martyrs—Compiled by Shua Ullah Behai	57
6. Selections from the Writings of Baha'u'llah Compiled by Shua Ullah Behai	67
7. Tributes to Baha'u'llah and His Mission—Compiled by Shua Ullah Behai	97
8. The Teachings and Will of 'Abdu'l-Baha—by Shua Ullah Behai	119
9. A Tribute to 'Abdu'l-Baha and Doubts About His Will by Kamar Bahai	141
10. The Station of Ghusn-i-Akbar Mohammed Ali Bahai by Shua Ullah Behai	147

11.	Message to the Believers in America—by Mohammed Ali and Badi Ullah Bahai	153
12.	Message upon the Passing of 'Abdu'l-Baha by Mohammed Ali Bahai	161
13.	On the Baha'i Vision of World Civilization: A Message to Mankind—by Mohammed Ali Bahai	165
14.	On Religious Conflict, Freedom and Unity: A Message to the People of Understanding—by Mohammed Ali Bahai	175
15.	An Interview with Ghusn-i-Akbar—by Shua Ullah Behai and Mohammed Ali Bahai	179
16.	Autobiography—by Mohammed Ali Bahai	183
17.	Will and Testament—by Mohammed Ali Bahai	227
18.	The Funeral of Mohammed Ali Bahai—by Shua Ullah Behai	251
19.	A Tribute to Mohammed Ali Effendi and Obituary by Kamar Bahai	255
20.	A Tribute to Ghusn-i-At'har Zia Ullah Effendi by Shua Ullah Behai	261
21.	Some Notable Baha'is—by Shua Ullah Behai	265
22.	Khadimu'llah's Epistle—by Aqa Jan Kashani	297
23.	Events After the Departure of Baha'u'llah by Mohammed Jawad Gazvini	309
24.	Letters About the Sons of Baha'u'llah—by Rosamond D. O. O. Templeton	329
25.	Autobiography—by Ibrahim G. Kheiralla	343
26.	Arguments Against 'Abdu'l-Baha—by Ibrahim G. Kheiralla	361

27.	Unitarian Baha'i Organizations and Teachings by Ibrahim G. Kheiralla	369
28.	Brief Baha'i History and Testimony—by Majdeddin bin Moussa Irani	383
29.	Against War: An Open Letter to World Leaders by Majdeddin bin Moussa Irani	389
30.	Memoirs—by Shua Ullah Behai	395
31.	The Importance of Unity: Messages to the Baha'is by Badi Ullah Bahai	417
32.	The Baha'i Faith under Shoghi Effendi Rabbani by Shua Ullah Behai	423
33.	Statements on the Dispute Between the Baha'i Family by Kamar Bahai	437
34.	Mousa Bahai and the Rotary Club of Haifa Compiled from Rotary Publications	449
35.	Messages in *Behai Quarterly* Magazine—by Shua Ullah Behai	455
36.	Address to an Occidental Gathering—by Shua Ullah Behai	473
37.	A Reminiscence: The Purpose, Condition and Potential of the Baha'i Faith—by Shua Ullah Behai	483

Epilogue by Eric Stetson	491
Appendix A: List of Writings of Baha'u'llah—by Shua Ullah Behai	543
Appendix B: Families of Baha'u'llah and the Bab	547

A Note on Middle Eastern and Baha'i Terminology

Baha'i is a religion that emerged in the Middle East in the 19th century—specifically Iran and the Levant—and as such, its history is filled with terminology peculiar to the Islamic society of that region and time. Throughout this book, the reader will notice frequent use of terms that are unfamiliar to most people without a background in the Arabic and Persian languages, Middle Eastern culture, or the Baha'i faith itself.

The word *Effendi* (e.g. in names such as Abbas Effendi, Shoghi Effendi, etc.) is not actually part of the name, but an honorific title that was used in the Ottoman Empire to mean roughly the equivalent of "Sir." Similarly, *Khanum* for women (e.g. in Samadiyya Khanum, Khanum Jani, etc.) means something like "Lady" or "Madam."

Mirza is a title that was prefixed to the names of men of Persian ethnic origin in the Baha'i faith (e.g. Mirza Husayn Ali Nuri, Mirza Aqa Jan Kashani, etc.), and simply means "Mister." In rare cases it is actually a name (e.g. Haji Siyyid Mirza Afnan).

Some names of early Baha'is and others involved in the religion's history include the titles *Aqa*, *Haji*, *Mulla*, *Siyyid*, or *Shaykh*. *Aqa* (or Agha) means "Master" and is a more honorific version of Mirza. *Haji* (or Hajji) honors a person who has made the *hajj*, the Islamic pilgrimage to Mecca. *Mulla* (or Mullah) means a Shi'ite Muslim clergyman. *Siyyid* (peculiar Baha'i spelling of Sayyid) identifies a descendant of the Prophet Muhammad. *Shaykh* (or Sheikh) means a revered elder, usually a Muslim cleric of Arab origin.

Pasha is a Turkish title for an important person, such as a high political official or dignitary (e.g. Namiq Pasha, governor of Ottoman Iraq). It is similar to the British "Lord."

The Baha'i tradition has also developed its own unique terms for certain concepts and activities. For example, many of Baha'u'llah's writings are called "tablets," and all of his writings are regarded as having been "revealed" by God through the "Supreme Pen" (i.e. Baha'u'llah channeling the divine voice rather than writing of his own accord). Baha'u'llah and other great prophets of history who founded religions (e.g. Moses, Jesus, Muhammad, etc.) are considered to be "Manifestations of God." Baha'is often refer to their religion as the "Cause of God" or simply "the Cause," and call fellow adherents "the Friends" (these terms usually appear in lowercase in this book with the same meaning). Baha'is "teach" the faith rather than preach or proselytize, according to their own terminology, and potential converts who are studying the Baha'i faith are called "seekers."

Behai is an old-fashioned spelling of Baha'i, and Baha'is were sometimes called *Behaists* (e.g. the Society of Behaists, which was a Baha'i denomination until about 1950). These forms are now obsolete. The term *Baha'ism* was commonly used through the early to mid 1900s as a noun to refer to the Baha'i religion—and it is used by some of the writers in this book—but this term fell out of favor, especially among Baha'is. It continues to be used occasionally by non-Baha'is in academic contexts.

Although Baha'is typically capitalize the word Faith in "the Baha'i Faith," this book generally refrains from such parochial usage, because the capitalized term is also used by most Baha'is today to refer to their membership-based religious organization, thus conflating the faith tradition with its currently normative administrative form. To refer to the Baha'i religion itself—including any and all organized manifestations it has had or may have, as well as aspects of the religion that do not depend on any organization—the lowercase *Baha'i faith* will be used, much as one would commonly refer to the *Christian faith* or any other faith.

This book mostly defers to established Baha'i spelling conventions in English. Exceptions include cases where the subject is more commonly known outside the Baha'i faith by a different spelling or variation of the name; this applies to historical figures and geographical locations. Also, in cases where individuals are known to have used or preferred a particular form of their name in English, or if their descendants use it, that choice will be respected and adhered to in this book. For example, the younger sons of Baha'u'llah used the surname Bahai, and their family and friends spelled their names Mohammed Ali and Badi Ullah when writing in English, and most people appended the title Effendi to their names according to the customary mode of address for gentlemen in early 20th century Palestine. This differs in every respect from how present-day Baha'i publications refer to these men. To assist Baha'i readers who might be confused by such differences, the "official" Baha'i spellings and versions of names are given parenthetically or in footnotes.

Throughout this book, diacritical marks are omitted from commonly used words such as Bahá'í, Bahá'u'lláh, the Báb, etc. They are also omitted in cases where their presence would not be particularly helpful or necessary for the average English speaker to pronounce a word correctly (e.g. Mírzá, 'Abbás, 'Alí, Shírází, etc.), but are retained where their absence would likely lead to mispronunciation.

In all of the primary source documents and out-of-print texts included in this book, spelling and capitalization have been regularized according to the standards and practices of this editor as described above. In quotations from sources with active copyrights, the original text is reproduced without change.

—The Editor

Foreword

By Maliha and Negar Bahai

We are great-granddaughters of Baha'u'llah. As sisters growing up in Haifa, in a house only a few blocks away from the Baha'i shrines on Mount Carmel, we witnessed the growth of the Baha'i faith firsthand. Our cousin, Shoghi Rabbani, was the recognized leader of the Baha'i community, and our home was filled with artifacts of the early days of the faith, such as original calligraphies of Baha'u'llah's tablets hanging on the walls.

We grew up surrounded by Baha'ism; we believed in the teachings of our distinguished ancestor—yet we, our parents and grandparents, aunts and uncles, and numerous cousins, were not allowed to be members of the religious organization bearing his name. We were excluded by our own relatives and their followers because of a difference of opinion about the religion. We were invisible Baha'is. Our very existence was unknown to most of the Baha'i world.

This did not deter us from practicing our faith. Our lives reflect the international and interfaith spirit of Baha'u'llah's teachings. Maliha married a Muslim man from India and has four children. One son lives in Canada, one daughter in England, one son in Germany, and one son still lives in the subcontinent. Negar married an Israeli Jew, whose distinguished career as an economist enabled them to travel all over the world during his life. Today, she lives in the same childhood home in Haifa, where she celebrates the holidays of Judaism, Christianity, and Islam with her diverse friends.

Our father, Mousa Bahai, was the head of the land registration office in Haifa, and was president of the Haifa Rotary Club for two years running, during the conflict between the Arabs and Jews in 1947-48.

Rotary wanted a neutral person and he accepted. He was called upon often to make peace between the two communities. We lived in the mixed quarter and the Jewish *Haganah* (defense) office was next door. Now the building is destined to be a "Diamond Hotel" which is fashionable in the German [Templar] Colony, inundated by European tourists.

Our mother, Kamar, was a very beautiful woman and had a feisty and assertive personality. She wrote pamphlets and letters to the newspaper about Baha'ism which you will read in this book. Not only that, she took Shoghi Rabbani to court because he had prohibited her and other family members from visiting Baha'u'llah's tomb. We are proud to say that our mother won; Shoghi settled the case. Because of her courageous action, the whole family now enjoys the right to pray at the Shrine of Baha'u'llah, which is located next to the house where our grandfathers lived much of their lives. Both of our parents were born in this mansion and were married there. We have pictures to that effect.

We are descended from Baha'u'llah on both sides of our family, because our parents were cousins. Marriage between cousins used to be common in the Middle East. In fact, our great-grandmother Fatimah was Baha'u'llah's cousin and became his second wife. He lived with her and their children in the mansion of Bahji in his later years and called her Mahd-i-'Ulya, the honorific title of the mother of the Shah of Persia. Our great-grandmother held a place of high honor in the Baha'i faith in those days, and Baha'u'llah was closely involved in the upbringing of their sons.

Our father was the youngest son of Mohammed Ali, who was the eldest son of Baha'u'llah and Mahd-i-'Ulya. Our mother was a daughter of Badi Ullah, who was Mohammed Ali's youngest brother. Both of our grandfathers were therefore half-brothers of Abbas Effendi, who was the eldest son of Baha'u'llah by his first wife.

We remember our elder grandfather, Mohammed Ali, as a quiet and prayerful man, a kind soul who never asked much for himself. Contrary to Middle Eastern tradition, he insisted that he and our grandmother not be given any special treatment or deference when they moved in with our parents in their old age; instead, he urged our parents to continue living their lives exactly as before.

This self-deprecating and generous spirit was characteristic of his personality. He was mild-mannered and avoided conflict. He rejected traditions that placed one human being above another. He studied the scriptures dutifully and was highly skilled in the art of calligraphy, and he created many beautiful inscriptions of the inspired verses revealed by his father whom he loved and served his whole life. We recall him always being down on his knees in prayer and among his artwork of calligraphy that he loved.

Negar remembers that when she was three years old, one day our grandfather Mohammed Ali was visiting and forgot to bring a gift that he had promised to bring on his visit. Negar was so disappointed that she slapped him in the face! But he asked our mother not to rebuke her, as he had not kept his promise. The same day, he wrote a verse of poetry especially for Negar, and in later years she appreciated it and was very flattered. It says in Persian, "From your visage springs the Spring."

Our grandmother, Laqa'iyya, was Mohammed Ali's cousin, the daughter of Baha'u'llah's faithful brother Moussa Kalim. She was given a choice to marry either him or Abbas Effendi, and according to the story she told, she chose our grandfather because of his mild manner and his wish to avoid religious debates.

At that time, the unfortunate conflict between Baha'u'llah's sons was already brewing. This was before Baha'u'llah passed from this world. The brothers had very different personalities and this undoubtedly contributed to their inability to cooperate with each other after their father's passing. For years beforehand, the branches of the family were drifting apart and preparing for what seemed like inevitable conflict after the unifying and overwhelming personality of the Great Master, Baha'u'llah, departed from the earth.

Jealousies may have played a significant role in the split between the brothers, because they had different mothers and Baha'u'llah lived with his second wife and second family. The story that has been passed down to us is that the families of Baha'u'llah's second and third wives were kept at a distance during his funeral, while Abbas Effendi's family was allowed to approach near to the body of Baha'u'llah. This was according to the Shi'ite custom of primogeniture and the primacy of the first wife, which the supporters of Abbas Effendi emphasized. Mahd-i-

'Ulya and her descendants thus saw their position suddenly downgraded and reversed, compared to the egalitarianism and close proximity to Baha'u'llah they enjoyed while he was alive.

Mohammed Ali had many friends of all faiths. One of his best friends was a Christian bishop. He was skeptical of absolute religious authority and did not want to see old patterns of authoritarian religion reemerge in Baha'ism after Baha'u'llah had given his life to free people from the Shi'ite clergy.

This skepticism and concern for individual freedom comes through in his writings, as you will read in this book, but he did not deny that his elder brother, Abbas Effendi, was the legitimate Baha'i leader. He did, however, believe that the focus of Baha'ism should be on the teachings of Baha'u'llah rather than on the charismatic leadership and opinions of any successor. This belief got him into trouble, because in the time and culture of the early Baha'i community—still heavily influenced by Shi'ite Islam—the eldest son was to be obeyed by the rest of the family, not questioned. As often happens between siblings even today, the older brother wanted more authority and respect, while the younger brothers wanted more freedom.

Our grandfather Mohammed Ali has been portrayed in Baha'i literature as a ruthless man who was obsessed with gaining power for himself and destroying Abbas Effendi. From the perspective of those who knew him personally, this is nothing but a laughable caricature. The man we knew was a gentleman whose religious beliefs were focused not on power or who should wield it, but on living according to the teachings of his father, Baha'u'llah, in his private life—a life of prayer, meditation, and cultivating a moderate lifestyle and a humble and kindly spirit.

The source of the dispute was in Baha'u'llah's will, which says that he had chosen Abbas Effendi as his first successor and then Mohammed Ali. Our grandfather often mentioned Baha'u'llah's teaching of the virtue of a gentle tongue and the danger of angry speech. Ironically, he was constantly slandered during his lifetime, and his rights and property were taken from him because it was not in his nature to fight back. He had opportunities to defend himself and his rights, but his devotion to Baha'u'llah's teachings was so uncompromising and his personality so meek that he preferred to endure the injustices he faced with silence and resignation, rather than bringing the Baha'i name into the law courts. This was out of respect, not weakness—respect for the Baha'i faith that was so instilled in his soul.

Our younger grandfather, Badi Ullah, was more outspoken and less willing to tolerate the injustices he saw in his own life and the lives of others in his family. He was a charismatic and gregarious man and resembled, both in personality and appearance, his eldest brother Abbas Effendi. Late in life, he wrote a long memoir in Persian about his experiences with Baha'u'llah and his elder brothers and how the unfortunate conflict developed between them. It has never yet been translated into English or published, but we hope this will be done in the future. We cannot read it—we could have read it in the modern Persian language, but it was written in classical style, which is difficult. We have been told that our grandfather Badi Ullah tells a story which would be very controversial, even shocking, and an important addition to the historical record. We also have a diary by our grandmother Laqa'iyya which we hope will someday be translated.

To sum up, our grandfathers were strong and devoted believers in the Baha'i teachings—just as we are sure our great-uncle Abbas Effendi was as well—and the noble and progressive principles they inherited from Baha'u'llah were passed down to their children and grandchildren. It is sad that all the brothers could not work together for the advancement of the faith they shared, but we hope this book may help to make a start toward healing the wounds of the past that have hindered the Baha'i faith from understanding its own history and potential.

Within the family of Baha'u'llah, some of the descendants of Abbas Effendi are now on friendly terms with us, after many years of the branches of the family having little or no contact because of the lingering religious dispute. Although they still see things differently from us, and even strongly disagree with much of the content of this book, at least we are able to see each other as fellow Baha'is. We hope that all the Baha'is of the world will be able to follow our example of tolerance and reconciliation. If we can do it, you can do it—it is not necessary that Baha'is must always agree on all points of religion, especially about what happened in the past!

Our uncle Shua Ullah, who was our father's eldest brother, was deeply in love with Abbas Effendi's daughter Ruha when they were young. He tells this story in the book, as you will read. They wanted to marry each other, but they had to break their engagement because their fathers would not consent to the marriage. The brothers sadly regarded each other as straying from the true path of Baha'i faith, and therefore they would not allow their children to be married.

Religious and family quarrels kept apart these young lovers, who continued to cherish each other for the rest of their lives even though they married other people. Ruha Shahid kept in touch with Negar until her dying day. Ruha herself was expelled from the Baha'i community by her own nephew, Shoghi Rabbani, along with all her sisters, children, nieces and nephews—ironically, because some of them married descendants of Baha'u'llah's third wife, who were also supposed to be shunned.

To think that this happened among Baha'is! And to think that it happened not just among any Baha'is, but among the immediate family of Baha'u'llah! We are all only human; that is the lesson of this disgrace. Even the people who were the closest to the founder of our great faith could not find a way to overcome their religious differences and they made their children suffer for it. If our uncle Shua and cousin Ruha had gotten married, perhaps this could have brought together the estranged brothers and they would have somehow resolved their disagreements, and the two sides of Baha'u'llah's family would have been reunited and reconciled. Generations of damage and heartbreak could have been avoided.

We will never know if such an alternative history would have been possible, but it is appropriate at this stage that we contemplate such things. It is beneficial that wounds that have been covered over and never fully healed be finally exposed to the open air of public discussion among the Baha'is, that they may achieve true healing once and for all. Allowing ourselves to reenvision the past might open a window to a better future for the Baha'is and for the world at large.

The lesson is that love is more powerful than doctrine; that humans should be human first and religious second. As our beloved grandfather Mohammed Ali wrote, but could neither fully realize in his own life nor find fully manifested in the life of his brother Abbas Effendi: "We are all from one root and we are, therefore, members of one universal brotherhood; and between brothers nothing should exist which might contradict equity and concord, and from which differences might arise."

Let the Baha'i faith finally live up to itself. Let it be true to the animating vision of Baha'u'llah—a vision of universal reconciliation for all the people of the world, putting aside the poisonous divisions of religion, the us-versus-them mentality and exclusivity that infects and debases religious organizations. Let the lessons of the past be the foundation of a better future, both for the Baha'is and for all other faiths. In our elder years, that is our hope and our prayer.

Comment by Maliha Bahai

In the mid 1940s, while attending the American University in Beirut, I helped edit and proofread my uncle Shua Ullah's manuscript about the history and teachings of the Baha'i faith. He wrote it in English with the hope that it should be read widely by a Western audience. After all these years, I am happy that a publisher in the United States has recognized the value of my uncle's work, and that the effort he put into writing his book can finally bear fruit.

Further Comments by Negar Bahai

In 2006 I was interviewed by two Israeli filmmakers for a documentary called *Baha'is In My Backyard*. They wanted to talk with a descendant of Baha'u'llah and they found me, even though Dr. Moshe Sharon, Chair of the Department of Baha'i Studies at Hebrew University, told them that there are no living descendants.

The Baha'i organization prefers that people not know that Baha'u'llah has dozens of descendants living all over the world today. Past leaders of the Baha'i community excommunicated nearly all of Baha'u'llah's children, grandchildren and great-grandchildren. Baha'is have been taught by those leaders to believe that the heresy they call "Covenant-breaking"—challenging the absolute authority of the Baha'i leadership—is passed from generation to generation. What is actually passed on are different facts, different memories, and different points of view that the present Baha'is would prefer not to be known and discussed. Therefore they tell their followers that anyone expelled from the Baha'i community must be shunned by the true believers. So they don't want to admit that people like me exist. Admitting my existence would be inconvenient for them, because it might cause the Baha'is to ask questions and find out things about the history of their religion that the present leaders don't want them to know. I think the whole thing is rather childish.

In 2010, I received a letter from a young American named Eric Stetson, who explained that he had seen my interview in that film, found my address in an Israeli phone book, and wanted to correspond with me about my family history and the Baha'i faith. He said that he was a former Baha'i who still had an interest in the religion and agreed with many of its teachings. Seeing my interview had caused him to do some research about my grandfather Mohammed Ali and his beliefs and writings, and he was eager to learn more.

Eric and I have corresponded and talked many times since then. I have found him to be humble, open-minded, and a sincere seeker of truth. For many years I had in my possession a manuscript written by my uncle Shua Ullah and pamphlets and letters by my mother—writings that had never been seen by the public—and Eric offered to edit them and find a publisher who would publish them as a book. I am very pleased that he was successful and this book is now in print. After many years, long after they passed from this world, the members of my family can tell their side of the story of the Baha'i faith, and hopefully their story will be heard by Baha'is and independent religious scholars.

I want to thank Eric Stetson for his efforts in editing the manuscripts I provided him, compiling them into this book, and seeing it through the publication process. I also want to thank the publisher, Vox Humri Media, and its president, Brent Mathieu, for agreeing to print this work and funding the project. I owe a debt of gratitude to the fine souls who made this project possible, and of course to my ancestors who wrote down their memories and thoughts about the Baha'i faith and events that happened in their lives, without which this book never could have existed. In my elder years, I can rest in the satisfaction of knowing that their stories will not go untold, their life's work was not in vain, and future generations will have the opportunity of learning the lessons of their lives and benefiting from their best ideas.

I am not a member of the organized Baha'i community, but that is not identical to the Baha'i Faith—even though they call it by that name, as if the religion were limited to an organization. The spirit of Baha'u'llah and his faith are present in the heart of every person who is a lover of humanity, who associates with the people of all religions with love and kindness, and respects both the diversity and the oneness of the human race. No excommunication is possible from such a broad and beautiful faith.

I was married for many years to Mordechai "Murad" Emsallem. As an Oriental Jew, he understood the Arab culture and spoke the language fluently. He had a company with his Arab friends during the [British] Mandate. Now, as always, I worship God together with my friends who are Jews, Christians, and Muslims. Sometimes I even invite them to hold meetings in my home, and I hold meetings on the Baha'i holy days and my friends attend. In my heart, my soul, my life, and my very genes, I am Baha'i. So were my grandfathers and all my relatives who believed in the faith of Baha'u'llah and lived accordingly.

I know it is difficult for people to change their minds about things they hold dear, especially when it comes to matters of religion and facts about the mythologized figures who were involved in historical dramas. Most people don't like to see their heroes revealed as less than perfect and their villains rehabilitated—it would ruin the stories they have become used to. I challenge the Baha'is of the world to read this book with an open mind and an unprejudiced heart, as hard as it may be. Readers may find that the story of their faith is actually richer, greater, and more real in light of the perspectives shared by the authors of this book. We cannot know the truth about the Baha'i faith until we are willing to see the important characters of the Baha'i story as human, not as caricatures—whether that means acknowledging their formerly hidden virtues or their flaws—and hear all of their voices.

Although I don't know whether the Baha'i faith will ever become what I believe my great-grandfather Baha'u'llah intended it to be, the publication of *A Lost History of the Baha'i Faith* makes it more likely that it could be reformed and the mistakes of its past be corrected. I trust that future histories will record that at least some of its followers and friends were sincere in the pursuit of truth, justice, and the highest principles and ideals.

Mohammed Ali Bahai, son of Baha'u'llah.

Badi Ullah Bahai, youngest son of Baha'u'llah.

Kamar Bahai, granddaughter of Baha'u'llah, as a young woman, c. 1940.

Mousa Bahai, grandson of Baha'u'llah, as a young man.

Mousa and Kamar Bahai at their daughter Maliha's wedding.

Preface

By Eric Stetson

The Paradox of the Baha'i Faith

In 1891, Mirza Husayn Ali Nuri, a Persian nobleman in exile who called himself Baha'u'llah ("The Glory of God"), wrote the following words, claiming to be revealing God's message for a new era of human civilization:

> The first Glad-Tidings... is that the law of holy war hath been blotted out from the Book [i.e. the scriptures of religion]. ... The second Glad-Tidings: It is permitted that the peoples and kindreds of the world associate with one another with joy and radiance. O people! Consort with the followers of all religions in a spirit of friendliness and fellowship.[1]

In his last will and testament, Baha'u'llah wrote:

> Every receptive soul who hath in this Day inhaled the fragrance of His garment and hath, with a pure heart, set his face towards the all-glorious Horizon [i.e. the highest heaven] is reckoned among the people of Baha [i.e. as Baha'is]... The religion of God is for love and unity; make it not the cause of enmity or dissension.[2]

---

[1] *Lawh-i-Bisharat* ("Tablet of Glad-Tidings"). Official Baha'i translation in *Tablets of Bahá'u'lláh Revealed After the Kitáb-i-Aqdas* (Wilmette, Ill.: US Bahá'í Publishing Trust, 1988 pocket-size edition), pp. 21-22.

[2] *Kitab-i-'Ahd* ("Book of the Covenant"). Official Baha'i translation in ibid., p. 220.

Baha'u'llah's first son and successor, Abbas Effendi, who called himself 'Abdu'l-Baha ("Servant of the Glory"), wrote the following in his own will:

> So intense must be the spirit of love and loving kindness, that the stranger may find himself a friend, the enemy a true brother, no difference whatsoever existing between them. For universality is of God and all limitations earthly. ...
>
> Consort with all the peoples, kindreds and religions of the world with the utmost truthfulness, uprightness, faithfulness, kindliness, good-will and friendliness, that all the world of being may be filled with the holy ecstasy of the grace of Baha, that ignorance, enmity, hate and rancor may vanish from the world and the darkness of estrangement amidst the peoples and kindreds of the world may give way to the Light of Unity. Should other peoples and nations be unfaithful to you show your fidelity unto them, should they be unjust toward you show justice towards them, should they keep aloof from you attract them to yourselves, should they show their enmity be friendly towards them, should they poison your lives, sweeten their souls, should they inflict a wound upon you, be a salve to their sores. Such are the attributes of the sincere! Such are the attributes of the truthful.[3]

However, in the very same document, 'Abdu'l-Baha also wrote:

> And now, one of the greatest and most fundamental principles of the Cause of God is to shun and avoid entirely the Covenant-breakers, for they will utterly destroy the Cause of God, exterminate His Law and render of no account all efforts exerted in the past. ...
>
> Beware lest ye approach this man [i.e. the chief of the "Covenant-breakers"], for to approach him is worse than approaching fire! ...
>
> A thousand times shun his company. ... Watch and examine; should anyone, openly or privily, have the least connection with

---

[3] *The Will And Testament of 'Abdu'l-Bahá* (Wilmette, Ill.: US Bahá'í Publishing Trust, 1990 reprint), Part One, pp. 13-14.

him, cast him out from your midst, for he will surely cause disruption and mischief.[4]

He was speaking of his own brother Mohammed Ali Bahai, and most of the rest of their family, their father's lifelong secretary, and numerous friends and supporters of Mr. Bahai, all of whom he had expelled from the new religious community. What was this "Covenant-breaking" that was so grave an offense that it would cause 'Abdu'l-Baha to make a special exception to his own teachings of universal fellowship and forbearance, and instead urge his followers to enter into the sort of adversarial stance he had described as the "darkness of estrangement"?

The specific accusations by 'Abdu'l-Baha against Mr. Bahai are outlined in his will, and were the basis for denying this younger brother the successorship that their father had envisioned for his second son,[5] who, like Abbas Effendi, had been an active leader in the formative years of the Baha'i faith. The accusations are serious and will be addressed in this book—both what 'Abdu'l-Baha alleged, which has been portrayed as unchallenged fact in official Baha'i histories and commentaries about the religion's "Covenant" of institutional authority, as well as Mohammed Ali Bahai's responses to the charges, which have never before been published—and furthermore, some of the counter-charges made by partisans of Mr. Bahai against 'Abdu'l-Baha.

Much more important than any of these accusations, however, is that in the formal excommunication of his brother, 'Abdu'l-Baha severed one of the most significant veins of Baha'i thought from the continued development of the faith. Mr. Bahai was an articulate and respected voice for an interpretation of Baha'ism centered on individual conscience and freedom from authoritarian religious leadership. His supporters called themselves "Unitarian" Baha'is, because of their emphasis on the oneness of God and the non-divinity and essential fallibility of the human leaders of religions—including 'Abdu'l-Baha. In

---

[4] Ibid., Part Two, pp. 20-21.
[5] Baha'u'llah wrote in his will, "We have surely chosen the Mightiest (*Akbar*) [i.e. Mohammed Ali Bahai] after the Greatest (*A'zam*) [i.e. Abbas Effendi] as a command from the All-Knowing, the Omniscient." See the last section of Chapter 6.

contrast, mainstream Baha'is today believe that 'Abdu'l-Baha and his chosen successor Shoghi Effendi Rabbani—known in Baha'i parlance as the "Master" and the "Guardian" respectively—were infallible and that their teachings can never be changed by future Baha'i leaders. This belief has locked in the mainstream Baha'i community to some interpretations and policies that are difficult to defend in the 21st century, most notably, the absolute exclusion of women from serving on the highest Baha'i institution, the Universal House of Justice.

The estranged relationship between Baha'u'llah's sons, more than any other fact or thread of Baha'i history, changed the Baha'i faith from what might have become an Islamic-inspired liberal spiritual tradition analogous to the Christian-sprung free-thinking pluralism of the Unitarian Universalist church, into what Dr. Juan R. I. Cole, professor of Middle Eastern history at the University of Michigan, has described as a faith community with strict "social control mechanisms" such as "mandatory prepublication censorship of everything Baha'is publish about their religion, administrative expulsion, blackballing, shunning and threats of shunning."[6] Dr. Cole, a former member of the Baha'i community who left in 1996 under threat of excommunication and shunning, is one of the foremost scholars of a faith he considers to be "curiously off-limits to careful investigation."[7] Other distinguished Baha'i scholars, such as Drs. John and Linda Walbridge, likewise have resigned their membership after being threatened by Baha'i officials for seeking greater openness of scholarly dialogue and administrative reform of the faith.[8]

---

[6] "The Baha'i Faith in America as Panopticon, 1963-1997." Originally published in *The Journal for the Scientific Study of Religion*, Volume 37, No. 2 (June 1998): 234-248. Available online at http://www-personal.umich.edu/~jrcole/Bahai/1999/jssr/bhjssr.htm

[7] Ibid.

[8] Dr. John Walbridge is a professor of Near Eastern Languages and Cultures at Indiana University. His late wife, Dr. Linda Walbridge, served as deputy director of the Middle East Institute at Columbia University in the 1990s and taught anthropology at Indiana University. The issues and events that led them, Dr. Cole and others to leave the Baha'i faith are described in an academic article by Karen Bacquet, "Enemies Within: Conflict and Control in the Baha'i Community," originally published in *Cultic Studies Journal*, Volume 18: 109-

The Need for Critical Baha'i Scholarship

Although Juan Cole and the other reform-minded Baha'i scholars did not call for a reevaluation of the great schism that occurred in the Baha'i faith between the followers of two of Baha'u'llah's sons—focusing instead on modern debates—a fresh and open-minded examination of the earliest debate about the nature and extent of Baha'i institutional authority is in fact long overdue, and could shed much light on how this religion, which paradoxically began as a movement against the stultifying authoritarianism of Shi'ite Islam, eventually adopted some similar characteristics. Other alternative Baha'i groups and reform movements have come and gone, none ever enjoying the kind of credibility and potential that the Unitarian Baha'is had in their heyday. After all, most of Baha'u'llah's own children and grandchildren were Unitarian Baha'is—a circumstance and significance that cannot be replicated.

The last books by adherents of Mohammed Ali Bahai were published in the early 1900s, before his sect gradually faded away into obscurity and disappeared. Since then, the only book I am aware of that even attempts a degree of objectivity in presenting their point of view was *The Baha'i Faith: Its History and Teachings*, by William McElwee Miller, published in 1974. Rev. Miller was a Christian minister whose purpose was, at least somewhat, to deter people from converting to the Baha'i faith, and therefore his book should not be taken as the last word on these issues. Moreover, it is a broad overview of the Baha'i religion which was not intended to delve deeply into the lives, testimonies, and arguments of the various members of Baha'u'llah's family and other key figures in the faith during the period of open schism—though to its credit, it does at least discuss the schism and the basic position of both sides, which is more than can be said for most introductions to the Baha'i faith. New and more extensive scholarship on this specific subject has been needed for decades, and finally is brought forward in *A*

---

140. Available online at http://www.angelfire.com/ca3/bigquestions/enemies.html. See also "The Talisman Crackdown" at http://www.angelfire.com/ca3/bigquestions/talisman.html

Lost History of the Baha'i Faith—which hopefully will not be the last book to cover this critical ground with the goal of objectivity.

What makes this new book special—other than the fact that its intriguing subject matter has mostly been ignored for nearly a century—is that most of its contents were written by the immediate family of the Baha'i prophet himself. It is thus a unique and crucially important compilation of the views and memories of people who intimately knew the founder of the Baha'i faith, who believed him to be the new messenger of God for modern times, yet who, because of some combination of doctrinal disagreements and personal quarrels, were not allowed by their own relatives to participate in the religious community bearing his name. I contend that it is impossible to have a clear and balanced understanding of the Baha'i faith, its historical development, its current challenges and future potential, without reading *A Lost History of the Baha'i Faith* with a sincerely open mind.

As editor, I have attempted to order and annotate the primary source materials that comprise this book in a way that presents a coherent narrative and which makes them accessible and understandable to everyone, including people who know little about the Baha'i faith. Thus, this book can serve as a first introduction to this fascinating religion of the modern era, while at the same time bringing to light—rather than avoiding or glossing over—some of the most controversial episodes and debates of its history.

Manuscript by Shua Ullah Behai

Most of the chapters of this book are reproduced, in some cases nearly verbatim, from an unpublished English-language book written in the mid 1940s by Shua Ullah Behai. The manuscript, titled simply *Bahai Faith*, included not only his own writings but also writings by other family members, especially Mohammed Ali Bahai, his father; 'Abdu'l-Baha, his uncle; and Baha'u'llah, his grandfather; as well as several other early Baha'is and historians of the faith. Many of these writings, including some of the words of Baha'u'llah, are original translations by Mr. Behai.

Shua Ullah Behai's manuscript was not a highly sectarian or polemical work. Although it is impossible for anything a believer writes about religion to be completely objective, Mr. Behai attempted to tell the Baha'i story in a way that was respectful of people he disagreed with, and focused on presenting facts rather than making judgments. Although his book reflected the overall perspective of the Unitarian Baha'i tradition he favored, it was not a one-sided account of the Baha'i faith but a compilation of various points of view including his own.

A Lost History of the Baha'i Faith includes most of the book Shua Ullah Behai wrote and compiled, as well as some additional texts that are relevant to the narrative. This book is an attempt to expand upon and update Mr. Behai's work in keeping with the spirit of his manuscript, letting key figures and witnesses of Baha'i history speak for themselves—especially those whose voices were suppressed and whose stories have been forgotten or neglected.

Some of the material I have added is more partisan in taking the side of Mr. Behai's father and portraying 'Abdu'l-Baha in a negative light, compared to Mr. Behai's own writings and especially those of the elder Mr. Bahai, who took pains to avoid harsh criticisms or judgments of his brother from whom he had been estranged. I have included the more partisan material for three reasons: First, the main purpose of Shua Ullah Behai's book was to provide important historical testimonies that would otherwise be ignored, and I feel that the passage of time and my distance from the Baha'i family feud make me capable of discussing material which he may have been reluctant to include out of respect for his famous uncle's reputation or for fear of coming across as personally biased—material which nevertheless ought to be presented in context and considered by anyone who wants to investigate the issues objectively. Second, I feel that it is instructional for the reader to observe the differences in tone and content between Mohammed Ali Bahai's own statements and some other critics of 'Abdu'l-Baha, as this sheds light on the character of the man Baha'u'llah intended to become his second successor and the significant and perhaps under-recognized role that other Baha'is played in the schism. Third, the testimonies of two of the writers I added, Mohammed Jawad Gazvini and Rosamond Templeton, corroborate Mr. Bahai's claim that 'Abdu'l-Baha sought to hide part of Baha'u'llah's will and would not permit the document to be disseminated without his own editorial control—a disturbing possibility that deserves scholarly consideration of all sources available which may either refute or confirm its likelihood.

The focus of *A Lost History* as I have reconstructed it is to relate the early history and teachings of the Baha'i faith through the eyes of some of its most intimate and marginalized adherents. To keep this the main focus and reduce distractions from the flow of the story, I have tightened up some chapters which contained lengthy unabridged selections from writings already published elsewhere. I have also somewhat reordered the contents of Mr. Behai's manuscript. Minor editing has been done to all the documents included in this new version of the book, to modernize and improve the English writing of the authors and translators, who were not native speakers; but I have tried to avoid the kind of editing that would significantly alter their writing style.

Throughout the book, text enclosed in parentheses is either original to the author of the primary source document or, in most cases, explanatory additions by the translator (e.g. Shua Ullah Behai). Bracketed text and footnotes have been added by this editor to further assist the reader. I have extensively annotated some chapters, in particular, where detailed explanations are needed either to clarify or raise doubts about the meaning of the author, or to provide relevant background information.

How Unitarian Were the Unitarian Baha'is?

Editing Shua Ullah's Behai's manuscript required grappling with an interesting theological issue. Both Mr. Behai and his father were native speakers of Persian and Arabic, the script of which does not have capital letters. As a result, Mr. Behai's English writings as well as his translations of his father's writings exhibit excessive and irregular capitalization of words. This has been corrected in the edited version. However, he was also inconsistent in capitalizing pronouns in reference to the religious leaders regarded by Baha'is as "Manifestations of God," including Baha'u'llah, which means that the editor could either leave the irregularities in the text (annoying the reader) or decide on a single, consistent style (obscuring the authors' diverse and complex views). Instead of these problematic options, I have edited the text to use either capital or lowercase "he" based on what I have been able to determine about the beliefs and intentions of the author at the time when each document was written. In some cases it depends on the tenor and purpose of a particular document or its intended audience. In other cases it depends on the author, since some authors demonstrated an obvious tendency to deify Baha'u'llah whereas other authors did not present him that way. For documents included in this book that have already been published elsewhere, I have been less inclined to change the capitalization of pronouns, but have done so occasionally.

The capitalization pattern in the original documents written or translated by Mr. Behai is worth noting: more frequent capitalization of pronouns in reference to Baha'u'llah, less frequent capitalization in reference to other Manifestations of God; more frequent capitalization in reference to Baha'u'llah in his earlier writings, and no capitalization at all of pronouns referring to Manifestations in the last extant document he is known to have written (a speech he gave in 1947). The theological significance of these facts may be debated, but it is my considered opinion that the observed patterns and changes are not accidental.

In the early 1900s, the Unitarian Baha'is tended to exalt Baha'u'llah's divinity as greater than that of other great religious leaders, with the possible exception of Jesus Christ. A prominent advocate of this view was Ibrahim Kheiralla, the first Baha'i missionary to the United States, who emphasized Baha'u'llah's station as the Return of Christ and the "Everlasting Father" of Biblical prophecy, and downplayed the station of Baha'u'llah's forerunner the Bab and other religious figures usually thought by Baha'is to be Divine Manifestations rather than mere prophets.

Mohammed Ali Bahai held and expressed what might, in Christian terms, be termed a "high Christology" regarding Baha'u'llah—perhaps to some degree as a way of drawing a sharper distinction between the station of the Manifestation and that of 'Abdu'l-Baha, his successor. Because Mr. Bahai was regarded by Unitarian Baha'is as an authoritative successor to Baha'u'llah, this view carried a lot of weight among his followers during his lifetime.

After his death, however, it appears that a true theological unitarianism began to emerge within the Unitarian Baha'i tradition. Among adherents of the tradition who left behind writings, both Baha'u'llah's grandson Shua Ullah and granddaughter Kamar Bahai seemed to humanize all the prophets, including Baha'u'llah, in their presentations of the Baha'i faith near the end of their lives. In the mid 1900s, both of them come across as spiritual progressives even by today's standards—fully embracing a liberal, open-minded view of religion while continuing to believe in its divine inspiration. Today, Negar Bahai Emsallem, daughter of Kamar and niece of Shua Ullah, could be fairly described as a liberal Baha'i, Unitarian and Universalist, who reveres but does not deify the founders of the great religions.

Motives and Intentions of the Editor

I feel that it would be appropriate for me to say a few words about why I have decided to compile and edit the primary source documents in this book and bring it to publication. The book was not published by a vanity press; I was paid for my work as editor. However, I would have been more than happy to serve in this capacity without compensation, and in fact I began compiling the documents and exploring options for publication more than a year before Vox Humri Media took on the project and hired me.

My interest in helping to get this book into print is for three reasons. First, I am a former member of the Baha'i faith community, but still believe in most of the principles taught by Baha'u'llah. I became a Baha'i in college and left the faith after about four years, in 2002, because I found organized Baha'ism to be too rigid in its doctrines and too focused on obedience to Baha'i religious leaders past and present. As a religious studies major who had been considering a career in academia, I was especially concerned about official Baha'i censorship of dissenting viewpoints, and the overall culture of intellectual conformity within the Baha'i community. It seemed inconceivable to me, for example, that any legitimate religious scholar could tolerate a policy such as "pre-publication review," in which a committee of Baha'i officials must censor and approve all books and academic articles written by Baha'is about their religion. I felt that the Baha'i faith needed to be reformed, but reform was not something that Baha'is were allowed to discuss. Feeling my spirit called in other directions, I eventually became a liberal Christian and Unitarian Universalist.

A few years ago I read some out-of-print books on the internet, and was fascinated to discover that the earliest "Covenant-breakers" were expelled from the Baha'i community precisely because they shared the desire for a more free-thinking, liberal Baha'i faith. It is not easy to learn this, because the evidence for this fact has been omitted from recently published histories of the religion; and even in the past, the reason for the rebellion of some early Baha'i insiders was glossed over as simply a stubborn refusal to obey legitimate Baha'i leaders. Although many Baha'is in recent times have left the Baha'i community or even the faith itself for the same basic reason they did—conscientious disagreement with Baha'i leaders' claims to be the infallible representative of God—surprisingly little has been written by religious scholars or historians about the fact that this kind of dissent is nothing new, but is part of a long, rich tradition of liberal-minded "dissident" Baha'is led by members of Baha'u'llah's own immediate family.

I believe this alternative Baha'i tradition of resistance to centralized, absolute religious authority, which dates back to the time of Baha'u'llah's passing, should be brought to light, fully researched and discussed, and critically examined for the important role it has played in Baha'i history and its potential significance for future developments of the faith. *A Lost History of the Baha'i Faith* is my attempt to get the ball rolling and contribute to this process. It is my hope that Baha'is may come to a more historically accurate and nuanced view of their religion's development and the key figures involved, why the Baha'i community struggles to attract and retain religious liberals among their membership, and how they might fix this problem by reevaluating internal debates of a century ago.

Secondly, after reading a variety of previously published and never-before-published primary source texts by Mohammed Ali Bahai, Shua Ullah Behai, and other writers in the Unitarian Baha'i tradition, I reached the opinion that regardless of whether their religious views were "right" or "wrong," these people have been unfairly maligned by mainstream Baha'i leaders and apologetic histories of the faith. Their character was attacked without sufficient evidence to support the allegations that led to their banishment from the religion they clearly loved. Therefore, because I was given exclusive access to unpublished documents they wrote, I felt I had a responsibility to help to bring these documents to print, so that their voices could be heard by the public. Only by studying their testimonies and teachings could Baha'is—or anyone else interested—even begin to form an intelligent and informed opinion about these historical figures, their beliefs, actions, values and motives. Only by considering the statements of both sides of a dispute can we attempt to move beyond hearsay and prejudice and strive for objectivity.

"Independent investigation of truth" has always been taught as a key principle of the Baha'i faith. *A Lost History* is a new and vital resource with which Baha'is may pursue such an investigation about some of the most important people and issues in their religious tradition—the children, grandchildren, and great-grandchildren of Baha'u'llah, and their sincere and passionate arguments with each other about the meaning and message of the faith they so intimately knew and shared.

A third reason for my involvement as editor of this book is a more personal one. Over the past few years I have become friends with Negar Bahai Emsallem, a great-granddaughter of Baha'u'llah who lives in Haifa, Israel. She is the person who provided me with the documents that have never before been seen by the public—not even by anyone outside of her immediate family. I first contacted Mrs. Bahai in 2010, after I saw her interviewed in a controversial Israeli film about the Baha'i faith called *Baha'is In My Backyard*, and I was curious to speak with a descendant of one of the ostracized members of Baha'u'llah's family to learn more about their point of view.

I am honored to count Mrs. Bahai as a friend. I have found her to be a woman of principle, decent, good-natured, kind and unassuming, with an open heart and an open mind. Her respect for all religions and habit of interfaith dialogue and fellowship are extraordinary for someone who grew up in her generation in the Middle East. Wishing to avoid fruitless sectarianism, she does not enjoy talking about, in her words, the "unfortunate conflict" between her grandfathers Mohammed Ali and Badi Ullah and her great-uncle 'Abdu'l-Baha; but she is firm in her conviction that they were good men and that her family's side of the story deserves to be told.

As a personal friend of Negar, I desire to see her quite reasonable wish fulfilled before she passes on from this world. Thus I have found a publisher for her family's writings and have done the best and fairest job I could as editor. In a better world, Baha'is on pilgrimage would disregard her status as an officially shunned "Covenant-breaker" and pay a visit to this dear elderly lady—living just a few blocks from Mount Carmel—who embodies a sensibility of mind and generosity of spirit of which her distinguished ancestor, the Baha'i prophet, would surely be proud.

Original Preface

The following message appears at the beginning of Shua Ullah Behai's manuscript, and seems to this editor to be a genuine expression of his character, his reasons for writing the book and an accurate description of its contents:

> Humbly I request every beloved Baha'i throughout the world to read this narrative unbiased and unprejudiced, irrespective of party affiliation, then to think and face the mirror of reality with the vision of investigation, answering this question: Am I a true Baha'i?
> In this narrative the reader will find many events which hitherto have been withheld or misrepresented by some of the past Baha'i writers—those who satisfied themselves with hearsay, and passed judgment without investigation. I did not attempt to rewrite the events, but I reproduced some of the articles which have been written by the well-known personages. I am not trying to prove the guilt or innocence of either party concerned. I am

merely presenting the hidden facts, for the enlightenment of the seekers of truth and future historians.

> O Son of Spirit!
> Justice is loved above all; neglect it not, if thou desirest me. By it thou wilt be strengthened to perceive things with thine own eyes and not by the eyes of men, to know them by thine own knowledge and not by the knowledge of any in the world. Meditate on this—how thou oughtest to be.
> Justice is of my bounty to thee, and of my providence over thee; keep it ever before thy sight.
> —Baha'u'llah[9]

---

[9] The Hidden Words, Arabic #2.

Shua Ullah Behai, eldest grandson of Baha'u'llah.

Kamar Bahai in the 1960s.

1

The Origin of the Baha'i Movement

By Kamar Bahai

Kamar[1] Bahai (October 5, 1904 – November 10, 1970) was a granddaughter of Baha'u'llah through his son Badi Ullah. This introductory essay about the origin of the Baha'i faith and its founder is compiled from part of a circular letter or pamphlet that she wrote in September 1952 called "The Bahai Movement" and the entirety of another one she wrote in January 1953 called "Baha U'llah." Both were originally written in English and Arabic versions, as were all the letters and essays of Mrs. Bahai that are reproduced in this book.

—The Editor

The Baha'i Movement

The reader has noticed that the local newspapers, Hebrew and English, have allotted space to writers who attempted insofar as they were acquainted with the subject to publish information regarding the essence of the Baha'i movement. ...

Now by virtue of my personal status as granddaughter of Baha'u'llah, the founder of the movement, and in response to many wishes expressed and questions set down in numerous letters I have received from Israel and abroad following the publication of my circular No. 2,[2]

---

[1] Also spelled Qamar.

[2] A previous circular letter by Mrs. Bahai, reproduced in Chapter 33.

I feel bound to put before the reader a concise and clear exposition of the essence and teachings of the movement. ...

Let me now take the reader back to Persia, the birthplace of the movement, to Persia the all powerful who bestowed an unrivaled civilization to the world, who produced great kings, statesmen, poets and philosophers, and let us together turn over the pages of history until we reach the end of the 18th and the beginning of the 19th century. Now we find that the kings are either too weak or too cruel, the religious heads fanatical to the extreme, and the people sunk into ignorance, for how could education be encouraged when science and knowledge were looked upon as hostile forces working against religion? Therefore with corruption prevailing in the government, with fanaticism replacing religion, and with an economy in confusion, the country was about to collapse.

Under the circumstances it was inevitable that a social revolution should occur. A distinguished reformer rose to lead the revolution against the then-existing evils. By virtue of his fiery spirit, his eloquence, convincing logic and peerless courage, he was able to enflame the feelings of the people and create an enthusiasm among the intellectual class whose members were scattered all over Persia but had long been waiting for the consummation of the prophecy which foretold the imminent appearance of a great reformer.

He laid down the foundations which afford a firm basis for unity, universal peace and goodwill, for the search after truth, the oneness of mankind, the unity of religion, of races, of East and West, the reconciliation of religion and science, the eradication of prejudice and superstition, the equality of men and women, the establishment of justice and righteousness, the setting up of a supreme [inter]national tribunal, the unification of languages and the compulsory diffusion of knowledge. This moral and spiritual reform and ideal progressive movement aimed at elevating humanity, socializing religion, unifying the fundamental ideals of the world and harmonizing the conflicting interests of nations.

Dear reader, if you scrutinize the above-mentioned ideal principles propounded by the founder of the movement, you will discover that they are for the interest and happiness of humanity. The Baha'i movement has preached these humanitarian principles from the beginning of the 19th century.

Baha'u'llah

God's revelation is like a crystal fountain that flows into the hearts of the prophets from time to time.

This fountain, crossing the life of Zoroaster, produced through his teachings great kings, experienced politicians, wise philosophers, inspired poets and outstanding men of art.

That same fountain inspired the great Buddha, who came as a huge cloud and showered his principles and quenched the thirst of millions of people.

It overwhelmed the quiet life of Confucius, and made the Chinese people a cultured and pious nation.

It found its way into Moses' heart, as a result of which the desert blossomed in fruit and flower.

It made a deep incision into Jesus Christ's soul, and then the scent of the flowers of love perfumed the lives of the believers.

It penetrated with violence and turmoil into the Arabian desert, where Muhammad, the irrigator watered the fields of knowledge, art and science.

And now this current of revelation struck the hearts of the Baha'i leaders. Mirza Husayn Ali, later named Baha'u'llah, was born in the city of Nur, Persia in the year 1817. He was the same reformer whose imminent appearance was prophesied by Mirza Ali Muhammad "Al Bab"[3] when the latter started his movement in May 1844, in which he declared that the world with its methods and worn-out traditions was about to collapse and a new free and strong world would replace it.

Baha'u'llah began his revolutionary mission in 1863 and waged a relentless war against the worn-out traditions and the forces of evil, as a result of which he was stripped of his hereditary title as a noble in the

---

[3] Generally known as the Bab, his title *al-Báb* means "the Gate" or "the Door" in Arabic.

Persian Court and suffered the loss of his vast estates through confiscation.

He proclaimed the end of the night of aggression and cruel fanaticism and prophesied the dawn of peace and brotherhood, preaching the oneness of Earth, race and religion.

And he is the one who said that all the human race springs from one source and the apparent differences result from differences of environment and degrees of culture, and that humanity is nothing else but one family. After all, God created the Earth without boundaries or frontiers.

The founders of the great religions in the world are but inspired people carrying holy messages to different corners of the world at different intervals of time.

Baha'ism is not an organization but a system of thought and a new way of living.

The effect of this was that the authorities of the state together with the authorities of religion combined, arrested and imprisoned Baha'u'llah and later exiled him with his family and a group of his followers across the Persian border. Baghdad then became his residence.

During the first twelve years of his exile in Baghdad, the Baha'i movement expanded and spread, for the suffering which he experienced and the hardships which beset him did not stop him from delivering his message. Men and women from various regions flocked to quench their thirst from this sweet and holy fountain.

Later he was exiled anew to Constantinople[4] and from there to [Adrianople][5] and at last to the fortress of Acre.[6] From that impenetrable fortress, this great prisoner spread his teachings of love, brotherhood, peace and justice to the East and West. From within the wall of this great fortress, Baha'u'llah sent his messages to the kings, emperors and rulers of the world, in which he showed them the way to salvation

---

[4] Present-day Istanbul.

[5] Present-day Edirne, Turkey. Mrs. Bahai erroneously wrote Adana, another Turkish city, in the original document.

[6] The city of Acre, Israel, is also commonly known as Akko in Hebrew and Akka in Arabic. It was the site of a Crusader fortress which was later rebuilt by the Ottomans and used as a prison.

and urged them to put an end to the rule of violence and establish a reign of justice and brotherhood, and to erect the foundations for a permanent international parliament.

These principles mentioned above, preached by Baha'u'llah with great power of Spirit, were transmitted to the President of the United States of America, to the King of Prussia, to the Emperor of Austria, to the Tsar of Russia, to Napoleon III, to Queen Victoria, to the Sultan of Turkey, to the Shah of Persia, and the Holy Pope.

After 40 years of exile and continuous labor and after the martyrdom of 20,000 of his followers, Baha'u'llah died in 1892, leaving a will to his eldest son, Abbas Effendi, to be succeeded by his second son, Mohammed Ali Effendi, assigning to them the spiritual leadership of the movement and the responsibility of carrying out his mission of brotherhood and peace.

Siyyid Kázim Rashti, forerunner of the Bab.

2

The Cultural and Religious Precursors of Baha'ism

By Shua Ullah Behai

Shua Ullah Behai (1878 – July 3, 1950), also known in the Baha'i tradition as Mirza Shu'a'u'llah, was the son of Mohammed Ali, son of Baha'u'llah. He was Baha'u'llah's eldest grandson. Mr. Behai was fluent in English and is the only known descendant of the Baha'i prophet to have become an American citizen.

This chapter contains most of the first two chapters of his book manuscript about the Baha'i faith. I have removed some Persian poetry and an excerpt from the writings of Professor Edward G. Browne about his meetings with the Bab's successor Subh-i-Azal, and condensed Prof. Browne's lengthy description of the execution of Babi martyrs, for the sake of brevity. Some of the section headings have been added.

—The Editor

The Great Culture of Iran (Persia), the Birthplace of the Baha'i Faith

The area of Iran is 1,648,000 square kilometers.[1] It is situated between the following countries: to the north, the Caucasus, the Caspian

---

[1] In 2014, it is exactly 1,648,195 square kilometers, which is 636,372 square miles.

Sea, and Russian Turkestan;[2] to the east, Afghanistan and British Baluchistan;[3] to the south, the Oman Sea and the Persian Gulf; to the west, Iraq and Turkey. Its population according to the last census is about 18,000,000.[4]

On account of the great mountains and wide plains, the climate of Iran is of two distinct types, that of the temperate regions and the tropical zones. Few countries of such a size enjoy such a diversity of climate.

According to history, Iran was a country of ancient civilization, great empire, and the center of the art of literature, producing such a historian-poet as Ferdowsi, who wrote the *Shahnameh* (Book of Kings),[5] which contains over fifty thousand verses of poetry and was completed by him in the 11th century A.D. His work has been acclaimed by modern judges of literature as one of the greatest, and his millenary was celebrated all over the world in 1934.

The following is from Ferdowsi's *Shahnameh* (reproduced from *The Oriental Caravan*[6]):

> A weary traveller sat to grieve
> By Gureng's gate, at early eve,
> Where fragrant gardens, filled with bloom,
> Cast forth their breath of soft perfume,
> And wandering o'er his brow and face,
> Relieved him for a moment's space.
> But sorrow weighed upon his breast,

---

[2] Russian Turkestan was a Governor-Generalship within the Russian Empire, which included the present-day countries of Turkmenistan, Uzbekistan, Tajikistan, Kyrgyzstan, and parts of Kazakhstan.

[3] A province of British India, which was located in the western part of the present-day country of Pakistan.

[4] This census would have been sometime in the 1940s. The population of Iran has grown dramatically since then, reaching over 75 million.

[5] The *Shahnameh* is the national epic poem of Iran. Including both mythology and history, it tells the story of the Persian empire from the creation of the world to the Islamic conquest of Persia in the 7th century.

[6] Sirdar Ikbal Ali Shah (Editor), *The Oriental Caravan* (New York: Claude Kendall, 1933), pp. 216-219. This book is a compilation of excerpts from various Middle Eastern and South Asian classical literature translated into English.

And dimmed the lustre of his eye;
He had no home—he sought but rest,
And laid him down to sleep—or die.

King Gureng's lovely daughter lies
Beside a fountain gently playing;
She marks not though the waves be bright,
Nor in the roses takes delight;
And though her maids new games devise,
Invent fresh stories to surprise,
She heeds not what each fair is saying; ...

But hark! soft whispers, questions gay,
Amongst the female train prevail;
A young slave, beautiful as day,
Blushes while she tells her tale. ...

The princess heard: "Go hence," she cried,
"And be the stranger's wants supplied:
Let him beneath our shades repose,
And find a refuge for his woes." ...

Meanwhile the princess mused alone,
And thus she sighed, in mournful tone:— ...
"That prince whose power was far above
All those who vainly seek my love; ...
His Kingdom gone, his fortune crost,
And he, perhaps, for ever lost!"

She ceased, when lo! The laughing train
Came dancing back, with song and jest,
And leading, in a flowery chain,
The stranger youth their welcome guest.
'Twas thus they met—they met and gazed,
Struck by the self-same power—amazed;
Confused, admiring, pleased, distressed,
As passion rose in either breast.

The princess spoke—soft as a bird

In spring to some dear partner sighing;
And the fair stranger's words were heard,
Sweet as the bulbul's[7] notes replying.

Her long hair, streaming to the ground
With odours fills the air around;
She moves to music and to song,
As the wild partridge steps along.

She leads him to her jasmine bower,
Midst fountains, birds, and blossoms sweet;
And her attendant maidens shower
The sparkling wave upon his feet; ...

My tale is told. Ye lovers, say,
Can ye not guess the blissful close?
How Jamshid[8] won a bride that day,
And found a balm for all his woes.

Another was the philosopher-poet Saadi, 13th century A.D., who wrote The Rose Garden (*Gulistan*) and The Orchard (*Bostan*). The following is the translation of a few verses from *Gulistan*:

In a public bath, one winter day,
A beloved presented me with a fragrant clay.
Amazingly said I! Art thou Musk or Amber?
To thine exquisite fragrance I slumber.
I was a common clay, humbly said he,
But I befriended the rose of Parsee.[9]

---

[7] *Bulbul* means nightingale in Persian.

[8] As the legend goes, Prince Jamshid became a great king who reigned for hundreds of years and commanded the powers of light and darkness. He became prideful and fell from grace, and roamed the earth as an outcast for a hundred years, but gained wisdom and regained his kingdom after marrying King Gureng's daughter.

[9] The *Parsees* (also spelled Parsis) are Persians who continued to follow the Zoroastrian religion, the original faith of Persia, after the arrival of the Islamic empire. A small number of Parsis remain in Iran today.

Chapter 2. The Cultural and Religious Precursors of Baha'ism

Sweet friendship of by-gone day,
Brought me the fragrance of to-day.
Take thou that fragrance from me away,
I am nothing but the same common clay.

The following is taken from Costello's *Rose Garden of Persia*:[10]

Contentment (from the *Bostan*)

Smile not, nor think the legend vain,
That in old times a worthless stone
Such power in holy hands could gain,
That straight a silver heap it shone.
Thy alchemist Contentment be,
Equal is stone or ore to thee.

The infant's pure unruffled breast,
No avarice nor pride molest:
He fills his little hands with earth,
Nor knows that silver has more worth.

The sultan sits in pomp and state,
And sees the dervish[11] at his gate;
But yet of wealth the sage has more
Than the great king, with all his store.

Rich is a beggar, worn and spent,
To whom a silver coin is thrown;
But Feridoun[12] was not content,
Though Ajum's kingdom was his own.

Hafez[13] was another well-known Iranian poet, of the 14th century

---

[10] Louisa Stuart Costello, *The Rose Garden of Persia* (London: Gibbings and Company, 1899), pp. 102-103.
[11] A *dervish* is a Sufi Muslim who follows a spiritual path of extreme poverty and asceticism.
[12] Feridoun (also spelled Fereydun) was a mythical king of Persian prehistory.
[13] Also spelled Hafiz.

A.D. The following verses by Hafez are translated by G.L. Bell:[14]

> The nightingale with drops of his heart's blood
> Had nourished the red rose, then came a wind,
> And catching at the boughs in envious mood,
> A hundred thorns about his heart entwined.
> Like to the parrot crunching sugar, good
> Seemed the world to me who could not stay
> The wind of Death that swept my hopes away.
>
> Light of mine eyes and harvest of my heart,
> And mine at least in changeless memory!
> Ah, when he found it easy to depart,
> He left the harder pilgrimage to me!
> Oh Camel-driver, though the cordage start,
> For God's sake help me lift my fallen load,
> And Pity be my comrade of the road!
>
> My face is seamed with dust, mine eyes are wet.
> Of dust and tears the turquoise firmament
> Kneadeth the bricks for joy's abode; and yet...[15]
> Alas, and weeping yet I make lament!
> Because the moon her jealous glances set
> Upon the bow-bent eyebrows of my moon,
> He sought a lodging in the grave—too soon!
>
> I had not castled, and the time is gone.
> What shall I play? Upon the chequered floor
> Of Night and Day, Death won the game—forlorn
> And careless now, Hafiz can lose no more.

Although Omar Khayyam's name springs readily to mind with the mention of Iranian poetry, in his native land his fame is surpassed by

---

[14] Gertrude Lowthian Bell (Translator), *Poems From the Divan of Hafiz* (London: William Heinemann, 1928), pp. 102-103.

[15] Ellipsis in original book by Bell.

that of Ferdowsi, Saadi and Hafez. The superb translation by FitzGerald[16] made him popular in the Western world as a poet.

Iran enjoyed great progress for many centuries, according to the Book of Kings (*Shahnameh*) which is the only [early] Iranian history in existence. Also the ancient examples of art and excavated discoveries prove this progress. Times passed as such, until the Arabs conquered the Persian empire and forced them to accept Islam by the sword.

After a long period of oppression, the Iranians became students of the Arabic language, devout followers of the Prophet [Muhammad] and strong believers in his book, the Qur'an. Eventually they surpassed the Arabs in their language. The first Arabic dictionary was compiled by an Iranian, named Abu Tahir Majdeddin Fairuzabadi, and it is still in existence today, bearing his name.

The following well-known personages are a few of the thousands of Iranians that served in the Islamic kingdom:

- The great Imam Abu Hanifa (founder of the Hanafi sect of Islam).
- Ibn Muqla (calligrapher of the Naskh alphabet, and powerful politician who served as Grand Vizier under three Abbasid caliphs).
- Abu Ishaq Estakhri (composer of the first book on geography in Arabic).
- Abu Ali Ibn Sina[17] (philosopher, physician, and founder of the science of medicine).
- Zamakhshari (logician and grammarian).
- Abu Bakr [Muhammad ibn Zakariya] Razi (physician and mathematician).
- Fakhruddin Razi (philosopher).
- Nasir al-Din Tusi (astronomer and founder of Maragheh observatory near Tabriz).
- Imam Muhammad Al-Ghazali (theologian, philosopher, and mystic).

---

[16] A selection of poems attributed to the 11th-12th century Persian intellectual Omar Khayyám was translated into English by Edward FitzGerald and published in 1859 under the title *The Rubaiyat of Omar Khayyam*.

[17] Also known as Avicenna.

Shi'ism, Theocracy, and the Descent of Persia into Darkness

As the years went by, the Iranians progressed greatly both socially and politically. Then a new idea appeared in their mind, and a decision was reached to control the government through the power of religion. They hoped to regain their freedom through that channel and to rebuild their empire. They tried on several occasions to fulfill their desire, especially during the Abbasid caliphate, but at every attempt they failed.

While the Safavid rulers controlled the throne of Iran during the 16th century, realizing their numerous unsuccessful attempts to overcome the Arabian kingdom, they encouraged the mullahs (leaders of theology) to renew the Shi'ite doctrine (which was originated after the reign of Ali, the fourth caliph after Muhammad) against the other Islamic denominations—thus building a strong wall between them, owing that no barrier could be stronger than religious superstition. By this means, they sowed the seeds of hatred in the hearts of the masses.

For the enlightenment of the reader I hereby explain some of the Shi'ite doctrine. The Shi'ites believe that the true spiritual leaders after the Prophet were his descendants, and they are called Imams. The Imam is the divinely ordained successor of the Prophet, one endowed with all perfections and spiritual gifts, one whom all the faithful must obey, whose decision is absolute and final, whose wisdom is superhuman, and whose words are authoritative. The Imams, the [chosen] descendants of the Prophet, were twelve in number; therefore it is termed "Creed of the Twelve."[18]

These twelve are as follows:
1. Ali, son-in-law of Muhammad.
2. Hasan, son of Ali and Fatimah [the daughter of Muhammad].
3. Hussein, [younger] son of Ali and Fatimah.
4. Ali, son of Hussein and Shahrbanu (daughter of Yazdegerd III,

---

[18] *Twelver* Shi'ism, as it is usually called, is the largest branch of Shi'ite Islam, but other types of Shi'ites also exist. For example, Zaidis believe in only five Imams, and Ismailis believe in seven.

the last Sasanian[19] king), generally called Zayn al-Abedin.
5. Muhammad Baqir, son of Zayn al-Abedin.
6. Ja'far Sadiq, son of Muhammad Baqir.
7. Musa Kazim,[20] son of Ja'far Sadiq.
8. Ali Reza,[21] son of Musa Kazim.
9. Muhammad [al-Jawad] Taqi, son of Ali Reza.
10. Ali [al-Hadi] Naqi, son of Muhammad Taqi.
11. Hasan Askari, son of Ali Naqi.
12. Muhammad, son of Hasan Askari and Narjis Khatun, called "Imam Mahdi."

Imam Mahdi was born in Surra Man Ra'a,[22] Iraq, and succeeded his father in the year 260 A.H.[23] [874 A.D.] The Shi'ites hold that he did not die, but disappeared in an underground passage in Surra Man Ra'a; that he still lives surrounded by a chosen band of his followers in one of the mystical cities called Jabulqa and Jabulsa;[24] and that when the fullness of time is come, when the earth is filled with injustice, and the faithful are plunged in despair, he will come forth to overthrow the infidels,

---

[19] The Sasanian dynasty ruled the last Iranian empire before the coming of Islam.

[20] Also spelled Musa Kadhim.

[21] Also spelled Ali Ridha or Rida.

[22] Present-day Samarra.

[23] *A.H.* (i.e. *anno hegirae*): The year according to the Islamic calendar, which starts at the *Hijra* or emigration of the Prophet Muhammad from Mecca to Medina in 622 A.D.

[24] Shi'ites believe the Imam Mahdi went into "occultation," i.e. disappeared from public view, and communicated his teachings through a series of deputies for several decades. After that, the "Hidden Imam" is believed to have continued to live somewhere unknown, on earth, and will reappear at a future time of divine judgment, heralding the return of Jesus Christ. Some Shi'ites taught that the Mahdi ascended to a mystical realm between heaven and earth, instead of remaining in hiding as a supernaturally long-lived man in the physical world. The 12th century Iranian Sufi philosopher Shahab al-Din Suhrawardi provided the basis for this alternative possibility with his teachings about the "emerald cities" of "Jabalqa and Jabarsa"—spiritual places that are only accessible through special gnosis in an altered state of consciousness. *Jabulqa and Jabulsa* is a variation of the same, and this concept was adopted by Shi'ites of the theological school that ultimately gave rise to the Baha'i faith.

establish universal peace and justice and inaugurate a millennium of blessedness. During the whole period of his Imamate, i.e. 260 A.H. until the present day, the Imam Mahdi has been invisible and inaccessible to the mass of his followers.

The renewal of the Shi'ite doctrine shattered the peaceful minds of Iranians, drowned them in the ocean of superstition and for two hundred years kept them in darkness. Students of history are aware of the unbearable conditions which existed in Iran from the 17th to the 19th centuries, especially during the Qajar rule. [Unnumbered people endured] extreme agonies for the freedom of their thoughts, and thousands of noble souls sacrificed their lives to free their fellow beings from the clutches of religious leaders and their superstitions.

The Shaykhi Reform Movement

The era of awakening for liberation from religious orthodoxy began in Iran (Persia) in the early 19th century. The first reformer was Shaykh Ahmad Ahsa'i, born 1741 A.D.[25] From his youth this great personage was a seeker of new light. He was a devout student of the Qur'an and the Shi'ite doctrine, a progressive teacher and [the founding] leader of the Shaykhi school.

At the suggestion of his spiritual advisors he journeyed to Karbala and Najaf[26] (the center for students of theology) where he resided and taught his progressive teachings. In a short time he acquired great fame and surrounded himself with many liberal-minded students. He was an advanced and independent thinker, and his explanations of doctrine appealed to the dissatisfied people. At the time, the horizon of the minds of Iranians was covered with the clouds of religious superstition; therefore the appearance of such a great sun of liberty and his sound explanation and interpretation of doctrine brought him fame and glory, and eventually he became a powerful leader. His sudden rise to popularity caused the Shah to extend to him an invitation to come to the

---

[25] The year of birth of Shaykh Ahmad is uncertain. Different sources report it as 1741, 1744, or as late as 1753.

[26] These cities are in present-day Iraq.

capital for counsel and advice. Then he proceeded to Kermanshah and from there to Yazd where he resided twelve years, devoting his entire time to progressive teachings.

He made several pilgrimages to Mecca, and on the last occasion he passed unto Eternity before reaching the Holy Shrine of the Kaaba in 1825 A.D.[27]

Shaykh Ahmad Ahsa'i was succeeded by his devoted disciple, Haji Siyyid Kázim Rashti, who came from a prominent merchant family.

While a young man, one night in a dream this future leader was authorized by a supposed "saint" to enroll himself under the spiritual guidance of the said Ahsa'i. He proceeded accordingly and eventually became a devout disciple of the great Ahsa'i, in whose doctrine he attained such a fame that after his death he was unanimously recognized as the leader of the Shaykhi school. He died at Baghdad, Iraq, in the year 1843 A.D. at the age of fifty.

This venerable teacher authorized his followers to expect the appearance of the Qa'im[28] or Imam Mahdi (said to be the spiritual return of Elijah)[29] after his departure. He did not appoint a successor and devoted the last few years of his life to paving the way for the coming of the Mahdi and his appearance on earth.

Siyyid Ali Muhammad Shirazi, the Bab

In May 1844 A.D. there appeared in Iran a young man of twenty-four years of age, whose name was Ali Muhammad, a descendant of the Prophet. He possessed the highest degree of the power of wisdom and spiritual inspiration. At the beginning he called himself the Bab, meaning the Gate (through which to gain knowledge of truth). Afterwards

---

[27] Different sources report the year of his death as either 1825 or 1826.

[28] The *Qa'im*, meaning "He Who Shall Arise," is another title for a prophetic figure expected by Shi'ite Muslims to appear on earth at the end of the age. The Qa'im is the return of the Imam Mahdi.

[29] Jews expected the prophet Elijah to return to earth to announce the advent of the Messiah and the Kingdom of God. In Islam, the Mahdi is expected to play a similar role prior to the return of Christ.

he claimed to be the Qa'im or Imam Mahdi, whom the Muslims expected.

In a short time he revolutionized the thoughts of the masses. He brought them from darkness to light and from extreme religious orthodoxy to liberalism. He paved the way for the coming of the Glory of God, "He Whom God Shall Make Manifest,"[30] Baha'u'llah.

One of the Bab's messages was thus: "O ye people of the earth, that which was prophesied by the holy men of ancient times will shortly come to pass. The Kingdom of God shall be established upon the earth."

His message spread rapidly throughout the land and thousands of theologians and learned students followed him. His followers were called Babis and were scattered all over Iran, but more prominently visible in the cities of Shiraz, Tabriz, Zanjan, the province of Mazandaran and the Persian province of Iraq.[31]

The rapid spread of his message and the progress of his cause aroused the anger of the mullahs, as they feared the downfall of their leadership. They organized against the Bab and his followers, calling him an impostor and a magician, and finally succeeded in sowing the seed of hatred in the hearts of the ignorant masses against the Babis. They allied themselves with the governors of many provinces and caused the persecution of thousands of innocent citizens. Faithful and prominent Babis were put to death without question or judgment, and many of the governors participated in these unfortunate events to satisfy the desire of the mullahs. In spite of severe persecution the Babis became more energetic and enthusiastic in their diffusion of the message throughout the land.

The clamor of this movement commanded the attention of the Shah, who sent Sayyid Yahya Darabi, one of the highest doctors of theology, to question the Bab as to his message. After his visit to the Bab, this learned man became convinced of the truth of the Bab's message

---

[30] In Persian, *man yuzhiruhu'llah*. This was the title by which the Bab referred to a coming messianic figure who would be even greater than himself. Baha'u'llah later claimed to be this figure.

[31] A western province of Persia, not the same as the present-day country of Iraq.

Chapter 2. The Cultural and Religious Precursors of Baha'ism

and allied himself with the cause as a zealous believer and preacher, so the Bab's cause became stronger as time passed.

The mullahs decided to try a new method to extinguish this great light by forcing the government to capture the Bab and put him in prison. Not satisfied with this, they finally caused his execution. The Bab and a devoted follower called Aqa Muhammad Ali[32] were together put to death in the city of Tabriz on July 9, 1850 A.D.

A noted Babi historian recorded this unfortunate event as follows:[33]

> Next day the chief of the *farráshes* (jail keeper) delivered over the Bab and a young man named Aqa Muhammad Ali who was of a noble family of Tabriz to Sam Khan, colonel of the Christian regiment of Urumiyyih,[34] at the sentences of the learned divine[35] Mulla Muhammad of Mamaqan, of the second ecclesiastical authority Mirza Baqir, and of the third ecclesiastical authority Mulla Murtaza-Quli and others. An iron nail was hammered into the middle of the staircase of the very cell wherein they were imprisoned, and two ropes were hung down. By one rope the Bab was suspended and by the other rope Aqa Muhammad Ali, both being firmly bound in such wise that the head of that young man was on the Bab's breast. The surrounding house-tops billowed with teeming crowds. A regiment of soldiers ranged itself in three files. The first file fired; then the second file, and then third file discharged volleys. From the fire of these volleys a mighty smoke was produced. When the smoke cleared away they saw that young man standing and the Bab seated… in the very cell from the staircase of

---

[32] Muhammad Ali Zunuzi, who is known as Anís ("companion") in the Baha'i tradition.

[33] Edward G. Browne (Translator), *A Traveller's Narrative: Written to Illustrate the Episode of the Bab*, Volume II. English Translation and Notes (Cambridge: University Press, 1891), pp. 43-45. The original Persian text of the book was written by 'Abdu'l-Baha. The translator was a British orientalist who studied the Babi and Baha'i faiths.

[34] Present-day Urmia, Iran.

[35] An old-fashioned term for a cleric or theologian.

which they had suspended them. To neither one of them had the slightest injury resulted.

Sam Khan the Christian asked to be excused (from the second attempt of the execution of the Bab); the turn of service came to another regiment, and the chief of the *farráshes* withheld his hand. Aqa Jan Beg of Khamsa,[36] colonel of the body-guard, advanced; and they again bound the Bab together with that young man to the same nail. ...

The colonel of the regiment appeared in person: and it was before noon on the twenty-eighth of [the Islamic month of] Sha'ban in the year [A.H.] one thousand two hundred and sixty-six (the 9th of July, 1850 A.D.) Suddenly he gave orders to fire. At this volley the bullets produced such an effect that the breasts of the victims were riddled, and their limbs were completely dissected, except their faces, which were but little marred.

Three days after the execution the remains were taken away by a few Babis in the darkness of night. Kept in a hiding place for years, they finally were brought to the Holy Land and buried on Mount Carmel in Haifa.

His Holiness the Bab is recognized as Mahdi and Elijah, and this is proven by his works and teachings entitled *Bayan*.[37] He says:

The whole *Bayan* revolves round the saying of Him Whom God Shall Make Manifest. A thousand perusals of the *Bayan* are not equal to one verse of what shall be revealed by Him Whom God Shall Make Manifest.[38] I swear by the most holy essence of God, Glorious and Splendid is He, that in the day of the appearance of Him Whom God Shall Make Manifest, if one should hear a single verse from Him and recite it, it is better than that he should recite

---

[36] A historical province of Persia, usually spelled Khamseh, which is part of the present-day province of Zanjan, Iran.

[37] The *Bayan* (Arabic: "exposition") is the principal scriptural text of the Bab.

[38] Cf. John the Baptist's statement regarding Jesus, the Messiah: "He is the one who comes after me, the straps of whose sandals I am not worthy to untie." (John 1:27). The Bab claimed to play a similar role as John the Baptist, who, in the Christian tradition, is regarded as the return of Elijah.

the *Bayan* a thousand times. The *Bayan* today is in the stage of seed but in the day of Him Whom God Shall Make Manifest it will arrive at the degree of fruition. All the splendor of the *Bayan* is "He Whom God Shall Make Manifest."

The Seven Martyrs of Tehran

The following narrative appeared in the works of the late Professor Edward G. Browne of the University of Cambridge, England, published in the year 1891:[39]

> "This year," says Lady Sheil[40] writing in September 1850, "seven Babis were executed at Tehran for an alleged conspiracy against the life of the Prime Minister [of Persia]. Their fate excited general sympathy, for every one knew that no criminal act had been committed, and suspected the accusation to be a pretence. Besides this Babism had spread in Tehran too. They died with the utmost firmness. Previously to decapitation they received an offer of pardon, on the condition of reciting the *Kalima*, or creed, that Muhammad is the Prophet of God. It was rejected, and these visionaries died steadfast in their faith. The Persian minister was ignorant of the maxim that persecution was proselytism."[41] Amongst these seven—"the Seven Martyrs" as they are called by the Babis—was the Bab's uncle Haji Mirza Seyyid 'Ali. The other sufferers were Haji Mulla Isma'il of Qum, Mirza Qurbán 'Ali the dervish, Aqa Seyyid Huseyn of Turshiz the *mujtahid*,[42] Haji Mulla Naqi of Kirmán, Mirza Muhammad Huseyn of Tabriz, and Mulla

---

[39] Edward G. Browne, *A Traveller's Narrative: Written to Illustrate the Episode of the Bab*, Volume II. English Translation and Notes (Cambridge: University Press, 1891), pp. 211-213, 215-216.

[40] Lady Mary Leonora Woulfe Sheil was the daughter of Stephen Woulfe, a Member of the British Parliament and Chief Baron of the Irish Exchequer, and the husband of Sir Justin Sheil, a British military officer and diplomat who served as envoy and minister at the court of the Shah of Persia.

[41] From Lady Sheil's book, *Glimpses of Life and Manners in Persia*.

[42] A *mujtahid* is a Muslim legal scholar with the authority to interpret Islamic law.

Sádiq of Marágha.[43] Of their martyrdom the *Tarikh-i-Jadid*[44] gives a long and touching account, on which I here append an abridgement.

What led to this tragic event was, as stated by Lady Sheil, a report conveyed to Mirza Taqi Khan[45] the Prime Minister that the Babis in Tehran meditated a rising. Thirty-eight persons suspected of belonging to the obnoxious sect were therefore arrested and cast into prison. After a few days it was decided that all of these who would consent to renounce or repudiate their connection with the Bab and his doctrines should be released, but that those who refused to do so should suffer death. ...

Accordingly of the thirty-eight prisoners seven... determined to adopt the more courageous course, while the others for various reasons were not prepared to forfeit their lives, and decided to recant. The latter were therefore released; the former were led out to die.

In spite of the wide-spread sympathy felt for the sufferers there were not lacking wretches to deride and mock them as they were led forth to the place of execution. Some of these threw stones at them; others confined themselves to abuse and raillery...

When the executioners had completed their bloody work, the rabble onlookers, awed for a while by the patient courage of the martyrs, again allowed their ferocious fanaticism to break out in insults to the mortal remains of those whose spirits had now passed beyond the power of their malice. They cast stones and filth at the motionless corpses... Nor would they suffer their bodies to be interred in a burial-ground, but cast them into a pit outside the Gate of Shah 'Abdu'l-'Azim,[46] which they then filled up.

After detailing the occurrences briefly set forth above, the Babi historian proceeds to point out the special value and unique character of the testimony given by the "Seven Martyrs." They

---

[43] Some sources list Haji Muhammad-Taqi Kirmani and Aqa Sayyid Murtada Zanjani among the seven martyrs, instead of Haji Mulla Naqi and Mulla Sádiq.

[44] A chronicle of the Babi movement written by the Babi historian Mirza Husayn Hamadani, which was translated into English by Edward G. Browne.

[45] Mirza Taghi Khan Farahani, also known as Amir Kabir, served as the chief minister to Naser al-Din Shah from 1848 to 1851.

[46] One of the entrances to the old city of Tehran.

were men representing all the more important classes in Persia—divines, dervishes, merchants, shop-keepers, and government officials; they were men who had enjoyed the respect and consideration of all; they died fearlessly, willingly, almost eagerly, declining to purchase life by that mere lip-denial, which, under the name of *kitmán* or *taqiyya*, is recognized by the Shi'ites as a perfectly justifiable subterfuge in case of peril; ... and they sealed their faith with their blood in the public square of the Persian capital wherein is the abode of the foreign ambassadors accredited to the court of the Shah. And herein the Babi historian is right: even those who speak severely of the Babi movement generally, characterizing it as a communism destructive of all order and all morality, express commiseration for these guiltless victims.

Fatimah Baraghani, Called Tahirih or Qurratu'l-'Ayn

The disciples of the Bab included many spiritual leaders of whom historians have spoken with great reverence. Among them was a great soul, a wonderful woman who discarded the veil[47] and preached the new message to the masses. She was called Qurratu'l-'Ayn ["Solace of the Eyes"], and Tahirih (meaning "Pure"). A daughter of a theologian and well-informed student, she served the cause of the Bab with great vigor and enthusiasm.

Of this noble soul an English author writes:

> The appearance of such a woman as Qurratu'l-'Ayn is in any country and any age a rare phenomenon, but in such a country as Persia it is prodigy—nay, almost a miracle. Alike in virtue of her marvelous beauty, her rare intellectual gifts, her fervid eloquence, her fearless devotion, and her glorious martyrdom, she stands forth

---

[47] Tahirih is best known for her radical act of removing her veil at a Babi religious conference, defying the strict interpretation of Islamic traditions of modesty which required women to cover their faces in front of men outside their family. The Bab supported Fatimah Baraghani's courageous action, which resulted in her arrest, and he gave her the new name Tahirih to affirm her purity. The Arabic word *táhira* means "pure one (female)." The alternative spelling Tahireh is closest to the preferred pronunciation among Baha'is (TAH-her-ay), which reflects a Persian dialect.

incomparable and immortal amidst her countrywomen. Had the Babi religion no other claim to greatness, this were sufficient—that it produced a heroine like Qurratu'l-'Ayn.[48]

This venerable lady was a poet also. The same author attributes the following verses to her:

> The effulgence of thy face flashed forth and the rays of thy visage arose on high;
> Why lags the word "*Am I not your Lord?*" "*Yea, that thou art*" let us make reply.
> "*Am I not's*" appeal from thy drum to greet what "*Yeas*" do the drums of devotion beat;
> At the gate of my heart I behold the feet and the tents of the host of calamity.
> That fair moon's love for me, I trow, is enough, for he laughed at the hail of woe,
> And exulting cried as he sank below, "The Martyr of Karbala am I."
> When he heard my death-wail drear, for me he prepared, and arranged my gear for me,
> He advanced to lament at my bier for me, and o'er me wept right bitterly.
> What harm if thou with the fire of amaze should'st set my Sinai-heart ablaze
> Which thou first mad'st fast in a hundred ways but to shake and shatter so ruthlessly?
> To convene the guests to his feast of love all night from the angel-host above
> Peals forth this summons ineffable "Hail, sorrow-stricken community!"
> Can a scale of the fish of amaze like thee aspire to sing of Being's Sea?
> Sit still like Tahirih, hearkening to what the monster of "No" doth cry.

---

[48] Edward G. Browne, *A Traveller's Narrative: Written to Illustrate the Episode of the Bab*, Volume II. English Translation and Notes (Cambridge: University Press, 1891), p. 309.

Qurratu'l-'Ayn, like many of the Bab's disciples, was executed in Tehran in the year 1852 A.D. The account of her execution varies but the most authentic is thus: After extreme tortures she was cast alive into a dry well which was filled with stones. Dr. Jakob Eduard Polak of Vienna, Austria, formerly physician to the Shah and professor at the Medical College of Tehran, happened to be an eyewitness to the execution. He writes of the horrible cruelties perpetrated on the Babis, their extraordinary fortitude, the tortures inflicted on the beautiful Qurratu'l-'Ayn, and the superhuman courage wherewith she endured her lingering death.[49]

Mirza Yahya Nuri, Called Subh-i-Azal

Mirza Yahya Subh-i-Azal[50] was born in 1828 A.D.[51]

He was appointed by His Holiness the Bab to be his successor, but when Baha'u'llah proclaimed himself the one "Whom God Shall Make Manifest," Mirza Yahya denied him, and therefore he lost the respect and support of the majority of the Babis.

In the summer of 1868 he was banished by the Turkish government to Famagusta, Cyprus. After the British occupation of that island in 1878 he was set free, but he preferred to remain there with the members of his household. He kept in seclusion and rarely made public appearances.

He passed unto Eternity on April 29, 1912 at Famagusta, Cyprus.

---

[49] These observations are recorded in Dr. Polak's 1865 book, *Persien. Das Land und seine Bewohner*.

[50] A younger half-brother of Baha'u'llah, who also made prophetic claims. His followers called him by the title *Subh-i-Azal*, which means "Morning of Eternity."

[51] According to most sources he was actually born in 1831.

3

A Brief Biography of Baha'u'llah

By Mohammed Ali Bahai

Mohammed Ali Bahai (December 16, 1853 – December 10, 1937) was the eldest son of Baha'u'llah's second wife, and the second son of Baha'u'llah who survived him. Baha'is today usually refer to him as Mirza Muhammad 'Ali.

This essay, originally titled "The Biography of Beha 'U'llah," was written in June 1934 and translated into English by Mr. Bahai's son Shua Ullah. The translation was published in the United States in a magazine called *Behai Quarterly*, a publication of the Society of Behaists. It was also included in Shua Ullah Behai's book manuscript, as part of a chapter called "Baha Ullah."

—The Editor

Whenever a mighty personage appears on earth and the news of his greatness spreads throughout the world, the intellectual people seek eagerly to be enlightened with the knowledge of his daily actions of life and his teachings.

In the past, many pilgrims, especially historians, who came to this sacred land and visited me, displayed an urgent fascination to know of the early life and actions of Baha'u'llah, Glory be to Him, and received such answers as time permitted on each occasion.

Of late, more inquiries have reached me through the mail from friends far and near. Therefore I deem it necessary to impart to the people of the world my experiences, through my constant personal contact with Baha'u'llah during the period of years from my childhood to the years that I had the privilege to serve Him as the inscriber of His utterances and promulgator of His teachings throughout the world.

Thus I will record herein His lineage, His early life and habits, His verbal messages to me and some of His teachings which I have copied from the numerous original volumes of His utterances in my possession. May the spirit of truth penetrate unto the citadels of the hearts, and the Sun of reality illumine the minds of men.

His Lineage

Needless to speak of the lineage of Baha'u'llah, His life and teachings are sufficient proof of His greatness and far above family connections; but knowing the fascination of past inquirers and for the guidance of future historians, I will state it briefly.

He was a descendant of the royal dynasty of Kian, who ruled in Persia centuries ago. The well-known Persian historian Mirza Abul-Fazl[1] Gulpaygani, after careful search of records available during his visit to Mazandaran,[2] the home of Baha'u'llah's forefathers, speaks with conviction of the family connection with the Kian Dynasty. Indeed the prophecy of Zoroaster was fulfilled as he spoke of the coming of "Mah Abad from the Kian Dynasty."[3]

The father of Baha'u'llah was Mirza Abbas Nuri, better known as Mirza Buzurg ("The Great")—scholar, theologian, and diplomat, politically powerful and socially prominent. He was connected with the

---

[1] Also spelled Abu'l-Fadl.

[2] A province of northern Iran, on the southern coast of the Caspian Sea.

[3] The Kian or Kianian Dynasty is an ideal, possibly mythological dynasty of ancient Persia, from which all the historically recorded Persian kings claimed to descend. Mah-Abad, in Persian tradition, was the most ancient prophet of the current world age, regarded as the "father of mankind." Thus, the prophecy that Mr. Bahai is speaking of presumably was that Mah-Abad would return at the end of the age as an ideal king, completing the great cycle of history that he had begun. This may be a variant of the prophecy of the Shah Bahram, a messianic figure of Zoroastrian eschatology. Baha'u'llah claimed to be the messiah of Zoroastrianism as well as the "King of Kings" prophesied in the Bible.

[government] ministry and the court for years, during the Qajar Dynasty, and to his last days served his country gallantly. He was calm, kind and fearless, always ready to help the needy, and made hosts of friends during his life.

The mother of Baha'u'llah was Khanum Jani.[4] Well known socially in the capital of Persia, she was a great help to her spouse during his life and career, and very active in the progress of her sex.

His Birth and Early Life

Baha'u'llah was born in the city of Tehran, the present capital of Persia [now Iran], on November 12, 1817, and in the same city grew to manhood.

As a young man He associated with nobilities, court officials, and the celebrities of the day, and always served His father faithfully. He spent some of His early days in Mazandaran in the Nur district, the original home of His forefathers.

When the Bab proclaimed himself the New Teacher, his message appealed to Baha'u'llah and He became an active worker for the new cause, and left Teheran for Karbala, where He remained a few months, then returned to Tehran.

The message of the Bab awakened the minds of the Persians, and thousands of learned people became his followers. This roused the anger of the mullahs, and fearing the loss of their leadership, they labored with all their might against this progressive new movement which was spreading rapidly throughout the land. Finally they succeeded in inducing the government to arrest the Bab and his devoted secretary and put them in prison, then suspend them both on a pole in the middle of the square in the city of Tabriz, and riddle their chests with hundreds of bullets.

After the Bab was put to death and two of his followers attempted the life of Shah Naser al-Din, through the influence of the same agitators, Baha'u'llah was arrested by the government and imprisoned for a period of four months.

---

[4] Baha'u'llah's mother is known to have been named Khadijah, so the name Jani is either a second name or nickname.

Then, through the protest of the Russian ambassador, Baha'u'llah was released and officially vindicated of all accusations, but was requested to leave His native land, to satisfy the desire of the mullahs.

By mutual agreement between Russia, Turkey, and Persia, He was sent to Baghdad, which is located near the border of Persia. Baha'u'llah remained in Baghdad nearly twelve years. While in Iraq He secluded himself in the mountains of Sulaymaniyah for two years, during which His whereabouts were unknown to all.

His Later Life and Ministry

After His return to Baghdad, Baha'u'llah proclaimed Himself to be the promised one of whom the Bab had spoken, "He Whom God Shall Manifest," the Glory of God. This proclamation renewed the new movement and the cause spread rapidly, in spite of the persecutions. In His tablet to the Shah of Persia, Baha'u'llah said, "I was asleep on my couch: the breaths of my Lord the Merciful passed over me and awakened me from sleep; to this bear witness the denizens of the realms of His Power and His Kingdom, and the dwellers in the cities of His Glory, and Himself the True."

After receiving this inspired message, Baha'u'llah arose with great power and energy, and devoted forty years of His life in revealing tablets and uttering verses, through which He commanded His followers to hold fast to the garment of the Everlasting Father and worship God alone, to live in love and unity with each other and with all the people of the world.

He suffered hardship, calamity, and banishment to bring us from the darkness of ignorance to the light of knowledge. Through the influence of the ambassador of Persia in the Ottoman capital, engineered by the same agitating group of mullahs, Baha'u'llah was invited to come to Constantinople, then the capital of Turkey, where He resided three months as the guest of the government, then was sent to Adrianapolis[5] where He remained five years. He was then banished to the fortress of

---

[5] Adrianople, present-day Edirne, Turkey.

Akka,[6] residing there for twenty-five years, until the time of His departure [from this world] on May 28,[7] 1892.

His Dignity in Exile

Baha'u'llah was reared in luxury while living in Tehran, and on account of the high station of His father in government circles, He had the respect of all His associates. After He was divested of all earthly possessions and was requested to leave Persia, though in financial distress, He made the journey from Tehran to Baghdad with great dignity. He was contented under all conditions and invested Himself with the garment of patience at all times.

Responding to the order of the government, Baha'u'llah, accompanied by His household and some of His followers, proceeded from the city of Baghdad to the other side of the [Tigris] river, remaining in the Garden of Najib Pasha[8] for a period of twelve days, delivering the New Message to all who came.

During these twelve days, thousands of persons of all classes, government officials, representatives of other nations, theologians, merchants, and the masses as well, came to His presence, paying Him homage and wishing Him farewell.

The news of His departure spread rapidly and caused such a commotion amongst the populace that Namiq Pasha, then governor of Iraq, deemed it his duty to pay Him his respects also, calling on Him in person, accompanied by another high official, though Baha'u'llah was his prisoner.

---

[6] Akka is the Arabic name for the city of Acre, Israel.

[7] May 29 is the officially recognized date of Baha'u'llah's passing, but several credible sources report it as a day earlier. In addition to Mr. Bahai, Baha'u'llah's nephew Majdeddin bin Moussa Irani and early Baha'i historians Mohammed Jawad Gazvini and Mirza Abu'l-Fadl Gulpaygani give the date as May 28 in their writings.

[8] Muhammad Najib Pasha was the *wali* (governor) of Baghdad from 1842 to 1847. He built a palace and the attached garden, which came to be known to Baha'is as the Garden of Ridvan ("Paradise"). When Baha'u'llah and his entourage camped there in 1863, the garden had passed to Najib Pasha's heirs. Today, a hospital complex stands on the site.

During the journey from Baghdad to Constantinople, which lasted about four months, He was cordially received by the people of the countryside wherever He camped, and was respected and loved by all. While confined in the fortress of Akka, not being permitted to leave the city gate, He was in great distress. However, He commanded His followers to be patient and satisfied with the Will of God; and to His last days on earth, He taught us to free ourselves from the bondage of earthly possessions, and to direct our efforts to the progress of mankind.

His Language

The native language of Baha'u'llah was modern Persian (Farsi). He also spoke the Arabic language fluently. The numerous volumes of His utterances which He left for the world bear witness to this statement. He spoke Mazandarani also, which is Persian of a different dialect, spoken in the Mazandaran province of His forefathers.

His Raiment

As far back as I can remember, Baha'u'llah adorned His head with a high-crowned round hat called a *taj*, made of fine felt, covered with materials embroidered with silk of the same shade—some were all white, others all red, green or gray—wound at the lower part with a small white turban. For informal occasions He wore a small cap called an *arakchín*, similar to the taj except shorter and lighter in weight.

He dressed in soft, light and pleasing shades. His outer robe, called a *jobba*, was of fine camel hair in natural or gray color. Under this He wore a second robe called a *ghaba* in white or gray, wound at the waistline with a white Persian belt called a *chaal*. His undergarments consisted of two pieces, always in white, white hose and handmade slippers.

His Nutriments

Baha'u'llah was very moderate in food. He partook of Persian prepared food consisting of sweets, fruits, vegetables, and some meat. He drank tea, milk, fruit juice, and very little coffee.

In His early days He smoked a Persian water pipe called a *nargilet*,[9] but no cigarettes. However, while still a young man, He began to abstain from smoking entirely. I remember when we were brought to the prison of Akka, and housed in the army barrack, He addressed me one day and said, "Do not get the smoking habit." Although this was but advice, it impressed me so strongly that I never had any desire for smoking.

His Recreation

Baha'u'llah enjoyed the open spaces, fresh air and natural views. In the spring when the hills and valleys were covered with a green carpet, occasionally we were fortunate enough to spend the entire day with Him either in the garden of Ridvan or the orchard called Junayna,[10] usually leaving at daybreak and returning after sunset, and often in the moonlight. I recollect many such wonderful days which I was privileged to arrange. He admired fragrant roses and used attar of rose and rose water frequently.

Baha'u'llah spent most of His last twelve years in the Palace of Bahja ("Joy"),[11] which is located on a hill near Akka, surrounded with miles of open fields. Here He passed unto Eternity and His shrine is located next to the palace which He occupied.

His Daily Routine

Baha'u'llah was an early riser, usually at daylight. His breakfast consisted of a small cup of tea and dry rusk,[12] served after sunrise. The pil-

---

[9] A type of hookah or narghile.

[10] Ridvan, originally called Nam'ayn, and Junayna (also spelled Junaynih) were garden retreats near Acre, frequented by Baha'u'llah after he was allowed to leave the prison fortress. The Garden of Ridvan in Israel is not to be confused with the historical location in Baghdad which was given the same name by Baha'is.

[11] Usually called the Mansion of *Bahji*, or simply Bahji, by Baha'is today. The area where the mansion is located was known as Al-Bahja, meaning "Place of Delight."

[12] A biscuit or twice-baked bread.

grims were then called to His presence, the audience lasting for an hour or longer. This was followed by the appearance of the inscriber, to take dictations, until the approach of lunch time.

While revealing utterances to the inscriber, Baha'u'llah walked slowly back and forth in the large chamber He occupied. On other occasions, He wrote His tablets in His own handwriting, while sitting on a divan.

After lunch He retired a while; then the inscriber was called to His presence again for dictation, lasting until afternoon tea was served. Again friends and pilgrims came to His presence to receive counsel, advice, and instructions.

Supper always was served around 9 p.m., and generally He retired before midnight.

This was His daily routine. In His later years, only the followers were granted the privilege to come to the presence of Baha'u'llah, as His entire time was devoted to revealing tablets and uttering verses for the enlightenment of mankind.

Conclusion

I hereby invite my brothers in humanity and all seekers after truth throughout the world, to come and partake of the spiritual food that is hidden in the volumes of the teachings of Baha'u'llah in my possession still unpublished.[13] My entire library is open for your study, and today the people of the world are in need of the knowledge contained therein. In this invitation my desire lies only in the elevation of the thoughts of mankind, and the progress of my brothers in humanity.

Baha'u'llah said:

> O people of Baha, ye have been and are the rising-places of love and the dawning-places of the grace of God. Pollute not the

---

[13] See Appendix A for a list of volumes of Baha'u'llah's writings as compiled by Mohammed Ali Bahai's son Shua Ullah. Some of the writings are well known to Baha'is, but numerous tablets of Baha'u'llah remain unpublished. Mr. Bahai's granddaughter, Negar Bahai Emsallem, has said that she thinks his private collection of Baha'i scriptures was passed down to one of her cousins, but is unsure of their present ownership or location.

tongue with execration and reviling anyone, and protect the eye from that which is unseemly. Show what ye possess; if it is accepted, the aim is attained. If otherwise, opposition would be futile; leave him to himself and face God, the Protector, the Eternal. Be not the cause of grief and much less the cause of corruption and strife. It is hoped that ye be brought up under the protection of the tree of Divine Grace and do that which God hath wished. Ye are all the leaves of one tree and the drops of one sea.[14]

With careful study of His utterances, humanity will realize Baha'u'llah's greatness. His teachings are in harmony with science, useful in our daily affairs, and satisfying our every need.

---

[14] *Lawh-i-Ishraqat* ("Tablet of Splendors"), Eighth Ishraq.

4

Baha'i Principles

By Shua Ullah Behai

This chapter contains most of the last chapter of Shua Ullah Behai's book manuscript. It is a summary of the basic principles of the Baha'i faith as understood by Mr. Behai.

Many of the quotations from Baha'u'llah's writings in this chapter are translations by Ali Kuli Khan published in the early 1900s, with minor changes. Some other quotations appear to be original translations by Shua Ullah Behai, or are from sources this editor was not able to determine.

For the most part, the author's presentation of Baha'i principles is similar to what would be found in any introduction to the Baha'i religion, but on two points, some significant differences can be observed. Firstly, he includes "Religion Without Clergy" as one of the most important teachings. Although this is a principle held by all Baha'is, it is not usually given such emphasis, perhaps because the Baha'i community has developed organizational hierarchies which approximate some of the roles traditionally played by clergy in other religions.[1] Mr. Behai cites historical examples of clerical leaders acquiring too much power,

---

[1] The Continental Boards of Counsellors and their subordinate bodies, the Auxiliary Boards for Propagation and Protection of the faith, are Baha'i institutions whose officials throughout the world are appointed to evangelize for the religion and to investigate and discipline adherents who dissent from standard Baha'i doctrine and practice. This system and its positions were established by the Universal House of Justice, the head of the Baha'i community, in 1968.

and places the blame for religious dissension and conflict on "the orthodoxy of religious organizations"—a stance that reflects his more liberal perspective compared to the mainstream Baha'i tradition which has, conversely, blamed those who resisted orthodoxy for disputes within the faith.

In the section prescribing a "Universal Tribunal," the author quotes one of Baha'u'llah's writings about the House of Justice, an institution which has usually been interpreted as a specifically Baha'i administrative body, but which Mr. Behai seems to have believed should also be a model for a world court as part of a secular international government. Some prominent Baha'is in the mainstream tradition have suggested that the supreme governing body of their own religious organization, the Universal House of Justice, should someday rule a global theocracy;[2] but Shua Ullah Behai, in contrast, presents Baha'u'llah's vision of the House of Justice as an inspiration for non-religious international political institutions such as the League of Nations (later revived as the United Nations), which he favors. Various statements by Mr. Behai throughout this book confirm his strong belief in the separation of religion and state.

—The Editor

This is the century of progress. The human mind is greatly advanced, education is universal, freedom of speech and the press is granted, and above all the freedom of thought and belief. But with all this progress we observe that Baha'ism, the most progressive movement of this age, has been shrouded by vagueness and generalities

---

[2] In fact, the proponents of this view have even included members of the UHJ itself, as discussed in Juan Cole's article entitled "Fundamentalism in the Contemporary U.S. Baha'i Community." Originally published in *Review of Religious Research*, Vol. 43, No. 3 (March 2002): 195-217. Available online at http://www-personal.umich.edu/~jrcole/bahai/2002/fundbhfn.htm. As Dr. Cole explains, the modern Baha'i belief in theocracy has little support in Baha'i scripture, which for the most part, actually contradicts it.

without due regard to the authentic teachings of the founder Baha'u'llah. Therefore some explanation is essential.

By delving carefully into the teachings of Baha'u'llah we discover numerous principles which, if practiced, will cause the betterment of humanity and the progress of mankind.

We, the Baha'is, should practice the same before preaching to others to do so.

For the enlightenment of the reader and a reminiscence to the Baha'is throughout the world, I hereby explain some of the major principles and precepts of Baha'u'llah.

The Oneness and Singleness of God

Before acknowledging the Oneness and Singleness of God, we must know what is the meaning of this word "God." In the dictionary it is explained thus: "God, god: The Supreme Being; a being possessing divine power; a divinity, a deity." From these definitions it appears that God is a name the English-speaking nations have given for the Supreme Ruler of the Universe.

From antiquity to this age, that great power which is behind everything movable and immovable has been called Supreme Being. The wise men, and the great Teachers that appeared on this earth from the beginning which had no beginning to this twentieth century, have called Him by different names and attributes. The Hindus, ["Brahma" or] "Buddha"; the Parsees, "Mah-Abad"; the Jews, "Jehovah"; the Christians, "Spirit of Truth"; and the Arabs, "Allah." That Great Power is a reality which is beyond the comprehension of man. We know Him not but by His traces, and His traces are His Messengers and their teachings which have been given to us from time to time.

With careful study of the life and teachings of the past Messengers we will observe that each one had an object in his appearance and a message for us. Adam spoke of the creation of the Universe and its beauties. Enoch taught eternal life. Noah saved humanity from the deluge of ignorance, restoring them to the Ark of knowledge. Moses saved the Israelites from Pharaoh. Buddha taught the brotherhood of man.

Zaradusht[3] guided the Iranians to the light of Truth. Jesus sacrificed his life for the sake of unity amongst humanity, and Muhammad saved the Arabs from idolatry. All of them bowed in reverence to the Supreme Ruler of the Universe, "God," and the essence of their teachings is the same: the elevation of the thoughts and morals of mankind.

According to archaeological research, man has progressed considerably from the stone age to this age of steel and electricity. With unbiased study we will observe that the great teachers, messengers, philosophers, and scientists have been immensely responsible for our progress of today. But from time immemorial, from antiquity, the cause of development of the minds of humanity has been the inspired teachings and belief in the Supreme Being—even when the sun was considered the example of that Great Power, and the idols representatives of the Supreme Ruler of the Universe.

If our progress of today seems useless in some way, we are to blame for misapplication. Everything in existence is good but can become evil through our actions. The power of speech is one of the faculties of man, through which we know his innermost. Truth and lies both are considered speech, and its creation was good, but when misused becomes evil. Fire produces heat, and it is very beneficial in our daily life, but dangerous when improperly used. Poison's nature is destruction, but also beneficial when used properly. It is true that mankind has progressed greatly scientifically, but has decreased considerably spiritually, through the misguidance of the leaders and the superstition driven into their minds by theologians: the belief that God is a certain personality sitting somewhere above, directing the affairs of the universe. This and other similar dogmas have kept people away from all creeds and finally caused the revolt against theology and religion.

Doubtless the progressive students will agree with me that the Great Power, the Cause of All Causes which is governing this universe, is worthy of our reverence, respect, adoration and love.

Baha'u'llah, the Great Sage of this age said, [speaking in the divine voice]:

---

[3] The Farsi name for Zoroaster, the great prophet of ancient Persia.

My outward speaketh to My innermost and My innermost to My outward, that there is no one else in the Kingdom beside Me... Verily the Branches (sons) who branched from the Tree [Baha'u'llah] are My fingerposts amidst My creatures, and My fragrances between heaven and earth. Do ye see that there is a partner or an equal to God, your Lord? By the Lord of the world, No! Therefore say not that which God doth not permit, fear the Merciful, and be of those who reason.[4]

The Oneness of Mankind

The students of science and religion both agree on this principle. Science's theory is that we are the evolved and developed issue of the first Atom. Religious belief is that we are the offspring of the first Adam. Therefore it is a fact that the origin was one but with diverse explanations. Our difference in color is due to the climatic conditions of various parts of the globe, and the superiority of a race or nation over another is the consequence of its advance in education. Extreme ortho-

---

[4] Shua Ullah Behai identifies the source of these verses as the Book of *Haykal*, a book compiled by Baha'u'llah which contained his *Suriy-i-Haykal* ("Surah of the Temple") and various other writings. However, these verses do not appear in the English translation of that work which has been published by the Baha'i community under the title *The Summons of the Lord of Hosts*. Mr. Behai's father, Mohammed Ali, quoted the same passage but referred to its source as simply "a tablet" by Baha'u'llah, without identifying which one (see the section entitled "Sons and Successors of Baha'u'llah Are Not His Equal" in Chapter 17). Therefore, it seems likely that Shua Ullah Behai was mistaken about the source of the text. However, it is also possible that the published translation of the Book of the Temple is incomplete, and that these verses do appear in the original version of that document. According to Mr. Behai, the original was 520 pages in length (see Appendix A: List of Writings of Baha'u'llah); but the translation in *The Summons of the Lord of Hosts* contains only 276 paragraphs, along with some other writings of Baha'u'llah which have been added. Multiple sources confirm that some of the verses included in the first printed edition of the Book of the Temple—which do not appear in the published translation—were recognized as authentic writings of Baha'u'llah only by the Unitarian Baha'is, but not in the mainstream Baha'i tradition (e.g., see the account of this controversy in Chapter 23, in the section entitled "Abbas Effendi Favors Those Who Most Exaggerate His Position").

doxy in religious belief and lack of learning often have kept a race or nation backward. To this, history bears witness.

Baha'u'llah said:

> O children of man! Do ye know why We have created you from one clay, that no one should glorify himself over the other? Be ye ever mindful of how ye were created. Since We created you all from the same substance, ye must be as one soul, walking with the same feet, eating with one mouth, and living in one land, that ye may manifest with your being, and by your deeds and actions, the signs of unity and the spirit of oneness. This is My counsel to you, O people of light. Therefore follow it, that ye may attain the fruits of holiness from the Tree of Might and Power.[5]

> The most splendid fruit of Tree of Knowledge is this exalted word: Ye are all the fruits of one tree and leaves of one branch. Glory is not his who loveth his own country, but glory is his who loveth his kind. In this connection We have formerly revealed that which is the means for the prosperity of the world and the unification of nations. Blessed are those who attain! Blessed are those who practice![6]

Equality of Races

Although we differ in our color, creed, habits, morals, mentality and belief, yet in humanity we are one and we should be on terms of equality. If some of us happen to be more fortunate in knowledge than others, it is the result of education; and we should share the same with the less fortunate, and with the language of love and kindness direct them to the fountainhead of truth, instead of avoiding them and glorifying ourselves over them.

Baha'u'llah said:

---

[5] The Hidden Words, Arabic #68.
[6] *Lawh-i-Ishraqat* ("Tablet of Splendors"), Sixth Ishraq. Translated by Ali Kuli Khan in *Tablets of Baha'o'llah Revealed at Acca, Syria* (Chicago: Bahai Publishing Society, 1917), p. 128.

The word of God in the Sixth Leaf of the Exalted Paradise:

The light of men is justice; quench it not with the contrary winds of oppression and tyranny. The purpose of justice is the appearance of unity among people. In this exalted word, the sea of God's wisdom is moving; all the books of the world are not sufficient to contain its interpretation.

If the world is adorned with this mantle, the sun of the saying "On that day God will satisfy them with His abundance" will appear and shine from the horizon of the heaven of the world. Know ye the station of this utterance, for it is from the loftiest of the Tree of the Supreme Pen. Happy is he who heareth and attaineth!

Truly I say, all that hath descended from the heaven of the Divine Will is conducive to the order of the world, and to the furtherance of unity and harmony among its people. Thus hath the tongue of this Wronged One spoken in His great prison (Acre).

The word of God in the Seventh Leaf of the Exalted Paradise:
O ye wise men among nations! Turn your eyes away from foreignness and gaze unto oneness, and hold fast to means conducive to the tranquility and security of the people of the whole world. This span-wide world is but one native land and one locality. Abandon that glory which is the cause of discord, and turn unto that which promoteth harmony. To the people of Baha, glory is in knowledge, good deeds, good morals and wisdom—not in one's native land or station. O people of the earth: Appreciate the worth of this heavenly word, for it is like unto a ship for the sea of knowledge, and is as the sun to the universe of perception.[7]

Equality of Men and Women

Readers of the world news are aware of the hardship that women have experienced in the most progressive republic, the United States of America, for the passage of the law of women's suffrage. They labored with great energy for years until they succeeded after the First World War, in 1920.[8]

---

[7] *Kalimat-i-Firdawsiyyih* ("Words of Paradise"). Ibid., pp. 52-53.

[8] The Nineteenth Amendment to the United States Constitution, which prohibits any U.S. citizen from being denied the right to vote on the basis of sex,

About forty years earlier, Baha'u'llah said:

> The blessing of God be upon you, O members of the Exalted Household.[9] Khanumi[10] (Samadiyya Khanum, second daughter of Baha'u'llah) should hold fast to the rope of the Oneness (of God) and be happy in the Divine Providence.
>
> Woman and man, before God, occupy one (equal) station. The most beloved people, before God, are those who are steadfast and upright. Peace and glory be upon you, O members of the Household. ...
>
> All should know and in this matter be enlightened by the lights of the sun of certainty. Females and males are one (equal) before God. The Dawning-place of the Light of God diffuseth its effulgence equally on all. He created them for one another.[11]

Harmony of Science and Religion

With careful analytical study of this little planet we call the world, its conditions and changes, we will observe that everything in existence had an origin and a maker.

There is no product without a producer, no building without a builder, and no invention without an inventor. Likewise the earth and its contents testify to the mighty power of a Creator whom the theologians call God, and the scientists Nature.

To the intellectual observer, both are pointing to the Supreme Architect of the Universe, the Mighty Power, the Great Governor of this cradle earth, who causes the mineral to mature through the processes of natural chemistry, vegetation to grow through the power of the sun, air and water, producing livelihood for the birds and animals, and blessing human beings with life and dominion over all.

---

was ratified on August 18, 1920, after several decades of activism by advocates for women's equality.

[9] Baha'u'llah's family.

[10] *Khanumi* means "my lady." Baha'u'llah is referring to his daughter with a respectful title rather than using her given name.

[11] From an unidentified tablet.

Saadi, the great Persian philosopher-poet said: "The clouds, the air, the moon and the sun are laboring so you may earn a loaf of bread and enjoy with gratefulness. All are humble under your command, therefore it is unjust of you to be disobedient."

Religion and science are two channels through which mankind has been endeavoring to reach the truth. Religion is based upon faith and its principles have been the same throughout the ages, only renewed in each cycle by the inspired teachers. Science works upon theory and has contradicted its discoveries from time to time.

Doubtless there is nothing in existence without an origin; therefore, a creator. If we take it for granted that all in existence originated itself, it must be thus: either it was in existence and became existent, or it was not in existence and still became existent. The first is unreasonable, and the latter is impossible, as from nothing comes nothing. If we consider that one of the substances in existence originated the others, it is also unreliable as each atom of matter individually testifies to its weakness.

If we claim the strongest atom among all types of matter produced the others, and all in existence depend on this, it is also unreliable, for the human being, though small in stature, possesses the highest station of all the creatures in existence, and should be called a creator, an originator, yet we observe his weakness also, for he cannot depend on his earthly existence a second hence. If we consider that one group of atoms originated the others, this also is impossible, for the four kingdoms—mineral, vegetable, animal and human—though equal in the line of progress, vary in function. If we claim a group of the strongest atoms originated the others individually or in units, this is also impossible, for if the said group possessed such a power, they should be able to prevent self-destruction.

It is an actual fact that we cannot produce something from nothing. We need a seed to produce a plant, an egg to produce a bird, etc. Science could not produce the numerous modern discoveries and achievements without some substance to work with, such as chemistry. Even the past sages did not produce the so-called miracles without an origin. The great Master Jesus produced wine from the water; the great personage Moses produced water from the earth.

Regardless of the arguments of our friends, the theologians, and the scientists, for whom I have the greatest admiration, we must confess that the Mighty Power which is governing this universe is worthy of our honor, devotion, adoration and love. To that great invisible power, which today is visible to the intellectual mind, we must be grateful for our progress and the knowledge that we have attained through His sages from time to time.

Religion and science both guide humanity to one great object, the Originator, the Beginner, the Creator; and both agree to the oneness and singleness of that object, The Mighty Architect of the Universe, Jehovah, Everlasting Father, The Prince of Peace.

If the students of theology and science could see the truth through each other's spectacles, without prejudice, they would reach perfect harmony and understanding, revering both disciplines, and with united effort labor on the greatest work before them: the progress of mankind.

Baha'u'llah said:

> The Third *Tajalli* ["Effulgence"] is concerning sciences, crafts and arts. Knowledge is like unto wings for the being (of man), and is as a ladder for ascending. To acquire knowledge is incumbent on all, but [only] of those [types of knowledge] which may profit the people of the earth, and not such sciences as begin in mere words and end in mere words. The possessors of sciences and arts have a great right among the people of the world, whereunto testifieth the Mother of Divine Utterance in the Day of Return. Joy unto those who hear! Indeed, the real treasury of man is his knowledge. Knowledge is the means of honor, prosperity, joy, gladness, happiness, and exaltation. Thus hath the Tongue of Grandeur spoken in this great prison.[12]

> The Eleventh Glad-Tidings: To study sciences and arts of all descriptions is allowable; but such sciences as are profitable, which lead and are conducive to the elevation of mankind. Thus hath the

---

[12] *Lawh-i-Tajalliyat* ("Tablet of Effulgences"). Translated by Ali Kuli Khan in *Tablets of Baha'o'llah Revealed at Acca, Syria* (Chicago: Bahai Publishing Society, 1917), pp. 76-77.

matter been decreed on the part of God, the Commander, the Wise.[13]

And We permitted you to study of the sciences that which benefiteth you, and not that which endeth in dispute. This is more advantageous to you, were ye of those who know.[14]

Religion Without Clergy

To the multitude such a venture seems impracticable—nay! unachievable—as we are accustomed by heritage to listen to the clergymen reading and explaining the Gospel rather than to study the Bible ourselves. In the dark ages, on account of the limitation of education, readers and instructors were essential. Today we are living in the age of progress. Education is compulsory and universal. We are able to read and study with reason, therefore we have no need for an explanator or interpreter of the words of God. We should study them carefully, analyze them cautiously and acquire the knowledge contained therein.

To appreciate the greatness of this principle, "Religion Without Clergy," we should study the past events of history. Thus we will observe that through the orthodoxy of religious organizations, dissension and strife has arisen amongst the followers after the departure of every Manifestation, usually ending with religious wars and the bloodshed of innocent individuals. The inspired teachings, which were revealed for the uplifting of humanity, became the whips of religious leaders, to fulfill their selfish desires and to rule over the oppressed masses.

Christianity made great progress during its early days. The monks collected the offerings from those who willingly gave and delivered them to those who were in need, even to the extent of carrying the offerings on their backs to the needy. Thus they performed the principles which Jesus commanded. As such, a period of time elapsed, until they began to build palaces called monasteries and lived the life of luxury and ease at the expense of the faithful followers, compelling them to

---

[13] *Lawh-i-Bisharat* ("Tablet of Glad-Tidings"). Ibid., p. 88.
[14] *Kitab-i-Aqdas* ("Most Holy Book"), paragraph 77.

accept their commands as supreme, equivalent to the words of the Master Jesus.

Not content with the spiritual rule which they possessed, the Christian clergy began to interfere with the affairs of state until they became the Supreme Ruler over the rulers. Then came the revolt of the state against the Church. King Henry VIII violated the law of the Vatican and proclaimed himself the head of the Church of England. Napoleon Bonaparte acted likewise, which eventually caused the division of state and church throughout the world. Martin Luther protested against the supremacy of the Holy See and founded the Protestantism of today, which in number of followers almost equals the Mother Church.

Islam also experienced the same phenomenon and its consequences, even to the extent of taking the life of the two grandsons of Muhammad. Hasan was poisoned and Hussein was beheaded. Caliph after caliph took control and in the name of religion ruled nearly fourteen hundred years, until the First World War, when the title of Caliph was abolished for the head of state, thus ending the Ottoman Dynasty.

All the past religions met the same fate after the departure of the Manifestation, through the selfishness of religious leaders, who corrupted the inspired teachings by misinterpretation and misguided the innocent masses. Grant us a survey of several churches on a Sunday morning. We will observe that each preacher is selecting a verse from the Gospel and interpreting it to harmonize with his sermon. The result is that many contradictory explanations of the same verse from the pulpit are causing confusion in the minds of the listeners.

According to the teachings of Baha'u'llah, the principles he commanded and the foundation he laid, the Baha'i organization should be composed of not less than nine members in each community,[15] elected by the vote of the members and subject to recall by popular vote. This duly-elected body shall appoint one of its members to be in charge of distribution of educational literature, free lectures, and promulgation

---

[15] See the *Kitab-i-Aqdas*, paragraph 30, in which Baha'u'llah writes: "The Lord hath ordained that in every city a House of Justice be established wherein shall gather counsellors to the number of Bahá [i.e. nine], and should it exceed this number it doth not matter."

of the teachings which are easy to understand and useful in our daily life, thus eliminating the need for clergy.

Baha'u'llah said:

> If ye differ in a matter, bring it to God, so long as the Sun is shining from the Horizon of this Heaven [i.e. while Baha'u'llah is alive on earth], but when He setteth, bring it to what was uttered by Him [i.e. his scriptures]. Verily it sufficeth the worlds.[16]

> Whosoever explaineth what hath descended from the Heaven of Revelation contrary to its obvious meaning, is of those who altereth the Supreme Word of God, and becometh of the losers in the manifest Book (the record of truth).[17]

> Blessed is he who cometh to the *Mashriqu'l-Adhkar* (rising-place of commemoration) in the early morning to glorify and praise God and ask forgiveness, and as he entereth in, he should sit down in silence and listen to the chanting of the scripture of God, the King, the Mighty, the Glorified. Verily the *Mashriqu'l-Adhkar* is every house built for My commemoration in cities and villages. Thus it was named on the part of the Throne, were ye of those who know.
>
> Those who chant the scriptures of the Merciful in beautiful melodies shall attain therefrom that which could not be equaled by the kingdoms of heavens and earths. By this they shall inhale the fragrance of My words which none knoweth today save those who are given the keen sight from this Beautiful Watchtower. Lo, verily they (the scriptures) attract the pure hearts into the spiritual realm, which could not be expressed, neither by writing nor by symbolizing. Blessed are those who hear.
>
> O people, help My chosen ones who rise up to commemorate Me amidst My creatures and elevate My Word in My Kingdom. They are the stars of the heaven of My Providence and the lamps of My guidance to all the people of creation. Whosoever teacheth contrary to what was revealed in My tablets is not of Me. Beware,

---

[16] *Kitab-i-Aqdas* ("Most Holy Book"), paragraph 53.

[17] Ibid., paragraph 105.

lest ye follow every wicked claimant. The tablets are adorned by the beautiful ornament of the Seal of the Breaker of Dawns, who speaketh amidst heavens and earths. Hold fast to My safe girdle and to the rope of My straight and firm command.[18]

Ye are forbidden from ascending upon pulpits. Whosoever wisheth to read to you from the scriptures of his God, let him sit down on a chair upon the platform and commemorate God, his Lord and the Lord of the worlds.[19]

It is decreed unto you to pray singly, whereas the congregational prayer[20] is abolished, save the prayer for the burial of the dead. Verily, He is the Commander, the Wise.[21]

Universal Tribunal

The establishment of a World Court is recommended here. The formation of the League of Nations was the fulfillment of this principle but unfortunately did not succeed, as it was without military power to enforce the laws agreed upon.

We hope that the present political leaders of the world will realize the importance of this principle and reestablish the Society of Nations for the sake of safeguarding the interest of the smaller nations.[22]

Baha'u'llah said:

---

[18] Ibid., paragraphs 115-117.

[19] Ibid., paragraph 154.

[20] Muslims traditionally have been encouraged to recite their daily prayers together in unison, led by an imam, at the mosque. Baha'u'llah abrogated this practice and directed Baha'is to pray individually. This, along with his ban of preaching from pulpits, indicates that Baha'u'llah envisioned the Baha'i faith as more of a personal spiritual practice rather than a religion with hierarchical forms.

[21] *Kitab-i-Aqdas* ("Most Holy Book"), paragraph 12.

[22] This part of the manuscript can thus be dated prior to 1945, when the United Nations was formed. The International Criminal Court has also been created since then. It is worth noting that the Baha'i vision of global governance is broader than any current or historical political institution, and has been interpreted in various ways.

The Eighth *Ishraq* ["Splendor"]:

This passage is written, at this time, by the Supreme Pen and is accounted [as part] of the Book of *Aqdas*.

The affairs of the people are in the charge of the men of the House of Justice of God. They are the trustees of God among His servants and the sources of command in His countries.[23]

O people of God! The trainer of the world is Justice, for it consisteth of two pillars, Reward and Retribution. These two pillars are two fountains for the life of the people of the world.

Inasmuch as for each day and time a particular decree or order is expedient, affairs are therefore entrusted to the House of Justice, so that it may execute that which it deemeth advisable at the time. Those souls who arise to serve the cause sincerely to please God shall be inspired by the invisible inspiration of God. It is incumbent upon all to obey (them, i.e. the House of Justice).

Administrative affairs are all in the charge of the House of Justice, but devotional acts must be observed according as they are revealed in the Book.

O people of Baha! Ye are dawning-places of the love and day-springs of the favor of God. Defile not the tongues with cursing and execrating anyone and guard your eyes from that which is not

---

[23] It is not clear whether Baha'u'llah envisioned the House of Justice to be a quasi-governmental or judicial body for only the Baha'is, or for all people regardless of religion. At the time when Baha'u'llah was writing, the Ottoman Empire had what was called the *Millet* system (from the Arabic word *milla*, "nation"), in which each religious group was viewed as a distinct national community which could manage its own affairs and exercise authority over its members in personal matters such as marriage, divorce, inheritance, etc. Religious courts were therefore a commonly accepted feature of life in the 19th century Middle East, and Baha'u'llah's conception of the *Bayt al-'Adl* (House of Justice) may have been simply the Baha'i analogue of this institution. However, some passages in his writings also indicate that he envisioned a global assembly that would be interfaith or secular in nature, perhaps as a House of Justice for all humanity. For example, in the *Lawh-i-Maqsud* he wrote: "The time must come when the imperative necessity for the holding of a vast, an all-embracing assemblage of men will be universally realized. The rulers and kings of the earth must needs attend it, and, participating in its deliberations, must consider such ways and means as will lay the foundations of the world's Great Peace amongst men." (*Gleanings From the Writings of Bahá'u'lláh*, 1990 pocket-size edition, section CXVII, p. 249).

worthy. Show forth that which ye possess (truth, etc.). If it is accepted, the aim is attained; if not, interference (with or rebuke of those who reject it) is not allowable. Leave him to himself, and advance toward God, the Protector, the Self-Subsistent. Be not the cause of sorrow (to anyone), how much less of sedition and strife! It is hoped ye may be trained under the shadow of the tree of divine favor and act in [accordance with] that which God desireth. Ye are all leaves of one tree and drops of one sea.[24]

Universal Language

Indeed this is the first cornerstone for the erection of the great temple of unity amongst humanity. The following are the commands of Baha'u'llah to the leaders of the world for the fulfillment of this principle:

> O people of the courts [of state, i.e. political officials] throughout the countries! Select one of the languages whereby all those who are on the earth should speak, and likewise one [script for] writing. Verily God elucidateth unto you that which benefiteth you and maketh you independent of others. Verily He is the Bounteous, the All-Knowing, the All-Wise. This is the cause of union, were ye of those who know, and the greatest means of concord and civilization, were ye of those who conceive.[25]

> The Sixth *Ishraq* is concerning union and harmony among servants [of God] (i.e. mankind). Through union the regions of the world have ever been illuminated with the light of the (divine) cause. The greatest means (for this end) is that the peoples should be familiar with each other's writing and language.
> We have formerly commanded, in the tablets, that the trustees of the House of Justice must select one tongue out of the present languages, or a new language, and likewise select one among

---

[24] *Lawh-i-Ishraqat* ("Tablet of Splendors"). Translated by Ali Kuli Khan in *Tablets of Baha'o'llah Revealed at Acca, Syria* (Chicago: Bahai Publishing Society, 1917), pp. 129-130.

[25] *Kitab-i-Aqdas* ("Most Holy Book"), paragraph 189.

the various scripts and teach them to children in the schools of the world, so that the whole world may thereby be considered as one native land and one place.[26]

Universal Peace

Advanced humanity is eagerly seeking universal peace and good will amongst mankind. The hearts are filled with the spirit of brotherly love, longing for lasting peace. The leaders of the world should realize the importance of this universal desire and use their efforts to bring it into being. Behold what became of the Egyptian, Persian, Roman, Macedonian, Babylonian and other great empires: The earth absorbed them all. Their empires were doomed, and their palaces ruined. A Persian philosopher-poet said, "Gaze with the eyes of recollection upon the palace of King Kesra; the cobwebs replaced the golden draperies and the owl is the lone musician."[27]

This land was given to us to live on it in peace and happiness, to produce from it our livelihood, to enjoy what nature has provided for us, and not to exploit or seek to possess it. The duration of our lives on this earth is limited, and sooner or later we will be absorbed by it, whether we are seated on the throne of gold and glory or on a ragged carpet.

Blessed is he who departs from this earth with a clear conscience and unstained hands. Blessed is he who leaves behind a monument of good acts and deeds. Blessed is he who shepherds the human flock to the pasture of knowledge and the pond of truth. Blessed is he who has sheltered the unfortunate under the dome of glory and served them with spiritual food. Blessed is he who crowned his head with the crown of justice, and adorned his temple with the garment of kindness.

---

[26] *Lawh-i-Ishraqat* ("Tablet of Splendors"). Translated by Ali Kuli Khan in *Tablets of Baha'o'llah Revealed at Acca, Syria* (Chicago: Bahai Publishing Society, 1917), pp. 127-128.

[27] According to legend, Kesra (also spelled Kisra or Kasra) was a great king of Persia who had an immense, lavish tomb like a palace. Today, the ruins of the *Taq-i Kisra* still stand near the town of Salman Pak, Iraq, as the only remains of Ctesiphon, the ancient capital of the Parthian and Sasanian Empires.

Blessed is he who occupied the throne of love and devoted his life to the service of his kind. Blessed is he who performed his duties to mankind and helped the needy generously. The glory of the Most Splendorous shall be with him forever and ever.

Baha'u'llah said:

> The Second *Ishraq*:
> We have commanded [the advent of] the Most Great Peace,[28] which is the greatest means for the protection of mankind. The rulers of the world must, in one accord, adhere to this command which is the main cause for the security and tranquility of the world. They (i.e. rulers) are day-springs of the power and dawning-places of the authority of God. We beg of God to assist them in that which is conducive to the peace of the servants (i.e. people).
>
> The account of this subject hath been previously revealed from the Supreme Pen. Blessed are those who act accordingly.[29]
>
> The word of God in the Ninth Leaf of the Exalted Paradise:
> Truly I say: Moderation is desirable in every affair, and when it is exceeded it leadeth to detriment. Consider the civilization of the people of the Occident, how it hath occasioned commotion and agitation to the people of the world. There hath appeared an infernal instrument, and such atrocity is displayed in the destruction of life, the like of which was not [before] seen by the eyes of the world, nor heard by the ears of nations. It is not possible to reform (or remove) these violent, overwhelming evils, except if the peoples of the world become united in affairs, or in one religion. Hearken ye unto the voice of this Oppressed One, and adhere to the Most Great Peace!

---

[28] The Baha'i concept of the "Most Great Peace" is a condition of the world in which all nations have united in a permanent accord, abandoning war and regarding all countries as one home for all. This alludes to the Biblical eschatological vision of a final, ultimate peace on earth brought about through the potent inspiration or presence of God.

[29] *Lawh-i-Ishraqat* ("Tablet of Splendors"). Translated by Ali Kuli Khan in *Tablets of Baha'o'llah Revealed at Acca, Syria* (Chicago: Bahai Publishing Society, 1917), p. 126.

A strange and wonderful instrument existeth in the earth; but it is concealed from minds and souls. It is an instrument which hath the power to change the atmosphere of the whole earth, and its infection causeth destruction.[30]

With careful study of the aforesaid principles, we the Baha'is should realize that we possess an ocean full of pearls of wisdom from which to gain knowledge, and a universe full of shining stars with which to be enlightened. Therefore we should meditate on the teachings and earnestly follow them.

---

[30] *Kalimat-i-Firdawsiyyih* ("Words of Paradise"). Ibid., p. 54. The "infernal," "strange and wonderful" instrument spoken of by Baha'u'llah is generally regarded by Baha'is as a prophecy of nuclear energy and nuclear weapons.

Above: Prof. Edward Granville Browne in Middle Eastern garb.
Below (L to R): Sayyid Hasan and Sayyid Husayn, Baha'i martyrs.

5

Stories of Baha'i Martyrs

Compiled by Shua Ullah Behai

This chapter is a compilation of stories of some of the most significant martyrs of the Baha'i faith in the late 1800s and the brutal persecution suffered by Baha'is, especially in Iran, during that period. All of these accounts were originally published by the British Orientalist Edward Granville Browne, a professor at Cambridge University, in two of his books about the Babi and Baha'i religions. Prof. Browne is generally regarded as the most important Western scholar of these new Middle Eastern faiths in the late 19th and early 20th century.

The four stories reproduced here—three from Persia and one from the Russian Empire—were selected by Shua Ullah Behai for inclusion in his book manuscript, appearing in a chapter called "Baha Ullah." I have divided the text of the first three sections into smaller paragraphs for ease of reading.

Note that in these historical accounts, the term *Babis* is used to refer to Baha'is, since Baha'ism was still usually considered a sect of Babism at the time of the events described.

—The Editor

In this faith, history repeated itself, and thousands of learned men sacrificed their lives for the enlightenment of their fellow-beings. The young progressive Iranians should realize the greatness of those noble souls, and their martyrdom for the freedom which they are enjoying today.[1]

The following articles are a few examples of the events that occurred.

The Martyrdom of Sayyid Hasan and Sayyid Husayn,[2] Recounted by 'Abdu'l-Baha[3]

[In 1879] there were amongst the inhabitants of Isfahan two brothers, Seyyids of Tabátabá,[4] Seyyid Hasan and Seyyid Huseyn, celebrated in those parts for piety, trustworthiness, and nobility; men of wealth, engaged in commerce, behaving towards all men with perfect kindliness and courtesy. And to all outward appearance no one had observed in either of these two brothers any swerving from what was best, much less any conduct or behaviour which could deserve torment or punishment; for, as is related, they were admitted by all (preeminent) in all praiseworthy and laudable qualities, while their deeds and actions were like exhortations and admonitions.

These had transacted business with Mir Muhammad Huseyn the Imam-Jum'a[5] of Isfahan; and when they came to make up their ac-

---

[1] In the mid 1900s, when Mr. Behai was writing, Iranian society and government were becoming more liberal and secular. This progress came to an end with the Islamic Revolution in 1979, which reestablished the political supremacy of conservative Shi'ite Muslim clergy. Since then, Baha'is in Iran have again faced severe persecution.

[2] These brothers are usually known to Baha'is as the *Núrayn-i-Nayyirayn* ("Twin Shining Lights"), and by the titles given to them by Baha'u'llah after their martyrdom, namely, *Sultánu'sh-Shuhadá* ("King of Martyrs") and *Mahbúbu'sh-Shuhadá* ("Beloved of Martyrs"), respectively.

[3] Edward G. Browne (Translator), *A Traveller's Narrative: Written to Illustrate the Episode of the Bab*, Volume II. English Translation and Notes (Cambridge: University Press, 1891), pp. 167-169.

[4] The *Tabataba'i* (also spelled *Tabatabaei*) are a family descended from Imam Hasan, the second of the Twelve Imams of Shi'ite Islam.

[5] The imam who leads the congregational prayers in one of Iran's major urban mosques.

counts it appeared that the sum of eighteen thousand *tumáns*⁶ was due to them. They (therefore) broke off (further) transactions, prepared a bond for this sum, and desired it to be sealed. This thing was grievous to the Imam-Jum'a, so that he came to the stage of anger and enmity. Finding himself in debt, and having no recourse but to pay, he raised clamour and outcry saying "These two brothers are Babis and deserve severe punishment from the king." A crowd at once attacked their house, plundered and pillaged all their goods, distressed and terrified their wives and children, and seized and despoiled all their possessions.

Then, fearing that they might refer the punishment to the step of the king's throne and loose their tongues in demand of redress, he (i.e., the Imam-Jum'a) fell to thinking how to compass their death and destroy them. He therefore persuaded certain of the doctors [of Islamic law] to co-operate with him, and they pronounced sentence of death. Afterwards they arrested those two brothers, put them in chains, and brought them before the public assembly. Yet seek as they might to fix on them some accusation, find some fault, or discover some pretext, they were unable to do so.

At length they said, "You must either renounce this faith [i.e. Babism and Baha'ism], or else lay down your heads beneath the sword of punishment." Although some of those present urged them saying, "Say merely 'We are not of this sect,' and it is sufficient, and will be the means of your deliverance and protection," they would by no means consent, but rather confirmed and declared it with eloquent speech and affecting utterance, so that the rage and violence of the Imam-Jum'a boiled over, and, not satisfied with killing and destroying them, they inflicted sundry indignities on their bodies after death to mention which is not fitting, and of which the details are beyond the power of speech.

Indeed in such wise was the blood of these two brothers shed that even the Christian priest of Julfá⁷ cried out, lamented, and wept on that

---

⁶ The translator notes that this amount of the Iranian currency at the time (also spelled *tomans*) was worth "about £5400" in 1891. In 2014 U.S. dollars, this would be nearly $800,000.

⁷ The Armenian quarter of the city of Isfahan. Present-day New Julfa.

day; and this event befell after such sort that every one wept over the fate of those two brothers, for during the whole period of their life they had never distressed the feelings even of an ant, while by general report they had in the time of famine in Persia spent all their wealth in relieving the poor and distressed. Yet, notwithstanding this reputation, were they slain with such cruelty in the midst of the people!

Further Martyrdoms in Isfahan Province, Recounted by Dr. Robert Bruce[8]

Aqa Mirza Ashraf of Abada was put to death for his religion in the most barbarous manner in Isfahan about October last [i.e. in 1888]. The hatred of the mullahs was not satisfied with his murder; they mutilated his poor body publicly in the *Maydán*[9] in the most savage manner, and then burned what was left of it.

Since then we have had two other persecutions of Babis, one in Sidih and the other in Najafabad.[10] In Sidih, where the Babi community is small, their houses were burned and their wives and children ill-treated. The men saved themselves by flight to Tehran, and I am told that about 25 of them have just returned to Isfahan and are in the Prince's stables in *bast* (i.e. sanctuary).[11]

In Najafabad there are about 2,000 Babis. They tried the same game

---

[8] Rev. Dr. Robert Bruce was an Irish Protestant evangelist and humanitarian worker for the Church Missionary Society, who lived in Julfa, Isfahan, in the late 1800s. This account of events in the area is an extract from a September 6, 1889 letter he wrote to Edward G. Browne. Published in Prof. Browne's book, *Materials for the Study of the Babi Religion* (Cambridge: University Press, 1918), pp. 291-292.

[9] The *Maidán-e Naqsh-e Jahán* ("Image of the World Square"), also called the Imam Square or Shah Square, is a large open plaza at the center of the city of Isfahan.

[10] Sidih was a village and Najafabad is a small city, both located near Isfahan.

[11] According to Sir Walter Townley, a British diplomat serving in Persia at the time, "On the return of these men to their homes about six weeks ago they were met and attacked by a mob headed by a man called Aqa Najafi, and seven or eight of them were killed and their bodies burnt with oil." (From a letter to Edward G. Browne, April 13, 1890, quoted in *Materials for the Study of the Babi Religion*, p. 294.)

with them, but some hundreds of them took refuge in the English Telegraph Office in Julfá, and the Prince[12] took their part and banished from Najafabad to Karbala the *mujtahid* who persecuted them, so the result is that they are freer now than they have ever been. I took very great interest in the poor people, not only for their own sakes, but for the sake of Persia also; as, if liberty is gained for them, it will be a great step towards breaking the power of the mullahs and getting liberty for all.

The Martyrdom of Haji Muhammad Riza, Recounted by Baron Rosen[13]

At 7 a.m. on September 8 (August 27, old style[14]), 1889, two fanatical Persian Shi'ites, Mashhadi 'Ali Akbar and Mashhadi Huseyn, threw themselves, dagger in hand, on a certain Haji Muhammad Riza of Isfahan, who was peaceably traversing one of the most frequented streets of Ishqabad,[15] and inflicted on him 72 wounds, to which he succumbed. Haji Muhammad Riza was one of the most respected of the Babis of Ishqabad. The crime was perpetrated with such audacity that neither the numerous witnesses of the occurrence, nor the constable who was on the spot could save the victim of this odious attack.

The assassins yielded themselves up to the police without any resistance; they were placed in a cab and conveyed to the prison. During

---

[12] Mass'oud Mirza, known as the *Zill-i Sultán* ("Shadow of the King"), was the governor of Isfahan. He was the eldest son of Naser al-Din Shah, but was not the heir to the throne because his mother was not from the Qajar family.

[13] Baron Victor Rosen (Viktor Romanovich Rozen) was a Russian Orientalist and professor of Arabic, who was one of the first Europeans to study the Babi and Baha'i faiths academically. This account of the assassination of a Baha'i in Russia was reproduced by Edward G. Browne in *A Traveller's Narrative: Written to Illustrate the Episode of the Bab*, Volume II. English Translation and Notes (Cambridge: University Press, 1891), pp. 411-412.

[14] The Julian calendar, which was superseded by the Gregorian calendar which is used today. Russia remained on the Julian calendar until 1918.

[15] Present-day Ashgabat, Turkmenistan. This city was near the border between Persia and the Russian Empire. It was under Persian control until 1881, when it was ceded to Russia.

the transit they fell to licking up the blood which was dripping from their daggers.

The examination, conducted with much energy by the military tribunal, gave as its result that Muhammad Riza had fallen victim to the religious bigotry of the Shi'ites. Fearful of Muhammad Riza's influence, the Shi'ites of Ishqabad, acting in accordance with the orders of mullahs who had come expressly for this purpose from Khurasan, [Persia] resolved to cut short the Babi propaganda by killing Haji Muhammad Riza. Knowing well, however, that the crime would not remain unpunished, they left it to chance to determine what persons should sacrifice themselves for the Shi'ite cause. Thus it was that the individuals named above became the assassins of Muhammad Riza, who had never injured them in any way.

The sentence of the tribunal was severe: 'Ali Akbar and Huseyn, as well as two of their confederates, were condemned to be hanged, but the penalty of death was commuted by His Majesty the Emperor [Alexander III of Russia] to hard labour for life.

This sentence was hailed by the Babis with an enthusiasm easy to understand. It was the first time since the existence of the sect, i.e. for nearly fifty years, that a crime committed on the person of an adherent of the new religion had been punished with all the rigour of the law. The impression produced on the chief of the sect, Baha['u'llah], appears to have been equally profound.

The Martyrs of Yazd, Recounted by a Baha'i in that City[16]

On the evening of the 23rd of the month of Ramadán A.H. 1308 (May 2, A.D. 1891) two persons, named respectively Aqa 'Ali Asghar Yuzdaruni and Aqa Gazargahi, went to the mosque of Amir Chaq-

---

[16] This account is reproduced by Edward G. Browne in *Materials for the Study of the Babi Religion* (Cambridge: University Press, 1918), pp. 304-308. Prof. Browne identifies it as a "translation of a letter written from Yazd on Shawwál 15 A.H. 1308 (May 24, 1891) by one Husayn to Hajji Sayyid 'Ali Shirazi at 'Ishqabad; and by him communicated to me." Its description of the persecution of Baha'is in Yazd, Iran, is similar to three other letters received and reproduced by Prof. Browne in the same book, including letters from Baha'u'llah's sons Abbas Effendi 'Abdu'l-Baha and Badi Ullah Bahai.

máq.[17] The people who were in the mosque recognised these two as Babis, and said to them, "You are Babis; why do you come to the mosque? Curse (the Bab), or we will torment you." They answered, "We are not Babis." "If you are not Babis," said their persecutors, "then curse." As they refused to curse or revile (the Bab), the people loaded them with abuse, and raised a clamour, crying, "These two men are Babis and have entered our mosque," and began to insult and maltreat them. Hajji Ná'ib, the *Farrásh-bashi*[18] of Prince Jalalu'd-Dawla,[19] who was present in the mosque, seized these two men and carried them before the Prince. They were severely beaten, cast into prison, and fined. Three days later they were released.

Three days after their release, Prince Jalalu'd-Dawla again demanded them at the hands of the *Farrásh-bashi*, who set himself to discover them. One Mahdi by name, the son of Ustad Báqir the druggist, offered his services to the *Farrásh-bashi*, saying, "I know where they are, and will point them out to you." So he accompanied the *Farrásh-bashi*, together with ten *farráshes*, as a guide, and led them to the house of Ustad 'Abdu'r-Rahim *Mushkí-báf*, where they arrested these two men and five others who were with them in the house. The seven they seized and brought before the Prince-governor, Jalalu'd-Dawla, striking them often on the way about the face and head, and finally casting them into prison. The names of the other five prisoners were, Mulla 'Ali of Sabzawar, Asghar, Hasan, Aqa Baqir, and Mulla Mahdi.

Next day Prince Jalalu'd-Dawla summoned them before him and interrogated them, bidding them curse and revile (the Bab), that he might set them free. They refused to do this, and frankly avowed that they were Babis.

The clergy, who have ever been mischief-makers and are always eager to provoke trouble and bloodshed, hastened to avail themselves of

---

[17] A major mosque in the city of Yazd. Also spelled Amir Chakhmaq.

[18] Chief of the *farráshes* (jail-keepers).

[19] Soltan Hossein Mirza Jalal ed-Dawleh was the son of Prince Mass'oud Mirza Zill-i Sultán and thus the grandson of Naser al-Din Shah. He was the governor of Yazd.

this opportunity, and urged Prince Jalalu'd-Dawla to kill these seven men. So far as can be ascertained, the Prince wrote his consent and desired the clergy to ratify it with their seals and signatures. So they agreed to make these seven pass beneath the sword of cruelty and injustice. While the Prince was interrogating them, some of his own attendants who were in his presence were filled with wonder and amazement, saying to themselves, "These have done nothing for which they deserve to incur wrath and punishment!"

On the morning of Monday the 9th of Shawwál (May 18, 1891) the following members of the clergy, Shaykh Hasan of Sabzawar, Shaykh Muhammad Taqi of Sabzawar, Mirza Sayyid 'Ali *Mudarris*, Mulla Hasan of Ardakan, and Mulla Husayn of Ardakan came to Prince Jalalu'd-Dawla's palace. They were concealed behind a curtain, and the seven Babis were then brought in. The Prince said to them, "I wish to set you free. Now by my head I conjure you to tell me truly whether you are Babis or not." "Yes," they replied, "we are Babis," confessing and acknowledging it. The clergy who were concealed behind the curtain of deceit heard their avowal, and at once wrote out and sealed the warrant for their death. The executioner was summoned forthwith and ordered to slay them. 'Ali Asghar was strangled with the bow-string in the Prince's presence in the most cruel manner. The other six were led through the bazaars with music and beating of drums to the marketplace, where they were killed one after another. The rabble of the people mobbed them, striking them with sticks, spitting on them, reviling them and mocking them. As the throat of each one was cut, the mob tore open the body to look at the heart, saying, "How bold they are in the presence of death and the death-warrant and the headsman! With what strength of heart do they yield up their life, while no word of cursing or reviling escapes their lips! We must see what sort of hearts they have."

When they had slain all the seven, they poured tar over their bodies and set fire to them. Never before this day have such behaviour, such malevolence and wickedness, been seen in any people as are seen amongst these Shi'ites in Persia. One of the Babis (he who was named Asghar) they bound to a tree in the marketplace, cut off his hands with the sword, then ripped open his belly, and finally beheaded him. Another, Hasan, they wounded in the head with swords and sticks, driving him about the marketplace and bidding him curse and revile (the Bab). "What should I say?" he answered, "do whatever is commanded you." So they cut him in pieces.

Till sunset of that day the bodies of these seven were in the hands of the roughs and rabble of the populace, and they brutally pelted them with stones, set fire to them, and burned them. After they had killed them and burned their bodies they asked permission of Prince Jalalu'd-Dawla to illuminate the city, and he gave them permission for two nights, but such was the disorderly conduct of the roughs and the exultation of the clergy on the first night that permission for the next night was withdrawn.

The widows and children of these seven men dared not, for fear of the mob, leave their houses or enter the bazaars even to obtain food and drink, and so remained without water or food until at length some Christian merchants of the Dutch nation sent provisions to them.

After the blood of these seven had been shed, a Babi named Hajji Mulla Muhammad Ibrahim *Mas'ila-gú*, who had gone to a place ten hours distant from the city towards the mountains, was followed and arrested by Hajji Ná'ib the *Farrásh-bashi*, severely beaten, brought back with every indignity to the city, carried before Prince Jalalu'd-Dawla, and cast into prison. His wife and children went to the Dutch merchants and entreated them to intercede and deliver him from the cruel clutches of his persecutors. These accordingly went before the Prince, but he would not admit their mediation, and declared that he had already sent the man to Tehran. On the following night he slew him with his own hands and had the body cast into a well.

By reason of these events many persons have fled into the surrounding country, and a strange commotion and disquietude prevail. The authorities have made it a pretext for extorting money, and have fined and mulcted many persons. They have also arrested several more, who are still in prison. They seized one named Aqa Husayn, a silk-merchant, who had in his possession nearly five hundred *túmáns'* (£150)[20]

---

[20] About $20,000 in 2014 U.S. dollars.

worth of silk belonging to himself and others, all of which they took from him. The clergy and Prince Jalalu'd-Dawla have made this thing a means of obtaining money, and have extorted large sums from all (the Babis), leaving their wives and children without bread.

Never before has such injustice been seen. Why should loyal and obedient subjects, who have been guilty of no offence, and who seek but to reform men's morals and to increase the welfare of the world, be subjected to such cruel persecutions by order of the foolish ones of the earth who show themselves under a garb of knowledge? Why should they be compelled to flee as outlaws and to wander as beggars from door to door, or be scattered abroad in mountains and deserts? Loyalty forbids us to appeal to foreign powers, and we can but cry in our anguish, "O God! We submit with patience and resignation to what we suffer at the hands of these godless, merciless and cruel people!" Thus do we tell our sorrow to our God, praying Him to take away from us the wickedness and oppression of the froward and ignorant ones of the earth. We have no helper but God, and none to support and succour us save Him.

6

Selections from the Writings of Baha'u'llah

Compiled by Shua Ullah Behai

This chapter is a compilation of some of the writings of Baha'u'llah in English translation, selected by Shua Ullah Behai and included in his book manuscript in a chapter called "Baha Ullah." All of these are among the better-known writings of the Baha'i founder, with the possible exception of the "Surah of the Branch,"[1] a document which was a source of controversy in the years following Baha'u'llah's death and was read by Baha'is more often in the past than today. Perhaps somewhat surprisingly, in this chapter Mr. Behai does not include any excerpts from the *Hidden Words* or the *Seven Valleys and Four Valleys*, which are among Baha'u'llah's most popular works; nor does he reproduce any of the laws of the central scriptural text of the Baha'i faith, the *Kitab-i-Aqdas*. Several of the Hidden Words and various teachings from the *Aqdas* are included elsewhere in the book, however.

Most of the writings of Baha'u'llah in this chapter are from translations that were publicly available at the time when Mr. Behai was compiling them, but a few are either his own translations or from sources this editor was unable to determine. None of them are the officially approved version of Baha'i holy writings used by Baha'is today, but some of these translations were used by Baha'is for many years.

Specifically, the "Glad Tidings" and "Book of My Covenant"[2] are

---

[1] More commonly known as the "Tablet of the Branch."
[2] Called the "Book of the Covenant" in the mainstream Baha'i tradition.

from a 1923 book called *Bahai Scriptures: Selections from the Utterances of Baha'u'llah and Abdul Baha*, with some minor changes by Mr. Behai. The epistle to the Shah of Iran is partly from *Bahai Scriptures* and partly from Edward G. Browne's translation of a portion of the document in *A Traveller's Narrative*. The epistles to Queen Victoria, Napoleon III, and the Pope are mostly from a translation by Prof. Browne in a long academic article entitled "The Bábís of Persia. II. Their Literature and Doctrines,"[3] with some small parts from *Bahai Scriptures*.

The epistles to the German Emperor and to the rulers of America, the "Words of Wisdom," and the "Surah of the Branch" are all probably original translations by Shua Ullah Behai. The translation of the latter document was somewhat based on the version in *Bahai Scriptures* but is significantly different in numerous places, presumably reflecting Mr. Behai's study of the Arabic original and his editorial judgment. He was fluent in Arabic, Persian, and English, and had access to his father's extensive library of Baha'u'llah's writings including original calligraphies, so he was capable of producing high-quality translations of his own.

In his translation of the Surah of the Branch, Mr. Behai indicates that the "Branch" described in the document is a reference to Baha'u'llah himself, thus rejecting the interpretation that it referred to his son Abbas Effendi, who was known by the title *Ghusn-i-A'zam* ("The Greatest Branch") or more commonly known today as 'Abdu'l-Baha. In the mainstream Baha'i tradition, this Surah is believed to be about 'Abdu'l-Baha, not Baha'u'llah, and has been used as a proof text for Baha'u'llah's purported intention that his eldest son should be regarded as occupying an extraordinarily lofty station—a station which would seem to be that of a "Manifestation of God" if the document is to be taken literally, though Baha'i doctrine today does not place 'Abdu'l-Baha in this metaphysical category. In Shua Ullah Behai's view, the Surah of the Branch describes Baha'u'llah's own claims about himself as a Manifestation of Divinity branching out from the Godhead—an interpretation that I consider to be more likely, especially since the document was written

---

[3] Published in *The Journal of the Royal Asiatic Society of Great Britain and Ireland*, Volume 21 (London: W. H. Allen & Co., 1889), pp. 881-1009.

in the 1860s, when Abbas Effendi was only in his early 20s and Baha'u'llah's ministry would continue on for yet another roughly 25 years.

One of the challenges of Baha'u'llah's writings is that he frequently switches back and forth from the divine voice to his own human voice. Often he seems to perceive the Manifestation of God as a divine agent who overtakes or merges with his own self, but other times he speaks as a servant of God, to whom the Deity is external. When speaking as God, he often refers to himself (i.e. Baha'u'llah) in the third person, which could mistakenly give the impression that he is speaking of someone else (as might be the case in the Surah of the Branch). These varied modes or styles of communication, and the difficult to discern transitions between them, can make the writings of Baha'u'llah somewhat confusing both for translators and readers—especially those with little or no background in Islamic mysticism. In the "authorized" translations used today, Baha'is have tended to obscure these subtle issues and regard all of Baha'u'llah's words as simply the Voice of God, but I don't think this does justice to the complexity of Baha'i metaphysics concerning the process of revelation. The translations presented in this chapter, though stylistically perhaps less elegant, seem to offer a more literal picture of Baha'u'llah's self-concept, relationship and sometimes identification with his God; and my notes on these texts identify and explore the religious background and key theological concepts that are essential to a nuanced understanding.

—The Editor

Baha'u'llah's "Glad Tidings"[4]

This is the Voice of El-Abha,[5] which is being raised from the Supreme Horizon, in the Prison Akka!

He is the Declarer, the Knower, the Omniscient!

---

[4] *Lawh-i-Bisharat.*

[5] Arabic *al-Abhá*, meaning "The Most Glorious." This title is the superlative of *Bahá*, "Glory," and refers to the Manifestation of God as revealed through Baha'u'llah.

God testifieth and the Appearance of His Names and Attributes beareth witness that, by the raising of the Voice and by the Exalted Word, it hath been (our) aim that the ears of the people of the world should be purified through the *Kawthar*[6] of Divine Utterance from false narrations and be prepared to hearken unto the blessed, pure, exalted Word which hath appeared from the treasury of the knowledge of the Maker of Heaven and Creator of Names. Blessed are those who are just!

O people of the earth:

The First Glad Tidings which is conferred in this Most Great Manifestation on all the people of the world, from the Mother Book,[7] is the abolishing of the decree of religious warfare from the Book. Exalted is the Beneficent One, the Possessor of Great Bounty—the One through whom the door of grace is opened before all in the heaven and earth.

The Second Glad Tidings: It is sanctioned that all the nations of the world consort with each other with joy and fragrance. Consort ye, O people, with (the people of) all religions with joy and fragrance! Thus hath the orb of permission and desire shone forth from the horizon of the Heaven of Command of God, the Lord of the creatures.

The Third Glad Tidings is the study of various languages. This command hath formerly flowed from the Supreme Pen. Their Majesties, the kings—may God assist them—or the counselors [i.e. government ministers] of the earth must consult together, and appoint one of the existing languages, or a new language, and instruct the children therein, in all the schools of the world; and the same must be done with respect to writing also [i.e. a common script]. In such case the earth will be considered as one. Blessed is he who heareth the Voice and fulfilleth

---

[6] A river in Paradise, mentioned in the Qur'an.

[7] In the Islamic and Baha'i traditions, the "Mother Book" or "Mother of the Book" (*umm al-kitáb*), also called the "Preserved Tablet" (*al-lawh al-mahfúz*) is envisioned as a heavenly book which is the source of all revelation, from which the scriptures of earth are derived. The "Supreme Pen" (*al-qalam al-a'la*), i.e. God in the role of revealer of truth to humanity, is believed to transmit the messages from this transcendent divine book through a revelatory agent, i.e. a prophet or Manifestation. In some mystical traditions of Islam which influenced the Baha'i faith, the Pen is seen in much the same way as Christians see Christ as the preexistent "Word" or *Logos*, through whom all things have been created.

that which is commanded on the part of God, the Lord of the Great Throne!

The Fourth Glad Tidings: Let every one of the kings—may God strengthen them—arise to protect and assist this oppressed community (i.e. the Baha'is). Each (Baha'i) must precede the other in serving and showing love unto them. This matter is obligatory upon all. Blessed are those who practice!

The Fifth Glad Tidings: In every country or government where any of this community reside, they must behave toward that government with faithfulness, trustfulness, and truthfulness. This is that which is revealed from the presence of the Ancient Commander! It is obligatory and incumbent on the people of the world in general to assist this Most Great Cause—which hath descended from the Heaven of the Will of the King of Preexistence—that perchance the fire of animosity which is ablaze in the hearts of some of the nations, may be quenched through the water of divine wisdom and lordly commands and exhortations, and that the light of union and accord may irradiate and illuminate the regions (of the world). It is hoped that through the favor of the appearances of the power of God (i.e. kings and rulers) the armaments of the world will be changed into peace, and corruption and conflict will vanish from among men.

The Sixth Glad Tidings is the Most Great Peace, the account of which hath been formerly revealed from the Supreme Pen. Joy unto whosoever adhereth thereto and practiceth that whereunto he is commanded on the part of God, the Knower, the Wise!

The Seventh Glad Tidings: Men are permitted to have their choice in the manner of attire, and in the cut of the beard and its dressing. But, beware, O people, not to make yourselves as playthings to the ignorant!

The Eighth Glad Tidings: The pious practices of the monks and priests among the people of His Holiness the Spirit (i.e. Christ)[8]—upon Him is the peace of God and His glory!—are remembered before God; but, in this Day, they must abandon solitude for open places (i.e. the society of men), and engage in that which may profit both themselves

---

[8] In Islam, Jesus is often referred to by the title *Ruh Ullah* ("Spirit of God").

and other men. We have conferred permission on them all to engage in matrimony, so that there may appear from them those (i.e. children) who may celebrate the praise of God, the Lord of the seen and unseen and the Lord of the Lofty Throne!

The Ninth Glad Tidings: The sinner, when in a state wherein he findeth himself free and severed from all else save God, must beg for (God's) forgiveness and pardon. It is not allowable to declare one's sins and transgressions before any man, inasmuch as this hath not been, nor is conducive to securing God's forgiveness and pardon. At the same time such confession before the creatures leadeth to one's humiliation and abasement, and God—exalted is His glory—doth not wish for the humiliation of His servants. Verily He is Compassionate and Beneficent!

A sinner must, (privately) between himself and God, beg for mercy from the Sea of Mercy and ask forgiveness from the Heaven of Beneficence, and then say:

> O my God! O my God! I beg of Thee—by the blood of Thy lovers, who were so attracted by Thy sweet utterances that they betook themselves unto the lofty summit, the place of Great Martyrdom, and by the mysteries concealed in Thy knowledge, and by the pearls deposited in the sea of Thy bestowal—to forgive me, and my father and my mother. Verily Thou art the Most Merciful of the merciful! There is no God but Thee, the Forgiving, the Beneficent!
>
> O my Lord! Thou beholdest the essence of error advancing toward the sea of Thy gift, and the weak one toward the kingdom of Thy power, and the poor one toward the sun of Thy wealth. O my Lord! Disappoint him not of Thy generosity and bounty; deprive him not of the graces of Thy days, and turn him not away from Thy door which Thou hast opened before all in Thy heaven and earth.
>
> Alas! Alas! My transgressions have prevented me from drawing nigh unto the court of Thy sanctity, and my trespasses have kept me afar from turning unto the tents of Thy glory. I have indeed wrought that which Thou hast forbidden me; I have neglected that which Thou hast commanded me! I beg of Thee, by

the King of Names, to decree for me from the Pen of Grace and Bestowal that which will draw me near unto Thee and will purify me from my sins which have intervened between me and Thy forgiveness and pardon. Verily, Thou art the Powerful, the Bounteous! There is no God but Thee, the Mighty, the Gracious!

The Tenth Glad Tidings: We have removed from the epistles and tablets the decree of effacing the books (i.e. the books of other religions)[9] as a favor from the presence of God, the Sender of this Great Message!

The Eleventh Glad Tidings: To study sciences and arts of all descriptions is allowable; but such sciences as are profitable, which lead and conduce to the elevation of mankind. Thus hath the matter been decreed on the part of God, the Commander, the Wise!

The Twelfth Glad Tidings: It is made incumbent on every one of you to engage in some occupation, such as arts, trades, and the like. We have made this—your occupation—identical with the worship of God, the True One. Reflect, O people, upon the mercy of God and upon His favors, then thank Him in mornings and evenings.[10] Waste not your time in idleness and indolence, and occupy yourselves with that which will profit yourselves and others beside you. Thus hath the matter been decreed in this tablet from the horizon of which the sun of wisdom and divine utterance is gleaming. The most despised of men before God is he who sits and begs. Cling unto the rope of means, relying upon God, the Causer of Causes. Every soul who occupieth himself in an art or trade—this will be accounted an act of worship before God. Verily this is from no other than His great and abundant favor!

The Thirteenth Glad Tidings: The affairs of the people are placed

---

[9] Islam traditionally viewed non-Abrahamic religions as pagan idolatry, and commanded that all idols be destroyed. Similar to Baha'u'llah's abrogation of the doctrine of holy war in the First Glad Tidings, here he appears to be instructing his followers to practice religious tolerance by respecting the scriptures of all faiths.

[10] Baha'u'llah may be suggesting that people should limit their prayers and reserve most of the day for work, rather than praying throughout the day. Islam mandates prayer at least five times a day for all Muslims, including twice during the middle of the workday.

in the charge of the men (i.e. members)[11] of the House of Justice of God. They are the trustees of God among His servants and the day-springs of command in His countries. ...[12]

The Fourteenth Glad Tidings: To undertake journeys for the sake of visiting the tombs of the dead is not necessary.[13] If those who have means and wealth should give to the House of Justice the amount which would otherwise be expended on such journeys, this would be acceptable before God. Happy are those who practice.

The Fifteenth Glad Tidings: Although a republican form of government profiteth all the people of the world, yet the majesty of kingship is one of the signs of God. We do not wish that the countries of the world should be deprived thereof. If statesmen combine the two into one form [i.e. constitutional monarchy], their reward will be great before God.

Agreeable to the requirements of former times, the former religions confirmed and commanded religious warfare, prohibited association and intercourse with other peoples, and forbade the reading of certain books, but in this Most Great Manifestation and mighty message, favors and gifts of God have pervaded all, and the irrefutable command is revealed in that which already hath been mentioned from the horizon of the will of the Lord of Preexistence. We praise God—exalted and glorified is He!—for that which He hath revealed in this Day, the blessed, the mighty, the wonderful! Were all the people of the world each to possess a hundred thousand tongues and speak in (God's) praise and glorification until the day which hath no end, verily all their thanks

---

[11] This parenthetical note may indicate that Shua Ullah Behai believed that Baha'u'llah's use of the word "men" in regard to the House of Justice was gender-inclusive, rather than intended to limit the membership of that institution to men only. Had he agreed with the mainstream Baha'i interpretation that prohibits women from serving on the Universal House of Justice, he likely would have seen no need to clarify the word "men" in the original text.

[12] The Thirteenth Glad Tidings is virtually identical to the Eighth *Ishraq* in the Tablet of *Ishraqat*. The text redacted here is quoted in full in the "Universal Tribunal" section of Chapter 4.

[13] Making pilgrimages to the tombs of Imams and other revered spiritual leaders was a common practice among Muslims at the time when Baha'u'llah was writing, especially in the Shi'ite tradition.

would not equal (what is due) even a single one of the favors mentioned in this epistle!—whereunto testifieth every man of knowledge and discernment and every man of wisdom and understanding. I beg of God—exalted is His glory!—and entreat Him to enable the kings and sovereigns, who are dawning-places of power and daysprings of might, to execute His precepts and commands.

Verily, He is the Powerful, the Mighty, and Worthy to grant.

From Baha'u'llah's Epistle to Naser al-Din Shah of Iran

O King of the earth, hear the voice of this servant. Verily I am a man who hath believed in God and His signs, and I have sacrificed myself in His way; to this do the afflictions wherein I am—the like of which none amongst mankind hath borne—testify, and my Lord the All-Knowing is the witness to what I say. ...

O King, verily I was as (any) one amongst mankind, slumbering upon my couch. The gales of the All-Glorious passed by me and taught me the knowledge of what hath been. This thing is not from me, but from One (who is) Mighty and All-Knowing. And He bade me proclaim betwixt the earth and the heaven, and for this hath there befallen me that whereat the eyes of those who know overflow with tears. I have not studied those sciences which men possess, nor have I entered the colleges; inquire of the city wherein I was, that thou mayest be assured that I am not of those who speak falsely. This is a leaf which the breezes of the will of thy Lord, the Mighty, the Exalted, have stirred. Can it be still when the rushing winds blow? No, by the Lord of the names and attributes! ...

As to this sect, it is twenty years and more that they have been tormented by day and by night with the fierceness of the royal anger, and that they have been cast each one into a (different) land by the blasts of the tempests of the King's wrath. How many children have been left fatherless! How many fathers have become childless! How many mothers have not dared, through fear and dread, to mourn over their slaughtered children! Many (were) the servants (of God) who at eve were in the utmost wealth and opulence, and at dawn were beheld in the extreme of poverty and abasement! There is no land but hath been dyed with their blood and no air whereunto their groanings have not arisen. And during these few years the arrows of affliction have rained down without intermission from the clouds of fate. Yet, notwithstanding all these visitations and afflictions, the fire of divine love is in such fashion kindled in their hearts that, were they all to be hewn in pieces, they would not forswear the love of the Beloved of all the dwellers upon earth; nay rather with their whole souls do they yearn and hope for what may befall (them) in the way of God.

O King! The gales of the mercy of the Merciful One have converted these servants and drawn them to the region of the (Divine) Unity... but some of the doctors (of theology) of Persia have troubled the most luminous heart of the King of the Age [i.e. the Shah] with regard to those who are admitted into the Sanctuary of the Merciful One and those who make for the *Ka'ba*[14] of Wisdom. O would that the world-ordering judgment of the King might decide that this servant should meet those doctors, and, in the presence of His Majesty the King, adduce arguments and proofs! This servant is ready, and hopeth of God that such a conference may be brought about, so that the truth of the matter may become evident and apparent before His Majesty the King. ...

We ask God to sanctify the hearts of certain of the doctors from rancor and hatred, that they may regard things with eyes which closure overcometh not; and to raise them unto a station where the world and the leadership thereof shall not turn them aside from looking toward the Supreme Horizon, and where (anxiety for) gaining a livelihood and (providing) household goods shall not divert them from (the thought of) that day whereon the mountains shall be made like carpets.[15] Though they rejoice at that which hath befallen us of calamity, there shall come a day whereon they shall wail and weep. By my Lord, were I given the choice between the glory and opulence, the wealth and dignity, the ease and luxury wherein they are, and the distress and affliction wherein I am, I would certainly choose that wherein I am today,

---

[14] Used here metaphorically, the Kaaba (*al-Ka'ba*) is the shrine in Mecca toward which all Muslims pray, and to which they make pilgrimage (*Hajj*).

[15] The day of the advent of the Messiah and the Kingdom of God. Cf. Isaiah 40:4-5, Luke 3:5-6.

and I would not now exchange one atom of these afflictions for all that hath been created in the kingdom of production! [i.e. the material world] ...

We ask God to extend His shadow, that the unitarians[16] may haste thereto, and that the sincere may take shelter therein; and to bestow on (these) servants flowers from the garden of His grace and stars from the horizon of His favors; and to assist him [i.e. the Shah] in that which he liketh and approveth; and to help him unto that which shall bring him near to the Dayspring of His Most Comely Names, that he may not shut his eyes to the wrong which he seeth, but may regard his subjects with the eye of favor and preserve them from violence. And we ask Him—exalted is He—to make thee a helper unto His religion and a re-garder of His justice, that thou mayest rule over (His) servants as thou rulest over those of thy kindred, and mayest choose for them what thou wouldst choose for thyself.

Verily He is the Potent, the Exalted, the Protecting, the Self-Subsistent.

From Baha'u'llah's Epistle to Queen Victoria of the United Kingdom

O Queen in London: Hear the voice of thy Lord, the King of (all) creatures from the Divine Lote-Tree that "There is no God but Me, the Precious, the Wise." Lay aside what is on the earth; then adorn the head of dominion with the diadem of thy glorious Lord; verily He hath come into the world with His Most Great Glory, and that which was mentioned in the Gospel hath been fulfilled. The land of Syria hath been honored by the advance of its Lord, the King of men, and the exhilaration of the wine of union hath seized upon the regions of the South and North: Blessed is he who discovereth the scent of the Merciful (i.e.

---

[16] Monotheists or believers in the oneness of God. Among Muslims, unitarianism is regarded as the central tenet of faith, as opposed to polytheism or idolatry, which is regarded as the greatest sin. Baha'u'llah's allusion here to the concept of unitarianism may have been intended to imply that the materialism of the clergy was a form of idolatry, preventing them from renouncing worldly comfort and position in the path of faith as Baha'u'llah had done.

God), and advanceth to the Dawning-place of Beauty in this clear morning. ...

It hath reached us that thou hast forbidden the selling of slaves and handmaidens: This is what God hath commanded in this marvelous Manifestation. God hath recorded unto thee the reward of this; verily He is the Discharger of the rewards of the well-doers. ...

And we have heard that thou hast entrusted the reins of deliberation into the hands of the Commonwealth. Thou hast done well, for thereby the bases of the edifices of (all) affairs are made firm, and the hearts of those who are under thy shadow (i.e. protection), both of the high and low, are made tranquil. But it behooveth them [i.e. the members of parliaments] to be (as) trustees amongst the servants (of God), and to regard themselves as guardians over whosoever is in all the earth. ... And when any one [of them] turneth towards the [parliamentary] assembly, let him turn his glance to the Supreme Horizon, and say, "O God: I ask thee by Thy Most Splendid Name to assist me unto that whereby the affairs of Thy servants may prosper, and Thy countries may flourish; verily Thou art powerful over all things." Blessed is he who entereth the assembly in the regard of God, and judgeth betwixt men with pure justice; is he not of those who prosper?

O ye leaders of assemblies, whether there [in England] or in some other country, think of results and speak of that whereby the world and its conditions may be reformed; were ye of those who deliberate. And look on the world as the body of a man who was created sound and whole, but diseases have attacked him from various and diverse causes, and his soul is not at ease for a day, but rather his sickness increaseth, in that he hath fallen under the control of unskillful physicians who are hurried away by vain desires, and are of those who stray madly. And if one limb of his limbs become sound in one age of the ages through a skillful Physician, the other limbs remain as they were: thus doth the Wise and Knowing One inform you. ... And that which God hath made the most mighty remedy and the most complete means for its health is the union of whosoever is upon the earth in a single matter, and a single law. This can never be possible except through a skillful Physician, perfect and strengthened (by God). By my life! this is the truth, and aught else is nothing but evident error.

From Baha'u'llah's Second Epistle to Napoleon III, King of France

O King of Paris! Tell the priest not to ring the bells. By God, the True One! the Most Glorious Bell hath appeared on the Temple of the Most Great Name, and the fingers of the will of thy Lord, the High, the Supreme, ring it in the World of Eternal Power, through His Most Splendid Name. Thus have the most mighty signs of thy Lord descended once more, that thou mayest arise to commemorate God, the Creator of the earth and the heaven... The Unconstrained hath come in the shadow of lights to vivify the beings by the fragrance of His merciful Name, to unite the people and bring them together at this Table which hath descended from heaven.

Beware not to deny the grace of God after its descent. This is better for you than that which ye have, because what ye have will vanish and that on the part of God will endure. Verily, He is the Ruler over that which He pleaseth. ...

We have sent one whom We have strengthened with the Holy Spirit, that he may give you tidings of this Light which hath shone forth from the horizon of the will of your Lord, the Exalted, the Most Splendid, and whose effects have appeared in the West, that ye may turn unto Him in this day...

Arise amongst the servants (of God) in My Name and say, "O people of the earth, advance toward Him, who hath advanced toward you, for verily He is the Face of God amongst you, and His evidence in your midst, and His proof unto you."...

This is that whereof the Spirit [Christ] gave you tidings when He brought the truth, and the Jewish doctors opposed Him, until they committed that whereat the Holy Spirit lamented and those who are near to God wept. ...

Say: O concourse of monks! Do not withdraw yourselves in churches and sanctuaries; come forth (thence) by my permission, then occupy yourselves with that whereby your souls shall be profited, and the souls of mankind. ... He who cleaveth to the house [i.e. the monastery or church] is indeed as one dead! It is meet for man that he should produce that whereby (other) beings shall profit; and he who hath no fruit is fit for the fire. ...

Verily, O King, we heard from thee a word which thou didst speak when the King of Russia asked of thee concerning what was settled as to the order of war; verily thy Lord is Wise and Informed. Thou didst say, "I was asleep in my bed (when) the cry of the servants (of God) who were wronged, even till they were drowned in the Black Sea, awoke me." Thus did we hear, and God is the Witness of what I say. Thou canst witness that it was not (their) cry, but (thine own) lust (of war) which awoke thee, inasmuch as we tried thee and found thee afar off. ... Hadst thou been the speaker of that speech, thou wouldst not have cast the book of God behind thy back when it was sent unto thee on the part of one Mighty and Wise.[17] Verily we tried thee therewith, and did not find thee in that state whereto thou didst pretend; arise and make reparation for what hath passed away from thee. The world shall perish, and what thou hast, and the Kingdom remain to God, thy Lord, and the Lord of thy fathers who were of yore. ...

Because of what thou hast done, affairs shall be changed in thy kingdom, and empire shall depart from thine hands, as a punishment for thine action; then shalt thou find thyself in manifest loss, and commotion shall seize the people there, unless thou arisest to assist in this matter and followest the Spirit in this straight path.

Thy glory hath made thee proud: By my life! Verily it shall not endure, but shall pass away, unless thou takest hold of this firm rope. We have seen humiliation hastening after thee, while thou art of those that sleep.

Epistle to King William I, German Emperor[18]

O King of Berlin! Hearken to the call issued from this Manifest Temple, that there is no God but Me, the Eternal, the Incomparable, the Ancient.

Let not self-conceit bar thee from the Dawning-Place of Appearance, or self-desire veil thee from the Ruler of the [heavenly] Throne and the earth. Thus the Supreme Pen admonisheth thee. Verily, He is the Clement, the Generous.

---

[17] A previous tablet sent by Baha'u'llah to Napoleon III.
[18] *Kitab-i-Aqdas* ("Most Holy Book"), paragraph 86.

Remember him who was greater than thee in influence and station [i.e. Napoleon III]: Where is he, and where are his possessions?[19] Awake, and be not of those who are asleep.

He cast the tablet of God behind his back when we informed him what hath befallen us from the hosts of tyranny. Thereupon, he was taken by humiliation from all directions until he returned unto earth with great loss.

O King! Think of him and of those who were like unto thee, who conquered countries and ruled over the creatures; how God made them descend from palaces unto tombs.[20] Be admonished and of those who remember.

Epistle to the Kings and Presidents of America[21]

O Kings of America[22] and the Presidents of Republics therein! Hear ye the chanting of the Great Spirit (*Varqa*, ["Dove"]) on the Eternal Branch, that there is no God but He, the Everlasting, the Forgiver, the Generous.

Adorn the body of the government with the ornament of justice and piety, and its head with the crown of glorifying your God, the Cre-

---

[19] As Baha'u'llah predicted, Napoleon III fell from kingship and the Second French Empire came to an end. Following his catastrophic defeat at the hands of William I in the Franco-Prussian War, the ousted French monarch died in exile in England in 1873.

[20] Only a few paragraphs later in the *Kitab-i-Aqdas*, Baha'u'llah again addresses Germany: "O banks of the Rhine! We have seen you covered with gore, inasmuch as the swords of retribution were drawn against you; and you shall have another turn. And We hear the lamentations of Berlin, though she be today in conspicuous glory." (paragraph 90). Baha'is interpret this as a prophecy of Germany's defeat in the two World Wars.

[21] *Kitab-i-Aqdas* ("Most Holy Book"), paragraph 88.

[22] At the time when Baha'u'llah was writing, some Central and South American countries had not yet gained their independence from European monarchies such as Spain. Furthermore, in North America, Canada was in the process of redefining its relationship with the United Kingdom, and became a "dominion" or self-governing colony within the British Commonwealth, under the sovereignty of the crown.

ator of Heaven. Thus the Dawning-Place of Names commandeth you on the part of the All-Knowing, the All-Wise.

The Promised One hath appeared in the Glorified Station through whom the face of the visible and the invisible existence hath smiled. Avail yourselves of the Day of God. Verily to meet with Him is better for you than all that upon which the sun shineth, were ye of those who know.

From Baha'u'llah's Epistle to Pope Pius IX

O Pope! Rend asunder the veil![23] The Lord of Lords hath come in the shadow of clouds, and the matter hath been decided on the part of God, the Powerful, the Unconstrained.

Disclose the (divine) splendors by the authority of thy Lord; then ascend into the Kingdom of Names and Attributes: thus doth the Supreme Pen command thee on the part of thy Lord, the Mighty, the Controller. Verily He hath come from heaven another time, as He came from it the first time;[24] beware lest ye oppose Him as the Pharisees opposed Him without evidence or proof. On His right side floweth the River of Grace, and on His left side the sweet Water of Justice; before Him go the angels of Paradise with the standards of signs.

Beware lest names withhold you from God, the Maker of the earth and the heavens; leave the creatures behind thee, then advance to thy Lord by whom all horizons were illuminated. We have adorned the Kingdom by our name, El-Abha (The Most Glorious); thus hath the matter been decided on the part of God, the Creator of all things. ...

Dost thou dwell in palaces, while the King of the Manifestation is in the most ruined of abodes (Akka)? Leave palaces to those who desire them, then advance to the Kingdom with spirituality and fragrance. ...

---

[23] This may be an allusion to Matthew 27:50-51. The veil or curtain in the Jewish Temple hid the Holy of Holies, the innermost sanctuary which contained the Ark of the Covenant, from sight of the people. Only the High Priest was ever allowed to pass beyond the veil, once a year on the Day of Atonement, thus entering into God's presence. According to the Gospel, the Temple veil ripped apart at the moment when Jesus died and his spirit left his body.

[24] Cf. John 3:13.

The breath of God is diffused throughout the world, because the Desired One hath come in His Most Great Glory. Lo! every stone and clod crieth, "The Promised One hath appeared, and the Kingdom is to God, the Powerful, the Mighty, the Pardoning." Beware lest theology prevent thee from the King of what is known, or the world from Him who created it and left it. Arise in the name of thy Lord the Merciful amidst the assembly of beings, and take the Cup of Life in the hand of assurance; drink therefrom, or not; then give to drink to those who advance of the people of (different) religions. ...

Remember when the Spirit came; he who was the most learned of the doctors of his age [i.e. the Jewish High Priest Caiaphas] gave sentence against Him in his city, while those who caught fish believed in Him. Be admonished, then, O people of understanding! ... And when We come unto you another time We see you fleeing from us; therefore doth the eye of My compassion weep over my people. Fear God, O ye who are in expectation.

Look at those who objected to the Son [of God] when He came unto them with dominion and power; how many Pharisees were awaiting His meeting and making humble supplications to God for His appearance; but when the fragrance of union diffused itself and perfection was disclosed, they turned from Him and objected to Him... Look likewise at this time. How many monks seclude themselves in churches in My Name; and when the appointed time was completed, and We disclosed to them perfection, they did not know Me;—after that they [still] call upon Me at eventide and at dawn [in their prayers]. We see them veiled from Myself by My Name (Jesus Christ). ...

Do ye read the Gospel, and (still) do not flee to the Glorious Lord? This beseemeth you not, O concourse of learned ones! ... The Word which the Most Faithful wrote hath appeared: It hath indeed descended into the form of man in this time.[25] Blessed is the Lord, who is the Father: He hath come with His most mighty power amongst the nations; turn towards Him, O concourse of the good! ... Lo, the Father hath come, and that which hath been promised unto you in the Kingdom is accomplished; this is a Word which was concealed behind the

---

[25] Cf. John 1:14.

veil of might, and when the promised (time) came, it shone forth from the horizon of the (Divine) Will with manifest signs.

My body was imprisoned to set you free, and We accepted humiliation for the sake of your glory; follow the Lord, the Lord of Glory and the Kingdom, and follow not every proud infidel. My body longeth for the Cross, and my head for the spear in the way of the Merciful One (i.e. God), that the world may be purified from sin… The people of the *Furqan*[26] (i.e. Muhammadans) have arisen, and tormented me with torments whereat the Holy Spirit crieth out; and the thunder roars, and the eyes of the clouds weep because of the unbelievers.

Whosoever imagineth that calamity will hinder Baha from that which God, the Creator of (all) things, willeth, say (unto him), No! by the descent of the rains, nothing shall prevent him from the mention of his Lord. By God the Truth! even though they burn him on the earth, verily he will lift up his head in the midst of the sea, and will cry "Unto God indeed belongeth whosoever is in the heavens and the earth." And even though they cast him into a dark pit, they shall find him on the summits of the mountains, crying "The Desired One hath come by the authority of Might and Sovereignty." And though they bury him in the earth, he will arise from the horizons of heaven, and will speak with the loudest voice, "Baha hath come to the Kingdom of God, the Holy, the Mighty, the Unconstrained." And though they shed his blood, every drop thereof shall cry out and call upon God by this Name whereby the perfumes of the Garment are diffused through (all) regions. …

O people of the Son [i.e. Christians]! We have sent unto you John (the Baptist) another time [as the Bab]. Verily he crieth in the wilderness of the *Bayan*, "O creation of beings! Make clear your eyes! The day of vision and meeting hath come nigh. Prepare then the way, O people of the Gospel. The day wherein shall come the Lord of Glory hath come nigh; prepare to enter into the Kingdom."[27] Thus was the matter decreed on the part of God, the Cleaver of the Dawn. …

---

[26] Arabic *al-Furqán*, "the standard" (for distinguishing between good and evil). This is a term used in Islam to refer to the Qur'an.

[27] Cf. Matthew 3:1-3.

This is indeed the Father, whereof Isaiah gave you tidings,[28] and the Comforter whom the Spirit (i.e. Christ) promised.[29] ... Hasten unto Him and follow not every denying infidel. And if the eye of any one oppose him in this, it behooveth him to pluck it out; and if his tongue oppose him, it behooveth him to cut it out.[30] Thus was it written by the Pen of Eternity on the part of the King of Contingent Being; verily He hath come another time for your deliverance, O people of creation. ... The Glorious One crieth continuously from the horizon of the Pavilion of Might and Greatness, and saith, "O people of the Gospel! He hath come into the Kingdom who was out of it; and today we see you standing at the gate. Rend the veils by the power of your Lord, the Mighty, the Munificent, and then enter into My Kingdom in My Name." Thus doth He command you who desireth for you enduring life; verily He is powerful over all things.

Blessed are those who have known the Light, and have hastened towards it! Behold, they are in the Kingdom; they eat and drink with the elect. And [yet] we see you, O children of the Kingdom, in darkness; this is not meet for you. Do ye fear to meet the Light because of your deeds? Advance thereto. ... Verily He said, "Come, that I may make you fishers of men;"[31] and today We say, "Come, that we may make you vivifiers of the world." Thus was the decree ordained in a tablet written by the Pen of Command.

"Words of Wisdom"[32] Revealed by Baha'u'llah

In the name of God, the Exalted, the Most High.

The essence of all good is trust in God, obedience unto His command, and contentment with His pleasure.

The essence of wisdom is apprehension of God, the dread of His power and judgment, and the fear of the appearance of His justice and punishment.

---

[28] Isaiah 9:6.
[29] John 15:26.
[30] Cf. Matthew 5:29.
[31] Matthew 4:19.
[32] *Asl-i-Kullu'l-Khayr.*

The essence of religion is to testify unto that which hath been revealed from God and follow that which hath been ordained in His mighty Book.

The essence of glory is the contentment of man with what hath been bestowed on him and satisfaction with that which hath been ordained for him.

The essence of love is for man to turn to the Beloved One, and detach himself from all else but Him, and desire naught save that which is the desire of his Lord.

The source of recollection is to make mention of the Remembered One and forget all else beside Him.

The essence of reliance is for the servant [of God] to pursue his profession and calling in this world, to hold fast unto the Lord, to seek naught but His grace, for in His hands lieth the destiny of the servant in his transformation and future abode.

The essence of detachment is for man to turn his face towards the Lord, to enter His presence, behold His countenance and stand as witness before Him.

The essence of creation is to testify to one's poverty and submit to the will of the Lord, the Sovereign, the Gracious, the Chosen.

The essence of benevolence is for the servant to recount the blessings of His Lord, and render thanks unto Him under all conditions and at all times.

The source of wealth is love for me; with my love all beings can dispense with everything and without my love everything is wanting for everything. Verily this is that which hath been written by the mighty and luminous Pen.

The essence of faith is scarcity of words and abundance in deeds; he whose words exceed his deeds is better dead than alive.

The essence of health is silence and looking forward to results and living in seclusion.

The origin of determination is in spending on one's self, on his family and the poor brothers in faith.

The source of power and courage is the promotion of the word of God, and steadfastness in His love.

The source of all evil is for man to turn away from his Lord and look forward to his own desires.

The origin of the burning fire is to question the revelations of God, dispute what hath been revealed from Him, turn away from Him, and show pride before Him.

The source of all learning is the knowledge of God, exalted be His Glory, and this cannot be achieved save through the knowledge of His Manifestation.

The source of humiliation is to pass by the shadow of the Merciful and seek shelter in the shadow of the evil one.

The source of impiety is disbelieving in the One God, reliance on aught else beside Him and fleeing from His decree.

The origin of all that we have revealed is justice, and that is for man to free himself from fancy and imitation, look forward unto the appearances of creation with the sight of Oneness and see with a searching eye into all matters.

Real loss is to him who spent his days not knowing himself; thus we have taught thee the Words of Wisdom, that thou mayest thank in thyself God thy Lord and glory therein amongst the people of the world.

The Surah of the Branch[33]

Revealed in truth from the heaven of the will of our Lord, the Merciful, the Compassionate.

He is eternal in My Most Glorious (Abha) Horizon!

Verily the cause of God hath come upon the clouds of utterances, and the polytheists are in this day in great torment. Verily the hosts of revelation have descended with banners of inspiration from the Heaven of the Tablets in the name of God, the All-Powerful, the Almighty! Then the monotheists rejoice in the victory of God and His Dominion, and the deniers will then be in great perplexity.

O ye people! Do you flee from the mercy of God after it hath encompassed the existent things created between the heavens and earths? Do not alter the mercy of God upon you, and deprive not yourselves

---

[33] *Súriy-i-Ghusn* or *Súrat al-Ghusn*.

thereof; and whosoever turneth away therefrom will be in great loss. Verily, mercy is like unto the verses which have descended from the One Heaven [i.e. closest to God's abode] and from them the monotheists are given to drink the wine of life, whilst the polytheists drink from the fiery water.[34] And when the verses of God are read unto them, the fire of hatred is enkindled within their hearts. Thus have they averted the mercy of God from themselves and are of those who are ignorant.

Enter, O people, beneath the shelter of the Word, then drink therefrom the choice wine of inner significance and elucidation, for therein is the Chalice of the Glorious One (God), and it hath appeared from the horizon of the will of your Lord, the Merciful, with wonderful lights.

Say: Verily, the sea of Preexistence hath branched forth from this Greatest Ocean. Blessed is he who abideth upon its shore, and is of those who are residing thereon. Verily, this Sacred Temple of Abha, the Branch of Holiness (i.e. Baha'u'llah Himself) hath branched forth from the *Sadratu'l-Muntaha* (the Lote-Tree).[35] Blessed is whosoever sought shelter beneath it and was of those who rest therein. Say: Verily, the Branch of the Cause hath sprung forth from this Root which God hath firmly planted in the Land of the Will,[36] and the Limb of which hath

---

[34] Cf. Qur'an 47:15.

[35] Also spelled *Sidrat al-Muntahá*, the "Lote Tree of the Limit" is a metaphor in Islam for the boundary in heaven beyond which no one in creation can pass, reserved for God alone. According to Islamic tradition, the Prophet Muhammad traveled to this uttermost limit in the "Night Journey" (known as *al-Isrá* and *al-Mi'ráj*), a visionary experience, and there received revelation from God. Baha'u'llah uses the term Sadratu'l-Muntaha in his writings to refer to the Manifestation of God in his preexistent and eternal divine station, with which the human personalities known as "Messengers" or "Manifestations" of God are identified as they speak and act as God's representatives on earth.

[36] The "Land of the Will" may be a reference or allusion to the realm of *Lahut*, which in Baha'i cosmology is the highest place before reaching God's own unreachable Essence (*Hahut*). It is the realm of the preexistent Word of God, the Supreme Pen, and the Lote Tree of the Limit—all of which are metaphors for the same basic concept: the first and highest emanation of God. Lahut is often translated as "Heaven/Kingdom of Command," "All-Glorious Horizon," and "Heavenly Court."

ascended to a station which encompasseth all the existence.[37] Therefore, exalted be He for this Creation, the Lofty, the Blessed, the Powerful, the Inaccessible.

O ye people! Draw nigh unto Him (i.e. the Branch, Baha'u'llah Himself) and taste therefrom the fruits of wisdom and knowledge on the part of the All-Powerful, the All-Knowing. And whosoever hath not tasted therefrom shall be deprived of the mercy of God, even though he hath partaken of all that is in the earth, were ye of those who know.

Say: Verily a Word hath been separated from the Greatest Tablet (i.e. God Himself) as a favor, and God hath adorned it with the Mantle of Himself and made it Sovereign over all in the earth and a sign of His grandeur and power among the creatures; that the people shall praise, through it, their Lord, the Almighty, the Powerful, the Wise; and that they shall glorify, through it, their Creator, and sanctify the Self of God that governeth all things. Verily, this is naught but a revelation on the part of the All-Knowing, the Ancient One.

Say, O people, praise God for His Manifestation, for verily He is the Greatest Favor upon you and the Most Perfect Blessing upon you, and through Him every decayed bone is enlivened. Whosoever turneth unto Him (i.e. the Manifestation Baha'u'llah) hath surely turned unto God; and whosoever turneth away from Him hath turned away from My Beauty, hath denied My Proof and is of those who transgress.

Verily, He is the Trust of God amongst you and His Charge with you, and His Manifestation unto you and His Appearance among the servants who are nigh. Thus have I been commanded to convey to you the message of God, your Creator, and I have delivered to you that which I was commanded, whereupon God testifieth thereunto, then His angels and His Messengers, and then His holy servants.

Inhale the fragrance of the *Rizwan*[38] (i.e. Paradise) from His Roses

---

[37] Baha'u'llah likens himself to a "Branch" or "Limb" on the Divine Lote Tree, i.e. a specific instance of the Manifestation of God reaching out through the appendage of a particular human appearance. This metaphor also calls to mind the Biblical prophecy of the Messiah as "a shoot" that "shall come out from the stump of Jesse, a Branch [that] shall grow out of his roots" (Isaiah 11:1), i.e. another branch of the Davidic Kingship of God's anointed ones.

[38] Also spelled *Ridvan*.

and be not of those who are deprived. Avail yourselves of the grace of God upon you and be not veiled therefrom, and verily, We have sent Him forth in the temple (i.e. form) of man; praise be unto the Lord, the Creator of whatsoever He wisheth through His command, the Inviolate, the Wise.

Verily, those who withhold themselves from the shelter of the Branch (i.e. Baha'u'llah Himself) are lost in the wilderness and are consumed by the fire of self-desire and were of those who perish.

Hasten, O people, unto the Shelter of God, that He may protect you from the heat of the Day [i.e. the Day of Judgment] whereon none shall find for himself any shelter or refuge save beneath the shelter of His name, the Forgiver, the Merciful. Clothe yourselves, O people, with the garment of certainty in order that He may protect you from the dart of imaginations and superstitions, and that ye may be of those who are assured in those days wherein none shall be firmly established in the Cause except by severing himself from all that is in the hands of the people and turning unto the Holy and Radiant Appearance.

O people! Do ye take the *Jibt* as a helper unto yourselves other than God, and do ye take the *Taghut* as a Lord besides your Lord, the Almighty, the Omnipotent?[39] Forsake, O people, their mention, and then take the Chalice of Life in the name of your Lord, the Merciful; verily, by God, through a drop thereof the universe is animated, were ye of those who know.

Say: In this day there is no refuge for anyone save in the Cause of God, and no retreat for any soul save in God. Verily this is the truth and there is naught after truth but manifest error.

Verily, God hath made it incumbent upon every soul to preach His Cause according to his means. Thus hath the command been ordained by the Fingers of Might and Power upon the tablets of majesty and greatness.

And whosoever enlivens a soul in this Cause is like unto one who hath enlivened all the people, and God shall send him forth on the Day

---

[39] *Jibt* and *Taghút* are idols mentioned in the Qur'an (4:51-52). Jibt was a literal idol. Taghut refers more generally to the arrogant, and to evil, Satan, and falsehood. Baha'u'llah's point seems to be that his followers should not turn to anyone else besides himself for spiritual guidance.

of Resurrection in the Paradise of Oneness in the garment of Himself, the All-Protector, the Almighty, the Generous. Verily this will be your assistance to your Lord, and naught else shall ever be mentioned in this Day before God, your Lord and the Lord of your forefathers.

And thou, O servant, hearken unto that by which We admonished thee in the tablet,[40] then seek thou the grace of your Lord at all times. Then spread the tablet among those who have believed in God and His verses, that they may follow that which is contained therein and be of those who are praiseworthy.

Say: O people! Cause no corruption in the earth and dispute not with the people, for verily, this hath not been worthy of those who have chosen in the shelter of their Lord a station which hath been secure in truth.

And if ye find one athirst, give him to drink from the Chalice of *Kawthar* and *Tasním*;[41] and if ye find one endowed with an attentive ear, read unto him the verses of God, the All-Powerful, the Almighty, the Merciful. Unloose the tongue with good utterance, then remind the people if ye find them advancing unto the sanctuary of God; otherwise leave them to themselves, then forsake them in the abyss of hell. Beware lest ye scatter the pearls of inner significance before every barren, blind one. For verily, the blind is deprived of beholding the lights and is unable to differentiate between the stone and the Holy Precious Stone.

Verily, wert thou to read to the stone for a thousand years the new and dear verses, will it understand in itself or will they take any effect therein? Nay! by thy Lord, the Merciful, the Compassionate. And if thou readest all the verses unto the deaf, will he hear a word thereof? Nay! by My Beauty, the Powerful, the Ancient. Thus have We delivered unto thee of the jewels of wisdom and elucidation, that thou mayest be gazing unto the direction of thy Lord and be severed from all the creatures.

---

[40] This appears to be addressed to the specific recipient of the document, Mirza 'Ali Rida Mustawfi. Baha'u'llah may be referring to a previous tablet sent to the same recipient, or to the Surah of the Branch itself.

[41] Like *Kawthar*, *Tasním* is a Qur'anic term for a source of holy water in Paradise.

May the Spirit rest upon thee and upon those who have dwelt in the abode of Holiness and were in manifest steadfastness in the Cause of their Lord.

The Book of My Covenant[42] (The Will of Baha'u'llah)

Although the Supreme Horizon is devoid of the vanities of the world, yet in the treasury of trust and resignation We have placed a priceless and unequalled inheritance for the heirs. We have not placed (therein) a treasure, neither have We added to the pain.

By God! In wealth fear is concealed and peril is hidden. Behold and then reflect upon that which the Merciful One hath revealed in the Qur'an: "Woe unto every maligner and backbiter who heapeth up riches and counteth them over."[43] There is no continuance in the riches of the world. That which is subject to mortality and undergoeth a change hath never been and is not worth regarding. But as is well known, the purpose of this Oppressed One in enduring these adversities and calamities, the revelation of the verses and the manifestation of the proofs [of prophethood], hath been to quench the fire of hatred and animosity, so that perchance the horizon of the minds of the people of this world may shine with the light of concord and attain the real tranquility. The sun of this explanation is shining and arising from the horizon of the divine tablet; all must look toward it.

O people of the world! I enjoin you to that which is the means of the elevation of your station. Hold to the virtue of God and grasp the hem of that which is just. Verily I say, the tongue is for mentioning that which is good; pollute it not with evil speech. God hath forgiven you that which is past; hereafter ye must all speak that which is befitting. Avoid execration, reviling, and that which is aggravating to man.

The station of man is high. A short while since, this exalted word was revealed from the repository of the Pen of Abha: "This is a great and blessed Day, but that which hath been hidden in man is and shall be disclosed (in this Day)." The station of man is great if he holdeth to

---

[42] *Kitáb-i-'Ahdí*, or *Kitáb-i-'Ahd* in the mainstream Baha'i tradition.

[43] Qur'an 104:1-2.

reality and truth, and if he be firm and steadfast in the [divine] commands. The true man appeareth before the Merciful One like unto the heavens: his sight and hearing are the sun and moon, his bright and shining qualities are the stars; his station is the highest one; his traces are the educators of the existence. Every believer who hath found the perfume of the Garment [i.e. the Manifestation of God] in this Day and turneth with a pure heart toward the Supreme Horizon, he is mentioned as one of the followers of Baha upon the Red Page [i.e. in the Book of Life].

Take the Chalice of My Favor in My name; then drink from it to My remembrance, the Dearest, the New.

O people of the world! The creed of God is for love and union; make it not the cause of discord and disunion. In the sight of the men of discernment and those who are holding to the Manifestation, that which is the means of preservation and the cause of the ease and tranquility of the servants [of God] is revealed from the Supreme Pen; but the ignorant of the earth who are fostered in ambition and lust are heedless of the matured wisdom of the True Wise One and are speaking and working in imaginations and fancies.

O saints of God and His loyal ones! Kings are the appearances of power and the daysprings of the might and wealth of the True One. Pray in their behalf, for the government of the earth is ordained to those souls; but the hearts He hath appointed for Himself.

He hath forbidden dispute and strife with an absolute prohibition in the Book. This is the command of God in this Greatest Manifestation, and He hath preserved it from any order of annulment and hath adorned it with the ornament of confirmation. Verily, He is the All-Knowing, the All-Wise.

It is incumbent upon all to aid those souls who are the daysprings of authority and the dawning-points of command, and who are adorned with the ornament of equity and justice. Blessing be upon the princes and learned ones in Baha. These are My trusted ones amongst My servants; these are the rising-points of My commandments amongst My creatures. Upon them be My glory, My mercy, and My grace which have surrounded all existence.

It is revealed in the *Kitab-i-Aqdas* concerning this, that which from the horizons of its words the light of the divine bounties gleam, rise, and glitter.

O My Branches (i.e. sons)! In this existence the greatest strength and the most perfect power is hidden and concealed; look towards it and gaze in the direction of its union and not in seeming differences. This is the Testament of God, that the Branches (*Aghsan*), Twigs (*Afnan*[44]), and relations (*muntasibín*) must each and every one look to the Greatest Branch (*Ghusn-i-A'zam*) [i.e. Abbas Effendi]. Reflect upon that which is revealed in My Book, the *Aqdas*: "When the Ocean of My Presence hath disappeared and the Book of Origin is achieved to the end, turn your faces towards him whom God hath purposed, who hath branched from this Pre-Existent Root."[45] The aim of this blessed verse hath been the Greatest Branch. We have likewise elucidated the command as a favor from before Us; and I am the Generous, the All-Dispensing.

Verily God hath ordained the station of the Mightiest Branch (*Ghusn-i-Akbar*) [i.e. Mohammed Ali Effendi] after the station of the former. Verily, He is the Ordainer, the Wise. We have surely chosen the Mightiest (*Akbar*) after the Greatest (*A'zam*) as a command from the All-Knowing, the Omniscient.

The love of the Branches is incumbent upon all, but God hath not ordained to any of them any right from the properties of the people.

O My Branches, My Twigs, and My relations! We enjoin you to the virtues of God, to follow that which is just and beneficial, and that by which your station will be exalted. Truly I say, piety is the greatest commander for the assistance of the divine religion, and the hosts that befit this commander have been and are good, pure, and pleasing qualities and deeds.

Say: O servants, make not the cause of order to be the cause of confusion, and make not the reason of union to be the occasion of discord! It is hoped that the people of Baha will look towards the blessed word, "Say: All are from the presence of God"; and this exalted word is like unto water for extinguishing the fire of hatred and animosity which is

---

[44] Relatives of the Bab.
[45] *Kitab-i-Aqdas* ("Most Holy Book"), paragraph 121.

deposited in all minds and hearts. The different creeds will attain the light of real union through this simple word. Verily, He speaketh the truth and guideth in the path, and He is the Merciful, the Mighty, and the Wonderful!

Respect and regard for the Branches is incumbent upon all for the honoring of the Cause and the exaltation of the Word; and this command hath been both previously and again recorded and mentioned in the books of God. Blessed is he who attaineth that which hath been commanded from the presence of the Commander, the Pre-Existent.

Also respect is (enjoined) for the ladies of the household of God, and the Twigs and the relations. I enjoin you to the service of the nations and the pacification of the world.

From the Kingdom of the revelation of the aim of the people of the world is revealed that which is the cause of the life of the world and the salvation of the nations. Hearken to the admonitions of the Supreme Pen with a true ear. Verily they are better unto you than all that which is upon earth. To this beareth witness My Book, the Mighty, the Wonderful.

7

Tributes to Baha'u'llah and His Mission

Compiled by Shua Ullah Behai

This chapter is a compilation of excerpts from three articles about Baha'u'llah, his life, teachings, and mission, written by important figures in the Baha'i faith in the early 1900s. These articles were selected by Shua Ullah Behai and included in his book manuscript in a chapter called "Baha Ullah." Considerably longer excerpts from the articles were originally included by Mr. Behai, but I have cut them further for the sake of brevity.

The authors of these tributes to Baha'u'llah are his eldest son ('Abdu'l-Baha), and two of the foremost teachers of the Baha'i faith at the time: one from the mainstream tradition (Mirza Abu'l-Fadl), the other from the Unitarian Baha'i tradition (Ibrahim Kheiralla). All of them were essentially in agreement in their celebration and characterization of the founder of their faith.

—The Editor

His name was Husayn Ali [Nuri], later Baha'u'llah. He was born in the city of Tehran, the capital of Iran, November 12, 1817 A.D. His ascension took place at Bahji, Acre District, Palestine, on May 29, 1892.

The following articles written by well-known personages briefly recount the life and claims of Baha'u'llah.

From an Address by Abbas Effendi, 'Abdu'l-Baha[1]

The Blessed Perfection Baha'u'llah belonged to the royal family of Persia. From earliest childhood he was distinguished among his relatives and friends. They said, "This child has extraordinary power." In wisdom, intelligence, and as a source of new knowledge, he was advanced beyond his age and superior to his surroundings. All who knew him were astonished at his precocity. ...

Until his father passed away, Baha'u'llah did not seek position or political station notwithstanding his connection with the government. This occasioned surprise and comment. It was frequently said, "How is it that a young man of such keen intelligence and subtle perception does not seek lucrative appointments? As a matter of fact every position is open to him." This is an historical statement fully attested by the people of Persia.

He was most generous, giving abundantly to the poor. None who came to him were turned away. The doors of his house were open to all. He always had many guests. This unbounded generosity was conducive to greater astonishment from the fact that he sought neither position nor prominence. In commenting upon this, his friends said he would become impoverished, for his expenses were many and his wealth becoming more and more limited. "Why is he not thinking of his own affairs?" they inquired of each other; but some who were wise declared, "This personage is connected with another world; he has something sublime within him that is not evident now; the day is coming when it will be manifested." In truth the Blessed Perfection was a refuge for every weak one, a shelter for every fearing one, kind to every indigent one, lenient and loving to all creatures.

He became well-known in regard to these qualities before His Holiness the Bab appeared. Then Baha'u'llah declared the Bab's mission to be true and promulgated his teachings. The Bab announced that the

---

[1] This speech by the son of Baha'u'llah on the "History of the Bahai Cause" was delivered on April 18, 1912, in New York City. Published in *Bahai Scriptures: Selections from the Utterances of Baha'u'llah and Abdul Baha*, edited by Horace Holley (New York: Brentano's, 1923), pp. 285-290.

greater manifestation would take place after him and called the promised one "Him whom God would manifest," saying that nine years later the reality of his own mission would become apparent. ... The Bab was martyred in Tabriz, and Baha'u'llah, exiled into 'Iráq-Arabí[2] in 1852, announced himself [as the new divine teacher] in Baghdad. For the Persian government had decided that as long as he remained in Persia the peace of the country would be disturbed; therefore he was exiled in the expectation that Persia would become quiet. His banishment, however, produced the opposite effect. New tumult arose and the mention of his greatness and influence spread everywhere throughout the country. The proclamation of his manifestation and mission was made in Baghdad. He called his friends together there and spoke to them of God. Afterward he left the city and went alone into the mountains of Kurdistan where he made his abode in caves and grottoes. A part of this time he lived in the city of Sulaymaniyah. Two years passed during which neither his friends nor family knew just where he was.

Although solitary, secluded, and unknown in his retirement, the report spread throughout Kurdistan that this was a most remarkable and learned personage gifted with a wonderful power of attraction. In a short time Kurdistan was magnetized with his love. During this period Baha'u'llah lived in poverty. His garments were those of the poor and needy. His food was that of the indigent and lowly. An atmosphere of majesty haloed him as the sun at midday. Everywhere he was greatly revered and beloved.

After two years, he returned to Baghdad. Friends he had known in Sulaymaniyah came to visit him. ... The Persian government [had] believed the banishment of the Blessed Perfection from Persia would be the extermination of his cause in that country. These rulers now realized that it spread more rapidly. His prestige increased, his teachings became more widely circulated. The chiefs of Persia then used their influence to have Baha'u'llah exiled from Baghdad. He was summoned to Constantinople by the Turkish authorities. While in Constantinople he

---

[2] Arab Iraq ('Iráq-i 'Arab in Persian), which was part of the Ottoman Empire. At the time, there was also a Persian region called Iraq, or 'Iráq-i 'Ajam, in western Iran.

ignored every restriction, especially the hostility of ministers of state and clergy. The official representatives of Persia again brought their influence to bear upon the Turkish authorities and succeeded in having Baha'u'llah banished from Constantinople to Adrianople, the object being to keep him as far away as possible from Persia and render his communication with that country more difficult. Nevertheless the cause still spread and strengthened.

Finally they consulted together and said, "We have banished Baha'u'llah from place to place, but each time he is exiled his cause is more widely extended, his proclamation increases in power, and day by day his lamp is becoming brighter. This is due to the fact that we have exiled him to large cities and populous centers. Therefore we will send him to a penal colony as a prisoner so that all may know he is the associate of murderers, robbers, and criminals; in a short time he and his followers will perish." The Sultan of Turkey then banished him to the prison of Akka in Syria.[3]

When Baha'u'llah arrived at Akka, through the power of God he was able to hoist his banner. His light at first had been a star; now it became a mighty sun and the illumination of his cause expanded from the east to the west. Inside prison walls he wrote epistles to all the kings and rulers of nations, summoning them to arbitration and Universal Peace. ...

The Blessed Perfection was a prisoner twenty-five years. During all this time he was subjected to the indignities and revilement of the people. He was persecuted, mocked, and put in chains. In Persia his properties were pillaged and his possessions confiscated. ...

He bore these ordeals, suffered these calamities and difficulties in order that a manifestation of selflessness and service might become apparent in the world of humanity; that the "Most Great Peace" should become a reality; that human souls might appear as the angels of heaven; that heavenly miracles would be wrought among men; that human faith should be strengthened and perfected; that the precious,

---

[3] In the Ottoman Empire, Syria was a large region which also included most of present-day Israel, Palestine, and Lebanon, beyond the borders of the modern nation of Syria.

priceless bestowal of God—the human mind—might be developed to its fullest capacity in the temple of the body; and man become the reflection and likeness of God, even as it hath been revealed in the Bible: "We shall create man in our own image."[4] ... [that] although [we are] pilgrims upon earth we might travel the road of the heavenly kingdom; although needy and poor we might receive the treasures of life eternal. For this has he borne these difficulties and sorrows.

From *The Behai Proofs* by Mirza Abu'l-Fadl Gulpaygani[5]

Although the calamities and afflictions suffered by the Blessed Perfection during His stay in Akka were beyond the endurance of man, yet, through the providence of God and His assistance, these torrents of disaster did not prevent Him from reforming the character of His followers, and the assault of hardships and grievances did not stop the spread of His teachings. For the tribulations of Baha'u'llah were not confined to the contradictions of the tyrannical clergy, or the calumnies of fanatical divines. Nor were His sufferings caused only by the injustice of statesmen and the covetousness of rulers, who accounted oppression of strangers and showing hostility towards those outside their faith as a religious duty. It was a greater task to beautify the character of His own people, than to defend Himself against exterior enemies. Guarding His followers from committing unseemly actions was more difficult than enduring the persecutions of the outsiders. For these people who had just embraced the Baha'i religion were formerly Babis, and... they had frequently departed from the limit of moderation, owing to the evil training of different leaders. ... This latitude and laxity of principle likewise extended to the conflict and bloodshed permitted by their former religion, Islam. The Babis generally were ignorant of the ordinances of the Bab, and supposed them to be similar to the doctrines of the Shi'ites, which they considered the source of the Babi religion. This ignorance was due to the fact that the Babis were

---

[4] See Genesis 1:26-27.
[5] Mirza-Abul-Fazl, *Hujaj'ul Beheyyeh (The Behai Proofs)*, translated by Ali Kuli Khan (New York: J. W. Pratt Co., 1902), pp. 62-70, 72-77, 79-81, 93-96.

strictly prohibited by the Persian rulers from holding intercourse with or visiting the Bab, while the latter was in prison. ...

When Baha'u'llah appeared, however, it was but a short time before His followers became noted for their good deeds and just characters. As a result of His training, they soon became successful in promoting His word, rendered spiritual assistance to His cause, and were grounded in admirable religious beliefs. Day by day, His followers increased in number and the power of His word became more and more manifest, so that in a short space of time it was introduced into other countries and penetrated other religions besides Islam. Even the Jews, Zoroastrians, Nusayrites,[6] and other remote peoples who were considered as being absolutely extinct and lifeless, attained, by thousands, the honor of accepting His Cause. For this they fell victims to the tyranny and persecutions of the Muslims and their own former co-religionists; quaffing the cup of martyrdom with joy, steadfastness, triumph, and forbearance. This was a matter of astonishment to sagacious men, for these people were many in number and belonged to the rich classes; numbers of them were merchants and traders, and thus could not be supposed to have embraced Baha'ism in order to gain riches or fame. For the followers of Baha'u'llah did not possess any wealth, affluence or material power which might induce people to join them. Moreover, after embracing this religion, they showed such steadfastness, that no fear of losing their lives and property could shake their faith. Therefore the Baha'is recognized this firmness, forbearance, and endurance of calamities to be a proof of the truth of this religion, and as the most manifest evidence and witness of the power of the word of Baha'u'llah. ...

The books, tablets, and divine revelations of Baha'u'llah contain treatises, written generally in answer to questions asked by people, both Baha'is and outsiders. For during His stay in Iraq, Adrianople, and Akka, when His name had become renowned in the world, and the penetration of His word attracted the attention of intelligent minds, the seekers after truth, who were earnest in the search for knowledge and wisdom, went to Him, asking intricate and abstruse questions. Those

---

[6] The Nusayris, more commonly known as the Alawites, are a mystical sect of Shi'ite Islam centered in Syria.

who were not able to visit Him on account of the strict prohibition of rulers and other obstacles, asked Him difficult questions through correspondence. He answered them instantly without delay or hesitation, although subject to rigorous calamities and afflictions. These answers were forwarded after a copy of them had been reserved. ...

He also wrote certain tablets which He sent to the crowned heads and to the chief religious doctors and divines. Thus, in a short time, His books and epistles were scattered like rose-petals throughout different cities, and the teachings given therein were poured forth like unto raindrops over all regions. So the voice of His Manifestation reached the West and East like a flash of lightning and His Cause penetrated other countries and nations. Some of the tablets He wrote in modern Persian, while others written in answer to the learned and leading Zoroastrians, are in pure Old Persian. Some He has written in eloquent Arabic, and others in ordinary Arabic of today, so that they may be comprehended by the common people. All of them are in the most graceful and elegant style, and although written without premeditation or reflection, are nevertheless in the most excellent form of composition. ...

The epistles and treatises of Baha'u'llah contain four different styles and classes of knowledge. Upon the understanding of these depends, as is believed by the Baha'is, the knowledge of the truth of all the divine religions. Without this understanding man cannot be thoroughly informed of the benefits of religion, nor can ideal refinement and civilization be realized.

[1.] Some of them contain laws and regulations whereby the rights and interests of all the nations of the world can be perpetuated, for these statutes are so enacted that they meet the necessities of every land and country and are acceptable to every man of intelligence. In this universality they resemble the laws of Nature, which secure the progress and development of all peoples; and they will bring about universal union and harmony. The most important and best known among these is the *Book of Aqdas* and its supplementary tablets, revealed in answer to questions asked concerning the texts of the *Aqdas*; also the Tablets of *Ishraqat*, *Tarazat*, etc. To this class belong the tablets written upon the conduct of the "ascetic" seekers and strivers after truth. Such is the Book of the *Seven Valleys*, written in answer to Sheikh 'Abdu'r-

Rahman of Kirkuk, one of the prominent Sufi sheikhs of Iraq-Arabi. Although Baha'u'llah has forbidden Sufism,[7] monkhood and inactivity—i.e., abandoning the practice of trade and profession—yet, in these tablets, He has explained the manner of real devotion.

[2.] Some others contain solutions of the intricate points of the heavenly books of former peoples, which, before His Manifestation, were "sealed" by the seal of the Prophets; God having decreed that their opening and interpretation should be effected at the Day of the Lord's Appearance.[8] As the learned attempted to interpret them before the appointed time, they fell into error in apprehension of their real purport, and thus misled people instead of enlightening them. The Baha'is believe that this very point caused the Jews to falsely deny our Lord Jesus Christ, and the Zoroastrians to consider all the Israelite [or Abrahamic] prophets as imposters. The Baha'is also believe that former interpretations of the Book are but false imaginations of man, and inversions of the Divine Word. To this class of [Baha'u'llah's] writings belong the well-known Book of *Iqan* and the book entitled *Jawahir u'l-Asrar* (Gems of Mysteries),[9] revealed in Baghdad at the request of one of the nobility of Fars [Province of Iran]; in which He has opened the seals of the former prophetic books.

[3.] Some others contain prayers and divine eulogies, which instruct men in the mode of worship; supplications and communes, which are means of communion between the worshipper and the Adored One. The benefits imparted by such devotional acts are the illumination and purification of man's conscience, by which the faculty of Divine apprehension is strengthened, the brutal qualities of man are refined, and the worshipper attains true realization and certainty.

---

[7] At the time, Sufism was associated with the extreme asceticism of dervishes, and was essentially an Islamic form of monasticism.

[8] In Islam, the Prophet Muhammad is regarded as the "Seal of the Prophets" (*Khátam an-Nabiyyín*), i.e. the last prophet before the Day of Judgment. The Bab and Baha'u'llah reinterpreted these concepts to mean that Muhammad was the last of a great cycle of prophecy which began in ancient times, and that the Day of Judgment is a metaphor for the next appearance of the Manifestation of God (i.e. "Him Whom God Shall Make Manifest" or Baha'u'llah), who inaugurates a new epoch of history.

[9] Usually called *Javáhiru'l-Asrár* ("Gems of Divine Mysteries") by Baha'is today.

[4.] Some others contain discourses and exordiums in which He has explained the real meaning of the Unity of the Divine Essence and has demonstrated and elucidated the original purpose of the mission of prophets, as well as the stations of the separation and union of those dawning-places of the command of God.

In other words, in these tablets, Baha'u'llah has solved intricate theological questions in the clearest way, whereby He not only has demonstrated the truth of the new cause, but also the truth of the founders of former religions. ...

During Baha'u'llah's residence in Baghdad, it was His custom to write the tablets with His own hand; but in Adrianople they were usually written by the pen of His eldest son, the "Greatest Branch of God" [i.e. Abbas Effendi]. During the exile at Akka they were dictated to different amanuenses, including Mirza Aqa Jan of Kashan (the servant of Baha'u'llah), Mirza Mohammed Ali, Mirza Zia Ullah, Mirza Badi Ullah (the children of His Holiness Baha'u'llah), and Mirza Majdeddin, his son-in-law. These amanuenses wrote them in His presence from His dictation, and after collating and revising them, copies thereof would be forwarded to the questioners. ...

As to the devotional ordinances instituted by Baha'u'llah, these comprise prayer, fasting, and the pilgrimage to the House of God, according to details explained in the Book [of *Aqdas*]. These are duties which are incumbent upon all, if circumstances permit their performance. There are also invocations and prayers which the Baha'is chant in their meetings as a blessing, or the pious recite in private, while communing with God. Most of these tablets are already collected and compiled.

His ethical ordinances comprise laws commanding good qualities and excellent virtues, such as sincerity, faith, devotion, love, integrity, chastity, purity, trustworthiness, and piety; and forbidding people from evil conduct and abominable deeds, such as lying, backbiting, slandering, murder, theft, fornication, disputing and striving, even with enemies, etc. ... Not only has He forbidden murder, conflict, and strife, but also slavery, self-exaltation, and all that may cause grief and offense to men; and He has commanded meekness and humility. It is revealed in the Book of *Aqdas* as follows:

> Ye are not allowed to buy male or female slaves. No servant [of God] hath the right to buy another servant, as this is forbidden in the Tablet of God; thus hath the matter been written through mercy with the Pen of Equity. No one should glory over another; all are servants unto Him, and show that verily there is no God save Him. Verily He is wise in all things.[10]

... He has commanded people to sincerely love every nation, without exception, as their own brothers—no matter to what religion and sect they may belong—and to consider it a most obligatory duty to purify their hearts and souls from former rancor. Therefore, He has commanded His friends to shun every word which might cause the slightest discord; to avoid cursing, execration, and all that gives offense; to serve all people; to glory not in loving our country, but rather in loving all the world. In this connection, He has said in the Book of *Aqdas*:

> Consort ye with all the religions with joy and fragrance, so that they may discover from you the odor of the Merciful. Beware not to be overtaken by the bigotry of the *Jahiliyyah*[11] among men. All come from God and will return to Him. Verily, He is the origin of the people and the goal of the creatures.[12]

... In a tablet written in answer to the questions of one of the prominent Zoroastrians, He says: "The Peerless Friend commandeth: Say, O friends, the Pavilion of Unity is erected; do not gaze at each other with the eyes of strangers. Ye are all the fruits of one tree and the leaves of one branch." ...

To sum up: In His tablets He has revealed wonderful words regarding the beautifying and perfecting of human characters and virtues which, as brilliant pearls, adorn and decorate the crown of the kings of

---

[10] *Kitab-i-Aqdas* ("Most Holy Book"), paragraph 72.

[11] Note by Mirza Abu'l-Fadl: "This term was applied by Muhammad, in the Qur'an, to the Pagan Arabs. Here it means fanatics among the nations who have not believed in the Cause of God."

[12] *Kitab-i-Aqdas* ("Most Holy Book"), paragraph 144.

the world, and from which people inhale the fragrance of roses. They have proved effective in training and reforming the character of the Baha'is and in straightening the crookedness of the Babis, so that, notwithstanding their greatly increased numbers, they have become universally celebrated for good conduct, noted everywhere for excellent morals; and nothing contrary to humanity or against the laws of the governments proceeds from them. ...

Were the leading men of the Persian government to justly reflect upon these points they would acknowledge the favor and providence of the Blessed Perfection, and open their mouth in His praise. Moreover, if those leaders and statesmen who still consider the Babis and Baha'is as one community and blame the innocent for the sin of the guilty, were to use sound judgment, they will clearly see that ... if different rulers in Persia had not, by the command of the ignorant clergy, prevented the Babis from intercourse with the Bab and had not so strictly repressed religious freedom, the Babis would not have remained ignorant of the ordinances and brilliant character of the Bab, and fought in self-defense, as required by their former religion. How is it that the Baha'is, while their number is now greatly multiplied and they are far more persecuted by the government than the former Babis, instead of defending themselves, do not even complain of any injustice? Why is it that their endurance and self-restraint is a matter of amazement to strangers, and their good conduct universally approved by all nations? It is because they are commanded to obey the government and to love the people of the world. Through Baha'u'llah's teachings the roses of grace and compassion have grown up in the grounds of their hearts, instead of the thorns of enmity and hatred, and by Him the breeze of obedience and peace has replaced whirlwinds of defense and resistance. So the Baha'is have increased and their tranquility, dignity, and constancy become renowned throughout all regions and climes, while obedience to government, love, and brotherhood with all the different nations have become their obligatory belief. ...

The author submits that the Beauty of El-Abha—exalted is His Glory!—has enacted laws and regulations concerning every point or subject referring to the preservation of society and the perfecting of human virtues; greater laws than which cannot be imagined by the possessors of intelligence. They concern manners and conditions of mutual intercourse, the founding of administrative organizations, the mutual rights of rulers and subjects, the spread of knowledge, respect due to philosophers and learned men, commands to refrain from rebellion against kings and princes, obedience and reverence to parents, the laws of marriage, and the mutual rights of the wife and husband, laws of inheritance, and other regulations. It is only through such laws that the union and harmony among nations of different religions and tongues can be effected; for, in enacting laws upon every subject, He has taken two points into consideration. First, that obeying and carrying them into practice may be possible for all peoples, notwithstanding the difference of their countries. Second, that they may not excite selfish prejudices and fanaticism. Through these laws, the breezes of ideal mercy and compassion will blow through hearts and souls, and the lights of real humanity will shine forth from all breasts. Thus, through the assistance of God, the spirit of disunion, discord, and hostility which divides nations, will be removed, and all the earth will be considered as one Paradise and one home. ...

In order to cause the spread of learning and enlightenment, He has made it incumbent to educate children of both sexes, and to train them in lofty morals. Should any one disregard these commands, and neglect the training of his children, the government shall educate and train them in the schools, and assess the expenses upon the father. Should the father be poor, the government must furnish the funds out of the money given to God, according to the law instituted in the Book [of *Aqdas*]; so that excellent morals may be universally spread throughout the world, and praiseworthy qualities may be firmly implanted in the hearts of both sexes from their childhood. He has so emphasized this command to educate children, that no righteous man will fail to realize the necessity of complying with it. He has included the teachers of children in the list of heirs, so that their care and fatherhood may be ever appreciated by the world, and they may be encouraged to educate their pupils. The substance of what He has said in the Book of *Aqdas* upon this subject is as follows: "Whosoever educates one of the children of the people who love God, it is as though he has educated one of the branches of the Blessed Divine Tree, and he is worthy of praise, blessing, and mercy of God."[13] When one reflects upon this point, he will find that as God has strictly commanded the spread of enlightenment and education, and as the power of the Word of God will assist it, this law of educating children will cause the removal of the darkness of ignorance and barbarity from all regions of the world, and the promise of God, "The earth shall be illumined with the light of its Lord,"[14] will be clearly realized.

In connection with occupations and professions, He has said that God the Almighty, during this great Manifestation, has made it obligatory for all to occupy themselves in professions which are praiseworthy, such as trade, agriculture, handicraft, etc. He has also stated that gaining one's living through means which benefit society is considered as worshipping God the Exalted. He has reinforced this command by enjoining upon the people of Baha, abstinence from monkhood, Sufism, and retirement, as well as from ascetic discipline. He has commanded them to marry[15] and to be engaged in the spread of knowledge which leads to the prosperity and welfare of peoples, and the restoration of the world.

From "Beha 'U'llah's Divinity" by Ibrahim G. Kheiralla[16]

I am of the opinion that the prophets and Manifestations of God must prove to the people of the earth the truth of their divine missions by producing the following four evidences in order that the people may believe and acknowledge them. Should they present such evidences and yet should we reject them, it would be our own fault and not theirs.

---

[13] This appears to be a loose paraphrase of the last part of paragraph 48 of the Aqdas.

[14] Qur'an 39:69. Also cf. Revelation 22:5.

[15] Baha'i law does not actually require people to marry, but strongly encourages it.

[16] Excerpted from a chapter with this title in a book by Ibrahim George Kheiralla, *O Christians! Why do Ye Believe Not on Christ?* (1917), pp. 97-100, 102-104, 106-108.

First: To utter verses which contain striking truths and principles, whereby the human race is uplifted and elevated, and the extremely wicked become upright and good.

Second: Their appearance is foretold by the prophets of yore.

Third: To display a divine knowledge, which is beyond that of man.

Fourth: To show a superiority in their lives and in their personalities.

These evidences were fully established in the person of Husayn Ali [Nuri], so as to leave no doubt that He was the Glory of God, and the Manifestation of the Father. In brief, all the prophecies concerning the coming of the Father were fulfilled in Him...

[H]is teachings are not visionary nor prophetic, but practical, final, and useful to the high and to the low, to the civilized and the uncivilized. At the same time they are in accord with reason and science and in harmony with the laws governing the world.

For instance, history proves that neither through Christianity nor Mohammedanism could peace be established upon earth, for the first shed blood, if not more, not less than the other, as the present horrible war[17] bears witness. But in the tablets which Baha'u'llah, the Prince of Peace, sent to the rulers of the world, He prohibited them from warring with each other, and commanded them to settle their differences by arbitration. He also strictly forbade the waging of war for differences in faith or otherwise. By His teachings, He established the foundation of peace and enlightened the world with the light of union, concord, and love. He urged His followers to rise up by the help of God, and deliver the world from religious hatred and enmity, which are a consuming fire devouring the human race. He came to unite all those who are upon earth and to save the world from the fetters of ignorance. He said: "Let justice be your army, and your weapon reason."

Baha['u'llah] said: "If ye follow me I will make you the heirs of My Kingdom, but if ye rebel against Me I will kindly be patient; I am the Forgiver, the Merciful."

Also Baha['u'llah] said: "Communicate to all people what ye know,

---

[17] World War I.

with the language of love and kindness." "Consort with people of all faiths, with fragrance and spirituality." "Allow not the zeal of bigotry to display itself in you, for every one cometh from God, and unto God shall he return. He is the Causer of their being, and the Center of their final attainment."

The verses written by the Supreme Pen of Baha'u'llah contain an ocean of sublime spiritual teachings, thrilling precepts and admonitions, excellent bases of religious principles, just and equitable laws and edicts. ... Through His teachings and commandments, the great peace shall come, capital and labor shall be conciliated, the wolf and the lamb shall live together, the unity of the [human] race shall be established, a universal language shall be adopted, and the people of the earth shall live as brothers, as one kindred, one family, loving not only their country, but the whole world.

All the prophets of yore foretold the coming of the Father and the establishment of His Kingdom on earth. They gave the signs of His coming, and that Elijah shall come as a forerunner. They located the city of Akka as the New Jerusalem. They predicted the year of His Manifestation, and described the condition at His day. Every prophecy in regard to the Manifestation of the Deity upon earth was fulfilled in Husayn Ali, and proved that He was the Glory of God.

Jewish rabbis, Christian theologians, Mohammedan doctors, and priests of other faiths, all expected the coming of the Kingdom of God on earth in the nineteenth century.[18] They were not mistaken, for the scriptures foretold His appearance. Jesus said: "the Lord of the vineyard cometh;"[19] "the Comforter will come;"[20] "when the Spirit of Truth is

---

[18] The most notable of the millennialist movements in the 1800s was led by William Miller, a Baptist preacher in the United States, who predicted that Christ would return in 1844, based on detailed calculations from his study of Bible prophecies. Although the Bab announced himself in that same year as a messianic figure expected by Shi'ite Muslims, the Millerites expected a literal, apocalyptic return of Jesus Christ which would be obvious to all the world, and they did not become Babis or Baha'is.

[19] Matthew 21:40.

[20] John 15:26.

come he will guide you into all truth."[21] He prayed: "Thy Kingdom come."[22] ...

All the signs of His coming which were mentioned in the scriptures of different religions were fulfilled in the nineteenth century. Jesus Christ said: "The Gospel of the Kingdom shall be preached in all the world for a witness unto the nations, and then shall the end come."[23] In the last century, the Christian missionaries preached the Gospel to all nations. Muhammad said: "When you behold the ships sailing upon the land, then he shall come." The trains sailed upon the land a few years before [Baha'u'llah] manifested Himself. Nahum said: "The chariots shall rage in the streets, they shall jostle one against another in the broad ways: they shall seem like torches, they shall run like lightning."[24] In this sign the material atoms declared the coming of the Glory of God. It is an accurate prediction of electric cars and modern vehicles, which throng our streets. "Behold I will send you Elijah, the prophet, before the coming of the great and dreadful day of the Lord." (Malachi 4:5). In 1844 Elijah the prophet came, for there appeared in Persia a young man who possessed great powers of wisdom and spiritual inspiration. He is known in history as Ali Muhammad [Shirazi]. He called himself "The Bab," meaning the "Gate" or "Door." ... He was [the return of] Elijah, the forerunner, and gave the glad tidings of the coming of the Kingdom of God, and the appearance of "Him whom God shall manifest," the Glory of God.

Akka is the New Jerusalem, the City of the Lord, unto which He was exiled as a prisoner of the Turkish government, and from whence He departed [from this world]. It is upon the Syrian coast, nine miles from the foot of Mount Carmel, and during the Crusades it was the headquarters of the Knights Templar, who called it Saint Jean d'Acre. It is a fortified city and notorious for its unhealthy climate and filthiness. It is the Turkish city of exile and the place of confinement for prisoners of the government.

---

[21] John 16:13.
[22] Matthew 6:10.
[23] Matthew 24:14.
[24] Nahum 2:4.

Isaiah (9:1) accurately located the New Jerusalem at Akka. [Here is a] literal translation of the prophecies of Isaiah by Professor [T. K.] Cheyne[25] of Oxford, England:[26]

> Surely there is (now) no (more) gloom to her whose lot was affliction. At the former time He brought shame on the land of Zebulun and on the land of Naphtali, but in the latter He hath brought honor on the way by the sea, the other side of Jordan, the district of the nations. The people that walk in darkness see a great light; they that dwell in the land of deep shade, light shineth brilliantly upon them. ... [A]nd his name is called Wonder-Counsellor, God-Mighty-One, Everlasting-Father, Prince of Peace...[27]

The spot described by the prophet between the land of Zebulun and the land of Naphtali is Akka; and to appoint the exact situation, he said: "But in the latter time, he hath brought honor on the way by the sea" (Akka).

From ancient times the highway to Damascus from the sea commenced at Akka. In [Prof. Cheyne's] *Prophecies of Isaiah* we read in a note on p. 60: "*Via Maris* ['Sea Way'], M. Renan observes, was the name of the high road from Acre to Damascus, as late as the Crusades. 'Way,' however, here means region." Thus literally, the Manifestation of Jehovah, Baha'u'llah, appeared in the latter days and brought honor upon the "way by the sea" (Akka). ...

The divine knowledge and wisdom which Husayn Ali displayed in epistles and tablets to his followers; in the just and beautiful laws he gave the world in the Most Sacred Book (*Kitab-i-Aqdas*); in the tablets which he sent to the rulers of the earth, inviting them to come to His Kingdom and partake of the spiritual banquet, to eat and drink with

---

[25] Thomas Kelly Cheyne was an Anglican minister and Biblical scholar who held the distinguished position of Oriel Professor of the Interpretation of Holy Scripture at Oxford University. In the early 1900s he converted to the Baha'i faith.

[26] Rev. T. K. Cheyne, M.A., *The Prophecies of Isaiah: A New Translation with Commentary and Appendices*, Vol. I (London: Kegan Paul, Trench, & Co., 1882, second edition), pp. 60, 62-63.

[27] Isaiah 9:1-2,6.

the elect; in His knowledge of the past and the future as was stated in His predictions, proved conclusively that He was the Glory of God, as such knowledge is beyond that of man.

For instance, in the second tablet sent to Napoleon III, he informed the Emperor concerning his past secrets, and judged him, because he cast aside the first tablet which Baha['u'llah] sent to him. The prediction was that the [French] Empire would depart from the hands of Napoleon, and humiliation would come upon him, and commotion would seize the people of France, and his glory would pass away. A few months later Napoleon declared war on Germany and was defeated, dethroned, humiliated as a prisoner of war, and finally died in exile in England. Also the commotion seized the French people at the revolution of the [Paris] Commune. ... [N]umerous written and verbal warnings of impending events which came to pass, are plain evidences of His divine knowledge.

The life and personality of Husayn Ali are convincing proofs that He was the Manifestation and the Glory of God. For forty years he suffered in jails and in exile; was oppressed and afflicted; was threatened with death by Mohammedan doctors and rulers; yet under the sword of the enemy He summoned all the people of the earth and their rulers, even those who imprisoned and exiled him, to come to God, the Creator of heaven and earth. At the same time he uttered volumes of wonderful teachings and precepts, vigorous in style, clear in argument, powerful in proof, displaying perfect acquaintance with the scriptures of different faiths. He spent his life for the salvation of our race, and suffered humiliation for our elevation. He was imprisoned to free us from the fetters of ignorance. ...

The wonderful and heavenly atmosphere of spirituality which shrouded the place of his presence, proved His Divinity. Professor Browne of Cambridge, England, the greatest historian of this faith, who recorded what the friends and adversaries said in favor or against Baha'u'llah, went himself and met Baha'u'llah in person, that he might be able to write from his own experience and knowledge, independently of what the others said. But he was attacked and blamed by Christian theologians and missionaries because he recorded his experience truthfully. While visiting Baha['u'llah], he wrote as follows:

I might, indeed, strive to describe in greater detail the faces and forms which surrounded me, the conversations to which I was privileged to listen, the solemn melodious reading of the sacred books, the general sense of harmony and content which pervaded the place, and the fragrant shady gardens whither in the afternoon we sometimes repaired; but all this was as nought in comparison with the spiritual atmosphere with which I was encompassed. ... Let those who have not seen disbelieve me if they will; but, should that spirit once reveal itself to them, they will experience an emotion which they are not likely to forget.[28]

---

[28] Edward G. Browne, *A Traveller's Narrative: Written to Illustrate the Episode of the Bab*, Volume II. English Translation and Notes (Cambridge: University Press, 1891), pp. xxxviii-xxxix.

Abbas Effendi (later known as 'Abdu'l-Baha), the eldest son of Baha'u'llah, as a young man. Photo taken in 1868.

'Abdu'l-Baha in his elder years, in 1915.

8

The Teachings and Will of 'Abdu'l-Baha

By Shua Ullah Behai

This chapter is taken from a chapter of Shua Ullah Behai's book manuscript in which he quotes extensively from the published teachings of his uncle Abbas Effendi, 'Abdu'l-Baha, and reproduces in its entirety the document regarded by all but a few Baha'is today as the Will and Testament of 'Abdu'l-Baha. Because that document is very long and repetitive, only some particularly relevant quotations from it have been retained here and most of it has been cut. Several quotations from speeches and writings of 'Abdu'l-Baha have also been removed for the sake of brevity. Section headings have been added.

The purported will of Abbas Effendi contrasts sharply with his public demeanor and rhetoric and the principles he taught Americans and Europeans who were interested in the Baha'i movement. 'Abdu'l-Baha was known to his Western admirers for his mild manner and high-minded teachings of peace, love, kindness, forgiveness, religious tolerance and reconciliation; but in the document considered to be his will, he rails against schismatic rivals led by his half-brother Mohammed Ali Effendi, whom he calls "The Center of Sedition" and whose goal, he says, is to "utterly destroy and exterminate" the Baha'i cause.[1] He accuses him of having broken the "Covenant" of Baha'u'llah by opposing 'Abdu'l-Baha, who was appointed as the leader of the faith in Baha'u'llah's will, and declares that this "grievously fallen" brother has thus

---

[1] *The Will And Testament of 'Abdu'l-Bahá* (Wilmette, Ill.: US Bahá'í Publishing Trust, 1990 reprint), Part Two, p. 21.

been "cut off" from the Baha'i faith, i.e. excommunicated.²

Laying out the case against Mohammed Ali Bahai, the Will and Testament of 'Abdu'l-Baha makes several specific accusations: that he once claimed to write verses with equal authority as the writings of Baha'u'llah—ironically, something that Abbas Effendi himself did throughout his ministry after Baha'u'llah's passing—and that he committed terrible acts of fraud and betrayal, such as tampering with Baha'u'llah's writings, submitting libelous reports about his activities to the Ottoman government, and conspiring with Shua Ullah Behai and unnamed others in a plot to have him killed. Embracing the possibility of assassination or execution, he asks God to "make me to drink from the Chalice of Martyrdom, for the wide world with all its vastness can no longer contain me"; and he envisions his excommunicated brother as "afflicted by the wrath of God, sunk into a degradation and infamy that shall be lasting until the Day of Doom."³ The author thus casts himself in the heroic role of innocent victim and defender of the faith in the face of the sinister machinations of those he believed to be enemies—the Unitarian Baha'is, whom he calls "Covenant-breakers"—who are cast as the embodiment of utmost evil.

Also in the will, 'Abdu'l-Baha appoints his grandson, Shoghi Effendi Rabbani, to a lofty station of infallible leadership as the "Guardian of the Cause of God." He asserts that anyone who opposes or disputes with Mr. Rabbani has "opposed God" and should be expelled from the Baha'i community, and calls for "the wrath, the fierce indignation, the vengeance of God [to] rest upon him!"⁴—much the same as his stance toward the Unitarian Baha'is. Surprisingly, he even goes so far as to say that "To none is given the right to put forth his own opinion or express his particular conviction."⁵

The overall tenor of the document makes it difficult to believe that it could really have been a celebrated progressive religious leader's last message to the world—especially when juxtaposed with some of the

---

[2] Ibid., Part One, p. 9.
[3] Ibid., Part Three, pp. 23, 24.
[4] Ibid., Part One, p. 11.
[5] Ibid., Part Three, p. 26.

other well-known writings, speeches and sayings of 'Abdu'l-Baha that Shua Ullah Behai presents in this chapter. Mr. Behai suggests the possibility of forgery, seemingly unwilling to accept that his uncle could have written a will laced with fierce accusations of moral and spiritual corruption against his father and himself, and criticizes the appointment of a "Guardian" for the Baha'i faith, which he likens to a "little pope." Mr. Behai praises 'Abdu'l-Baha as a great Baha'i leader and teacher, and emphatically denies the charge made in the will that he conspired to assassinate him.

Shua Ullah Behai was not the only person to suspect that the Will and Testament of 'Abdu'l-Baha may have been forged. A few years after the Baha'i leader's death, an American Baha'i named Ruth White arose in opposition to the appointment of Shoghi Effendi Rabbani as Guardian—a position that was not called for in Baha'u'llah's writings and which, in her view, seemed to contradict some of the teachings of 'Abdu'l-Baha. In 1930, she arranged for an expert to examine the handwriting of the document in which this appointment was made. Dr. C. Ainsworth Mitchell, a British forensic scientist with experience in cases of suspected forgery, was commissioned to analyze a photographic copy of the will in question and samples of 'Abdu'l-Baha's handwriting provided by Mrs. White. In his report, he concluded that he had "failed to detect in any part of the will the characteristics of the writing of Abdul Baha, as shown in the authenticated specimens," i.e. the samples provided for comparison. Dr. Mitchell further stated that "the writing does not agree with the hypothesis that it was all written by one person," suggesting that the will itself may have been written by more than one hand.[6]

Although C. Ainsworth Mitchell's report does lend some credence to the possibility that the "Will and Testament of 'Abdu'l-Baha" was forged, either in whole or in part, it certainly does not prove it. For one thing, even if the document was not written by 'Abdu'l-Baha's own hand, he could have had secretaries or relatives take dictation. Also, two important points have been raised against the conclusions of Dr.

---

[6] A complete copy of Dr. Mitchell's report is available online at http://www.fglaysher.com/bahaicensorship/CAMitchell_Report.htm

Mitchell: first, that he was not experienced in analyzing handwriting in the Persian script, and in fact was illiterate in that language in which the will was written; and second, that the other samples submitted to him by Ruth White may not have been 'Abdu'l-Baha's handwriting at all.[7]

The validity of the will was never contested in a probate court, and Baha'is have been asked to trust Shoghi Effendi and other supporters of 'Abdu'l-Baha who asserted that it was authentic—and nearly all, both historically and in the present day, have done so. As later chapters of this book reveal, there is a great deal of testimony from various early Baha'i insiders which would support the mainstream belief that the alleged will of 'Abdu'l-Baha was consistent with his views and therefore probably his own—especially the parts about rejecting Mohammed Ali Effendi as a wicked heretic. No final conclusions can be drawn, however, without rigorous forensic examination and analysis of the original document and verified handwriting samples of Abbas Effendi and others who might have had access to it.

Also of note in this chapter is the fact that Shua Ullah Behai says that Abbas Effendi was born in 1841. This conflicts with the commonly accepted Baha'i tradition which places the birth of 'Abdu'l-Baha in the year 1844 on the same day that the Bab declared his prophetic mission, suggesting that this story may be mythological.

—The Editor

——✧——

Ghusn-i-A'zam, the Greatest Branch, Abbas Effendi, 'Abdu'l-Baha—The greatness of this personage no one could deny, as he was the eldest son of Baha'u'llah, and the appointed leader of the Baha'is, according to the Will of Baha'u'llah, entitled *Kitab-i-'Ahdi*.[8]

---

[7] Sen McGlinn, "Mitchell's mistake," blog article at http://senmcglinn.wordpress.com/2009/05/27/mitchells_mistake/

[8] Unitarian Baha'is referred to Baha'u'llah's will as *Kitab-i-'Ahdi* ("Book of My Covenant"), whereas in the mainstream Baha'i tradition it is called *Kitab-i-'Ahd* ("Book of the Covenant") in English. Technically, *Kitab-i-'Ahdi* () is correct, as shown by the use of this version of the title on an Arabic-language

The pages of Baha'i history are covered with his praise. Numerous books have been published about him, by the believers and admirers, and all are testimonials to his greatness. Therefore I do not think that I could possibly add to what has been written.

His life, his orations, and his efforts in the diffusion of the sacred teachings of Baha'u'llah should be an example for the devoted followers.

He was born in Tehran, Iran, in the year 1841 A.D.[9] and passed away at Haifa, Palestine, 1921 A.D.

The following are some of his messages to mankind, and his will.

Teachings of 'Abdu'l-Baha

'Abdu'l-Baha says in a letter to the Baha'is of America:

> Beware! Beware! Lest ye offend any heart!
> Beware! Beware! Lest ye hurt any soul!
> Beware! Beware! Lest ye deal unkindly toward any person!
> Beware! Beware! Lest ye be the cause of hopelessness to any creature!
> Should one become the cause of grief to any one heart, or of despondency to any one soul, it were better to hide oneself in the lowest depths of the earth than to walk upon the earth.[10]

---

page of the Baha'i organization's own website (http://info.bahai.org/arabic/covenant.html, accessed November 12, 2014).

[9] Cambridge University Professor Edward Granville Browne, one of the greatest early scholars of the Babi/Baha'i faith, also gives 1841 A.D. (1257 A.H.) as the year of 'Abdu'l-Baha's birth, in his 1918 book *Materials for the Study of the Babi Religion* (p. 320). This is the same year given by Mohammed Jawad Gazvini in *An Epitome of Babi and Bahai History to A.D. 1898*, translated in full by Prof. Browne in *Materials* (p. 47). Ibrahim G. Kheiralla relates in his autobiography (see Chapter 25) that 'Abdu'l-Baha said he had been 27 years old in 1867, which would place his birth in 1839 or 1840. However, Baha'is today believe that 'Abdu'l-Baha was born on May 23, 1844, on the night when the Bab declared his prophethood.

[10] Quoted by J. E. Esslemont in *Bahá'u'lláh and the New Era* (Wilmette, Ill.: US Bahá'í Publishing Trust, 1980 edition), p. 81.

Again 'Abdu'l-Baha says:

> Among the teachings of Baha'u'llah is one requiring man, under all conditions and circumstances, to be forgiving, to love his enemy and to consider an ill-wisher as a well-wisher. *Not that he should consider one as being an enemy and then put up with him, or to simply endure him... This is declared to be hypocrisy. This love is not real.* Nay, rather, you must see your enemies as friends, ill-wishers as well-wishers and treat them accordingly. That is to say, your love and kindness must be *real*. Your well-wishing must be reality, not merely forbearance, for forbearance, if not of the heart, is hypocrisy.[11]

'Abdu'l-Baha tells us:

> To be silent concerning the faults of others, to pray for them, and to help them, through kindness, to correct their faults.
> To look always at the good and not at the bad. If a man has ten good qualities and one bad one, to look at the ten and forget the one; and if a man has ten bad qualities and one good one, to look at the one and forget the ten.
> Never to allow ourselves to speak one unkind word about another, even though that other be our enemy.[12]

To an American friend he writes:

> [T]he worst human quality and *the most great sin is backbiting*; more especially when it emanates from the tongues of the believers of God. If some means were devised so that the doors of backbiting could be shut eternally and each one of the believers of God unsealed his tongue in the praise of the other, then the teachings of His Holiness Baha'u'llah would be spread, the hearts illumi-

---

[11] Address delivered in Oakland, California, October 3, 1912. Published in *Star of the West*, Vol. IV, No. 11, p. 191. *Emphasis in original*. Available online at http://starofthewest.info

[12] Quoted by J. E. Esslemont in *Bahá'u'lláh and the New Era* (Wilmette, Ill.: US Bahá'í Publishing Trust, 1980 edition), p. 83.

nated, the spirits glorified, and the human world would attain to everlasting felicity.[13]

'Abdu'l-Baha says:

Truthfulness is the foundation of all the virtues of the world of humanity. Without truthfulness, progress and success in all of the worlds of God are impossible for a soul. When this holy attribute is established in man, all the divine qualities will also become realized.[14]

'Abdu'l-Baha says:

Everyone must do away with false prejudices and must even go to the other churches and mosques, for, in all of these worshiping places, the name of God is mentioned. Since all gather to worship God, what difference does it make? None of these worship satan. The Mohammedans must go to the churches of the Christians and [the synagogues] of the Jews, and vice-versa, the others must go to the Mohammedan mosques. They hold aloof from one another merely because of unfounded prejudices and dogmas. In America, I went to the Jewish synagogues, which are similar to the Christian churches, and I saw them worshiping God everywhere. In most of these places I spoke to them about the original foundations of the divine religions and I explained to them the proofs of the validity of the divine prophets and of the holy Manifestations. I encouraged them to do away with blind imitations. All of the leaders must, likewise, go to the churches of one another and speak of the foundation and of the fundamental principles of the divine religions. In the utmost unity and harmony, they must worship God, in the worshiping places of one another and they must abandon these false fanaticisms.[15]

---

[13] "Tablet to Doctor M. G. Skinner, Washington, D.C.," 1913. Published in *Star of the West*, Vol. IV, No. 11, p. 192. *Emphasis in original.*

[14] *Tablets of Abdul-Baha Abbas*, Vol. II (Chicago: Bahai Publishing Society, 1909 edition), p. 459.

[15] Quoted in *Star of the West*, Vol. IX, No. 3, p. 37.

'Abdu'l-Baha says:

God has given man the eye of investigation by which he may see and recognize truth. He has endowed man with ears that he may hear the message of reality, and conferred upon him the gift of reason by which he may discover things for himself. This is his endowment and equipment for the investigation of reality. Man is not intended to see through the eyes of another, hear through another's ears, nor comprehend with another's brain. ... Therefore, depend upon your own reason and judgment and adhere to the outcome of your own investigation; otherwise, you will be utterly submerged in the sea of ignorance and deprived of all the bounties of God.[16]

'Abdu'l-Baha's definition of "What is a Baha'i?":

When asked on one occasion: "What is a Baha'i?" 'Abdu'l-Baha replied: "To be a Baha'i simply means to love all the world; to love humanity and try to serve it; to work for universal peace and universal brotherhood." ... In one of [h]is London talks [h]e said that a man may be a Baha'i even if he has never heard the name of Baha'u'llah. He added:—"The man who lives the life according to the teachings of Baha'u'llah is already a Baha'i. On the other hand, a man may call himself a Baha'i for fifty years, and if he does not live the life he is not a Baha'i. An ugly man may call himself handsome, but he deceives no one..."[17]

['Abdu'l-Baha says:]

We are commanded to quicken the souls, to train the characters, to illumine the realm of man, to guide all the inhabitants of the

---

[16] Talk given in Malden, Massachusetts, August 29, 1912. Published in *The Promulgation of Universal Peace* (Wilmette, Ill.: US Bahá'í Publishing Trust, 1982 second edition), p. 293.

[17] Quoted by J. E. Esslemont in *Baha'u'llah and the New Era* (Wilmette, Ill.: US Bahá'í Publishing Trust, 1980 edition), p. 71. Pronouns referring to 'Abdu'l-Baha have been changed to lowercase (see bracketed text), but were capitalized in Esslemont's book according to official Baha'i policy.

earth, to create concord and unity among all men, and to lead the world of humanity to the Fountain of the Everlasting Glory. The reformation of one empire is not our aim; nay, rather we invoke from God that all the regions of the world be reformed and cultivated; the republic of men become the manifestors of the bounty of the most glorious Lord; the East and the West be brought nearer together... in brief, all the nations and peoples of the world become as one soul and one spirit, in order that strife and warfare be entirely removed and the rancor and hostility disappear, so that all become as the waves of one ocean, the drops of one sea, the flowers of one rose-garden, the trees of one orchard, the grains of one harvest, and the plants of one meadow.[18]

['Abdu'l-Baha says:]

The Baha'i Movement is not an organization. You can never organize the Baha'i Cause. *The Baha'i Movement is the spirit of this age.* It is the essence of all the highest ideals of this century. The Baha'i Cause is an *inclusive movement*: The teachings of all the religions and societies are found here; the Christians, Jews, Buddhists, Mohammedans, Zoroastrians, Theosophists, Freemasons, Spiritualists, et. al., find their highest aims in this Cause. Even the Socialists and philosophers find their theories fully developed in this Movement.[19]

['Abdu'l-Baha says:]

Be ye not seated and silent! Diffuse the glad-tidings of the Kingdom far and wide to the ears, promulgate the word of God... arise ye with such qualities and attributes that ye may continually bestow life to the body of the world, and nurse the infants of the

---

[18] *Tablets of Abdul-Baha Abbas*, Vol. III (Chicago: Bahai Publishing Society, 1909 edition), p. 490.

[19] Shua Ullah Behai notes the source of this quotation as "from a booklet N. 9." This editor was unable to locate an extant copy of the booklet or determine its title and publisher. However, the same quotation with slightly different wording was also published in *Star of the West*, Vol. V, No. 5, p. 67. This version is reproduced here; *emphasis* indicated in all caps in the original.

universe up to the station of maturity and perfection. Enkindle with all your might in every meeting the light of the love of God, gladden and cheer every heart with the utmost loving-kindness, show forth your love to the strangers just as you show forth to your relations. If a soul is seeking to quarrel, ask ye for reconciliation; if he blame you, praise (him); if he give you a deadly poison, bestow ye an all-healing antidote; if he createth death, administer ye eternal life; if he becometh a thorn, change ye into roses and hyacinths. Perchance, through such deeds and words, this darkened world will become illuminated, this terrestrial universe will become transformed into a heavenly realm, and this satanic prison become a divine court; warfare and bloodshed be annihilated, and love and faithfulness hoist the tent of unity upon the apex of the world.[20]

In his farewell address to the Baha'is in New York, USA, 'Abdu'l-Baha said:

> You must manifest complete love and affection toward all mankind. Do not exalt yourselves above others, but consider all as your equals, recognizing them as the servants of one God. Know that God is compassionate toward all; therefore, love all from the depths of your hearts, prefer all religionists before yourselves, be filled with love for every race, and be kind toward the people of all nationalities. Never speak disparagingly of others, but praise without distinction. Pollute not your tongues by speaking evil of another. Recognize your enemies as friends, and consider those who wish you evil as the wishers of good. ... Act in such a way that your heart may be free from hatred. Let not your heart be offended with anyone. If some one commits an error and wrong toward you, you must instantly forgive him. Do not complain of others. Refrain from reprimanding them, and if you wish to give admonition or advice, let it be offered in such a way that it will not burden the bearer. Turn all your thoughts toward bringing joy to hearts. Beware! Beware! lest ye offend any heart. Assist the world of humanity as much as possible. Be the source of consolation to every sad

---

[20] *Tablets of Abdul-Baha Abbas*, Vol. III (Chicago: Bahai Publishing Society, 1909 edition), pp. 503-504.

one, assist every weak one, be helpful to every indigent one, care for every sick one, be the cause of glorification to every lowly one, and shelter those who are overshadowed by fear.

In brief, let each one of you be as a lamp shining forth with the light of the virtues of the world of humanity. Be trustworthy, sincere, affectionate and replete with chastity. Be illumined, be spiritual, be divine, be glorious, be quickened of God, be a Baha'i.[21]

Excerpts from the Alleged Will of 'Abdu'l-Baha

[Three years after 'Abdu'l-Baha's death, his grandson Shoghi Effendi Rabbani allowed the leaders of the North American Baha'i community to distribute to the members a document purported to be the last will and testament of the deceased successor of Baha'u'llah, forbidding them from publishing any part of it or disseminating it to non-believers:]

> I feel that the conditions are now favorable for the circulation of the Will and Testament of 'Abdu'l-Baha only in manuscript form and among recognized believers in America. Every such believer should be trusted with a single copy with the express understanding that no duplicate copies or extracts of it be made or published anywhere.[22]

The will was issued in accordance with the conditions laid down by Shoghi Effendi, by the National Spiritual Assembly, in February, 1925. [The following are excerpts from the will, which was eventually made available to the general public.]

---

[21] Talk given in New York City, December 2, 1912. Published in *The Promulgation of Universal Peace* (Wilmette, Ill.: US Bahá'í Publishing Trust, 1982 second edition), p. 453.

[22] From a letter written by Mr. Rabbani to the American National Spiritual Assembly of the Baha'is, dated November 27, 1924. The full letter can be found in a "Compilation of Letters and Extracts of Writings from the Guardian Published in the *Baha'i News* of the United States, December 1924 – November 1934," and was published in the January 1925 issue of that periodical. Available online at http://bahai-library.org/books/bahainews.guardian/

[The document contains serious charges and a statement of excommunication pronounced against Mohammed Ali Effendi, the eldest surviving son of Baha'u'llah:]

> O ye that stand fast and firm in the Covenant! The Center of Sedition, the Prime Mover of mischief, Mírzá Muhammad 'Alí, hath passed out from under the shadow of the Cause, hath broken the Covenant, hath falsified the Holy Text, hath inflicted a grievous loss upon the true Faith of God, hath scattered His people, hath with bitter rancor endeavored to hurt 'Abdu'l-Bahá and hath assailed with the utmost enmity this servant of the Sacred Threshold. Every dart he seized and hurled to pierce the breast of this wronged servant, no wound did he neglect to grievously inflict upon me, no venom did he spare but he poisoned therewith the life of this hapless one. ... [I]t is incumbent upon everyone to hold fast unto the Text of the clear and firmly established blessed verse, revealed about him. None other transgression greater than his can be ever imagined. He (Bahá'u'lláh) sayeth, glorious and holy is His Word:—"My foolish loved ones have regarded him even as my partner, have kindled sedition in the land and they verily are of the mischief-makers. ... Should he for a moment pass out from under the shadow of the Cause, he surely shall be brought to naught." ... Ere long will ye behold him and his associates, outwardly and inwardly, condemned to utter ruin.
>
> What deviation can be greater than breaking the Covenant of God! ... What deviation can be greater than calumniating the Center of the Covenant ['Abdu'l-Baha] himself! What deviation can be more glaring than spreading broadcast false and foolish reports touching the Temple of God's Testament![23] What deviation can be more grievous than decreeing the death of the Center of the Covenant, supported by the holy verse:—"He that layeth a claim ere the passing of a thousand years...,"[24] whilst he (Muhammad 'Alí)

---

[23] The "Temple of God's Testament" appears to be a reference by 'Abdu'l-Baha to himself, similar in meaning to the "Center of the Covenant," i.e. the person in whom Baha'u'llah invested authority in his will and testament, known as the Book of the Covenant.

[24] Baha'u'llah strictly prohibited anyone from claiming to be a new messenger of God during the next one thousand years after his own ministry: "Whoso

without shame in the days of the Blessed Beauty [Baha'u'llah] had advanced such a claim as this and been confuted by Him in the aforementioned manner, the text of his claim being still extant in his own handwriting and bearing his own seal. ...

[I]n concert with others, he that hath broken the Covenant, hath prepared a document teeming with calumny and slander wherein, the Lord forbid, among many similar slanderous charges, 'Abdu'l-Bahá is deemed a deadly enemy, the ill-wisher of the Crown. They so perturbed the minds of the members of the Imperial Government that at last a Committee of Investigation was sent from the seat of His Majesty's Government which, violating every rule of justice and equity that befit His Imperial Majesty, nay, with the most glaring injustice, proceeded with its investigations. ... One of their many calumnies was that this servant had raised aloft a banner in this city, had summoned the people together under it, had established a new sovereignty for himself, had erected upon Mount Carmel a mighty stronghold, had rallied around him all the peoples of the land and made them obedient to him, had caused disruption in the Faith of Islam, had covenanted with the following of Christ and, God forbid, had purposed to cause the gravest breach in the mighty power of the Crown. May the Lord protect us from such atrocious falsehoods! ...

In like manner, the focal Center of Hate [Mohammed Ali], hath purposed to put 'Abdu'l-Bahá to death and this is supported by the testimony written by Mírzá Shu'á'u'lláh [i.e. Shua Ullah Behai] himself and is here enclosed.[25] It is evident and indisputable that they are privily and with the utmost subtlety engaged in conspiring against me. The following are his very words written by him in this letter:—"I curse at every moment him that hath kindled this discord, imprecate in these words 'Lord! have no mercy upon him' and I hope ere long God will make manifest the one that shall have no pity on him, who now weareth another garb and

---

layeth claim to a Revelation direct from God, ere the expiration of a full thousand years, such a man is assuredly a lying impostor." (*Kitab-i-Aqdas*, paragraph 37).

[25] This alleged testimony by Mr. Behai is not included in the book version of *The Will And Testament of 'Abdu'l-Bahá*. As far as this editor has been able to determine, it has never been published.

about whom I cannot any more explain." Reference he doth make by these words to the sacred verse that beginneth as follows:—"He that layeth a claim ere the passing of a thousand years..."[26] Reflect! How intent they are upon the death of 'Abdu'l-Bahá! ...

In short, O ye beloved of the Lord! The Center of Sedition, Mírzá Muhammad 'Alí, in accordance with the decisive words of God and by reason of his boundless transgression, hath grievously fallen and been cut off from the Holy Tree [i.e. excommunicated]. Verily, we wronged them not, but they have wronged themselves![27]

[The document also refers to a charge made against Mohammed Ali Effendi in a letter distributed by 'Abdu'l-Baha, which was written by Badi Ullah Effendi when he briefly switched sides in the conflict between his elder brothers, and accuses the latter of materialistic motives, duplicity and spying:]

Adversities have waxed still more severe as they rose with unbearable cruelty to overpower and crush me, as they scattered far and wide their scrolls of doubt and in utter falsehood hurled their calumnies upon me. Not content with this, their chief [Mohammed Ali], O my God, hath dared to interpolate Thy Book [i.e. Baha'u'llah's "Book of the Temple"], to fraudulently alter Thy decisive Holy Text and falsify that which hath been revealed by Thy All-Glorious Pen. He did also maliciously insert that which Thou didst reveal for the one that hath wrought the most glaring cruelty upon Thee, disbelieved in Thee and denied Thy wondrous Signs [i.e. Subh-i-Azal], into what Thou didst reveal for this servant of Thine that hath been wronged in this world.[28] All this he did that he

---

[26] Later in the verse, Baha'u'llah warns that a false prophet will experience a "merciless" punishment sent by God, but the specific nature of the punishment, and whether it is carried out by a supernatural or human agent, is not specified.

[27] *The Will And Testament of 'Abdu'l-Bahá* (Wilmette, Ill.: US Bahá'í Publishing Trust, 1990 reprint), Part One, pp. 5-9.

[28] The allegation is that Mohammed Ali Bahai changed one of Baha'u'llah's writings which criticized Mirza Yahya Subh-i-Azal, a half-brother of Baha'u'llah who refused to follow him and who made prophetic claims of his own, by

might beguile the souls of men and breathe his evil whisperings into the hearts of Thy devoted ones. Thereunto did their second chief [Badi Ullah] testify, confessing it in his own handwriting, setting thereupon his seal and spreading it throughout all regions. ...

Gracious God! After Mírzá Badí'u'lláh had declared in his own handwriting that this man (Muhammad 'Alí) had broken the Covenant and had proclaimed his falsification of the Holy Text, he realized that to return to the True Faith and pay allegiance to the Covenant and Testament would in no wise promote his selfish desires. He thus repented and regretted the thing he had done and attempted privily to gather in his printed confessions, plotted darkly with the Center of Sedition against me and informed him daily of all the happenings within my household.[29]

[Here the Will and Testament of 'Abdu'l-Baha commands the Baha'is to shun Mohammed Ali Effendi, his supporters, and anyone who has any connection at all with him:]

> And now, one of the greatest and most fundamental principles of the Cause of God is to shun and avoid entirely the Covenant-breakers, for they will utterly destroy the Cause of God, exterminate His Law and render of no account all efforts exerted in the past. ...
>
> [S]hould this man [Mohammed Ali] succeed in bringing disruption into the Cause of God, he will utterly destroy and exterminate it. Beware lest ye approach this man, for to approach him is worse than approaching fire! ...
>
> [I]t is incumbent upon the friends that are fast and firm in the Covenant and Testament to be ever wakeful lest after this wronged one [i.e. 'Abdu'l-Baha] is gone this alert and active worker of mischief may cause disruption, privily sow the seeds of doubt and sedition and utterly root out the Cause of God. A thousand times

---

substituting the name of 'Abdu'l-Baha to make it appear as if Baha'u'llah's criticism was directed at him. This is in addition to the previous allegation of interpolation, which is regarding the text of a book by Baha'u'llah that Mr. Bahai prepared for publication.

[29] *The Will And Testament of 'Abdu'l-Bahá* (Wilmette, Ill.: US Bahá'í Publishing Trust, 1990 reprint), Part Two, pp. 17-18, 21.

shun his company. Take heed and be on your guard. Watch and examine; should anyone, openly or privily, have the least connection with him, cast him out from your midst, for he will surely cause disruption and mischief.[30]

[T]he beloved of the Lord must entirely shun them [i.e. the followers of Mohammed Ali], avoid them, foil their machinations and evil whisperings, guard the Law of God and His religion, engage one and all in diffusing widely the sweet savors of God and to the best of their endeavor proclaim His Teachings.[31]

[Having given the reader reasons to believe that Mohammed Ali Effendi should not become the second successor of Baha'u'llah as envisioned in his will, the author of the Will and Testament of 'Abdu'l-Baha appoints Shoghi Effendi Rabbani to a position of "Guardianship" with supreme authority as the representative of God and chairman of the Universal House of Justice, and decrees that he should be succeeded by his lineal descendants:]

Salutation and praise, blessing and glory rest upon that primal branch of the Divine and Sacred Lote-Tree [i.e. Shoghi Effendi], grown out, blest, tender, verdant and flourishing from the Twin Holy Trees [the Bab and Baha'u'llah]; the most wondrous, unique and priceless pearl that doth gleam from out the Twin surging seas; ... [and] upon them that have believed, rested assured, stood steadfast in His Covenant and followed the Light that after my passing shineth from the Dayspring of Divine Guidance—for behold! he [Shoghi Effendi] is the blest and sacred bough that hath branched out from the Twin Holy Trees.[32] Well is it with him that seeketh the shelter of his shade that shadoweth all mankind. ...

---

[30] Ibid., Part Two, pp. 20-21.

[31] Ibid., Part Three, p. 25.

[32] Shoghi Effendi Rabbani was descended both from Baha'u'llah (as his great-grandson) and from the family of the Bab (as his great-grand-nephew). See Appendix B for genealogical lists of these two families and the intermarriages between them.

Chapter 8. The Teachings and Will of 'Abdu'l-Baha

O my loving friends! After the passing away of this wronged one, it is incumbent upon the *Aghsán* (Branches) [i.e. sons of Baha'u'llah], the *Afnán* (Twigs) of the Sacred Lote-Tree [i.e. relatives of the Bab], the Hands (pillars) of the Cause of God [i.e. highest appointed Baha'i leaders] and the loved ones of the Abhá Beauty [i.e. followers of Baha'u'llah] to turn unto Shoghi Effendi... as he is the sign of God, the chosen branch, the Guardian of the Cause of God... He is the Interpreter of the Word of God and after him will succeed the first-born of his lineal descendents.

The sacred and youthful branch, the Guardian of the Cause of God, as well as the Universal House of Justice to be universally elected and established, are both under the care and protection of the Abhá Beauty [Baha'u'llah], under the shelter and unerring guidance of the Exalted One [the Bab] (may my life be offered up for them both). Whatsoever they decide is of God. Whoso obeyeth him not [i.e. the Guardian], neither obeyeth them [the House of Justice], hath not obeyed God; whoso rebelleth against him and against them hath rebelled against God; whoso opposeth him hath opposed God; whoso contendeth with them hath contended with God; whoso disputeth with him hath disputed with God; whoso denieth him hath denied God; whoso disbelieveth in him hath disbelieved in God; whoso deviateth, separateth himself and turneth aside from him hath in truth deviated, separated himself and turned aside from God. May the wrath, the fierce indignation, the vengeance of God rest upon him! The mighty stronghold shall remain impregnable and safe through obedience to him who is the Guardian of the Cause of God. It is incumbent upon the members of the House of Justice, upon all the Aghsán, the Afnán, the Hands of the Cause of God to show their obedience, submissiveness and subordination unto the Guardian of the Cause of God, to turn unto him and be lowly before him. He that opposeth him hath opposed the True One, will make a breach in the Cause of God, will subvert His Word and will become a manifestation of the Center of Sedition. Beware, beware, lest the days after the ascension (of Bahá'u'lláh) be repeated when the Center of Sedition [Mohammed Ali] waxed haughty and rebellious and with Divine Unity for his excuse deprived himself and perturbed and poisoned others. ...

It is incumbent upon the Guardian of the Cause of God to appoint in his own life-time him that shall become his successor, that differences may not arise after his passing. ... [S]hould the first-born... not inherit of the spiritual within him... then must he (the Guardian of the Cause of God) choose another branch [i.e. male descendant of Baha'u'llah] to succeed him.

The Hands of the Cause of God must elect from their own number nine persons... [who] must give their assent to the choice of the one whom the Guardian of the Cause of God hath chosen as his successor. ...

And now, concerning the House of Justice which God hath ordained as the source of all good and freed from all error... the Guardian of the Cause of God is its sacred head and the distinguished member for life of that body. ... Should any of the members commit a sin, injurious to the common weal, the Guardian of the Cause of God hath at his own discretion the right to expel him, whereupon the people must elect another one in his stead.[33]

To none is given the right to put forth his own opinion or express his particular conviction. All must seek guidance and turn unto the Center of the Cause [i.e. the Guardian] and the House of Justice. And he that turneth unto whatsoever else is indeed in grievous error.[34]

[The "Guardian" is empowered to appoint and oversee a body of Baha'i religious leaders called "Hands of the Cause of God," who are given the power of excommunication:]

[T]he Hands of the Cause of God must be ever watchful and so soon as they find anyone beginning to oppose and protest against the Guardian of the Cause of God, cast him out from the congregation of the people of Bahá and in no wise accept any excuse from him. ...

O friends! The Hands of the Cause of God must be nominated and appointed by the Guardian of the Cause of God. All must be under his shadow and obey his command. Should any, within or

---

[33] *The Will And Testament of 'Abdu'l-Bahá* (Wilmette, Ill.: US Bahá'í Publishing Trust, 1990 reprint), Part One, pp. 3, 11-12, 14.

[34] Ibid., Part Three, p. 26.

without the company of the Hands of the Cause of God disobey and seek division, the wrath of God and His vengeance will be upon him, for he will have caused a breach in the true Faith of God.[35]

[Baha'is are instructed to donate 19% of their wealth to the Guardian of the faith:]

The Lord, as a sign of His infinite bounties, hath graciously favored His servants by providing for a fixed money offering (*Huqúq*), to be dutifully presented unto Him[36]... It is to be offered through the Guardian of the Cause of God, that it may be expended for the diffusion of the Fragrances of God and the exaltation of His Word, for benevolent pursuits and for the common weal.[37]

Reaction to the Alleged Will

When this will was published, I hoped that eventually it will be considered invalid, for the following reasons:

First, it is in violation of the commands of Baha'u'llah, and the laws laid down by him.

Second, it is contradictory to 'Abdu'l-Baha's own teachings, and Baha'i principles which he so nobly advocated.

Third, it is the destroyer of the foundation of liberty of thought, faith, belief, speech, and the press.

---

[35] Ibid., Part One, pp. 12-13.

[36] Baha'u'llah encouraged his followers to give him 19% of their wealth to be used for the benefit of the faith, a tithe he called *Huququ'llah*, meaning the "Right of God" (*Kitab-i-Aqdas*, paragraph 97). He did not provide specific instructions regarding how the practice of Huquq should continue after his own passing, although he did write in his will that "The love of the Branches is incumbent upon all, but God hath not ordained to any of them any right from the properties of the people." (See "The Book of My Covenant" in Chapter 6). Nevertheless, some Baha'is gave Huququ'llah to 'Abdu'l-Baha during his lifetime.

[37] *The Will And Testament of 'Abdu'l-Bahá* (Wilmette, Ill.: US Bahá'í Publishing Trust, 1990 reprint), Part One, p. 15.

But my hopes were shattered and my expectations were in vain, when one of the Baha'i communities, namely "The National Spiritual Assembly of the Baha'is of the United States and Canada," attributed such a prominence to this will, by incorporating the same into the by-laws of their organization, and compelling the members to become loyal and steadfast adherents to every clause of this will. Thus, reproducing the "catechism" of the old Roman Church:

- Baha'i Trinity [i.e. a trinity of divinely inspired chiefs of the faith: the Bab, Baha'u'llah, and 'Abdu'l-Baha].
- Baha'i Elders [i.e. the Hands of the Cause].[38]
- Guardians of the Cause, little popes, perpetual representatives of God on earth.[39]
- Excommunications.
- Absolutions.
- etc. etc. etc.

I firmly believe that 'Abdu'l-Baha was too wise to leave such a will, and I am in doubt of its authenticity.

Denial of Accusations

In this will, I am accused that, "God forbid," I have conspired against the life of 'Abdu'l-Baha.

How could it be possible that I should contemplate such an unlawful action towards my beloved uncle, my father's brother, and the father of the dearest lady [Mr. Behai's cousin Ruha Khanum] to whom I was engaged in my young days, and whom, despite the elapse of years, still I respect, cherish, and honor?

I emphatically deny the accusations against me in this will, and I

---

[38] The institution of the Hands of the Cause of God, as described in the Will and Testament of 'Abdu'l-Baha, is somewhat similar in function to the College of Cardinals in the Roman Catholic Church.

[39] A more accurate comparison for the Baha'i Guardianship would actually be the Shi'ite Imamate rather than the Catholic Papacy, since the Guardians were to be descendants of Baha'u'llah in each generation as the Twelve Imams were lineal descendants of the Prophet Muhammad. However, in terms of functioning as an officially chosen, supposedly infallible representative of God on earth, the offices were similar.

believe that they are fabricated by those who wrote the will, for the sole purpose of gaining control of leadership, as it is evident today.

Complying with the commands of Baha'u'llah, I forgive my accusers. Thank God, my conscience is clear, my character is clean, my name is unstained, and I know that the accusations are falsehood.

'Abdu'l-Baha in 1912.

9

A Tribute to 'Abdu'l-Baha and Doubts About His Will

By Kamar Bahai

This short essay is a circular letter or pamphlet that Kamar Bahai wrote in early 1953 called "Abdul Baha Abbas." Section headings have been added.

Mrs. Bahai praises 'Abdu'l-Baha effusively and does not mention his long-term unresolved feud with Mohammed Ali Effendi. She alleges that the Will and Testament of 'Abdu'l-Baha was forged and expresses concern that the content of the will, if accepted as his own, would undermine his reputation. In light of the conflict between her uncles which she ignores in this essay, her rejection of the purported testamentary document seems motivated in part by a desire to protect 'Abdu'l-Baha's image and that of the Baha'i faith, since he was a much-admired public figure who spoke for the new religion.

Kamar Bahai claims that "certain persons looking after their own private material benefit" wrote the will attributed to 'Abdu'l-Baha, but she does not identify these persons. According to her daughter Negar Bahai Emsallem, the story passed down in their family is that the appointment of Shoghi Effendi Rabbani to a position of "Guardianship" was the idea of his grandmother, Munirih Khanum, the wife of 'Abdu'l-Baha. It is conceivable that she, perhaps along with her daughter Zia'iyya Khanum (the mother of Shoghi Effendi) or other close relatives, could have forged all or part of the Will and Testament of 'Abdu'l-Baha with the intention to become powers behind the throne in Shoghi Effendi's ministry, since as Kamar Bahai points out, he was just a boy when the will was written.

However appealing this possibility may be for those who have disagreed with the institution of Guardianship of the Baha'i faith or Mr. Rabbani's exercise thereof—or who would prefer to purge 'Abdu'l-Baha's harsh and combative last words from the historical record—the forgery theory remains mostly conjecture, unsupported by any convincing evidence.

—The Editor

The Life of Abbas Effendi

'Abdu'l-Baha Abbas was born at midnight on the 23rd of May, 1844, in Tehran, the same year that "The Bab" proclaimed his mission to the world.[1]

When Abbas Effendi was scarcely nine years old, his father was arrested and imprisoned in Tehran. The mob attacked his house and looted it; the family was stripped of its property and left to suffer the sting of hardship and poverty.

'Abdu'l-Baha Abbas was so attached to his father that he almost appeared to act as his bodyguard. Being constantly around him, his father educated him as he wished and brought him up as he saw fit, sowed in him the seeds of his principles, built in him a strong personality, imbibed him with the spirit of humanitarianism, and taught him that those who serve humanity achieve victory in the end. He told him that to be a good Baha'i, he should love the world and humanity in general and try to serve it and labor for universal peace and brotherhood.

'Abdu'l-Baha Abbas graduated from his father's school a strong spiritual personality; he was wise and generous, a father to the needy and a guide to those who went astray. He drew his sublime principles and humanitarian ideals from the school of life and the hardships of experience.

---

[1] See Chapter 8, note 9.

Chapter 9. A Tribute to 'Abdu'l-Baha and Doubts About His Will

The despotic rule of Abdul Hamid having terminated in 1908 and the then young Turkey having extended a general amnesty for all prisoners, 'Abdu'l-Baha Abbas was released [in his mid or late 60s] from the prison which he had entered as a boy.[2]

At that age Abbas Effendi took upon himself the responsibility to propagate his father's mission, proceeded to Egypt, Switzerland, France, Germany, Hungary, Great Britain, the United States of America, and Canada, and there preached his father's principles and humanitarian ideals which were deeply rooted in him. In the course of his visits to those countries, thousands of people heard him preach the principles of his father, in churches and in every type of religious institution, and millions of people read about the teachings of Baha'u'llah in the local newspapers; and so in virtue of his magnetic personality he was able to attract men and women of every belief and religion.

His followers loved him greatly and he reciprocated their love, he lifted their standards morally, spiritually, and materially to the limit of his capacities, and he endeavored with all his might to come to the rescue of those who were materially in need as well as to those who sought moral assistance.

Allegation of Forgery of 'Abdu'l-Baha's Will

This beloved religious leader who called himself 'Abdu'l-Baha—meaning the servant of Baha'u'llah, his father—who was led by his father's personality in darkness and guided in solving problems; this leader who carried out his father's teachings almost literally without originating anything new himself or misconstruing; do you believe, dear reader, that this servant of Baha'u'llah, this honest and good man

---

[2] The Young Turk Revolution overthrew Sultan Abdul Hamid II, who had imprisoned many people in the Ottoman Empire who were regarded as political and social reformists. 'Abdu'l-Baha, along with the rest of Baha'u'llah's family, had been confined for decades to the vicinity of Acre in present-day Israel (then under Ottoman control), and at times in the prison-fortress in that city. The age of 'Abdu'l-Baha when he was released is either 64 or anywhere from 67 to 69, depending on which of several purported years of birth is accurate.

could in any way deviate from the path his master drew for him for the advancement and leadership of the Baha'i movement?

Certain persons looking after their own private material benefit originated what they called a will and attributed its issue to Abbas Effendi, in which he was supposed to have nominated his grandson [Shoghi Effendi Rabbani] to the spiritual leadership of the movement. This grandson who was at that time a young boy[3] and therefore unable to realize the extent of the great responsibility that was being entrusted to him by those persons, is, in my opinion—and I have undeniable evidence to this effect—unable to realize it up to the present moment.

Those persons, whether they intended or not, have certainly committed an unforgivable sin against Abbas Effendi. A will contradicting his father's Will! This is to Shame, Shame itself, especially as the sacred nature of a will is respected not only by the Easterners but also by the nations of the world. Moreover is it believable that Abbas Effendi should have tampered with [i.e. contradicted] his father's Will so long as he knew that he had no right whatever to change any-thing in it, especially as his father had limited the succession, in case of death, to his brother, Mohammed Ali Effendi?

Those persons who originated the will and pretended to venerate Abbas Effendi attached to him a disgrace which the commonest of people would have resented; so how much more with him, the great religious leader, for they have pictured him as a disobedient boy violating his father's Will, the same Will which gave him the right to the leadership. His brothers respected the holiness of their father's Will and accepted it and extended their help in the struggle for the propagation of the movement.

On Friday the 25th of November, 1921, 'Abdu'l-Baha Abbas as usual attended Friday prayers[4] and personally distributed alms to the poor and needy and returned to his residence. Three days later, on the 28th

---

[3] Part One of the Will and Testament of 'Abdu'l-Baha—in which the author appoints Shoghi Effendi to the position of "Guardian of the Cause of God"—is generally believed to have been written sometime between 1904 and 1907, when he was anywhere from seven to ten years old.

[4] 'Abdu'l-Baha attended weekly Islamic worship services throughout his life.

of November, he died, leaving according to his father's Will the spiritual leadership of the movement to his brother, Mohammed Ali Effendi.[5]

---

[5] 'Abdu'l-Baha certainly did not do so—the brothers had been feuding for years—although in the absence of an authentic will contradicting the Will and Testament of Baha'u'llah, the leadership of the Baha'i faith would have passed to the younger brother automatically according to Baha'u'llah's instructions.

Tablet of Baha'u'llah which praises his son Mohammed Ali, entitled Ghusn-i-Akbar. Image from *Behai Quarterly* magazine.

10

The Station of Ghusn-i-Akbar Mohammed Ali Bahai

By Shua Ullah Behai

This is the first part of a chapter of Shua Ullah Behai's book manuscript in which he introduces his father and reproduces several of his writings in English translation. It includes Mr. Behai's translation of a tablet written by Baha'u'llah in which he praises Mohammed Ali Effendi, who was entitled *Ghusn-i-Akbar* (the Greatest or Mightiest Branch).

The word *akbar* means "Greatest" in Arabic, being the superlative of *kabir*, "great," and in a religious context it can be taken as a reference to the almighty greatness of God (e.g. the Islamic affirmation *Allahu Akbar*, meaning that God is the Most Great or the Almighty). However, Baha'u'llah called Abbas Effendi by the title *Ghusn-i-A'zam*, which also means the Greatest Branch. To avoid confusion, Unitarian Baha'is usually translated Mohammed Ali Effendi's title as "the Mightiest Branch," reserving the title "the Greatest Branch" for 'Abdu'l-Baha, acknowledging the fact that Abbas Effendi was given the first position of leadership according to Baha'u'llah's will.[1]

The meaning and significance of the tablet of Baha'u'llah reproduced in this chapter was a matter of dispute between the followers of

---

[1] In the mainstream Baha'i tradition, 'Abdu'l-Baha is called either the "Most Great Branch" or "Most Mighty Branch," while Mohammed Ali Bahai is called the "Greater Branch." Both traditions thus indicate the primacy of the first son over the second son, though using a different nomenclature.

'Abdu'l-Baha and Mohammed Ali Bahai. Mr. Bahai and his supporters sometimes called it the "Holy Tablet" or "Sacred Tablet" and considered it an important proof text for the station of the younger son of Baha'u'llah as one of the Baha'i prophet's intended successors. They believed that the entire tablet was about him, Ghusn-i-Akbar, who is mentioned by name in the document. Abdu'l-Baha, on the other hand, reportedly argued that the first part of the tablet was about him, not Mr. Bahai, or that both brothers shared in that part of the tablet. One prominent Unitarian Baha'i accused 'Abdu'l-Baha of rejecting the tablet completely[2]—perhaps because it had become a source of sectarian tension—and in fact, it is generally unknown among Baha'is today.

In this editor's opinion, 'Abdu'l-Baha was likely correct in his belief that the tablet was about Baha'u'llah's successorship as a whole, beginning with Abbas Effendi and then continuing to Mohammed Ali Effendi, rather than referring only to the latter individual. The arrangement of the verses in the illuminated manuscript shown on page 146 is suggestive of two successors being identified and praised by Baha'u'llah. Most of the verses in the tablet would logically be applicable to any chosen "branch" appointed by Baha'u'llah to succeed him—and he is known to have appointed his two eldest sons in his will, first Ghusn-i-A'zam, then Ghusn-i-Akbar, rather than only one or the other. The tablet's ambiguity about the identity of the "branch" being referred to, in all but a few verses, is problematic. However, both the Unitarian Baha'is and the mainstream Baha'is have taken extreme positions in response to this confusion: the former insisting, despite some reasonable arguments to the contrary, that the tablet referred only to their own preferred leader; and the latter allowing this significant tablet to fade away into obscurity, having largely forgotten about its existence, presumably because some verses clearly praise and honor a man whom they consider the worst of heretics.

—The Editor

---

[2] See Chapter 22.

Chapter 10. The Station of Ghusn-i-Akbar Mohammed Ali Bahai

Ghusn-i-Akbar, the Mightiest Branch, Mohammed Ali Effendi—The second son of Baha'u'llah,[3] who was appointed in his Will entitled *Kitab-i-'Ahdi*, i.e. The Book of My Covenant, successor to Ghusn-i-A'zam, Abbas Effendi, 'Abdu'l-Baha.

Baha'u'llah says, "Verily God hath ordained the station of the Mightiest Branch (Ghusn-i-Akbar) after the station of the former [Ghusn-i-A'zam]; verily He is the Ordainer, the Wise. We have surely chosen the Mightiest (Akbar) after the Greatest (A'zam), as a Command from the All-Knowing, the Omniscient."[4]

This venerable son of Baha'u'llah was grossly misjudged, wronged, abused, and falsely accused by the so-called Baha'is—those who satisfied themselves with hearsay and passed judgment without investigation. His message to mankind, his will and autobiography which follow, explain the events, and no one could be a better defender of his case than himself.

He was born in Baghdad, Iraq, December 16, 1853, and passed unto Eternity at Haifa, Palestine, December 10, 1937.

He was a chosen branch and was favored with numerous tablets by the Supreme Pen of Baha'u'llah. The following is a translation of one of them:

THE GREATEST, THE MOST GLORIOUS.
O my God! Verily this is a Branch who hath branched from the lofty tree of Thy Singleness and the *Sadra* (Lote Tree) of Thy Oneness. Thou seest him, O my God, looking unto Thee and hold-

---

[3] Baha'u'llah's second-born son was actually Mirza Mihdi, a full-brother of 'Abdu'l-Baha who died in his youth and predeceased Baha'u'llah, and therefore Mohammed Ali Effendi has often been referred to as the second son, especially in the Unitarian Baha'i tradition.

[4] The word translated here twice by Shua Ullah Behai as "after" is *ba'da* in the original Arabic text of Baha'u'llah's will. This word can mean either "after" in time or after (beneath) in status. The official Baha'i translation is "beneath" in both places where the word appears—overemphasizing the other meaning of *ba'da* which Mr. Behai omits completely. An objective reading of the text would capture both meanings that Baha'u'llah seems to have intended: that (1) Mohammed Ali Effendi, his second son, should occupy a lesser status under the leadership of 'Abdu'l-Baha, his first son; and (2) after the death of the eldest, the primary leadership position should pass to the younger son.

ing fast to the rope of Thy benevolence. Therefore keep him in the vicinity of Thy mercy. Thou knowest, O my God, that I desire him not save because Thou hast desired him; and I have chosen him not save because Thou hast chosen him. Assist him with the hosts of Thy earth and heaven, and help, O my God, whosoever helpeth him, then choose Thou whosoever chooseth him, and forsake whosoever denieth him and desireth him not. O my Lord! Thou seest that at the time of elucidation my pen moveth and my limbs tremble. I ask Thee by my perplexity in Thy Love and my longing to reveal Thy Cause, to ordain for him whatsoever Thou hast destined for Thy Messengers and the faithful to Thy divine inspirations; verily Thou art God, the Almighty, the All-Powerful.

HE IS THE GREATEST:

O my God! Assist Thou Ghusn al-Akbar[5] (the Mightiest Branch) to Thy remembrance and Thy praise, then cause to flow from his pen the marvels of Thy sciences and secrets. My Lord! Verily he hath hastened unto Thy pleasure and hath fasted for the love of Thyself, and in obedience to Thine order. Destine for him every good revealed in Thy Book; verily Thou art the All-Powerful, the Omnipotent.

Blessed is he who hath rested in the shelter of the Branch of God, his Lord, Lord of the Throne and Lord of the Worlds.

O My Branch! Be thou the cloud of the Spring of My Generosity; then rain upon the things in My Name, the New.

O My Branch! We have chosen thee because the Chosen One hath chosen thee; say: praise be unto Thee, O God of all the worlds.

O Ghusn-i-Akbar! (Mightiest Branch) Verily We have chosen thee for the help of My Cause; rise thou in a marvelous assistance.

Conquer thou the cities (strongholds) of the names in My Name, the Ruler over all that He wisheth.

O Sea! wave in My Name, the Rising, the Great!

Verily every action dependeth on thy love; blessed is he that winneth that which hath been desired by his Lord, the All-Knowing.

Blessed is he that hath heard thy call and hath come forward unto thee for the love of God, the Lord of the worlds.

---

[5] *Ghusn al-Akbar* is the Arabic spelling of *Ghusn-i-Akbar*, which is Persian.

Mohammed Ali Bahai in 1900.

Badi Ullah Bahai in 1900.

11

Message to the Believers in America

By Mohammed Ali and Badi Ullah Bahai

This circular letter, written eight years after the passing of Baha'u'llah by the eldest and youngest sons of his second wife, was sent to Ibrahim G. Kheiralla to be read by the Baha'is of the United States.

Dr. Kheiralla had become a Baha'i during the ministry of Baha'u'llah and was the recipient of several tablets addressed to him. He was the first Baha'i missionary to the United States and became the founder of the American Baha'i community. After Baha'u'llah's passing, he initially supported 'Abdu'l-Baha, but later became convinced of the Unitarian interpretation of the Baha'i faith as taught by the younger sons of Baha'u'llah.

This message by Messrs. Bahai was translated into English and printed by Dr. Kheiralla in a book he compiled and published in 1901, entitled *Facts for Behaists*. Section headings have been added, and some paragraphs have been combined or divided.

—The Editor

A message to the believers from the younger Branches, the Mightiest Branch [i.e. Ghusn-i-Akbar], Mohammed Ali Effendi, and the Most Luminous Branch [i.e. Ghusn-i-Anwar], Badi Ullah Effendi.

TO THE BELIEVERS:

By the Sacred Name of our God, who has no equal. O children of the Kingdom! The Sun of Divinity has shone upon you when It appeared upon the horizon of the world, clothed in the garment of the Greatest Name [i.e. Baha'u'llah], and the Supreme Pen revealed that our God, El ABHA, accepted the sufferings, calamities, imprisonment, exile, and persecutions for the salvation of the creatures, for all people, and for developing them to the highest position; and that He sacrificed himself for the peace of the world, passed His days in guiding the people of the world, revealed in His holy books that which will exultingly expand the hearts of the people of knowledge and understanding and will guide His creatures to the horizons of virtue and mercy.

Baha'u'llah's Greatest Teaching

Hark to what He pronounces in the Tablet of Wisdom![1] where His tongue gives utterance to most perfect precepts and complete wisdom: "The glory is not in loving yourselves, but rather in loving the children of your kind [i.e. humankind]; the virtue is not to the one who loves his native land, but rather to him who loves the world."

This utterance satisfies those of understanding and brings those who are seekers to a higher attitude and a universal reward.

There is no doubt that if any man would attain this chief glory and will acquire this transcendent virtue he will realize that all creatures are brothers, will find that the countries are as one native land, will see the lights of the Kingdom shining forth toward humanity, will receive the protection of the Beneficent and Everlasting Father surrounding all His children and the Kingdom of that Eternal God pervading all directions.

Also see the greatness and wisdom of the following text: "Make your mornings better than your evenings and your tomorrows better than your yesterdays." I bear witness that He perfected the wisdom, completed the grace, and revealed to His favorites that which will cause them to reach to the highest degrees and attain the most honorable attitudes. [Baha'u'llah continues:] "Blessed be he who will be enlightened by the lamp of His revelation and will ascend to the heavens of His knowledge, and will stand forth to mention His perfection, which irradiates and shines upon His creatures."

---

[1] The *Lawh-i-Hikmat*.

The Duty of Every Baha'i to Teach the Faith

O brothers, pure in heart and with lights shining from the horizon of love and faithfulness, what are the duties of the children of this Father, who suffered the direst calamities for the salvation of nations and yielded to imprisonment for the liberation of the world? Is it our duty to be silent or inactive after His Supreme Pen cried every morning and every evening, calling His creatures to the Everlasting Paradise? Is it meet that we sit down and rest after we discover that the Lord has suffered innumerable calamities, exile and imprisonment by the hands of His creatures? By your lives, I say unto you, NO![2]

O brothers, we must endeavor in every way to spread the fragrances of His Word and raise the standard of His knowledge and wisdom everywhere, and thus attract the pure in heart toward the Highest Kingdom and enlighten the world by the radiance of unity and truthfulness.

I ask from the benevolence of this Living One, "The Ancient of Days," to sustain you all in the service of His Great Cause, and to guide the children to the Father, the Loving and the Merciful.

Turn to the Scriptures of Baha'u'llah

Think of those who, after the ascension of the Redeemer [i.e. Jesus], arose for the spreading of the lights of unity! How they opened every country and attracted the hearts of their people. If their uprising was caused by the appearance of the Holy Spirit, seen in the "likeness of a dove,"[3] now that Spirit is transfigured in the form of the highest utterance to the people of Baha, and shines from the horizons of the books of our God, El ABHA, which swells the hearts, gives rest to the eyes, and

---

[2] Mohammed Ali Effendi and Badi Ullah Effendi are saying that in the same way as all Baha'is should work to spread the faith of Baha'u'llah, they themselves should do likewise, rather than remaining "silent or inactive" in the cause because of their theological disagreement with their elder brother, Abbas Effendi.

[3] When Jesus was baptized, God's Spirit is said to have descended upon him in the form of a dove, and thereafter he began his ministry (see Luke 3:21-23, John 1:32-37).

gladdens the innermost soul. There can be no doubt that the Most High deposited in every word of the texts in the books a Spirit which sustains and confirms all people of discernment, strengthening them in every good and perfect word.

Ponder well upon this [verse], which is shining from the horizon of His Most Holy Book: "If you differ concerning any matter, carry it to God, so long as the Sun of Revelation is shining from the horizon of this Heaven; but after this Sun has set, then bring the differences unto His utterances, which suffices the worlds."[4]

In the above quotation He has substituted His great texts in the place of His Supreme Self and has commanded everyone to go to them when in difficulty, after the setting of the Sun of Truth from the horizon of humanity and its shining in the horizon of the Heavenly Kingdom. His Word is the balance for our fullness and fineness. Weigh well everything in this great balance, which has descended from your God, the All-Wise.

Respect for Baha'i Leaders

In the exalted position and attitude, respect the one who has been the means of guiding you to this highest Kingdom [i.e. Ibrahim Kheiralla]—who has brought you to the knowledge of your God, El ABHA.

Let it be known to you also that the position and attitude of the Branches of the Tree of Life [i.e. the sons of Baha'u'llah] are those of absolute servitude (to God and His people). They are the finger-posts pointing the way toward the Sun of Truth. God has created them and raised them up to continually spread the knowledge of the Word and to elevate His commands among His creatures; has commanded everyone to honor them and respect them and to appreciate their position, to look upon them as an example in the shadow of the Word of God in disseminating the fragrances of His utterances and raising the standards [i.e. banner] of His revelations. That is to say—provided they (the Branches) are faithfully rising to serve the cause of God and endeavoring to spread the lights of the Word of God, then it is meet that the

---

[4] *Kitab-i-Aqdas* ("Most Holy Book"), paragraph 53.

people of understanding and wisdom and the believers shall take them as examples and follow in their footsteps. The texts of the Book and the tablets of our Merciful God bear witness to what I say.

Baha'u'llah Is the Messiah[5]

O you who are turning toward God, "The Ancient of Days," be assured that your Lord the All-Knowing has named His Most Glorious Temple [i.e. Baha'u'llah] as the Branch in many different tablets, e.g. the "Branch of Command," the "Branch of Holiness" and the "Branch of Eternity." These are grandly beautiful titles, confined to His great and glorious Temple—His Temple which was promised in the holy scriptures—and He built it with the Hand of Might after He reached the prison at Acre, which was called in the prophecies "The Land of Judgment" and "The White City." This was a symbol of the appearance of "The Ancient of Days,"[6] and all things mentioned in the holy scriptures were and are attributed only to His absolute perfection and Glorious Temple.

Likewise He called Himself "The Servant," a fulfillment of what was said in the books of the prophets of all times.

The Cause of Schism Among Baha'is

O sons of the Kingdom, let it be known to you that after that great calamity, the departure of the beloved El ABHA [i.e. the death of Baha'u'llah], had befallen us, we were continually dealing with everyone

---

[5] This section of the message appears to be a rebuttal to claims of divinity for 'Abdu'l-Baha that Messrs. Bahai were concerned were circulating. In the early years of 'Abdu'l-Baha's ministry, many American Baha'is considered him as the return of Christ. Messrs. Bahai are arguing that any messianic titles or prophecies belong only to Baha'u'llah.

[6] The "Ancient of Days" is a term used in the Old Testament to refer to God as the Judge of humanity: "Thrones were set in place, and the Ancient of Days took his seat. His clothing was as white as snow; the hair of his head was white like wool. His throne was flaming with fire, and its wheels were all ablaze." (Daniel 7:9). The Book of Daniel continues with a prophecy of the Ancient of Days raising up the Messiah and God's Kingdom on earth (vss. 13-14).

in kindness and in peace and with purity of thought and intention. In the spirit of obedience to the command of the Supreme Pen [to turn to Abbas Effendi] we used to harmoniously accompany them [i.e. his followers] in every question which is in accordance with the revelations in the Holy Book, until we discovered the odor of departure from the safety found in the shadow of the Word, and we realized that there was disobedience to or departure from the sacred texts—evident endeavor to attain personal desires and especial purposes; the promulgation of ideas and tenets which our God, "The Ancient of Days," prohibited, and the spreading of teachings contradictory to those found in the tablets of our Great God. Then we were quick to give voice to the utterances of God in the ears of the people; we published the books of the Mighty and the Giver of All Things [i.e. Baha'u'llah]; we taught the people what we found in the tablets and what we learned from the writings traced by the Pen of the Father.

If God wishes, we will send to you that which will give you a clear understanding of the whole question [of the schism]. For this reason we are now writing in brevity: Hoping that the Holy Spirit will confirm you in all conditions and that the angels of victory will help you in the dawn and in the evening, and that the Lord, Most High is He, will endow you with the divine power to spread the lights of the Kingdom now established on the earth.

Closing Salutation and Prayer

Greetings and El Baha (the Splendor [of God]) be upon you, O children who are following the Father, who is transfigured in the horizon of His Splendor [i.e. Baha'u'llah].

O my Lord, thou seest those who have been attracted by the fragrances of Thy Word and who have labored in heralding Thee amongst Thy creatures. Thou knowest that they confessed the greatness of Thy name, El ABHA, and the Oneness of Thyself, the Most High. I ask Thee to enroll them in Thy services and in Thy work with such steadfastness that expands the heart of the Son [i.e. Jesus], who is standing on the right hand of Thy Majesty, and which makes the innermost of the pure in heart to tremble with joy in the Kingdom of Thy Might; that the world may be flooded with the light that is shining from the horizon of Thy Greatest Name, and the souls and hearts of all shall be drawn to the horizon of Thy name, the Mighty and the Beloved.

>   (Signed by:)   Mohammed Ali
>   Badi Ullah
>
> April 1, 1900.

Mohammed Ali Bahai in the 1920s.

12

Message upon the Passing of 'Abdu'l-Baha

By Mohammed Ali Bahai

This circular letter by Mohammed Ali Bahai was written soon after the death of his elder half-brother Abbas Effendi in 1921 and was intended to be read by all Baha'is. It is not known how many people actually read the letter, since the majority of Baha'is shunned Mr. Bahai as a "Covenant-breaker," but presumably it was read by adherents of the Unitarian Baha'i tradition, which included most of Baha'u'llah's family and some others. This document was included in a chapter of Shua Ullah Behai's book manuscript in which he compiles several of his father's writings in English translation. Section headings have been added.

This letter can be considered the opening statement of Mohammed Ali Effendi's ministry as the second successor of Baha'u'llah, as he saw himself according to Baha'u'llah's will. Even though he was never recognized as such by most Baha'is, he comes across in this message as a man whose values and leadership style focused on avoiding sectarian conflict and learning from the mistakes of the past, rather than continuing to pour salt in old wounds. Although some might perceive his very brief reminiscence on the career and character of 'Abdu'l-Baha as damning him with faint praise, Mr. Bahai displays no desire to downplay the importance or legitimacy of 'Abdu'l-Baha's leadership of the Baha'i faith, or even to offer any public criticism of the brother with whom he contended over matters of religious doctrine for nearly 30 years.

—The Editor

TO THE BAHA'IS FAR AND NEAR:

I deeply regret to have to record the great and unspeakable bereavement we have recently sustained by the departure of the venerable Ghusn-i-A'zam, Abbas Effendi, Sir[1] 'Abdu'l-Baha, who was the backbone and support of his friends and the pride of his followers. Indeed I feel that the more I try to describe him and show my deep grief for his loss, the more I feel my utter inability by word or pen, to give an exact description of his personality. I pray God to grant us patience and to comfort us with His mercy and to follow the right course laid down by our Great Master Baha'u'llah, namely the unison of hearts and complete unanimity of opinion to act in accordance with what our Great Master wrote in the Book containing His last Will written in His own honorable autography, entitled the Book of My Covenant.

Overcoming Hatred Through Forgiveness and Good Speech

Dear friends:

I have addressed you twice before[2] and wish hereby to address you for the third time, as I feel it my much desired duty, much more than ever it was before. My only aim is to remind you of the precepts and admonitions which we have been given to follow. You, as well as all the

---

[1] 'Abdu'l-Baha had been honored as a Knight of the British Empire for his charitable aid to the poor of Palestine, hence the title "Sir." This title has only rarely been used by Baha'is in reference to 'Abdu'l-Baha, since he did not use it himself.

[2] This statement would appear to indicate that Mohammed Ali Bahai wrote two previous circular letters to the Baha'i community. The first one is probably the epistle called "The Essence of Unity" which resulted in Mr. Bahai's immediate excommunication by 'Abdu'l-Baha (see Chapter 16, the sections entitled "Unitarian Baha'is Excommunicated and Shunned" and "Comments on Excommunication and Baha'i Leadership"). The second one might be the "Message to the Believers in America" he co-authored with his younger brother Badi Ullah (Chapter 11), but this is uncertain; it could be a different document. Neither of the first two epistles of Mr. Bahai were included among the texts his son Shua Ullah compiled in his book manuscript.

world, are aware that our Great Master and Example Baha'u'llah spent all His days and exerted His energies in educating and uniting the hearts, and guiding His followers to what would benefit them all over the world. Further, in the Book of His Will referred to above, He reminds them all of His desires and His great aim, wherein He mentions that His purpose in all His [i.e. God's] mortal Manifestations and bearing troubles and hardships was to quench the fire of hatred latent in the hearts of the parties, and wherein He also orders all to follow His footsteps.

Among His counsels are the following precepts: "The tongue is for utterance of good; defile it not with bad speech. May God forgive the past. Everyone henceforth should speak decently and avoid cursing, backbiting, and any word that might grieve a man."

The Book [of My Covenant] is full of such precepts and as you all have gone through it, I will be short and come to the point. I do not intend by these words to acquaint you with my right mentioned therein as you have surely read it often for many years, and you are well aware that [Baha'u'llah] appointed two positions and defined their personalities, namely, firstly the Greatest Branch [Ghusn-i-A'zam, Abbas Effendi] and secondly the Mightiest Branch [Ghusn-i-Akbar, Mohammed Ali Effendi]. Therefore there is no need for either bringing the point home to you or even making mention of it, but I have today wished to address you by virtue of my moral position, in order to call upon you to act in accordance with the statutes relating to the uniting of the hearts of mankind and harmonizing their thoughts and struggling to remove hatred from the hearts of the parties.

The Duties of Being a Baha'i

Good friends:
You are aware of mortality and that death might come any moment, and that everything might be deferred and made light of with the exception of one's duties, for if a man neglects them he is sure to regret it and stand responsible therefore before God and himself as well.

O ye that know: Do ye in accordance with your knowledge that which shall please your Master.[3] Ponder ye the history of bygone days and take it as a lesson, lest it might be written thus about you on the pages of time. Our Great Master's commands go to educate the character, improve the reputation, establish unity, love, and good morals, and remove hatred. In short they approve all attributes becoming of human beings and condemn all attributes unseemly. If ye, therefore, strive after these things, you shall be the recipient of all goodness and rewards, the greatest of which is the pleasure of our Great Master, who sacrificed His rest and struggled for fifty years for our instruction and education, and bore afflictions and troubles in order to maintain the cause of this noble aim and to give it publicity.

This is what occurred to me; and I believed it to be my duty of love and sincerity. I have mentioned it in the above lines, hoping that you will do your very best to fulfill your duties and avoid all things forbidden in the writings of our Great Master Baha'u'llah, so that we might have a name more gentle than light, and a memory more fragrant than perfume.

May God the Almighty strengthen you to do His Will, and protect you from what He abhors. PEACE BE WITH YOU.

---

[3] Mohammed Ali Bahai frequently refers to Baha'u'llah as "Master" or "Great Master." He never refers to 'Abdu'l-Baha as "Master," as became customary among Baha'is of the mainstream tradition.

13

On the Baha'i Vision of World Civilization: A Message to Mankind

By Mohammed Ali Bahai

This chapter is compiled from two messages by Mohammed Ali Bahai that were translated into English by his son Shua Ullah and published in *Behai Quarterly* magazine, the periodical of the American Unitarian Baha'i community. The first one, written in January 1934, was untitled and is reproduced here in its entirety. The second one, written in November 1935, was called "A message to mankind," and most of it is included here, with the exception of a concluding invitation to peruse the author's personal library of Baha'u'llah's writings. The first of these two messages was also included in Shua Ullah Behai's book manuscript. Section headings have been added, and the last section is from the November 1935 message.

—The Editor

Corrupt Theocracy and the Baha'i Movement for Reform

Nothing takes place in this world without a cause, and no matter of importance displays itself without some reason to necessitate it. The physician is generally required when maladies and diseases prevail, and the need for a just and noble ruler is more strongly felt when disorder and injustice dominate.

Readers of the world news know well how far discord and inequity invaded the Near East in the 19th century, especially Persia. Religion, which was established solely for the purpose of the betterment of the nations and the promotion of the manners and morality of mankind, was made the greatest cause for the attainment of personal interests and selfish desires, and used as a stepping stone for gaining power and ruling the people. The influence and power of the religious leaders were so great that government itself was but a tool in their hands, and thus fulfilled the orders they would dictate. Therefore no act of the government could be passed and executed without its being first sanctioned by these religious authorities. The poor nation, being powerless and wholly in the hands of these authorities, had no choice but to abide by their wishes and thus be deprived of promotion and success. They were completely overcome and unable to take a single step for their own welfare or even breathe of any reform of civilization.

Because these corruptions were carried out under a moral pretext, and as the religious authorities had found in and made of religion a means of furthering their worldly interests and desires and of spreading their deviancy, there was no other alternative but to remove these diseases by uplifting the morality and strengthening the spiritual tendencies of the people. It was an instructive cause and a natural tendency that brought about the renewal. It was a spiritual reality that appeared in corporeal form, and a luminous state [of being] that worked to reform the defects and remedy the diseases.

As soon as these spiritual matters became publicly known in the country, the religious heads began to raise their voices in opposition as was their habit for ages past. They attacked from all sides and caused numerous difficulties, doing deeds which neither the tongue nor the pen can record or enumerate.

When these injustices became very great, Baha'u'llah rose with a strong will and a still stronger energy, wisdom, and eloquence, and began to educate and instruct the people. He made great advances in bettering both their moral and material condition and spent his entire time seeking to remove the existing problems and controversies. His beautiful speeches and honorable words speak of his greatness and open the way to righteousness, rectitude, and salvation.

For the benefit of all people, I briefly quote hereunder some of his statements, so that the reader will realize his motive in bearing all hardships and difficulties to which he was exposed during his time on earth. It is undoubtedly clear that had his motive been to attain greatness and accumulate riches, the means for doing so were not lacking prior to his arising [in his mission], and so there would have been no need for bearing all these hardships and difficulties. It is then quite clear that there was a spiritual motive behind his actions, which were the means of showing forth all this power and steadfastness.

Baha'u'llah's Teachings for a New World

There is no doubt that every matter or cause in this [plane of] existence appears in the context of the necessities of the time and the tendencies of the people. Thus in these days in which the effects of the Great War[1] still prevail and are not forgotten, we see that more efforts are being spent on inventing instruments of destruction and means of devastation. I, therefore, consider it a moral obligation to disclose some of the words of Baha'u'llah which I find most useful and relevant in these trying times.

It is evident that so long as discord reigns among the governments, the public will remain troubled and unable to find rest. Every day brings new problems and at any time political disagreements may be further inflamed.

For this reason Baha'u'llah invited all the governments to the Most Great Peace and admonished the reduction of arms and the improvement of the world, so that there should remain no need for the government to keep large armies which would only be a burden. He recommended only the keeping of a force sufficient to guard and protect the people.

He prohibited the increase of all government expenditure to prevent burdening the people with it, and says that the public is the treasury of the government. "Do not burden them (the public) lest they should be ruined, and do not entrust that treasury to the thieves, that it might be saved"—that is, do not appoint dishonest officials to govern the people.

---

[1] World War I.

Baha'u'llah says: "Repair the broken with the hand of justice"—that is, look after the oppressed and deal with them in justice and moderation. "Break the agent of the oppressor with the power of just orders"—that is, punish the powerful oppressor with justice and equity.

Baha'u'llah also says that governments should know perfectly well the affairs of their officials, and should give the position to those who deserve it and are both capable and honest.

A ruler who governs different colonies must rule each of them with regulations suitable and convenient to the customs and usages of the people, not according to the rules and laws of the mother country. Care must be taken that the appointed governor or ruler be one learned in the ways, habits, and language of the people whom he governs so that he may be able to perform his duties efficiently.

Governments should observe the common interest in justice and equity, making no exceptions because the people are of different nationalities and creeds. Before the law all are equal. Their treatment must be based on equality and justice; none should be given preference to others. This principle must be strictly observed.

The League of Nations[2] is one of the best schemes adopted by the world powers, only on condition that its program should guarantee and protect peace among the nations; not that it should be confined to the special interest of some of the great powers. A special force should also be appointed for the execution of the decisions of the League and should be in a position to inflict punishment on any of the powers exceeding the limits of the program.

Another principle of Baha'u'llah is the choosing of one of the existing languages or the invention of a new one [as a common means of communication], so that the people will not spend years of this life in studying languages to be able to understand one another. Here this writer wishes to state that to choose one of the existing languages would seem difficult, because no nation would agree to give up its own language and adopt another. Therefore, it would seem advisable to invent a new language. It is evident that the existing languages, not having been specially composed, are not free of difficulties either in pro-

---

[2] Predecessor of the United Nations.

nunciation or grammatical rules. It would therefore seem advisable to elect certain learned persons from every nationality both Occidental and Oriental, who would jointly invent a new language which would be altogether free from the difficulties observed in the existing languages, and which would also be easy to master. This language would then be adopted as a secondary language in all the schools of the world.

Baha'u'llah says it is incumbent on all fathers to educate their children, and if the fathers desist from it, those who are in a position to do so should bring them up and educate them, charging the expenses to the fathers; and if these be poor and unable to pay the expenses, then the House of Justice should be responsible for the payment, because the House of Justice has been established as a refuge for the poor and the needy.

Baha'is must treat the government of any kingdom [or country] in whose dominion they live with honesty, truth, faithfulness, and righteousness.

It is evidently clear to all people of understanding that the more the intellectual powers of a nation are increased, the stronger and greater the government of that nation becomes, because nations are the backbones of the governments.

In the "Book of My Covenant" (*Kitab-i-'Ahdi*), his Last Will, Baha'u'llah says:

> O saints of God and His loyal ones! Rulers are the manifestations of power and the day-springs of the might and wealth of the True One. Pray for them, for the government of the earth is ordained to these souls; but the hearts He hath appointed for Himself. He hath forbidden dispute and strife with an absolute prohibition in the Book. ...
>
> It is incumbent upon all to aid those souls who are the day-springs of authority and the dawning-places of command, and who are adorned with the ornament of equity and justice.
>
> O people of the world! I enjoin you to that which is the means of the elevation of your stations. ...
>
> Verily I say, the tongue is for mentioning that which is good; pollute it not with evil speech. ...

> O people of the world! The religion of God is for love and union; make it not the cause of discord and disunion. ...
>
> We enjoin you to the service of the nations and to the pacification of the world.

In another tablet Baha'u'llah says:

> O people of Baha! Consort with all the people of the world with love and spirituality. If ye have a word or a jewel of which others are deprived, say it with the tongue of love and tenderness. If it is accepted and the effect produced, the object is attained; otherwise leave him to himself and pray on his behalf and be not harsh to him. The tongue of tenderness attracts the hearts and is food for the soul.

Baha'u'llah also says:

> Be a good example amongst the creatures, and a book of admonition which they long to copy. Say: Let your word be one word and your thought one thought. Let your mornings be better than your evenings and your tomorrows better than your yesterdays. The glory of man is in his service and perfection, and not in decoration, wealth, or money. Sanctify your speech from falsity and lust, and purify your deeds from doubts and hypocrisy. Squander not the achievements of your precious lives on selfish desires, and confine not your efforts for your personal benefit. Spend when ye gain, and be patient when ye lose. Verily there is ease after every hardship, and clarity after every disturbance. Beware lest ye sow the tares of contention among the creatures and the thorn of doubt in good and pure hearts. Ye have been created for love, and not for hatred and strife. The honor is not in loving yourselves, but in loving your kind; and the glory is not to him who loveth his native land, but to him who loveth the world. Let justice be your army, and your weapon reason. Be characterized with forgiveness and charity, and with that which giveth pleasure to the hearts of the angels.[3]

---

[3] *Lawh-i-Hikmat* ("Tablet of Wisdom").

Proposal for a Representative Democratic World Assembly

The present state of affairs in the world at large obliges me to suggest a proposal which I hope will meet with the approval of the civilized world; and I further hope that those who hold in their hands the future of the nations will assist me in this matter, because in making this proposal, my only goal and aim is the good of the nations and the betterment of the affairs of the world.

All laws, whether spiritual or civil, are to be bringing about union, brotherhood, liberty and equality. The union of the nation is the foundation on which the pillars of politics are erected and its laws promulgated; and union is only obtained through brotherhood, liberty, and equality.

The world is not devoid of differences in ideas, beliefs, and aspirations, but I think that the differences of [religious] belief must be confined to places of worship. Every person is free to believe however and in whomsoever he wishes, and these different doctrines have nothing to do with human society. After finishing our prayers in our different places of worship, we are all one in humanity and brotherhood, and must consequently be on terms of equity in our mutual relations and in civil rights. In this respect Baha'u'llah says, "Ye are all the fruits of one tree, and the drops of one sea."

It is true that our languages, morals, manners, habits, and usages differ, but the human world includes us all. We are all from one root and we are, therefore, members of one universal brotherhood; and between brothers nothing should exist which might contradict equity and concord, and from which differences might arise.

Circumstances sometimes necessitate the union of two or more powers of the political world into a compact or agreement which is only carried out for the general welfare of the powers so uniting. The results and ends arrived at by such union cannot be denied. I would, therefore, suggest to my brothers in humanity to follow in this matter the footsteps of the political leaders of the world, and appoint a special place for meetings to be held, in order to discuss all matters of importance. The following conditions should apply to the meetings and must be observed:

1. That the assembly be held with the permission of the government.
2. That regular meetings be held therein at specified intervals.
3. That representatives of all classes of the people of the different nationalities and religions attend the meetings. These representatives should be qualified persons nominated by their respective nations and sects, and having full power to discuss and decide matters which would tend to promote the welfare of the nations.
4. That the representatives of all classes, nationalities, and creeds should be treated in the assembly on the same standing, no preference being given to the representatives of any nation or group over others.
5. That the decisions arrived at in these meetings be morally binding on the representatives themselves and on the nations they represent. These decisions should be properly arranged, signed, printed, and distributed among the nations.
6. That in case any deviation from these rules and decisions is noticed, the person or persons found guilty be warned and treated in the manner found most suitable by the representatives themselves, because no betterment of the world would be possible if the rules and laws laid down by the governing authorities are not observed and obeyed.

We can come to perfect agreement only if we revere and honor our mutual opinions, although some of them may be contrary to our own habits and usages. From disregard and disrespect of other people's opinions nothing would result but harm and injury.

Baha'u'llah says: "O different creeds! Look forward unto agreement and be enlightened by the light of concord. For the sake of God, assemble in a place and remove from amongst you that which is the cause of dissension."

This led me to lay out the above-mentioned proposal, and my only hope and desire is that if my proposal is met with approval and carried out, the assembly may not be temporary, but continue on indefinitely.

The affairs of the world, as witnessed, are not promising in the least, and the moral obligations have never been so binding as they are today. So let all who can, rise up and act, that the world may be better and its inhabitants happier.

A Plea for Universal Peace and Brotherhood

My brothers in humanity:

These are critical days in which the entire world is threatened with another conflict, socially, economically, and politically.

The hearts of the individuals are filled with hatred towards one another through the spirit of nationalism.

The sun of peace is covered with the clouds of preparedness for war.

The lamp of unity is dimmed, treaties violated, covenants broken, natural laws discarded, moral obligations forgotten, and discord substituted for harmony.

I sincerely request every seeker of truth throughout the world to pray in his own way for universal peace and better understanding amongst the children of man.

Ponder over this message of our Great Master Baha'u'llah: "Let justice be your army and your weapon reason. Be characterized by forgiveness and virtue, and do what brings happiness to those who are near to God."

"The glory is not in loving yourselves but rather in loving your kind; the virtue is not for him who loves his native land, but rather for him who loves the world."

Humanity is in need of his instructive principles today more than ever. Through their adoption and practice mankind will become better and live in greater happiness and harmony with one another. Therefore, I invite you my brothers to come, search, and study his wonderful teachings.

14

On Religious Conflict, Freedom and Unity: A Message to the People of Understanding

By *Mohammed Ali Bahai*

This essay by Mohammed Ali Bahai, originally titled "A message to the people of understanding throughout the World," was written in January 1935 and translated into English by his son Shua Ullah. The translation was published in the United States in *Behai Quarterly* magazine. Section headings have been added.

—The Editor

The Fountainhead of Knowledge said: "O different creeds! Look forward unto agreement and be enlightened by the light of concord. For the sake of God, assemble in a place and remove from amongst you that which is the cause of dissension."

From where did these rare jewels of wisdom come? The speaker—who was he, and what was his object? Who are the different creeds, and what is it that must be removed before mankind may hope to live in harmony?

A voice arose from the ancient fortified city of Akka, in Palestine. A voice of infinite wisdom and knowledge, patience and love for all mankind: our Master Baha'u'llah. One who gave freely of His great understanding, with no object save the elevation and progress of His fellowmen.

Religious Leaders Are a Source of Conflict and Suffering

"O different creeds," who are the cause of dissension [among you]? Are they not the religious leaders of the great nations and peoples, followed in kind by the religious leaders of smaller ones? We have but to recall the events of the last World War. With our own eyes and ears, we observed and heard the enslavement, martyrdom and suffering of countless souls in all parts of this globe, wrought in the name of the different creeds by the religious leaders, who misguided the innocent followers and used the inspired teachings for their personal desires and aims, causing conflict amongst the people of the world, dividing the brothers of humanity—and as in the innumerable wars of the past, destroyed life and property, cities and nations.

Religious conflict is like a blazing forest fire, which starts with a spark and ends, generally beyond control, destroying green and dead vegetation alike. To this the history of the world bears witness.

Although each different creed teaches unity, accusing others of dissension and strife, if they would observe with a keen eye and speak with the tongue of justice, they must testify that now, as in ages past, religious hatred is the foundation and cause of many unspeakable events.

The spiritual teachings given to mankind through the inspired sages, which are revealed for the purpose of enlightening the understanding and elevating the souls of humanity out of the mire of ignorance and superstition, became the whips of the leaders of the many creeds—whips which were used upon innocent, undeveloped, and unenlightened individuals, exploiting and oppressing the people who sincerely followed them. Paying dearly with their lives and fortunes. O Religion! what atrocious crimes have been committed in thy name!

The result is here, as we observe today: Humanity en masse has rebelled against all the religious creeds, understanding them only as a medium through which the leaders receive benefit, elevating their status in life, fulfilling their desires, and giving the right to rule over the oppressed masses.

Freedom from Clergy

Behold! a great principle: "Religion Without Clergy." Baha'u'llah commanded that His teachings are our leaders, and we accept them literally without interpretation. Indeed by this command He released us from the bondage of the clergy.

In these days of fast material progress, modern scientific discoveries have proven to be of great service to the inhabitants of this world; humanity with its great unlimited power of thought has also advanced greatly, imaginations become realities, and the hidden mysteries are no longer hidden to those who understand. Yet in this age of fast progress with such advance in human development, it is pitiful to observe that the so-called intellectual people belittle their true station, that divinely endowed individuals lack confidence and self-understanding.

Free souls, yet remaining enslaved, allowing themselves and others to be caught in the meshes of religious superstition, to be ruled over by a small group of hand-picked leaders. O friends and brothers, withdraw from your deluded seclusion and become your noble selves. Arise with great energy and vigor and fly in the vast and unlimited space of freedom. Think, and allow not yourself or your brothers to become entangled in the cobwebs of imagination and religious intrigue.

Baha'ism: A Progressive and Inclusive Spiritual Cause

The aforesaid tablet of our Great Master [quoted at the beginning of this message] was revealed for the elevation of all mankind, yet it behooves those of us who are endeavoring to follow His commands to be the first to eliminate the cause of dissension and all practices which are in violation of His teachings. We are in truth all members of one family and brothers in humanity. Be friendly with one another, and consider no one your enemy—especially those noble souls who traveled with you in the Valley of Knowledge,[1] in search of truth, and received the spiritual food from the Fountainhead of Knowledge.

---

[1] In the *Seven Valleys*, Baha'u'llah describes the mystical journey of the seeker finding oneness with God. The Valley of Knowledge is the stage in which a per-

Should anyone be unfriendly, befriend him, and with the language of love and kindness guide him and bid him come and share with you the unlimited fruit of knowledge which you have attained.

In many of his tablets Baha'u'llah repeatedly said that His only object in enduring untold hardships and calamities was to be able to reveal from His great understanding the way to extinguish the fires of hatred and animosity and to bring unity and harmony amongst people of the earth. O friends: Arise, noble souls, and fulfill His commands! Become the shining stars of the heaven of kindness and reflect as such upon all beings. Follow His footsteps, and with united efforts, using the weapons of His commands, endeavor to awaken and save your brothers in humanity from the ever-renewed web of religious prejudice and its vicious corruption.

In this message I have no other motive but to awaken and elevate the thoughts of my brothers in humanity. THINK! my brothers; and may peace and happiness encompass you at all times.

---

son apprehends the Divine Manifestation and rises to a higher state of consciousness based on this knowledge. Mohammed Ali Bahai's comments about friendliness and brotherhood may be an allusion to this verse: "Yet those who journey in the garden land of knowledge, because they see the end in the beginning, see peace in war and friendliness in anger." (*The Seven Valleys and the Four Valleys*, 1991 pocket-size edition, p. 15). Mr. Bahai is challenging Baha'is—those among humanity who have attained the knowledge of the manifestation of Baha'u'llah—to see the bigger picture of their faith and rise above sectarian quarrels.

15

An Interview with Ghusn-i-Akbar

By Shua Ullah Behai and Mohammed Ali Bahai

This formal interview of Mohammed Ali Bahai by his son Shua Ullah, originally titled "My Interview with Ghusni Akbar Mohammed Ali Behai,[1] The Eldest Living Son of Beha 'U'llah," was published in the United States in the First and Second Quarter 1937 issue of *Behai Quarterly* magazine. This is presumably a translation of the dialogue that took place, since the elder Mr. Bahai was not fluent in English. Some excerpts from this interview also appear in the younger Mr. Behai's book manuscript.

In *Behai Quarterly*, Shua Ullah Behai appended to the transcript of the interview a letter he wrote to 'Abdu'l-Baha in 1912 with the approval of his father, as evidence supporting Mohammed Ali Effendi's statement that he attempted to seek dialogue to resolve the religious differences that had divided the sons of Baha'u'llah. This letter is omitted from this chapter but is reproduced in Chapter 30 as part of Shua Ullah Behai's memoirs, since that is where he included it in his book.

Mohammed Ali Effendi passed away only a few months after this interview. These are the last statements he made that were published for an English-speaking audience during his lifetime.

—The Editor

---

[1] Mohammed Ali's surname was sometimes spelled "Behai." The family now uses "Bahai" as the standard English spelling; only Shua Ullah's name continues to be spelled Behai, because this was his legally registered name as an American citizen.

[Shua Ullah Behai]: I come from the United States of America bringing to your Excellency greetings, love and best wishes, from the members of the Society of Behaists,[2] and assuring you of their devotion to the teachings of our Great Master Baha'u'llah, and their steadfastness in his cause which you so nobly advocate.

A. [Mohammed Ali Effendi]: O confessors of the Oneness of God! Your sincere message which explains of your steadfastness in the cause of Baha'u'llah, Glory be to Him, and of your devotion to His teachings, brings me happiness. Every believer who has achieved this blessing and tasted its fruit and pleasure will have to do his best to impart it to others. It is incumbent on every believer to try, so far as it is in his power, to awaken the others and guide them to that which is revealed by God, glorified be His Greatness.

O Gracious and Merciful God! Assist Thy servants who have confessed Thy Oneness and Singleness, to spread Thine utterances amidst Thy creatures. I ask Thee to grant them success, and to inspire them with that which would attract the hearts and enlighten the eyes; and help them to plant in the gardens of the hearts the flowers of knowledge and friendship, union and love. That they may remove the rust of ignorance, differences, and hatred from the smooth mirrors of the consciences; that they may adorn them with that which Thou hast commanded, and prevent them from that which Thou hast forbidden; because the commands revealed in Thy Book are for the progress, welfare, and salvation of the people of the world. Whatever Thou hast said, Thou hast wished thereby good for Thy servants; and Thou hast ordained unto the Manifestation of Thy Cause, hardships and calamities for the welfare and the salvation of the people. Indeed Thou art the Mighty, the Generous, the Merciful.

Q. [Shua Ullah Behai]: For the satisfaction of the past questioners, and the enlightenment of the readers of the *Behai Quarterly*, I have

---

[2] The Society of Behaists was the organized community of Unitarian Baha'is in the United States at the time.

some important questions to ask your Excellency. Will you kindly grant my humble request?

A. [Mohammed Ali Effendi]: I am very happy to answer them, proceed.

Q: A lengthy document has been printed and circulated in the United States of America entitled the "Will of Abdul Baha, Abbas," your late brother; have you read the same?

A: I have read the copy in the original language.

Q: In the said will you are accused of unpardonable crimes, or hostilities against him, of interpolating and falsifying the words and verses of the [Baha'i scriptural] text?

A: All the accusations in the said will and by other individuals towards me are hearsay, gross misrepresentation, and without foundation. I have always lived in accordance with the commands of Baha'u'llah, Glory be to Him, and thus fulfilled my duties. I devoted my entire life to the service of the cause and the promulgation of His teachings. I have faced my enemies with a smile, hardships and calamities with endurance, and for those who wronged, misjudged, and accused me falsely, I bear no feeling of animosity, but sincerely pray that God may forgive and guide them to the truth; He is the Merciful, the Forgiver.

Q: Mrs. Ruth White, a rebel member of [the Baha'i organization led by] the National Spiritual Assembly of the United States and Canada, in her published book entitled *The Bahai Religion and Its Enemy, the Bahai Organization*, emphatically denies the authenticity of the Will of 'Abdu'l-Baha, and with firm conviction states that your Excellency assisted Shoghi Effendi in fabricating the said will?[3]

A: Shoghi has never been in my presence, and I do not know him personally. Mrs. Ruth White's accusations are untrue. It is indeed surprising to observe that progressive Occidentals satisfied themselves with hearsay, and passed judgment without investigation.

Q: It is evident that a dissension existed between you and 'Abdu'l-

---

[3] This bizarre conspiracy theory was quickly disproved, since Shoghi Effendi Rabbani, after becoming Guardian of the Baha'i faith, continued 'Abdu'l-Baha's policy of shunning and denouncing the Unitarian Baha'is. There is no evidence that Mr. Rabbani ever sympathized with Mohammed Ali Bahai or his followers.

Baha after the departure of Baha'u'llah. What was the cause, material or spiritual?

A: The cause of our misunderstanding was on account of the principles of our religion, and not for earthly possessions. It grieves me to state that 'Abdu'l-Baha's teachings are not in accordance with the commands of Baha'u'llah, Glory be to Him, and by comparing his writings with the utterances of Baha'u'llah you will agree with me.

Q: After the misunderstanding occurred, did your Excellency endeavor to eliminate the cause by private or public conferences?

A: I regret that my numerous requests met with resistance. I pleaded with him time after time, for a conference to discuss our differences, and to solve the problems in accordance with the teachings of Baha'u'llah, as we are commanded, but unfortunately my requests were not granted and my pleadings were in vain.

16

Autobiography

By Mohammed Ali Bahai

This memoir by the second son of Baha'u'llah who survived him—the first child of his second wife—was included in Shua Ullah Behai's book manuscript. It was likely written in the early to mid 1930s, when the author was around 80 years old. Some long paragraphs have been divided for ease of reading, and section headings have been added.

This important historical testimony has never before been seen outside of Baha'u'llah's family. It provides a window into the life, beliefs, and personality of the man who, according to Baha'u'llah's will, was intended to become the next successor to leadership of the Baha'i community after his elder half-brother Abbas Effendi; his significant role in the new religious movement during Baha'u'llah's ministry; his perspective on the disagreement which led to his excommunication; and the roles played by other key figures in the faith at the time, with whom he was intimately associated, some of whom not only shared his views but actually urged him to take a stand, according to the story he tells.

Mohammed Ali Effendi denies the charges leveled against him in the Will and Testament of 'Abdu'l-Baha and explains, from his point of view, the spurious basis and motivation for the allegations. He also makes a charge of his own: that 'Abdu'l-Baha concealed part of Baha'u'llah's will from everyone except his brothers, and that the omitted text specially recognized Baha'u'llah's assistant, Mirza Aqa Jan Kashani, who served as the Baha'i prophet's chief secretary and scribe for over 40 years but was excommunicated by 'Abdu'l-Baha.

Another, related charge made by Mohammed Ali Bahai is that 'Abdu'l-Baha led his followers to believe that he had the authority to suppress any of Baha'u'llah's writings he felt should be set aside. In particular, Mr. Bahai mentions the *Kitab-i-Aqdas*—one of the central scriptural texts of Baha'ism—which, curiously, was not released in official English translation by the Baha'i community until about 120 years after it was written, likely because it contains some teachings that might seem objectionable to a Western audience. Mr. Bahai alleges that a Baha'i publishing company established according to Baha'u'llah's instruction during his lifetime, which printed the first books of Baha'i holy writings, was forced out of business by 'Abdu'l-Baha, presumably because he did not want some of the writings to be made widely available.

The main thrust of Mr. Bahai's objections to his elder brother's leadership style, as gleaned from this document, is that 'Abdu'l-Baha seemed to want Baha'is to follow him personally, with a similar kind of devotion as they previously followed Baha'u'llah, and for Baha'u'llah and his writings to recede into the background. The younger son expresses a preference for emphasizing Baha'i scripture and glorifying Baha'u'llah rather than his successors. He seems to have thought that the proper role for Abbas Effendi (and later himself) was merely as a community organizer and spokesperson for the Baha'i movement; not a quasi-prophetic type of leader with a station of infallibility, which is what 'Abdu'l-Baha became in the mainstream Baha'i tradition.

Overall, Mohammed Ali Bahai's autobiography serves to humanize the man, revealing the authentic voice of one who was once a central figure in the Baha'i faith, and who could have quite believably gone down in history as the revered successor to 'Abdu'l-Baha, were it not for their tragic feud. He recounts his desire from an early age to travel the world to teach the faith, and his journeys to Egypt and India for that purpose and to help build up Baha'i institutions as Baha'u'llah's trusted representative. He presents himself as a dutiful worker in his father's inner circle in Acre, and a devoted Baha'i who lived according to his conscience and accepted some unpleasant consequences for himself and his family as a result of standing up for his beliefs after Baha'u'llah's death. He claims to have sought compromise and reconciliation with the brother from whom he was estranged.

Regardless of what we may think of the controversial choice he made in refusing to defer to 'Abdu'l-Baha's expansive interpretation of his authority when he became the new Baha'i leader—a debatable decision for which he forfeited his place in the Baha'i faith as it has developed—Mohammed Ali Effendi emerges in this memoir as a genuine and complex human being with whom many might be willing to sympathize, perhaps even admire. The man, speaking for himself and his values, stands in stark contrast to the cartoonish portrayal of an ever-scheming "Center of Sedition," bent on "utterly destroy[ing] the Cause of God," who appears in 'Abdu'l-Baha's will.

—The Editor

HE IS GOD: THERE IS NO GOD BUT HIM.

Early Childhood

This servant of the threshold of the Great Baha'u'llah was born in the "City of Peace," Baghdad, in the year 1270 A.H. (1853 A.D.) and was named by the Supreme Tongue [i.e. God or Baha'u'llah], Mohammed Ali (Ghusn-i-Akbar). I was brought up, reared and educated under the shadow of His favor and Divine Providence.

When I was a little over four years of age, Her Grace Mahd-i-'Ulya (the Supreme Cradle) traveled to Iran to visit her brother and relations. Therefore my little sister Samadiyya and myself joined our mother and proceeded to Tehran and Mazandaran. We spent some time there, enjoying the hospitality of our relatives, then we returned to the City of Peace and we were fortunate to be in the service of His Resplendent Glory [i.e. Baha'u'llah] again. Although this journey was for visiting relatives, especially the Red Leaf,[1] yet there were other matters that Her

---

[1] Baha'u'llah's cousin and sister-in-law Maryam, usually called the "Crimson Leaf" by Baha'is today. She was Mahd-i-'Ulya's sister and the wife of Baha'u'llah's half-brother Haji Mirza Rida-Quli. She was a devoted follower of Baha'u'llah, but her husband did not share her religious views. Baha'u'llah called his wives and daughters "leaves," and his bestowal of this title on Maryam indicated their close relationship and her station as one of the most important female believers.

Grace had to attend to in person which could not be accomplished by correspondence. After completing this mission we returned to Iraq and, complying with [Baha'u'llah's] commands, brought with us Mirza Mihdi (Ghusn-i-At'har)[2] who was at Tehran.

In those days when the Blessed Abode (of Baha'u'llah) was at Baghdad, He made a journey to Salman Pak[3] and remained there a few days. The following are those who were honored to be at His service: Ghusn-i-A'zam Abbas Effendi ('Abdu'l-Baha), Mirza Moussa Kalim, Aqa Mirza Muhammad-Quli,[4] Aqa Mirza Aqa Jan (the servant of Baha'u'llah)[5] and Aqa Muhammad Ibrahim Amir. This humble servant (i.e. Mohammed Ali) submitted a petition to His Sacred Presence, and in reply I received a sacred tablet written by the Supreme Pen, addressed thus: "This letter should reach the hands of Mirza Mohammed Ali, of Baghdad and of the Spiritual Dwelling-place." At the beginning He says: "(The petition) arrived to the place where the Merciful is seated upon the Throne, reached the point where to God belongs the Kingdom of the heavens and the earth, and arrived to the right hand, that is the possessor of the Universal Kingdom. Realizing that He is the Greatly Merciful, the petition was accepted. Upon observing and hearing the chanting of the *Wagha* (Dove) from the Eternal Throne 'that came to those who are near their portion,' the reply will be sent from the treasured Blessing, the invisible Banquet and the hidden Words..."

Studying with the eyes of intellect the said holy tablet, it will be observed that in those days the blessed cause was made evident by the Pen of Might [i.e. Baha'u'llah revealing divine verses], but as the ap-

---

[2] Ghusn-i-At'har (Arabic: *ghusn al-athar*), meaning "the Purest (or Most Chaste) Branch," was the title given by Baha'u'llah to his second son, Mihdi. However, this son died in his youth and the same title was then passed to Baha'u'llah's third living son, Zia Ullah, who was a younger brother of Mohammed Ali.

[3] A city about 15 miles south of Baghdad.

[4] Moussa Kalim (known to Baha'is today as Mirza Musa, Aqay-i-Kalím) and Muhammad-Quli were brothers of Baha'u'llah.

[5] Mirza Aqa Jan Kashani was Baha'u'llah's chief secretary and scribe. He was often referred to as Khadim or Khadimu'llah, meaning "servant (of God)" in Arabic.

pointed time, i.e. the year 1280 A.H. (1863 A.D.) mentioned by the Bab (the Forerunner) in the Book of *Bayan* had not yet arrived, [Baha'u'llah's] General Proclamation was recognized only by a few of the chosen followers.[6] Most of the special tablets, [such as] the Arabic and Persian *Hidden Words* were revealed in Baghdad, and all of them were testimonials to the greatness of the cause, but as the appointed time had not yet arrived those present were prevented from the knowledge of His Appearance until such a time that the complete declaration was made when the Blessed Procession[7] moved to the Garden of Ridvan and later at Adrianople. Then the Supreme Tongue delivered the message and opened the gate of knowledge to those who were both far and near.

When the city of Baghdad was blessed with His presence, by His command, assistance and encouragement I began to read and write, and gradually I composed some articles in the Arabic language. Our Great Master (Baha'u'llah) mentioned this in the Epistle of Badi, the reply to Ali Muhammad Sarraj, and in some other tablets, that I wrote Arabic while I was only six years old. I shall explain this in detail later.

Departure from Baghdad to Turkey

In the year 1280 A.H. (1863 A.D.) it was ordained that the Sacred Procession should leave Baghdad and proceed to Istanbul (Constantinople). I petitioned to [Baha'u'llah] in favor of two of the believers requesting His consent for them to join us and render their services during this journey so that they may be considered as pilgrims. My humble request was granted, and both Aqa Husayn, son of Aqa Muhammad Jawad, and Aqa Muhammad Hasan, son of Aqa Abdu'r-Rasul Shahid, both of Kashan, joined us to Adrianople and thence to Acre, and now

---

[6] Baha'u'llah had yet to declare himself publicly as the next Manifestation of God, whom the Bab had prophesied to appear in 1863 A.D. Nevertheless, he was already writing tablets in the style of divine revelation and sending them to some of his close companions, such as family members and selected followers of Babism, and these people were thereby able to understand that he was claiming a divine station.

[7] The Blessed (Sacred, Supreme, etc.) Procession means Baha'u'llah with his family and companions.

both have passed unto Eternity. The offspring of the said Husayn are now residing at Acre.

Another friend was Sheikh Sádiq of Yazd, who was a very faithful follower, and was by day as well as by night ready and prepared to hasten to the Holy Abode [i.e. Baha'u'llah's presence] in order to offer his sincere services. To this ardent believer I was very much attached, but I did not dare to petition to our Great Master for a third person; nevertheless, after the departure of the Blessed Procession, the said Sádiq could not remain behind and followed us on foot with the post caravan. Unfortunately the hardship of the trip made him ill, and he was released from the earthly world and its troubles. May the mercy of God and His Divine Providence rest with him.

In the said journey the resting places were short and well nigh to each other, therefore we traveled with ease. Some were traveling on horseback, others were walking, and the ladies of the household were riding in *kajavas* (saddle with small tent on it). Ghusn-i-A'zam ('Abdu'l-Baha) was riding a horse; Mirza Mihdi and myself, being still very young, went into kajavas especially arranged for our Great Master's blessed use—the right side was occupied by [Baha'u'llah] and in the left were seated Mahd-i-'Ulya our mother, my sister Samadiyya and myself. Thus we traveled up to Samsun on the Black Sea, then we took a boat to Istanbul, and thence to Adrianople in a carriage which was especially arranged for our Great Master (Baha'u'llah). My mother, my little sister and myself were fortunate to be with Baha'u'llah during this journey, and served Him until we reached Adrianople.

There was a nice horse called Saoudi which Baha'u'llah, Glory be to Him, used to ride, one hour before reaching each resting place. The Supreme Procession was accompanied by an escort of ten Arab horsemen with their long spears who were sent by the *Wali* (i.e. the Ruler) of Iraq and followed by the members of the household in kajavas and the believers on horseback and on foot. Namiq Pasha [the Wali] ordered the said detachment of Arab horsemen to accompany the Supreme Procession and also supplied them with letters of introduction to all the Governors and Sub-Governors of the cities and towns on their way which were marked out as resting places. These letters authorized them to render honor and service to the Supreme Procession during the journey from Baghdad to Istanbul, as they [i.e. Baha'u'llah's entourage] were the guests of the government.

Mohammed Ali Serves the Cause as a Child

In Adrianople the sacred tablets revealed were taken down by the Khadim (the servant of Baha'u'llah), [Mirza Aqa Jan Kashani], in a sort of shorthand; they were afterwards copied by Ghusn-i-A'zam ('Abdu'l-Baha) and sometimes by Moussa Kalim (the brother of Baha'u'llah). These tablets were then copied by some of the believers for preservation and the first copy was mailed to the owner or sent by a special messenger.

During the last days of the sojourn at Adrianople I used to copy the revealed tablets by [Baha'u'llah's] command, and at times I used to write, also by His order, personal letters to the believers. I recollect that on one occasion I wrote about eighty letters to the Arab believers who resided at Baghdad and the vicinity, and all these letters were presented to His Resplendent Glory and corrected by His Blessed Pen after which I copied them for mailing. These letters contained nothing but the remembrance of His Blessed Cause, its greatness, and invitations to all to believe in Him, loyal and steadfast in His Cause, and attain the knowledge of His Oneness. It is obviously clear that in those days I was only a child, that I was acting only according to His commands, obeying His orders and writing only to those I was commanded by Him, and in the manner laid down by Him.

During the sojourn at Adrianople, sometimes when the followers and pilgrims were ushered into the presence of Baha'u'llah, by His command I used to write an article on the greatness of the cause, and the Khadim after chanting the holy text [i.e. verses of Baha'u'llah], used to read to them my humble compositions. It is evident that this was simply to make those who were steadfast in their belief to become more animated and inflamed in the cause, for to see a child praising the Cause of God in such a manner, inviting those who seek to come forward and partake of the Banquet of His Presence, would certainly kindle the fire of love in their hearts and make them more steadfast in the cause.

I recollect that once Sheikh Salmán Hindiyani[8] had come to Adrianople and was the guest of one of the believers. One day Baha'u'llah commanded me to visit the said Salmán and while there ask for paper and pen and to write an epistle in Arabic for him. Obeying His commands, immediately I visited him and while there I wrote an article in the Arabic language. After I left the premises, Salmán asked, "I wonder if he knows the meaning of what he has written?" This remark reached the presence of Baha'u'llah and with a smile He commanded me to visit Salmán again, ask for what I had written and translate it in his presence from the Arabic into Persian. Again I followed His orders, visited Salmán, asked for what I had written before, wrote its contents in Persian and delivered it to him. These commands were as I explained earlier, to show to the followers the greatness of the Manifestation, to kindle their enthusiasm and to keep them steadfast in the cause.

Young Mohammed Ali Wishes to Teach the Faith Abroad

In those days I submitted a petition to His Blessed Presence for permission to travel, accompanied by one of the believers, to some part of the world for the purpose of delivering the message of glad-tidings to mankind, and to the best of my ability preach to them the appearance of the Great Manifestation. Replying to my humble petition, [Baha'u'llah] commanded the believers to hold a meeting and discuss the matter, and follow whatever their decision may be. In the meeting some of the believers disagreed on account of my age and lest some bodily harm would befall me. The humble petition which I had presented to Him was kept by Him (Baha'u'llah) until the days when the Palace of Bahji was blessed with His Presence.

One day He gave it to me and commanded me to preserve it. The said supplication reads thus:

Thou Art the Dear, the Everlasting, Praise be to Thee O God, Verily
Thou Art the One who Hath Created me and provided for me. In-

---

[8] Shaykh Khánjar Hindiyani, named Shaykh Salmán by Baha'u'llah in honor of a loyal disciple of the Prophet Muhammad, was one of Baha'u'llah's devout followers who dedicated his life to delivering the writings of Baha'u'llah to Baha'is.

deed Thou Art the Powerful to do what Thou choosest. In Thy Name O Thou Who Art free from everything besides Thee, Thou Art the God, there is no God but Thee, Thou Art the Single, there is no equal to Thee, and Thou Art the Observer of All things. Praise be to Thee O God, O my God, forgive me, my sins, my errors and my mistakes. I shall be in everlasting loss if I am not blessed with Thy forgiveness and Mercy. O Lord; Pardon me: Indeed Thou Art able to do whatsoever Thou choosest, Thou Art God, there is no God but Thee. Verily Thou Art in the creation, the Only, the Lasting, the Eternal, the Single, the One. O my God, My Master and my Lord, Permit me to leave this place and go to some other country accompanied by one Thou choosest from Thy devoted believers, who have traveled with Thee and pilgrimed to Thine Abode, to deliver the glad-tidings and guide the people of the world to Thy Straight Path.

To the learned and intellectual people, it is evident that the portion allotted is according to the capacity of the container. I mean that while writing and presenting the petition I was a child and had not reached the age of puberty, so the sentences in my petition were therefore bereft of the rules of composition and grammar. It proves that they were written in all simplicity and plainness and that I had no object but confessing His Singleness and Greatness and securing permission to go out in the world and promulgate His message.

Baha'u'llah's Offspring Should Not Be Regarded as His Partner

During our stay in Adrianople, a sacred tablet was revealed by the Supreme Pen and by His command was sent to Qazvin, [Iran] in my name. This caused disturbance among the believers, dividing them into two parties. Agha Ali, for whom the said tablet was revealed, and some of them followed me, while others remained steadfast in the cause, confessing His Oneness. This blessed tablet was sent to Qazvin for the sole purpose of testing the faithfulness of the believers there. Later on another tablet was revealed, again in my name, which abolished the imagination caused [i.e. the misunderstanding that Mohammed Ali was revealing divine verses].

The object of this incident was that thereafter the friends [i.e. the Baha'is] should realize the station of the Manifestation of God and should not choose a partner for Him or an equal to Him.[9] The original of the first tablet, which is in my handwriting and signed by me, is [still] existing, and the name of the person for whom this tablet was revealed is inscribed on it by the Supreme Pen of Baha'u'llah; the copy of the second tablet is also existing, and both bear witness to the genuineness of this statement. Some other tablets were also revealed which rent asunder the imaginations, such as the tablet which begins with "We endowed Nabil Qable Ali[10] (i.e. Mohammed Ali) with the power of speech in his teens"; also in the Epistle of Badi: "We endowed him to utter (verses) when he was six years of age..." I shall explain this subject in detail later.

The everlasting kindness of Baha'u'llah, Glory be to Him, did not permit the said Agha Ali and his family to be deprived of their portion of nearness [i.e. they were forgiven for their mistaken belief], and while His Blessed Presence was at Acre, He commanded them all to come and reside there. They were sheltered under the Dome of His Mercy and received His blessings. And to this day the beloved son of the late Agha Ali, Aqa Mirza Abdullah Bahhaj and his family are present [in the Holy Land]. He is one of the confessors to the Oneness and Singleness of God, who performed his [religious] duties, and he has written many poems and essays to that effect. May God be with him, grant him His satisfaction and bless him with His mercy in Eternity as He hath blessed him in this world.

---

[9] In recounting this incident as being orchestrated by Baha'u'llah, Mr. Bahai is defending himself from the charge made in 'Abdu'l-Baha's will that he "without shame in the days of the Blessed Beauty had advanced such a claim" to be a Manifestation. Mr. Bahai is also laying the groundwork for his own argument that 'Abdu'l-Baha's writings and teachings do not have the same authority as those of Baha'u'llah. In his view, Baha'u'llah was illustrating the point that even his own son cannot legitimately reveal divine verses, regardless of how eloquent and inspiring the verses may be.

[10] Arabic: the "noble (one) before Ali." The "noble one" presumably means the Prophet Muhammad, who came before the Imam Ali. Muhammad and Ali are the two greatest figures in Shi'ite Islam. *Nabíl qabl 'Alí* is therefore a play on words indicating the name of Baha'u'llah's son Mohammed Ali.

During the last year at Adrianople, some of the pilgrims were there, amongst them Mishkín-Qalam, who requested me to compose a supplication for him, so that he might copy it in his own handwriting, as he was known for his calligraphy.[11] Complying with his request I wrote a short supplication and presented it to Baha'u'llah. His Resplendent Glory, after reading my supplication, glanced at my humble signature "*Abdu'llah-ul-Ali* (i.e. the servant of the Great God) Mohammed Ali." Although this was according to His instructions, He commanded me to sign in the future thus: "*Al-Mustashriqu min Núru'llah al-Bahí* (i.e. the one illumined by the Resplendent Light of God) Mohammed Ali." Both signatures were by His commands and not in accordance with my humble wishes; but alas, after His ascension these signatures were taken (by my opponents) as a cause for objection, and in some cases they took them as proof that I had made a claim [to a divine station].

Baha'u'llah and His Family Imprisoned in Acre

When the Blessed Procession arrived at the great prison of Acre [in 1868] and was housed in the army barracks, the duty of copying the holy tablets revealed [by Baha'u'llah] was given to me. Mirza Mihdi (Ghusn-i-At'har) and Khadim used to take down what was revealed, and this humble servant used to copy them in the form prescribed for the tablets and sent to their owners [i.e. recipients] in Iran and other countries. Ghusn-i-A'zam ('Abdu'l-Baha), after the arrival at Acre, did not [transcribe or copy] the tablets anymore and contented himself with associating with government officials and members of the public. I also recollect that when staying at the barracks he used to give lessons to the friends on the meanings of the chapters of the Qur'an.

During the first and second year of our imprisonment in the barracks at Acre, the Supreme Pen revealed several tablets in which He foretold that the gates of the prison shall be opened and the prisoners shall be freed. Amongst these tablets were the following verses which

---

[11] Mirza Husayn Isfahani, known to Baha'is as Mishkín-Qalam, was a prominent Baha'i who was posthumously designated as one of the nineteen Apostles of Baha'u'llah. His artistic calligraphy was widely renowned in 19th century Persia.

according to the commands of Baha'u'llah were copied by me in large type and good penmanship and were mailed to Iran: "Very soon, that which is closed shall be opened and that which is torn shall be repaired; those who are prevented shall enter and those who are scattered shall be gathered; that which is hard shall be made easy and that which is invisible shall become manifest. Think ye, O possessors of inner sight, that ye may comprehend the recorded secrets." In other tablets He says, "Very soon the gate of the prison shall be opened and those who surround this Sun shall be released." When the appointed time arrived and the gates of the prison were opened to all, those who were there traveled to wherever they desired and those who were thirsty advanced to the Fountainhead of nearness and quenched their thirst.

Mohammed Ali Effendi Visits Egypt as a Young Man

In the year 1295 A.H. (1878 A.D.), by the command of Baha'u'llah I visited Alexandria and Cairo, Egypt, accompanied by Aqa Siyyid Ali Yazdi and Mirza Mustafa bin-Shahid, and for nearly two months enjoyed the association of the numerous believers who resided in those places. The late Haji Mirza Hasan Shirazi, generally known as Khorasani,[12] received the [Baha'i] message in those days; his [teachers of the faith] were Haji Mulla Ali Tabrizi and Haji Abdu'l-Karim Tehrani. One night the said Khorasani and Abdu'l-Karim came to my abode and a discussion ensued regarding the blessed cause. Finally he accepted and rendered his petition to Baha'u'llah [i.e. declaration of faith] and received His message.

Later on the numbers of the believers in that land increased. While on this journey I was favored with many sacred tablets [from Baha'u'llah], among them the following which is written by the Supreme Pen:[13]

---

[12] Also spelled Khurasani.

[13] All of Baha'u'llah's communications—even simple letters such as this one—were regarded by his followers as divine "tablets." Baha'is did not, and still do not today, make any distinction between scriptural and non-scriptural writings of Baha'u'llah; every word he ever wrote is considered part of the Baha'i scriptural corpus.

He is the Dear: O My Branch, thy letter from (Port Said) arrived; God willing it shall always arrive. Thou shalt receive rock sugar from Egypt, sugar from India, and from the school garden of the world thou shalt partake of knowledge, forbearance, art and perception. Although the separation from thee hath caused a burning in the hearts of the beloved ones of God, haply God shall produce results therefrom, and the fragrance of thy faithfulness to God may spread over there and diffuse its fragrance in the cities and their surroundings. Verily He is the Powerful to do whatsoever He desireth. Peace be with thee and with those who advance toward the Supreme Horizon, and believe in God, the Possessor of the Names and the Creator of Heaven.

Entrusted with Essential Duties in Acre

After spending two months [in Egypt] this humble servant returned to the Holy Land, and resumed my duties of copying the holy tablets as in the past. This time, to my duties was added another service: [making] the preparations for occasional outings of the Blessed Procession to the orange groves or other points of interest such as Mazra'a and its vicinity, the *Birka* (i.e. the water pool), the village of Kabri and other places which were visited by Baha'u'llah. Always I took the greatest care in arranging for these journeys. Some of the believers have written about these places which were blessed with His presence. If time permits me I shall record hereafter some of the places which I recollect.

All the places which the Blessed Procession intended to visit, I had to go first and examine, and if they were found suitable they would be blessed with His presence. The following is part of a tablet which was revealed for me while I was in Tiberias and which proves my statement. He said:

He is the Dear: O Ghusn-i-Akbar, on account of thine absence the affairs of the tablets [i.e. transcribing Baha'u'llah's revelations and managing his correspondence] are suspended, the departure of Mulla Muhammad Ali is delayed, the cause of *Tabárakallah* ["God's blessing"] is stayed, and the Birka and Yirka[14] are in grief. Indeed by thine absence most of the affairs are at a standstill, nay they appear to be disturbed. It was well said, "From his rising and submersion two cities are upset."[15]

This Mulla Muhammad Ali who is mentioned in the tablet was from Dahaj of Yazd,[16] and made several journeys to Acre bringing petitions from the faithful followers and returning with tablets to them in Iran; and whereas the copying of the holy tablets in good calligraphy was my personal duty, He said "the departure of Mulla Muhammad Ali is delayed." Also, as the preparations for the movements of the Blessed Procession were my responsibility, He says "the cause of *Tabárakallah* is stayed and the Birka and Yirka are in grief."

Travels to India and Publication of Baha'u'llah's Writings

After the elapse of some time, and by the commands of Baha'u'llah, Glory be to Him, I made a journey to East India [in 1882]. This was during the winter season, and I was accompanied by the late Mirza Abu'l-Qasim Nazir and his Kurdish wife, upon them be the Glory of God. The main object of my journeys to Egypt and India was to visit the friends and make preliminary plans for the spread of the cause, the guidance of the seekers[17] and the diffusion of the light of knowledge. This object was not attained in Egypt as was expected at that time, but the result appeared later. The [Baha'i] community grew in enthusiasm and number, and believers from Iran and other places assembled there. The sa-

---

[14] Yirka, more commonly spelled Yarka, is a village near Acre.

[15] Mohammed Ali Effendi is making the point that Baha'u'llah relied on him greatly as an administrative leader in the new religious community, and copiously lamented even his brief absence. He is building the case that Baha'u'llah expected him to play a leadership role in the faith and would not have wanted him to be sidelined.

[16] Dahaj, also spelled Dehaj, is a city located in the present-day Kerman Province of Iran. It is near Yazd and may have been part of that province in the past.

[17] People studying and considering conversion to the Baha'i faith are often referred to by Baha'is as "seekers."

cred tablets revealed by the Supreme Pen in honor of this humble servant while I was in Egypt and India explain the main object clearly. They prove that there was no other purpose than the spreading of the teachings, and no other aim than to serve the cause of God. My journey to India lasted six months, and by the command of Baha'u'llah I received a telegram from Afnan of Beirut to return at once and appear in His Presence.

After returning from the said voyage and remaining a few years under the shadow of the Great Sun of Truth, Baha'u'llah, again by His command I journeyed to Bombay[18] (East India) [in 1889]. This time my son Shua Ullah and the late Haji Khavar accompanied me. The previous voyage was for the purpose which I have already explained, and this time also the object was to serve the cause of God. The existence of a printing press was essential, in order to publish some of the blessed revelations [of Baha'u'llah] and spread them abroad, that the ears of those who seek may hear the call of the Supreme Pen. It was difficult to attain this object in this land [i.e. Palestine] and I therefore humbly petitioned to Baha'u'llah to grant me permission to fulfill this important service during my visit to India.

The Supreme Will commanded [it], and after my arrival at Bombay I held a meeting with the late Haji Siyyid Muhammad Afnan, upon him be His Mercy and Glory. He showed a great deal of enthusiasm, and though it was financially difficult for him at that time, he arranged it eventually, and opened the Naseri Press. I petitioned to Baha'u'llah and explained the situation. Permission was granted with one understanding, that the said Afnan should control the press and I should have no interest in it whatsoever.

When the project was carried out and the printing press was in full action, the Book of *Aqdas* and the Book of *Haykal* were copied by the late Haji Mirza Husayn Shirazi, better known as Khartumi, and the late Mulla Ahmad Ali Nayrizi. I carefully compared them with the original manuscripts, then sent them to the printing press. When the proofs of both books came, I presented them to Baha'u'llah through the mail and again secured His permission for the final printing. Also an epistle

---

[18] Present-day Mumbai.

which was composed by Ghusn-i-A'zam ('Abdu'l-Baha) and which I asked the late Mirza Muhammad of Isfahan, who was the caretaker at the pilgrim house in Acre, to inscribe. This was also printed. Later on, other holy books [by Baha'u'llah] were printed, namely the Book of *Ishraqat*, the book inscribed by Mishkín-Qalam, the Book of *Aqdas* in modern type, the book of supplications [i.e. Baha'i prayer book] inscribed by Haji Mirza Husayn Khartumi, and the small book of supplications in modern type.

All the above-mentioned books were printed by the said Naseri Press. The owner was Haji Siyyid Muhammad Afnan and the manager [was his cousin] Aqa Mirza Ibrahim Afnan.[19] Doubtless Baha'u'llah considered this as one of the most important events [in his ministry], and the said Haji Siyyid Muhammad Afnan was bestowed with the great favor to be the pioneer in this service. Indeed he did everything in his power either in the way of service or in spending capital to arrange this printing press. He lost a considerable amount of money in this enterprise, as after the ascension of Baha'u'llah, they ('Abdu'l-Baha and his supporters) did not let him receive any earthly benefit from it, and finally he was obliged to sell the printing press at a loss and return to Shiraz, Iran. His heart was broken, and in grief he became ill and passed unto the Eternal Realms. May the mercy of God be with him and place him in the Paradise of contentment. Exalted be his station in the end as it was in the beginning.

My second journey to India was my last travel during the days of our Great Master [Baha'u'llah], although I made many small trips to Tiberias, etc., but as they were short distances they are not worth mentioning. My object is not to relate historical events but rather the meaning of the events, and the most important of them all is the question of the printing of the holy books, which if time permits I shall explain in more details later.[20]

---

[19] Messrs. Afnan were both nephews of the Bab.

[20] In relating the story of Naseri Press, Mr. Bahai is explaining some of the background for his contention that 'Abdu'l-Baha inappropriately attempted to shift the focus of the Baha'i faith away from Baha'u'llah's writings and toward himself and his own ministry.

Organizing Baha'i Communities in Egypt and India

My second voyage to India lasted fifteen months. I spent several days on the way visiting Port Said, Alexandria, and Cairo [in Egypt]. While going we had to wait many days in Port Said for the arrival of the steamer. On our return, as I was invited by Haji Mirza Hasan Khorasani and other friends, and with the permission of Baha'u'llah, I spent a few days in Cairo and Alexandria.

While at Port Said many friends from Cairo and Alexandria were present. We discussed many subjects pertaining to the service of the cause and its progress. I made a suggestion, that the Baha'i merchants of Egypt agree to donate a certain percentage of their daily sales, say one *piastre*[21] out of a hundred, to a community chest, and that at the end of the year what has been saved would be used for the spread of the teachings and the service of the cause. Those who were present held several meetings amongst themselves and finally decided to carry out the plan. This plan was carried out very successfully and was backed heartily, especially by Haji Khorasani. After my return to Acre, he wrote many letters to me regarding the progress of the plan, and petitioned to Baha'u'llah for a name [for the Baha'i organization in Egypt], and [Baha'u'llah] named it "The Spiritual Association." The said Haji desired me to become a member of this Association, but I refused to do so and informed him that any amount so collected was the property of the Association which they could use in the best way they thought fit for the service of the cause.[22]

---

[21] The *piastre* was one penny, or one hundredth of an Egyptian pound.

[22] This appears to have been, in modern Baha'i terminology, the first National Spiritual Assembly of the Baha'is of Egypt. The author claims to have been instrumental in its establishment, and by declining to join that institution and exercise influence over its expenditures, he apparently also helped to establish the principle that local and national Baha'i communities should run their own affairs without micromanagement from international Baha'i leadership. It is especially interesting that Baha'u'llah gave Mohammed Ali Effendi a great deal of independent authority and latitude to work with the Egyptian Baha'is to establish their first Spiritual Assembly and assist them to develop some prin-

While I was in Bombay on my second journey I advised the friends to open a meeting place, as was usual, in India. The friends responded warmly, the house was opened and was called "The Consultation House." Haji Mirza Husayn Khartumi rendered his services to the same and arranged the house in which the friends met regularly once a week, remembering the Lord and chanting the holy revelations. In a short time the community grew in number and many nationalities were represented, mostly Persian Zoroastrians who immigrated to India and earned their livelihood there.

Author's Motivation for Writing These Memoirs

The enlightened and intellectual people should know that the object of this humble servant, in writing these words and reporting the past events, is neither self-glorification nor any idea of the exaltation of my personal station; I am only explaining the facts to add knowledge to those who seek the truth and desire enlightenment. Many false and untrue statements have been circulated, and it is therefore my duty to relate the facts in as brief a manner as possible so that it might not bore the readers.

What I am recording is not designed to prove my innocence nor to satisfy my readers. I am indeed stating what I know to be the real truth. Blessed is he who understands and acknowledges the truth, and may God forgive him who insists on his own conviction without investigation.

I do not interfere with anyone and ask favor from none. Saadi, may God's mercy rest with him, has justly said, "I have no right to meddle in an affair which takes place without my participation, but if I see a blind person approaching a well, and remain silent, then I would be committing a sin." It is the study of this point that moves the pen, raises the voice and obliges me to speak.

---

ciples for how it would be funded and carry out its work. If the story is accurate, it indicates a high level of trust by Baha'u'llah for this son, and would partly explain why so many important early Baha'is followed him after his excommunication by 'Abdu'l-Baha.

The Changing Roles and Duties of Baha'u'llah's Family Members

While the Blessed Procession proceeded from Iran to the City of Peace, Baghdad, as some of the well-known historians have recorded, Ghusn-i-A'zam ('Abdu'l-Baha) and our sister Bahiyyih Khanum were in His service and our brother Mirza Mihdi was, as explained before, left at Tehran. Those three were born in Tehran.

In Baghdad, Ghusn-i-A'zam was sometimes associating with the Muslim natives, among them 'Abdu's-Salám Effendi,[23] and sometimes used to inscribe the revealed tablets, and I have seen the copies of the following in his own handwriting: the Epistle of *Sulúk*, the Book of *Iqan* and some special tablets. After the departure of the Supreme Procession to Istanbul and the arrival at Adrianople, Ghusn-i-A'zam began to study the Turkish language and associate with the Turks. He was also engaged in inscribing the holy tablets, and His Excellency the Kalim (i.e. Mirza Moussa, the brother of Baha'u'llah) assisted him now and then.

In those days, on account of my age, my handwriting was weak, but later on it improved, and during the last year of our stay at Adrianople I began to inscribe some of the holy tablets. When we were placed in the army barracks of the prison at Acre, Ghusn-i-A'zam gave up altogether the inscribing of the holy tablets and started to associate with the natives and government officials. During our stay in the army barracks our interaction with the public was limited, but after we were housed in the city of Acre outside the barracks, association was increased. Ghusn-i-A'zam secured a special reception house, and devoted his days and evenings in entertaining the government officials and the natives. My duties were the improvement of my handwriting and copying in good calligraphy the holy tablets.[24]

Khadim [i.e. Mirza Aqa Jan Kashani] and Mirza Mihdi were engaged in taking down the holy tablets as they were revealed by Baha'u'l-

---

[23] Probably Shaykh 'Abdu's-Salam ash-Shawwaf, a teacher at a theological college who studied under the Iraqi Islamic scholar Mahmud al-Alusi.

[24] Mohammed Ali was a teenager at this time.

lah. After the departure [of Mirza Mihdi, i.e. his death, in 1870] the inscription of the revealed tablets was confined to Khadim. In those days the Branches Zia Ullah Effendi and Badi Ullah Effendi were yet very young. Among our cousins, Mirza Majdeddin[25] was a better calligrapher; knowing his capacity for this service I petitioned to Baha'u'llah and He permitted him to inscribe the holy tablets, and gradually he was taking down the revealed tablets also, and some of the holy revelations are in his handwriting. Later on, Zia Ullah Effendi and Badi Ullah Effendi were also engaged in copying the holy tablets and sometimes taking them down while they were revealed. Communication was greatly increased on account of the rapid spread of the cause, and we were all busy. Khadim's occupation became greater, inscribing the holy revelations and personal communications which also were revealed by Baha'u'llah in his (i.e. Khadim's) name.

While the Palace of Mazra'a[26] was blessed with the Presence of Baha'u'llah, the members of the household were there, including Khadim, and we were all performing our duties. Ghusn-i-A'zam and his family were living at Acre, as the said palace was rather small and could not comfortably house the entire family. Wherever the Supreme Procession moved to, my younger brothers and I, and Khadim, accompanied [Baha'u'llah] to render our services; Aqa Mirza Majdeddin was also with us. Conditions remained as such until the year 1309 A.H. (1892 A.D.).

The Passing of Baha'u'llah

I wish that I was not in existence to see that dark day. I do not know what to say and to write, and how to explain, as it is beyond the endurance of human strength. (A poet said,) "as the pen moves to inscribe the events, the pen is broken and the paper is torn." The Pen of Grandeur [i.e. Baha'u'llah], in one of the revealed tablets said, "The Supreme Pen is agitated, and with lamentations and weeping sayeth, 'There is no praise after Thee, O Thou Ruler of Names, and no Pen, O Thou, in

---

[25] Majdeddin bin Moussa Irani, son of Mirza Moussa (Kalim).

[26] Also spelled Mazra'ih. A country house used by Baha'u'llah in the summers from 1877 to 1879, before he moved to Bahji.

whose Name all praises are effaced'..." To keep silent is better, to quench the fire burning in my innermost, and thus [I merely] record the events in brief.

One day in the Palace of Bahji, a slight fever attacked Baha'u'llah, but this did not prevent the regular routine and some of the faithful followers were admitted to His presence. The next day the fever increased, and immediately I wrote a letter to Ghusn-i-A'zam ('Abdu'l-Baha) at Acre informing him of the event; he came, and we both served Him to the last. During those days [while Baha'u'llah was ill], all the members of His household were at the Palace (of Bahji). Ghusn-i-A'zam and some members of his family divided their time between the house at Acre and the Palace, as discontinuing the association with the natives and the government officials would not have been a wise step.

When the Sun of Reality submerged in the ocean of disappearance [i.e. when Baha'u'llah passed away], according to His commands Ghusn-i-A'zam, myself, and Mirza Majdeddin attended to the holy remains, and Khadim assisted us. The other two younger branches[27] could not stand the ordeal and did not join us. Indeed our task was beyond endurance, but we obeyed His command and performed our duties, though burning with the fire of separation.

The owner of the Garden of Bahji, our neighbor, was a Christian from Lebanon whose name was Eskandar Jammal, and who by chance one day had paid his respects to Baha'u'llah. On that day, on which the horizon of our hearts was covered with the dark clouds of grief and sorrow, Ghusn-i-A'zam asked me to see the said Eskandar Jammal and secure a parcel of land under the pine trees outside of the Palace [for Baha'u'llah's tomb]. During this conversation Aqa Mirza Ali Reza, son of [Moussa] Kalim, suggested that the house of [Siyyid Ali] Afnan was more suitable, and we all agreed with him as this house belonged to the family and was free from all encumbrances.

In Adrianople a holy tablet had been revealed for one of the believers containing a special supplication for those who desire to face east

---

[27] Baha'u'llah called all of his sons "branches" (Arabic: *aghsán*, plural of *ghusn*). The two youngest sons, mentioned here, were Zia Ullah (*Ghusn-i-At'har*, the "Purest Branch") and Badi Ullah (*Ghusn-i-Anwar*, the "Most Luminous Branch").

[i.e. towards the Holy Land] and recite it; also in the days of Acre a smaller and similar supplication was revealed. Janab-i Nabil Zarandi copied these two holy supplications and selected from two other tablets two short supplications and brought them to Ghusn-i-A'zam, who showed them to me, and we agreed that these should be chanted in the Sacred Shrine [of Baha'u'llah], and to this day [this selection of prayers] is used by all.

In those days, every morning and evening we all used to visit the Sacred Shrine, Ghusn-i-A'zam chanting the supplications melodiously, and afterwards we spent one hour with the followers in the main reception hall, visiting and chanting the holy tablets, and then returned to our apartments.

Abbas Effendi Conceals Part of Baha'u'llah's Will

The days passed as such, until the ninth day after the ascension of Baha'u'llah, when Ghusn-i-A'zam ('Abdu'l-Baha) authorized Mirza Mustafa to go to the city of Acre and bring with him a small box which contained "The Book of My Covenant," the will of Baha'u'llah. Ghusn-i-A'zam invited several of the believers to my private reception room that he was occupying while staying here, and asked Aqa Riza Shirazi to chant the will.

After the said followers heard the will and left, Ghusn-i-A'zam sent for me from where I was sitting in the adjoining room and then for the first time I read the will of our Great Father Baha'u'llah. I observed the last part of the will was covered with a dark paper so that no one could read it. But as I raised the will to read it, which was written on two pages, the dark paper which was not stuck slipped. Ghusn-i-A'zam said, "It shall not be a secret from you, only I do not wish as yet that the believers should read it and know its contents [i.e. the hidden part]." I read it all, and it (i.e. the part covered) was regarding Khadim and his services, and at the end addressed both Ghusn-i-A'zam and the Khadim enjoining them to be faithful to Him.[28]

---

[28] Mr. Bahai claims that the hidden portion of the will included two points: special recognition of the service of Baha'u'llah's chief secretary, Mirza Aqa Jan

Zia Ullah Effendi also read the will. Afterwards Ghusn-i-A'zam asked Aqa Mirza Majdeddin to chant the will to the members of the household and to the believers. Then a copy was sent to Bombay, India, where Aqa Mirza Muhsin Afnan[29] wrote it in his handwriting and printed the same in the Naseri Press and spread it abroad.[30]

The hiding of the last part of the Book of My Covenant caused me uneasiness and great surprise, as a will is written for being spread and for carrying out its contents, and hiding it is contrary to the intention for which it is written. But under the circumstances I kept silent and did not raise an objection, hoping that later on it (i.e. the entire will) would be produced and the station of Khadim ordained in the will be made known, so that Baha'u'llah's wish in this respect be known to everyone, and that all may know that none shall be deprived of the recompense of their services, and the forty years service of Khadim be not lost and considered as vain.[31]

Abbas Effendi Regarded as Superseding Baha'u'llah

In those days it became evident that secretly they were singing another song (i.e. the wind was blowing in a different direction), and that

---

Kashani (Khadim), and an enjoinder to Abbas Effendi and Khadim to continued faithfulness. The latter point is very significant, since it would imply that Baha'u'llah did not intend for the Baha'is to regard his successor as perfect or infallible, as Baha'is today believe about 'Abdu'l-Baha. Instead, calling for him to be faithful—together with such a call to another important figure in the cause—presupposes the possibility that, in Baha'u'llah's view, 'Abdu'l-Baha could err in his practice of Baha'i faith, like anyone else.

[29] One of the brothers of Haji Siyyid Muhammad Afnan, the owner of Naseri Press. Mirza Muhsin married one of 'Abdu'l-Baha's daughters.

[30] If Mohammed Ali Bahai's story is to be believed, this will that was read to the Baha'is, printed and distributed, is an incomplete version of the document originally written by Baha'u'llah. It is known today as the *Kitab-i-'Ahd* ("Book of the Covenant"). To this editor's knowledge, no other version with additional verses has ever been published or circulated, and the original handwritten will (if extant) has not been made available for forensic analysis.

[31] 'Abdu'l-Baha excommunicated Khadim, and as a result, his long career of service to Baha'u'llah and role in the Baha'i faith have been downplayed in mainstream Baha'i histories.

in some special gatherings a certain conversation was current which was hidden from us. Some of those present were planning something new, of which myself and the members of the [late Baha'u'llah's] household were kept in the dark. Although aware of the secret intentions we disregarded them and remained silent. We were extremely anxious lest something would crop up and cause dissension.

Here is an example: One evening after we rendered our supplications at the Sacred Shrine, we all gathered in the reception hall, all the believers present. It was said that one of the pilgrims by the name of Bassar of Rasht had written a poem in praise of Ghusn-i-A'zam ('Abdu'l-Baha) which would be recited that evening. Haji Niaz who was living at Cairo was present, and after receiving permission from Ghusn-i-A'zam he recited the poem. The melodious chanting and the contents of the poem left the impression as if a king had departed and now reigned in his place a Great King with Might and Glory.

To be brief, this meeting surprised me and the [other] members of the household, that at such a time in which we were all surrounded with grief and sorrow, the friends should meet and instead of showing their grief and sorrow, they should act in this manner. This meeting exposed to a certain degree the object of the secret gatherings, and the curtain of secrecy was raised. [When] the meeting was over, Ghusn-i-A'zam rose and said, "O Bassar, write a poem and tell of my servitude." This suggestion somewhat explains the true meaning of the poem.[32]

---

[32] Mr. Bahai may be alluding to the later claim of Abbas Effendi to be 'Abdu'l-Baha ("the Servant of Baha['u'llah]"). This title was not given to him by Baha'u'llah, and it was somewhat ambiguous in that it could be interpreted either as a mark of humility, or as indicative of a station of perfect servitude to God's will as the exemplar for all other Baha'is (a type of infallibility). Throughout this document, Ghusn-i-Akbar repeatedly refers to Abbas Effendi by the title Baha'u'llah gave him (i.e. Ghusn-i-A'zam), implying that he felt it was inappropriate for Abbas Effendi to claim any additional titles and that he should have contented himself with the title he received from their father. In juxtaposing the poem Abbas Effendi allowed to be read at a Baha'i meeting describing him as "a Great King with Might and Glory" and his subsequent response to "write a poem and tell of my servitude," Mr. Bahai seems to be accusing Abbas Effendi of false humility and of encouraging the Baha'is put the focus of the faith on himself, one way or another, rather than keeping the focus on Baha'u'llah.

Conditions remained as such, and day by day increased; meetings were held and discussions took place which caused great discord and dissension. In one of the meetings Mulla 'Ali-Akbar[33] was the principal speaker, and some of his preaching was thus: "If Ghusn-i-A'zam commands that we must wash (destroy) the Book of *Aqdas* we must do it." This kind of preaching which was in violation of the teachings [of Baha'u'llah] increased, and wrong ideas became widespread, wounding the hearts and souls.[34]

Believers Ask Mohammed Ali Effendi to Defend the Original Faith

Although we observed these things and heard such conversations, we ignored them and pretended that we did not hear or observe them, depending on God the Merciful, that we may not be the cause of dissension and strife among the followers. Also I decided to keep away from the [Baha'i] community and secluded myself in my private abode for a long time, [hoping] that they might keep quiet and repent, but alas, it did not produce any result.

Finally some of the believers raised their voices, saying that Ghusn-i-Akbar is indifferent regarding the Cause of God, as he hears of the gross violation of the teachings of Baha'u'llah but keeps silent. Some of the faithful held a special meeting outside the gate of the city of Acre in which the Khadim was also present. After a long conversation and debate, they informed me through the two branches Zia Ullah Effendi and Badi Ullah Effendi that my silence and seclusion was not agreeable

---

[33] Mulla 'Ali-Akbar Shahmirzadi, also known as Haji Akhund, was a prominent Baha'i who taught the faith in Iran and was arrested and imprisoned on multiple occasions for his religious beliefs. Baha'u'llah called him a "Hand of the Cause," a very high honor. He made several trips to Acre and lived there for some years in the late 1880s and 1890s.

[34] Mr. Bahai does not directly accuse 'Abdu'l-Baha of encouraging such preaching, but he implies that 'Abdu'l-Baha either approved of it or tolerated it, despite the fact that it was antithetical to the core Baha'i belief that the writings of a Manifestation of God cannot be abrogated until the dispensation of a new Manifestation.

and that I must express my ideas and spread the truth.[35] I replied that if I raise my voice, affairs would become difficult, hardship and calamities will follow, and then you would not endure them. They insisted with great vigor and energy to such an extent that one of the honorables present said, "This is a case of our religion; even if we are persecuted and killed, whatever happens, we are ready and satisfied."

Unitarian Baha'is Excommunicated and Shunned

This servant of God was compelled to raise his voice. I therefore wrote a very mild epistle, thinking that Ghusn-i-A'zam will agree with me after reading it, as it was only a testimonial to the Oneness and Singleness of God. But alas! The day Zia Ullah Effendi read my epistle to the believers, Ghusn-i-A'zam was in the Sacred Shrine, and Aqa Siyyid Hadi immediately notified him about it. From that day Ghusn-i-A'zam cut off all relationship with us and authorized the followers to avoid us to the extent of not even greeting us, and thus we were excommunicated.

Not satisfied with this, he also compelled them to write vulgar and repulsive replies. Aqa Riza Qannadi and others wrote such replies which showed what was hidden in their innermost.

My epistle was printed at Bombay, India. One half of it explained the situation and the other half was only from the teachings of Baha'u'llah, which proved the truth of my statement, and there was not one word in the said epistle which deserved repulsive replies. That printed epistle is available to those who would like to examine it and judge for

---

[35] Apparently Mr. Bahai did not attend the meeting himself, but his younger brothers did. The reference to Khadim's presence at the meeting may indicate that he was a key figure in the developing conflict between 'Abdu'l-Baha and other members of Baha'u'llah's inner circle, in light of the respected position he had held. To what degree the power struggle originated from Mr. Bahai's personal opposition to 'Abdu'l-Baha is unclear. Traditionally he has been understood as the prime instigator of the schism, but he himself frames it as a broad-based movement of important believers who looked to him to assert their views. He may have faced something of a no-win situation, either challenging his elder half-brother or losing the respect of his younger brothers and other co-workers in the faith.

themselves.³⁶ Is it allowed that those who claim to be true believers should write repulsive replies to the revelations of the Supreme Pen, and yet consider themselves faithful and steadfast in His cause?³⁷

The said epistle was mailed and distributed abroad. Some of the believers accepted it and joined me, (among them) well-known personages such as [the] Honorable Ismu'llah Jamal [Burújirdi] and Haji Muhammad Husayn of Kashan and other friends from Tehran, Aqa Mirza Khalil, Haji Muhammad Ali and son, Mirza Abdu'l-Husayn Khan and other friends from Azerbaijan.³⁸ Numerous friends from Khorasan, and many other provinces of Persia responded to my call, some of whom are still alive. Aqa Siyyid Mirza Afnan, Haji Siyyid Muhammad Afnan, Haji Mirza Husayn Khartumi, Haji Husayn Ali Jahrumi, Haji Muhammad Avazi and numerous well-known personages from Bombay, India, also joined me.

In the Holy Land the two Branches [Zia Ullah Effendi and Badi Ullah Effendi], the two Holy Leaves [Samadiyya Khanum and Foroughiyya Khanum, their sister and half-sister], Her Grace our mother [Mahd-i-'Ulya, widow of Baha'u'llah], and all the members of the household,³⁹ the Khadim who served Baha'u'llah for forty years, the nephews of Baha'u'llah, and some of the believers remained with me.

Some of these friends wrote pamphlets proving their point of view, although later on some of them contradicted, for worldly desires, their own statements and acted contrary to their previous actions. Some of the believers in the above-mentioned countries, after receiving the said epistle, returned them and wrote repulsive replies. The reason for their

---

³⁶ Unfortunately, this editor has not been able to locate any extant copies of this first epistle of Mohammed Ali Effendi, without which there is no way to know whether his description of its tone and contents is accurate.

³⁷ As can be seen in his messages included in this book, Mohammed Ali Bahai did have a habit of quoting the scriptures of Baha'u'llah extensively. Here he expresses incredulity that any Baha'is would respond in a hostile manner to a letter filled with quotations from Baha'u'llah.

³⁸ Probably the region of northwestern Iran called Azerbaijan, not the present-day country of the same name.

³⁹ Not including 'Abdu'l-Baha and his sister Bahiyyih Khanum, and their mother Navvab, who predeceased Baha'u'llah.

action was this: The leaders appointed by Ghusn-i-A'zam, like Haji Mirza Haydar Ali[40] and others, were traveling for years throughout the land, sowing the seeds of hatred in the hearts of the [Baha'is] and directing them to refuse our letters or epistles, and causing them to write vulgar and repulsive replies.

Later on, unexpectedly two pilgrims from Bombay, India, namely Jahrumi and Avazi came to Acre for the sole purpose of making investigations. They arrived at Acre without announcing their coming and stopped at a local hotel. They visited first Ghusn-i-A'zam and his followers whom they met repeatedly and asked questions. Then they interviewed me and those who were with me, and after careful examination of the claims of both parties, left this land; and wherever they went and whomever they met, they explained to them in detail what they had learned.

While they were here, I wrote a short epistle which was lithographed by the said Jahrumi. I sent a copy of this epistle with one of the faithful followers, Aqa Muhammad Qaeni,[41] to Ghusn-i-A'zam, but alas! he refused to accept it and asked the bearer [of the letter] what he (Ghusn-i-Akbar) wanted. The bearer humbly explained that he desires the removal of the present dissension, whereupon Ghusn-i-A'zam said, "If he desires the removal of the dissension, let him come in the same manner that Mirza Badi Ullah came."

Badi Ullah Effendi Switches Sides, Is Excommunicated Again

Before the coming of the two pilgrims from India for the purpose of investigation, the separation of my brother Badi Ullah Effendi took place. The details in brief are thus: At the time of my first epistle as mentioned above [i.e. the one that resulted in their excommunication],

---

[40] Probably Haydar Ali Isfahani, who is known to have been a staunch supporter of 'Abdu'l-Baha and critic of the Unitarian Baha'is. However, 'Abdu'l-Baha also had a prominent follower by the name of Haydar Ali Usku'i. It is not clear which man was intended by Mr. Bahai.

[41] Not to be confused with Aqa Muhammad Qá'iní, a distinguished Baha'i known as Nabíl-i-Akbar, who died in 1892. The surname Qaeni is the same, though spelled differently to avoid confusion.

and thereafter, we were in financial difficulties; but later on these difficulties became worse, because Ghusn-i-A'zam had closed all the sources of our income and thenceforth did his utmost to keep us in hardship, so that we might become exhausted and agree with him in his principles which were contrary to the teachings of Baha'u'llah.[42]

Meanwhile Zia Ullah Effendi became ill and left this earthly world, departing to the Eternal Realm. This brother was very near and dear to me and his separation was very hard for me. Praise be to God! His Will is above all, and we must be contented. [Zia Ullah] was a pure soul, an ardent lover of humanity, a faithful and zealous promulgator of the [Baha'i] teachings and steadfast in the cause. He was my coworker in our common fight for the freedom of the thoughts of mankind, and their release from the clutches of religious leaders.

To be brief, our mode of living did not suit Badi Ullah Effendi. He could not stand the hardships, as we were in a very bad financial situation. He piled up debts and the debtors pressed him. Ghusn-i-A'zam was watching the opportunity. Poor living, the accumulation of debts, lack of patience, and the watchful waiting of Ghusn-i-A'zam paved the way [for Badi Ullah to switch sides].

Meanwhile Badi Ullah Effendi became a little ill. Our family physician was a Greek, and the friend of all. One day, he informed me that Ghusn-i-A'zam desired to come and visit Badi Ullah Effendi; I said very well and we are grateful. The next day Ghusn-i-A'zam came in the company of the said doctor and went directly to the room of Badi Ullah Effendi, and during the conversation said to him that a change of cli-

---

[42] The sons of Baha'u'llah were political prisoners and had worked their whole lives in the service of the Baha'i movement—a cause that was still regarded as heresy by most members of the society around them—and thus they did not have the opportunity to find normal employment to earn a living. All of Baha'u'llah's sons, like their father before them, depended for their livelihood on a stipend from the Ottoman government, donations from Baha'is around the world, and revenue from lands that had been acquired with these funds. 'Abdu'l-Baha, the eldest son and duly appointed leader of the Baha'i community after Baha'u'llah's passing, held the purse strings; his younger brothers relied on his willingness to provide them with their portion of income. This situation gave 'Abdu'l-Baha considerable leverage, which according to Mr. Bahai, he used to full effect, attempting to compel his brothers to submit to his interpretation of the Baha'i faith.

mate was necessary: "I am ready to arrange for everything, only tell me where you would like to go." He insisted on this change, using all his efforts to win him, and then left.

This visit gave my brother Badi Ullah Effendi an excuse; although up to that time they had secret relations, after this visit the relations became more open. They met often and discussed the situation. Ghusn-i-A'zam agreed to pay all Badi Ullah Effendi's debts, and provide for him and his family their needs of livelihood, with one condition: that whatsoever Ghusn-i-A'zam desires, he (Badi Ullah Effendi) should write about me, and separate himself from me and those who confessed the Oneness of God, and report anything improper about me.

This brother wrote,[43] and Ghusn-i-A'zam provided him with a house. He allied himself with Aqa Siyyid Ali Afnan (husband of Foroughiyya Khanum); they came to me together, argued with me for an hour and then left. Afterwards he (Badi Ullah Effendi) sent carriers and removed his belongings.

But alas! none of them received what they had expected. Badi Ullah Effendi was sent away.[44] Afnan was thrown out. My poor sister was forced to leave me, but did not receive any benefit by doing so, and on account of ill treatment and grief became ill, and passed away at an early age.[45] Her husband the said Afnan followed her to Eternity later.

---

[43] Badi Ullah Effendi wrote a short confession in 1903 and a longer essay, probably in 1904. These were widely circulated by 'Abdu'l-Baha, who ordered them translated into English and published together in the United States in 1907 under the title "An Epistle to the Baha'i World." In this document, also known simply as "Badi'u'llah's Epistle," he portrays Mohammed Ali Effendi as obsessively opposed to their elder half-brother and plotting to ruin his reputation and gain power for himself through underhanded schemes. 'Abdu'l-Baha used this epistle as the primary basis for the allegations he made against Mohammed Ali Bahai in his will. It is unknown to what degree Badi Ullah's epistle reflected his real observations and concerns, or to what degree he was just writing what 'Abdu'l-Baha wanted him to say, as Mr. Bahai claims.

[44] After being excommunicated by 'Abdu'l-Baha for the second time, Badi Ullah Effendi again became a Unitarian Baha'i and remained so for the rest of his life.

[45] Foroughiyya Khanum was the daughter of Baha'u'llah by his third wife, Gawhar. She died of breast cancer. Mr. Bahai speculates that her early death may have been related to the stress she endured as a result of the conflicts

Suspected Motive for Slander of Unitarian Baha'is

Now let us consider what these two brothers said and what was their aim. My appointment by the Supreme Pen in the "Book of My Covenant" (The Will of Baha'u'llah) [to be second in line to the leadership of the Baha'i faith] was not agreeable to Ghusn-i-A'zam, as he desired complete independence. He wanted to appoint whomsoever he wished after him and to say what he desired without opposition. The fulfillment of this object was impossible with my presence, as I was appointed by Baha'u'llah after him. How could he refute the clear text? There was no other way but to spread false accusations against me, my mother, and the members of the holy household, so that these slanderous accusations might destroy the affections and respect of the believers towards us and refute the clear text.

The slanders reached to such a stage that they even said that there were no other offspring of Baha'u'llah except Ghusn-i-A'zam ('Abdu'l-Baha) and his sister [Bahiyyih Khanum]. If so, who are those who were mentioned by the Supreme Pen in the Book of My Covenant and other tablets, and where are they? Indeed such mischief and misrepresentations never happened before and were not heard of from any [past religious] sect.

When conditions reached this stage, the tongues became loose, and everyone said what he desired. The seekers after leadership grasped the opportunity and flooded the land with the claims of exalted position for Ghusn-i-A'zam and false accusations towards me and my associates. With these unfounded claims they poisoned the minds of the people, and caused the present dissension and violation of the great principles commanded by Baha'u'llah.

Response to Allegation of Interpolation of Sacred Text

Among the accusations towards me, which they have made Badi

---

within Baha'u'llah's family. According to her granddaughter Bahiyeh Afnan Shahid, 'Abdu'l-Baha reconciled with her and Mr. Afnan and was kind to her during her terminal illness (see http://www.abdulbahasfamily.org/writings/sayyid-ali-afnan-forough-khanum-and-their-sons/).

Ullah Effendi the medium of its confirmation, is the interpolation of the sacred text. At first they said that the Book of *Haykal* (which had been printed in Bombay, India) was interpolated. When I heard this, at once I proved the falsity of their statement. When they saw that their accusation met with resistance and proved futile, the song was changed; through the testimony of my younger brother, they state that there was a tablet in the blessed handwriting [of Baha'u'llah] which I have interpolated.[46] Where is that tablet? To whom does it belong and with whom is it [i.e. who was the recipient of the original]? I have no knowledge of, have never seen, nor possessed or produced such a tablet. If the brothers ('Abdu'l-Baha and Badi Ullah) possess it, why did they not produce it, and if others have it let them show it, "That he who is dishonest may be disgraced." It is not sufficient [merely] to make an accusation, and no civil or religious court will pass a judgment without [a] hearing, or give a decision without questioning or investigation.

[Something like] [t]he interpolation which they have accused me of is reflected on Ghusn-i-A'zam himself. Although I do not like to admit it, in a booklet which they have printed—and a copy of the same is in our possession—a letter is published which is attributed to Ghusn-i-A'zam ('Abdu'l-Baha), addressed to the American Baha'is. In this letter is copied the first part of a holy tablet which was revealed for me (by Baha'u'llah) and which they claim to be for him ('Abdu'l-Baha). Later on they stated that we, i.e. myself and Ghusn-i-A'zam, were partners in the said tablet [i.e. that Baha'u'llah revealed it in praise of both of them]. It is really amazing: they claim partnership in the Holy Tablet,[47] which was revealed by the Supreme Pen specially for me, and they want to deprive me of my portion of the "Book of My Covenant," which is the

---

[46] In "Badi'u'llah's Epistle," Mohammed Ali Bahai is accused of deliberately misinterpreting a tablet by Baha'u'llah regarding Mirza Yahya Subh-i-Azal as a prophecy of Abbas Effendi falling into heresy. Moreover, the epistle accuses him of altering the text of the tablet to support this slanderous interpretation.

[47] This tablet, reproduced in Chapter 10, was also called the "Sacred Tablet" by some Unitarian Baha'is. Both "holy" and "sacred" are probably translations of the same word. It is not clear whether this was actually the title of the tablet or just a description.

last will of Baha'u'llah and in which my name is repeatedly mentioned in very clear words.

Response to Allegation of Complaint to Turkish Government

Among the accusations is another hearsay, that I have complained to Istanbul and was the cause of the Turkish government sending out a commission of inquiry [to investigate the Baha'i community and the activities of 'Abdu'l-Baha]. While Ghusn-i-A'zam was at Alexandria, Egypt, a Christian named Salim Qub'ayn visited him and asked several questions. The said questions and answers were published in the *Mokattam* weekly edition, a well known Arabic newspaper in Cairo. The answers prove the incorrectness of what has been stated in his (i.e. 'Abdu'l-Baha's) will.[48] Both are the words of Ghusn-i-A'zam and one contradicts the other. Now which one shall we accept? Doubtless the answers in the said weekly represented the truth, as they were published years before the departure [i.e. death] of Ghusn-i-A'zam and he did not deny them, and the non-denial proves the truth of the statements published in the above-mentioned weekly.

Furthermore, when the said commission was here, my cousin Aqa Mirza Majdeddin met Riza Qannadi (one of the supporters of 'Abdu'l-Baha) and asked him to obtain permission from Ghusn-i-A'zam and join him [i.e. Mirza Majdeddin] in interviewing the commission and demand officially a copy of the alleged complaint by Ghusn-i-Akbar, so that either the truth or the falsity of the accusations might be revealed. Unfortunately the request was not granted [by 'Abdu'l-Baha and Mr. Qannadi] and no reply was given [by them]. Indeed, in the field of accusations they are fast workers, but when they are asked to search for the truth, they are negligent and careless.

---

[48] In his will, 'Abdu'l-Baha claims that Mohammed Ali Effendi and his supporters "prepared a document teeming with calumny and slander wherein... 'Abdu'l-Bahá is deemed a deadly enemy, the ill-wisher of the Crown. They so perturbed the minds of the members of the Imperial Government that at last a Committee of Investigation was sent... [and] with the most glaring injustice, proceeded with its investigations." See Chapter 8.

The members of the commission were residing at the house of Messrs. Beydoun, from the day of their arrival up to the time of their departure. I therefore wrote a letter to the Beydoun family regarding the matter, and this is their reply:

> To His Excellency Mohammed Ali Effendi Bahai:
>
> After expressing our fondest respects we state in reply to your epistle dated Safar 8, 1345 A.H. [August 18, 1926] that we have not heard from the commission of Inspectors or from any of them individually, during their stay at our house, a word which would indicate or prove the correctness of the said circulated accusations against you, i.e. that you or any of your followers presented a petition to the Sublime Court[49] or to the representatives of the said Government in the Province or County against your deceased brother Abbas Effendi ('Abdu'l-Baha), and that the commission's presence had anything to do with this matter. This is the truth of the situation which we are explaining. Please accept our fondest respect.
>
> (Dated)   Safar 10, 1345 A.H. [August 20, 1926]
> (Signed) Zaki Beydoun
>   Shafik Beydoun
>   Sahel Beydoun
>   Sadik Beydoun

Comments on Excommunication and Baha'i Leadership

Among the accusations is their allegation that I have violated the Book of My Covenant.[50] On what occasion was this violation (commit-

---

[49] Presumably this is a variant of "Sublime Porte," which was a term for the central government of the Ottoman Empire.

[50] 'Abdu'l-Baha accused Mohammed Ali Bahai of being a "violator" of "the Covenant"—a "Covenant-breaker" in modern Baha'i parlance. From the way Mr. Bahai refers to this allegation, he clearly did not regard the covenant of Baha'u'llah as anything more than the *Kitab-i-'Ahd(i)* itself, i.e. Baha'u'llah's last will and testament. The word *'ahd* in Arabic means covenant or testament; the will, therefore, *was* the covenant, in Mr. Bahai's view, and the only way to violate it would be to violate its stipulations, the expressed wishes of the deceased. 'Abdu'l-Baha, on the other hand, interpreted "the Covenant" as a Baha'i religious concept based on Baha'u'llah's clear appointment of a successor: a promise by

ted), which they allege, and when did it take place? If it is in the commandments like fasting, prayer, and others, these were according to the Most Sacred Book [i.e. the *Kitab-i-Aqdas*] and were obeyed long before the Book of My Covenant was revealed. If they have seen any violation, let them explain it. I know that I have obeyed them all. I have devoted all my life to inscribing and calligraphing the revealed holy books [of Baha'u'llah] and promulgating His teachings, and by thorough reading of the holy books I have obtained the meanings contained therein.

If they say that the violation is on account of disagreement with Ghusn-i-A'zam ('Abdu'l-Baha), let them state, where was it and how did it happen? If they gaze with the eyes of justice at my first epistle, entitled "The Essence of Unity," they will learn what was the cause of discord. This delicate situation must be carefully observed: although [Baha'u'llah] has said to turn towards Ghusn-i-A'zam, this is confined to the limitations mentioned in the holy books and is subject to the words of God and not above them. The Book [i.e. the scriptures of Baha'u'llah] has the sovereignty over all, and the two appointed Branches (i.e. 'Abdu'l-Baha and Mohammed Ali) are its promulgators. No one can change what has been revealed, neither can he add thereto, until the next Manifestation; then He may change what He wishes. He alone is the Law-giver and all the rest are subject to the commands of His words and must obey Him. Indeed He is God, there is no God but Him.

Yet some of the selfish people and seekers of leadership attributed an unlimited station to Ghusn-i-A'zam and considered the words to "turn towards" as a glad-tidings [i.e. an announcement of a new Manifestation].[51] They made a manifestation of him and interpreted in his

---

God to humanity that the Baha'i faith would never be divided into sects, through absolute obedience to the "Center of the Covenant" ('Abdu'l-Baha himself), and to the institutional system of succession he spelled out in his own will.

[51] Mohammed Ali Effendi is expressing his belief that to "turn your faces toward" Abbas Effendi, as Baha'u'llah commanded, means simply to acknowledge his leadership of the Baha'i community after Baha'u'llah's passing, not a prophetic or divine station. In his will, Baha'u'llah tells his family and followers to "turn, one and all, their faces towards Ghusn-i-A'zam. ... 'When the ocean of My presence hath ebbed and the Book of My Revelation is ended, turn your faces toward *Him Whom* God hath purposed, *Who* hath branched from this

favor the contents of some of the holy tablets which refer only to the appearance of the coming Manifestation.[52] With their mischievous acts they misguided the innocent followers and held them under their control. Their main object was to attain the station of leadership, collect earthly possessions and live the life of ease and luxury like some who have lived in the past and others who are living at present.

The kind of leadership that they have originated is being observed by you today[53] and no doubt you are hearing about their corrupt actions and the violation of the commands [of Baha'u'llah]. Today one person is rejected, tomorrow another is expelled [from the Baha'i community]. What was his fault? and what did he do to deserve rejection or expulsion? Did he deny the existence of the Creator, the Great Manifestation?[54] Nay by God, perhaps he contradicted the personal desires

---

Ancient Root.' [i.e. the Greatest Branch, Abbas Effendi]." Readers should note the pronouns italicized by this editor, which refer to 'Abdu'l-Baha; they are capitalized in the official English translation of the text. All officially approved Baha'i publications in English use capitalized pronouns to refer to 'Abdu'l-Baha (e.g. "He" instead of "he"). This has long been the standard practice among Baha'is to refer to God, the Manifestations of God, and 'Abdu'l-Baha—but no other human beings—and this was the case even during 'Abdu'l-Baha's own ministry. The capitalization is a doctrinal decision or a form of interpretation, since Baha'u'llah wrote in Arabic and Persian, neither of which has capital letters. This is probably the most obvious example of the phenomenon noted by Mohammed Ali Bahai, i.e. his contention that Baha'is deified or at least inappropriately idolized 'Abdu'l-Baha. Mainstream Baha'i doctrine does not technically consider him to be a Manifestation of God, but does regard him as infallible, the "true exemplar" of a holy life, and considers his writings as scripture. Before this formulation was developed, some Baha'is in the early years of 'Abdu'l-Baha's ministry did believe he was a Manifestation.

[52] Mr. Bahai attributes this idea to some of 'Abdu'l-Baha's followers, rather than to 'Abdu'l-Baha himself. Although this may largely be true, it may also be somewhat of a diplomatic interpretation of what occurred. See the section in the Epilogue entitled "'Abdu'l-Baha and the 'Covenant-Breakers'" for an in-depth discussion of this issue.

[53] This is presumably a reference to the appointed branch of the Baha'i Administrative Order established in 'Abdu'l-Baha'is will, i.e. the Guardianship and Hands of the Cause, and the collection of *Huququ'llah* to fund their organization.

[54] According to the "Book of My Covenant," the sole criterion for being recognized as a Baha'i is defined as sincerely recognizing the Manifestation of God

of a certain individual and therefore deserved the hardship and calamities imposed on him.

Where is that freedom of thought which is the cause of the progress of the world, and what became of the commands of the Supreme Pen? He said, "O people of the world! The creed of God is for love and union; make it not the cause of discord and dissension." Today we hear and observe nothing but malice and hatred, and the condition [of the Baha'i faith] has reached to such a state that the commands are openly violated and the Book of My Covenant is (being) disregarded.

What are our sins? Because we did not accept Ghusn-i-A'zam ('Abdu'l-Baha) as a new manifestation? We obeyed all his wishes and desires, only we could not interpret the word "turn towards" as they have done and overlook all the revealed books. The foundation of religion is the confession of the Oneness and Singleness of God, and if we interpret the word "turn towards" as they have done, we would be violating that foundation and those principles. We could not be polytheists and ruin the work of our lifetime. We have lived many years under the blessed shadow of our Great Master Baha'u'llah and have heard the commands from His Ancient Tongue. How could we forget what we have heard and observed in those blessed days, and for the sake of the seekers of earthly possessions and leadership keep silent?

Efforts for Reconciliation and Unity of Faith

[Baha'u'llah] says, "Religious malice and hatred is a world-burning fire." O friends! Come and use your efforts to quench this burning fire, and if you cannot extinguish it, the admonitions of God are numerous. And although He says "to extinguish it will be very difficult," yet if we follow His blessed commands and arise to serve Him with united efforts, free from the hope of personal benefit, we shall be assisted with

---

for this era, i.e. Baha'u'llah: "Every receptive soul who hath in this Day inhaled the fragrance of His garment and hath, with a pure heart, set his face towards the all-glorious Horizon is reckoned among the people of Bahá in the Crimson Book." (*Tablets of Bahá'u'lláh Revealed After the Kitáb-i-Aqdas*, 1988 pocket-size edition, p. 220).

the hosts of the unseen, providing that we do not desire anything for ourselves nor follow our own opinion. Our aim should be to serve the Cause of God, and to promulgate what was revealed by the Supreme Pen, devote our time to the remembrance of His days, and give to the [spiritually] needy the pearls of wisdom which are hidden in His teachings; to enlighten those who are in darkness and to awaken those who are asleep.

Well-informed people should know that this servant always desired to establish unity and love amongst the different faiths, that religion may not be the cause of dissension and enmity, especially among the Holy Family [of Baha'u'llah], the friends and believers. When dissension took place amongst us, I did all I could to bring about unity and several times communicated with Ghusn-i-A'zam regarding this important duty, either verbally or in writing, or through special messengers who were the most devoted, the most earnest, and the most steadfast Baha'is; but unfortunately my pleadings were not accepted.

When Ghusn-i-A'zam returned from the United States, I heard that he was visiting Acre. Without hesitation I proceeded to his house and paid him a visit. Many Baha'is and native friends were present. The object of my visit was to remove the dissension and hard feelings. I did not make any conditions and did my duty, and if he desired the removal of those hard feelings, he would return my call and gradually the past events would be forgotten—that perchance we might sit together and with the language of love and kindness discuss the most vital subject on which we differ, so that the subsequent difficulties would not have taken place. My object of that visit was to renew unity and love, but alas! he did not desire to do so and thus the desired object could not be attained.

Response to Allegation of Pride and Divine Rejection

One of the accusations attributed to me, which has been repeatedly mentioned, is that I claimed a station [of divine authority]. They have used this for their personal objects. First, the Tablet to Qazvin and then some Arabic writings which I had written in my childhood.

Chapter 16. Autobiography of Mohammed Ali Bahai

The Tablet of Qazvin which bore my name and signature was revealed by the Supreme Pen (of Baha'u'llah). They were two tablets and not one: one in Arabic and another in Arabic and Persian, and both of them were revealed by Baha'u'llah. By sending the first tablet to Qazvin, He tested the followers in that land, and the second tablet eliminated the existing imaginations. His only aim was that the followers should know the station of the Manifestations, that God has no equal and no partner, and that we are all His creatures. The said tablet which is in my handwriting is preserved and the name of the addressee is written on it by the Supreme Pen of Baha'u'llah. The copy of the second tablet is also preserved.

What I did compose in Arabic in those days was presented to the blessed presence of Baha'u'llah, and after having been corrected by the Supreme Pen, they [the compositions] were copied by me, and by His command were sent abroad. Baha'u'llah revealed the details of this question in the Epistle of Badi, in the reply to Ali Muhammad Sarraj, and other blessed tablets. By studying the above-mentioned tablets the seekers of truth will comprehend the purpose clearly.

The object of my accusers was to keep the innocent followers in the dark, and prevent them from reading the holy books [of Baha'u'llah] by the mention of interpolation [i.e. accusing Ghusn-i-Akbar of altering Baha'u'llah's writings], as by reading the revealed books they would learn the truth. Since my name is repeatedly mentioned in the Book of My Covenant, the Will of Baha'u'llah, therefore by these false accusations they wanted to misguide the followers, and belittle the greatness of the Book of My Covenant.

Now let us study the tablet in which [Baha'u'llah] mentions the sons;[55] He says, "he and his likes." Which branches (sons) were my likes at that time? When this tablet was revealed, of the two younger branches (i.e. Zia Ullah Effendi and Badi Ullah Effendi) one of them was very little and the other had just been born. Doubtless my likes at that time were my two older brothers, Ghusn-i-A'zam and Mirza Mihdi.

---

[55] The identity of the tablet is difficult to determine from this brief description. It is likely one of the many writings of Baha'u'llah that have never been translated into English.

Also they point to the tablet which specifies the rejection [i.e. of verses sent in Mohammed Ali's name], but they ignore what has been revealed [by Baha'u'llah] later. He said in several tablets "that God made him utter [those verses] in his childhood." Therefore what God has made me to do was not my own act and does not prove that I had any claim. Furthermore I am accused that I was a claimant while I was a child in the days of Baha'u'llah. The numerous blessed tablets revealed for me ever since, and my appointment in the Book of My Covenant, repudiate this accusation.

They also point to what has been revealed: "If for a second he leave the shadow of the cause of God, he will cease to exist completely." It is true that whosoever leaves the shadow of His cause will become non-existent, but to cease to exist cannot take place except for two reasons: one is by command of the Supreme Pen, and from the Supreme Pen we have nothing in our hands save extreme favor and divine providence. He has not mentioned or revealed one word which indicated my non-existence. On the contrary, in several tablets and in the Book of My Covenant my existence was confirmed with great favor and divine providence, and He said to those who may oppose me and the other branches, "Fear God and be not of those who are tyrants."

Now what excuse have my opponents in violating His commands and His will? There is not a verse in which they could hope for forgiveness without repentance. If they say that I have been violating the commands of God, where is that and which (one of them) is it? All these years they have satisfied themselves with hearsay and none of them approached me or communicated with me to investigate the truth and weigh these hearsays with the scale of search and inquiry. They contented themselves with what they heard from Ghusn-i-A'zam, the members of his household and their relations. And by this careless act, they have violated the commands of Baha'u'llah in His will and many other tablets. It is an established fact that accusations must be proved before the accused can be held responsible for them, and no court of justice will pass judgment without a hearing, be the accused a prince or a pauper.

Baha'is Must Consider Both Sides and Have an Ecumenical Dialogue

O friends! When they informed you that a dissension existed amongst the branches, it was incumbent upon you to investigate and hear what the two appointed branches [i.e. Ghusn-i-A'zam and Ghusn-i-Akbar] had to say and what are the causes of dissension, not that you should side with one party without question and condemn the other without investigation. The two appointed positions [i.e. the first and second successor of Baha'u'llah] are one and have no differences save in time. Both are under His laws and not above them, and our dissension could be eliminated through His teachings only.

Hearken to my impartial suggestion and discard your selfishness and extremism, and according to the admonitions of the Supreme Pen, hold a conference of peace and study in spirituality what you have heard, and investigate the truth. Compare the stories of both sides with the commands of God in the Book of *Aqdas* and other revealed books, then accept what is in accord with them and reject what does not agree. It is obvious that in such an unselfish conference the dissension could be eliminated and the light of unity shall brighten the horizon of the Baha'i world.

Undoubtedly the leadership-seekers detest this kind of meeting, as it will shake the (apparent) firmness of the foundation of their leadership and prevent them from performing their corrupt objects. The seekers after leadership desire to keep their followers in darkness, that they might attain their object, as whosoever becomes enlightened cannot be misguided, and will not exchange the complete freedom which God has willed for him, for the bondage of their servitude. The leadership-seekers are after the unfortunate, ignorant people who would listen to whatsoever they are told and obey their commands, although these may be contrary to the commands of God. Such leaders do not desire to have around them open-minded and intelligent people.

Baha'u'llah, Glory be to Him, said: "O different creeds! Look forward unto agreement and be enlightened with the light of concord; for the sake of God assemble in a place and remove from amongst you that which is the cause of dissension." Doubtless what has been revealed shall appear and will be the cause of unity, but it is more desirable that you may succeed today in performing this service. Arise for the sake of God and be the cause of freedom for the unfortunate; then you shall become the examples of the holy verse, "The proceeders, the proceeders, they are those who are favored."

Abbas Effendi Dies Estranged from His Brother

I mentioned previously that I tried repeatedly to come to an understanding with Ghusn-i-A'zam, and upon his return from America I visited him without announcement or reservation, with the hope that after visiting the foreign lands his ideas may have changed and his heart become more lenient, but unfortunately things did not change and the expected result was not attained; therefore I kept silent and held fast to the rope of patience and resignation.

One day as usual (when) I was going to Acre, I noticed a commotion among the followers and after investigation I learned that Ghusn-i-A'zam had passed away suddenly the night before at Haifa. They had informed the followers but kept it a secret from us. Alas! he passed away suddenly and left us in despair; the wounds of the hearts are still unhealed, unity has disappeared and now all the efforts to bring about peace are futile.

With a burning heart and eyes full of tears I proceeded to Haifa with the intention of saying my last farewell and consoling myself. When I reached the door of the house, I saw a policeman sitting outside and in the doorway standing Ruhi, son of Aqa Mirza Muhsin Afnan (the husband of Touba Khanum, one of the twin daughters of 'Abdu'l-Baha).[56] When Ruhi saw me, he said a few words, closed the door in my face and stood behind it refusing me admittance. Therefore I was compelled to return [home] full of grief and sorrow, and did not raise any objection. While on my way to my deceased brother's house, the son of

---

[56] Ruhi Afnan, a grandson of 'Abdu'l-Baha and cousin of Shoghi Effendi Rabbani, served for many years during Mr. Rabbani's Guardianship of the Baha'i faith as his corresponding secretary and a well-respected international spokesperson for the religion. In 1941, Mr. Rabbani excommunicated Mr. Afnan from the Baha'i community.

an old Turkish Pasha, Ali Mansour Pasha by name, who was a friend of the family, had joined me, and when he observed their ill treatment became disappointed and returned [home] also. The next day my sons and cousins met with the same treatment from Ruhi, who also used wild language during the funeral.

After the departure [i.e. death] of Ghusn-i-A'zam, I communicated repeatedly with the Baha'is and explained to them what I deemed necessary. The copies of all my communications are preserved. I did not desire a high station for myself and never mentioned my religious rights, nor my personal rank. Every Baha'i has read the Will of Baha'u'llah, heard and observed the text of the Supreme Pen regarding this servant. It is up to them to obey or to disobey Him. I do not interfere with anyone, and I have no object but to serve the cause of God and spread His teachings. I have been patient under all circumstances and have left everything in God's hands. I hope that up to the end I shall pass the days in patience. Exalted be His Glory, to assist me to serve His cause and grant me that which is the desire of my heart.

17

Will and Testament

By Mohammed Ali Bahai

This is the spiritual will and testament of Baha'u'llah's son Mohammed Ali Bahai, who passed away on December 10, 1937 at the age of 84—approximately 16 years after the passing of his elder brother, 'Abdu'l-Baha. Mr. Bahai was the leader of the Unitarian Baha'i community and, according to the belief of his supporters, the legitimate successor of 'Abdu'l-Baha based on his appointment in Baha'u'llah's will.

The will of Mohammed Ali Bahai has never before been made available to the public. It was translated into English by his son Shua Ullah, who included it in his book manuscript. Some long paragraphs have been divided and section headings have been added by this editor.

Mr. Bahai's last message to the world is strikingly different in tone than the Will and Testament of 'Abdu'l-Baha, containing no direct attacks on his late brother's character and closing with a prayer for Baha'is to tolerate each other's differences of opinion rather than letting these disagreements become a cause of hatred. The author does, however, criticize some aspects of Baha'i belief as it had developed under 'Abdu'l-Baha, thus making the case that Baha'u'llah's first successor erred in his interpretation of the religion.

This document is, more than anything else, a theological treatise and summary of Mohammed Ali Effendi's view of the Baha'i faith. In many ways it is a counterpoint or alternative vision of Baha'ism based not on a supposedly infallible succession of divinely inspired authority, as 'Abdu'l-Baha argued for and implemented through his creation of the institution of Guardianship in his will, but instead on reverence for

Baha'u'llah as the only source of divine revelation in the present historical era. Mr. Bahai did not appoint a successor, and claimed that the idea of a "Guardian" for God's cause was unnecessary and contrary to Baha'u'llah's teachings. He mentioned the House of Justice as the appropriate administrative authority for the Baha'i community, but rejected the notion that any religious leadership or institution is in any way infallible—reserving this lofty station of command for the Manifestation of God alone.

Overall, Mohammed Ali Bahai presents a relatively simple vision of the Baha'i faith, based on obeying the scriptures of Baha'u'llah and rejecting any further claims of divine inspiration for the next one thousand years, and expresses concern that the "imagination" of religious leaders who desire excessive authority can "cause endless harm."

—The Editor

IN THE NAME OF GOD, THERE IS NO OBJECT OF WORSHIP BUT HIM.

The Oneness of God, the Manifestations and Religions

The book of Revelation [i.e. all scripture], from the beginning to the end, is adorned with the Oneness of God, and what has been revealed by the Supreme Pen in each cycle [of history], although different in tongue, confesses as to His Oneness and Singleness.

By gazing with the eyes of discernment, in the book of the Creation [i.e. the physical world], we will observe the signs of His might and the banners of His greatness apparent and exalted everywhere. The great examples in creation testify as to the Oneness of the unequal Creator, and direct the intellectual people to the knowledge of the Eternal Being. Hatef (the poet)[1] said well, "If you open the heart of each atom, You will find a sun hidden in the bosom." Also Saadi said, "The green

---

[1] Hatef Esfehani was an 18th century Iranian poet.

leaves of the trees, to the intellectual observer, Each leaf is a booklet, glorifying the Creator."

Each impression in the world of existence guides to the impresser, and each craft directs the learned to the knowledge of the craftsman. The beauty of the garden shows the capability of the gardener, and the firmness of the building proves the power of the builder. If you see a finger-ring, you will speak of a jeweler, and if you look at a chair, you will know of a carpenter. It is said that a philosopher passed by an aged woman, who was busy at her spinning-wheel, and asked: "What proofs have you of the existence of the Creator?" The aged woman in reply, silently detached her hands; the wheel stopped; then she commenced to work. Indeed by her action, she proved the existence of the Creator without a murmur.

There is nothing in the world of existence without a cause, and as existence varies the cause varies too; therefore we are in need of the cause of all causes, to open the gate of knowledge and tranquility to the people of intellect. That first cause and remote goal, which is called by some the Lord of Lords, the Light of Lights, the God of Gods, and by others described as Nature, is a reality which is above the grasp of the human mind, and an entity which is beyond the comprehension of the intellect. This Reality could not be known but by His traces and will not be understood but by His deeds. The greatest of His traces and the most important gifts of His knowledge are His Manifestations who have appeared in human garments at various times and places. Each time they spoke in a new tongue, and although they used different languages, yet the revelations were always the same. They varied in forms and customs, but always had the same effulgence and appeared in the different rising-places with one Light.

The Indians worship Him according to their knowledge and customs, the Chinese have other explanations, the Parsees call Him Abadian,[2] the Jews have other names for Him, the Christians sing a different song in His praise, and the Muslims have other beliefs. If we study

---

[2] Probably a variation of Mah-Abad, a messianic king of Persian mythology, whom the Zoroastrians expected to return at the end of the age to establish God's kingdom on earth.

this point justly and take into consideration the [underlying] realities, the changes of the phrases [i.e. religious terminology] and the variety of the interpretations will not prevent us from the knowledge of the original Reality. Hakim Sanai,[3] regarding this object said, "If you search for a language for the words of God, no matter which, Hebrew or Assyrian; If you desire a place for God, no matter where, Jabulqa or Jabulsa?"[4]

His Holiness Adam, whom we call the father of mankind, preached to his human children the Oneness of God. He taught them unity, equality, good morals and kind manners. His Holiness Noah, whom we know as the owner of the Ark, saved humanity, in the ark of knowledge and belief, from the deluge of ignorance and disbelief. His Holiness Abraham, whom we call the conqueror of Nimrod, saved himself and his fellow beings from the erring polytheists, exchanging the fire of the imagination and the superstition of Nimrod, and guided them to the praise and commemoration of the reality of God. His Holiness Moses annihilated the misguided followers of Pharaoh with the might of the Book of Law [i.e. the Torah], and with extreme humbleness and poverty fed the seekers of truth with the manna and quail of knowledge. His Holiness Jesus destroyed the cross of ignorance and temptation with the glorious and luminous Temple of guidance.

Then arrived the time of the Kaaba of the free and the Qibla[5] of the just (i.e. Muhammad); the hand of power worked wonderfully and the sun of Reality shone with full light. He broke the idols, severed the connections, and in the book of Revelation and Creation left nothing but the knowledge and belief in the Oneness and the Glory of the Great and Only One [i.e. God]. Although he was invested with great power, glory, and might, yet he called himself only a servant, a messenger and a member of the human family. Indeed his action was a lesson to man-

---

[3] Hakím Saná'í Ghaznavi was a Persian poet of the 11th and 12th century.

[4] Note by Shua Ullah Behai: "Two imaginary sacred cities in the Shi'ite doctrine." See note 24 in Chapter 2.

[5] In Islam, the *Qibla* is the direction to which all Muslims pray, i.e. facing toward the Kaaba in Mecca. Here the term is used metaphorically to refer to the Islamic prophet as the source and focal point of divine inspiration.

kind: that they might know their limitations and not exceed their position of servitude (towards God).

But alas! that some (leadership-seekers) took advantage of God's effulgence, and blow the trumpet of "It is I, and there is no one else beside me,"[6] binding the unfortunate masses with the strong chains of restrictions. In the name of Truth, they hold meetings, and enjoy earthly pleasures, while they know Him not. The [religious] leaders are enjoying their leadership and predominance, and the followers are dazed with vanishing fancies and vain imaginations, considering themselves the fortunate saved and the rest of humanity condemned, but they do not realize that their acts and deeds are repudiated by the Book, precepts, commandments, and laws [of true religion].

The Bab, the Forerunner

When the fixed time elapsed and the proper era drew nigh, the Temple of light and glory in the name of the one prophesied in Hijaz (Arabia) [by the Prophet Muhammad] appeared and unveiled himself in Shiraz (Iran). The personage called the Qa'im and named the Mahdi (i.e. the Bab) came and said, "O thou who art in expectation, I am your promised one, the object of the friends and the beloved of the faithful." He produced what the other Manifestations of Reality had produced, and explained what they had explained. Those who were earnestly and righteously seeking after the Truth investigated his claim and accepted his mission, and their hearts were illumined with the light of the Sun of Reality.

That Light of Truth, although he possessed of greatness, perfection, might and power, yet he called himself a Forerunner and preached the glad-tidings of the arrival of a most Perfect Temple, and a most glorious one [i.e. Baha'u'llah]. For great wisdom beyond our capacity he concealed the name [of the new Manifestation] and called Him "He Whom God Shall Manifest." He explained [his teachings] in detail and opened the gates of reality, but the selfish [Muslim] leaders rose in en-

---

[6] In other words, claiming to be the representative of God or mediator of human salvation.

mity, caused disturbances, enabled his assassination, and crucified him in a public square.

Although the evidence showing the truth of [the Bab's] claims was numerous, the signs [i.e. divine proofs] of his cause countless, and his messages and revelations beyond [worldly] explanation, [most compelling is] the achievement at the time of the martyrdom: An unusual incident occurred, and that is, from the rifles of a detachment of eight hundred soldiers, not a bullet touched him, and his illumined temple was not harmed. Even with this unusual occurrence, they did not repent; they called another detachment and with extreme cruelty sent that pure soul and enlightened personage to martyrdom—thinking that by this dreadful injustice and hideous act, both the noble and the humble (i.e. the people) will disregard the cause of God, repudiate the truth and uphold falsehood. They were unaware of the fact that the Hand of Might is open and the Lamp of Knowledge is [still] giving light. They were rejoicing in their act of injustice and desired to extinguish the Lamp of Knowledge.

Baha'u'llah, the Fulfiller

Suddenly the blessed verse (in the Qur'an), "God is reluctant unless He completes His Light"[7] was fulfilled and the great Sun of Reality (Baha'u'llah) made His appearance in Iraq, blessing the seekers with His effulgence. The appointed day arrived and the light of knowledge appeared in the hearts, and its illumination became beyond explanation. The prophecies of the Forerunner were fulfilled, as he said, "In the ninth year ye shall be blessed with meeting God."[8] Also what the noble [Shaykh Ahmad] Ahsa'i had said became evident: "Ye shall hear His news *ba'd hín* (i.e. after a while)." The year 69 (i.e. 1269 A.H. [1853 A.D.])

---

[7] This may be a paraphrase of Qur'an 61:7-8: "… And God guides not those who do wrong. Their intention is to extinguish God's Light (by blowing) with their mouths: But God will complete (the revelation of) His Light, even though the unbelievers may detest (it)."

[8] The ninth year after the Bab began his movement was 1853. In that year, Baha'u'llah began telling some of his companions that he was the new Manifestation of God.

was equal to the words *ba'd hin* (in the Arabic *Abjad* system of numerology[9]), and both prophecies were fulfilled together. He Whom God Shall Manifest, mentioned in the *Bayan* (the book of the Bab) that He shall appear in the day of resurrection of the *Furqan* (Qur'an),[10] lifted the veil from His glorious face. But this appearance was only special [i.e. private, restricted to his close companions], and in the year 80 (1280 A.H. [1863 A.D.]) He made His universal appearance. Tablets and epistles were uttered and proofs produced.

The Supreme Pen, moving with the fingers of the Greatest Name [i.e. al-Abha, Baha'u'llah], worked in such a degree that His example filled the world, His Light encompassed humanity, and His secrets untied the knots of calamities. Homai, the poet, speaking of his beloved said, "There is only one resurrection, but thou, Every time that thou makest thine appearance, is a resurrection." Although the poet is praising the visible [i.e. earthly beloved], yet this poem is in harmony with the appearance of the Manifestations of God, as in the past cycles, whenever a Manifestation appeared a resurrection took place, and the world of humanity underwent a test. Accounts and books, judgment and rewards, heaven and hell, recompense and penalty all were settled through His appearance.

O friends! those of you who are assembled under the canopy of His utterances and are following God, Glory be to Him: In the Book of *Aqdas* He said that every person should write a will, confessing the Oneness of God; therefore this humble servant, obeying His commands, will write these few words, explaining in brief some of the events, and hope that they may meet with the approval of the friends.

In this glorious century[11] when the great sun of Truth and Reality

---

[9] *Abjad* is a system in which numerical values are assigned to the letters of the Arabic alphabet, similar to Hebrew *Gematria*. Abjad was used in Islamic mysticism, and in the Babi faith, to derive hidden meanings and relationships between words, by calculating and comparing the sum of their letters according to their Abjad value.

[10] As in Christianity, the Qur'an prophesies a "day of resurrection" at the end of the age. This was interpreted metaphorically in the Babi and Baha'i faiths.

[11] Baha'u'llah was still alive in the 14th century A.H., the same century of the Islamic calendar in which the author was writing his will.

illumined the horizon of the universe, the Supreme Pen (of Baha'u'llah) was always moving. For years, with the language of love and kindness, He directed humanity to the right path. He explained in the numerous epistles and tablets the station of the Creator and the position of the creatures: so that the people may know their own limitations, that they may not go beyond that which has been ordained by Him. His blessed appearance was the Greatest Manifestation and the axis of the circle of all the Manifestations. In the Book of the Prophets[12] of the children of Israel, He is called God the Powerful, the Everlasting Father, and the Prince of Peace;[13] in the New Testament, the Lord,[14] the Comforter, and the Spirit of Truth;[15] in the Qur'an the Manifestation of God is clearly explained, and in the *Bayan* as He Who Shall Appear and Him Whom God Shall Make Manifest.

Sons and Successors of Baha'u'llah Are Not His Equal

O spiritual brothers: Sanctify such a Promised One from a like or an equal. Study what has been revealed by Him, and according to His revelations, confess His Oneness and ennoble His Resplendent Singleness. All else beside Him are His servants, and under the shadow of His words. In a tablet He said:

> My outward speaketh to My innermost, and My innermost to my outward, that there is no one in the Kingdom besides Me, but the people are in deep ignorance. Verily the Branches (sons), who are branched from the Tree [i.e. Baha'u'llah], are My fingerposts amidst My creatures, and My fragrance between heaven and earth. Do ye see a partner or an equal to God, your Lord? By the Lord of the worlds, No: Therefore speak not that which God hath not permitted you; fear the Merciful and be of those who reason.

---

[12] The *Nevi'im* (Hebrew: "Prophets") is one of the three sections of the Jewish Tanakh. The same writings are contained in the Christian Old Testament, but are arranged in a different order.

[13] Isaiah 9:6.

[14] Several verses, such as 1 Thessalonians 5:2, refer to the second coming of the Messiah as the "day of the Lord."

[15] John 15:26.

In this blessed revelation, [Baha'u'llah] has called the branches (sons) His fingerposts and His fragrances, and sanctified Himself from a partner or an equal, and prohibited us from uttering a word which He did not command.

[Regarding] the *tavajjoh* (i.e. turn your face) revealed in the blessed Book of My Covenant (i.e. the Will of Baha'u'llah):[16] The object of the same is unity in the service of the cause and the promulgation of the words of God. The leadership and the following [of Baha'u'llah's successor] are both for this exalted object; do not consider it a servitude and do not appoint a partner for God.[17] In the Qur'an [God] says, "If in the heaven and the earth, beside God, were other gods, doubtless both (heaven and earth) would have become disordered."[18]

The great glory in each appearance [i.e. each dispensation of divine revelation] belongs to the Manifestation of God, and all else besides Him are under His shadow. The exalted station of Oneness and the Great Infallibility are the attributes of that sanctified Manifestation. His command is the command of God, obedience to Him is obedience to God, and disobedience to Him is rebellion against God. Through Him we know God, and from Him we hear the commands of that Unseen Entity and the Hidden Mystery. He is the Dawning-place of Divine inspiration, the Origin of Divine guidance and the Mine of [God's] commands and laws. By knowing Him, gaining the knowledge of His station and confessing His Oneness, we must obey His commands and

---

[16] The Persian word *tavajjoh* (Arabic: *tawajjuh*) means "turn your face toward" or "pay attention to." In Baha'u'llah's will, it was used in reference to his eldest son and successor, Ghusn-i-A'zam (Abbas Effendi), as an instruction to the Baha'is to look to him as their leader. See Chapter 16, note 51.

[17] In Mr. Bahai's view, Baha'u'llah's will that his followers "turn [their] face toward" Abbas Effendi was intended to provide the Baha'is with a community organizer and spokesperson for the writings and teachings of the new faith, not to establish a master-servant relationship between the new Baha'i leader and his followers. Mr. Bahai evidently regarded this as a key distinction, and felt that in idolizing 'Abdu'l-Baha, many Baha'is had fallen into the grave sin known in Islam as *shirk*: joining partners with God.

[18] Qur'an 21:22. In quoting this verse, Mr. Bahai may be alluding to Baha'u'llah's admonition in his will, "Say: O servants! Let not the means of order be made the cause of confusion and the instrument of union an occasion for discord."

accept all His utterances to be from God. Knowledge without obedience is fruitless and obedience without knowledge is useless, and neither one could be accepted without the other, as has been revealed by the Supreme Pen in the beginning of the Book of *Aqdas*.[19]

Furthermore we must consider [the Manifestation of God], in all His stations and conditions, free from an equal or a like. The revelations [of scriptures] are His specialty and belong to no one else beside Him. What has been uttered by His tongue and revealed by His Supreme Pen are revelations, although they may be in the common language; and the conversation and composition of all others besides Him are the words of the creatures, though they may resemble the revelations.[20] What we observe in His actions and movements are signs and miracles, although they may resemble the actions of the creatures; and the actions of all else besides Him are examples of weakness, though they may appear to us great.

By this explanation I do not mean that we should accept without knowledge or obey blindly, but the object is that we must pay our tribute to God, and after knowing Him perform our duties towards Him. Knowledge of Him cannot be attained without careful search and study.

The Incomparable Station of Baha'u'llah

After being inwardly satisfied [of the truth of the Manifestation], it

---

[19] "The first duty prescribed by God for His servants is the recognition of Him Who is the Dayspring of His Revelation and the Fountain of His laws... It behoveth every one who reacheth this most sublime station, this summit of transcendent glory, to observe every ordinance of Him Who is the Desire of the world. These twin duties are inseparable." (*Kitab-i-Aqdas*, paragraph 1).

[20] In stating his view that eloquent writings and oratory by Baha'u'llah's successors are only human compositions, not from God, Mr. Bahai is implicitly disapproving of the inclusion of 'Abdu'l-Baha's books, letters, prayers, and speeches in the Baha'i scriptural corpus. These were and are, in fact, considered scripture in the mainstream Baha'i tradition, rather than merely commentary. For example, in the devotional portion of "Feast" meetings, Baha'is are allowed to recite the words of 'Abdu'l-Baha alongside the writings of Baha'u'llah, the Bab, the Qur'an, the Bible, and the holy writings of other religions; but non-scriptural texts are not permitted to be read.

Chapter 17. Will and Testament of Mohammed Ali Bahai

is our duty to sanctify Him in all conditions, because confessing His Oneness and glorifying Him is glorification of God. Through Him we know God, and by His appearance [i.e. the theophanic nature of the Manifestation] we learn of the Unseen Entity and the Hidden Mystery. With His aid we have received the commands and the laws of God.

[God] and the Manifestation are one. He is the example of God amidst His creatures; although he appears in human garment in the world of limitation and the qualities of the creatures, He is sanctified and exalted above all limitations—like the light of the lamp, which appears with limitations, and if it does not appear with the limitations of the lamp, the limited eyes of the individuals cannot observe it. The limitations of the lamp belong to the created world, and the Eternal Light belongs to God. Gaze to the effulgence of the sun, in a clear mirror: that effulgence comes from the unlimited world [i.e. the heavens], and the clear glass is subject to the limitation of the [earthly] world.

When the Effulgence [of God] is partial and does not appear in a complete form, He is called by the names of Messenger and Prophet; and when the great Sun of Reality appears in complete effulgence, He is qualified by the name of God and Lord; and in both effulgences He is exalted above the limitations of the human creation and being.[21]

By careful study of the tablets, the chapters [surahs] and the epistles revealed by the Supreme Pen, we understand that we should expect

---

[21] This is different from mainstream Baha'i theology, which identifies the "Messengers" (Arabic: *Rusul*, singular *Rasúl*) as fully Manifestations of God, and the "prophets" (*anbiyá'*, singular *nabí*) as inspired humans who are not Manifestations. Mohammed Ali Bahai seems to be presenting an alternative metaphysics of divine revelation in which both the Messengers (e.g. Abraham, Moses, Muhammad) and the prophets (various lesser religious figures) are "partial" Manifestations of God, perhaps to differing degrees, but none of them is a "complete" Manifestation such as Baha'u'llah. Some Unitarian Baha'is seem to have included Jesus in the category of "God and Lord" alongside Baha'u'llah, contrary to both Islam and mainstream Baha'ism which regard Jesus as having essentially the same station as all the other Messengers—*not* divine in Islam, or *all* divine in the Baha'i faith. Compared to standard Baha'i doctrine, Mr. Bahai's metaphysical system might be more open to accepting the human imperfections of most of the great spiritual leaders of history, since it does not regard them as completely or perfectly divine. Furthermore, it tends to draw more of a distinction between the Manifestation or "Effulgence" of God and the human vessel through which it appears.

the appearance of a Manifestation in each cycle [i.e. historical era], either with partial or complete effulgence. We must accept Him, the Manifestation of Him Who Doeth That Which He Chooseth. He is the Judge and all else besides Him are judged. The great infallibility and the great Oneness are His special and inseparable attributes. It is incumbent upon all to obey His commands; if we think otherwise, His commands are not worthy of consideration. Because if we do not consider the informer to be infallible and free from limitations, how can we accept His information and rely upon it?

His great appearance (in this cycle) is the Complete Effulgence, adorned with the mantle of the greatest distinction according to the text of the Supreme Pen. [Baha'u'llah] is exalted and exempt from a partner, an equal, a like, or a minister. His commands could not be changed and His laws cannot be altered, and shall remain in force a thousand years. He is the axis of the Cycle of the Appearances [i.e. all the Manifestations of God in a great epoch of human history], and if a Manifestation should appear in a thousand years, He shall be speaking in His name, and shall rise in commemoration of His attributes. Also in *Mustaghath* (i.e. 2001 [of the Baha'i Era], in the [*Abjad*] language of numerology) there shall appear One who will testify to His Oneness and Singleness.[22]

This Complete Effulgence that we have accepted as the axis of all the Manifestations of God according to the supreme revealed text, appears only once in five thousand years,[23] and will make Himself known to His creatures, and all the previous and subsequent Manifestations circumambulate Him, belong to Him and speak of Him.

---

[22] *Mustaghath* literally means "He who is invoked for help." It is a title of another Manifestation of God that Baha'is expect to appear far in the future. The Abjad value of this word is 2001, which Baha'is believe is the year of this Manifestation's advent, i.e. another thousand years after the Manifestation who is expected to appear one thousand years after Baha'u'llah.

[23] In some other Baha'i sources the duration of Baha'u'llah's great epoch is given as five hundred thousand years, not five thousand. In any case, the point is that Baha'is are to believe he is the greatest Manifestation of God in all of recorded history and will remain so for ages to come.

Baha'u'llah Is the Branch, the Tree, the Temple, and the Servant

The Great Unequal, in each of His stations, chose for Himself a name; hence He called Himself a Branch, at another time the *Sadra* (i.e. the Tree),[24] on one occasion the Sun, and in another the Servant.

Regarding the Branch, in a sacred tablet written by His Supreme Pen to the late Mirza Mahdi Kashani,[25] upon him be the Glory of God and His Mercy, He says:

> Hear ye, O people, the voice of God from this Blessed Branch, that was planted in the Eternal Paradise by the Hand of God, the Sovereign, the Unseen and the Seen, the Invisible and the Visible. Verily, there is no God but Me, the Protector, the Self-Subsisting.

And in another tablet by His Supreme Pen, He says:

> Say, by God! We have already bestowed on the existence, also on the subsistents [i.e. God's creatures], from the mercy that encompassed the entire universe, that the great favor of this justice be conferred on all the worlds. He who wisheth may hear the melodies of the birds of the Throne on this Branch that hath risen in truth and hath encompassed the existence with a power known to be the Truth.

And in the Surah of the Branch, revealed in Adrianople, He says: "and hath branched from the Eternal Tree, this Sanctified Resplendent Temple, the Holy Branch; blessed is he who hath sought shelter under His shade, and was of those who are reclined (contented)."

The Great Oneness [i.e. God] has called by the name of "the Branch" every Temple [i.e. human being] that has been destined by Him to be the recipient of His Effulgence. Therefore the headings of

---

[24] The *Sadratu'l-Muntaha* ("Lote Tree of the Limit"). See Chapter 6, note 35.

[25] Also spelled Mirza Mihdiy-i-Kashani. He was a brother-in-law of Baha'u'llah, and a devout Baha'i who followed him to Iraq and later to Acre. His sister, Gawhar Khanum, was Baha'u'llah's third wife.

many of the tablets were revealed thus: "He is the Warbler on the Branches," "He is the Singer on the Branches," and likewise, meaning that the Exalted, Incomprehensible and Unseen [God] is singing on the Branches of the Eternal Tree, which are the Temples of the Manifestation of His commands and the Rising-place of His revelations. Similarly, the Rising-place of His commands in each epoch and every era spoke of Him and delivered His commands to mankind.

The Great Unequal has named His Sanctified Temple "The Branch," and that Branch of Truth has built the Temple of the Lord, in the form of "The Book of the Temple," in fulfillment of the prophecies of the prophets of yore. At the end of the Book of the Temple, He says:

> Thus We have built the Temple with the hands of Might and Power, were ye of those who know. Verily this is the Temple that ye were promised in the Book;[26] seek ye His nearness. This is meet for thee, were ye of those who comprehend. Be just, O people of the earth, is this better for you, or the temple which is built with clay? Turn your faces towards Him. Thus ye were commanded by God, the Protector, the Self-Subsisting. Follow the command and be thankful to God, your Lord, for what He hath conferred upon you. Verily He is the True God; there is no God but Him, the Discloser of what He wisheth, by His words, "Be and it will be."[27]

---

[26] The Bible, e.g. Revelation 21:22-24: "I did not see a temple in the city [the mystical New Jerusalem], because the Lord God Almighty and the Lamb are its temple. The city does not need the sun or the moon to shine on it, for the glory of God gives it light... The nations will walk by its light, and the kings of the earth will bring their splendor into it." Baha'u'llah's Book of the Temple consisted of messages to the kings and rulers of various nations, inviting them into his new faith.

[27] Baha'u'llah appended this paragraph to his Tablet to Naser al-Din Shah, which was the last part of the expanded version of the Book of the Temple that Baha'u'llah had published near the end of his life. It is thus the concluding paragraph of that book, although it did not appear in the original letter to the Shah. The Book of the Temple should be distinguished from the *Suriy-i-Haykal* ("Surah of the Temple") which is only part of the compilation. An English translation with some additional documents has been published by the Baha'i community under the title *The Summons of the Lord of Hosts*.

In the above revelations He spoke of the building of the Temple, and said this is the Temple which you were promised to be built in the Book, and is not this better for you than the temple which is built with clay?[28]

With regards to His calling Himself the *Sadra* (i.e. the Tree), the Eternal Tree, the Blessed Tree, the Tree of Oneness, the Godly Tree, the Sun of Truth and the like: all these refer to the Origin of His Reality [i.e. God].

The words Branch and Servant refer to the Temple of His Manifestation [i.e. the human person]. The servitude which He mentions for Himself is in its essence Divinity, as has been said in the past, "Servitude is an essence, the substance of which is Divinity."[29] If we mention the word servitude as an attribute of anyone else beside Him, its substance will, according to the blessed text (of Baha'u'llah), remain servitude.[30]

Limitations of 'Abdu'l-Baha's Authority

At this point, it is necessary to mention certain facts, and this humble servant, in narrating them has no object but the enlightenment of the friends. What I am writing is in accord with the holy revelations, and in harmony with the words of God. Whosoever studies them justly will bear witness that I am not stating anything visionary, and I am ex-

---

[28] In repeating this verse, Mohammed Ali Bahai apparently wishes to emphasize his belief in the superiority of Baha'u'llah and his revelations over any man-made religious institutions—a theme underlying his opposition to some of the ideas of 'Abdu'l-Baha, which he mentions in the next section of his will.

[29] This *hadith* (saying or tradition) is attributed to Ja'far al-Sádiq, the Sixth Imam of Shi'ite Islam.

[30] This may be a veiled reference to Abbas Effendi calling himself by the title 'Abdu'l-Baha ("Servant of Baha['u'llah]"). Mr. Bahai seems to have believed that Abbas Effendi's choice of this moniker was a disguised form of self-glorification. In his view, only the Manifestations of God may glory in their servitude, which for them is an attribute of divinity; but for everyone else, serving God is only an attribute of humility and should not be claimed as a special station. Mainstream Baha'is regard 'Abdu'l-Baha as the perfect exemplar of human servitude to God, but Mr. Bahai saw this role as restricted to Baha'u'llah and the past and future Divine Manifestations.

plaining nothing but what I have found to be in accord with the blessed revelations.

When the waves of the Ocean of elucidation became quiet (i.e. after the ascension of Baha'u'llah), some statements were circulated which caused dissension of ideas and disturbances of thoughts (of the believers). Now with regards to the Branch [i.e. Ghusn-i-A'zam]: If we consider the place which has been built on Mount Carmel (i.e. the Tomb of the Bab) as the promised Temple, and we accept Ghusn-i-A'zam ('Abdu'l-Baha) as the builder, and thus interpret in this what has been prophesied before [i.e. by the Hebrew prophets regarding the rebuilding of the Temple by the Messiah], the possessors of justice and intellect, after reading the supreme text [of Baha'u'llah] regarding the same in the Book of the Temple, would surely consider our suppositions as worthless words and contrary to the commands of God; as He said: "This [i.e. himself and his book] is the Temple that ye were promised in the Book."[31]

Likewise, if we interpret the word *tavajjoh* (i.e. turn your face) which is revealed in the Book of My Covenant (i.e. the Will of Baha'u'llah) according to our imagination and we appoint him (i.e. 'Abdu'l-Baha) an equal to God, and in testimonial mention the verse of ablution,[32] and if we exaggerate to the extent of calling him God Him-

---

[31] In the mainstream Baha'i tradition, the Shrine of the Bab, the terraced gardens and Baha'i administrative buildings on Mount Carmel in Haifa, Israel, are regarded as a fulfillment of Biblical prophecies about the glorious days of the Messiah. 'Abdu'l-Baha was a strong proponent of developing Mount Carmel as something of a New Jerusalem for the Baha'i faith, and began construction on the mountain during his lifetime. Mohammed Ali Bahai apparently objected to this interpretation and favored a more esoteric view, in which Zion is rebuilt in the mystical power of Baha'u'llah's revelations, not any physical edifice or location.

[32] In the Medium Obligatory Prayer prescribed by Baha'u'llah, Baha'is are to recite this verse while washing their face as a ritual ablution: "I have turned my face unto Thee, O my Lord! Illumine it with the light of Thy countenance. Protect it, then, from turning to anyone but Thee." Mr. Baha'i seems to be suggesting that some Baha'is used this prayer as evidence for equating 'Abdu'l-Baha with God, because the same expression ("turn your face") was used by Baha'u'llah in his will regarding the Baha'is turning to Abbas Effendi for guidance.

self, how can we consider ourselves the followers of His (Baha'u'llah's) commands? In the Qur'an [God] says: "Obey God, obey the Messengers, and the people in command amongst you."[33] With all their lofty station, no one considered them (i.e. the people in command) to be a partner of God and His Messengers. It is evident that the object was to create unity between the governors and the governed in performing their service to the cause.[34]

There are three stations for *tavajjoh*. The first is the tavajjoh of the creatures to the Creator, which we are commanded to perform during our prayers, and many revealed tablets confirm this fact. The second is the tavajjoh of the Creator to the creatures, as has been revealed in several tablets: "Thus, We have turned Our face to thee." The third is the tavajjoh of the creatures to the creatures, and of this last station is that which has been revealed in the Book of My Covenant: Because He (Baha'u'llah) repeatedly calls His Branches (i.e. the sons) the most noble of the creatures, and sanctifies Himself from a partner, an equal, a like, or a minister, the object [of Baha'u'llah commanding the Baha'is to "turn your face" toward Abbas Effendi] is therefore cooperation between the followers and those higher to them [i.e. the leaders of the Baha'i community], in order to serve the cause with great unity and energy, and diffuse the light of the truth.

Likewise the words "The Branch that hath branched": If we restrict these to one person [i.e. Abbas Effendi] and consider him equal to the Pre-Existent Root [i.e. the Manifestation of God], how can we prove

---

[33] Qur'an 4:59.

[34] Mr. Bahai is presenting what is essentially a *Sunni* view of Islam (the majority Islamic tradition), in which the successors of the Prophet Muhammad (caliphs) were seen as governors of the Muslim community, not spokespersons for God. However, in the *Shi'ite* view (the minority Islamic tradition out of which Baha'ism evolved), Muhammad's successors—a hereditary line called the Twelve Imams—were seen as speaking with some degree of divine inspiration. Many Shi'ites revere the Imam Ali and Imam Hussein as occupying a station almost equivalent to that of the Prophet. The theological difference between Abbas Effendi and Mohammed Ali Effendi therefore boils down to this historical analogy: the elder brother envisioned the Baha'i faith developing along Shi'ite lines, while the younger brother favored a Sunni interpretation of the Baha'i succession.

that we are right? The word "branched" has been revealed on many occasions and was not confined to the Branches only, but was revealed in honor of some distinguished personages.[35] Doubtless the only object in these revelations was to bestow His grace and mercy on His servants (mankind), as His Holiness the Messenger (i.e. Muhammad) referring to one of His believers has said: "If he had preceded me, I would have followed him, but I have preceded him, so he followed Me," whilst there was no similarity or likeness between them.

If we accept the position of "The Branch that hath branched" (i.e. 'Abdu'l-Baha) as it is [interpreted and] circulated by the tongues (of the followers), how can we consider God sanctified from a partner, an equal, an adversary, or a like? And how can we interpret the revealed tablets regarding His Great Oneness? Because if we desire to consider two as one, He (Baha'u'llah) says, "In the Name of the Beloved of the world. This day is the day of God, and all besides Him testify as to His Pre-Existence, His Greatness and His Power. ... The unification is to know one as one, and sanctify Him from numbers, but not to know two as one."[36]

If we consider him ('Abdu'l-Baha) a manifestation, as someone has said (referring to 'Abdu'l-Baha), that "the great Sun of Reality disap-

---

[35] The author's point here seems to be that the station of Baha'u'llah's sons, or any specific one of them, is not metaphysically higher than that of any other person who might be a leader in the Baha'i community. In his view, the metaphor of a branch coming out of a tree and its root cannot logically imply a divine or elevated nature for Abbas Effendi but a lower nature for other "Branches" or people whom Baha'u'llah has referred to as "branched" from him; the difference in station would only be functional, not a metaphysical difference. Baha'is today do, in fact, believe that 'Abdu'l-Baha is ontologically superior to the other "Branches," occupying a station in the Baha'i system of metaphysics uniquely between the Manifestations of God and all other human beings—a position which, though not as exalted as what Mr. Bahai alleges that 'Abdu'l-Baha's followers claimed for him in his own time, is still significantly beyond what Mr. Bahai would have considered appropriate.

[36] Shua Ullah Behai's book manuscript accidentally omits the closing quotation mark, so this editor cannot be certain that the last sentence of this paragraph is Baha'u'llah's words. However, the ellipsis appears in the original manuscript, suggesting that the sentence which follows is probably from Baha'u'llah, later in the same tablet that Mohammed Ali Bahai is quoting.

peared from the Sanctified Temple, and has appeared in another Temple," how could we be able to interpret and explain the clear text revealed in the Book of *Aqdas* and other tablets, that we should not accept him who shall put forward a claim (i.e. [divine] mission) before the completion of one thousand years?[37] And on what grounds could we call ourselves the followers of the Great Oneness (Baha'u'llah) and His utterances?

Similarly, if a partner is appointed to the Infallibility of God, and mention of "greater" and "lesser" infallibilities is made, and anyone else besides Him is considered infallible and chosen [for such a station], how could these [doctrines] be in harmony with the holy revelations?[38] In the Book of *Ishraqat*, extensive explanations regarding infallibility are revealed, in which God is considered the possessor of the Great Infallibility and the power to do what He chooses, and all else besides Him are considered to be under His command and judgment, and under the shadow of His utterances.

Also, if we consider the Expounder [i.e. the interpreter or commentator on Baha'i scripture] as one person only and restrict this station to ['Abdu'l-Baha] alone, in the Epistle to [Varqa],[39] in reply to a questioner [Baha'u'llah] says: "By 'the Book' is meant the Book of *Aqdas*, and by

---

[37] See *Kitab-i-Aqdas*, paragraph 37, quoted in Chapter 8, note 24.

[38] Baha'is today believe that 'Abdu'l-Baha, Shoghi Effendi, and the Universal House of Justice have degrees of "lesser" or "conferred" infallibility which are not as extensive in scope as the "most great" infallibility of Baha'u'llah, but that they all are truly infallible, and their opinions and decisions may not be questioned by adherents of the faith within their respective scope of authority. Basically, the degree or scope of infallibility is regarded as diminishing somewhat with each successor to the Manifestation: total divine infallibility for Baha'u'llah, a near-divine level for 'Abdu'l-Baha, a somewhat more restricted level for Shoghi Effendi, and so on. Mohammed Ali Bahai is disagreeing with this idea of partial levels of infallibility for Baha'u'llah's successors, believing it to be contrary to teachings of Baha'u'llah which limited infallibility to God alone (through His Manifestation).

[39] The name is difficult to read and spelled differently in the manuscript copy provided to this editor. My best guess is Varqa, an eminent follower of Baha'u'llah who is known to have been the recipient of several tablets.

'the Branch that hath branched' (is meant) a Branch."[40] He did not say the Great (i.e. [Ghusn-i-A'zam] 'Abdu'l-Baha) or the Mighty (i.e. [Ghusn-i-Akbar] Mohammed Ali), but He did designate the Book [of *Aqdas*], and not all the revealed tablets and surahs. Furthermore, the authenticity of explanation [or interpretation] is proved when it is in harmony with the words of God; if what the expounder mentions is in accord with what has been revealed by God, then what he says is worthy of acceptance, otherwise it is unworthy of any consideration. The duty of the expounder is to explain the truth, and not to follow his own inclinations and make the words of God an excuse to oppress the followers, forcing them to accept his orders and fulfill his desires.

There Cannot Be a "Guardianship" of the Baha'i Faith

Also, if we mention the Guardianship,[41] and imagine a guardian for God, in the blessed epistle to Ali Muhammad Sarraj, [Baha'u'llah] says:

> These are the days of the Manifestation and God is manifest like unto the sun in the midst of heaven, and in the courtyard of His sanctity, nothing of the vanities of the world existeth which would necessitate a guardian to divide it. And if ye say that He is in need of a guardian for His cause, verily this is an injustice on your part with regard to God, the Protector, the Eternal. For the cause is, and shall be going round Himself and shall never separate from Him. Beware lest ye create for God a minister, an equal, an adversary, a like, a guardian, a companion, or a match.

Briefly I say, whosoever studies carefully these blessed revelations will

---

[40] Mr. Bahai is arguing that Baha'u'llah did not intend to restrict the right of interpretation and commentary on all of his writings to one specific son. Baha'is came to believe that only 'Abdu'l-Baha had this right, that it extended beyond merely the *Kitab-i-Aqdas* to encompass all the words of Baha'u'llah, and that it was inappropriate for the younger sons of Baha'u'llah to write and circulate their own commentaries on Baha'i teachings such as Mr. Bahai did.

[41] At the time when Mr. Bahai was writing, his grand-nephew Shoghi Effendi Rabbani was leading the mainstream Baha'i community as the "Guardian of the Cause of God," an office of successorship created by 'Abdu'l-Baha in his will.

bear witness that the mere idea of a guardian [of the Baha'i faith] is insignificant imagination and doubtless in violation of the words of God.

Follow the Scriptures, Not the Pretensions of Religious Leaders

If we take the verse in the Book of *Aqdas* [about turning to the Branch] as a glad-tidings [i.e. a prophecy of the advent of a Manifestation] and consider the Book of My Covenant (i.e. the Will of Baha'u'llah) its interpreter [about which Branch to turn to], how could our heart be contented to call the Lord and Master [Baha'u'llah] a forerunner of His servant ['Abdu'l-Baha], and what distinction is then left for the Great Resplendent Manifestation? Is it permissible that the Root should give glad-tidings about the branch or the Sovereign call the subjects to his servant? The falsity of this notion is evident and everyone will comprehend it, because the promised one should be greater than the promisor.

Yes, it is customary for the predecessor to speak about his successor, and the appointment is only for bringing about friendship and amity. This is not a glad-tidings. The glad-tidings belong to Manifestations only. If the friends study carefully the tablets of the Great Merciful [i.e. Baha'u'llah], they will bear witness that they are not in need of a Manifestation after His great appearance. He says: "The Forerunner came and foretold, the Fulfiller came and fulfilled. Wherefore and for whom another Manifestation?"

The laws revealed in the Book will not be changed for a thousand years, and each word that has been uttered by the Supreme Pen, in honor of anyone, cannot be effaced. Negation and confirmation are particular stations belonging to God, in which no one else has the right to intrude. The greatest scale is the Book of God, and by that the truth and falsity of every statement will be known. Each word and action which the Book of God will confirm, is true, and those in violation of that (Book) are false. "God shall efface and confirm that which He chooseth."[42] In the days of the Manifestation, the cause is in the hands

---

[42] Qur'an 13:39.

of the Owner of the Day, and after His disappearance everything is referred to the Book.

O friends, the cause of God was completed in His Blessed Appearance [i.e. Baha'u'llah] and nothing was left incomplete. Religious duties are subject to what has been revealed in the Book, the administration of affairs was left to the House of Justice, and the completion of the appearances [in this cycle] by His Great Manifestation was repeatedly mentioned in His revelations.

With the might of the holy tablets, use your efforts to improve the present defects [in the faith]. Do not allow any further spread of vain imaginations, that the friends may not suffer martyrdom again. The past is a mirror of the future. You have observed that at the beginning of the cause, what great harm the old imagination caused, and how many martyrdoms took place. According to the revelation of the Supreme Pen, those imaginations became bullets and poured into the pure body of the Primal Point (i.e. the Bab), thus piercing His blessed chest. A grain of imagination today will become a dome in the future, will gradually spread and cause endless harm.[43] Hakim Ferdowsi (the Persian poet who wrote the *Shahnameh*) said well, "A narrative will cause war, Time will make out of a toothpick a pole. A mischievous person, through his conversation, will destroy well constructed homes."

This humble servant of His threshold has no aim but the welfare of the friends, and all my statements are under the shadow of His ordinances and according to His counsel. Compare them, and if you find them to be in accord with the sacred laws and counsels, kindly accept them.

Response to Charges of Interpolation of Baha'u'llah's Writings[44]

The question of interpolation (of the [sacred] text), which has been

---

[43] Mr. Bahai is warning of the dangers posed by religious leaders who arrogate to themselves excessive power over the people. The "imaginations" he speaks of are pretensions to divine authority that can grow from small and seemingly innocuous beginnings, ultimately becoming so grandiose as to serve as a rationalization for violence against people with different religious beliefs.

[44] For more by Mr. Bahai on this subject, see also the section entitled "Response to Allegation of Interpolation of Sacred Text" in Chapter 16.

widely circulated, is insignificant, weak, and based on false imagination. The Book of the Temple which is said to have been interpolated, two manuscript copies of the same, bearing different dates, exist in the handwriting of Zaynu'l-Muqarrabín,[45] who has inscribed them in His (Baha'u'llah's) blessed days, and which do not vary a word with the printed copy of the said book. Come and search, and make this examination the cause of the elimination of the dissension over the revelation.

Also it is stated that certain tablets have been interpolated. Have you seen or received such a tablet? If anyone should produce a tablet and claim that it is written by the Supreme Pen (of Baha'u'llah), examine it carefully through the medium of modern methods of examination and testing practiced among progressive nations; and after such examination, decide for yourselves either to accept [it] or refuse. A well-known proverb says, "Do not go to judge alone." God says, "Do not believe every speaker, and do not depend on every comer." Also it has been said in the past, "A fame may be without foundation."

Motives and Intentions; Closing Prayer

In this world the intentions are numerous, there is a great deal of disagreement in thought, and everyone with a bad intention tries to impress his impartiality on the people. I am speaking for the sake of God, and I am explaining these facts for the welfare of the [Baha'i] cause. I ask you to read them, for the sake of God; also that, complying with His commands, you may rise with all tenderness and love and with great vigor, to eliminate the cause of the existing dissension and hatred (i.e. among the followers): that perchance the gates of calamity may be closed to the innocent among humanity, and so far as possible, prevent the introduction of new difficulties which may cause hardship to mankind in future generations.

O Thou, Unequal Creator! Thou art aware of the conscience of this needy one, and bear witness to his sincere intentions.

---

[45] Zaynu'l-Muqarrabín was a Muslim preacher who joined the cause of the Bab and later Baha'u'llah, and became one of the most important scribes in Baha'u'llah's inner circle of companions.

I ask Thee to assist the friends in carrying out justice and equity, and aid them to consider what I have explained above, that they may understand the said events and comprehend the revealed truths, that they may not be prevented from what Thou hast revealed by Thy Supreme Pen in the tablets; to take hold of Thy signs, and with the light of Thine evidence, illumine the world; to place Thy revelation before their eyes, and rise with good deeds, satisfactory actions, love, faithfulness, kindness, tenderness, and great compassion, calling and guiding mankind:

That perchance the disagreement in thoughts may not become the cause of dissension of hearts, and differences in actions and deeds may not produce hatred and animosity.

That with Thine endless mercy, the world become the Paradise of Abha (i.e. the Most Glorious), and what Thou hast willed in Thy great days and considered as the distinction of Thy Cause may become manifest; and that love and unity encompass mankind.

Indeed Thou art the Omnipotent, the All-Knowing, the Omniscient, the All-Observing.

18

The Funeral of Mohammed Ali Bahai

By Shua Ullah Behai

This chapter was the last part of Shua Ullah Behai's memoirs (the rest of which is reproduced as Chapter 30). Besides simply honoring his late father, the point of this description of the elder Mr. Bahai's funeral seems to be to show that he was well regarded by many people, including some prominent religious leaders and intellectuals—perhaps intended by the author as an indirect rebuttal to the assertion in the Will and Testament of 'Abdu'l-Baha that Mohammed Ali Bahai had "sunk into a degradation and infamy that shall be lasting until the Day of Doom."

—The Editor

The following is the announcement of [Mohammed Ali Effendi's] departure made by the family to the friends throughout the world.

> The members of the household of Baha'u'llah inform you with the deepest grief and sorrow of the departure of their most beloved and revered leader—
> Ghusn-i-Akbar, the Mightiest Branch, Mohammed Ali Effendi—
> Who left this earthly world and departed to the Eternal Realm on the morning of Friday, December the Tenth, 1937, at Haifa, Palestine. The last services were held on the following afternoon and the sacred remains were carried by hand from the house to King's Way, a distance of one mile, where the remains were placed on a

vehicle and escorted with great honor to Acre, where again carried by hand to the last resting place at Bahji near the Sacred Shrine [of Baha'u'llah].

The procession was preceded by an escort of unarmed police detachment with their officers, followed by the members of the household, government officials, notables, and religious heads. Muslims, Jews, Christians, and Baha'is walked silently side by side in reverence to that great personage who lived the life of a saint, and who was the most ardent lover of peace and harmony and a real friend of humanity.

Memorial services will be held at Haifa on Tuesday, January the 18th, 1938. We humbly ask the friends throughout the world to join us in commemoration on that or any other convenient day.

In his memory we shall recite the following supplication revealed by the Supreme Pen of Baha'u'llah for His departed Branch:—

THE GREATEST, THE MOST GLORIOUS.

O my God, verily this is a branch who hath branched from the firm and lofty tree of Thy Singleness and Oneness. Thou seest him, O God, gazing unto Thee and holding fast to the rope of Thy bounty. Therefore keep him in the shadow of Thy mercy. Thou knowest, O my God, that I desire him, as Thou hast desired him. Therefore assist him with the hosts of earth and heaven, and help, O my God, whosoever helpeth him, choose whosoever chooseth him, and assist whosoever cometh to him. Then forsake whosoever denieth him and desireth him not. O my Lord, Thou seest that while inspired my pen moveth though my limbs tremble. I ask Thee, by my longing for Thy love and my anxiety to manifest Thy cause, to ordain for him, and to those who love him, what Thou hast destined for Thy Messengers and the faithful of Thy divine inspiration. Verily Thou art God the All-Powerful.

The sad news was broadcasted by the Oriental radio stations, also by the British Broadcasting Corporation, London, England. Messages of condolence reached us from all parts of the world.

Memorial services were held at Haifa, which was well attended. Many notables delivered memorial speeches and sermons. Among them the Muslim representative was Abdullah Bey Mokhles.[1]

The Christian leader, Bishop Hajjar,[2] who was [the late Mohammed Ali Effendi's] personal friend for thirty-five years, delivered the most impressive sermon. His subject was "Virtue." For nearly an hour he spoke on the "Excellence of Virtue," ending each paragraph with this remark: "The departed soul was invested with all these virtues."

Wadi Effendi Boustani,[3] the Arabian philosopher-poet and prominent advocate, recited his memorial poetry [i.e. in commemoration of the deceased]. Likewise the well-known poet known as "Abu Salma," this being his nom de plume.[4]

Among those who could not attend in person was Sheikh Ass'ad esh-Shukeiry, a well-known Muslim religious leader, who sent in his speech to be read at the day of the memorial.

---

[1] Also spelled 'Abdu'llah Mukhlis. He was a professor and the Secretary of the National Muslim Society.

[2] Gregorios Hajjar (also spelled Gregorius) was the Archbishop of Acre for the Melkite Greek Catholic Church, a Byzantine-rite Eastern Catholic denomination in full communion with the Roman Catholic Church. He was much beloved in Palestine and came to be known as "Christ of the East."

[3] Wadi al-Bustani was a Lebanese poet, attorney, and intellectual. He co-founded an organization for Islamic-Christian dialogue and translated classical Hindu and Persian literature.

[4] Abu Salma's real name was Abdel-Karim al-Karmi. He was a celebrated 20th century Palestinian poet.

Mohammed Ali Effendi Bahai.

19

A Tribute to Mohammed Ali Effendi and Obituary

By Kamar Bahai

This short essay is a circular letter or pamphlet that Kamar Bahai wrote in February 1953 called "Mohammad Ali Effendi." Section headings have been added.

While eulogizing her uncle Mohammed Ali, Mrs. Bahai claims that some "intriguers" schemed to drive a wedge between him and her uncle Abbas Effendi "by magnifying trifling incidents" so as to "increase the misunderstanding between them." Although she doesn't specifically identify these intriguers, presumably they would have been members of the family or other important Baha'is who knew the brothers personally. Based on Mrs. Bahai's concluding remark about the appointment of Shoghi Effendi Rabbani as "a boy whom they were able to handle as they pleased," the obvious implication is that she believed some members of 'Abdu'l-Baha's immediate family wanted power in the faith to remain with themselves and their descendants, and thus had a motive to foster animosity between 'Abdu'l-Baha and his half-brother Mohammed Ali, who represented a different branch of Baha'u'llah's family originating from a different wife of the prophet.

I am reluctant to embrace this as a full explanation of the sectarian conflict; it seems to shift too much of the responsibility away from the central actors, the sons of Baha'u'llah themselves. However, Mrs. Bahai's scenario does seem plausible as a significant contributing factor in the dissension, especially since the brothers' disagreement was about subtle issues of theology and authority, on which relatively minor differences could have been magnified through repeated misunderstandings encouraged by people who did not wish to see them reconcile and work together.

In this regard, I should mention that Kamar Bahai's daughter Negar Bahai Emsallem made it clear to me that her family did not believe 'Abdu'l-Baha's side of the family were the only ones to blame. She says that one other relative, in particular, was regarded by her family as sharing much of the blame for keeping 'Abdu'l-Baha and Mohammed Ali Bahai apart, because he wanted his daughters to marry Mr. Bahai's sons. She asked me not to name this person, but even without the name, the story is relevant because it provides an example of how private interests may have motivated various family members to influence Baha'u'llah's sons to maintain and deepen their feud.

Kamar Bahai's further claim that the Will and Testament of 'Abdu'l-Baha was forged seems much less likely than the obvious kinds of family intrigues, for the simple reason that the "intriguers"—to the degree that they existed—succeeded in causing 'Abdu'l-Baha and Mohammed Ali Bahai to distrust each other and regard each other as heretics. Thus, they would not have needed to forge a will to strip Mr. Bahai of the successorship, because 'Abdu'l-Baha would probably have seen fit to do that himself.

—The Editor

The Baha'i Movement Was Sabotaged from the Inside

The records of history instruct us about the worldwide social movements and about the intrigues that centered around earnest reformers; they also bring to light conspiracies which were hatched by consummate plotters for no other reason than considerable personal benefit.

If it were possible for me to mention here instances of such intrigues as accompanied the social movements referred to above, I would have done so, but considering the limited space of this circular, this is clearly impossible. If interested, the dear reader could turn over the pages of history and discover for himself innumerable instances of the existence of such intrigues.

The Baha'i movement itself did not form an exception to the rule. The basest form of intrigue was minutely wound up around the movement and to a large extent succeeded in achieving its vicious aim, and, in my opinion, not without besmirching the reputation of loyal and good leaders. The intriguers, acting jointly to create a chasm in the Baha'i family, aimed at separating the two brothers, 'Abdu'l-Baha Abbas and Mohammed Ali Effendi, the legitimate leaders of the Baha'i movement. They sowed the seeds of discord between them by magnifying trifling incidents in such a way as to affect adversely the hearts of the two brothers and increase the misunderstanding between them. They succeeded in their dark purpose, for the misunderstanding which they planted grew as the years went by.

To complete their wickedness those same intriguers prevented Mohammed Ali Effendi from seeing his dying brother, Abbas Effendi, pretending that the latter did not wish to be disturbed by his own brother from paying his last respects to his dying brother! And need there be the clearest manifestation of Mohammed Ali's noble character, when he submitted to the intriguer's will and desisted from seeing his dying brother in order to prevent further dissension in the movement.

Obituary of Mohammed Ali Bahai

As I am now presenting to the reader a picture of the life of the Baha'i leaders [in this series of pamphlets], I feel bound to put on record a [few] short paragraph[s] on the life's work of the second son of Baha'u'llah, Mohammed Ali Effendi—this son who was usurped of his right, whose good heart and noble character followed the principles of Baha'ism to the letter, whose humanity was boundless, this man of peace whose very virtues enabled the intriguers to take full advantage of his adherence to Baha'ism in order to destroy the last bridge that linked him with what they called the followers of Abbas Effendi, who were in fact the intriguers themselves and a few of their supporters.

I would like to quote extracts from the then local Arabic, English, and Hebrew newspapers when they mourned Mohammed Ali Effendi's death. In this connection it is noteworthy to mention that even the famous review *Great Britain and the East*, which is regarded as the mouthpiece of the British government in matters of foreign policy, published an article on the occasion of his death bearing the heading "Bahai Leader Dead." The kind reader will now read the quotations taken from *Al-Difa, Filastin, Al-Jamiya Al-Islamiya, Post News, Palestine Post, Haboker, Haaretz,* and *Davar*.

The picture of the deceased Mohammed Ali Effendi, the renowned and noble leader of Baha'ism, son of the great Baha'u'llah, the founder of Baha'ism. Mohammed Ali Effendi, whose father Baha'u'llah entitled him "The Mightiest Branch" [i.e. Ghusn-i-Akbar] was born in Teheran, the capital of Iran, in the year 1853.[1] [He] accompanied his father to Baghdad and then to the capital of the caliphs [i.e. Constantinople] and finally to Acre where the founder of Baha'ism established his permanent residence.

His father educated him so profoundly that for all controversial matters regarding Baha'ism and other religions, he was consulted as an authority. Moreover he edited books and wrote messages. As shown by his father's letters and messages, Baha'u'llah specially favored him, and so much so that he nominated him to the leadership of the [Baha'i] movement to follow his elder brother, the late Abbas Effendi, entitled "The Greatest Branch" [i.e. Ghusn-i-A'zam].

Mohammed Ali Effendi was a personality with a noble character, lofty heart and soul; a man of peace and above petty family quarrels, he instructed his followers to remain peaceful and quiet. He was the inseparable secretary and confidant of his father.

Mohammed Ali Effendi's Qualities and Leadership Abilities

Truly he was his father's confidant, for his father during his lifetime entrusted him with the mission of preaching Baha'ism in India and Egypt. He was the only son, among Baha'u'llah's sons, to have been honored with such a responsible and weighty mission while the movement

---

[1] This conflicts with what Mr. Bahai wrote in his autobiography (Chapter 16), in which he reported his birthplace as Baghdad, Iraq.

Chapter 19. A Tribute to Mohammed Ali Effendi and Obituary

was still in its infancy and needed strong and imposing men. He succeeded in his mission and achieved the aims set out by Baha'u'llah, his father.

The fact that the founder of Baha'ism assigned the weighty responsibility of carrying out the mission to his son, Mohammed Ali Effendi [from] among [all] others, clearly proves that he had great confidence in his abilities to carry out such a mission.

It is not an exaggeration to say that with all his inherent qualities Mohammed Ali Effendi would have been an ideal leader to succeed his brother, 'Abdu'l-Baha Abbas.

This symbolic picture of the ideal leader, this noble heart, this wonderful character and elevated soul, this leader who loved Baha'ism and devoted his whole life to its service, his care for the edifice he had helped to set up [i.e. the Baha'i faith], his earnestness to prevent it from cracking and crumbling—all these obliged him to swallow in silence the great lie regarding the forged will [of 'Abdu'l-Baha] which the malicious intriguers had fabricated, and who made use of the alleged misunderstanding [between the brothers] which they themselves invented in order to mislead public opinion and achieve their vicious ends. Consequently they tarnished the reputation of 'Abdu'l-Baha Abbas and succeeded in discarding Mohammed Ali Effendi from the leadership, and entrusted it to a boy [i.e. Shoghi Rabbani] whom they were able to handle as they pleased—on account of his youth.

Zia Ullah Effendi, entitled Ghusn-i-At'har, son of Baha'u'llah.

20

A Tribute to Ghusn-i-At'har Zia Ullah Effendi

By Shua Ullah Behai

This chapter is taken from a chapter called "The Two Younger Branches, the Leaves, and Their Spouses" in Shua Ullah Behai's book manuscript. A section heading has been added.

Not many details are known about Zia Ullah Effendi,[1] who died anywhere from age 30 to 34 (year of birth is uncertain). After his half-brother Mirza Mihdi died in his youth, he was called by the same title that the former had been given (i.e. Ghusn-i-At'har, "The Purest Branch").[2]

Mohammed Ali Bahai mentions in his autobiography (see Chapter 16) that Zia Ullah Effendi was allowed to read Baha'u'llah's will. He says that this son of Baha'u'llah was one of the key figures involved in persuading him to state openly his concerns about Abbas Effendi's style of leadership, and helped share Mr. Bahai's controversial epistle to the believers. He describes his brother Zia Ullah as "very near and dear to me," "a pure soul, an ardent lover of humanity, a faithful and zealous promulgator of the [Baha'i] teachings and steadfast in the cause... my

---

[1] In the Baha'i community today, Zia Ullah Effendi is called Mirza Diya'u'llah or Ziya'u'llah (alternate spelling which more accurately reflects pronunciation).

[2] The title Ghusn-i-At'har does not actually contain the Arabic letter *hamza*—typically represented as (') in English transliterations—and is therefore usually spelled Ghusn-i-Athar. This can be confusing, as the word is supposed to be pronounced "at-har," not "a-thar"; hence we have spelled it with an apostrophe to denote the appropriate separation of syllables.

coworker in our common fight for the freedom of the thoughts of mankind, and their release from the clutches of religious leaders."

According to some sources, 'Abdu'l-Baha reportedly forgave Zia Ullah Effendi for supporting Mohammed Ali Effendi's side in their argument,³ but other sources recount that 'Abdu'l-Baha and his supporters actually celebrated his death.⁴ He is generally considered a "Covenant-breaker" in the mainstream Baha'i tradition. In fact, his body was removed from the Shrine of Baha'u'llah where it was originally buried next to his father, as an act of "purification... from past contamination," in the words of the Universal House of Justice.⁵

—The Editor

Zia Ullah Effendi, Entitled Ghusn-i-At'har

This noble son of Baha'u'llah was born in Adrianople on August 14, 1868,⁶ and accompanied his great father to the prison of Acre. He grew to manhood under the shadow of Baha'u'llah, and received his education from him.

When he reached the age of maturity, he joined the several amanuenses and engaged himself in inscribing the revealed tablets. During the later years of Baha'u'llah, he also copied the tablets in nice calligraphy.

He was greatly attached to his father and was very despondent after his ascension. He was most holy and spent the major part of his time in

---

³ Adib Taherzadeh, *The Covenant of Baha'u'llah* (Oxford, UK: George Ronald, 1992), p. 165.

⁴ See Chapter 23.

⁵ *Messages from the Universal House of Justice 1963-1986: Third Epoch of the Formative Age* (Wilmette, Ill.: Baha'i Publishing Trust, 1996), p. 66. Available online at http://bahai-library.com/uhj_messages_1963_1986

⁶ Other sources give different birthdates. For example, Hasan M. Balyuzi, a prominent Baha'i author of the mid 20th century, reported it as August 15, 1864, and this is regarded by Baha'is today as the correct date. Mohammed Jawad Gazvini, a Unitarian Baha'i writing in in the early 1900s in *An Epitome of Babi and Bahai History to A.D. 1898*, reported that Zia Ullah was born in 1865.

commemoration and spreading the [Baha'i] teachings, and followed Baha'u'llah to the Eternal Realms after six years, on October 30, 1898.

The following is the translation of one of the several tablets revealed for him by Baha'u'llah:

> HE IS THE EVERLASTING.
>
> God beareth witness that I have believed in Him who, in His commemoration, the chosen have partaken from the chalice of life, and the sincere [have partaken] of what all (the people) in the heavens and the earth are unable to comprehend, save those whom your Lord, the All-Knowing, the Wise, wished.
>
> O Zia! Be thou patient in calamities, content in all conditions, a believer in Reality, swift in charity, submissive to God, a concealer of (the faults of) the people, opposer of imagination and follower after truth.
>
> Be thou a cloud (of mercy) to humanity, kind to the transgressor, forgiving to the sinner, firm in the covenant and steadfast in the cause.
>
> Thus commandeth thee this Wronged One, moreover to serve God with piety. Likewise We command thee to be trustful and truthful, and to practice both of them [i.e. these virtues] always.
>
> Blessing be upon thee and upon them who love thee nobly, and woe unto him who hateth thee and turneth away from that which hath been decreed in the Book.

Soraya Khanum, the Widow of Zia Ullah Effendi

She is the daughter of Shaykh Kazim Samandar, a well-known Baha'i teacher of Qazvin, Iran.[7] Although she lost her husband in her youth, she has remained faithful to him to this day, making her home with the members of the household of Baha'u'llah.

---

[7] Born Muhammad Kazim Qazvini to a prominent Babi family, he became a Baha'i as a young man and was given the name Samandar by Baha'u'llah. An eminent teacher of the new faith, he was posthumously identified in the Baha'i tradition as one of Baha'u'llah's nineteen Apostles.

21

Some Notable Baha'is

By Shua Ullah Behai

This chapter contains excerpts from "The Two Younger Branches, the Leaves, and Their Spouses" and most of another chapter called "Bahai Personalities" in Shua Ullah Behai's book manuscript. The last section is from a chapter called "Shoghi Effendi Rabbani." The quotation from Edward G. Browne in the first section did not appear in the manuscript, but was taken from an editor's note by Mr. Behai in the First and Second Quarter 1936 issue of *Behai Quarterly*.

The original ordering of the sections in the "Bahai Personalities" chapter seemed somewhat haphazard, so I have rearranged them to list the Persian believers first; followed by Ibrahim Kheiralla, who brought the Baha'i faith to America; and lastly, the American converts.

All the children of Baha'u'llah who survived him are mentioned, as well as their spouses, with the exception of 'Abdu'l-Baha Abbas and Ghusn-i-Akbar Mohammed Ali, whose stories are told in other chapters; and Baha'u'llah's son Zia Ullah and his wife (see Chapter 20), who were originally included with the rest of the family mentioned here.

Beyond the family, most of the Baha'is profiled by Shua Ullah Behai in this chapter were supporters of the Unitarian Baha'i tradition, with the exception of Nabil Zarandi, Mirza Abu'l-Fadl Gulpaygani, Abdu'l-Ghaffar Isfahani, Haji Mirza Siyyid Hasan Afnan "Kabir"; Lewis Stuyvesant Chanler, who followed 'Abdu'l-Baha but not Shoghi Effendi; Abdullah Bahhaj, who followed 'Abdu'l-Baha during his lifetime but whose later views are unclear;[1] and possibly Mirza Abu'l-Qasim Nazir, whose sectarian allegiance I was unable to determine. Mr. Behai does not include any of the important Western converts who joined the mainstream Baha'i community, a significant omission. On the other hand, the inclusion of various early Baha'is who supported the Unitarian interpretation of the faith—most of whom are nowhere to be found in popular Baha'i histories, or whose role and contributions have been minimized as a result of their perceived heresy—is a welcome addition to the historical record.

—The Editor

———✧———

Family of Baha'u'llah

Badi Ullah Effendi, entitled Ghusn-i-Anwar[2] ["The Most Luminous Branch"], is the youngest and only surviving son of the Great Baha'u'llah. Although he has passed the age of seventy-five,[3] he is hale and healthy, active and vigorous. He is kind and sociable, always ready to meet visitors with a smile and to give them good advice when it is needed.

Alia Khanum is the wife of Badi Ullah.

Bahiyyih Khanum was the eldest daughter of Baha'u'llah. She accompanied her father from Tehran to Acre. She was a great help to 'Abdu'l-Baha, also to Shoghi Effendi after the death of 'Abdu'l-Baha. She did not choose a spouse and remained unmarried all her life.

Samadiyya Khanum was the second daughter of Baha'u'llah. She was a great supporter of Mohammed Ali and remained faithful to him to the last.

---

[1] Mohammed Ali Bahai, in his autobiography (Chapter 16), praised Mr. Bahhaj and described him as "one of the confessors to the Oneness and Singleness of God," which suggests that he may have become sympathetic to Unitarian Baha'i ideas after 'Abdu'l-Baha's death.

[2] Also spelled Ghusn-i-Anvar.

[3] Badi Ullah Effendi was born in 1867, 1868, or 1871, depending on the source, which is consistent with this manuscript being written in the mid 1940s.

Her husband, Aqa Mirza Majdeddin, was the son of Mirza Moussa entitled Kalim, brother of Baha'u'llah. Therefore, Mirza Majdeddin is [both] nephew and son-in-law of Baha'u'llah. Regarding this venerable gentleman, the late Prof. Edward G. Browne, in his introduction to the book entitled *A Traveller's Narrative*, said:

> Towards evening I received another visitor, whose mien and bearing alike marked him as a person of consequence. He was a man of perhaps thirty or thirty-five years of age, with a face which called to one's mind the finest types of Iranian physiognomy preserved to us in the bas-reliefs of Persepolis,[4] yet with something in it beyond this, which involuntarily called forth in my mind the thought, "What would not an artist desirous of painting a saint or an apostle give for such a model!" My visitor (who, as I afterwards discovered, was a son of Baha['u'llah]'s deceased brother Musa[5]) was clothed, save for the tall red fez which crowned his head, entirely in pure white; and everything about him, from his short well-trimmed beard and the masses of jet-black hair swept boldly back behind his ears, to the hem of his spotless garment, was characterized by the same scrupulous neatness. He saluted me very graciously, and remained conversing with me all the evening.[6]

Foroughiyya Khanum was the youngest daughter of Baha'u'llah. Haji Siyyid Ali Afnan[7] [was her] husband.

Mirza Aqa Jan, Khadim, the Amanuensis

Mirza Aqa Jan [Kashani, i.e.] of Kashan,[8] in his youth became a devoted follower of the Bab and zealous worker in his cause. After the

---

[4] Persepolis was a capital city of ancient Persia.

[5] Moussa Kalim.

[6] Edward G. Browne, *A Traveller's Narrative: Written to Illustrate the Episode of the Bab*, Volume II. English Translation and Notes (Cambridge: University Press, 1891), pp. xxxiv-xxxv.

[7] He was one of the sons of Haji Mirza Siyyid Hasan Afnan "Kabir" (see section about the elder Mr. Afnan later in this chapter).

[8] Kashan is a city in central Iran.

Bab's martyrdom, he searched for the promised one of whom the Bab had foretold, "Him Whom God Shall Make Manifest." This devoted follower discovered the fulfillment of the prophecy of the Bab in the person of Baha'u'llah, and thus he was among the early believers in his mission.

He joined Baha'u'llah in Baghdad, migrated with him to Istanbul, then to Adrianople and from there to the great prison of Acre. He served him faithfully to the last, as inscriber of his utterances and diffuser of his teachings.

He was given the titles of "the servant" [i.e. *Khadim*], "the servant always present," and "the servant who is present before the Throne," and is mentioned as such in hundreds of tablets by Baha'u'llah. There are numerous volumes of correspondence to the followers throughout the world which were revealed by Baha'u'llah in his name.

He passed unto Eternity on May 17, 1901, at Bahji, Acre district, Palestine, and was buried at Abu Ataba, which is located near the Holy Shrine of Baha'u'llah. ...

The following is the translation of a tablet written by the Supreme Pen of Baha'u'llah, which [among other things] explains the station of Mirza Aqa Jan, the servant. A photograph of the original tablet appears on page [blank].[9]

O CREATOR OF EVERY BEING.

This is what hath been revealed from the heaven of Eternity, and herein is described the place wherein abideth the Beauty of God on the throne of a Great Name. And verily, He is the Promised One in all the tablets in all names, were ye of those who know. And He was named in the *Bayan* by "Him Who Shall Appear,"[10] and He shall appear in the *Mustaghath* (i.e. 2001 [of the Baha'i Era], after

---

[9] The manuscript provided to this editor does not include photographs, although in several places the author mentions that they would be included in the book and leaves blank spaces for them. In this case, Shua Ullah Behai apparently had a photograph of the original tablet by Baha'u'llah, but I have not been able to determine if that photograph or the tablet itself is still extant.

[10] This is presumably a reference to the Bab, the author of the *Bayan*, who claimed to be the one expected to appear according to messianic traditions of Islam.

the elapse of 2000 years) in manifest power [i.e. as another Manifestation of God].

Say: By God! this is the day the like of which the eyes of the invisible [i.e. the people in heaven] have not beheld, and how much more the eyes of these deprived ones [the people on earth].

Then blessed is he who shall come forward on that day, unto the Presence of God in full obedience; and he who shall read this tablet before the Throne, that the Hearing of God (i.e. the ears of the Manifestation) may hear these melodies that have appeared of yore between the heavens and the earth. And thereby this name [Baha'u'llah] shall be mentioned in a seat that God hath sanctified from the remembrance of all the worlds.

Verily, We have not wished by what hath been mentioned in this tablet save Myself, the Protector of the worlds. He who shall expect a Manifestation after Me [before the appointed era] is verily of those who have lost. And He who shall appear after the one thousand (years after Baha'u'llah) shall be speaking in My name; and in the *Mustaghath*, there shall come One who shall bear witness that I am God, the Lord of the heavens and the earth.

No one hath ever understood this Manifestation save to a certain degree; verily He is the All-Knowing.

O people! Hold fast, after Me, unto the Branches [i.e. sons], who have branched from this Pre-Existent Root. Verily, through them the fragrances of My Garment are spread among the people of the world and none shall find them save every steadfast believer.

It behooveth you, O people of Baha, to be, in every case, steadfast in the Cause of God. Beware lest ye follow every ignorant transgressor.

And after the Branches, a distinguished station is ordained for the Servant who is present before the Throne (i.e. Mirza Aqa Jan the Amanuensis). And it behooveth you to honor the family wherefrom the Beloved of the world hath appeared; those who have believed in God, the Mighty, the Praiseworthy. Thus hath it been revealed in the *Bayan* and this brilliant tablet. And whosoever turneth away from them, verily he is of those who disbelieve in God and hath become a polytheist. Verily he is of those who have gone astray, unless he repenteth; verily He is the Forgiver, the Merciful.

Ismu'llah Jamal

Better known in Iran as Mullah (the most learned) Jamal Burújirdi, before he became a Baha'i he was a powerful Shi'ite Muslim leader and a great theologian with over 25,000 followers.

He accepted the new faith in the early days of Baha'u'llah, and to the last he was a true disciple of him. When the news spread throughout the land that Mullah Jamal Burújirdi had joined the Babis, it caused a great commotion amongst the populace. Indeed by his act [of conversion to Babism, later Baha'ism], he relinquished a great leadership. His earnest belief in the appearance of the Qa'im and the Manifestation [i.e. the Bab and Baha'u'llah] was so strong that he sacrificed wealth and leadership for the sake of truth.

Eventually he became one of the prominent Baha'i teachers during the days of Baha'u'llah; also he was a medium of correspondence between him and the followers. He was honored with numerous tablets by Baha'u'llah. He made several pilgrimages to Adrianople and to Acre and he was given a lengthy audience with Baha'u'llah on each occasion.

After the ascension of Baha'u'llah, when Ismu'llah Jamal was over the age of eighty, he made a pilgrimage to Acre from Tehran, Iran, on horseback by the way of Turkey. This journey was made in three months. I remember the day of his arrival as he came directly to Bahji to pay his homage to the Holy Shrine of Baha'u'llah. After a few years he made another pilgrimage to the Holy Land; this was his last visit.

Although a former Muslim theologian and somewhat of a fundamentalist, nevertheless he was very broad in his ideas. In one of his numerous messages addressed to the Baha'is, he begs them to become united, demanding the formation of a spiritual gathering by the different Baha'i parties for the sole purpose of the elimination of dissension. His last remark is so wonderful that I will reprint its translation in his memory. He says, "If we cannot agree to bring unity amongst ourselves, in our great religion, let us unite on the elimination of religion entirely and free the innocent humanity from the bondage of religious superstitions in the future."

He passed unto Eternity on May 30, 1911, at Tehran, Iran.

Haji Mirza Husayn Shirazi, Better Known as Khartumi

Haji Mirza Husayn was born in Shiraz, [Iran,] the birthplace of the Bab. In his youth he became a Baha'i.

In 1886 he left his native land accompanied by Haji Mirza Haydar Ali Isfahani. They journeyed to Adrianople and paid their homage to Baha'u'llah for the first time. After remaining there a few months, with the permission of Baha'u'llah they left for Egypt and resided in Mansoura, preaching the new faith.

In a short time, several of the Iranians who lived in that locality accepted the message. One of the new converts named Haji Abu'l-Qasim Shirazi, a well-known merchant, made pilgrimage to Adrianople and paid tribute to Baha'u'llah. After his pilgrimage he returned to Egypt, and with dynamic force and great enthusiasm, openly gave the glad-tidings [of Baha'u'llah] to his fellow merchants, converting several of them to the new faith.

This caused a commotion among some of the merchants who were [fundamentalist] fanatics, those who were opposed to this movement. The agitators raised their voices in protest, calling the Baha'is violators and infidels. They held meetings and demanded an explanation and proofs of their claims. During these meetings, they received convincing replies, logical proofs according to their scripture [e.g. the Qur'an], which caused several of those who were present during the debates to accept the [Baha'i] message.

This news reached the ear of the Iranian Consul General at Cairo, namely Mirza Hassan Khan. He tried to become acquainted with the progressive group [i.e. the Baha'is], showing them a friendly attitude. After a few days the Consul invited them to the consulate for dinner through Mirza Husayn Nadim Hakkak Shirazi. During the evening they exchanged views on several questions pertaining to the new faith, and the Consul was agreeable and friendly to his guests.

Late that evening, when the departing hour arrived, the host disregarded the command of his Prophet Muhammad, who said, "Honor thy guest, though he be an infidel," and ordered the capture of his guests, chained and held them prisoner in the consulate. In the same evening he ordered the search of their homes and confiscated all the Baha'i literature they possessed.

The next morning, the Consul of Iran hastened to the Khedive[11] of Egypt, Isma'il Pasha, and explained the situation. By the order of the Khedive, the Muslim theologians called a meeting, examined the Baha'i literature which had been confiscated, and without question, further investigation, or hearing the testimony of the prisoners, rendered a verbal final decision for their permanent banishment to Sudan. So the following seven Baha'is—namely, Haji Mirza Husayn Shirazi Khartumi, Haji Mirza Haydar Ali Isfahani, Haji Ali Kirmani, Mirza Hasan Kashi, Abdu'l-Vahhab Zanjani, Aqa Muhammad Hashim Naraqi, and Haji Abu'l-Kazim Isfahani—the same day, accompanied by gendarmes, were marched on foot to the river Nile, to Fammel Bahr (i.e. the seashore), and kept in chains for one month in an underground prison. Then a special Khedivi steamship arrived for their deportation; and a detachment of Egyptian soldiers took possession of the prisoners, sailing for their destination.

From the night of their imprisonment until they reached their final place of confinement, Khartoum, the capital of Sudan, six months had passed. The duration of their exile lasted nine years with severe hardship, but they were contented and happy under these calamities and steadfast in the cause.

During the term of their exile, Baha'u'llah sent two messengers for their comfort and for news: The first was Jasim the Arab; the second, Aqa Sheikh Ali Yazdi. After the elapse of nine years, the prisoners were released by the order of Gordon Pasha[12] in the year 1873.

After their release, Haji Mirza Husayn Khartumi and his cellmate, Haji Mirza Haydar Ali Isfahani, made pilgrimage to Mecca and from there to Acre, where they paid their homage again to their Master

---

[11] A *khedive* was a viceroy of the Ottoman Empire. At the time, Egypt was an autonomous tributary state under the Ottoman umbrella.

[12] Major-General Charles George Gordon was a British army officer and administrator who, with the approval of the British government, entered the service of the Khedivate of Egypt and became Governor-General of the Sudan. *Pasha* was an honorary title in the Ottoman Empire, equivalent to the British Lord.

Baha'u'llah. Then Haji Mirza Husayn went to Bombay, India, and engaged himself in spreading the new message there. In 1890 when the writer [i.e. Shua Ullah Behai] was in Bombay, the said Haji Mirza Husayn was residing there, and he calligraphed the Book of the Temple which was printed in Bombay with other books by the commands of Baha'u'llah. Also through his efforts the first Baha'i Assembly was organized in Bombay, during the blessed days of Baha'u'llah.

After the ascension of Baha'u'llah, he came to the Holy Land on several occasions, sometimes remaining here a few months or a year. He served the cause with great vigor and energy to the last. In his later years he was residing in Alexandria, Egypt, and he passed unto Eternity in the same city, August 14, 1907.

Janab-i Nabil Zarandi[13]

In his youth he left his native land [Iran] in the search after truth. He came to Baghdad, Iraq, while Baha'u'llah was in seclusion in the mountains of Sulaymaniyah. Nabil was dissatisfied with the conditions then existing among the Babis at Baghdad; therefore he left for Karbala and remained there until the return of Baha'u'llah to Baghdad.

During his stay in Baghdad, by the commands of Baha'u'llah, he made several journeys to Iran for the sole purpose of spreading the new message, and he was successful in his mission.

After the Blessed Procession [i.e. Baha'u'llah and his companions] had left Baghdad for Constantinople, Nabil invested himself with the garment of a dervish and followed on foot, joining them on the way. In Constantinople he was commanded by Baha'u'llah to go to Iran and promulgate the message. He performed his duties energetically, and made an extensive tour throughout the land, giving the glad-tidings of the coming Manifestation.

When Baha'u'llah universally [i.e. publicly] claimed to be the one "Whom God Shall Make Manifest," Nabil hastened to Adrianople, and

---

[13] Mr. Zarandi's given name was Muhammad, but he is usually known among Baha'is as Nabil-i-A'zam or simply Nabil. *Janab* is a Persian title meaning "Excellency," used here by the author to show great respect.

after paying his homage to Baha'u'llah, he left for Egypt. He arrived in Egypt a few months after the arrest and deportation of the seven Baha'is to Sudan through the efforts of the Consul General of Iran; so Nabil was arrested and placed in prison in Alexandria, Egypt.

When the Blessed Procession was passing through Alexandria en route to the great prison of Acre, Nabil was in prison and was deprived of the pleasure of visiting his Great Master Baha'u'llah. After his release from the prison, Nabil journeyed to Acre and joined his Master, and remained under his blessed shadow to the end.

He was a true Baha'i, a faithful follower of the teachings, a zealous worker and staunch supporter of the great cause. He was a natural-born poet, and he composed several volumes of poetry, consisting of Baha'i historical events and the daily routine of Baha'u'llah. I remember that noble soul well, [from] when I was in my teens, and have observed him composing poetry on short notice on several occasions. Indeed he spent years in commemoration of his Master.

After the ascension of Baha'u'llah, Nabil made a vow, that he shall not compose poetry in the future, but Ghusn-i-A'zam 'Abdu'l-Baha suggested that he should compose a poem for a well-known Baha'i teacher who was then confined in the prison of Tehran, Iran. Complying with the orders he composed a few pages all in commemoration of Baha'u'llah, explaining the events from his birth to his ascension, ending with a few verses to the aforesaid prisoner. Also he composed a short poem after that, and a much shorter one a few days later.

Nabil was very despondent after the ascension of Baha'u'llah. He could not be separated from him; he was greatly attached to his Master and willfully joined him in the Eternal Realms, by drowning himself on the seashore north of Acre, looking towards the Shrine of Baha'u'llah.

The following is the translation of the last few verses which the noble soul Nabil wrote. May the blessing of the Most Merciful be with him.

A REMEMBRANCE by Nabil Zarandi

The essence of my heart, life, and soul,
Bones, flesh, veins, and all,

Testifies with bow and prostration:
Baha'u'llah is the promised Manifestation;

One! In Self, in name and attribute,
Single and Unequal in His attitude.

The prophets gave glad-tidings of Him,
Saints and sages spoke reverently of Him,

That in the Holy Land He shall appear,
As the sun, bright and visible far and near.

This world of tyranny and oppression,
Through the appearance of the Manifestation,

Shall become the land of justice and equality,
Paradise, incomparable to this sublimity.

Behold, He came and brightened the Universe,
And rebuilt this old worn-out earth.

[For] [t]heir progress and advancement He tried,
Finally their inner-soul He occupied.

Through Him, the earth and heaven advanced,
And the stations of the faithful enhanced.

The gate of mercy became wide open;
On everyone, He bestowed his portion.

Seventy-five years, that Treasure, invisible,
With unequal beauty of Yusuf,[14] [was] visible.

---

[14] Yusuf is the Arabic name for Joseph, the son of the Hebrew patriarch Jacob. There is a Surah of Yusuf in the Qur'an, and he is considered in Islam to have been a model of prophetic virtue and patience in the face of injustice. The first scriptural text written by the Bab was the *Qayyum al-Asma*, a book-length commentary on the Surah of Yusuf.

In Iraq, Turkey, and Syria, appeared He,
In every corner an inspired devotee.

Heads on the spears,[15] in His path loudly cheer,
"O Thou Most Resplendent, Glorious, and Most Dear."

When the appointed time was ended,
To the Eternal Realms He ascended.

The Day of Judgment appeared on this earth;
Peoples of earth covered their heads with earth.[16]

O Thou the Blessed, the Sacred Whole,
Thou art aware of my burning soul.

My eyes in tears, my blood boiling,
Like a fish on fire I am broiling.

Ninety-five days from Thine ascension passed,
And I am still with this earth encompassed.

By Thy Branches and Thy faithful,
O Thou, Most Generous, and Most Merciful,

Open Thou a way to my heart's aching,
And drown me in this year of drowning.[17]

By Thine Ocean of Mercy, I pray,
May they some kind words towards me say:

---

[15] "Heads on the spears": This is presumably a reference to Baha'i martyrs.

[16] "covered their heads with earth": This could mean either that they felt shame and repented of their sins, or that they fell to the dust because of God's judgment.

[17] Shua Ullah Behai mentions in a footnote that "year of drowning" equates to 1310 in the Arabic *Abjad* system of numerology. Nabil Zarandi drowned himself in 1310 A.H., i.e. late 1892 A.D.

Those spiritual nightingales[18] may sing to me,
"O strange Nabil, our thoughts are with thee;

Under the shadow of nearness you remain,
In the Great Baha'u'llah's Eternal Domain."

On Safar the ninth, Tuesday evening,[19]
At Bahji, I write this, with yearning.

So shall remain with the faithful friends,
From this disturbed one, a "Remembrance."

Aqa Mohammed Jawad Gazvini, Entitled Ism-i Jud

He was a Baha'i historian, a staunch supporter of the cause and a devout follower of Baha'u'llah. He migrated with Baha'u'llah to the prison of Acre, and he was a medium of correspondence with the followers during the days of Baha'u'llah.

He was one of the nine persons chosen by Ghusn-i-A'zam 'Abdu'l-Baha to hear the reading of the Book of My Covenant, the Will of Baha'u'llah, the ninth day after his ascension.

He is the author of *A Brief History of Beha U'llah*, translated into the English language and published in 1914.

He departed unto Eternity on [blank][20] and is buried at Abu Ataba near the Sacred Shrine [of Baha'u'llah].

Ismu'llah Mahdi[21]

He was an early believer in the faith, and one of the Baha'i teachers

---

[18] "spiritual nightingales": The nightingale (Arabic: *bulbul*) is frequently used in Sufi and Baha'i writings as a symbol of the divine voice, e.g. prophets, angels, or other beings inspired by the Holy Spirit.

[19] The 9th day of the month of Safar, 1310 A.H., was September 2, 1892. It was actually a Friday.

[20] A blank space was left in the original manuscript by Mr. Behai, and this editor was not able to determine from other sources when Mr. Gazvini died.

[21] Also known as Sayyid Mahdi or Siyyid Mihdi Dahaji.

during the days of Baha'u'llah, who traveled extensively throughout Iran for the spread of truth.

Mirza Abu'l-Fadl of Golpayegan, Iran

According to records available, Mirza [Muhammad] Abu'l-Fadl [Gulpaygani] accepted the Baha'i faith in 1875.[22] He was a great student of Aristotelian as well as rational Islamic philosophy.

Several times he was placed in prison by the order of the Shah of Iran, with many other faithful Baha'is, during the years from 1882 to 1886.[23]

He spent years spreading the [Baha'i] teachings, traveling in remote countries. He journeyed northward through Iran, Turkey, the Caucasus, Tartary[24] and Russia as far as Moscow; eastward as far as the confines of China and Kashgar;[25] to Syria, Palestine, and Egypt; and westward to Europe and America.

He spent his later years in Cairo, Egypt, and passed unto Eternity there.

Mirza Abu'l-Qasim Nazir

This noble soul accepted the Baha'i faith during the days of Baha'u'llah and served the cause faithfully to the last. He was in the service of the government of Iran and served as governor of several provinces during the Qajar Dynasty. In his capacity as governor, he assisted the Baha'is considerably in those trying days of oppression and religious fanaticism.

---

[22] Most other sources say 1876.

[23] The arrests were actually ordered by Kamran Mirza, the governor of Tehran. It is possible that the Shah was involved in the matter, but other Baha'i sources hold the governor responsible, as well as a Tehrani religious leader named Sayyid Sadiq Sanglaji.

[24] An old-fashioned name for the central Asian steppe. Specifically, Abu'l-Fadl traveled to the present-day countries of Turkmenistan and Uzbekistan.

[25] Kashgar is the westernmost city of China, located near the border with Tajikistan and Kyrgyzstan.

He retired from government service and migrated to Acre, Palestine, during the latter part of the 19th century, to be near his Master Baha'u'llah.

In 1882 he accompanied Ghusn-i-Akbar Mohammed Ali to Bombay, India, returning to Acre with him.

For a short time he resided in Egypt, and afterward returned to Acre and was there during the ascension of Baha'u'llah. A few years later he left for Tehran, Iran, and he passed away there.

Aqa Mirza Abdullah Bahhaj

He was a devout Baha'i, philosopher, writer and poet. He migrated to Acre with his father and family during the days of Baha'u'llah. He has composed many constructive and inspiring verses of poetry and prose in the great Baha'i cause.

He was appointed a teacher by 'Abdu'l-Baha for Shoghi Effendi and his other grandchildren, and served in this capacity during the First World War.

Abdu'l-Ghaffar Isfahani

He was one of the devotees of Baha'u'llah who migrated with him to the prison of Acre. Upon reaching the port of Haifa, while still on the steamship, Abdu'l-Ghaffar was informed by the Turkish authorities that he was not allowed to land at Haifa, and that he was banished to the island of Cyprus. Abdu'l-Ghaffar, learning that he would be separated from his Master Baha'u'llah, immediately threw himself into the sea, exclaiming, "O Baha! O Baha!" and so preferring death to separation. But he was saved by the sailors standing on the deck and was taken to his prison in Cyprus.

However, after a few years he joined Baha'u'llah at Acre,[26] and was happy again. A short while after the ascension of Baha'u'llah, he left for the city of Damascus, Syria, and passed unto Eternity there.

---

[26] He escaped from prison in Cyprus in 1870.

Haji Mirza Siyyid Hasan Afnan

Better known as Afnan Kabir (i.e. the Great), he was given this title as he was the oldest among the relatives of the Bab. He was a philosopher and astronomer. Of this great personage Professor Edward Browne said:

> [A] very old man with light blue eyes and white beard, whose green turban proclaimed him a descendant of the Prophet [Muhammad], advanced to welcome me, saying, "We know not how we should greet thee, whether we should salute thee with '*as-salamu alaykum*' or with '*Allahu abha*.'"[27] When I discovered that this venerable old man was not only one of the original companions of the Bab but his relative and comrade from earliest childhood, it may well be imagined with what eagerness I gazed upon him and listened to his every utterance.[28]

Haji Siyyid Muhammad Afnan

He is the son of Afnan Kabir. He was a zealous worker in the Baha'i cause to the last. In 1889 he organized the Naseri Press in Bombay, India, for the sole purpose of publishing the teachings of Baha'u'llah. Through his earnest endeavor several books of the teachings were printed by Naseri Press, by the commands of Baha'u'llah. Among them, The Book of *Aqdas*, The Book of *Haykal*, The Book of *Ishraqat*, The Book of *Iqan*, and The Book of the Tablets, inscribed by the famous calligrapher Mishkín-Qalam.

Ibrahim George Kheiralla

Ibrahim Kheiralla had the great honor of being the first person who

---

[27] *As-salámu 'alaykum*, meaning "peace be upon you," is the traditional greeting among Muslims. *Allah-u-Abhá*, meaning "God is Most Glorious," is the customary greeting among Baha'is.

[28] Edward G. Browne, *A Traveller's Narrative: Written to Illustrate the Episode of the Bab*, Volume II. English Translation and Notes (Cambridge: University Press, 1891), pp. xxxvii-xxxviii.

delivered the message of Baha'u'llah to the people of the United States of America. He was a true Baha'i, an earnest believer in Baha'ism, and he taught [the faith] according to his understanding with great energy to the end of his days. He was converted into the Baha'i faith in 1890 A.D. when he was honored with the following tablet from Baha'u'llah:

> TO IBRAHIM WHOM GOD CONFIRMED.
> HE IS THE LISTENER AND THE ANSWERER.
>
> A remembrance issued from the Presence of the Oppressed, to the one who confessed the Oneness of God and His Singleness, and that He is the Beginning and the End, the Visible and the Invisible. There is no God but He, the Single, the One, the All-Knowing, the All-Wise.
>
> Verily, We heard thy supplications, and granted them to thee, and remembered thee with such remembrance, whereby the hearts will be attracted to thee. We command thee and My redeemers (those who redeemed themselves) to be charitable, upright and pious, holding fast to that which will draw you nearer to God your Lord, and the Lord of all the worlds.
>
> Say: Praise be to Thee, O God my Lord; I ask of Thee, by Thy prophets, Thy chosen and Thy redeemers, to send down upon me, from the heaven of Thy bounty, Thy special providence and Thy particular mercy; and open, before my face, the doors of Thy gifts and blessings.
>
> Indeed Thou art the Rich, the Compassionate, the Giver, the Generous. There is no God but Thee, the Forgiver, the Merciful.[29]

During the summer of 1898, while Ibrahim Kheiralla was visiting Acre with some of the American believers, 'Abdu'l-Baha conferred upon him the titles of "Peter of Baha," "The second Columbus and discoverer of America." Indeed, the latter title was fulfilled to the letter, as unfortunately, like Columbus, he received the same treatment.[30]

---

[29] Quoted in *Beha 'U'llah (The Glory of God)* by Ibrahim George Kheiralla (Chicago: 1900), p. 545.

[30] Presumably this is a reference to the fact that Columbus was removed from his position as governor of the Spanish colonies in the New World, much like Kheiralla was removed from his role as chief teacher and organizer of the Baha'i faith in the United States. See Chapter 25 for Ibrahim Kheiralla's account of

Regardless of the past events and the existing prejudice of some of the so-called Baha'is toward that great soul, we cannot deny the fact that he was the first who brought the message of truth to the New World, and in spite of this prejudice his noble name shall remain as such on the pages of Baha'i history. When the present book of dissension is closed and the existing prejudices are eliminated, his name will shine again and he shall be accorded great honors and will always be remembered with reverence.

There is a marble statue of that noble soul, the work of a great sculptor, in the possession of his son, Dr. George Kheiralla. The Baha'is who are in control of the affairs of the Baha'i temple in Wilmette, Illinois, should secure that statue and place it outside the entrance of one of the gates of the temple in memory of that noble soul, who brought them the message which gave them the power and the energy to build it. This is going to be done eventually; why not now? By this act they will eliminate the existing prejudice and fulfill what His Excellency 'Abdu'l-Baha said:

> To be silent concerning the faults of others, to pray for them, and to help them, through kindness, to correct their faults.
> To look always at the good and not at the bad. If a man has ten good qualities and one bad one, to look at the ten and forget the one; and if a man has ten bad qualities and one good one, to look at the one and forget the ten.
> Never to allow ourselves to speak one unkind word about another, even though that other be our enemy.[31]

Dr. Ibrahim Kheiralla wrote several books on Baha'ism, the most important of which is the book entitled *Beha 'U'llah*. He answered his Master's call and left this earth for Eternity on March 6, 1929, at Beirut, Lebanon.

---

how this happened. It should be noted that at the time when Shua Ullah Behai was writing this book, Christopher Columbus was still generally regarded as a hero, rather than the much more negative assessment of more recent historians.

[31] Quoted by J. E. Esslemont in *Bahá'u'lláh and the New Era* (Wilmette, Ill.: US Bahá'í Publishing Trust, 1980 edition), p. 83.

Frederick Olin Pease

Mr. Pease was born August 17, 1852, on a farm near Stoughton, Wisconsin. He was the third of ten children. His father was a Methodist exhorter,[32] as well as a farmer. He was of English extraction, though the Pease family had been in America since 1625.

About 1870 the family moved to southwestern Minnesota, taking up a homestead of 160 acres near the town of Pipestone. Farm life was not for him, and so after a few years he left to make his own way in the world. His first venture was to own and run a photography studio. He took pictures of people and scenes. In those days you had to make your own photographic plates, as there were no factories making them. Later he started a factory to make them, but his partner skipped out with all the money.

In 1878 he and Allie J. Hankinson were married. There were four children, all boys. Only one of the entire family is now left.

The practice of medicine had always appealed to Mr. Pease, so in 1880 he entered the Chicago Homeopathic Medical College, graduating, as valedictorian, in 1885. He practiced as a physician for forty-five years.

In 1895, Mr. William F. James, who was the fourth[33] of the Chicago converts of Dr. Kheiralla to the truth of Baha'u'llah, interested Dr. Pease [in the faith]. He accepted [it] and became an ardent believer and worker in the cause. He taught many classes in his home, as well as working in the [Baha'i] Assembly, helping to make it known to the people of Chicago.

I had the pleasure of meeting this noble soul the first time in 1904 when I visited the Chicago Assembly, and after that we communicated with each other occasionally. Indeed he was a true follower of Baha'u'llah and promulgator of his teachings to the end.

---

[32] Now known as a "lay speaker," an *exhorter* was a layperson who served as an assistant preacher in the Methodist church.

[33] Ibrahim Kheiralla actually identifies Mr. James as "the first of the American believers." See the section entitled "Bringing Baha'ism to the U.S.A." in Chapter 25.

Dr. Pease died in early April 1933, being 80 years and eight months old. He is buried near Pipestone, in a beautiful spot sloping to the east.³⁴ He is survived by a son, Mr. Leslie E. Pease, who is also one of the early Baha'is and a devout follower of Baha'u'llah.

Count Gaspar Bela Daruvary

While I was in the Golden State of California, I met a very charming personality, the Magyar American philosopher-poet, who composed many constructive verses in commemoration of the Manifestation. In one of his communications to me, he said:

> Forty years ago in my beautiful native land, Hungary, when I was only a boy, my noble grandfather,—Count Andras Geza Daruvary, who was one of the most brilliant statesmen (three times Minister of Foreign Affairs in the Cabinet of King Francis Joseph³⁵), who was revered even by his political opponents—before he passed unto Eternity, stroking my head most affectionately, told me the following: "My little lamb," (that was my pet name by him), "in far away Persia there was born a Great Soul, who is even greater than a wise man; He is an avatar of mankind! When you are grown up to manhood, then my little son, go and search for this Great One; for our king has failed to heed his wise admonitions."³⁶
>
> These last parting words of my deeply beloved grandfather were indelibly engraved in my tender boyish mind, such that

---

³⁴ Baha'i burial practice is for the grave to face towards the Shrine of Baha'u'llah in Acre, Israel (i.e. with the feet of the deceased pointed in that direction). This is also the direction towards which Baha'is turn to pray. In the United States, this direction is east.

³⁵ Franz Joseph I, Emperor of Austria and King of Hungary.

³⁶ In 1867, Baha'u'llah wrote the *Suriy-i-Muluk* ("Tablet to the Kings"), in which he addressed the world's monarchs collectively and counseled them to seek peace, reduce their expenditures on weapons and the military, lighten the burden of taxation on their people, and show compassion towards the poor. In the *Kitab-i-Aqdas*, completed in 1873, Baha'u'llah addresses certain monarchs individually, including Emperor Franz Joseph of Austria-Hungary (in paragraph 85), whom he rebukes for ignoring him.

eleven years later I went to your ancient and historical native land, Persia, in search of that great man.

From Tehran in the company of the Hungarian Consul General, Baron Sandor Imre Almady, I traversed through Luristan, the Valleys of the Assassins, the castles of Lamasar, the mountain of the Throne of Solomon,[37] and also the Persian hinterland, as well as the great temples of the forgotten glories which was once Persia. Alas! Alas! my weary quest was all in vain.

But near the city of Zanjan, a humble farm worker by the name of Aga Jan made a most profound salutation to me and said in solemn pronunciation: "Young Effendi, I greet in thee the Divine Spark which guided thee here, from the far, far away land of thy forefathers! Verily, He is the Guide of all things to the Right Path."

Not until 1920 did the realization dawn upon me that perhaps that farm worker was a bitterly persecuted, devout follower of the one for whom I searched even in the Valleys of the Assassins, our Great Master Baha'u'llah. (That extraordinary greeting, of course, I was able to understand through my interpreter, Baron Almady.)

I hereby end these memories with the following verses contributed by Gaspar B. Daruvary:

TOLERATION

Cast aside your old prejudice,
Give no thoughts to race or creed,
Worry not 'bout Jews or Cath'lics,

---

[37] These places mentioned by Mr. Daruvary were popularized by explorer Freya Stark in her 1934 book, *The Valleys of the Assassins: and Other Persian Travels*. Luristan (present-day Lorestan Province) is a remote, mountainous region of western Iran. Lamasar (also spelled Lambasar or Lambsar) was a fortified stronghold of the Nizari Ismaili sect of Islam in medieval times, whose opponents derisively called them "Assassins." The Takht-e Suleyman Massif ("Throne of Solomon" mountain range) is located in the central Alborz mountains, in northern Iran. According to legend, the so-called Assassins, also called the *hashishiyya*, were hashish-smoking terrorists who inhabited the various mountain valleys of these parts of Persia. This characterization of Ismaili Muslims, largely fictional, captured the imagination of Western visitors.

Protestants, or other breed.
Just remember, all are wand'ring
On the path to one same goal,
Living, hoping, trusting, wond'ring,
If they'll get there in the Soul.

Cease your fighting, quarr'ling, frowning,
Talks of doctrines, sects bewail.
Think of Oneness in religion,
Let One God, for all, prevail.
Just remember that the Spirit
Permeating all of life,
Is impartial, favors no one,
Looks with pity on all strife.

Christian, Jew, Mohammedan,
Are God's children, one and all.
Buddhist, Hindu and Brahmin,
Neither rise, nor can they fall.
Baha'u'llah never favors
No particular sect or plan,
All are struggling on the Pathway
Toward TRUTH, the best they can.

Cast aside then ancient bias,
Aim together for the Truth,
Spark of which hold all religions,
Regardless of name, forsooth.
Sweetest thing that should be practiced
By each race and ev'ry nation,
That would make of world a heaven,
Is the creed of Toleration.

Frederick Arthur Slack

He was born in Nottingham, England, December 26, 1866. He immigrated to the United States in 1888 and took up residence in Trenton, New Jersey. He moved to Kenosha, Wisconsin, in 1897.

Mr. Slack accepted the Baha'i faith in 1900. He assisted in organizing the Society of Behaists, in Kenosha in 1903, and served as its President and spiritual guide, faithfully to his last day on earth.

Indeed he was a true Baha'i, an earnest worker and a great teacher. He was the cause of the guidance of many seekers to the message of our Great Master Baha'u'llah. He passed unto Eternity on March 28, 1943, in Kenosha, Wisconsin.

[The following is a poem by Frederick A. Slack:]

A MIRROR

This world is a wonderful mirror,
    A reflection of things unseen,
Of pictures that stamp them forever,
    As a shaft from God's golden beam.

What is below the surface?
    What is above the blue?
Treasures for mankind's service,
    Stars that eclipse the view.

Creation is one of God's mirrors,
    A gift from the God of love,
Where myriads of sparkling rivers,
    Leap forward to join us above.

Rivers of light and of mercy,
    Speeding us all on our way,
Guiding our thoughts from the earthy,
    To a mirrored and cloudless day.

Rivers of joy, peace and knowledge,
    That God intends us to share;
When man shall return to God's Vintage,
    And receive what is waiting him there.

Man is the mightiest of mirrors,
    Reflecting the God unseen,

Rivaling the hues of the rainbow,
    The image unraveling God's skein.

Then are we true mirrors of God,
    Do we obey the Divine behest?
Are we using aright His divining rod
    Which giveth His people rest?

Then let us be perfect mirrors of God,
    Let Him mold us as He think best,
Then the earth sublime that God hath trod
    Will mirror God's "Eden of rest."

Joseph G. Hamilton

He was born October 14, 1870, in Paboda, Söderåkra, Kalmar, Sweden. He immigrated to the United States in 1888 and resided in Chicago, Illinois. He accepted the Baha'i faith in the early days when the message reached the Western Hemisphere.

Mr. Hamilton devoted the greater part of his life to the service of the cause, conducted a Baha'i mission in Chicago, and published numerous booklets, in English and Swedish, spreading the teachings of Baha'u'llah. He passed away on August 6, 1942, in the city of Chicago.

The following is one of his numerous recitations:

RESTORATION

O Thou Most Resplendent Glory,
    Praise to Thee for ever more,
For Thy sacred inventory
    Of Thy truths, which were of yore.
Thine they are and so shall be,
    Proving Thy authority.

Thine they were and so regarded
    By the Guides who walked Thy Way.
Now by Thee they are rewarded
    In Thy own and Promised Day.

Praise to Thee for this Thy deed;
    Now they all Thy truths can heed.

Praise to Thee for this Thy "favor,"
    To "divines"[38] that come to Thee.
By Thy truths and their endeavor
    They "may win the victory."
This we now perceive as true,
    For Thou hast made all things new.

Now we know these truths descended
    "On the prophets of the past."
This "divines" have comprehended
    And attained by what Thou hast.
Praise to Thee for this Thy care.
    Now "divines" Thy truths can share.

Praise to Thee for this redemption
    Of the hosts whom Thee adored.
No one now can claim exemption
    For Thou hast Thy truths restored.

Lewis Stuyvesant Chanler

In memory of the late Honorable Lewis Stuyvesant Chanler, and his services to the cause, I hereby reprint [excerpts from] an article written by John Goodrum Miller, Esq., published in the *New History* magazine,[39] April 1942, entitled "A Knight Has Ridden Away."

> The Honorable Lewis Stuyvesant Chanler died on February 28, 1942 at his residence, 132 East 65th Street, New York City. After services on March 3, at the Church of St. Mark's-in-the-Bouwerie, the burial took place at Glen Cove, Long Island, in the family plot that had belonged to S.L.M. Barlow, grandfather of Mrs. Chanler.

---

[38] This poetic-sounding term has often been used in Baha'i writings to refer to clergy or religious leaders.

[39] A periodical of the New History Society, a liberal Baha'i organization that existed at the time.

In recognition of Mr. Chanler's long official and public service in Dutchess County, as a member of the [New York State] Assembly from Dutchess County and as Lieutenant-Governor, the Chief Executive of the State, Governor [Herbert H.] Lehman, ordered that flags on all public buildings in Albany be lowered to half-staff until after the ceremony.

Thus closed the earthly career of a man whose life neither began with the birth of his body nor ended with its death. I believe Mr. Chanler's credo of human experience did not deem that excursion other than a short span—*un petit pas*—in the perpetual motion of a vaster life. ...

Born September 24, 1869, and brought up in the open space of Dutchess, a rural county, where the fresh smell of plowed earth filled his breathing passages and the chirping of birds and the neighing of horses were early sounds in his ears, the young squire, the country gentleman, observed life as a strong, clean current to battle or ride with a robust way, as good conscience might determine at the moment. ...

Fine tutors, Cambridge [University], England, and Columbia [University] in New York, the political example of his father and forebears returned him to Dutchess County and sent him later to New York City, fit for the pew of the vestryman, the forum of politics and the bar.

After a successful and useful course in Dutchess County politics and in the courts of New York, Mr. Chanler was nominated by the Democratic Party of New York State, in 1906, for the office of Lieutenant-Governor, the nominee for Governor of both the Democratic Party and an organization called the Independent League being William Randolph Hearst.

A campaign ensued of national interest in which Charles Evans Hughes, the Republican nominee, was elected Governor over Mr. Hearst, a most spectacular feature of the campaign being that Mr. Chanler was elected Lieutenant-Governor in a split election in which Mr. Hearst was defeated for the governorship.

This political feat was of conspicuous importance and caused Mr. Chanler's nomination by the Democratic Party for the governorship against Governor Hughes in 1908, resulting in discussion of Mr. Chanler as Presidential timber for the future. However, the great prestige of the Hughes administration and the nationwide sweep of the Republican Party in favor of Mr. [William Howard] Taft for the Presidency brought Democratic defeat in New York. ...

Mr. Chanler's course must be re-traced a bit to pick up certain romantic threads that glisten in his silken garment. Completing a law course at Columbia, he entered the practice of the criminal law and became the Knight Errant[40] of the New York bar; and, during a long period of professional experience, there was none so poor in New York that he was without able and voluntary counsel. Mr. Chanler was regarded as one of the most distinguished lawyers at the criminal bar, trying more than one hundred murder cases with but one client paying the death penalty.

In commenting upon his own career, Mr. Chanler said that he had boyhood dreams of being the defender of the unfortunate in the courts of justice and he turned these dreams into actuality when the chance came. ...

One should hesitate to invade the privacy of another's soul and yet I do not think that this departed gentleman would object to the comments I am about to make. I believe he was much of a mystic and that there was within him a deeply religious vein which, unimprisoned by dogma, gave inner peace and security.

I speak of something that was revealed by manner rather than words, for I have heard him mention such matters but few times. I recall vividly a poetic glow upon his countenance when he did let drop a word or two—once when he spoke of having been a vestryman of Trinity Church; again when he mentioned his Masonic Lodge, and notably when he referred to 'Abdu'l-Baha, in whose philosophy he found satisfaction in later life.

I fancy, this man felt as I feel about prophets and founders of religion—that they are highly attuned, sensitized beings who state or re-state the same eternal truths in different eras; who are, in fact, of a great Brotherhood working in common for the elevation of mankind. As a lawyer, I can understand that he as a lawyer approved the statement of the case by 'Abdu'l-Baha—the case for the eternal truth and cosmic order.

---

[40] An expression signifying a man of honor who seeks out opportunities to serve a noble cause without thought of personal gain.

We disagreed about many things. Unable to accept all his opinions on politics and religious philosophy, I have often wondered if he did not possess a wisdom and perspective far in advance of mine, and if he did not see more deeply in the past and further into the future than my own experience and vision permitted. ...

St. Mark's-in-the-Bouwerie is probably the closest existing link between the New York of this day and the Dutch Colony of New Amsterdam. Beneath its floors lies the dust of Petrus Stuyvesant,[41] the last and most picturesque of the Dutch governors. Strikingly, this quaint structure surrounded by an immense Jewish population in a locality long deserted by New York's fashionable world, is noted for its catholicity, its willingness to take a chance on God and man. Fitting therefore, it was that the casket of Lewis Stuyvesant Chanler, the descendant of old Petrus, should rest before its altar, and that his funeral service was jointly Episcopalian and Baha'i. I question whether or not such a circumstance could take place in any other edifice belonging to the Episcopal Church, and believe that the scene on the morning of March 3rd was rare.

Upper Fifth Avenue knelt with Union Square.[42] Judge Samuel Seabury, indefatigable nemesis of Tammany Hall,[43] bent the knee with more than one good Tammany brave. I sat in the same pew with a famous portrait painter. A former German diplomat occupied the seat in front of me and there were not a few of New York's East Indian population to be seen.

And so the funeral of Lewis Stuyvesant Chanler brought together in a Christian church cavalier and yeoman, Jew and Gentile, Hindu and Mohammedan, Catholic and Protestant, all listening wistfully and willingly while an Episcopal clergyman and a Baha'i representative read from the teachings of their two Masters, finding no conflict of creed or practice.

The Christian service was conducted by Rev. C.A.W. Brocklebank and the Baha'i readings were offered by Mirza Ahmad Soh-

---

[41] Also known as Peter Stuyvesant.

[42] Union Square has historically been a site for radical political demonstrations, including the first Labor Day parade in 1882.

[43] Tammany Hall was the Democratic Party political machine in New York City in the late 1800s and early 1900s, known for helping immigrants.

rab,[44] Mr. Chanler's close friend. Unquestionably, the service and the gathering were exactly as Mr. Chanler would have chosen.

The birds and squirrels in Central Park could not come, but I am sure they kept very quiet and still during the service hour. They will miss the tall friend who fed them seeds and peanuts as a daily rite, even in the dead of winter. ...

[Condolences to Mrs. Chanler from the President of the United States:]

> I am deeply distressed to hear of the passing of Lewis— my heartfelt sympathy goes out to you and to all who mourn with you.
> Franklin D. Roosevelt.

---

[44] Mr. Sohrab, a former secretary of 'Abdu'l-Baha, was the founder of the New History Society and one of the leading advocates for a broad-minded interpretation of the Baha'i faith.

Above: Group photo of early Baha'is taken in Adrianople, mid 1860s.
Below (L to R): Closeups of Mohammed Jawad Gazvini, 'Abdu'l-Ghaffar Isfahani (standing) and Ismu'llah Mahdi.

Standing (L to R): Nabil Zarandi, Mirza Aqa Jan Kashani (Khadimu'llah), Mishkín-Qalam, Mirza 'Ali Sayyah.
Seated (middle row, L to R): Mirza Mihdi (son of Baha'u'llah), Abbas Effendi, Mirza Muhammad-Quli (half-brother of Baha'u'llah) holding one of his children.
Seated (bottom row, L to R): Majdeddin (nephew of Baha'u'llah), Mohammed Ali Bahai.

22

Khadimu'llah's Epistle

By Aqa Jan Kashani

This incomplete circular letter by Mirza Aqa Jan Kashani, Khadimu'llah, was written in 1900, according to Shua Ullah Behai, and was translated into English and printed by Ibrahim G. Kheiralla in a book he compiled and published in 1901, entitled *Facts for Behaists*. Section headings have been added.

Mr. Behai included a small part of this document (the invocation, the next two sentences, and the whole next paragraph after that) in a chapter called "Bahai Personalities" in his book manuscript. Most of the epistle was omitted, however, as Mr. Behai tended to refrain from sharing material that strenuously criticized 'Abdu'l-Baha. Dr. Kheiralla, on the other hand, published a much larger part of the document, and the entirety of that portion is reproduced here. In *Facts for Behaists* he wrote, "As we have not enough space here for the complete publication of this long epistle, the balance will be published later on." However, I have not been able to locate any additional parts of the epistle published in English.

It is important that we consider Aqa Jan Kashani's observations and point of view regarding the conflict between Baha'u'llah's sons—including the combative and controversial things he said—because he was a key figure in the Baha'i movement whose role has been largely ignored in mainstream Baha'i histories. His title, Khadim(u'llah), means "servant (of God)," and he was the longest-serving and most important of all believers who served in Baha'u'llah's inner circle besides his eldest sons Abbas Effendi and Mohammed Ali Effendi. His occupation was as Baha'u'llah's chief amanuensis and corresponding secretary.

Mohammed Ali Bahai claims in his autobiography that Mr. Kashani was mentioned in Baha'u'llah's will alongside Abbas Effendi, but that the latter prevented all other Baha'is from reading that part of the will. This allegation seems at least plausible because of Baha'u'llah's statement in a tablet quoted in Chapter 21, that "after the Branches [i.e. sons], a distinguished station is ordained for the Servant who is present before the Throne," i.e. Khadim. Mr. Bahai also says that Mr. Kashani was involved in an effort to persuade him to voice his concerns about 'Abdu'l-Baha to the Baha'i community, in the early days of the dissension.

It seems likely that 'Abdu'l-Baha and Aqa Jan Kashani saw each other as rivals, since both were highly responsible and respected figures in the early Baha'i community, and therefore it would not be surprising if they both sought to weaken each other's position very soon after Baha'u'llah's passing. The fact that Mr. Kashani's responsibilities had been focused on inscribing and disseminating the writings of Baha'u'llah may have deepened the split, since one of the main concerns of the Unitarian Baha'is was that 'Abdu'l-Baha placed more emphasis on his own writings than on Baha'u'llah's.

Khadimu'llah's epistle portrays 'Abdu'l-Baha in a harsh light and contains very serious allegations against him. It would be easy to regard it as, at least in part, the product of bitterness at his loss of position when 'Abdu'l-Baha became the new leader of the Baha'i faith. However, this does not necessarily mean that Mr. Kashani's portrayal of 'Abdu'l-Baha is untrue. As in all cases in which an important, well-respected employee is dismissed or demoted when a new boss takes charge of an organization, it is difficult to evaluate the credibility of negative statements made by old personnel against the agent of organizational change.

—The Editor

In the name of the Everlasting and Self-Sustaining God. Glory be to His Splendor!

This epistle is written by the mortal servant who has been for forty years in the service of his Lord, El Abha ["The Most Glorious," i.e. Baha'u'llah], and who has always been occupied in inscribing His great utterances. It is sent for those whose hearts have been enlightened by the Supreme Word of God, and those whose souls were gladdened when listening to His voice, while He was on the throne of His earthly Kingdom. In it I wish to explain to them the events which have taken place since the waves of the Ocean of the Revelations were stilled and the enjoyment of meeting the King of Command was ended, that they may understand the dissensions, differences and disobediences which have arisen and made themselves manifest in many countries, and know what was commanded by the Supreme Pen in the sacred books which He designated to be the lamp of guidance for the world.

O people of God, living in different countries, to whom the gifts of love and faithfulness were entrusted! The Lord, Most High is He, commanded us to be affectionate to each other and be united like one man; and to consort with peoples of different faiths with love, spirituality and fragrance [i.e. pleasantness]. These wise commands are written in the *Kitab-i-Aqdas* and in many other sacred tablets. Baha'u'llah expressly said in His texts and verses that He suffered calamities and persecutions in order that the fires of hatred and enmity might be extinguished among the inhabitants of the earth. This is the remarkable virtue of His appearance and the great mark which distinguished His days and commandments, and He repeated and emphasized this great teaching in His books and tablets, and designated it to be the only means of progress and prosperity of mankind.

But, alas! I see these commandments are ignored and the light of love and affection is hidden behind the clouds of hatred and enmity. It appears as if the Lord, Glory be to Him, had never moved the Pen of Wisdom and Admonition to write these great utterances and precepts from the Kingdom of Command. I wish I had not been born; thence I would not have seen the Branch—Abbas Effendi—instead of being a guide for the nations and a lamp of righteousness and faithfulness for the world, rising up and spreading hatred and enmity, ignoring the Father's plea for a universal unity, doing what was prohibited by Him, and ordering his followers not to keep the commandments which are laid down in the holy and sacred tablets. I cannot understand how you could be pleased and satisfied with such actions, while you know and you testify that the Lord, Most High is He, warned and prohibited us in His Supreme Word from renewing hatred, enmity, and the superstitions of the past and dark ages. Alas! Alas! Abbas Effendi has caused his followers to display such vehemence of hatred and rancor, the like of which has never been shown by barbarous nations, and even the most ignorant tribes would detest it.

'Abdu'l-Baha's Policies of Shunning and Censorship

Abbas Effendi knows well that the Branches of the Tree of Life [i.e. sons of Baha'u'llah], the family, relatives, and those who were honored in the presence of Baha'u'llah have more knowledge and greater understanding concerning the commandments of God and His laws than anyone else. If his followers will come in contact with them and discuss the teachings and the differences they will be awakened to the truth of the utterances of the Father and will rise up to awaken those who follow him [i.e. 'Abdu'l-Baha] blindly. Abbas Effendi has prohibited his followers from correspondence, discussion, talking, or even trading with those who do not admit his claims, calling them *Naqizin* (violators), while in truth they believe in the Oneness of God and worship none else besides Him. For this, relatives were separated, parents hated their children, husbands disagreed with their wives, and families were ruined.

One of Abbas Effendi's strange actions is his strict orders to his followers at Akka, that none of them be allowed to write a letter even to his friends or relatives unless he first give it to Abbas Effendi, by him to be read, corrected, and sealed with his own seal. Every reasonable man dislikes such an action. There are personal things between friends and especially between husbands and wives, which none else ought to know. A godly man must adopt the right principles which distinguish him from others. It is not proper for him who claims to have the truth and is a relative of the Blessed Tree of Life to perform such an action. In adopting this course of action, fidelity will cease and dishonesty prevail among peoples and nations.

Baha'u'llah's Writings Suppressed

Another of the strange things which Abbas Effendi has done: He prohibited the spreading and publication of the utterances of the Manifestation. He ordered his followers to read and spread only his [own] epistles and writings throughout the countries.

On the contrary, all the true believers know and testify that their Lord Baha'u'llah was very anxious to spread the light of His works, and has commanded the publication of His Sacred Word. Also, He expressly said in many tablets that He had sent letters to the kings and rulers of the earth at the time when He was in the prison at Akka:

> We have sent to the kings the epistles of their Lord. Their might and what We have suffered of calamities have not prevented Us from so doing. Thus, in truth, the decree was written in the Tablet of Judgment by the Pen of El Abha. We have uttered for them the powerful texts which were sent to them with might from Our presence. Whereby they know that calamities cannot prevent Baha-['u'llah] from uttering, even in prison, that which has enlightened the hearts of the righteous and disturbed the one who is kept away from the fragrance of the revelations.

There is no doubt that the Word of God was uttered to guide the creatures and attract their hearts toward their Creator. Baha'u'llah on many occasions commanded us to publish it. In 1890 He issued an order to establish a printing press in India for this great purpose. In that country several of His sacred books were published. But, although the utterances of Baha'u'llah refute all untrue claims and all false doctrines and teach the Oneness of God and that there is no equal to Him, yet Abbas Effendi has destroyed the said press and prevented the spreading of the Word of God among his followers, that they may remain ignorant of the facts, which are in direct contradiction to his claims.

Again, Abbas Effendi has rejected the "Sacred Tablet,"[1] written in the handwriting of Baha'u'llah, and cast it away. This happened when

---

[1] This was a tablet which praised Mohammed Ali Effendi, reproduced in Chapter 10.

one of the Unitarians presented the said tablet to Abbas Effendi, in the presence of many believers, on the Sacred Tomb of Baha'u'llah. Have you heard, O people of discretion, of this event or not? Is it meet for you to be indifferent and yield to the one who refuses to acknowledge the great tablet, which was written in the handwriting of your Lord? Can it be said that he who does this is a believer in God? If anyone were to deny [that] this action of Abbas Effendi [occurred] it would be easy to prove it, merely by presenting the same tablet to Abbas Effendi at another time in the presence of some faithful believers [i.e. to see if he accepts or rejects it].

Another of the sacrilegious actions of Abbas Effendi is that he issued a strict order to his followers to reject every sacred tablet from the utterances of the Manifestation which is not approved by him and sealed by his seal. It is known that the existence of Abbas Effendi depends upon a word from the Mouth of God. In order to be just we must testify that the Lord's Word is high in itself and sublime, that it is not in need of the approval of one of His servants, for the existence of the servant depends upon the word of the Creator. This false claim of Abbas Effendi [to possess the authority to approve or reject Baha'u'llah's writings] is a daring breach of fidelity and leads his followers into a great loss. We ask God to help them to return to Him and be faithful and obedient.

His greatest offense to the Cause of God is this: Abbas Effendi ordered his followers to burn all the sacred tablets of the Manifestation which were written by His scribes, the [younger] Branches of the Tree of Life.[2] I should like to mention the following event, which took place at the city of Akka: While the followers of Abbas Effendi were holding a meeting in the house of one of them, a certain man, seeing on the

---

[2] All the sons of Baha'u'llah were at one time or another involved in inscribing Baha'u'llah's writings. However, most of the writings were inscribed by the younger sons (and Khadim), not 'Abdu'l-Baha, who spent most of his time during Baha'u'llah's ministry dealing with government officials and other external affairs. See Appendix A for a list of the inscribers of Baha'u'llah's writings, and the section of Chapter 16 entitled "The Changing Roles and Duties of Baha'u'llah's Family Members."

wall the words "Ya Baha'u'l-Abha"[3] written and signed by Mohammed Ali Effendi, rushed in and knocked down the motto with his fist, breaking it with its frame and glass into pieces. One of those present did not like this action and complained. To know if such action was right or wrong, the question was brought to Abbas Effendi. His answer was: "Blame not the man for so doing and rebuke him not, because he has done this for his great love for me."

Still another of the strange actions of Abbas Effendi is that he has hidden the last part of the "Testament" (The Book of My Covenant) entrusted to him by Baha'u'llah. The Branches, relatives, many believers and friends asked him time and again to show forth the "Testament," that all differences may be settled and all believers reunited. But to no avail, for he insisted on hiding it and refused everyone and every request regarding it. This action is a treachery to the "Testament." He cannot claim to be the appointed one of the "Testament," while he does not dare to show the last part of it, and furthermore, he has misinterpreted some of its contents.

Strange Behavior of 'Abdu'l-Baha

One of the events which took place before the development of the dissension is the following: To excite the believers and plant in their hearts the seeds of hatred against the younger Branches, Abbas Effendi pretended to leave for Jerusalem. His purpose was to prejudice the believers against the Branches, the family and the relatives [of Baha'u'llah]. He succeeded in creating a disturbance in the minds of the believers who were living in Akka, and some of them, by his actions and speeches, began to hate the Branches. His claim[4] was not known at first

---

[3] This Arabic phrase, meaning "O Glory of the Most Glorious," is commonly used by Baha'is as an exclamation of praise, similar to *hallelujah* in the Christian tradition.

[4] It is unclear what, specifically, Aqa Jan Kashani is suggesting that 'Abdu'l-Baha claimed. One possibility may be that 'Abdu'l-Baha believed (or if Mr. Kashani's story is accurate, maliciously wanted his followers to believe) that the rest of Baha'u'llah's family was conspiring to harm him in some way and therefore it would be unsafe for him to remain in Acre; but more information would be needed to confirm such a speculation. The way Mr. Kashani tells the

to his brothers, but when they discovered it they at once came to Akka and made great efforts with kindness and love to persuade him not to leave the Sacred Place, yet they understood that in reality Abbas Effendi was not intending or wishing to leave, but planned this scheme to gain his point, for he plainly showed that he was expecting the opportunity to give up the idea of leaving. With all that, the brothers, fearing the dissension of the believers, did their best to quiet things. This event is briefly written, and if the full details are wanted I will write them on demand.

Abbas Effendi repeated his successful scheme and created a great disturbance when he traveled alone to Tiberias. One afternoon he suddenly drove in his special carriage into the Palace [of Bahji]. On entering the Sacred Tomb [of Baha'u'llah] he delivered to the believers a speech, which excited his followers. Then he went out and drove in his carriage with the intention of departing alone for Tiberias. At once some of the Branches and their relatives came and begged to accompany him, but with harsh words he refused their request. Zia Ullah, the Holiest [or Purest] Branch [i.e. Ghusn-i-At'har], clung to the carriage; Abbas Effendi ordered the coachman to drive with speed; the brother was thrown to the ground and narrowly escaped being crushed by the wheels.

Zia Ullah; Shua Ullah, the son of Ghusn-i-Akbar; and [Ali] Reza Effendi, the son of Moussa, the brother of Baha'u'llah, followed Abbas Effendi on horseback. When they reached him on his way to Tiberias they found that his carriage was stalled, and he did not know what to do. Seeing the difficulty which he was in, they galloped to the nearest neighborhood and hired some men, who came and lifted the carriage out of the mire. They all together spent that night in the nearest village. Next morning Abbas Effendi, with his shrewd strategy, persuaded the Branches to return to the Palace, that he might arrive at Tiberias alone and be able to assert that he was left without any help or assistance, thereby claiming that a certain prophecy concerning the Manifestation referred to him personally. Reasonable people cannot accept such a

---

story in such a vague and abbreviated fashion, it seems as though the events in question may have been familiar to many of the Baha'is at the time.

claim and cannot believe that he was there alone.[5] By this journey he caused a great disturbance among the believers, and at the same time he had in doing so a hidden purpose, which shall be fully explained on another occasion.

After a short sojourn at Tiberias the local government ordered him to return to Akka. While coming back, Zia Ullah and the sons of his brother [Mohammed Ali Effendi], [namely] Shua Ullah and Amin Ullah Effendi, and his cousin Majdeddin Effendi, went to Nazareth to meet him. But by force he prevented them from accompanying him to Haifa. Before his arrival at the city of Haifa, Badi Ullah Effendi, the youngest brother, met him on the way with some of the inhabitants of the city, but Abbas Effendi paid no attention to him and did not treat him as a brother should. Also he refused to come to the place which Badi Ullah Effendi prepared for him, but instead he went to the house of one of his followers. When his brothers and relatives came to Haifa to salute and congratulate him, he met them with harsh language and treated them cruelly.

Cursing Baha'u'llah's Wife and Children

Then Abbas Effendi lived in a building situated half a mile west of Haifa, which belongs to the Mohammedan Church,[6] erected close to the cave in which, it is claimed, Elijah the Prophet used to live in ancient times. This place, to which the Muslims pay religious visits, is called [Al-]Khader. There he stayed until the government forced him to return to Akka. While Abbas Effendi was at Tiberias and at Khader he plainly urged, on every occasion, his followers, who visited him in these places, to disregard the Branches, the family and the relatives [of Baha'u'llah], and to despise, execrate, and curse them.

Abbas Effendi has intrigued so skillfully as to convince his followers that it is their duty to curse the [younger] Branches, the wife of the

---

[5] Note by Ibrahim Kheiralla: "A certain one of his followers, named Mohammad Ali, who was appointed by Abbas Effendi to be with us in Haifa while visiting, told us that he was with Abbas Effendi in Tiberias."

[6] It is unclear whether this means a mosque or the Muslim community in general.

Manifestation [Baha'u'llah's widow Mahd-i-'Ulya] and the Holy Leaves [i.e. Baha'u'llah's daughters, except Bahiyyih Khanum who supported 'Abdu'l-Baha], openly in their meetings and writings. None of them can deny this statement, for their epistles, written in their own handwriting, bear witness that they have cursed the wife of the Manifestation, His daughters and the Branches. The Lord, Glory be to Him, strictly commanded us in many tablets to honor, respect, and follow them. He made the respect of the Branches a condition for strengthening His Cause and a means of elevating His Word. Therefore, whosoever breaks this commandment is not obeying the Supreme Word, but on the contrary, belittling the Cause of God.

'Abdu'l-Baha's Furious Temper

On one occasion the wife of the Manifestation, accompanied by her sister and daughters, honored Abbas Effendi by paying him a visit at his house in the city of Akka. Abbas Effendi treated her harshly. After a discussion concerning present conditions and differences of faith, Abbas Effendi, finding her to be steadfast and faithful to her Lord and His commandments, which refute his schemes and purposes, rose up and furiously attacked her with the intention of doing her bodily harm. Seeing the danger, she left his house and returned to the Palace of Bahja. This event was a source of great sorrow to his brothers and sisters. It is strange that Abbas Effendi dared to so treat the wife of his Father, the Manifestation, when he knew that Baha'u'llah commanded that she be treated with all proper respect. If the one who claims to be the head of this religion breaks the commandments himself, how can we expect the obedience of the followers?

At times Abbas Effendi used to meet his brothers and sisters at the Sacred Tomb of Baha'u'llah and speak to them in harsh language and treat them cruelly, in order to compel them to believe that which is against the laws of the Lord, Glory be to Him. On one occasion, by force, he seized the hand of the youngest sister [Foroughiyya Khanum] and repeatedly struck her with her own hand upon her head. This took place in the presence of many believers and relatives. Her two little ones [i.e. her children] and those who were present, men and women, wept for her and supplicated him for mercy. Abbas Effendi took no heed to them, but continued beating her, and with a loud voice uttering very harsh words. On account of these continued indignities, the abused sister being very sensitive, suffered from mental prostration, and since then has had a stroke of paralysis, and for five years has been confined to her bed. Can it be said that such actions were in accord with the commandments of the Lord, which He uttered on behalf of His wife and daughters? Can the faithful and righteous people consent to these doings?

Mohammed Jawad Gazvini.

23

Events After the Departure of Baha'u'llah

By Mohammed Jawad Gazvini

Mohammed Jawad Gazvini, also known as Muhammad Javad Qazvini, was one of the inner circle of Baha'u'llah's companions, and was given by him the title *Ism-i-Júd* or *Ismu'lláhi'l-Júd* ("The Name of God, Bounty"). Originally from Qazvin, Iran, he accompanied Baha'u'llah in his exile to Baghdad, Adrianople, and Acre, and served as one of his corresponding secretaries. After Baha'u'llah's death, he sided with Mohammed Ali Bahai in the sectarian dispute against 'Abdu'l-Baha, and in 1914 wrote one of the most important books of the Unitarian Baha'i tradition, a history of the Baha'i faith entitled *A Brief History of Beha U'llah*.

This chapter is reproduced from a portion of Mr. Gazvini's historical narrative which was translated from the original Arabic into English by Edward G. Browne and published in his *Materials for the Study of the Babi Religion*, as Chapter 1 of that book, "An Epitome of Babi and Baha'i History to A.D. 1898." Most of the section headings appear therein. The same narrative appears in *A Brief History of Beha U'llah*, but in a different English translation.

Although Mohammed Jawad Gazvini's testimony was not included in Shua Ullah Behai's book manuscript, I have added it here because it is one of the most significant testimonies by a devout follower of Baha'u'llah who worked closely with him for years, who became a Unitarian Baha'i. Mr. Behai omitted some of the more partisan writings, such as this one, from his manuscript, probably because he did not wish to focus on the allegations against his uncle 'Abdu'l-Baha. Such omission may have been intended not only to protect 'Abdu'l-Baha's image, but also perhaps the image of the leading figures of his own Unitarian Baha'i tradition, some of whose writings were inflammatory at times.

If we wish to consider objectively the traditions that developed under the leadership of Abbas Effendi and Mohammed Ali Effendi, we should be aware of the deep animosity that existed between their respective supporters. Just as it may be disturbing to read the Will and Testament of 'Abdu'l-Baha and perceive the vitriol directed at the Unitarian Baha'is and their leader, some of the material in Mohammed Jawad Gazvini's testimony in this chapter is similarly vitriolic, indulging in the same kind of demonization of the other side that the Unitarian Baha'is deplored when it was directed at them. For example, Mr. Gazvini says that 'Abdu'l-Baha's followers "manifested joy and gladness and quaffed the drinks commonly used on festivals," upon the death of Zia Ullah Effendi, one of Baha'u'llah's sons who had sided with the Unitarians.

However, we must also be open to the possibility that Mr. Gazvini was describing the real attitudes of some Baha'is. Even more disturbingly, he claims to have been an eyewitness to an attempted abduction of Zia Ullah's widow, Soraya Samandari, orchestrated in person by 'Abdu'l-Baha's wife. Some of the thuggish behavior described in this document make the Baha'i community of Acre under 'Abdu'l-Baha look frankly like a cult—if Mr. Gazvini's account is to be believed.

Regardless of whether one wishes to believe or reject his portrayal, Baha'is should understand that Mohammed Jawad Gazvini was one of the closest and most respected of Baha'u'llah's companions; his version of events cannot simply be dismissed because it is unpleasant for adherents of the Baha'i faith to contemplate. Mr. Gazvini was, in fact, in such an elite group of early Baha'is that he was one of only nine persons chosen by 'Abdu'l-Baha to hear the reading of Baha'u'llah's will, before it was released to the whole Baha'i community. Speaking of which, Mr. Gazvini corroborates Mohammed Ali Bahai's claim that part of that will was concealed by 'Abdu'l-Baha under a sheet of paper to prevent its entire contents from being read.

Another of the more interesting parts of this chapter is a selection of quotations from a treatise by 'Abdu'l-Baha, quoted by Mr. Gazvini and juxtaposed against writings of Baha'u'llah, which in his opinion demonstrate an inappropriately lofty claim of Divinity by the successor of the Baha'i prophet. In this editor's opinion, Mr. Gazvini's argument on this point seems somewhat stretched or exaggerated, though not without merit. In one of the quoted verses 'Abdu'l-Baha does describe his station as "explicitly differentiated, like the Sun in all its phases, from all that is on the earth." If this is an authentic quotation, then it should come as no surprise that some Baha'is found it inappropriate and protested against such claim, since the metaphor of the Sun is commonly used in Baha'i scriptures to refer to the Manifestation of God. Mainstream Baha'i doctrine ultimately settled on the idea of 'Abdu'l-Baha as the Moon, perfectly reflecting the light of the Sun[1]—not in essence a Manifestation of God, yet revealing the Divine Light—but there may have been a period during which beliefs about Abbas Effendi's station were open to more grandiose interpretations, perhaps in part due to his own writings and utterances.[2]

—The Editor

Gentle Character of Baha'is in the Time of Baha'u'llah

The loftiness of the teachings and counsels of His Holiness our Great Master Baha'u'llah in His days produced a great effect on the

---

[1] Shoghi Effendi called 'Abdu'l-Baha "the stainless Mirror of [Baha'u'llah's] light... the Moon of the Central Orb of this most holy Dispensation." (*The World Order of Bahá'u'lláh*, 1991 first pocket-size edition, p. 134).

[2] Juliet Thompson, a well-known American devotee of 'Abdu'l-Baha who is regarded by mainstream Baha'is as a credible source, corroborates Mohammed Jawad Gazvini's claim that 'Abdu'l-Baha called himself the "Sun." As she wrote in her diary in 1912, remembering her pilgrimage to the Holy Land in 1909: "I was on the roof of the House in 'Akká with the Master [i.e. 'Abdu'l-Baha] and [his daughter] Munavvar Khánum. The Master was pointing to the moon. 'The East. The moon. No!' He said. 'I am the Sun of the West.'" (*The Diary of Juliet Thompson*, Kalimat Press 1983 edition, p. 232).

character of His companions and showed far-reaching results, so that they attained in virtuous attributes, good manners, humane conduct, and spiritual qualities to a station where they were seen, on occasions of afflictions, sorrows, calamities, and troubles, (to be) patient, acquiescent, thankful, acting according to the purport of this blessed verse of the *Kitab-i-Aqdas*: "Whosoever is angered against you, meet him with kindness, and he who revileth you, revile him not." And this verse: "That ye should be slain for His good pleasure is better than that ye should slay."

In short, by the elevating influence of His Holiness our Master Baha'u'llah they used to meet the oppressor with gentleness, the aggressor with pardon, and the vituperator with love. In many lands they were slain but did not slay, notwithstanding their power so to do on some occasions, as happened at 'Ishqabad (Ashgabat) in Russia, where the Shi'ites dwelling there one day murdered one of this community named Haji Muhammad Riza of Isfahan in the public thoroughfare with cutting, wounding iron weapons, such as daggers, knives, and the like. The crime was proved against them in the law-court, and sentence was pronounced by the Russian government that the two murderers should be hanged. But when the gallows was erected for their execution, the companions (i.e. the Baha'is) went to the governor and begged that intercession might be made with His Majesty the Emperor for their release and pardon. So the governor interceded, and the sentence of death was commuted, by command of the emperor, to banishment to Siberia.

Degeneration of Baha'is under Abbas Effendi

But alas, alas for what we see today! All these spiritual virtues and humane practices have undergone a complete change. Concord has been replaced by dissension, constancy by cruelty, and affection by enmity. Dissent and mutual avoidance have appeared in this community, and their concatenation has been dissolved and their assembly dispersed. All this that has been mentioned has happened by reason of the love of self and seeking after supremacy emanating from "Ghusn-i-A'zam" Abbas Effendi, and his opposition to the last Testament of His

Chapter 23. Events After the Departure of Baha'u'llah   313

Holiness our Great Master Baha'u'llah. For He (Baha'u'llah) says in Persian—may my life be sacrificed to His utterance!—"Every soul from which the scent of existence (i.e. love of self) is perceived today is the cause of discord."

He has also informed us in most of His tablets that His object in making manifest His dispensation was to cause religious hatred to disappear from the world, and to diffuse love and concord and kindliness amongst the nations. But after His ascension (i.e. His death) events took place and sayings became current which produced great discord and mutual avoidance within the [Baha'i] community, by reason of what issued from Abbas Effendi, as has been stated, so that antagonism and separation arose between father and son, brother and sister, husband and wife, and so forth; nay, God be our refuge! even enmity and hatred.

In this connection I will mention certain events and matters which gradually came to pass after the death of His Holiness our Great Master Baha'u'llah, some of which I beheld with my own eyes, while others I heard from trustworthy witnesses. These I will mention briefly, lest the reader be wearied, so that the Guardians of the Divine House of Justice and all just and fair-minded people may be the better informed and admonished, and may set themselves to amend what has happened.

Part of Baha'u'llah's Testament Held Back by Abbas Effendi

The first difference which happened after the death of His Holiness our Great Master within this community was that Abbas Effendi concealed some part of the book of (Baha'u'llah's) Testament entitled "the Book of My Testament,"[3] which book was given to him by Baha'u'llah in His own holy writing.

The detail of this is that on the ninth day after the ascension (i.e. the death of Baha'u'llah) Abbas Effendi chose nine persons from amongst the companions, one of whom was the author (of this book) [i.e. Mr. Gazvini], and disclosed to them this document, concealing, however, a portion of it with a blue leaf (of paper) without any reason

---

[3] Or "Book of My Covenant," i.e. *Kitab-i-'Ahdi*.

or justification, and gave it to them that they might enjoy the blessing of its perusal. One of them, named Aqa Riza of Shiraz, read it at a sign from him down to the place concealed by the blue leaf, whereupon Abbas Effendi said to the persons above mentioned, "Verily a portion of this book is concealed for a good reason, because the time doth not admit of its full disclosure." On the afternoon of that day Majdeddin Effendi read it again, by command of Abbas Effendi, in the Holy Place [i.e. the Shrine of Baha'u'llah], before a company of the *Aghsan* (sons of Baha'u'llah), *Afnan* (kinsmen of the Bab), *Muhajirin* (exiles), *Mujawirin* (settlers in Akka) and *Musafarin* (temporary visitors), down to the afore-mentioned passage, as narrated above.

Let it not be hidden from persons of discernment that the injunctions set forth in the above-mentioned book all refer to this community generally; how then could it be right for Abbas Effendi to disclose what he wished and conceal a portion thereof? For there is no doubt that if what was so concealed had not been suitable (for general publication) His Holiness Baha'u'llah would not have written it in His august writing.

The duty of sons is to carry out the testamentary instructions of their father, not to reveal a portion and conceal a portion thereof, according to their private ideas and opinions or personal inclinations; for His Holiness Baha'u'llah says: "O (Divine) Beauty! Verily I have spent my soul and my spirit for the glorification of the Word and the exalting of the Dispensation of thy Glorious and Beneficent Lord. If we see one of the 'Branches' (*Aghsan*, that is sons) otherwise than as God willeth, we will rightfully drive him away: verily I am the Mighty, the All-Powerful."

Abbas Effendi's Claim

The second difference was that His Holiness our Great Master has said in numerous places in His holy scriptures, plainly and explicitly, that no fresh Manifestation shall take place until a full thousand years shall have passed from this Theophany; and that if anyone advances a claim to any such position before the completion of this period, whosoever he be, and from whatsoever place he be, he is a vain pretender

Chapter 23. Events After the Departure of Baha'u'llah

worthy of rejection; as when He says in the "Most Holy Book" (*Kitab-i-Aqdas*): "Whosoever layeth claim to a (new) Dispensation before the completion of a full thousand years is a liar and prevaricator. ... And whosoever construes this verse or interprets it otherwise than as it hath been obviously revealed is deprived of the Spirit of God, and of His mercy which encompasseth all the worlds."[4]

But Abbas Effendi, after he had attained to supremacy, clearly and explicitly adopted the position of originality,[5] and claimed such lofty stations and high degrees as belong exclusively to Divine Theophanies, and even proclaimed in public in America that he was the Messiah and the Son of God, and in India that he was the promised *Bahram*.[6]

Thus he says in one of his writings: "The Dispensation in its entirety hath reverted to this visible place (i.e. himself), and it is not (permissible) for anyone to stir save after his permission." And again: "Whosoever calls on men in my Name, verily he is from me."

(But) His Holiness our Great Master says: "Whosoever layeth claim to any station, rapture, ecstasy or craving otherwise than in this (my) Name, verily he is of (the number of) the most lost, though he speak with all utterance,[7] and cause rivers to burst forth from rocks, and control the winds, and cause the clouds to rain."

And Abbas Effendi says in Persian: "Say, 'the Goal and Sum of all are the products of this Pen, and the proof is that which this tongue utters.'"

(But) His Holiness our Great Master says in Persian: "What this Oppressed One desireth of all is justice and equity. Let them not be satisfied with listening, but let them ponder on what hath been manifested by this servant. By the Sun of the *Bayan* arising from the horizon of the heaven of the Kingdom of (God) the All-Merciful, had there been found anyone (else) to explain or to speak, we would not have made ourselves the object of men's revilings and calumnies." And again, in

---

[4] *Kitab-i-Aqdas* ("Most Holy Book"), paragraph 37.

[5] Note by E. G. Browne: "i.e. of being the bearer of a new Revelation, and not merely the interpreter and maintainer of that given by Baha'u'llah."

[6] Note by E. G. Browne: "The expected Saviour of the Zoroastrians or Parsees."

[7] Note by E. G. Browne: "Or, 'with all the *Bayan*,' i.e. all the utterance of the Bab."

the "Chapter of the Pen" (*Suratu'l-Qalam*): "Say, 'Into the heart of whomsoever it entereth to rival this Pen (i.e. Baha'u'llah himself), or to associate himself therewith, or to approach it, or to know what is revealed by it, let it be surely known that the Devil hath whispered into his soul: thus hath the matter been revealed, if ye would know it.'"

Abbas Effendi says in Persian: "This servant is the expositor of the perspicuous Book, and whatever of God's writings is not confirmed by this servant is not worthy of credence."

His Holiness our Great Master says: "The Covenant was taken at the time of the Dawn from those who believe that they should not worship (aught) save God, nor work mischief in the earth."

Abbas Effendi ascribes all the covenants and vows mentioned in the sacred books to himself, as his words prove. Thus he says in Persian: "In short, verily from the beginning of Creation until now there hath not happened or appeared any plain covenant or clear promise like unto this. Yea, there have been promises, but they were not beneath the shadow of the Tree of Prophecy and the Lote-Tree of the Limit, but were only suggested by allegories. But in this great cycle and luminous epoch the Object of the Covenant is visible in the horizons and the Center of the Promise is known amongst the people of the world."

His Holiness our Great Master says in Persian: "Though one should adduce all the scriptures in the world, yet speak otherwise than as God willeth, he is mentioned in God's Book as of the Fire [i.e. hell], and is (so) inscribed by the Supreme Pen."

Abbas Effendi says in Persian: "The Dispensation in its entirety reverts to the recognized and acknowledged place, and this Station is distinguished, witnessed, and explicitly differentiated, like the Sun in all its phases, from all that is on the earth."

And he has many other utterances of this sort in his treatise, available to all in a text lithographed from a copy made by one of his well-known disciples. Let him, therefore, who desires (further) information peruse this treatise entitled "the Production of the Proof,"[8] for therein is what amply suffices.

---

[8] Note by E. G. Browne: "*Ityanu'd-dalil li-man yuridu'l-Iqbal ila siwa'i's-Sabil*, lithographed (in Egypt?) on Safar 1, 1318 (May 31, 1900). See pp. 188-9 infra. [in *Materials for the Study of the Babi Religion*]."

Enmity and Dissension Fostered by Abbas Effendi

The third difference is that His Holiness our Great Master Baha'u'llah in many passages of His writings, as also in the book of His (last) Testament, commanded this community to do away with discord, to extinguish the fire of sectarian hatred, and to consort with all religions with kindness and friendliness, as He says in Persian:

> By the Sun of Truth arising from the horizon of the heaven of this prison (i.e. Akka), never did the Beauty of Eternity desire strife and discord, or aught whereby (men's) hearts are troubled! Refer to the tablets: He saith, "Consort with (all) religions with spirituality and fragrance." The object of this Theophany is the extinction of the fire of hatred kindled in the hearts of the creeds, and the abatement thereof by the *Kawthar* of the utterance of divine counsel and celestial admonition. In this very year, A.H. 1306 (1888-9 [A.D.]), a tablet was revealed in the writing of this Oppressed One wherein this sublime word shone forth from the horizon of the Supreme Pen: "O people, speak well of (God's) servants, and speak not of them evil, or that whereby their souls may be troubled." The mention of evil hath also been forbidden in this law, because the tongue is for the commemoration of the truth, and it is pitiful that it should be defiled by backbiting or uttering words which cause sadness and grief to (God's) servants.

He says also in Persian in "the Book of My Will" [i.e. *Kitab-i-'Ahdi*]: "The object of this Oppressed One in bearing hardships and afflictions is the revealing of verses and the showing forth of proofs, so that the fire of malice and hatred may be quenched; then perhaps the horizons of men's hearts may be illuminated with the light of concord and may attain to true peace." And again in the same Book: "O people of the world! God's religion exists for love and concord: do not make it a means to enmity and discord!"

But Abbas Effendi has nullified this most great gift and most high and glorious aim, since he, for his private ends and personal aims, has instituted hatred and discord amongst the people of Baha, in such wise that he has introduced division and separation between brother and sister, fathers and sons, husband and wife, friend and old comrade; and whosoever does not agree with him in his ideas and statements, and does not speak evil concerning his brother Mohammed Ali Effendi "Ghusn-i-Akbar" and the Holy Family [of Baha'u'llah] is accounted a "violator" (*Naqiz*) of the Covenant and a "vacillator" (*Mutazalzil*), nay, an infidel, wherefore they avoid him and hold it unlawful to speak, or converse, or have any dealings with him. Let it not be hidden from the intelligent that the causes of discord are numerous, but the author has not touched on them fully from a desire for brevity.

The sum of the matter is that this schism took place on account of what has been mentioned, and for (other reasons) which have not been mentioned, so that this cleavage resulted, and this community became two communities. On the one hand are the followers of Abbas Effendi, who constitute the majority. Most of these believe him to be possessed of the Supreme Immaculacy [or Infallibility] and to be the Mirror of "He doeth what He will,"[9] as is witnessed by their published treatises in handwritings well-known (to all). They ascribe to him the high degrees and lofty stations peculiar to the Divine Manifestations, and name themselves "the steadfast" (*ath-thabitun*).

On the other hand are the minority, who find Abbas Effendi and his claim, his sayings, and his ideas at variance with the commands of His Holiness our Great Master; who regard Mohammed Ali Effendi as submissive to God and obedient to the commands of His Holiness Baha'u'llah; and who conceive of him as of a finger who points to his Master, so that they agree and unite with him, and are called "Unitarians" (*ahlu't-Tawhid*).

Mohammed Ali's Followers Demand a Conference

When it became certain that a schism had taken place, Mohammed

---

[9] This is a reference to the infallibility of the Manifestation of God. As Baha'u'llah wrote: "He Who is the Dawning-place of God's Cause hath no partner in the Most Great Infallibility. He it is Who, in the kingdom of creation, is the Manifestation of 'He doeth whatsoever He willeth.' God hath reserved this distinction unto His own Self, and ordained for none a share in so sublime and transcendent a station." (*Kitab-i-Aqdas*, paragraph 47).

Ali Effendi and those who were with him, in conformity with the commands of His Holiness our Great Master, where He says in the *Kitab-i-Aqdas*: "If ye differ in any matter, refer it to God, so long as the Sun continueth to shine from the horizon of this heaven (i.e. so long as Baha'u'llah is alive); and when it hath set, then refer to what hath been revealed by Him: verily that sufficeth the worlds"; and in another place in Persian: "O divers peoples, turn towards unity, and become illuminated with the light of concord: meet in some place in godly fashion, and put away from amongst you whatever is the cause of difference"; (—In accordance with these precepts, I say) they repeatedly communicated with Abbas Effendi asking him to appoint a sitting in godly fashion and to choose a few representatives from both sides to discuss the matter with the utmost loving-kindness as regards the disagreement and its causes; to make the efforts necessary to remove it; to weigh words and thoughts in the balance of God's scripture; and to distinguish the truth from all else by the criterion of His (Baha'u'llah's) words.

Moreover they besought the acceptance of this proposal with the extreme of supplication and sincerity, and repeated their request many times, but obtained no answer from him (i.e. Abbas Effendi), nor would he in any wise consent to this, perceiving that reference to the verses explanatory (of this question) would be contrary to his private ideas and personal advantage, and knowing that the truth would be revealed by reference to them, and that all men would recognize the vanity of the ideas and expressions current in the assemblies of Abbas Effendi and his followers and contained in their writings.

So hatred and aversion increased between the two parties, and matters reached a pitch which one dislikes to describe in detail, and they uttered with regard to Mohammed Ali Effendi and the family of the House of Greatness (i.e. members of Baha'u'llah's family who rejected the claim of Abbas Effendi) statements and allegations at which reasonable people were horrified, paying no heed to the injunctions of His Holiness our Great Master where He enjoins in His honorable writings respect for the "Branches" (*Aghsan*), wives and family, even as He says in the Book of His Testament, "respect and heed for the 'Branches' (*Aghsan*, i.e. sons) is incumbent upon all for the glorifying of the Dispensation and the uplifting of the Word."

Abbas Effendi Favors Those Who Most Exaggerate His Position

The fourth difference was that the more the followers of Abbas Effendi increased in the exaggeration of his praise, and described him by names and attributes proper only to the Divine Majesty, the more he magnified his gifts to them and the more graciously he treated them. So they exaggerated the more, and carried matters to the point of polytheism,[10] exceeding all limits in respect to him. Thus they took certain verses of the *Suratu'l-Amr* and made them a separate tablet, which, they asserted, was Abbas Effendi's, so that they might establish for him a glory proper only to Divine Theophanies.[11] And Abbas Effendi himself made alterations in one of [Mirza Aqa Jan] the Servant's letters to Muhammad Mustafa of Baghdad in Beirut, that is to say added to it and diminished from it, saying that it was a tablet which the Lord had revealed to him.[12] Moreover he claimed that the Holy Tablet specially addressed to his brother Mohammed Ali Effendi[13] was shared by himself.

Again the Servant (i.e. Mirza Aqa Jan of Kashan, commonly called Janab-i-Khadimu'llah), during the days when His Holiness our Great Master sojourned at Adrianople, had written a tract wherein he made mention of the mischief [i.e. opposition or persecution] of the days of the Manifestation. This tract Abbas Effendi named "the Tablet of the

---

[10] Note by E. G. Browne: "[The sin in Islam called] *Shirk*, i.e. associating partners with God."

[11] The *Suratu'l-Amr* or *Súriy-i-Amr* ("Tablet of Command") is known to have been written by Baha'u'llah to his brother Mirza Yahya, announcing his claim to be a new Manifestation of God.

[12] This document is known as the *Lawh-i-Ard-i-Ba* ("Tablet of the Land of Ba")—sometimes called the "Tablet of Beirut"—and is regarded as an authentic revelation of Baha'u'llah in the mainstream Baha'i tradition. Unitarian Baha'is considered it to be a letter written independently by Mirza Aqa Jan Kashani to one of the Baha'is in Beirut, and accused 'Abdu'l-Baha of altering it, falsely attributing its authorship to Baha'u'llah, and falsely claiming to be its recipient. Some of the language in the *Lawh-i-Ard-i-Ba* seems to exalt Abbas Effendi to a station of divinity.

[13] The document reproduced in Chapter 10, sometimes called the "Sacred Tablet" by Unitarian Baha'is.

Mischief," saying that it was a holy tablet revealed from the Supreme Pen, and ordered it to be read in the assemblies, his object therein being to cast doubts into men's hearts, so that they might imagine that the utmost importance belonged to his days. Again our Great Master, before He made known His mission, warned us of the advent of "the grievous days," meaning thereby the days of His Manifestation. But after the Manifestation He declared in one of the holy tablets that they had come to an end. But Abbas Effendi said in answer to a question concerning "the grievous days" that they were the year of the ascension [i.e. death of Baha'u'llah], in order to establish the importance of his own days, as has been mentioned.

And notwithstanding all that we have mentioned, he asserted that his brother Mohammed Ali Effendi had tampered with the published divine verses, I mean the (edition of the) *Kitabu'l-Haykal* ["Book of the Temple"] lithographed in the days of His Holiness our Great Master, whereof many copies exist in the writing of Zayn (u'l-Muqarrabin)—who is well known amongst this community and who collated this lithographed edition—and said that the verses which were not confirmed by him [i.e. Abbas Effendi] were not to be relied on, intending thereby to prevent his followers from referring to these divine verses, lest they should become aware of his (Abbas Effendi's) opposition to the holy writings in word, deed, declaration, and writing.

Abbas Effendi Deprives His Brothers of Their Allowances

In the fourth year after (the death of) His Holiness our Great Master (i.e. about 1896), the partisans of Abbas Effendi held a meeting in his audience-chamber at his suggestion, took counsel with one another, and agreed that what was given of the necessaries of life to the Holy Family and to his brothers was on no account permissible; wherefore Abbas Effendi cut it off completely, so that he compelled them to borrow for household expenses, because they were deprived of means. This was a wrongful act on his part, because whatever (revenue) reached him from the different countries was not his private property, but belonged to the entire Holy Family, as will not be hidden from the discerning. Yet he cut it off from them, and spent it on whom he would of the officials and men of influence,[14] in order to effect his personal aims, not acting conformably to truth, justice and equity.

Death of Zia Ullah

In the sixth year after (the death of) His Holiness our Great Master (i.e. 1898) a grievous sickness overcame Zia Ullah Effendi, by reason of the vehement emotion caused in him by the existing events and differences. After some days he went for change of air to Haifa, where the malady increased in gravity. And during the days of his illness neither Abbas Effendi nor any of his family or followers came to visit his sick brother or to enquire after him; until the signs of dissolution appeared, on the afternoon of the 14th of Jumada II, A.H. 1316 (October 30, 1898), when Abbas Effendi came, stayed a few minutes, and then returned to his lodging. Next morning he came, accompanied the corpse to the gate of the town (Akka), and after a short while went to the Palace (of Bahja), tarried a while there, and returned to Akka, but was not present at the funeral, nor anyone of his family and followers.

They did not even close their shops and offices on that day, as is customary, but on the contrary manifested joy and gladness and quaffed the drinks commonly used on festivals. This behavior (on their part) astonished all, whether present or absent, kinsmen or strangers.

Attempt to Abduct the Widow of Zia Ullah

Zia Ullah Effendi had a wife [Soraya Khanum] whose parents and brothers were followers of Abbas Effendi, who summoned them to his presence, desiring by their means to draw her to himself. But since after her husband's death she chose faithfulness (to his memory) and the service of Her Holiness his mother [i.e. Baha'u'llah's widow Mahd-i-'Ulya], with whom she dwelt in the Palace of Bahja, Abbas Effendi sent her parents and her brother to the Holy Place. They sent a certain

---

[14] This is presumably a reference to the practice of *baksheesh* (legal bribery), which was rampant in the Ottoman Empire as a means to gain favorable decisions from government officials.

Chapter 23. Events After the Departure of Baha'u'llah

woman of the partisans of Abbas Effendi to her mother-in-law, demanding an interview with the girl, that is, the widow of Zia Ullah Effendi, in the Holy Place; which request being granted, she came in company with the above-mentioned woman to the Holy Place and met her parents and her brother, who held her in conversation with enquiries as to her condition and declarations of affection, walking meanwhile towards the gate, on emerging from which her parents and brother seized her by force, and carried her off, holding her hands and feet to drag her to the place where a carriage was in readiness to carry her away. Abbas Effendi's wife [Munirih Khanum] was present in person to superintend the arrangements described above, while some of her relations and followers were helping the parents in her abduction, she being bareheaded and bare-footed, crying out and asking for help, and saying "O Baha, help me! They have taken me by force!"

This event happened at a time when Mohammed Ali Effendi and Badi Ullah Effendi were absent, and no one was present except the Servant of the Presence [Khadimu'llah], and a few of the Unitarians. The author of this history and some others of the companions were proceeding towards the Holy Place to visit it, and we happened to be there when they brought her out crying for help. We and the Servant hastened to the spot and delivered her out of their hands. But Abbas Effendi, when he perceived that he was foiled in his scheme and saw that it had not succeeded, ordered some of his followers to write a pamphlet in which the matter was entirely misrepresented, and sent it with the signature of the ill-used lady's father (I mean the widow of Zia Ullah Effendi) to Egypt to Hajji Mirza Hasan of Khurasan [i.e. Khorasani], who printed and published it in the lands by his command.

Protest of Mirza Aqa Jan (Janab-i-Khadimu'llah); Ill Treatment and Death

In the fifth year (after Baha'u'llah's death), on the 26th of Dhú'l-Hijja, A.H. 1314 (May 28, 1897),[15] the Servant of God [Khadimu'llah] invited all the companions to the neighborhood of the Holy Place in

---

[15] Note by E. G. Browne: "This was the fifth anniversary of Baha'u'llah's death."

Bahja, where, after they had partaken of food and drunk tea, he stood up about the time of the afternoon (prayer) and addressed the people, saying:

> This servant has been silent all this time and has not uttered a word, for fear of giving rise to dissension. Now, however, I perceive that my silence causes increase of discord in God's religion; therefore I say unto you that the deeds and words which have issued from Abbas Effendi and his company are all contrary to God's commands, and at variance with His injunctions revealed in the holy scriptures. The Covenant and Promise mentioned aforetime in the immaculate writings refer exclusively to previous and subsequent Theophanies, but Abbas Effendi has appropriated them to himself, and you have so accepted them, wherein you have greatly erred.

One of Abbas Effendi's followers (Sayyid Hadi) informed him of the Servant's words, whereupon he at once appeared on the scene, seized him by the hand and expelled him from the house bareheaded and bare-footed, while his followers beat him on the head and face, he crying out meanwhile in a loud voice, addressing them, "Verily ye are now in the neighborhood of the Holy Place, while I am speaking to you with discriminating signs (verses), that thereby the true may be distinguished from the false and the polytheist from the Unitarian." Yet not one of them listened to him, but they continued to beat him and to drag him to the Holy Place, where Abbas Effendi struck him with his hand a painful blow. From the Holy Place they took him by command of Abbas Effendi and imprisoned him in a stable, after they had taken from him such writings and letters as he had on him. After that they denounced him as reprobate, apostate, croaker, hypocrite, and devil, notwithstanding the recommendations of His Holiness our Great Master concerning him and His command to them in the Book of the (last) Testament,[16] and in other tablets also, to honor the Servant, even as He

---

[16] Here Mr. Gazvini is corroborating Mohammed Ali Bahai's claim that the original text of the Will and Testament of Baha'u'llah included a recognition of the station of Khadimu'llah. See the section entitled "Abbas Effendi Conceals Part of Baha'u'llah's Will" in Chapter 16.

says in a tablet in His own holy writing: "And after the 'Branches' (*Aghsan*, i.e. the sons of Baha'u'llah) show honor to the Servant who stands before the Throne in a laudable station."[17]

In short, after this event the Servant attached himself to the Place of our Great Master [i.e. the Shrine of Baha'u'llah], and used to spend his time with Mohammed Ali Effendi and the Holy Family in commemorating the Lord—glorious in His State—and in the service of the Universal Word, as is proved by his writings in his own well-known hand.

And after a time he went one morning to the house of Abbas Effendi at Akka to discuss and confer about the actual conditions and existing differences; but they shut the door in his face and prevented him from entering, and he sat before them on the ground for the space of two hours, begging Abbas Effendi and his partisans to produce the holy verses and tablets in their possession, so that he might discuss with them and they with him according to their purport, in order that it might appear what actions and words were conformable or contrary to them, and which thereof were acceptable in God's sight and which displeasing. But none would give ear; and finally Abbas Effendi sent his son-in-law named Mirza Muhsin [Afnan] to the government to say to the (Turkish) officials that the Servant had come to make mischief. Thereupon an officer came and took the Servant to the Government House, where they detained him for a while, after which they drove him out from the Palace.

So he continued worshipping and commemorating God and elucidating the Supreme Unity until he fell sick. His sickness lasted fifteen days, and on the 29th of Muharram, A.H. 1319 (May 17, 1901) he responded to the call of his Master in the Palace of Bahja, and was buried with the utmost reverence at Abu Ataba, Mohammed Ali Effendi and the Unitarians seeing to what was necessary for him in the way of washing, shrouding, and burial.

---

[17] Note by E. G. Browne: "The events here narrated form the subject of a separate tract of 16 pages, lithographed, entitled *Waqi'a-i-ha'ila-i-Khadim-i Abha dar Rawza-i-Mubaraka-i-'Ulya* ('The Dreadful Calamity of the Servant of Baha in the Blessed and Supreme Garden'). The persecutors were twelve in number, of whom eight are named."

Janab-i-Khadimu'llah's Books and Papers Appropriated by Abbas Effendi

The Servant during his days (of life) had repeatedly expressed his wish to the friends [i.e. the Baha'is] that all of the holy writings which belonged to him should return to God, and that after his death they should all be deposited in the Holy Place. So after his death Mohammed Ali Effendi, Badi Ullah Effendi, and some of the Unitarians, including the author, went one day to a house in the neighborhood of the Holy Place and examined the sacred mementos which the Servant had left. These included twelve holy portraits, two hundred and seventeen holy tablets produced by the Supreme Pen, and a number of the holy headdresses,[18] garments and hairs, besides many sacred books and a mass of correspondence, bound and unbound, and private possessions, and a number of tracts composed by the Servant concerning the Divine Unity and the Supreme Immaculacy. All these they wrote down (in a list), and placed in three boxes, which they sealed with two seals and deposited as a trust in the house of Sayyid 'Ali Effendi [Afnan], the son-in-law of His Holiness our Great Master, because he was a Russian subject (and therefore not liable to be molested by the Persian or Turkish government), so that they might be protected from interference at the hands of tyrants.

Recently, however, it appears that Abbas Effendi in the month of Safar, A.H. 1326 (March, 1908) obtained the consent of the Blessed Leaf and the Holy Spouse,[19] and of Sayyid 'Ali Effendi Afnan, and sent his son-in-law Mirza Muhsin [Afnan] and Aqa Riza of Shiraz by night in his private carriage to Bahja to bring him the three boxes deposited in trust as above mentioned, without the knowledge of anyone. And there is no doubt that the carrying out of this transaction secretly by night is a clear proof that it was contrary alike to the holy law and its ordinances, and to the common law and its provisions, for it was effected

---

[18] Note by E. G. Browne: "*Tijan* [plural of *taj*], literally 'Crowns,' i.e. the tall felt caps which Baha'u'llah used to wear."

[19] These terms probably refer, respectively, to Foroughiyya Khanum, the wife of Ali Afnan, and her mother Gawhar Khanum, the third wife of Baha'u'llah.

by theft and larceny. For Mohammed Ali and those who were with him had left the boxes there under seal as a trust, for the carrying out of the Servant's last testament and in order to give effect to it. How then could it be right for Abbas Effendi to appropriate them in this fashion, or that this treachery should be committed by him?

Increased Stringency of Control by Turkish Officials

After Abbas Effendi had attained to supremacy, he made a great display, by reason of the moral and material prestige which he now possessed. So likewise his followers did not observe prudence, wisdom, or moderation in affairs,[20] whence arose many troubles and difficulties, so that orders were issued by the Ottoman government to confine him and his brothers in the fortress of Akka. After a while there appeared four inspectors to investigate and enquire into the circumstances of certain of the officials and exiles, and they examined his (Abbas Effendi's) affairs also. After a while Khalil Pasha, the Governor of Beirut, appointed an inspector to watch him and ascertain who associated with him of the people of the country and others; and when he chanced on such a one, he used to bring him to the Government House, where he was examined to ascertain the cause of his frequenting the society of Abbas Effendi.

He, however, ascribed all that had happened to his brother Mohammed Ali Effendi, spreading this report abroad in the country, and thereby filling the hearts of his followers with hatred, enmity and aversion, so that they used to display the extreme of dislike and detestation in regard to Mohammed Ali Effendi and the Holy Family, and used to speak unseemly words concerning them.

But when Mohammed Ali Effendi discovered that his brother ascribed these occurrences to him, he communicated with him repeatedly by means of some of the officials and inhabitants of the city and some of his followers, and begged him to agree to appoint a time and

---

[20] The suggestion here may be that Baha'is in the Holy Land under 'Abdu'l-Baha's leadership were too open about preaching their faith, which was considered a heresy against Islam and a liberal social reform movement, and thus politically suspect in the conservative Muslim Ottoman Empire.

men to enquire into the truth of these matters, investigate these events, and ascertain their reasons and causes. This happened during the presence of the inspectors, and he requested him to appoint two persons on his behalf that they might go together to the local government and to the Board of Inspectors and formally demand (the production of) a note of complaint, if such were in their possession, on the part of Mohammed Ali against his brother Abbas Effendi, or an assertion that they were cognizant of some direct complaint on his part. For all official papers and legal complaints are preserved in the originals as well as in copies by the government in its records.

But Abbas Effendi would not accept this or agree to it, because he sought by these falsehoods and slanders to give effect to his plans [i.e. to discredit Mohammed Ali Effendi], and if he had appointed such persons and they had gone to the above-mentioned official quarters and made investigations, it would have become plain to all that these accusations were false, and these reports devoid of truth and reality. For it is not hidden that the false loves the darkness and hates the light, lest its evil circumstances and deeds should become apparent.

In short, this schism and its results were manifold, but space does not allow more (to be said) than what I have mentioned, so I have contented myself with this summary, having already set forth most of (the facts connected with) it in another treatise.

24

Letters About the Sons of Baha'u'llah

By Rosamond D. O. O. Templeton

Rosamond Dale Owen Oliphant Templeton (1846 – 1937) was a granddaughter of Robert Owen, founder of the utopian socialist community of New Harmony, Indiana. Rosamond's first husband, Laurence Oliphant, was a British author, world traveler, diplomat, and Member of Parliament. After the end of his political career, he took a keen interest in mysticism, Zionism, and new religious movements. Mr. Oliphant became a devotee of Thomas Lake Harris, a preacher and commune organizer with a background in Universalism, Swedenborgianism and Spiritualism, but later broke with his movement. Laurence Oliphant died only a year after marrying Rosamond. She then married James Murray Templeton, another disciple of Harris who was an artist and poet, but this marriage was also short-lived, as he committed suicide two years later.

Rosamond Templeton spent many years in the Middle East, and wrote a book about her experiences called *My Perilous Life in Palestine*. Throughout her life she was an idealistic intellectual and was interested in various utopian and progressive religious movements, including the Baha'is.

Mrs. Templeton is a key witness in Baha'i history, since she is a rare example of a non-Baha'i who developed personal relationships with both 'Abdu'l-Baha and his younger brothers and wrote about them. In fact, I have not come across any other testimonies by outside observers who were closely connected with Baha'u'llah's family as a whole, rather than only one side or another in the sectarian dispute that tore the family apart. Rosamond Templeton's observations are thus of tremendous significance in attempting to determine the truth about this crucial aspect of the history of the Baha'i faith. Although no one can be completely free of bias, her perspective may be as close as we can get to an objective account of the sons of Baha'u'llah, their personalities and stances toward one another.

The letters of Rosamond Templeton reproduced in this chapter were originally published by Ibrahim G. Kheiralla in *Facts for Behaists*. In that book, Dr. Kheiralla wrote:

> It happened that some of the believers, on our side, were well acquainted with Mrs. Templeton, an American, who has been residing in Haifa, Syria, for a long time. Personally, she had known Baha'u'llah and all His family. Her friends thought that as she is a faithful and devoted Christian, and as she is not a believer in our religion and therefore not partial, her testimony would be valuable. For this reason many believers in Chicago and New York wrote to her letters of inquiry, all of which she answered.[1]

Mrs. Templeton's overall point of view about the conflict between Baha'u'llah's sons and its tragicomic nature can perhaps be best summed up by her amusing rhetorical question: "With regard to the accusation that Mohammed Ali strokes his beard, I shall have to acknowledge that he does, but if Abbas Effendi intends to regulate the conduct of his brothers as to the innocent act of stroking their beards, need we wonder that they object to the unbounded authority which he claims?"

—The Editor

---

[1] Ibrahim George Kheiralla, *Facts for Behaists* (Chicago, 1901), p. 6. Available online at http://www.h-net.org/~bahai/diglib/books/K-O/K/kheiralla/Facts.htm

Letter to the Leaders of the Baha'i Faith in Persia (January, 1900)[2]

To the Chief Representatives of the Religion of the "Bab"[3] in Persia—Honorable and Venerable Effendis:

During a recent visit to Abbas Effendi to discuss certain business matters, which will be explained in the letter which follows, he asked me to examine and to judge the differences between himself and his two younger brothers, Mohammed Ali Effendi and Badi Ullah Effendi.

He made this request because I am writing a history of my sojourn in Syria,[4] including an account of my acquaintance with the sect of the "Bab" at St. Jean d'Acre,[5] and also because of the friendship, lasting during ten years, which has existed between the family of the sainted Baha'u'llah and myself.

This task I accepted and prayerfully considered, sending him the following letter after an interview with Mohammed Ali Effendi and Badi Ullah Effendi:

> Haifa, Syria, November 30, 1899.—To Abbas Effendi, the Chief of the Religion of the "Bab" at St. Jean d'Acre—Venerable Effendi:
>
> I came to see you to discuss money matters, without consulting your brothers, Mohammed Ali Effendi and Badi Ullah Effendi. When I said to them that I had asked for this money they were very much pained. I, therefore, have the honor to inform you that it is not necessary to trouble you further concerning my financial affairs.
>
> As Badi Ullah Effendi has rendered me many services he would have the right, in truth, to accept a pecuniary recompense, but your two brothers insist that they will not accept this recompense, although they are in great need. Therefore, it is not necessary to put you to any pains concerning this wrong.

---

[2] Ibid., pp. 19-24.

[3] At the time when this letter was written, the Baha'i faith was still usually considered to be a sect of Babism and referred to as such by Western observers.

[4] The Holy Land was part of Ottoman Syria.

[5] An old-fashioned name for the city of Acre.

During the visit which I made to you, you were good enough to ask me to judge between you and your brothers, in order that the history I am writing should be a trustworthy one, a history which will be read, probably, in Europe, in America, in Syria, and in Persia. After due reflection I find that I have only one request to make at present:

The principal accusation which you made against your brothers was that they have refused to obey you as the chief of the religion of "Bab" at d'Acre. You state that your authority is based on a Testament given by your venerable father, and you say that this Testament is in your possession and that it has been read by Colonel Bedri Bey.[6] On leaving your house I went directly to the house of your brothers in order to present to them your objection. Their answer is that they are absolutely ready to obey the Testament, which has been given by their father on condition that they can see this Testament written by the hand of Baha'u'llah.

This question, therefore, is a simple one. Effendi: I propose that you, Abbas Effendi, Mohammed Ali Effendi, Badi Ullah Effendi, and myself, with three witnesses chosen by you and three chosen by your brothers, an interpreter, an English photographer whom I will bring—I propose that these twelve persons shall meet at the sacred tomb of your father at noon on the 7th of December to read the Testament of Baha'u'llah and to take a photograph of that Testament. You said that I had judged between you and your brothers without hearing the two sides, your side and theirs; therefore, Effendi, in order to avoid this fault with which you justly reproached me I have written to Mohammed Ali Effendi and to Badi Ullah Effendi, asking that they also shall present their Testaments[7] during the reunion at the tomb of your father. Will you be

---

[6] Bedri Bey (also spelled Badri Beg) was an Ottoman colonel named Hasan Bedreddin and commonly known as Bedri Pasha. Because of his reformist views, he was removed from Istanbul to Palestine by Sultan Abdul Hamid II. There he became a friend of 'Abdu'l-Baha. After the Young Turk Revolution, he served as governor general (*vali*) of a province in present-day Albania.

[7] The specific nature of these "testaments" in the possession of Baha'u'llah's younger sons is unclear. They may have been copies of the will that was circulated among the Baha'is under the title "The Book of the Covenant," but it's possible that they were completely different documents instead. If they were different documents, they could have been tablets addressed by Baha'u'llah to

good enough to give me your answer, written in Arabic, in your own handwriting, as I have asked the same courtesy from your brothers?

If you refuse to show and to photograph the Testament upon which you found your authority, you cannot require the acceptance of that authority, for it is certain that if the Testament gave you this authority you would be quite ready to read it before witnesses and to send photographic copies of it to Persia.

Rosamond Templeton.

Emin Abdul Nour Effendi, the honorary dragoman of the English Consulate of Haifa, was good enough to present this letter to Abbas Effendi, and the English Consul was so courteous as to pay a visit to Abbas Effendi in order to set the matter before him, both these gentlemen having agreed to help me, not in an official, but in a friendly capacity, as the question is a moral and not a political one.

Abbas Effendi said to these gentlemen, in the presence of Ferrick[8] Pasha, the military commander of St. Jean d'Acre, of Colonel Bedri Bey and others, that he refused my request to read the Testament, and Emin Abdul Nour Effendi brought me this answer in person, as Abbas Effendi had not acceded to my prayer to send a written answer.

I also wrote to the two younger brothers the following letter:

Haifa, November 30, 1899.—To Their Excellencies, Mohammed Ali Effendi and Badi Ullah Effendi:

Your venerable brother, Abbas Effendi, has had the goodness to ask me to examine and to judge the differences between himself and you. As the principal accusation of Abbas Effendi against

---

each of his sons, such as the one quoted in Chapter 10. However, the most likely explanation, taking into consideration Mr. Bahai's autobiography (see the section entitled "Abbas Effendi Conceals Part of Baha'u'llah's Will" in Chapter 16), is that each son had a copy of the *Kitab-i-'Ahd* but that they believed their copies were not identical to the original version. Mrs. Templeton would therefore have requested all of Baha'u'llah's sons to "present their testaments" so that the original document, in 'Abdu'l-Baha's possession, could be compared to the copies which he had made and distributed to other Baha'is such as his younger brothers.

[8] Usually spelled Fariq.

yourselves is that you have refused to obey his authority, and that the authority he claims is given him by the Testament of Baha'u'llah, your sainted father—this being the accusation, there is one sole means of satisfactorily judging these differences—namely, to examine the three Testaments, that of Abbas Effendi and the two which you possess.

As Abbas Effendi has begged me to examine these differences, he has given me the right to ask that his Testament be submitted to an examination, but you, Effendis, have not accused your brother to me, and I have no right, therefore, to ask that your Testaments should be inspected. But, knowing that you desire an honorable peace between you and your brother and that you are ready to take any legitimate means of establishing that peace, I take the liberty of asking that you also, Effendis, shall submit your Testaments to an examination, although, in truth, I have no right to make this request, as I have in the case of Abbas Effendi.

I beg you, therefore, to meet us at the sacred tomb of your father on the 7th of December, at noon, with Abbas Effendi, three witnesses chosen by him, three witnesses chosen by you, an interpreter, a photographer to photograph the Testament, and myself. Will you have the goodness to give me an answer, written by each of you in your own handwriting, as soon as possible? May I present to you, Effendis, my sincere good wishes?

Rosamond Templeton.

To this letter I received the following reply, in Arabic, with a translation in French, which I translate into English, as follows:

Acre, the Castle, December 2, 1899.
Virtuous and Celebrated Authoress, Madame Templeton—May God preserve your person!

We have received with gratitude your amiable letter and have carefully considered your gracious proposal, which has enhanced your charm and has lighted in the urn of our hearts a brilliant flame, because it manifests your pacific disposition and your eagerness to do good. We pray the All-Powerful God to assist your person to bring to a successful issue [i.e. result] your generous initiative and wise intention and to accord to you a worthy reward.

With regard to your invitation to attend a reunion on the 7th of December, 1899, at noon, to examine the noble Testaments and to take a photographic copy, we accept willingly, and we shall repair to the meeting with much pleasure, because Testaments are destined for publication and not destined to be hidden away. As we two are agreed and of the same opinion, we have thought it best to address you together, in order to avoid repetition, and we pray you to accept the assurance of our perfect respect and our desire that you shall always be enriched by Divine blessings.
MOHAMMED ALI EFFENDI.
BADI ULLAH EFFENDI.

The original of this letter in Arabic is in my possession, and if anyone in Persia desires to see it I can send them a photographic copy.

The facts and letters above cited I desire to present to the representative men of the religion of the "Bab" in Persia, adding the following suggestions: The only reason Abbas Effendi could have for refusing to read the Testament would be that it contained secrets sacred to his father and himself which he is not allowed to divulge, but as he has read this Testament to Colonel Bedri Bey, so he (Abbas) stated to me, this statement being confirmed by Colonel Bedri Bey himself, and as he (Abbas) stated to Emin Abdul Nour Effendi that he had sent copies of the Testament to the Sultan of Turkey and the Padishah[9] of Persia, he cannot refuse, on this plea, to read the Testament to his two brothers, the children of the sainted Baha'u'llah.

Will your Society in Persia allow me to suggest that all good persons would approve of a request sent by representative men among you to Abbas Effendi, asking him to read and to photograph his Testament, in order that this difference existing during several years may be adjusted? I am taking the liberty of writing you this letter and of asking an answer addressed to Checri Effendi, Cardahi, pour Madame Templeton, Haifa, Syria, because I wish to record in my history the decision of your honorable society.

---

[9] A more respectful title that was sometimes used for the Persian Emperor, i.e. Shah.

Will you permit me to say, in conclusion, venerable Effendis, that in the beginning of my long acquaintance with the family of the sainted Baha'u'llah I respected and admired all the brothers, one as much as the other? During these years I have seen them often, and gradually my respect for Abbas Effendi has decreased and my respect for the Effendis Mohammed Ali and Badi Ullah has increased, both these younger brothers following strictly the religion of their father, no matter how difficult it has been for them, whereas Abbas Effendi has failed to be true to the noble principles of his noble father.

I have seen Badi Ullah Effendi more than any of the brothers and now have a true friendship for him, founded on many experiences in which he has been most honorable.

I am sure all good and wise persons would rejoice to see this worthy youngest son of your revered Baha'u'llah relieved from the many anxieties he has suffered—anxieties which would be removed by a clear and explicit understanding of the will of Baha'u'llah, as expressed in his last Testament to Abbas Effendi, a Testament the younger brothers are willing to obey in every detail, as they have said to me many times.

If Abbas Effendi is, in truth, the noble person which he claims to be, can he refuse this legitimate request?

Will you accept, Effendis, my sincere good wishes, desiring that your venerable days may be long and prosperous?

Rosamond Templeton.

Excerpt from Reply to Mr. and Mrs. W.[10] (March 10, 1900)[11]

And now for the question between Abbas Effendi and the younger brothers. Abbas Effendi is a remarkable man, and might have been a noble one except for one defect. His pride, alas! is very great. In the beginning I had a true affection and esteem for all the brothers and Abbas Effendi was, naturally, the prominent figure among them, but as the years have passed, I have esteemed him less and the others more,

---

[10] Remainder of the surname redacted in Ibrahim Kheiralla's publication of this letter.

[11] *Facts for Behaists*, pp. 6-8.

although the Spirit of God may at any time awake the original character, which was a fine one. For the present, however, he seems to be blinded, and I am very sorry.

Some months since a saintly old man named Agha Jamal came from Persia on horseback (the ride taking three months and three to return), for the sole purpose of reconciling Abbas Effendi to his brothers; it was a touching act of devotion, and I have rarely seen a man to whom I was more drawn. The Spirit of God was upon him.

Abbas Effendi refused to give him any satisfaction and paid no heed to his requests. A short time after I called upon Abbas Effendi and told him some disagreeable truths (which, by the way, he received with a perfect courtesy, the courtesy of the Orient we westerners would do well to copy). In this interview he asked me to look into and to judge the differences between himself and his brothers, a request which astonished me, as many notables among the Persians and Turks had asked to do this and were refused by him.

I accepted the task. He stated during this interview, first, that his chief accusation against the younger brothers was that they failed to recognize and to obey his authority; second, that this authority was founded on the Testament given him by his father, Baha'u'llah; third, that several persons had seen this Testament, but his brothers were not among these.[12] Each of the other brothers has a Testament from their venerated father.[13]

The matter, then, was a very simple one. I wrote letters to the three brothers, the Effendis, Abbas, Mohammed Ali, and Badi Ullah, asking them to meet at the tomb of their father, which is their shrine, on a certain day, and there to read the three Testaments before witnesses selected by either side and myself, and also that I might be permitted

---

[12] This conflicts with Mohammed Ali Bahai's claim, in his autobiography, that 'Abdu'l-Baha did show him the original will and testament of Baha'u'llah.

[13] This statement by Mrs. Templeton is ambiguous. She could be referring to their copies of the document that was circulated under the title "The Book of the Covenant," or perhaps to some other unspecified writings of Baha'u'llah. Mrs. Templeton herself might not have known exactly what documents Messrs. Bahai had in their possession, only that they said they had something different than what 'Abdu'l-Baha possessed.

to bring a photographer to photograph the Testaments, in order that copies might be sent to Persia. Abbas Effendi refused this request, and the two younger brothers accepted it, saying that they were willing to obey to the letter the Testament of Baha'u'llah belonging to Abbas Effendi, any commands their venerable father had issued being sacred, but that they must see the Testament with their own eyes 'ere they could obey it.

This was certainly a most reasonable demand and one which Abbas Effendi should have been only too happy to grant. With regard to business matters, Abbas Effendi has not been just to his brothers, who have suffered a great deal, and very nobly and uncomplainingly, in consequence.

This, then, my dear friends, is a concise history of my relation to the Babists [i.e. Baha'is]. Badi Ullah is one of my best friends here, a man of a singularly sweet and pure nature whom all must respect who know him well. Nevertheless, as I have said, the noblest Christians I have known have been the noblest people I have met on earth; although many among us may learn great lessons from this people [the Baha'is], I, among others, being grateful to them for the good they have done me. Will you remember me kindly to Mr. Kheiralla and accept the good wishes of your sincere friend,

Rosamond Templeton.

Excerpt from Reply to Dr. Frederick O. Pease (March 23, 1900)[14]

The morning after your letter came, Mohammed Ali Effendi called on me and I read it to him. His sole answer was, "We must pray that the Spirit of God shall return to my brother." I said, "There is one way only whereby Abbas Effendi can find his true, his noble self—namely, by humiliating his pride." "That," said Mohammed Ali, "will be very difficult for him, I fear." The charitable gentleness of his manner as he spoke of his brother filled me with respect and admiration, knowing as I do how much the younger brothers have suffered at the hands of the elder during the past eight years.

---

[14] *Facts for Behaists*, pp. 8-9.

With regard to the personal questions in your letter, let me say:

1st. That Badi Ullah Effendi is one of the most temperate men I know. In dress, in speech, in manner, in food, in drink, he practices the restraint of a balanced nature. I do not wish to accuse Mr. G.[15] of a deliberate falsehood, for it is quite possible that he may have mistaken someone else for Badi Ullah, but it is quite certain that Mr. G. is mistaken. The Effendi has dined with me many times and has never even taken a glass of wine, contenting himself with my own beverage, cereal coffee. The Babist religion does not forbid the use of wines,[16] as does the Mohammedan, but it enjoins moderation in all things, and the younger sons of Baha'u'llah obey this instruction strictly.

2nd. With regard to the sale of personal effects, I can say nothing, as I have no information, but if the younger brothers sold these effects they were compelled to do so by the conduct of Abbas Effendi. The family has an income from the government, as well as a revenue from three villages. These funds Abbas Effendi has appropriated for eight years, and with these has made his charitable gifts, leaving the forty dependents of the younger brothers to live as best they could; the anxiety of these years has marked the faces of the younger brothers with deep lines of care. The government money they could have reclaimed simply by presenting a request to the Mutasarrif[17] of St. Jean d'Acre, but they refused to take those steps, believing that a legal accusation of their brother, Abbas Effendi, would be against the spirit of their father's wishes.

3rd. With regard to the accusation that Mohammed Ali strokes his beard, I shall have to acknowledge that he does, but if Abbas Effendi intends to regulate the conduct of his brothers as to the innocent act of

---

[15] Remainder of the surname redacted in Ibrahim Kheiralla's publication of this letter.

[16] Mrs. Templeton apparently was unaware that Baha'u'llah did prohibit his followers from drinking alcoholic beverages. It was not a major teaching, however, and some early Baha'is might have ignored it or not even known of Baha'u'llah's position on the subject.

[17] A *mutasarrif* was an administrative official who governed a district in the Ottoman Empire, such as a city or small region.

stroking their beards, need we wonder that they object to the unbounded authority which he claims?

4th. As to the accusation that they are "profligate," it is wholly untrue. The whole tenor of the lives of these pure and high-minded gentlemen disproves this assertion.

Ibrahim G. Kheiralla.

25

Autobiography

By Ibrahim G. Kheiralla

Ibrahim George Kheiralla[1] (November 11, 1849 – March 6, 1929) was the first Baha'i missionary to the United States of America, made the first American converts to the Baha'i religion, and organized the first Baha'i spiritual assemblies in the U.S. After clashing with 'Abdu'l-Baha over matters of doctrine and leadership style, he was stripped of his role as the chief spokesperson and organizer of the Baha'i faith in America. He switched his allegiance to the Unitarian Baha'i movement of Mohammed Ali Bahai, leading hundreds of American Baha'is into that sect, at least temporarily.

This chapter is taken from a 1917 book by Dr. Kheiralla entitled *O Christians! Why do Ye Believe Not on Christ?* The titles of some sections have been added, removed, or altered from the original by this editor. Most of this autobiography was included in Shua Ullah Behai's book manuscript, although Mr. Behai omitted some parts. In the "Visit to Akka" section, the omitted portion begins with "Now, I will relate some of those sad events for the sake of presenting the truth…" and ends just before the paragraph that begins, "Abbas Effendi urged me and my wife to live together in peace…" In the "Beginning of the Dissension in America" section, the omitted portion begins with "Since 1900, many communications have taken place between me and his Excellency, Mohammed Ali Effendi, El-Akbar…" All sections of the autobiography after that were omitted by Mr. Behai completely.

---

[1] Also spelled Khayru'llah.

I have pulled three of the omitted sections from the original document and included them separately in Chapter 27, because I felt they would fit better there; and I have restored the other omitted portions here in this chapter. Between these two chapters, I have reproduced Dr. Kheiralla's entire autobiography in this book. The key role he played in spreading the Baha'i faith to the United States—and its great schism—makes his testimony very historically significant and worthy of an unabridged reprinting.

The portrait of Ibrahim Kheiralla that emerges in his autobiography is that of a vigorous, extraordinarily effective Baha'i teacher or evangelist who had a strong interest in theology, an argumentative personality, and little tolerance for a people-pleasing approach to religion. He appears to have been driven by a desire to discover absolute truth through the study of scripture, and was unwilling to submit to charismatic authority, instead demanding the production of Baha'u'llah's writings and open debate about religious ideas. As a new immigrant to the United States, he easily associated with people of substance and was able to convert some of them to an exotic Middle Eastern religion—some of whom went on to become important and celebrated figures in the Baha'i faith even after they no longer supported their first teacher's interpretation of it.

Dr. Kheiralla's impressions of 'Abdu'l-Baha, gleaned through his personal interactions with him during a visit to the Holy Land, are particularly interesting in this chapter. He describes Abbas Effendi as "a powerful and shrewd Turkish and Romish diplomat combined," a master of emotional manipulation who played upon his followers' desire for an all-knowing guru figure and demanded and received their absolute loyalty and submission. Dr. Kheiralla describes how, at first, 'Abdu'l-Baha lavished him with extravagant titles, praise, and attention, but then cut him out of the loop when he began to argue with him about doctrines. Both men were clearly intelligent and talented religious leaders who thought highly of themselves, their beliefs and abilities, and the clash of egos predictably led to a falling out. Ibrahim Kheiralla seems to have been doctrinaire and inclined to endless, perhaps fruitless debate, whereas 'Abdu'l-Baha is presented as the type of leader who cared more about consolidating his power, who would say and do whatever is necessary at any given time to win or impress a follower or to turn a situation to his advantage. Dr. Kheiralla accuses 'Abdu'l-Baha of being an "artful fawner" and shares examples he claims to have witnessed of his deceptiveness and calculated methods of affecting the Baha'is to gain their sympathy and devotion.

The author goes on to describe his relationship with Baha'u'llah's younger son Mohammed Ali Bahai and decision to join his sect. He claims to have received "not less than 150 letters from him wherein you cannot find one single word against his brother Abbas Effendi." In contrast, he describes 'Abdu'l-Baha as "full of accusations against his brother, El-Akbar, Mohammed Ali Effendi," and criticizes the elder brother for "threaten[ing]" Baha'is "with hell fire if they dare to disobey him."

Ibrahim Kheiralla makes two very serious, specific charges against 'Abdu'l-Baha in this document: First, that he sent one of his followers to offer a large cash bribe to Dr. Kheiralla if he would once again join 'Abdu'l-Baha's side in the schism; and secondly, that some of 'Abdu'l-Baha's followers threatened to murder him when he refused. Just as with 'Abdu'l-Baha's accusations of criminal intent by his brother Mohammed Ali and his followers, there seems to be no way, so long after the fact, to prove or disprove these charges; no convincing evidence has ever been presented by either side for the most heinous allegations they hurled at each other.

—The Editor

Introduction

I was born of Christian parents at the village of Bhamdoun, Mount Lebanon, Syria,[2] November 11, 1849. My father died before I was two years old, and my mother took the burden of raising and educating me

---

[2] Bhamdoun is located in the governorate of Mount Lebanon in the present-day country of Lebanon. This region was part of Ottoman Syria at the time of the author's birth.

and my only sister. My ancestors were Chaldeans[3] and fled to Mount Lebanon from the city of Antioch[4] because of persecution by the Turks. I got my diploma as a B.A. from the Syrian American College at Beirut, 1870 A.D.

I left for Egypt, where I spent one year as a teacher in an American Protestant academy, and then opened a business of my own. At Alexandria, Egypt, I married a Syrian girl, born in the suburbs of the city of Sidon, who was the mother of my three children: Nabiha, who married the Amir (prince) Hani Ali Schehab; Labiba, who married R. G. Saleeby; and George I. Kheiralla, who graduated as a Doctor of Medicine from the Northwestern University in Chicago.

I was somewhat prosperous in Egypt, traded in cotton and grains, and had cotton and sugar plantations. For eight years I was the contractor of the sugar factory at the city of Biba in upper Egypt. Also I had a drygoods store at Cairo called "London House," which I sold to Mr. and Mrs. Cole, an English couple.

After the death of my first wife I married a Coptic[5] widow whom I divorced before I believed in Baha'u'llah. I embraced the Baha'i religion in 1890 and married a Greek girl. In that same year a tablet was revealed to me by Baha'u'llah which I inserted at the end of my work entitled *Beha 'U'llah*.[6]

On June 19, 1892 A.D., I left my family in Cairo, Egypt, for St. Petersburg, expecting to return to them in the course of three months. My object in going to Russia was to sell to the government a walking apparatus which I had invented for preventing fatigue. For I hoped to regain the losses I suffered in a case against Abdul Malik Beyk through the interference of Lord Cromer,[7] who made the case a stepping stone

---

[3] Chaldeans are ethnic Assyrian adherents of the Chaldean Catholic Church, a branch of the Assyrian Church of the East which entered communion with the Roman Catholic Church in the 17th century.

[4] Present-day Antakya, Turkey.

[5] Copts are the native Christians of Egypt.

[6] Dr. Kheiralla was the recipient of several tablets of Baha'u'llah, who often wrote such epistles to teach and inspire important followers of the new faith.

[7] Evelyn Baring, 1st Earl of Cromer, who served as the British Controller-General and Consul-General in Egypt.

for the English to control the Egyptian local tribunes. When the deal with the Russian minister of war was off, I left for Germany, then for France. At last I crossed the ocean to the United States of America in a German vessel called *Swavia*, and landed at New York City three days before Christmas, 1892.

Bringing Baha'ism to the U.S.A.

In the winter of 1893, I taught my faith to a few Syrians in New York City, and discussed some of its principles with Prof. Briggs,[8] to whom the Presbyterians attributed heresy on account of his religious views. Also I visited Dean Hoffman[9] of Chelsea Square, a theological institution, and discussed with him the Baha'i principles and Prof. Briggs's views. There I met Ernest Jewell, whom I met while he was touring in the land of Egypt. He took me with him to Grand Rapids, Michigan, then to Petoskey, where he was ordained as the Deacon of the Episcopal Church by both Bishop Tuttle of Missouri and Bishop Gillespie of Michigan. I tried to convert him to my faith, but later I heard that he became a Catholic priest. I lectured in Grand Rapids concerning religion and Egypt, and also in Kalamazoo and Dowagiac on my way to Chicago, which I reached in February, 1894. Then I began to preach the appearance of the Father and the establishment of His Kingdom on earth.[10]

Although it was hard work for me to make the Americans understand my deficient English speech, yet in 1894 and in the beginning of 1895, I converted many intelligent and well-educated persons. They were all convinced and persuaded of the truth of the Baha'i religion,

---

[8] Charles Augustus Briggs, an American Presbyterian scholar and theologian from New York City, who was a professor of Hebrew and Biblical theology at Union Theological Seminary. He was excommunicated from the Presbyterian Church in 1893 for his liberal religious views.

[9] Eugene Augustus Hoffman was a wealthy and prestigious Episcopal clergyman who in 1879 was appointed dean of General Theological Seminary, which is located in the Chelsea neighborhood of Manhattan.

[10] Dr. Kheiralla regarded Baha'u'llah as the manifestation of God the Father, in Christian terms, and the fulfillment of Biblical prophesies of the coming (or second coming) of the Messiah.

and that it was the fulfillment of Christ's predictions and the prophecies of the old prophets. Among them were Mr. William F. James, Mr. [Edward] Dennis, Mrs. Wilcott, Mrs. Kendall, the late Mr. Arthur Dodge,[11] Dr. Straub and Dr. Augusta Linderborg and so forth.

Upon realizing my success in teaching, I made up my mind to become a United States citizen and live the rest of my life in America. So I sent word to my Greek wife twice to join me, and each time her answer was an absolute refusal. On these grounds the State Court at Chicago granted me a decree of divorce. This divorce was known and declared to all believers men and women. In the summer of 1895, Miss Marian Miller and myself married at the house of Mr. William F. James, the first of the American believers. We both left for Europe and there I became acquainted with her relatives in France and in England, and converted her aunt, Miss Browne of London, to the Baha'i religion.

In the same year we returned and lived on the west side of Chicago on Monroe Street, and I began the teachings again. Many new seekers after the truth came and I taught them in classes with from five to twenty-five persons in each class. I used to deliver open lectures Friday evenings and Sunday afternoons and gave the hearers nearly an hour at the end of the lectures, to ask questions which were all answered to the satisfaction of the whole audience.

In 1896, I published *Bab-ed-Din*, which contained several chapters on "The Identity of God," "The Oneness and Singleness of God," "The Vicarious Atonement," which were combined and published in my work *Beha 'U'llah*. In the same year Mr. Lane of Kenosha, Wisconsin, induced me to go once a week to his home, where I taught a class the same lessons I gave in Chicago, and the whole class, with the exception of one member, embraced the faith. I sent Mr. Dealy to Kenosha to teach in my place when the seekers crowded me in Chicago. For nearly two years, I used to teach classes, one after the other, from one o'clock p.m. to eleven and twelve p.m., and retired to my bed tired out and exhausted. Then I organized an assembly in Kenosha and appointed Mr.

---

[11] Arthur Pillsbury Dodge was an attorney, inventor and entrepreneur, and publisher of *New England Magazine*.

Lane as its teacher. Another assembly was organized in Racine, Wisconsin, most of whose members took the teachings first at Kenosha.

I never taught the Baha'i religion secretly as Dr. Wilson alleged,[12] but in a manner as you see the lessons arranged in *Beha 'U'llah*. The first lesson, "Immortality." The second, "Mind." The third, "Life," and so forth. Also I taught privately; that is to say, I did not allow beginners to attend the lessons which were to be given to the advanced members. Each class and person of all those who took the lessons, took them without deviation or variance as they were arranged and published in *Beha 'U'llah*.

In the summer of 1897, myself, my wife and son spent the vacation in the city of Enterprise, [in the] state of Kansas. We spent two months there, during which I taught a class and converted twenty-one persons to the Baha'i faith.

Mrs. Lida H. Talbot and the late Mr. Arthur Dodge (both took the teachings in Chicago and moved to New York City) requested me, in 1898, to come and teach New York seekers and a few others from New Jersey. Through the influence of Mrs. Talbot and her friend, Miss Kern, the number of those seekers was about two hundred. They were divided into three classes: one of them took the lessons at the home of the late Dr. Gurnsey, the second at the Nineteenth Century Hall, and the third at the boarding house where we and the late Arthur Dodge's family were boarding. At the end of four months 141 souls out of the three classes were converted into the Baha'i religion. Later I organized them as a Baha'i assembly and appointed Mr. Howard MacNutt as their teacher.

On my way from Chicago to New York City, I stopped for a few days at Ithaca, New York, by the request of the late Mrs. Getsinger,[13] whom I authorized to give the teachings to a class while she was visiting her

---

[12] Samuel Graham Wilson was acquainted with Ibrahim Kheiralla and wrote a 1915 book criticizing the Baha'i faith, called *Bahaism and Its Claims*. In that book he alleges that Dr. Kheiralla "first taught Bahaism in secret lessons, as a religion of mysteries, a secret order..." (p. 266 in 1970 reprint).

[13] Lua Getsinger went on to become a prominent Baha'i teacher in the mainstream tradition and was posthumously designated as one of nineteen "Disciples of 'Abdu'l-Baha" by Shoghi Effendi Rabbani. She died in 1916.

relatives. I helped her in giving the class the final lessons, and then I gave them the Greatest Name of God[14] and taught them how to practice it.

During my stay in New York City for teaching, I frequented the city of Philadelphia and helped Mrs. Sara G. Herron, whom I sent to teach a class which I formed there. The outcome of our endeavors was the conversion of about twenty-five souls into our new faith.

Writing *Beha 'U'llah*

To safeguard and protect my teachings from changes and misrepresentations by the teachers whom I appointed to teach, and also by the others who studied them, I made up my mind to put them in black and white in the form of a book and publish them. In the summer of 1898, I rented a typewriting machine and took my wife and Mrs. Anna Bell with me to the north part of the state of Maine, to a city called Lubec.[15] Nine weeks I spent there walking to and fro in my room and reciting the lessons as I gave them to the classes, and Mrs. Bell wrote them on a typewriter as I dictated. We worked from six to nine hours every day until I finished twenty-one chapters of the book, which I named after the name of the Manifestation [of God], *Beha 'U'llah*. I kept of the work two copies typewritten by Mrs. Anna Bell as a remembrance of that event. One of them was entrusted to the care of Mr. Hoar[16] in New York and the other I took with me when I went to Akka.

While I was dictating the twenty-second chapter to Mrs. Bell, Mrs. Kheiralla, who seldom visited the room when we were working, entered

---

[14] *Allah-u-Abha*, which means "God is Most Glorious." Islam has 99 names for God, and the Baha'i faith adds *Abha* as the 100th and supposedly greatest name. Another commonly used form of the Greatest Name is *Ya Baha'u'l-Abha!* which means "O Glory of Glories!" i.e. as an invocation to God. The title Baha'u'llah comes from the same Arabic root, *bahá*, meaning glory or splendor. Baha'u'llah instructed his followers to recite the Greatest Name ninety-five times a day.

[15] The town of Lubec is actually located at the easternmost tip of Maine.

[16] William H. Hoar owned and operated a sanatorium in New Jersey. He became a speaker and administrator in the mainstream Baha'i community and was posthumously designated as a Disciple of 'Abdu'l-Baha.

and exclaimed, "Good news, very good news!" Then she read a telegram sent by Mrs. Getsinger from California, that Mrs. P. A. Hearst[17] accepted the teachings and wanted me and my wife to go with her as her guests to Akka, to visit the Tomb of Baha'u'llah and his family. We were urged to be in New York on the 20th of July, in order to cross the ocean to France. In a few days we arrived at New York, which I left for Chicago and Kenosha to bid the believers goodbye. At the appointed time, 20th of July, my wife and myself were in New York ready to sail with Mrs. P. A. Hearst and her company of guests.

During all this time I did not receive any money for the lessons I gave to the pupils, but I taught and lectured gratis. Also I made it a rule that all the teachers I appointed in different places should not receive wages or even presents for teaching the truth. I earned my living from my profession as a healer and on many occasions I refused to accept Christmas presents. Many times from my own pocket I paid the rent of the places of meetings for the Assembly which they never paid back to me.

Visit to Akka

In July, 1898, we sailed on the German steamship *Fuerst Bismarck*. I stayed in Paris a few days, during which I completed the teachings to Mrs. P. A. Hearst and companions, and gave them the Greatest Name and taught them how to practice it. In the meantime I enjoined on those who accepted the teachings with Mrs. P. A. Hearst, who lived in England and in France, to preach the appearance of the Kingdom of God on earth; and thus the Baha'i religion began to be taught in Europe.

I left Paris alone for Akka, and passed through Alexandria, Egypt, to see my two daughters, who were living there with their grandmother. I stopped twenty-one days with them until the German Emperor returned from Palestine, for strangers were not permitted to land at Haifa

---

[17] Phoebe Apperson Hearst was the wife of U.S. Senator George Hearst and the mother of newspaper magnate William Randolph Hearst. She was a noted philanthropist and advocate of women's suffrage.

so long as his Majesty was still in the Holy Land. My daughters were converted into the new faith and followed me later to visit the Tomb of Baha'u'llah. Also Mrs. P. A. Hearst and her companions reached Akka in succession, and the number of visitors who were originally Christians was sixteen persons. I stayed at Akka and Haifa more than six months, during which important events took place, which were as follows:

The next day after landing at Haifa I went to Akka with Huseyn Irani, the person appointed to meet the visitors at Haifa. In his drawing room on the second floor, Abbas Effendi entered and exclaimed: "Welcome, O beloved. O Peter of Baha, O second Columbus," and embraced me to his bosom. Then I sat beside him on a divan, and he talked with me and showed me a great deal of love and kindness, and asked me to stay at his home as a guest for which I sincerely thanked him. Next day a Turkish officer, a believer, visited me and placed on my head a fez in place of a hat and said: "Abbas Effendi has ordered this fez for Peter of Baha, the second Columbus, and discoverer of America." Henceforth believers congratulated me for this distinction and repeated my new names as Peter of Baha and so forth.

On my first visit to the room at Bahja in which the sacred remains of Baha's Temple [i.e. his body] were entombed, Abbas Effendi said that I was the first believer who ever entered the room for prayers. But afterwards other believers were allowed to pray therein.

One day at Haifa he took me with him to Mount Carmel in order to take the place of his second brother, Mohammed Ali Effendi, and I began to dig with him the foundation of the building he intended to erect for entombing the sacred remains of the Bab, which were expected to be brought soon from Persia. There we were furnished each with a pickaxe and dug out the ground, whilst a servant removed the earth. He then ceased to dig and ordered me to do the same and told me that I was the only believer upon whom this great honor was bestowed. He praised my teachings and declared their correctness to his followers; and in his writings to me called me "the shepherd of the people of God in America." Likewise his followers were very amiable to me, and even Bahiyyih Khanum, his sister, gave me her special book as a token of respect and said that this was a present from her to "Peter of Baha, the discoverer of America, who did for the Cause what the other teachers failed to do." I sincerely thanked her, and kept the book among what sacred relics I have.

Before visiting Akka I begged Abbas Effendi many times to send me some of the utterances of Baha'u'llah, so that I might compare my teachings with them, and correct them if there were mistakes; but all my appeals failed. When I was at Akka I ardently asked him again to give me some of the teachings of Baha, but he denied their existence saying, "All the writings were removed from Akka so that the Turkish officials could not find them, so as to make them a cause to persecute the followers." Then I translated a few chapters of my book, *Beha 'U'llah* into the Arabic language, so that he might correct them if they were wrong. But he approved them and praised them highly in the presence of the Western and Eastern followers.

One day Mrs. Kheiralla and Mr. and Mrs. Getsinger requested me to ask Abbas Effendi, 'Abdu'l-Baha, what was the symbolic meaning of the two unclean animals which were allowed to enter the Ark of Noah.[18] His answer was that they were ungodly people who pretended to be believers and deceitfully joined the Assembly of the faithful. Then I said to him, "Inasmuch as the Ark symbolically means God Himself, and as they cannot deceive God, so they cannot enter nor be allowed to come into it." He asked then, how did I explain it? I said, "The two unclean animals represented the parents whom God will kindly favor in this appearance [i.e. the manifestation of Baha'u'llah] for the sake of their children who believed in Him." Then he turned to them and said to me, tell them, "Every subject has two meanings, one spiritual, the other material; what I explained to you is right, and what Kheiralla explained, is also right."

Since then Abbas Effendi avoided answering any of the many questions which I asked him in order to gain more knowledge. This forced me to ask and discuss many subjects with the guides who were visiting there, like Ibn Abhar with whom I differed regarding immortality, the

---

[18] See Genesis 7:2.

return of the soul [i.e. reincarnation],[19] and the attributes of God Almighty. Because of this, 'Abdu'l-Baha appointed a meeting to discuss these subjects before him, that he might judge and adjust our differences. After a long discussion, Abbas Effendi said to me, "Your logic is good, but you must not limit God and clash with the Persian Doctors." I said, "Everything known is limited and as by the Infinite Knowledge of God He knows Himself, therefore God is limited Himself to Himself." He rejoined, "This is an error, you should not limit God, say He is independent and sanctified from His creatures." I retorted, "Is not the saying, 'God is independent from His creatures' a kind of limitation also?" Abbas Effendi's face turned white and frowned at me, then he rose up and smilingly said, "We shall discuss this question another time." Here ended the first and the last meeting on these subjects.

After this meeting a change took place in the conduct of the Persian and American believers; and even my wife turned against me. When I used to ask a question they answered, "Abbas Effendi alone can explain such subjects." And when I asked him personally, his answer was to wait for a better opportunity. I frequently asked for the books published in Bombay, India, by the order and in the lifetime of Baha'u'llah, but Abbas Effendi claimed that there were no copies of them to be found at Akka. At last I purchased them in Egypt on my way back to America.

Many other events of the same nature took place, yet they did not shake me nor make me nor my daughters deviate from the right path, because our belief was strongly founded on the predictions and promises of the Old and New Testaments. But we were very much grieved and surprised concerning the conduct of the Greatest Branch, 'Abdu'l-Baha. After our return to America and reading *Kitabu'l-Aqdas*,[20] God opened our eyes and we perceived the truth. It always takes time and patience to comprehend and realize facts. Now, I will relate some of

---

[19] Some passages in Baha'u'llah's writings speak of the return of prophets and saints of past religious dispensations in the present era. Ibrahim Kheiralla interpreted this as evidence for reincarnation of the soul. The mainstream Baha'i tradition, however, interpreted these verses metaphorically and rejected the idea of reincarnation.

[20] The *Kitab-i-Aqdas*.

those sad events for the sake of presenting the truth, and veil many others as it is not meet to mention them.

Abbas Effendi is a powerful and shrewd Turkish and Romish diplomat combined; and his policies are put in practice with such management and tact as to overwhelm even his most intelligent followers, to say nothing regarding the simple-minded among them. He meets all his visitors with love and kindness and surrounds them with some of his adherents at Akka and Haifa, who move with them wherever they move and humbly serve and obey them, and never leave them alone until they go to bed. Then they report to him all the events of the day. This system of spying is used in all countries where there are followers. He keeps his followers from reading the revelations of Baha'u'llah, that they may remain ignorant of the true teachings of the Baha'i religion.

His talks and writings are pathetic and full of accusations against his brother, El-Akbar, Mohammed Ali Effendi; and he relates that the suffering he is enduring from the Turkish government was brought about by the intrigues of this brother. In this way he gains their sympathy and estranges them from his good brother, so they may not meet him and learn the truth.

He made rules to interfere in all the actions, dealings, and correspondence of his followers with each other, and always tried to split them into parties against each other in order that all of them might appeal to him and ask his assistance.

The worst thing he has done is to put himself between his followers and their God, and to threaten them with hell fire if they dare to disobey him, thus creating in their hearts and simple minds the fear which was and shall be the worst enemy of mankind. Also he is drilling his grandson, Shoghi, the son of his daughter, to occupy his place after his death. This action alone proves beyond a doubt that he fell from grace, for it is a gross violation of the Last Will of Baha'u'llah, in *Kitabu'l-'Ahd*,[21] wherein Mohammed Ali Effendi was chosen to be his successor as a command from the All-Knowing.

One day Abbas Effendi invited Bedri Bey, a Turkish military officer, to dine with him and with the American visitors. Before going to the

---

[21] The *Kitab-i-'Ahdi*.

dining room he told my daughter Nabiha to tell the Americans to deny knowledge of the French language if Bedri Bey should ask them to speak it with him. When we sat at the table, Bedri Bey asked whether any of the ladies could speak French as he could not converse in English. According to the wish of Abbas Effendi, they denied being able to speak it, though several of them like Mrs. Kruper of London, and the late Mrs. Thornbourg, her mother, and Miss Aberson were able to speak it fairly well. Lying is detested by God, and whatever the reason may be, it is not permitted.

Once at the dining table, Abbas Effendi began to tell two of the ladies the important past events of their lives. I knew at once that he was informed of these events by an American visitor, for Mr. Getsinger gave me a list of those events written in English, and according to his (Getsinger's) request, I translated them into Arabic. Then Abbas Effendi looked at the most revered lady and said, prophesying, "After ten thousand years the newspaper of your son will be sent as a valuable present from one king to another." When we left the table I plainly showed Abbas Effendi my displeasure at such an action, but he laid his hand upon my shoulder and said, smilingly, "It is done for a wisdom which you cannot comprehend at the present time."

Again at the table, Mr. Getsinger asked Abbas Effendi to permit him to take his photograph. He answered that he was photographed once only when twenty-seven years old, in 1867,[22] at Adrianople, and he would be photographed once more when he puts the Taj of his Father on his head while they lead him to martyrdom, and where thousands of bullets would pierce his body. This made a great effect on us all and some wept bitterly. He has been photographed many times since, and his prophecy has not been fulfilled.

Abbas Effendi urged me and my wife to live together in peace when we bade him goodbye. But my wife laughed loudly when he said so and her laugh was interpreted when we arrived at Port Said, Egypt; she left me and my daughters without bidding us farewell, and without uttering a single word, to the astonishment of those who were present.

---

[22] This would place Abbas Effendi's birth in 1839 or 1840, contrary to the 1844 date in official Baha'i biographies.

Return to America; Decision to Join Mohammed Ali Effendi

Two months after my arrival in America [in 1899] I received a letter from Abbas Effendi written in his own handwriting, which I kept with the relics, signed [A. A.],[23] wherein he praised me and said, "Thou art the center of the circle of the love of God and the axis around which the souls revolve in their imploring and supplication to God." This letter settled me and I made up my mind that he was an artful fawner, because his letter was an answer to my inquiry [regarding] how and in whose name a rich person could send money to him. At the same time I was informed that the Getsingers, who came to America shortly after my own return, were circulating the story among the American followers that Abbas Effendi was not pleased with me and that my teachings were wrong and that Mr. Getsinger had been appointed as the head of the Baha'i movement in America, and had proved his claims by showing his credentials signed by Abbas Effendi.

Pondering over these sad events and studying the sacred texts of Baha'u'llah, which prove the fallacy of the claims, deeds, and teachings of Abbas Effendi, I abandoned Abbas Effendi and joined the lines of Mohammed Ali Effendi in obedience to the command of *Kitabu'l-'Ahdi* (The Book of My Covenant) and began to correspond with him.[24] I have in my possession not less than 150 letters from him wherein you cannot find one single word against his brother Abbas Effendi, but he urged us to pray for him that he may repent and return to God.

Beginning of the Dissension in America

Seven months after my return to America, in a meeting held in the

---

[23] 'Abdu'l-Baha typically signed his initials, standing for 'Abdu'l-Baha 'Abbas, both of which begin with the Arabic letter *'ayn*.

[24] The *Kitab-i-'Ahdi* appoints Abbas Effendi as the first successor of Baha'u'llah and Mohammed Ali Effendi as the next in line after him. Apparently Dr. Kheiralla, having decided that 'Abdu'l-Baha was a heretic, believed he was justified in transferring his allegiance to the latter son of Baha'u'llah even though the first son was still alive. Dr. Kheiralla's defection from 'Abdu'l-Baha and embrace of Mohammed Ali Bahai was a key event that confirmed the sectarian split between the brothers and enabled it to spread.

Masonic Temple, Chicago, I declared my separation from Abbas Effendi and my adherence to his brother Mohammed Ali Effendi. I asked those who were of my opinion to join me. About 300 in Chicago and Kenosha and many others in different places united with me. But the great majority remained with Abbas Effendi because the wealthy Americans were still of his party. In those days I gave my work *Beha 'U'llah* to the printers, Hollister Brothers of Chicago. Here I must express my gratitude to Mr. Howard MacNutt of New York City and sincerely thank him for editing and polishing the language of many chapters of that work.

A few months later, Abbas Effendi sent first Haji Abdu'l-Karim Tehrani[25] to restore me to him, but he failed to convince me [even] though he promised me that I should receive $50,000 as compensation from a wealthy American person.[26] Then Mirza Asadu'llah, a brother-in-law of Abbas Effendi,[27] and Mirza Hasan Khorasani were sent to restore me to Abbas Effendi or remove me out of the way. Several warnings came to me from Akka, and three detectives were appointed by the government [i.e. American police] to look after my safety. Asadu'llah, who is the father of Dr. Ameen Fareed,[28] informed the American followers of 'Abdu'l-Baha that I should die and appointed the day of my funeral should I disobey. The same day I met downtown an American follower who expressed surprise because I was still alive. Later Abul-Fazl [Gulpaygani] was sent and we never agreed nor met each other as Mrs. Getsinger was the messenger between us.

The bitter persecution, the sufferings, and the false accusations which were brought upon me by the followers of 'Abdu'l-Baha and his

---

[25] Mr. Tehrani (also spelled Tihrani) was the person who had first taught the Baha'i faith to Dr. Kheiralla.

[26] In 1900, $50,000 would have been worth over $1 million in 2014 U.S. dollars.

[27] Mirza Asadu'llah Isfahani was a prominent Baha'i teacher and organizer who married the sister of 'Abdu'l-Baha's wife.

[28] Dr. Ameen U. Fareed (also spelled Aminu'llah Farid or Amin Fareed) worked as a secretary and translator for 'Abdu'l-Baha. Their relationship deteriorated as 'Abdu'l-Baha reportedly disapproved of some of his actions such as unauthorized fundraising. Finally, 'Abdu'l-Baha excommunicated Dr. Fareed for moving to America against his orders to remain in Haifa.

envoys, and the most important events which took place after my return from Akka, are all recorded by the historian of the Baha'i movement in America, Frederick O. Pease, M.D. He intends to publish them before long, hence there is no need of inserting them in this brief autobiography.[29]

Since 1900, many communications have taken place between me and his Excellency, Mohammed Ali Effendi, El-Akbar; and her Grace the widow of Baha'u'llah, Mahd-i-'Ulya; and Khadimu'llah, Mirza Aqa Jan; and Mohammed Huseyn Shirazi and several others of the Holy Household, concerning the teachings of Baha'u'llah, which refute the claims and actions of Abbas Effendi, the Greatest Branch. This was plainly stated in my two works, *Facts for Behaists* and *The Three Questions*, published between 1901 and 1902.

Mohammed Ali Effendi, the Mightiest Branch, supplied me with hundreds of sacred tablets revealed by Baha'u'llah and many precious manuscripts written in the handwriting of Baha's scribes. Also he gave me valuable information in regard to the revelations and granted me priceless gifts such as a sacred tablet written in the sacred handwriting of the Father himself, and two tufts of his hair besides several sacred relics, and bestowed on me the title of "Doctor" in correspondence.

I continued to teach and hold meetings with those who joined me in different places in Chicago. In 1904 I married Miss Augusta Linderborg and went to the Exhibition at St. Louis, and thence to New York City. In 1906, we returned to Chicago, and I began to teach as usual and also taught two classes in the suburbs of Chicago, one in Evanston and the other in Wilmette. My wife passed away in 1912, a faithful and staunch believer in Baha'u'llah, and her last words on her death-bed were the Greatest Name of God, *Allah-u-Abha*.

In 1914, I returned to Chicago from the Black Hills, Rapid City, South Dakota, where I spent about eighteen months with my son, Dr. George I. Kheiralla. Here in Chicago I held some meetings with believers in Baha and decided to form an Association under the laws of the

---

[29] This editor has not been able to find a published document by Dr. Pease recording such events.

State of Illinois, known as the "National Association of the Universal Religion." ...

Joyful Close

For many years, my earnest desire and longing was to know, for a certainty, the existence of God, the Creator, and the hereafter, and personal immortality, and a distinct line separating intelligence from matter, and right from wrong. Through the grace of God, I came to the realization of these facts in my researches and studies, as is plainly shown in the teachings of both of my works, *Beha 'U'llah* and this one [i.e. *O Christians*, which contained this autobiography]. Every reasonable and just man can find in their contents strong scientific and logical proofs, which will convince and satisfy him that the above-mentioned facts were established. But even if we disregard all these proofs, and keep only what was mentioned in my works of the prophecies and predictions from the Bible, the Qur'an, and other scriptures, which are beyond the knowledge of man, and were fulfilled in the appearance of Baha'u'llah, it is enough to persuade every soul of the veracity of these facts. That is to say, that there is a Creator who sent prophets and messengers to mankind and taught personal immortality and the hereafter, and at the latter days He came Himself and established His Kingdom on earth, whereby our redemption became the established certainty, which we were promised by our Lord Jesus Christ.

Now, let us close this by raising up our hands to Heaven as Jesus did and joyfully say, "Praise be to Thee, O Father, for Thou hast granted us life-eternal by manifesting Thy Supreme Self and made us know that Thou art the only true God"; the Glory, the Kingdom, the Might, and the Power belong to Thee forever and evermore.

26

Arguments Against 'Abdu'l-Baha

By Ibrahim G. Kheiralla

This chapter is a short statement by Ibrahim Kheiralla, originally untitled, which was published in his 1901 book *Facts for Behaists*. Section headings have been added. It is a convenient summary of some of the most significant criticisms and complaints by Unitarian Baha'is against 'Abdu'l-Baha during the early years of the schism. Notably absent from this list is the charge that 'Abdu'l-Baha concealed part of Baha'u'llah's will.

The most shocking assertion in this chapter is that some of 'Abdu'l-Baha's favored teachers taught that he is "God Himself" and that "his position is superior to that of the Father," i.e. Baha'u'llah. It seems unlikely that 'Abdu'l-Baha would have approved of this—it certainly never became Baha'i doctrine—but if such ideas ever were circulated it could have been a factor in worsening the divide with the Unitarian Baha'is. As for 'Abdu'l-Baha himself, Dr. Kheiralla says that he "claimed to be a Manifestation... by hints and in obscure words and phrases." Whether or not that is a fair assessment of his claims, the basic thrust of the Unitarian Baha'i critique of 'Abdu'l-Baha—both by Ibrahim Kheiralla and other authors—is that he inappropriately sought to magnify his own station and dealt harshly with Baha'is who wanted to keep the focus on Baha'u'llah and his writings.

—The Editor

This is a brief answer to him who inquired concerning the actions of Abbas Effendi (the Greatest Branch) and his followers, which are repugnant to the commandments and laws that Baha'u'llah established during his sojourn here [on earth]:

Shunning

1st. Baha'u'llah expressly said that the distinguishing feature of His teachings during His earthly dispensation was the prohibition of discord and hatred and the establishment of union and love. He commanded His servants to associate with people of all religions with spirituality and fragrance [i.e. pleasantness].

The Greatest Branch strictly forbade his followers to associate, speak or correspond with the Unitarians, with whom they are not even allowed to have the slightest business transactions. All the inhabitants of Akka can bear witness to this.

Excessive Claims

2nd. Baha'u'llah said: "Whosoever claims to be a Manifestation (a prophet) is a lying impostor."[1]

Abbas Effendi, in his epistles, has claimed to be a Manifestation, not always in express terms, but by hints and in obscure words and phrases. Those who preach him throughout the countries explain these obscure phrases to mean that he is God Himself; sometimes they say that the Father and the Son are one and that Abbas Effendi is a new Manifestation, and that his words are to be received as inspired texts. They have written many epistles to this effect and have even said that his position is superior to that of the Father.

We have many epistles in the handwriting of his most advanced teachers which bear witness to what we state. Every honor, respect, and help are bestowed upon these teachers by Abbas Effendi. He praises and glorifies them in all his writings and sends them to different countries in order to accomplish his aims and spread his erroneous doctrines.

---

[1] This is a paraphrase of a verse from the *Kitab-i-Aqdas*, paragraph 37.

Disrespect for Baha'u'llah's Family

3rd. Baha'u'llah commanded everyone to respect the Branches, in order to strengthen the Cause. He expressly said that this command applies to the past as well as to the future. He also commanded that everyone should honor His family and relatives.

But Abbas Effendi ignored this command. Indeed, it would appear that Abbas Effendi wished the Cause to be suppressed, for Baha'u'llah, in the "Book of My Covenant," commanded us to respect the Branches in order to strengthen and elevate the faith.

Disrespect for Baha'u'llah's Secretary

4th. Baha'u'llah commanded us to respect and take care of His servant (Khadimu'llah, Mirza Aqa Jan).

But Abbas Effendi insulted and beat this servant at the Sacred Place (the tomb of the Manifestation) when he rose up to defend the Cause of God. Abbas Effendi was not satisfied with what he himself had done to this faithful man, but ordered his followers to imprison and cruelly beat him, which they did on the same day, and, had they not been in fear of the local government, they would have slain him. To the present day they curse and slander him and invent and spread false stories against him.

Cursing and Slander

5th. Baha'u'llah prohibited backbiting and slander, execrating and cursing, etc., but Abbas Effendi caused his followers to commit all these crimes, in order that he might attain his purpose. This can be proved by attending their meetings or by reading their writings, which are now in our possession.

Trusting Unreliable People

6th. Abbas Effendi neglected the relatives and others whom Baha'u'llah had relied upon and had confidence in. He slighted them upon all occasions and also ordered his followers to do likewise. On the other hand, he displayed great confidence in and reliance upon those whom the Father in his day had considered to be unreliable. These people Abbas Effendi allowed to do in all matters as they pleased.

Spreading His Own Writings, Not Baha'u'llah's

7th. Baha'u'llah commanded us to publish His Sacred Word and spread it as soon as possible, but Abbas Effendi tried by all means in his power to prevent this order of Baha'u'llah from being carried out. His followers are only allowed to read those parts of the works of Baha'u'llah which, according to his interpretation of them, support his claim. Should it happen that someone is present in their meetings whom they believe to be still a firm adherent of Baha'u'llah they will then read some of the shorter communes of the Father. Otherwise, all they read and circulate at the present time are the writings of Abbas Effendi. His believers are prohibited from reading the important tablets and books of Baha'u'llah.

Shutting Down Baha'u'llah's Publishing Company

8th. By the command of Baha'u'llah, signed by His written command, a lithographic press was established in India for the publication of the holy books and for the purpose of spreading them throughout the world. Some of the books were published at that time and some after His departure [i.e. death].

Abbas Effendi did his utmost to destroy that press and prevent his followers from having or using the sacred books printed by it.

Disbanding the Spiritual Assembly of Egypt

9th. By the command of Baha'u'llah, signed by His hand, a company was established in Cairo, Egypt, and its vicinity, called "The Spiritual Company,"[2] for the sole purpose of serving the Cause of God. Abbas

---

[2] Mohammed Ali Bahai calls it "The Spiritual Association." See Chapter 16, the section entitled "Organizing Baha'i Communities in Egypt and India." These are likely two different translations of the same word in Arabic.

Effendi struggled hard for its destruction and eventually succeeded.

In this manner he destroyed the most important works established during the lifetime of Baha'u'llah, in order that no traces of what was done in those days might remain.

The above is a brief statement of what Abbas Effendi has done against the commandments of the Father, but we have seen and heard many things of what he has done and said of which it is not wise to write—things which can only be imparted verbally.

Fabricating and Distorting Baha'u'llah's Writings

In answer to the question, "Has Abbas Effendi ever dared to change the texts uttered by Baha'u'llah?" we say, most certainly, "yes"; and we have no doubt that whenever he and his followers find a change of the texts necessary they will alter them, for when a man dares to alter one word of the texts he is liable to change whatever he desires.

We have in our possession many of the texts of Baha'u'llah which have been changed by Abbas Effendi. We send you a few of the most important ones.

1st. The so-called Tablet of Beirut. Abbas Effendi's family produced a paper which at first they claimed was written by the servant of Baha'u'llah, Khadimu'llah (Mirza Aqa Jan), and sent to the Greatest Branch (Abbas Effendi) when he was at Beirut. Later they claimed it to be one of the utterances of Baha'u'llah and called it the "Tablet of Beirut." But Khadimu'llah, the servant of Baha'u'llah, denies that it ever was written by him and says that it is not one of the utterances of Baha'u'llah. Abbas Effendi does his utmost to impress his followers with a belief in the authenticity of this document.[3]

2nd. They took one of the sacred surahs (tablets), which is called the "Tablet of Command,"[4] and omitted from the middle of it some of its verses and then claimed it to be a special tablet to the Greatest Branch (Abbas Effendi). They have written this tablet in their epistles. It so happened that we saw these tablets and we refuted their claim, for

---

[3] See Chapter 23, note 12 for more about this disputed document.

[4] *Súriy-i-Amr*. See Chapter 23, note 11.

we have this very tablet in the handwriting of Baha'u'llah, and then they were silenced. It is still read secretly to those who have not this knowledge of the works of Baha'u'llah, as the special tablet to Abbas Effendi.

3rd. They have taken texts from two different tablets and made out of them one tablet, called "The Treasure Tablet," and claim that it was given specially to Abbas Effendi. When we received a copy of this we produced the two tablets from which it was taken and explained that clearly in our epistles. Then Abbas Effendi denied having composed it, and actually said that we, the Unitarians, had written it! But to this day some of his followers and teachers in India still produce this so-called "tablet" as proof of his claim.

4th. He misinterpreted the Arabic word *tawajjuh*, which means "to look to"; he said that it means "to look to him (Abbas Effendi) from all directions," and as we should look to God, so we must look to him. This interpretation is always so used by him and his followers.[5]

5th. Abbas Effendi has attributed [as referring] to himself a paragraph from a tablet called the "Sacred Tablet," which belongs entirely to the Mightiest Branch (Mohammed Ali Effendi), and his followers use that paragraph as a further proof of his claims. But when we spread photographic copies of the original tablet[6] among the people they frequently asked Abbas Effendi about it and his answer invariably was that this paragraph referred to him as well as the Mightiest Branch (Mohammed Ali Effendi). His answer is an untruth, for no one with any common sense, upon reading the original, can see in it any reference to Abbas Effendi.

6th. Baha'u'llah (Glory be to Him) said the "Book of My Covenant" (*Kitab-i-'Ahdi*), and did not say the Book of *the* Covenant of somebody

---

[5] The specific interpretation of the word *tawajjuh* (or Persian *tavajjoh*) in Baha'u'llah's will, regarding the appointment of Abbas Effendi as his successor, was a key point of contention between the supporters of 'Abdu'l-Baha and those who felt that he went too far in his claims. See the section entitled "Limitations of 'Abdu'l-Baha's Authority" in Chapter 17 for an in-depth discussion of this issue by Mohammed Ali Bahai.

[6] See image on page 146, and an English translation of the tablet in Chapter 10.

else.⁷ Abbas Effendi declares that this book is the book of his own covenant. He teaches his followers that the Speaker with God (Moses) took the covenant of the Spirit (Jesus Christ), and the Spirit (Jesus Christ) took the covenant of the Point of *Furqan* (Muhammad the Prophet), and the Point of Furqan (Muhammad) took the covenant of the Point of *Bayan* (the Bab), and the Point of Bayan (the Bab) took the covenant of "Him whom God shall manifest" (the Everlasting Father), and "He whom God shall manifest," the Father, Baha'u'llah, took the covenant of "him whom God has chosen" (Abbas). By this Abbas Effendi claims to be a Manifestation of God and greater than Baha'u'llah.

7th. The servant of Baha'u'llah, Khadimu'llah, wrote an epistle, while Baha'u'llah was in exile at Adrianople, in which he described the disturbance which took place at that time (the great time of testing humanity), when Baha'u'llah declared Himself [as the Manifestation of God]. These days are called in the holy books, "the days of difficulties," and that year was called "the year of difficulties." The days, or year, of difficulties were mentioned in several tablets. Baha'u'llah expressly said in some of these tablets that the days, or year, of difficulties have passed away. Abbas Effendi explains that the "year of difficulties" is the year after the departure of the Father, and he calls this paper, written by Khadimu'llah, a tablet, and insists that it was written by the command of Baha'u'llah, and in this way he uses this paper for the furtherance of his own aims.⁸

---

⁷ The original title of Baha'u'llah's will was *Kitab-i-'Ahdi* ("Book of My Covenant"), but this has been changed to *Kitab-i-'Ahd* ("Book of the Covenant") in the mainstream Baha'i tradition. Unitarian Baha'is preferred the former title, emphasizing that Baha'u'llah's testamentary document was his own instructions for the benefit of his family and followers, rather than "the" Covenant of God promising a new source of divine revelation. This subtle difference tends to either reduce or elevate the significance of the successorship after Baha'u'llah, depending on which title for his will is used. Unitarian Baha'is did not see Baha'u'llah's successors as speaking for God or fulfilling a great covenant between God and humanity—only as duly appointed leaders of the Baha'i community according to Baha'u'llah's wishes.

⁸ If Baha'u'llah wrote a tablet predicting that the year after his own passing would be a "year of difficulties," this could be considered as a prophecy of the bitter sectarian split that occurred among his family and companions. If Dr. Kheiralla is correct and there was no such tablet written by Baha'u'llah, then

8th. Baha'u'llah, the All-Wise, uttered the first sentence of the Sacred Book, *Kitab-i-Aqdas*, for His Holy and Supreme Self, but Abbas Effendi claims that that first sentence descended in his favor, and he considers himself to be the representative of God.[9] Baha'u'llah expressly declared in many of His utterances that the glorious temple of His appearance was the representative of God, the Being. Abbas Effendi has changed the real meaning of several texts of Baha'u'llah to suit himself by giving them a false interpretation. But our space is too limited to give them.

---

the implication is that 'Abdu'l-Baha constructed this narrative to lend credence to his contention that the excommunication of Mohammed Ali Bahai and his supporters was anticipated by Baha'u'llah and part of the divine plan.

[9] The first verse of the *Kitab-i-Aqdas* is as follows: "The first duty prescribed by God for His servants is the recognition of Him Who is the Dayspring of His Revelation and the Fountain of His laws, who representeth the Godhead in both the Kingdom of His Cause and the world of creation." Dr. Kheiralla's assertion is that 'Abdu'l-Baha claimed it is an essential duty of Baha'is to recognize his own station as, in his view, the next representative of God after Baha'u'llah, and to obey him as the equivalent of obeying God or Baha'u'llah.

27

Unitarian Baha'i Organizations and Teachings

By Ibrahim G. Kheiralla

This chapter contains writings by Ibrahim Kheiralla about the Unitarian Baha'i organizations he helped to found and lead in the United States. The first section, about the Society of Behaists, is from his book *Facts for Behaists*. The remainder of the chapter, about the National Association of the Universal Religion, is from Dr. Kheiralla's autobiography which was published in his book *O Christians!* (see Chapter 25 for the rest of the autobiography).

These two organizations appear to have had much the same purpose, although there are indications that the NAUR may have been more Universalist and perhaps designed to appeal to a broader audience. For example, the name of the organization itself does not include the word Baha'i, and Dr. Kheiralla states that its main object was "to promulgate the amalgamation of all different religions into one Universal Religion," rather than to spread the Baha'i religion specifically. Also of note is that universal salvation is included in its list of principles.

It is unclear whether the Society of Behaists and the NAUR were intended to complement each other or whether the latter was intended to supplant the former. Regardless, it appears that the Society of Behaists remained as the primary religious organization for Unitarian Baha'is, since in 1937, Shua Ullah Behai mentioned it but did not mention the NAUR in his summary of "The Three Baha'i Sects" (see the section by that name in Chapter 35).

—The Editor

The Society of Behaists

Those [among the Baha'is] who were of my opinion and myself, on seeing clearly the unreasonable claims and teachings of Abbas Effendi and his messengers, decided to take this stand: To strictly follow the commandments of the Father in *Kitab-i-Aqdas*, depend upon God only, seek no help from anyone besides Him, and to allow no created being to stand between our Creator and ourselves. At the same time we made up our minds to investigate the cause of the dissension among the Branches and learn the truth and follow it. It was very difficult for us to believe the teachings we heard—i.e., that Abbas Effendi alone of the four Branches of Baha'u'llah and his sister [Bahiyyih Khanum] are the favorites of God, and the rest of the family and the relatives, numbering over thirty people, are all cut off and considered infidels, and with their followers are called *naqizin* (violators) simply because they do not obey and believe in the claims of their half-brother, the eldest son of Baha'u'llah, Abbas Effendi.

According to the *Kitab-i-Aqdas*, our Assembly kept all the festivals and anniversaries which the followers of Baha'u'llah are commanded to keep, and organized the House of Justice, of not less than nine members, to manage the affairs of the cause of God and the spreading of His word. We also incorporated the Society of the Behaists (the followers of Baha'u'llah) in America, according to and under the protection of the laws of the government, as Baha'u'llah commanded us strictly to obey the laws of the country in which we live and be loyal citizens thereof. We conducted our meetings and performed all our religious duties in accordance with the *Kitab-i-Aqdas*, which we have constantly made our special study. Besides the organization of the First Assembly of Behaists in Chicago, we organized the Second Assembly in Kenosha,

Wisconsin, under a charter granted to them from the Society of Behaists in America.

The National Association of the Universal Religion

[In 1914, some Baha'is in Chicago] decided to form an association under the laws of the State of Illinois, known as the "National Association of the Universal Religion." We received the charter the same year, and the chosen officers of the National Association were myself as President and Chief-Instructor; Frederick O. Pease, M.D., Vice President; Harry R. Reynolds, Secretary and Treasurer.

The National Association of the Universal Religion and all its branches work under the headship of his Grace, El-Akbar, Mohammed Ali Effendi, whom I represent in the United States of America. He was chosen by Baha'u'llah in the "Book of My Covenant" as the trustee and diffuser of its teachings, principles, and laws throughout the world after Abbas Effendi. The directors of this Association are authorized to confer the title of "Doctor" in the teachings of the Universal Religion to those who deserve, and no Baha'i teacher in this country is considered [an] authority nor competent unless he is a member of the National Association of the Universal Religion.

The main object for which this Association was formed is to promulgate the amalgamation of all different religions into one Universal Religion, that differences in faith and race may be annulled in order to establish peace and unity with God and with each other. The following requisitions inserted in the "Guide" are enjoined on members of this Association:

Requisitions of the N.A.U.R.

1. It is required of every member of this corporation to believe in the oneness and singleness of God, the Supreme. For He is Infinite Perfection and nothing can be taken from nor added to Him; hence, He is Most High and sanctified from being divided into persons, parts, and sparks.

2. Our God is a living God, known and knowable. For it is an estab-

lished fact that everything in existence is known by its qualities, powers, attributes, and manifestations, and especially through His greatest manifestation and Face entitled the Everlasting Father. The nothing is the only unknown, because it has no qualities, no powers, no attributes, neither manifestations; hence, the nothing does not exist and it is the unknown God or rather the God of ignorance. Besides this, God wished to be known and created us to know Him. Should He be unknowable, there would be no object of our creation, and such an aimless action cannot be attributed to the All-Wise.

3. Members of this corporation must not allow any party or parties to stand between them and God. For He is the Ocean of Light and Intelligence and we are like unto fishes therein. We live in Him, exist in Him, move in Him, breathe in Him, and are sustained by Him. So, He is nearer to us than we are to ourselves. Therefore, we must be on our guard and never allow anyone to stand as a barrier between us and Him.

4. The duty of each one of us is to rise up by the help of God and urge the others to rise up likewise and assist in uprooting from the hearts of the peoples of this world the hatred and rancor wrought therein by differences of faith and race. This hatred and rancor are like unto consuming fire devouring mankind and destroying the organization of the human family and the preservation of our [one human] race. The past and present horrid wars are sufficient evidences of what hatred has done in the way of ruination and destruction to the people of the earth.

5. We shall live for the world that the world may live for us, and teach others to do the same. We are all brothers and sisters, one family, one kindred, one race, and the offspring of the same parents, as taught by the scriptures of nearly every religion. Besides this, nature and its laws teach us that we are one race, one [human] family, as it was conclusively proved in bringing children by [inter]marriage of all kinds of peoples of different countries and climates. So each one is a member of the same family and must live for the family that the family may live for him.

6. One of the chief works of this corporation is to labor and help in formulating an easy and short language for mankind all over the world. It should be taught to children in schools everywhere, in order that in

the near future, each human being can talk the same language with all the others. This would be the cause of unity and accord among all nations and strengthen the ties of brotherhood thereof. For it would destroy from our minds the conception of being aliens to each other as we feel when we cannot converse in the same language with people of other countries.

7. Spirituality is to know the Spirit of Truth, the Fountainhead of Revelations, who spoke in Jesus and in all the prophets of yore. He is the Everlasting Father, the Face of the Infinite and His Self-Representative in the world of command and creation. He is the Manifestation of the Eternal Identity and the only true God, and to know Him is life eternal as Christ said in His prayers for His disciples. He is standing behind the doors of the hearts of His seekers, ready to enter therein and make them die for what they have and live for what He has for them, that they may become heirs of His Kingdom. This lofty station cannot be attained unless we obey His commandments, for both achievements [i.e. faith and works] are inseparable and the one cannot be accepted without the other.

8. Morality: Inasmuch as mankind is the vineyard which the Everlasting Father planted, and inasmuch as He organized it as a family of two sexes, male and female; He wished to guard and protect it; He laid [down] laws and established commandments whereby the human family can live in unity, peace and prosperity, if they obey them and walk accordingly. So you see that every action which is performed for the protection of the organization of the human family and the preservation of mankind is good, and that which is a violation of its protection and preservation is evil, i.e., it is an immoral deed. For instance, to kill a cow [to eat] is good, but to kill a man is evil. Then murder, adultery, theft, slander, backbiting, etc., are immoral [to] our fellow creatures, and spirituality is our duty and obligation to our Heavenly Father. Consequently, it is supposed that every spiritual man is also a moral one, but many moral people are devoid of spirituality. Morality cannot uplift and elevate our souls into a Divine state, because to neglect our most important duties is a sin against the Spirit of Truth, though we [may] do all good actions. Those who depend on morality only, are likened

unto a tree bearing delicious fruits which benefit those who eat them, but do no benefit whatsoever to the tree itself which produced them.

9. The greatest purpose of man's life on this earth is to prepare and fit himself for the life hereafter; that is to say, to be naturalized into and characterized by the nature and characteristics of his Heavenly Father. To do good because it is good and abstain from evil because it is evil, and not for reward nor fear of punishment. Our Father wished that His children be like unto Him, so let us eat of the fruits of the Tree of Knowledge (the Manifestation of the Deity), of good and evil, and become like God.

10. No eternal punishment was decreed unto man, though the punishment of God is severe. Man is a soul and the soul is the breath of God, which cannot perish forever. From God man emanated and unto God shall he return. The prodigal son (mankind) shall return to his Father's home.[1] The Father said, "O people of the earth, if ye believe in Me, I will make you the heirs of My Kingdom, and if ye reject Me I will kindly be patient. I am the Generous, the Forgiver."[2]

11. Though there is no hell-fire and brimstone, yet there is a hell which is worse and more severe than that. It is a real horrible hell, when man is far away from God, the Father. The real heaven of the Universal Religion is more excellent and more sublime than the heaven which is decorated with silver, gold, jewels, gems, and all kinds of precious stones. Our heaven is when we are near to God, the Father of mankind. In both cases of hell and heaven we must remember that there is no condition without a position and no position without a condition.

12. Inasmuch as the Everlasting Father is the Manifestation of the Infinite throughout the creation, and as the Infinite is known and knowable by His Face which is inseparable therefrom, therefore, the Father is the Self-Representative of God Almighty and the same One. Whosoever comes to the Father comes to God and who knows Him knows the Infinite, and who rejects Him rejects the Eternal Identity and the Creator of heaven and earth.

---

[1] See Luke 15:11-32. The parable of the Prodigal Son has been used by some Christians as an argument for universal salvation.

[2] Presumably a quotation by Baha'u'llah from an unidentified tablet.

Chapter 27. Unitarian Baha'i Organizations and Teachings 375

13. It is enjoined on each member to pray privately alone. The congregational prayer is prohibited[3] for these reasons: No one should be allowed to stand between you and your Heavenly Father. No one should be considered superior to others before God. Though we can pray for each other, yet it is impracticable for one to pray in the place of the others, for each must do it for himself.

14. It is demanded from us to toil with energy and sincerity that we may conquer our selfish desires and bad emotions, and also subdue those which are good, in order to avoid doing wrong. For instance, we must conquer hatred and rancor to save ourselves from committing evil. Likewise, we must subdue love to save ourselves from doing injustice. "Justice is the best thing before God."[4] Love was, is, and shall be the root of many wrongs and miseries in this world, for if we do love ourselves, our relatives, or our countrymen more than we love the others, we do wrong and commit injustice against them. "Love not thyself more than thy neighbor."[5] So we must tone down and moderate even our good desires [such] as love; otherwise, they lead us astray.

15. Begging and giving to beggars both are strongly prohibited.[6] It is impossible for a beggar to attain the lofty station of elevating himself to become like his Father in Heaven, and those who give to beggars are encouraging them to remain abased in that position, practicing this low and degraded craft. Those who are not able to work and earn their living should be provided for by local governments or states.

16. The rulers of the earth and all nations thereon are strictly commanded by the founder of the Universal Religion to cease warring

---

[3] Islam and Christianity both have traditions of congregational prayer, in which an imam, priest or minister recites a prayer on behalf of an entire congregation. In the *Kitab-i-Aqdas* (paragraph 12), Baha'u'llah prohibited this practice except in the case of funerals. Moreover, the Baha'i faith does not have clergy, because Baha'u'llah did not believe there should be intermediaries between man and God except the Manifestations of God.

[4] This is likely a paraphrase of the first sentence of the Hidden Words, Arabic #2, by Baha'u'llah.

[5] Cf. Leviticus 19:18, Luke 10:27.

[6] This prohibition, unusual among religions, was taught by Baha'u'llah in the *Kitab-i-Aqdas* (paragraph 147).

against each other for any reason whatsoever. The command is, they must settle their differences by submitting them to an international court composed of judges and delegates representing the governments of the world, and all nations must abide by and obey the decisions of said international court. If a government should insist on waging war against another, the rest of the world should unite together to prevent such an occurrence. But, if their warning were not heeded they are commanded to compel that government to yield even though it were necessary to use force.

17. No other means to remove the three causes of war—differences of faith, differences of race, and selfishness—exists save the Universal Religion, whose flag of "Love not thyself more than thy neighbor" shall be raised over every city in the world.

18. Every person must take hold of some work or profession and toil honestly, physically or mentally, to earn a living for himself and for those for whom he is responsible. This is paramount to worshipping God. Idleness and mendicancy are prohibited, for to live on the labor of others is against the organization of the human family and a deed of injustice and selfishness.

19. Parents are commanded to educate their children, and he who educates other children is considered as if he were educating the children of God Himself.

21. Cleanliness in body and garments is strictly decreed unto everyone. It is impossible for him who is not clean to be acceptable as an equal associate by those who observe and practice cleanliness. Cleanliness joins mankind in brotherhood and paves the way of unity and concord, besides being beneficial and sanitary.

22. We are requested to consort with all peoples of different faiths and countries with love and pleasantness, using the language of kindness, which is the lodestone of hearts, whereby unity and peace may be established.

23. One of the important objects of our association is that every member shall gain and grow in knowledge and wisdom in order to be able to expel ignorance from among his fellow creatures and lead them to the truth. Knowledge is to gather and know more established facts,

and wisdom is to use said knowledge and apply it rightly for uplifting and elevating mankind.

24. Everyone should expel from his heart the fear of death and cease to grieve and bewail the separation from his dear ones. For it is not pleasing to the departed souls and at the same time it is a lack of confidence in the power and love of the Father. The happiest moment of man's life is the time of leaving this earth for his Father's home. When the soul comes [at birth] she cries and those who are around her smile, but when she departs, she smiles, leaving others behind her in tears. If we had the faintest idea of what perfect power and happiness the sanctified souls shall have in the spiritual realms, we would prefer to go there today. Indeed, death is a feast to the sanctified soul.

25. Burial of the dead and funerals shall be conducted with pomp and splendor as an act of respect to the Image of God and His Likeness[7] and an object lesson to those who remain behind.

26. The edict of the Universal Religion is to practice honesty and truthfulness in all our dealings with our fellow creatures, abandoning hypocrisy, false pretenses, and holding fast to justice and reason. We are urged to use the eyes seemly, the hands honestly, the tongues truthfully, and the hearts purely, and be characterized with forgiveness and charity.

Organization of Newark Branch

Mr. William E. Dreyer of the city of Newark, New Jersey, formed with some other Baha'is a Branch Association called "The Newark Branch" of the National Association of the Universal Religion. The National Association granted them a charter to work for the same purposes and under the same stipulations, requisitions, and laws in the "Guide," which was written to be adopted by the National Association and all its Branches, and work was commenced accordingly. Mr. Dreyer was appointed President and Instructor of said Branch, and also he was given the degree of a Trustee of the Baha'i teachings, on account of his

---

[7] The human being whose life is being celebrated, who was created in God's image and likeness (see Genesis 1:26-27).

faithfulness and the valuable service which he had already rendered for the Cause of God. Likewise, Frederick O. Pease and Harry R. Reynolds of Chicago, both attained the degree of Trustee for their faithfulness and good services to the Cause. These three Trustees were the first Trustees to achieve this important degree in the United States of America. Negotiations are pending for other Branches and we anticipate that before long we will have many Branches organized in different cities of the United States.

Ibrahim G. Kheiralla in his elder years.

Baha'i family photo taken in 1923.
Standing (L to R): Majdeddin bin Moussa Irani, Mirza Jamil (Majdeddin's younger brother), Salah Bahai, Alia Khanum, Laqa'iyya Khanum, Maryam (Majdeddin's daughter), Amin Ullah Bahai.
Bottom row (L to R): Mousa Bahai seated between Ismat and Iffat, Shua Ullah Behai crouching over Kamar and Sazij (all daughters of Badi Ullah); Samadiyya Khanum, Zaranguise (Maryam's sister), unknown child.
Closeup below: Alia Bahai (wife of Badi Ullah), Laqa'iyya Bahai (wife of Mohammed Ali).

Baha'i family photo taken circa 1933.
L to R: Amin Ullah Bahai, Laqa'iyya Khanum, Mousa Bahai, Mohammed Ali Bahai (seated), Maryam, Majdeddin bin Moussa Irani, Zaranguise, Mirza Jamil, Soraya Khanum Samandari.
Below: Closeup from previous page: Samadiyya Khanum with daughter Zaranguise. From photo above: Mirza Majdeddin.

28

Brief Baha'i History and Testimony

By Majdeddin bin Moussa Irani

Majdeddin bin Moussa Irani (before 1945 – 1955), usually known to Baha'is as Mirza Majdi'd-Dín, was a nephew and son-in-law of Baha'u'llah. He was the son of Baha'u'llah's brother Moussa, known as Aqay-i-Kalim, who was a strong supporter of the Baha'i cause. He was married to his cousin Samadiyya, the second daughter of Baha'u'llah.

Majdeddin Irani was one of the inner circle of Baha'is until Baha'u'llah's passing, and is reported to have been given the honor of reading Baha'u'llah's will to a group of relatives and important believers. Later, he became one of the most significant opponents of 'Abdu'l-Baha and sided with Mohammed Ali Bahai in the schism. He lived to be over 100 years old and continued to support Unitarian Baha'ism until the end.

This essay, originally entitled "Brief Behai History," was written in March 1936 and published in the First and Second Quarter 1936 issue of *Behai Quarterly* magazine. Section headings have been added.

—The Editor

Origins of the Baha'i Faith

In the year 1844 A.D. a young man appeared in Iran (Persia) whose name was Ali Muhammad, but as he claimed to be the gate of knowledge, he was called "Bab" (Gate) and his followers "Babists."[1]

---

[1] Or "Babis."

He declared himself to be the one whose appearance was expected by Islam, called "Mahdi," and his great mission was the glad-tidings of the coming of the greatest manifestation [of God] on earth.

He mentioned Him in his utterances with supreme deference, just as John the Baptist spoke of the appearance of Jesus. Although he claimed the highest state of spirituality, yet he considered himself as naught and a humble servant in comparison with the appearance of He [in whom] God shall manifest "The Glory of God."

The message of the Bab awakened the minds of the Persians and thousands of learned people became his followers. This aroused the anger of the Islamic theologians, and fearing the loss of their leadership, they labored with all their might against this progressive new movement which was spreading rapidly throughout the land. Finally they succeeded in inducing the government to arrest the Bab and his devoted secretary and put them in prison, then suspended them both on a pole in the middle of the square in the city of Tabriz, province of Azerbaijan,[2] and riddled their chests with hundreds of bullets. This unfortunate event took place in the year 1850 A.D.

Baha'u'llah, "The Glory of God" of whom the Bab had spoken, was born November 12, 1817 A.D. in the city of Tehran, the present capital of Iran (Persia). His name was Husayn Ali, later Baha'u'llah. When the Bab proclaimed himself the new teacher his message appealed to Baha'u'llah and he became an active worker in the new cause and a prominent figure among the Babists. After the Bab was put to death, through the influence of the same agitating group [i.e. the mullahs], Baha'u'llah was arrested in the outskirts of Tehran, brought to the city and placed in a dungeon for the period of four months. Then through the protest of the Russian ambassador, he was released, but was requested to leave his native land.

By mutual agreement between Russia, Turkey, and Persia he was sent to Baghdad, Mesopotamia, then a Turkish possession. Baha'u'llah resided in Baghdad nearly twelve years. While there he secluded himself in the mountains of Sulaymaniyah and for two years his wherea-

---

[2] A province of Iran, not to be confused with the present-day country also called Azerbaijan.

bouts were unknown to all. After his return from seclusion, Baha'u'llah proclaimed himself to be the promised one of whom the Bab had spoken, "He whom God shall Manifest," The Glory of God. This proclamation renewed the movement and under his gracious leadership the cause progressed in spite of persecutions, and ever since the followers of this religion are called Baha'ists.[3]

Baha'u'llah devoted forty years of his life to uttering verses and revealing tablets for the progress of his fellow men. In chains and exile he sent epistles to all the rulers of the world, including the pope of Rome, inviting them to come to the Kingdom of the Father. He suffered hardship, calamity, and banishment to bring us from the darkness of ignorance to the light of knowledge.

Through the influence of the ambassador of Iran (Persia) to the Ottoman court, Baha'u'llah was requested to come to Istanbul, then capital of Turkey, and from there was sent to Adrianapolis[4] where he remained five years. He was then banished to the prison of the fortress of Acre, residing there twenty-five years.

Completing his mission on earth, he departed unto Eternity on May 28, 1892 A.D.[5]

Testimony to the Greatness of Mohammed Ali Bahai

Baha'u'llah in his will entitled the Book of My Covenant (*Kitab-i-'Ahdi*) appointed two of his sons [to be] leaders after him, both occupying the same position one after the other: his eldest son the Greatest Branch, Abbas ('Abdu'l-Baha), who passed away in 1921, and his second son the Mightiest Branch, Mohammed Ali Bahai, who is living and resides at Acre, Palestine.

This great personage, the eldest living son of Baha'u'llah, is the head of the Society of Behaists throughout the world and the legal spir-

---

[3] This term, also spelled "Bahaists" or "Behaists," was common at the time when the author was writing, although "Baha'i" eventually became the standard term for an adherent of the faith of Baha'u'llah.

[4] Adrianople, present-day Edirne, Turkey.

[5] Or May 29. See note 7 in Chapter 3.

itual leader of all the Baha'i organizations according to the aforesaid will of Baha'u'llah.

He was reared in the bosom of Baha'u'llah and served him faithfully to the last, as inscriber of his utterances and promulgator of his teachings. He is the chosen son and received the highest honors by Baha'u'llah.

Hereunder is the translation of a tablet written to him by the Supreme Pen of Baha'u'llah, which showers upon him the highest honors and love.[6]

THE GREATEST, THE MOST GLORIOUS

O MY GOD! Verily this is a branch who hath branched from the firm and lofty tree of Thy singleness and oneness. Thou seest him, O my God, gazing unto Thee, and holding fast to the rope of Thy bounty. Therefore keep him in the shadow of Thy mercy. Thou knowest, O my God, that I desire him, as Thou hast desired him, and I have chosen him as Thou hast chosen him. Therefore assist him with the hosts of earth and heaven, and help, O my God, whosoever helpeth him, choose whosoever chooseth him, and assist whosoever cometh to him. Then forsake whosoever denieth him and desireth him not. O my Lord! Thou seest that while inspired, my pen moveth though my limbs tremble. I ask Thee by my long-

---

[6] This is the same tablet that appears in Chapter 10, but the translation is quite different. The most notable difference is that in this version, the last sentence appears to refer to God, whereas in the other one it refers to Mohammed Ali Bahai. Even in this version it is unclear, however, because the distinction is based entirely on capitalization of pronouns, and there are many inconsistencies of capitalization in the unedited text. Based on the capitalization pattern loosely followed in both the translated tablet and the rest of the essay by Majdeddin bin Moussa Irani, it is the opinion of this editor that the intended usage was to capitalize pronouns referring to God and not to capitalize pronouns referring either to Baha'u'llah or his son; and I have edited the text to conform strictly to that pattern, as best as I could determine. The reader should bear in mind that Baha'u'llah's writings were originally in Arabic and Persian—languages that use a script which has no capital letters—and as a result, the meaning of certain statements is ambiguous and has been interpreted differently in different translations.

ing for Thy love and my anxiety to manifest Thy cause, to ordain for him, and to those who love him, what Thou hast destined for Thy messengers and the faithful of Thy Divine Inspiration. Verily Thou art God, The All-Powerful, The Omnipotent.

HE IS THE GREATEST

O my God, assist the Mightiest Branch (*Ghusn-i-Akbar*) in Thy remembrance and Thy praise. Then cause to flow from his pen the marvels of Thy science and secrets. O my God, verily he hath hastened unto Thy pleasure, and hath fasted for the love of Thyself, and in obedience to Thy commands. Destine for him all good revealed in Thy book. Verily, Thou art the All-Powerful, the Omnipotent.

Blessed is he who hath rested in the shelter of the branch of God, his Lord, Lord of the Throne, and Lord of the Universe.

O my branch! Be thou the spring cloud of my mercy, then shower upon all things in my name, The New.

O my branch, We have chosen thee, as the chosen one hath chosen thee. Say praise be to Thee, O God of the Universe.

O Mightiest Branch, We have chosen thee to serve my cause; arise with marvelous assistance. Conquer the cities of all names, in my name, The Ruler over all He wishes.

O ocean, wave in my name, The Rising, The Great.

Open the cities of the hearts in my name, The Beloved, The Dear, The Bountiful. Verily every action depends on Thy love. Blessed is he who accepted the Will of his Lord, the All-Knowing. Blessed is he who hath heard Thy voice and hath come to Thee for the love of God, The Lord of the Universe.

This chosen son is a devout follower of the [Baha'i] teachings and a staunch believer in them.

He is kind, gentle, patient, and always ready to help the needy. Although he occupies the highest position among us, yet he considers himself our elder brother.

He is misjudged, wronged, and falsely accused by so-called friends, those who satisfied themselves with hearsay without investigation.

I have been fortunate to be in his service the major part of my life and pray to God to grant me strength to write his biography as a testimonial for the future historians, so the sun of truth will not remain covered under the clouds of falsehood.

29

Against War: An Open Letter to World Leaders

By Majdeddin bin Moussa Irani

This originally untitled document by the nephew and son-in-law of Baha'u'llah, dated September 18, 1944, was included in a chapter called "The Two Younger Branches, the Leaves, and Their Spouses" in Shua Ullah Behai's book manuscript. Mr. Behai described this open letter as "his [i.e. Mirza Majdeddin's] recent message to the world." Written near the end of World War II, it is a short but forceful essay about Baha'u'llah's teachings of peace, the dangers of excessive industrialization and the decline of religion.

According to Mr. Behai, the letter was "forwarded through the office of the High Commissioner of Palestine to His Majesty King George of Great Britain. Also a copy was sent by registered mail to His Excellency Franklin Delano Roosevelt, President of the United States." The letter received a polite, brief reply from the British government, which stated that "your message has been laid before His Majesty the King but that the Secretary of State was unable to advise His Majesty to take any action on it."

—The Editor

To Their Majesties the Kings and Honorable Leaders of State:

I do hereby lay before you an urgent plea that you soften your hearts and agree to decide on a general armistice for the establishment of peace. The wails of suffering humanity are loud and unto the heavens crying "it is enough." The whole of this planet earth has become as one fierce flaming volcano spilling death and destruction all around. If there is a little corner somewhere that has escaped the fire, it has not escaped the scorching blinding smoke of its burning sides.

The underlying intention of all nations is peace. Had they not formed in the League of Nations a tribunal for the solution of international problems? This was what Baha'u'llah willed and advised long before its formation. There is no doubt that if all the sister nations, together and in agreement, solved the world's problem, the waking fire of war would have been safely lulled back to sleep.

Thus spoke Baha'u'llah unto the kings:

> Settle ye your disputes amicably among yourselves and ye shall have no need to equip and keep huge armies. For order and peace in your cities and kingdoms ye shall need but little. Unite, all ye mighty sovereigns, and the storm of dissension will abate: Unite so that your people may live and prosper in peace and comfort.

He also says:

> Blessed is the ruler that hath ruled his own self. Blessed is the king that hath mastered his temper. For he that is thus blessed is a lover of peace and a friend to equity; he is an enemy to all that is unjust and tyrannous. The finest fruit that the tree of wisdom hath ever borne is this celestial word: "Ye are all the fruits of one tree, and unto each other like the leaves of one branch. The glory is not to him who loveth his own land only, but to him who loveth the whole world."
>
> The Divine and Holy Pen to you hath writ: O ye kings and sultans, O ye partners of fate, ye princes, sages, and leaders of state, revere and uphold religion. For religion is the cause of all that is just and orderly on the face of the earth. Without it ye shall have no peace. Uphold it with all your might for if its pillars tremble, the wicked multiply and breed, its weakness lends them courage, its absence fame. I tell you in truth that ye may have faith in me, that the little that religion loseth from itself, the evildoers and sinners gain a hundredfold. Hearken unto me, [the] All-Seeing and

mark my words, for if ye heed them not, there will be nothing save turmoil and the discord of chaos.

Taking away the life of a useless cumbersome old man is a crime the whole world abhors and severely punishes. But on the other hand we witness all around the merciless slaughter of millions of men in the bloom of their youth. Their pure and sacred blood is shed, the hearts of their weeping mothers are wrung and bled, their kin scattered, their children starved and homes destroyed. We witness an endless chain of misery and suffering but the world seems to stand aside as if in wonder.

No matter what the outcome of war may be, does it balance the cost? The aims of wars are in fact mere hopes and illusions, that are indefinite at best and so grossly vague in themselves. One outcome and one end only is certain: it is misery, destruction and suffering on a grand scale, a heart-rending epic in so eloquent a style. Is this what the Father, Son, and The Holy Spirit ordain?

The tide of this unebbing sea is overflowing with the corpses of the guiltless and the rotting food of the starving and homeless. At the bottom of the sea lies the shattered framework of the world's construction. And yet there is no shimmer of hope to reflect the radiance of peace. Whither from here and when is the end?

There is hardly a spot on the face of the earth that has not felt the guns of the sea, or the bombs of the air; hardly a plot that has not suffered, from mountain or plain. The aim is bent and energies focused on one sole object, which is the mass destruction of civilization and humanity.

If you have lost the track of truth and become blind to the light of peace, do not forget temperance in your every action. Of temperance Baha'u'llah in one of his tablets says:

> The process of civilizing that is being followed by the sages of the industrial countries, if carried to excess and made to overstep the limits of temperance, will lead the people of the world to ruin. Thus speaketh the All-Knowing. For in its excess it doth become a process of vice and sin as much as it was in its temperance a way of new life and betterment. Ponder over these words, ye people,

and reflect lest ye be followers in the footsteps of the rash and perish. With temperance follow it [i.e. industrial development], for if ye run after it your cities shall burn with the fire of its speed. The Tongue of Omnipotence hath spoken that sovereignty is God's, the Merciful and Almighty.

How bitterly true these words have been. The cities now burn over the heads of their builders.

It gives me great pain to see the world's leaders of state who are the most civilized indulge in wars with one another. Though they know the policies and intentions of one another, from the dawn of history until now they have not ceased this interminable struggle for mutual destruction. This has come as a result of their own man-made laws along which they are trying to run the universe. Their misery and that of their peoples increases day by day and generation after generation in spite of their professed intention of peace for all on the earth. Even now, though they are rich with the experience of thousands of years, they have not as yet changed what they have become used to. It is time for them who hold the right of life and death over their people to return to the Law of God—that divine law which He has given us so that we may enjoy His gifts and adore His works and so live in peace in happiness.

Listen, O ye mighty kings, to this my call to you. I am but one of the weak and powerless. I send you this plea, in the eyes of God, seeking no recompense. Hearken unto it, for it embodies the hopes of the suffering millions that like me are weak and powerless.

Hoist unto the heavens the banner of armistice; unfold on the earth the healing wing of peace. May you in justice long rule and prosper.

This is from a supplicant that boasts nothing for himself save the power to plead unto God that He may have mercy on him. I humbly pray unto His Almighty Throne that you feel with the weak like me, and may He touch your hearts with the compassion that is His. And may His will be done.

Seated: Shua Ullah Behai as a 12-year-old boy. ***Standing:*** Mirza Hadi Afnan, who later became the son-in-law of 'Abdu'l-Baha and father of Shoghi Effendi Rabbani. Photo taken in Bombay, India, 1890.

Shua Ullah Behai in the late 1930s, about 60 years old.

30

Memoirs

By Shua Ullah Behai

This autobiographical chapter was included by Shua Ullah Behai as the introduction to his book manuscript. Section headings have been added.

Mr. Behai surveys the main events of his life from childhood until the death of his father, Mohammed Ali Bahai, in 1937. He describes the heartbreak and long-lasting depression he suffered after being obliged to break his engagement with his beloved cousin Ruha Khanum, 'Abdu'l-Baha's daughter, because of their fathers' religious feud, and his subsequent failure in love. He discusses some of his own efforts to promote Unitarian Baha'i beliefs after emigrating to the United States, such as his publication of *Behai Quarterly* magazine, and a strongly-worded open letter he wrote to 'Abdu'l-Baha calling for a public conference to discuss and resolve the sectarian differences, which was published in American newspapers and was met with a nasty rebuke from the Baha'i leader. Shua Ullah Behai also mentions a planned pilgrimage to the Holy Land with a prominent Baha'i couple who were loyal to 'Abdu'l-Baha, for the purpose of attempting to bring his father and uncle together to end their dispute—a plan which unfortunately was thwarted by the outbreak of the First World War.

A large portion of this memoir is Mr. Behai's travel diary from his month-long return journey by ship from California to his family home in Haifa, where he retired after having spent most of his adult life in America. This is an eye-opening account of various tourist destinations along the way, as they appeared in the 1930s.

—The Editor

In the path of faith, millions of humanity have met their fate. But nothing in comparison with the lives lost and homes destroyed under the banners of nationalism. May peace come on earth and good will amongst mankind.

Introduction

I am the son of Mohammed Ali, son of Baha'u'llah. I was born in Qasr al-Mazra'a,[1] Acre District, Palestine, 1878 A.D. and grew to maturity under the shadow of the Great Baha'u'llah.

Needless to speak of my connection with the Baha'i faith, as I am born and bred in it. Although I am molded with the teachings, and firmly believe that the Baha'i principles are the most essential to practice in these trying days, yet I am [still] open for conviction otherwise. I am explaining this so that my readers should not think that I am following the Baha'i faith blindly or [only] on account of my birth.

Travels with Father to Egypt and India

In 1889 while I was at the age of eleven, I was commanded by Baha'u'llah to accompany my father on his journey to Egypt and India. Haji Khavar joined us also as attendant. We embarked on a steamer from Haifa, Palestine, to Port Said, Egypt. Upon entering the steamer that evening I was greatly amazed by the electric lights, as that was my first view of this kind of lighting. The short voyage was not a pleasant one for me, as I was seasick most of the way.

At our arrival to Port Said we were received by a Baha'i delegation from Egypt headed by Aqa Mirza Aqa Afnan,[2] and after the completion

---

[1] The *Qasr al-Mazra'a* ("Palace of Mazra'a") was a summer house in the town of Mazra'a, near Acre, where Baha'u'llah lived at the time. Baha'is today usually spell it Mazra'ih.

[2] Also known by the title of Nuri'd-Din. He was a nephew of the Bab who became a follower of Baha'u'llah and later served as one of 'Abdu'l-Baha's secretaries.

of custom house formalities, we were ushered to the house of the aforesaid Afnan, where we were entertained royally by our host during our sojourn there, which lasted twenty-one days. Faithful Baha'is arrived daily from all over Egypt to receive counsel and advice from my beloved father, and I as a boy used to enjoy immensely their conversation and extreme politeness.

For the enlightenment of the young readers I must illustrate that from my childhood I was reared with grown people and I had a very limited number of selected boys of my age to play with; therefore it was natural for me to associate with young and old, especially as in those days most of the followers were former theologians, Sufis, scientists and philosophers.

From Port Said we boarded an Italian steamer, passing through the Suez Canal and from there to Aden, Yemen, where our steamer docked the whole day. We landed for a few hours and enjoyed a cup of coffee and some dates.

On the twelfth day we reached our destination, Bombay, India. Upon landing in Bombay I had another surprise, observing the nudity of the natives.[3] This seems natural nowadays.

At our arrival to Bombay we were received by Haji Siyyid Mirza Afnan, his brother Haji Siyyid Muhammad Afnan, and others, among them Siyyid Hadi Afnan (who later married the eldest daughter of my uncle 'Abdu'l-Baha, and is thus the father of Shoghi Effendi).[4] We stayed at the abode of Haji Siyyid Mirza Afnan, which was located in Byculla, Bombay.

After a few weeks we secured a nice little bungalow house surrounded with a flower garden near the Mahalakshmi railway station. At that time the horse race track was in that section. We spent over a

---

[3] As people in India did not appear literally naked in public, the author is likely referring to the fact that traditional Indian attire allowed significantly more exposed skin than that of Persians and Arabs, especially for women, who were expected to cover even their hair in Islamic cultures. The relatively liberal customs of Bombay, a predominantly Hindu city of India, may have seemed to a Middle Eastern boy of that time as verging on nudity.

[4] Mirza and Muhammad Afnan were nephews of the Bab, and Hadi Afnan was a grand-nephew.

year in the city of Bombay, occasionally traveling to the nearby countryside, [such] as Poona,[5] Khandala, etc. My beloved father was occupied receiving visitors and arranging the printing of several books of the teachings of Baha'u'llah. I was studying French under a private teacher, as at that time the French language was the most popular in our country, which was then called Syria, under the Ottoman rule. I was greatly impressed by the natives of India, their sincerity, simpleness, humbleness and kindness.

On our return to Acre, Palestine, we stopped at Cairo, Egypt. We were the guests of Haji Mirza Hasan Shirazi, better known as Khorasani. I had the opportunity to see the points of interest in Cairo also. After a few days we arrived at home and again I was privileged to be with my mighty grandfather Baha'u'llah after the elapse of fifteen months.

During our preparation to leave Bombay the aforesaid Siyyid Hadi Afnan begged my father for permission to join us, so we had an extra companion on our return voyage from Bombay to Egypt. On the steamer, Haji Khavar prepared our meals and the said Siyyid Hadi Afnan took care of several large flat baskets, each containing three pots of different flowers and young trees that my father brought with him from India. Indeed, it was through his assiduous care of watering them regularly and moving them from place to place when needed that they reached their destination safely.

Two years after our return from India the ascension of Baha'u'llah took place. The events which happened after his ascension are recorded briefly in my father's Autobiography, and I refer my good readers to them.

More Childhood Memories

A few years before my journey to India, Siyyid Asadu'llah of Qum was appointed as a tutor for my brother Mirza Amin Ullah, who is four years my junior, and myself. Although he was a companion more than a teacher, yet he served us faithfully to the best of his ability until a few

---

[5] Present-day Pune.

months after the ascension of Baha'u'llah, when he had to leave us and return to his native land, Iran, to become a Baha'i missionary. The following years I had several private teachers, and occasionally I took English lessons also.

During my young days I was very fond of horseback riding and hunting. In those days the means of transportation were confined to horses, mules, donkeys or camels, as modern vehicles were not in existence in the Orient; therefore we all grew up learning horse riding. Also hunting was the only sport available as we had no golf or tennis grounds, nor were there any cinemas or theatres.

Engagement to 'Abdu'l-Baha's Daughter Ends in Heartbreak

After reaching the age of maturity I became engaged to my cousin Ruha Khanum, one of the twin daughters of my uncle 'Abdu'l-Baha. We were extremely in love with each other, but on account of the sudden dissension between our fathers and our due respect for them, we were obliged to give up each other, so my first and childhood love affair ended with disappointment. This incident in my life seems [like] a fiction nowadays, as the modern young people will not sacrifice their lifelong happiness for the sake of their parents. After this separation I was depressed and brokenhearted, but I tried my utmost and kept it to myself.

Visit to the United States as a Young Man

Years passed as such until 1904, when I received an invitation from relatives and friends in the United States of America to visit the World's Fair of St. Louis, Missouri, USA. I was greatly encouraged by this invitation for the following reasons: first, to forget my grief and sorrow, and second, to see the New World and to study the Western civilization.

With the permission of my father and my grandmother, the widow of Baha'u'llah, I left Palestine for Egypt and from there boarded a steamer for Marseilles, France, arriving in Paris July 12 of the same year. On July 14 the people of France celebrated their Independence Day [i.e. Bastille Day]. It was a great experience for me to go from Acre, Palestine, to Paris and to attend such a jubilant celebration. The following day I secured a passage with the American Line on the steamship *New York*, arriving at the port of New York the last week of July.

After two days rest in the great city of New York I went to St. Louis, Missouri. I spent the summer months there, observing the wonders of the Exposition, which were a great education for me. During the same summer I made a visit to the Baha'i friends in Chicago, Illinois and Kenosha, Wisconsin, accompanied by Dr. Ibrahim Kheiralla. Notices of my arrival to the United States appeared in numerous daily newspapers and magazines. The first two winters and summers I spent in St. Augustine, Florida and Atlantic City, New Jersey. While I was in New York I visited the Syrian colony in Brooklyn. During my stay there I had the pleasure of the visit of Mr. Howard MacNutt, and on my return visit to him I met Mrs. MacNutt also. We had a sociable visit, but later on I was informed that Mr. MacNutt was reprimanded by the Baha'i higher authorities for his association with me.[6]

Living in America

During my residence in the United States I served the Baha'i cause to the best of my ability, in my spare time, earning my livelihood through trade. I have had several opportunities to commercialize our teachings but I refrained from doing so, as I believe truth should be

---

[6] Howard MacNutt was a prominent early American Baha'i who was threatened with excommunication by 'Abdu'l-Baha for his liberal theological views and for associating with the Unitarian Baha'is. According to Baha'i author Robert Stockman, "Howard MacNutt had an extremely high regard for the ability of persons to fulfil their own potential, to the extent of becoming like Christ in one's spiritual abilities. One consequence was a belief that 'Abdu'l-Baha had no extraordinary spiritual station" by nature, but instead "that through works and service and overcoming all He attained to [such a] station." (Source: http://bahai-library.com/stockman_macnutt). Most Baha'is did not share Mr. MacNutt's unitarian theology and stopped inviting him to speak at their meetings. 'Abdu'l-Baha ordered him to cut off all communication with Ibrahim Kheiralla, his first Baha'i teacher, and other Unitarian Baha'is. Initially he disobeyed, but when warned that he would be excommunicated, he decided to remain with 'Abdu'l-Baha and submitted to a lengthy process of reeducation. He went on to become a dedicated teacher of the mainstream Baha'i faith, and was posthumously designated as one of nineteen Disciples of 'Abdu'l-Baha.

given gratis. For several years I edited and published *The Behai Quarterly* at my own expense and distributed it absolutely free of charge.

I traveled extensively in the United States, crossing the continent from Florida to Oregon, Maine to California. I have visited the most prominent winter and summer resorts. I have met people from all walks of life, the elites of Fifth Avenue, now Park Avenue, to the humbles of the Bouwerie,[7] the snobs of New England to the sociables of New Orleans. I have conversed with philosophers, scientists, politicians, communists, theologians, Theosophists, Christian Scientists, and Spiritualists and found some good in all of them, by discarding personal prejudice and respecting their viewpoints.

While in Southern California I married a charming American young lady of English stock, whose maiden name was Brewster, a descendant of William Brewster who came to America with the ship *Mayflower*. I regret that my second venture in love was unsuccessful also, as I have lost her. Ever since, I hesitated in making a third attempt and I presume that I shall leave this world without issue.

Open Letter to 'Abdu'l-Baha

During the winter of 1910-1911 I was visited by Mrs. L[ua] Getsinger and Dr. Ameen Fareed, while they were touring the States as Baha'i missionaries. The object of their visit was to guide me to the path which both of them believed then to be the right one. However they were unsuccessful in their mission.

In 1912 while my uncle 'Abdu'l-Baha was visiting the United States, by the authority of my father I humbly wrote him a letter and asked him for a conference to settle the existing differences in our cause. I hereby reproduce the copy of the same:

> To His Excellency Abbas Effendi 'Abdu'l-Baha.
> Dear Sir:
> Inasmuch as your views and doctrines in our religion are radically different from those of my father, your younger brother, Mo-

---

[7] This neighborhood of New York City is now spelled Bowery.

hammed Ali Effendi, who was chosen in the "Book of My Covenant," the Last Will of Baha'u'llah, to occupy after you the same position you occupy now;

And inasmuch as this difference between both of you spread among the followers of Baha'u'llah and divided them into two parties, one following you and believing in your personal teachings, and the other party which joined your brother believing in the teachings of Baha'u'llah only and considering them final as He declared;

And, inasmuch as we were all commanded in the "Most Holy Book," *Kitab-i-Aqdas*, to bring our differences to the utterance[s] of Baha'u'llah, which sufficed the world, whereby they should be settled;

And, inasmuch as our duty is to establish peace at home, among ourselves first, before we preach others to do so;

I hereby beg your Excellency to appoint a conference of peace and spirituality to hold its meetings at the city of Chicago, or some other place, at a certain time, in order to discuss with the language of love and kindness the differences between the said two parties and settle them in accord with the utterances of Baha'u'llah and His commandments.

If it please you, said conference would be composed of your Excellency with some learned ones of your followers, myself and Dr. I. G. Kheiralla, who introduced Baha'ism into America and Christendom, with a few of our party.

My father, Ghusn-i-Akbar, authorized me to state that he will accept and sanction whatever your Excellency would establish with me and with his representative Dr. I. G. Kheiralla.

The official language of said conference shall be the U.S. language; a neutral interpreter should be hired to translate from the Arabic language all that you would like to say and in the meantime to translate to you all the discussions of the conference. Also to ask the Associated Press to send a reporter to write the minutes of the conference; and to invite three American savants to attend the meetings and act as witnesses and judges.

I suggest the questions and discussions to be the following:

First: Why your Excellency concealed a part of the "Book of My Covenant," the Will of Baha'u'llah? That will was entrusted to you that you might give all of it to the followers of Baha'u'llah.

Second: Ghusn-i-Akbar was chosen to occupy after you the same position you occupy, but your Excellency claimed that he was cut off and fell. How is it possible that he fell from the said position before having had a chance to occupy it?

Third: What grounds have you to claim that you are the Center of the Covenant? God only is the Center of the Covenant.

Fourth: Why do you claim to be the Interpreter of the utterances of Baha'u'llah? He declared in the Book of Wisdom that there is no Interpreter to them save Himself.[8]

Fifth: How could it be that you are the manifestation of servitude and Baha'u'llah declared it to Himself only? Also He taught there are no manifestations after Him until one thousand years have passed from His appearance.

Sixth: Why do you claim the great infallibility, calling your letters sacred tablets and revelations? Baha'u'llah said: "Whosoever claimeth a mission before the completion of one thousand years (from His Manifestation) is a lying impostor."[9]

Seventh: Why do you teach that this greatest Manifestation has three chiefs, the Bab, Baha'u'llah and yourself? Baha'u'llah said: "There is no one else beside Me in the Kingdom." Likewise the Bible taught that at the latter days we shall have one shepherd,[10] only one chief and not three. Also Baha'u'llah said: "He hath no agent, no successor, and no son."

Eighth: Why do you claim and in the same breath deny that which you claim?

Ninth: Why do you not teach and spread the teachings of Baha'u'llah as you were commanded to do, instead of spreading your own?

I close this open letter, appealing to your Excellency by justice, love and unity to grant my request.

Your humble servant,

---

[8] This may be a reference to the following verse in the *Lawh-i-Hikmat* ("Tablet of Wisdom"): "This is a Tablet wherein the Pen of the Unseen hath inscribed the knowledge of all that hath been and shall be—a knowledge that none other but My wondrous Tongue can interpret." (*Tablets of Bahá'u'lláh Revealed After the Kitáb-i-Aqdas*, 1988 pocket-size edition, p. 149).

[9] *Kitab-i-Aqdas* ("Most Holy Book"), paragraph 37.

[10] John 10:16.

The grandson of Baha'u'llah,
Shua Ullah

I forwarded the above letter to 'Abdu'l-Baha in Chicago, Illinois, where he was staying, but unfortunately I did not receive a reply. When I heard of 'Abdu'l-Baha's arrival in California I addressed him the same letter again, this time through the press as an open letter, a copy of which appeared in several newspapers throughout the United States.[11]

A reporter from the *Los Angeles Examiner* interviewed 'Abdu'l-Baha and the following reply appeared in that newspaper, October 20, 1912:

"Would you listen to the talk of the drunkard in the street?" [said 'Abdu'l-Baha]

"Do you class your nephew as one no better than a drunkard?" he was asked.

"Worse," he benignly replied.

Indeed I was very surprised by his unkind and untimely statement, and to this day I am in doubt of its authenticity.

Conversations about Baha'i Family Dispute

In 1912 while my uncle 'Abdu'l-Baha was in Chicago, Mr. M. H.

---

[11] For example, in the *San Francisco Call*, an article appeared on October 13, 1912, in which Shua Ullah Behai is quoted addressing 'Abdu'l-Baha as follows: "Last May, through an open letter, I begged of your excellency for a peace conference to settle the differences between you and your younger brother, Ghusn Akbar Mohammed Ali… but, to my regret, the request was not granted, and since then false accusations have been circulated against your brother. … For the sake of truth, grant my request and appoint the peace conference. May the Almighty guide us all to understand His will and wish." Portions of Mr. Behai's open letter to 'Abdu'l-Baha are reproduced thereafter. In the next day's edition of that newspaper, an article appeared in which 'Abdu'l-Baha dismissed the matter as "unworthy of the slightest consideration" and compared Mr. Behai to a man coming out of "a saloon on the corner." (Scanned copies available online at http://www.h-net.org/~bahai/docs/vol14/San_Francisco_Call_13-14_Oct_1912.pdf).

Dreyfus[12] of Paris, France, unexpectedly called on me with a fighting spirit; most of his conversation was appertaining to the unfounded accusations towards my father regarding the petition to the Ottoman government and the arrival of the investigators, etc. I patiently listened to him until he was exhausted; then I said: "All your statements are hearsay and absolutely without foundation. I am ready to go with you to Palestine for the sole purpose of investigation there in the governorate or to go to the Vilayet[13] at Beirut, or to go to the headquarters of the Ottoman government in Constantinople if necessary, and if we find a petition presented to the government by my father or any of his followers as you have stated, then all what you said is correct. But I am positive that we will not find even a complaint whatsoever, from my father or any of his followers against His Excellency 'Abdu'l-Baha." Mr. Dreyfus remained with me until late that evening and somehow he was satisfied with my explanations as he left me.

One year later, on a Sunday afternoon I answered the doorbell and to my surprise I saw Mr. Dreyfus standing at the door. After exchanging greetings and after he had rested, I discovered that he was in California with Mrs. Dreyfus, the former Miss Laura Clifford Barney[14] of Washington D.C. and her mother, on their way to the Far East. On this visit our conversations were more sociable and mostly incidentals. He remained with me all afternoon, returning to his hotel in Los Angeles in the evening. Two days later I went to Los Angeles, returning my friend's call, and I had the pleasure of meeting Mrs. Dreyfus and her mother.

---

[12] Hippolyte Dreyfus, who changed his surname to Dreyfus-Barney after marrying Laura Clifford Barney in 1911, was designated by Shoghi Effendi Rabbani as one of the nineteen Disciples of 'Abdu'l-Baha. He was the first French convert to the Baha'i faith and translated numerous writings of Baha'u'llah into French. He held a doctorate in law and was involved in legal efforts to protect the Baha'i community from persecution.

[13] *Vilayets* were the first-order administrative divisions or provincial governments of the Ottoman Empire. The Vilayet of Beirut included much of present-day Israel, Palestine, and Lebanon. Each vilayet was ruled by a *vali* (Arabic: *wali*).

[14] Laura Clifford Barney, who later took the surname Dreyfus-Barney, was an American Baha'i who is best known for having compiled the book *Some Answered Questions* from her interviews with 'Abdu'l-Baha.

During this meeting the existing dissension between my uncle and my father was discussed but very mildly, and we arranged that they shall go to the Far East, and the following winter in 1914 we should all meet in Palestine and try to bring unity among the two brothers and their followers; but unfortunately the following year the war [i.e. World War I] was declared in Europe and we could not make our pilgrimage as we planned.

Disappointment with Baha'i Community; Association with Liberal Baha'is

In 1923 I made a visit to the Holy Land. This journey lasted six months; also I visited Egypt. I regret that I found the true Baha'i spirit that was in existence in the past had been diminished, and the offspring of those noble souls that sacrificed their lives for the spread of truth were entangled in the cobwebs of earthly possessions, eagerly seeking false leadership for the accumulation of riches, originating new names and titles for the control of leadership and the collection of dues which were [originally intended] for the widows and orphans; their ears deaf to the words of God, and following the golden calf as they did in the time of Moses; intoxicated by false promises and drowned in the sea of superstition; their hearts filled with hatred toward those whose only faults were the confession of the Oneness and Singleness of God.

During my last sojourn in the city of New York, I had the pleasure of meeting Mrs. Lewis Stuyvesant Chanler and her coworker Mirza Ahmad Sohrab,[15] while I was attending a reception which was arranged by

---

[15] Ahmad Sohrab was a secretary and interpreter for 'Abdu'l-Baha who founded an educational organization called the New History Society and later the Caravan of East and West, which connected people around the world for interfaith and cross-cultural dialogue as pen-pals. These organizations were intended to spread the Baha'i principles without being officially connected to the Baha'i faith. In 1939, Mr. Sohrab was expelled from the Baha'i community by Shoghi Effendi Rabbani, because he refused to allow his organizations to come under the oversight of the Baha'i Spiritual Assembly of New York, as ordered by Mr. Rabbani. Julie Chanler, the wife of New York politician Lewis Stuyvesant Chanler, attempted to bring about a reconciliation but was unsuccessful, and the Chanlers were also expelled. Ahmad Sohrab continued to teach the Baha'i

the natives of India, in honor of the well-known Muslim leader Maulana Shaukat Ali.[16] I was invited by the aforesaid lady to attend the meetings of the New History Society. Complying with her kind request I attended a few of the Baha'i gatherings, and I had the pleasure of meeting The Honorable Lewis Stuyvesant Chanler also.

Journey from California to the Holy Land

In 1933 I left New York for California again, and the mild climate of the Golden State lured me to remain there.

In the summer of 1936 I received news from home that my beloved father was ill and demanded my presence; therefore I left California and made a pilgrimage to the Holy Land. I hereby invite my readers to enjoy the minutes of that journey with me.

Our pilgrimage began from San Diego, California, USA at 10 a.m. on Sunday, October 25, 1936. We journeyed in two motor cars with our luggage via the Coast Highway, arriving at the Terminal Island port of Los Angeles at 1:30 in the afternoon. After placing our luggage in our staterooms with the Panama Pacific Liner S.S. *Pennsylvania*, a thirty-three thousand ton steamer, we left the Terminal Island for Ocean Park, a suburb of Los Angeles, and visited a delightful couple there, where we spent a few hours. Then we motored to Hollywood to the abode of other beloved friends, a newly and happily wedded couple, where we enjoyed their kind hospitality of a royal farewell dinner. At ten o'clock in the evening we motored to the pier, some of the friends joining to

---

faith in his own way, publishing an anthology of the scriptures of world religions (including Baha'i) called *The Bible of Mankind*, and also wrote books criticizing Shoghi Effendi's leadership style and excommunications of prominent Baha'is. With the support of Mr. and Mrs. Chanler and other liberal Baha'is, Mr. Sohrab's organizations enjoyed considerable success during his lifetime. In 1956, he wrote that the Caravan of East and West "numbers 1,300 chapters in 37 countries, with an aggregate membership of 100,000 children, young people and adults." (*Living Schools of Religion*, edited by Virgilius Ferm. Chapter entitled "The Baha'i Cause" available online at http://bahai-library.com/sohrab_ferm).

[16] Maulana Shaukat Ali was a prominent activist for Indian independence and later for political self-determination for India's Muslims.

wish us farewell and unanimously desirous to accompany us on our pilgrimage. Being late we insisted on their departure, so the friends left us with the wonderful wish "Bon Voyage!" No need to state our mutual feelings when the parting time arrived; all I can say is: "May God bless them and keep them safe for me." We are at the deck of the liner watching the multitude of humanity ebb and flow like the waves of the sea.

A short time before the departing hour we suddenly become cognizant of the presence of some other friends, who motored 150 miles to see us and faithfully remained at the pier until our steamer sailed and we disappeared in the darkness of the night.

Although we are surrounded with joy, being on the pilgrimage to the Holy Land, yet the parting with our friends and beloved ones is trying, and, I must confess that there is an emptiness in my heart while we are sailing and gradually the illuminated lights of the great city are getting dimmer and dimmer.

The last two days passed pleasantly in good weather and smooth sailing. Today we are passing through the gulf streams of Lower California [i.e. Baja]; it is a little rough and unpleasant for those who are not good sailors.

October the 29th, we reached a seaport in Old Mexico, a quaint little place called Acapulco. The liner anchored, and through the courtesy of the Panama Pacific Company we landed and spent a few hours here. The town is unusual, the roads are rough, narrow and uneven. The buildings are ununified and the street vendors are visible everywhere. Women and children go around in their bare feet carrying provisions on their heads to their homes. Señoritas of the better classes are going to the market in pajamas. Men are enjoying their siesta on street benches and on the sands of the seashore. Everyone is carefree, enjoying the tropical climate. A town far behind the present progressive age. The only modern objects we observed were American-made motor cars of the latest models, and the reason for their popularity, as explained to us, is the existence of a fine paved highway completed recently between here and Mexico City, the capital of the Mexican Republic. Therefore many visitors motor to this place on weekends. There is a nice hotel and some cottages on the top of the hill for the convenience of the tourists. Indeed, there is some contrast between this place and

California in architecture and customs—their life and habits are amusing, although in very humble circumstances, they are happy and contented. We enjoyed a drink of fresh coconut juice which was served in its original shell; the natives boasted graciously of this delightful drink. The scenery is marvelous; the hills are covered with green vegetation. A thought sparked in my mind: how anxious an American real estate developer would be to hold and operate such a land and what a seaside resort this spot would make, if some hotel association could secure and improve it.

Acapulco was a great seaport and enjoyed commercial progress during the 16th, 17th and 18th centuries, while Mexico was under the dominion of Spain. Being the only Mexican seaport to the Philippines and Asia, the Manila galleys anchored here bringing rich wares from Asia and in return loading spices, rice, etc., from India; their cargo being carried on the back of the caravan of burros to and from Veracruz, the Mexican seaport of the Atlantic Ocean where the Spanish galleys carried them to the fatherland.

Three more days on the ocean, we passed the shores of Guatemala, Honduras, Nicaragua, and Costa Rica. Tropical weather and pleasant sailing, lots of sports on deck, congenial passengers, officers and crew very thoughtful, good service, fine food, and all on board happy.

Monday, November 2, we reached Panama and Balboa. We took an interesting sightseeing tour, passing through a section of Balboa, the spotless American town which is the seat of the Panama Canal administration. Thence to Fort Amador, a United States military port at the entrance of the canal; through Balboa Heights and Ancón, residential quarters for canal employees; the American hospital grounds; Bella Vista, the modern residential section of Panama. The statue of Balboa, the discoverer of the Pacific Ocean. Club Miramar, the race course, the golf club. And the old Panama, the ruins of the cathedral and the site of the city which was destroyed by fire in the year 1671. Our guide suggested strolling in the shopping district of Panama City if we desired and unfortunately we followed his advice. The narrow and winding streets were full of shops of all sizes, owned and run mostly by the natives of East India and China, overstocked with luxurious and inferior merchandise from East India, Japan, and China. All displaying the same line, hungry for business, pulling the visitors into the shops and trying their utmost to part them from their cash.

November the 3rd, we passed through the great engineering enterprise, the Panama Canal. It took eight hours to go through this wonderful monument representing the mighty power of the human mind which linked the great oceans together, the Pacific and the Atlantic. Our steamer docked at Christóbal, we strolled for a while, the city is calm and quiet. Being the Panama Independence Day,[17] all the business concerns were closed, by mutual agreement; American Independence Day and this day are observed by all in the Canal Zone.

Two days at Caribbean Sea, pleasant weather, the passengers on the deck enjoying sun baths and the tropical climate.

The morning of November 6 found us at the island of Cuba and the historical city of Havana. Upon disembarking we engaged the services of a guide and a motor car and proceeded to the Plaza de Armas, the ancient central square. Here are the palaces of the old Spanish Governor Generals, the "Little Temple" (El Templete) marking the spot where the first mass was said in Cuba, and the oldest fort in the Western Hemisphere, [Castillo de] La [Real] Fuerza. Nearby we saw the cathedral where rested the ashes of Columbus from the year 1791 to 1898, when they were removed to Spain. The drive continued to the President's Palace; the tobacco factory, the home of the Havana cigars; the [Paseo del] Prado, world-famous avenue with a fine view of Morro Castle from its foot; to the Malecón, a seaside drive extending three miles in a beautiful crescent beside the blue Gulf of Mexico; to Vedado, a modern suburb of palatial homes.[18] En route we saw the bronze statue of [Antonio] Maceo [Grajales], one of Cuba's liberators, and the tall twin shafts of the [USS] *Maine* Memorial. Next we visited the University Heights, and to our surprise, we learned that the university itself has been closed by the order of the government on account of Soviet propaganda amongst the students. Thence we motored to the cemetery with its many beautiful monuments; Camp Columbia, where the American army spread

---

[17] Separation Day, celebrating Panama's separation from Colombia.

[18] Vedado is now part of downtown Havana.

its tents in the year 1898; the beautiful tropical gardens with their romantic atmosphere, the country club with velvety golf links, the yacht club with bathing beach, the casino with Monte Carlo reputation, then back to the business section of the city. Here we dismissed our guide and car and strolled in the busy streets. We found most of the shops displaying American-made merchandise. While wandering in the picturesque streets near the waterfront we sought some information from three different Cuban policemen, and to our surprise none of them understood one word of the English language.

Two more days on the ocean, we passed the coasts of Florida and the Carolinas, the weather getting colder as we are approaching the East Coast.

November 9, we reached New York City, and after completing custom-house formalities, we motored through the busy section of the great city, and passed the Hudson Tunnel[19] to Jersey City Pier of the American Export Lines. Placing our luggage with the representatives of the company, we returned to New York. While at the custom house we met some dear friends who extended to us the courtesy of using their car, and through their kindness we motored in the metropolitan city that afternoon and rested the night at a hotel in the heart of the bright light section of Broadway. I regret that the time allotted to us here is limited and we are unable to visit the numerous friends who reside in this locality.

November 10, at 4 p.m., we embarked on one of the Four Aces of the American Export Lines, S.S. *Exochorda*, and a while later we sailed. Five days passed on the great Atlantic Ocean, no land is visible, occasionally we pass a steamer. Nice weather, plenty of entertainment, sociable passengers, fine food, and all on board are thankful.

Today is November 16, and we are at the Azores islands, the vessel anchored at Ponta Delgada, the first interlude of this voyage. Here history goes back to the days of the Phoenicians and Moor rovers, where later Portuguese navigators laid the foundation for the islands' Portuguese aristocracy. Ponta Delgada is the harbor city of St. Michael, the

---

[19] Now called the Holland Tunnel.

largest island of the group, which is beautifully decorated with rich vegetation. From the bay the approach is an exciting prelude to the bewitching landscape that dots the shores of the Mediterranean. In the foreground is an operatic picture of homes of primrose, yellow, pink and white walls resting in green valleys and perched on summits that pierce the azure sky.

Two more days on the Atlantic Ocean, and on November the 18th we were extended the hospitality of the Captain's dinner and afterwards with a dance in the social hall for those who desired to attend.

November 19, we arrived at Gibraltar, the natural fortified rock which the European dictators gaze at with envy and for its possession sigh in vain. The steamer stopped a sufficient time to disembark passengers and mail and we bid farewell to the Atlantic Ocean, entering the picturesque Mediterranean. We enjoyed the first day on this alluring sea immensely.

November 21, we docked at the city of Marseilles, the ancient seaport of the French Republic. We spent a very interesting day at this cosmopolitan and commercial city. Occasionally we came in contact with the natives who are known for their extreme politeness. Here we observed people of all walks of life rubbing elbows with one another peacefully with the feeling of utter detachment from worry. We motored in and around the city, visiting the Cathedral of La Major, Abbey of St. Victor, City Hall, Longchamp Palace, the Prado, and Notre-Dame de La Gard. The day was completed with a boat trip to the famous Chateau d'If, rendered immortal by Dumas in his *Count of Monte Cristo*.

November the 22nd, we passed between the islands of Corsica and Sardinia, and on November the 23rd, we arrived at the famous city of Naples. There can scarcely be a more interesting port in the world; not only does it possess romantic beauty in its incomparable bay with its waters of the deepest blue, and the stately [Mount] Vesuvius, but it also has a stirring history which began with the Greek settlers who founded the city and gave it its name, "Neopolis." Our visit to the beautiful National Museum explained the wonders we saw afterwards in the great excavation of Pompeii. Crossing the Mediterranean we experienced only one unpleasant night on account of disturbed weather; the rest of the voyage passed delightfully. Fine weather, comfortable accommodations and excellent food. Officers and crew extremely courteous and doing their utmost to please the passengers. A floating first-class American hotel with all the conveniences of home one desires. Fine group of passengers, amongst them His Excellency the American Minister to the Kingdom of Egypt, His Excellency the Belgian Minister to Iran (Persia), an Arabian Pasha, and other notables.

On November the 25th, we enjoyed the delicious farewell dinner, especially the greeting extended to us by the Commander and the crew printed on the last page of the menu which touched the heart. Showing my appreciation, I reprint here the same: "Bidding farewell to our Mediterranean passengers. The Commander, officers and crew bid adieu to their passengers, shipmates of the voyage, and extend the heartiest of best wishes and Godspeed.—S.S. *Exochorda*, Wenzel Habel, Commander."

After a day at sea we approached the dean of seaports, Alexandria, the oldest harbor in the world and the gateway to Egypt. On the island at bay stands the remnant of the Pharos Lighthouse built in the third century. Passing its northern tips we are reminded that it is an even 5,000 miles to New York, yet we feel a million miles away and are carried back to the Egyptian splendor. Three hours by railroad from this historic port and we are at Cairo, which is called the queen of the cities of Islam, crossed by the silver ribbon of the Nile; the eye is lost in the sea of its roofs, domes, and minarets. In the modern quarter, the streets are lined with trees and fine buildings; gardens and monuments adorn the squares. In the medieval quarters of the caliphs, we entered a city of the Arabian nights, with narrow crooked alleys, bazaars, mosques, and coffee houses, the secret look of which tells how East is East and West is West. The visit to the cities of the pyramids, the Sphinx and the Temple of the Sphinx at Giza added a valuable chapter to our book of thoughts. What a glorious heaven this world will be when East and West will become united considering mankind one kindred. The Great Master, Baha'u'llah said: "Ye are all leaves of one tree and the drops of one sea."

Our last night at sea passed with anxiety as we were approaching our goal. Sunday morning, November 29, we anchored at the ports of Jaffa and Tel Aviv, the latter being the largest modern city built by the children of Israel since the World War. In a few hours we sailed for our destination, arriving at the port of Haifa at 6 p.m., after thirty-five days of travel by water. We humbly thank the Almighty for our safe arrival to the Holy Land, where the Manifestations, prophets, and great Messengers appeared; where the wise men saw the Star of Bethlehem, and where the Prince of Peace, the Everlasting Father established His Kingdom. The shrines of the nations, the fountainhead of truth, the land of our dreams and boyhood days.

The steamer docked and at our landing I found myself in the arms of my two beloved brothers surrounded with relatives and friends, by whom we have been entertained ever since. Our pilgrimage was completed by a visit to the Sacred Shrine [of Baha'u'llah] where we rendered our supplications, remembering our Western friends as well.

A year later my beloved father passed away.

Shua Ullah Behai wearing traditional Middle Eastern robe (*abaya*) and felt hat (*tarboosh*).

Badi Ullah Bahai in his elder years.

31

The Importance of Unity: Messages to the Baha'is

By Badi Ullah Bahai

Badi Ullah Bahai (1871[1] – November 1, 1950), known as Mirza Badi'-u'llah in the mainstream Baha'i tradition, was the youngest son of Baha'u'llah. This circular letter by Mr. Bahai was included in a chapter called "The Two Younger Branches, the Leaves, and Their Spouses" in Shua Ullah Behai's book manuscript. A section heading has been added by this editor.

Shua Ullah Behai described the untitled document as Badi Ullah Effendi's "latest message to the friends throughout the world." Based on the fact that the leader of the Unitarian Baha'i community, Mohammed Ali Effendi, died in 1937, and Mr. Behai's manuscript was compiled in the mid 1940s, this message was therefore most likely written in the late 1930s or early 1940s.

The author also includes a previous message which he quotes, saying that he wrote it to the Baha'is after the death of 'Abdu'l-Baha. Interestingly, he refers to him by that title, which may suggest a less staunch opposition than his brother Mohammed Ali, who avoided using Abbas Effendi's preferred epithet and hinted in some of his writings that he found it inappropriate.

Although Badi Ullah Effendi was a Unitarian Baha'i, he had at one time sided with 'Abdu'l-Baha and may not have entirely agreed with

---

[1] Most published sources say he was born in 1867 or 1868, but members of the Bahai family report his year of birth as 1871.

either of his elder brothers. Some of the statements and tone of this document suggest that he saw the death of Mohammed Ali Effendi as opening the door for reconciliation and reunification of the Baha'i sects that had developed as a result of the long-standing dispute between the late leaders of the two factions. The "new era" he refers to is presumably an era in which, in his view, Baha'is could move beyond the arguments of the two rival sons of Baha'u'llah who had passed into history.

—The Editor

HE IS GOD.

With the grace and bounty of the Blessed Perfection, Baha'u'llah, it is hoped that this new era will provide a blessing to all the Baha'is in both the Orient and the Occident, that they may be destined to carry out and perform that which benefits this great cause.

Revered Baha'is! Arise in thanks to this era, to eliminate the existing dissension in accordance with the precepts laid down in both the *Kitab-i-Aqdas* and the *Kitab-i-'Ahdi*, so that all may be gathered under the canopy of the all-uniting word [of Baha'u'llah].

In the *Kitab-i-Aqdas*, The Most Holy Book, He says: "O people of the earth! When the Sun of My Beauty sets and the Heaven of My Temple is screened [i.e. obscured], be not disturbed, but arise to assist My cause and to raise My word among the creatures. Verily, We are All-Powerful."

He also says: "And We behold you from Our Most Glorious Horizon and assist those who arise to assist My cause with the hosts of the Unseen and the chosen angels."

As this assistance is not possible except by referring to what has been revealed by His Most Glorious Pen, He says: "If ye differ in any matter, refer it to God [i.e. Baha'u'llah] so long as the Sun is shining from the Horizon of this Heaven, and when He sets, refer to what hath been revealed from His presence; verily this suffices the worlds."[2]

---

[2] *Kitab-i-Aqdas* ("Most Holy Book"), paragraph 53.

O friends! The cause is being weakened because of the present dissension, and the essential intention of the Blessed Perfection, Baha'u'llah, is no more visible.

In the Most Holy Book, He says: "Beware lest the propensities of selfishness and desire disperse you; be like fingers on a hand and limbs on a body. Thus the Pen of Revelation admonisheth you, if ye are of those who believe."[3]

In the Book of My Covenant, *Kitab-i-'Ahdi*, He says:

> The object of this Oppressed One in enduring hardships and calamities and revealing texts and bringing forth proofs [of his mission] is to extinguish the fire of rancor and hatred, that the horizon of the hearts of the people may be illumined with the light of unity and attain perfect tranquility. The star of this elucidation hath dawned and risen from the horizon of the Tablet of God; therefore it behooveth everyone to contemplate it.

He also says: "O people of the earth! The religion of God is love and concord; make it not the cause of enmity and strife." And He says:

> O people! Do not make the elements of discipline a cause of disorder, and make not the essence of concord a stepping stone to discord. It is meet for the people of Baha to contemplate this blessed verse: Say, from God everyone hath come! This great word is like unto water which extinguishes the fire of rancor and hatred, which is inherent and hidden in the hearts.

I have the greatest hope that the divine followers of Baha'u'llah place before their eyes the admonitions of the Supreme Pen, and hold fast to that which is the cause of unity and turn away from what causes dissension and discord. There is no doubt that dissension and discord produce only weakness as may be seen in the cases of the nations of yore.

---

[3] Ibid., paragraph 58.

Badi Ullah Effendi's Message upon the Passing of 'Abdu'l-Baha

After the departure of 'Abdu'l-Baha, the Greatest Branch [Ghusn-i-A'zam], I wrote a short notice which is hereinafter repeated for the benefit of those who did not read it then:

> A little attention to the book of creation [i.e. the natural world] shows us clearly the benefits and powers derived from unison and concord.
>
> When God ordained [it] and all the requirements for creation were ready, the particles scattered in the nebula slowly gained heat and motion and joined together with the help of this powerful attraction of love, and all the present creatures found existence. Had these particles remained apart, no being would have existed.
>
> Likewise, if we consider the book of inscription [i.e. the written word], we find that all the existing books, sciences and teachings have come to light with the help of the union of the alphabetical letters. Had these letters remained apart, neither words nor sentences could be formed. These thousands of books filled with teachings and sciences would not have been spread and published in the human world.
>
> It is therefore certain that power lies in unison and love, and weakness lurks in separation and contention. For this reason Baha'u'llah enjoined in most of His blessed tablets unison and concord, and prohibited strife and contention.
>
> O spiritual brothers! Arise, unfold the banner of union and concord and do away with dissension and discord, so that you may hear, from the Kingdom of God, the call of "Well done my friends" and be considered among God's own people.
>
> Peace be with you all.

Shoghi Rabbani, great-grandson of Baha'u'llah. This photo was taken in 1921, around the time of 'Abdu'l-Baha's death, when the young Shoghi Effendi became Guardian of the Baha'i faith.

32

The Baha'i Faith Under Shoghi Effendi Rabbani

By Shua Ullah Behai

This chapter is reproduced from a chapter in Shua Ullah Behai's book manuscript called simply "Shoghi Effendi Rabbani." Section headings have been added. A long section about Lewis Stuyvesant Chanler at the end of the original chapter has been omitted from this edited version and can be found, in abbreviated form, in Chapter 21.

Shoghi Rabbani, usually called Shoghi Effendi by Baha'is, was the eldest grandson of 'Abdu'l-Baha. He was born in 1897 and died in 1957, more than ten years after Shua Ullah Behai's manuscript was written. Even though Mr. Rabbani's leadership of the Baha'i faith continued for a considerable time beyond the scope of this chapter, the major themes of his "Guardianship" as perceived by the Unitarian Baha'is are all addressed: his appointment to the office in violation of Baha'u'llah's appointment of Mohammed Ali Bahai to succeed 'Abdu'l-Baha; the clash between, on the one hand, his loyal followers who created a more tightly regulated Baha'i organization, and on the other hand, various liberal Baha'is who resisted this development; his expulsion of all his relatives and numerous other Baha'is from the faith community; and his organization's failed attempt to sue dissenting Baha'is into silence or submission.

—The Editor

The Shocking Appointment of Shoghi Effendi

Shoghi Effendi Rabbani was the son of Mirza Hadi Afnan and Zia'iyya Khanum,[1] eldest daughter of His Excellency 'Abdu'l-Baha.

Shoghi Effendi was appointed in the will of 'Abdu'l-Baha as supreme leader of the Baha'is, in defiance of the commands of the Great Baha'u'llah in his will entitled *Kitab-i-'Ahdi* (i.e. the Book of My Covenant), wherein the second son of Baha'u'llah, Ghusn-i-Akbar, Mohammed Ali, is designated as successor to Ghusn-i-A'zam, 'Abdu'l-Baha.

Baha'u'llah says: "Verily God hath ordained the station of the Mightiest Branch (Ghusn-i-Akbar) after the station of the former [i.e. Ghusn-i-A'zam]. Verily He is the Ordainer, the Wise. We have surely chosen the Mightiest (Akbar) after the Greatest (A'zam) as a command from the All-Knowing, the Omniscient."

It appears that the will of 'Abdu'l-Baha was written when Shoghi Effendi was only ten or eleven years of age.[2]

Setbacks and Dissent

Many unfortunate events took place since Shoghi Effendi has presided over the Baha'i affairs. Dissatisfaction prevailed among the Baha'is everywhere, in the East as in the West. Numerous prominent Baha'i teachers severed their connections with the Baha'i centers. Baha'ism was suppressed by the governments of several countries, namely Iran, Turkey, and Germany.

Two Iranian Baha'i teachers, 'Abdu'l-Husayn Avara[3] and Hasan

---

[1] 'Abdu'l-Baha instructed Mr. and Mrs. Afnan to give their children the surname Rabbani, which means "godly" or "divine" (from the Arabic word *rabb*, meaning "Lord").

[2] The Will and Testament of 'Abdu'l-Baha was written in three parts over a period of several years. Part One of the document, in which Shoghi Rabbani was appointed to the position of "Guardian" of the Baha'i faith, is thought to have been written when he was seven to ten years old. The exact year is uncertain.

[3] 'Abdu'l-Husayn Ayati, known to Baha'is as Avarih (also spelled Avareh or Avara), was an Iranian Baha'i missionary, writer, and secondary school teacher. 'Abdu'l-Baha appointed him to the position of Hand of the Cause of God and

Niku,[4] left the cause entirely. The former even changed his surname to Ayati, and both of them wrote several books and pamphlets against this movement, and flooded the Eastern Hemisphere with their antagonistic propaganda.

In the United States of America, the *Reality* magazine[5] was the first Baha'i publication that revolted against the supremacy of the Baha'i organization, and finally the dispute was ended with an unfortunate decision, namely the excommunication of the members of that publication.

Baha'i Organization Legally Established Under the Guardianship

In 1926 the Declaration of Trust and the By-Laws of the National Spiritual Assembly of the Baha'is of the United States and Canada were formed, after several years of hard labor, by a few selected regular officials of that organization. The following is part of the Declaration of

---

commissioned him to write an authorized history of the Babi and Baha'i faith in Persian, which was published in 1923. He later renounced his Baha'i faith and was designated as a "Covenant-breaker" by Shoghi Effendi. In a book he wrote explaining his apostasy, Mr. Ayati claimed that 'Abdu'l-Baha had instructed him to distort some historical facts in his earlier book in order to conform with 'Abdu'l-Baha's preferred account of events. Baha'is have attempted to expunge the memory of Avarih's important position and contributions to the faith, as documented by Vance Salisbury in "A Critical Examination of 20th-Century Baha'i Literature" (available online at http://bahai-library.com/salisbury_critical_ examination_literature).

[4] Hasan Niku was a leading Iranian Baha'i missionary who, after leaving the Baha'i faith, published a book explaining why he became disillusioned with the movement. Among other things, he accused 'Abdu'l-Baha of excessive worldly ambition and desire for money, and criticized him for writing flattering epistles to wealthy and powerful people whom he hoped to win as disciples.

[5] *Reality* was a commercial magazine founded by liberal Baha'is in 1919, which covered the Baha'i faith and other topics of interest to spiritual progressives of the day such as metaphysics and socialism. The magazine grew increasingly critical of some of the beliefs and leadership of the organized Baha'i community, especially when Shoghi Effendi Rabbani became the Baha'i Guardian in the early 1920s. After 1926, the magazine shifted its attention away from Baha'i issues and towards other subjects, and in 1929 it ceased publication.

Trust and part of the By-Laws of the aforesaid organization.[6]

DECLARATION OF TRUST

We... the National Spiritual Assembly of the Baha'is of the United States and Canada, with full power to establish a Trust as hereinafter set forth, hereby declare that from this date the powers, responsibilities, rights, privileges and obligations reposed in said National Spiritual Assembly of the Baha'is of the United States and Canada by Baha'u'llah, Founder of the Baha'i Faith, by 'Abdu'l-Baha, its Interpreter and Exemplar, and by Shoghi Effendi, its Guardian, shall be exercised, administered and carried on by the above-named National Spiritual Assembly and their qualified successors under this declaration of Trust. ...

Article II.

... [W]e declare the purposes and objects of this Trust to be to administer the affairs of the Cause of Baha'u'llah for the benefit of the Baha'is of the United States and Canada according to the principles of Baha'i affiliation and administration created and established by Baha'u'llah, defined and explained by 'Abdu'l-Baha, and amplified and applied by Shoghi Effendi and his duly constituted successor and successors under the provision of the Will and Testament of 'Abdu'l-Baha. ...

BY-LAWS OF THE NATIONAL SPIRITUAL ASSEMBLY

Article II.

The Baha'is of the United States and Canada, for whose benefit this trust has been established, shall consist of all persons resident in the United States and Canada who are recognized by the National Spiritual Assembly as having fulfilled the requirements

---

[6] Published in *The Bahá'í World: Volume 03 (1928-1930)*, compiled by the National Spiritual Assembly of the Bahá'ís of the United States and Canada (New York: Bahá'í Publishing Committee, 1930), pp. 96-104. Available online at http://bahai-library.com/usnsa_bahai_world_3. The same text, with minor changes, has been used as a model for Baha'i National Spiritual Assemblies around the world. See http://bahai-library.com/nsa_bw_18.

of voting membership in a local Baha'i community. To become a voting member of a Baha'i community a person shall ...

c. Have established to the satisfaction of the local Spiritual Assembly, subject to the approval of the National Assembly, that he possesses the qualifications of Baha'i faith and practice required under the following standard: Full recognition of the station of the Forerunner (the Bab), the Author (Baha'u'llah), and 'Abdu'l-Baha the True Exemplar of the Baha'i Cause; unreserved acceptance of, and submission to, whatsoever has been revealed by their Pen; loyal and steadfast adherence to every clause of 'Abdu'l-Baha's sacred Will; and close association with the spirit as well as the form of present-day Baha'i administration throughout the world. ...

Article VII. ...

Section 3. Among its more specific duties, a local Spiritual Assembly shall have full jurisdiction of all Baha'i activities and affairs within the local community, subject, however, to the exclusive and paramount authority of the National Spiritual Assembly as defined herein. ...

Section 6. The local Assembly shall pass upon and approve the qualifications of each member of the Baha'i community before such members shall be admitted to voting membership; but where an individual is dissatisfied with the ruling of the local Spiritual Assembly upon his Baha'i qualifications, such individual may appeal from the ruling to the National Assembly, which shall thereupon take jurisdiction of and finally decide the case. ...

Section 12. ... All differences of opinion concerning the sphere of jurisdiction of any local Spiritual Assembly or concerning the affiliation of any Baha'i or group of Baha'is in the United States and Canada shall be referred to the National Spiritual Assembly, whose decision in the matter shall be final. ...

Article IX.

Where the National Spiritual Assembly has been given in these By-Laws exclusive and final jurisdiction, and paramount executive authority, in all matters pertaining to the activities and affairs of the Baha'i Cause in the United States and Canada, it is understood that any decision made or action taken upon such matters shall be subject in every instance to ultimate review and approval by the Guardian of the Cause or the Universal House of Justice.[7]

The power invested to the leader [i.e. Shoghi Effendi, the Guardian] and the officials of the National Spiritual Assembly by the above-mentioned Declaration of Trust and By-Laws, caused great anxiety to the intellectual Baha'is throughout the world, as they considered them in violation of the Baha'i principles. Indeed, it worked like dynamite and shattered the minds of the free thinkers, and caused many good and godly souls to keep in seclusion and to be silent. Others revolted to the extent of denying the authenticity of the will of 'Abdu'l-Baha.

The Beliefs and Allegations of Ruth White

In 1929, while I was on a visit to Wisconsin, a dear Baha'i friend handed me a book, written by Mrs. Ruth White, entitled *The Bahai Religion and Its Enemy, the Bahai Organization*. The object of my friend in presenting me this book was that I may answer to some of the accusations contained therein towards my beloved father, Ghusn-i-Akbar, Mohammed Ali.

After reading the contents of the book carefully, I discovered that the author was entirely in the dark about the actually existing conditions and had passed judgment without investigation. After a long debate with my innermost, I could find no other course to pursue, but to hand over the case to an attorney, with instructions to bring a libel suit against the author for slander. But as this action would have been in violation of the Baha'i principles and the spirit of the teachings of Baha'u'llah, therefore I kept silent and left the matter to God's hands.[8]

In 1937, when I visited the Holy Land, during my interviews with

---

[7] The Universal House of Justice did not yet exist at the time when these bylaws were written, but was described by Baha'u'llah and 'Abdu'l-Baha in their writings.

[8] Baha'u'llah did not prohibit civil lawsuits. However, the Bahai family was reluctant to use the court system to fight over matters of religion, perhaps because they felt that such a course of action would be too contentious and potentially harmful to the Baha'i faith, and Baha'u'llah had prohibited conflict and urged peaceful relations among his followers.

Ghusn-i-Akbar, Mohammed Ali, I asked him several questions which he graciously answered. I hereby reproduce the question and the answer appertaining to this matter.

> Q. Mrs. Ruth White, a rebel member of the [Baha'i organization led by] the National Spiritual Assembly of the Baha'is of the United States and Canada, in her published book entitled *The Bahai Religion and Its Enemy, the Bahai Organization*, emphatically denies the authenticity of the will of 'Abdu'l-Baha Abbas, and with firm conviction states that your Excellency assisted Shoghi Effendi in fabricating the said will?
>
> A. Shoghi has never been in my presence, and I do not know him personally. Mrs. Ruth White's accusations are untrue. It is indeed surprising to observe that progressive Occidentals satisfied themselves with hearsay, and passed judgment without investigation.

Indeed the name of the said book is very appropriate, but I regret that I cannot agree to all it contains. I personally sympathize with Mrs. White in her allusions [i.e. regarding the danger of the Baha'i organization to the religion itself], but she should have exercised the law of investigation before passing judgment. No court of law, whether judicial or theological, would render judgment without a hearing.

Independent investigation of truth is one of the great Baha'i principles, but unfortunately it is not practiced.

Public Debate Discouraged by Baha'i Officials

Some years ago, in 1923 to be exact, I noticed a discussion among the Baha'is which substantiated my aforesaid assertion. In the *Reality* magazine, Vol. VI No. 12, pages 33-34, December 1923, a letter addressed to Reality Publishing Co. by one of its Consulting Editors, Dr. Richard M. Bolden,[9] was published. [Here is an excerpt:]

---

[9] Rev. Richard M. Bolden served both the Church of Emmanuel as well as the Baha'i Spiritual Assembly of New York. He is an example of an early 20th century liberal Baha'i who, like many, retained their ties to Christianity while embracing belief in the principles of the Baha'i movement.

Hence a few days ago when I was waited upon by an official of the Bahai Cause in America, who reported to me that in consultation with other officials they had decided that my position as Consulting Editor of the *Reality* Magazine made me appear as an enemy to the Bahai Cause, ...

I said to the representative that such things as were being told to me in order that I might withdraw what little influence I have from the *Reality* Magazine ought to be published in that magazine and all other magazines or papers that the friends of the Cause read, so that the truth of the Cause of God might prevail. The answer to this was that the true Bahai's method of combating falsehood and evil was to be in the manner that I was dealt with rather than in the open arena of public opinion.

Controversial Renovation of the House of Baha'u'llah

Another occurrence concerned the possession of the house which was occupied by Baha'u'llah during the last ten years of his appearance on earth. This house was called Qasr al-Bahji (i.e. Palace of Joy or Delight). The lower floor was built by Abdullah Pasha, who ruled this district during the last part of the 18th century, for his mother.

In the 19th century, the said house was purchased by a Christian and he built the upper floor and the surrounding houses, as shown on the sketch drawn on page [blank].[10]

During the days of Baha'u'llah the Qasr was rented from the Christian. The ascension of Baha'u'llah took place in the Qasr, and the Shrine of Baha'u'llah was placed in the northwestern corner house, which at that time was owned by Haji Siyyid Ali Afnan, husband of Foroughiyya Khanum, youngest daughter of Baha'u'llah. That house was purchased by the said Afnan from a relative of the above-mentioned Christian, and this was the first house on this locality which was purchased during the days of Baha'u'llah. Later on, the second house, which is located south of the Shrine, was also bought by Siyyid Ali Afnan, and at the present time both houses are registered in the name of his heirs.

---

[10] A sketch was not included with the copy of the manuscript provided to this editor.

Chapter 32. The Baha'i Faith Under Shoghi Effendi Rabbani

After the ascension of Baha'u'llah, gradually Qasr al-Bahji was purchased from the heirs of the said Christian by 'Abdu'l-Baha, Mohammed Ali, and two nephews of Baha'u'llah—namely Aqa Mirza Majdeddin, husband of Samadiyya Khanum, second daughter of Baha'u'llah, and one of the amanuenses; and his brother Aqa Mirza Ali Reza—and at the present time the Qasr is registered in the names of the heirs of 'Abdu'l-Baha, the heirs of Mohammed Ali, and the two above-mentioned nephews of Baha'u'llah.

After the ascension of Baha'u'llah the Qasr al-Bahji was occupied by Her Grace Mahd-i-'Ulya, the widow of Baha'u'llah; the three Branches (sons), Ghusn-i-Akbar Mohammed Ali, Zia Ullah Effendi and Badi Ullah Effendi; the Holy Leaf Samadiyya Khanum, and the members of the household.

Six years after the departure of 'Abdu'l-Baha, in 1927, Shoghi Effendi requested Mohammed Ali and the members of the household of Baha'u'llah to vacate the Qasr, with the excuse that the house was in need of repair. As the heirs of 'Abdu'l-Baha controlled the greater share in the Qasr, the request of Shoghi Effendi was granted and the place was surrendered after removing the contents of the house, although repairs were possible while occupied.

Since the ascension of Baha'u'llah, the room which had been occupied by him was always kept in order by the members of the household, and the visitors who came were welcomed to visit the sacred room.

Before the removal of the contents of the room of Baha'u'llah, Shoghi Effendi sent a photographer and took the photograph of the room, and after the removal, sent a cabinet maker and duplicates of the furniture were made, namely two sofas and a bureau. He also requested, through the Holy Leaf Bahiyyih Khanum, the pattern of the lace which covered the cushions and the divan on the south side of the room, and a duplicate of the same was made.

Thus the sacred room is refurnished with reproductions. All the original furniture, floor coverings, bed, etc. are at present in the possession of the heirs of Mohammed Ali, and arranged carefully in a room in the northwest upper house, which is occupied by the heirs of Mohammed Ali, adjoining the Holy Shrine of Baha'u'llah.

The remaining rooms of the Qasr al-Bahji are changed into a Baha'i library and museum. Four rooms are converted into modern bedrooms for the use of selected pilgrims, whenever they come. In fact none of the rooms resemble the original, as it was in the days of Baha'u'llah, with the exception of the room which was occupied by him, and unfortunately the contents of that sacred room are all reproductions.

The gross misrepresentation in this case compelled me to state the facts for the enlightenment of the progressive Baha'is and future historians. The photograph of the articles belonging to that sacred room, which are in our possession, appears in this book,[11] and the original sacred contents of that room are ready for inspection at any time at the above-mentioned location.[12]

Truthfulness is the duty of every honest individual. We, the Baha'is that advocate truth, should practice the same.

A visible sign should be placed in the sacred room of Baha'u'llah in the Qasr al-Bahji, to indicate that the contents of that room are reproductions, for the guidance of the public, to know the truth.

Shoghi Effendi Excommunicates His Family

Another occurrence was the excommunication and the expulsion of the members of the household of 'Abdu'l-Baha and the majority of the followers in the cities of Acre and Haifa, Palestine.

A few years after the departure [i.e. death] of the Holy Leaf Bahiyyih Khanum, sister of 'Abdu'l-Baha, and after Shoghi Effendi was invested with the supreme and infallible power by the above-mentioned Declaration of Trust and By-Laws, by the National Spiritual Assembly of the Baha'is of the United States and Canada, the air of dissension appeared among the members of the household of 'Abdu'l-Baha. His twin daughters Touba Khanum and Ruha Khanum with their families took up residence in Beirut, Lebanon, and the youngest daughter Mu-

---

[11] This photograph was not included with the copy of the manuscript provided to this editor.

[12] Presumably some relative of Mr. Behai inherited these furnishings, but their present owner or location is not known by this editor.

navvar Khanum with her husband Aqa Ahmad Yazdi resided mostly in Europe and Egypt.

When the war [i.e. World War II] started, they were all obliged to return to Palestine, and ever since they have made their homes in Nazareth and on Mount Carmel, and none of them associate with Shoghi Effendi.

Practically all the family of 'Abdu'l-Baha, including the two brothers and sisters of Shoghi Effendi and their husbands and wives, are either excommunicated or expelled from the community circle by Shoghi Effendi.[13]

Shoghi Effendi Orders Mass Emigration or Excommunication

In addition to the above-mentioned family, there are over seventy persons, Baha'i-born men, women and children, residing at Acre and Haifa who are excommunicated.

Most of the excommunicated persons who live at Acre and Haifa are offspring of those faithful followers who migrated with Baha'u'llah from Baghdad to Adrianople and from there to the great prison of Acre, and the manner of their excommunication is thus:

A few years ago while Shoghi Effendi was in Europe, through his brother Hussein Effendi, he ordered a few of his followers and their families who had no business connections in Acre and Haifa and were mostly a burden on him financially, to leave for Iran, Syria, Lebanon, or Egypt, with the promise that they should be taken care of by the Baha'i Assemblies at their destinations. Those who left for Iran were to be paid

---

[13] These relatives were mostly expelled for marrying people that Shoghi Effendi did not approve of, or for refusing to shun their children, siblings or cousins who entered into such marriages. Doctrinal differences may also have played a role, especially concerning the degree of authority of the Guardian and the personal freedom of Baha'is. However, unlike the previous generation of relatives who were excommunicated by 'Abdu'l-Baha, 'Abdu'l-Baha's own descendants who were excommunicated by Shoghi Effendi did not attempt to start a competing Baha'i tradition or organization; in fact, they avoided making any public statements about the Baha'i faith for decades. Writings by the descendants of 'Abdu'l-Baha about issues related to the expulsions were finally published in 2013, at http://www.abdulbahasfamily.org.

P.L.[14] 50, equivalent to $200 traveling expenses,[15] and those who left for Syria, Lebanon, and Egypt were to be paid P.L. 20, equivalent to $80.

Some of the families obeyed and left Palestine. Those who migrated to Iran received no assistance as promised and were left destitute. When they applied for help from the Assemblies, they were informed that they had been banished from Palestine and under the circumstances, what did they expect! Finally, after severe hardship, a few of them secured employment and are earning a simple living. Others pleaded by mail to Shoghi Effendi to be permitted to return to Palestine, but were refused.

After a few months, another order came, for more families to leave Acre and Haifa. This time the order affected those who were in business, shopkeepers of old standing, some who had inherited their businesses from their fathers. A few of the faithful followers obeyed the orders, disposed of their merchandise at a loss and left. But a few families made excuses and pleaded for mercy, explaining that they were born and bred here, and could not go to a foreign land and make a living. But their pleadings were rejected and they were threatened with excommunication if they disobeyed; and so, they were all excommunicated.

After a while came the turn of the rest of Shoghi Effendi's followers, who were property owners and government employees. This time the majority revolted and disobeyed; and so, they were all excommunicated.

Shoghi Effendi's Denomination Sues Dissenting Baha'is, Loses Case

Another event which happened: In 1939 a lawsuit was initiated by the National Spiritual Assembly [of the United States and Canada] and authorized by Shoghi Effendi, against the New History Society, to prevent the latter from using the name of "Baha'i" and teaching Baha'ism.

---

[14] The currency in Palestine during the British Mandate was the Palestine pound.

[15] In 2014 U.S. dollars, this would be worth approximately $3,000.

In 1941 a decision was pronounced by the Supreme Court of New York in favor of the New History Society; also the Appellate Division upheld the decision in the same year.[16]

For full information regarding this case I refer my good friends and readers to the remarkable book written by Mirza Ahmad Sohrab, entitled *Broken Silence: The Story of Today's Struggle for Religious Freedom*, published in 1942 by Universal Publishing Co., New York, for the New History Foundation, 132 East 65th Street, New York, N.Y.

Although it is unfortunate that the Baha'is should allow their differences to reach the courts of justice, yet for the future progress of the Baha'i movement this event was most fortunate.

The Baha'is should read the above-mentioned book, unbiased and unprejudiced, regardless of their party affiliation. Indeed it is an exposition of truths so far untold, and a great testimonial about the present activities under the leadership of Shoghi Effendi.

I congratulate Mrs. Lewis Stuyvesant Chanler and her coworker Mirza Ahmad Sohrab on their triumph [in the court case]. Indeed, they labored energetically for the accomplishment of the great task.

---

[16] In the decision, the Supreme Court of New York County wrote that "The plaintiffs have no right to a monopoly of the name of a religion," thus invalidating Trade-Mark 245,271 (simply the word "Baha'i") which had been registered with the United States Patent Office in 1928. Despite this ruling, the mainstream Baha'i denomination has twice more filed lawsuits against dissenting Baha'i communities not under their umbrella, attempting to legally ban them from describing themselves as "Baha'i." Most recently, they lost a case in 2010 against a small Baha'i denomination calling itself the Orthodox Baha'i Faith.

33

Statements on the Dispute Between the Baha'i Family

By Kamar Bahai

This chapter contains two parts: The first section is an undated circular letter or pamphlet by Kamar Bahai entitled "A Statement on the Dispute Between the Behai Family,"[1] which was the first in her series of six such letters. The second section is the second in the series, also undated, called simply "Statement No. 2." Section headings have been added.

Mrs. Bahai praises 'Abdu'l-Baha and focuses all of her opposition towards the person and policies of Shoghi Effendi Rabbani. She makes some questionable statements such as that the will of 'Abdu'l-Baha is "counterfeit" and that "Mohammed Ali's group were the true believers in Abbas Effendi"—part of a consistent pattern in her writings of attempting to protect the public image of both of her uncles rather than acknowledging the deep distrust that existed between them during

---

[1] It should be noted that the spellings "Bahai" and "Behai" were used interchangeably by Baha'u'llah's descendants, who were transliterating the word from their native languages of Arabic and Persian. Even in English the spelling of the word "Baha'i" did not come to be standardized until the latter part of the 20th century, and sometimes the apostrophe is still omitted, though the "Behai" spelling is now obsolete. I have chosen to refer to the entirety of the descendants of Baha'u'llah as the "Baha'i family" (with apostrophe)—i.e. the first family or holy family of Baha'is—since many of them did not use the surname Bahai/Behai, and had other surnames instead such as Rabbani, Afnan, Shahid, etc. The "Bahai family" (without apostrophe) would refer only to the members of the Baha'i family who used the Bahai/Behai surname.

their lifetimes. Mrs. Bahai explains the reasons for the lawsuit she filed against Mr. Rabbani, and speculates that he settled it out of court because of fear that a trial could have opened up larger and more difficult to resolve issues concerning his legitimacy as the world Baha'i leader.

—The Editor

Letter to *El Youm*

In its issue of May 23, 1952, the daily newspaper *El Youm* published an article under the following heading: "The Ministry of Religious Affairs settles a dispute between the Baha'i Family." This article is a gross misrepresentation of the facts. In order, therefore, to do justice to history and proclaim the truth of the matter, I requested the newspaper *El Youm* to publish the following statement, but, taking a stand inimical to the principles of freedom of the press and for some other reasons, the said newspaper refused to accede to my request.

> The dispute between the Baha'i family is deep-rooted and cannot be settled as easily as may be inferred from the published article.
>
> The Baha'i movement was born amidst vicissitudes and worn-out traditions. Its leaders started in all sincerity a relentless social revolution against the rotten system then existing in Persia for the purpose of achieving social justice and general reform. In the initial stages of the movement they sacrificed worthy position for the sake of maintaining their struggle and spreading their principles. When defeated, they were banished to Acre where they were imprisoned in the citadel and severely tortured. At the head of these leaders was Baha'u'llah and his companions.
>
> Prior to his death Baha'u'llah nominated his eldest son Abbas Effendi, called "The Greatest Branch" to succeed him and to be followed by his second son, Mohammed Ali Effendi, "The Mightiest Branch."
>
> The followers loved Abbas Effendi, obeyed his orders willingly and faithfully, as a result of which the movement attained its zenith during his lifetime, spread widely both in spirit and truth. Ab-

Chapter 33. Statements on the Dispute Between the Baha'i Family 439

bas Effendi was also respected by the Muslim community, fulfilled his Muslim obligatory prayers in the Jarina Mosque in Haifa uninterruptedly, distributed alms to the Muslims and Christians as well as to the other denominations who may have stood in need, and convened Muslim religious personalities, who highly esteemed him, to discuss with them the interpretation of the holy Qur'an.

Abbas Effendi was fulfilling the commandments of his father "El Baha" to the letter and was faithful and trustworthy in his mission. His followers were conscious of his sympathetic regard towards them which he demonstrated by elevating their educational and social standard, sending their children to universities for higher studies, and further extending his financial help to those of his own community who were in need. For all these humanitarian acts, Abbas Effendi was greatly beloved and adhered to by his followers who carried out his wishes conscientiously.

Following the death of Abbas Effendi, Shoghi Rabbani, who was then still young, claimed that he was holding a will from his grandfather on his mother's side, as Abbas Effendi did not beget any male children. In accordance with this will, which is counterfeit, Shoghi Rabbani was nominated successor. The Baha'is subsequently split among themselves: of them there were adherents of Mohammed Ali Effendi, the son of Baha'u'llah who was to be the legal successor to his brother in accordance with their father's will, while Shoghi Rabbani had few supporters among his relatives.

Mohammed Ali's group were the true believers in Abbas Effendi. In his time, remarkable advancement in the movement was made, because he carried on along the lines of his father's teachings. Combined with his qualities, the most holy respect with which Easterners regard wills [means that] Abbas Effendi, whom they believed and trusted, could not possibly have entertained the idea of the non-fulfillment of his father's will. It is therefore illogical that Abbas Effendi should have committed the blunder of appointing his young grandson as his successor and set aside his experienced brother who bore great suffering and struggled hand-in-hand with him to advance the movement.

As a first step to safeguard himself against the Baha'i family, Shoghi Rabbani excommunicated the adherents of Mohammed Ali Effendi by introducing a reign of terror which deprived them of their basic rights such as the right to pay their respects to their grandfather's tomb [i.e. the Shrine of Baha'u'llah].[2] He further threatened his immediate followers and sympathizers, [ordering them] to discontinue any contact with the other group [i.e. the Unitarian Baha'is] and considered their presence in his [i.e. Baha'u'llah's] vicinity as disturbing to his divinity. He therefore dispersed and banished them [from the Holy Land], thus causing a serious social and economic loss to his followers.[3]

By now the reader would have realized how deep rooted lies the dispute between the Baha'is and how far it is from easy solution, for how could a settlement be achieved when such settlement should begin by deposing the world Baha'i leader, as the newspaper called Shoghi Rabbani.

Shoghi Rabbani is not the grandson of El Baha nor is he the legal heir of the Baha'i movement; he does not represent the Baha'i family or sect—the men of the movement and the members of the Baha'i family are separated from him.[4] In America there are thousands of followers of El Baha who hold dignified positions, own newspapers, publish books, maintain their teaching, and consider Shoghi Rabbani as a usurper, diverted from the policy originally laid down by the leaders of the movement.[5]

---

[2] The Unitarian Baha'is were already regarded as heretics by 'Abdu'l-Baha, but he did not prevent them from visiting the Shrine of Baha'u'llah. Shoghi Effendi Rabbani's attempt to prevent them from performing an important ritual act of Baha'i faith may be taken to signify a more formal excommunication.

[3] As Shua Ullah Behai describes in greater detail (see Chapter 32), Mr. Rabbani ordered most of the large number of Baha'is who were living in Palestine (now Israel) to leave the country. Most of those who followed his orders and emigrated to other lands—reluctantly in most cases—were in fact supporters of 'Abdu'l-Baha, not Mohammed Ali Bahai. However, Mr. Rabbani may have been motivated by a desire to consolidate his position as the new Baha'i leader, fearing that any Baha'i living in Haifa or Acre who might disagree with some of his decisions or leadership style could be easily influenced by the members of Baha'u'llah's family who lived in the area and supported Mr. Bahai.

[4] By the time when Kamar Bahai was writing this letter, Shoghi Rabbani had expelled from the Baha'i community all descendants of Baha'u'llah who were still living, except himself.

[5] The numbers are an exaggeration, but the Society of Behaists and the New History Society—both of which rejected Shoghi Effendi's Guardianship—did include various erudite and distinguished members and supporters.

Chapter 33. Statements on the Dispute Between the Baha'i Family

Shoghi Effendi would have declined to accede to the wishes of the Ministry of Religious Affairs to permit Mohammed Ali Effendi's followers to visit their holy places—a visit prohibited to them for the last 30 years—had he not feared to be brought before the Israeli courts where justice is delivered in ideal measure, and had he not anticipated the emergence of other serious complications, the settlement of which would have been impossible.[6]

Although I feel in what critical position Shoghi Rabbani is placed and know that the permission to visit the holy places was extorted from him [i.e. through the threat of a trial]—his agreement to it disparages his position and dignity among his followers—yet on the other hand, Shoghi Rabbani was unscrupulously callous towards the afflictions of his followers when he was ordering their banishment and dispersion.

It had not been my intention to raise the matter up to courts in order to stop the demolition of two small rooms situated at the entrance of El Baha's grave[7] except for the following reasons:

1. To preserve the historical aspect of the building.
2. To apprise Shoghi Rabbani of the necessity of consulting his partners in the estate when he proposes to undertake any constructional change.

I fail to understand how Shoghi Rabbani denounces a group as heretics and sets out to demolish their property by force without sanction. Under the circumstances, I had no alternative but to lay the matter for adjudication before the public through the medium of newspapers and to resort to litigation if necessary.

---

[6] One of these complications which might have come up in court had the case gone to civil trial was the fact that the authenticity of 'Abdu'l-Baha's will had been challenged by a forensic scientist. Furthermore, the wills of Baha'u'llah and 'Abdu'l-Baha conflicted with each other on the matter of the succession, and 'Abdu'l-Baha had never allowed Baha'u'llah's will to be reproduced photographically to confirm the accuracy of its contents as reported to the Baha'is. Both of these issues might have been reopened in a court case, with the outcome uncertain.

[7] This matter must have been mentioned as a key point of the Baha'i family's legal dispute in the newspaper article to which Mrs. Bahai is responding. For more information on renovations at the Bahji property ordered unilaterally by Shoghi Effendi Rabbani, see Chapter 32.

Kamar Bahai
Granddaughter of Baha'u'llah

Article by Giladi in *Ma'ariv*

In its issue No. 1353 dated June 6, 1952, the evening Hebrew newspaper *Ma'ariv* published a lengthy article by the well-known writer N. Giladi[8] on the Baha'i movement and the history of its founder and its leaders, in which he discusses the existing dissensions between the members of the family. I quote hereunder for information a verbatim translation of the article for the particular attention of the Baha'i family and the Baha'is all over the world.

While I do not concur with all the views expressed in the article, I must point out that the writer pronounced the mere truth about the malevolence of Shoghi Rabbani, his usurpation of the spiritual leadership of the Baha'i movement and the harsh treatment and exile inflicted by him on its leaders. However, I leave it to every reader of the article to form his own judgment.

> The Brotherhood Celebrates Its Jubilee in Dissension
>
> The Baha'i religion, called religion of brotherhood, religion of light or Persian religion, will celebrate shortly the centennial anniversary of its founder Baha'u'llah (the Light of God), thanks to whose inspiration the center of the fourth world religion has been instituted in Palestine.
>
> This event is to be celebrated in the midst of a great schism besetting the Baha'i family, whose sixty members oppose the self-imposed leadership of Shoghi Rabbani.
>
> While the nature of the dispute within the sect is spiritual, yet it has a material and social aspect as well.
>
> While his antagonists contend that in the founder's will his son, Abbas Effendi is nominated as successor to be followed by his second son Mohammed Ali Effendi, they claim that Shoghi Rab-

---

[8] A man named David Giladi was one of the founders of *Ma'ariv*, but this editor, who cannot read Hebrew, was unable to determine the identity of "N. Giladi."

Chapter 33. Statements on the Dispute Between the Baha'i Family

bani violated the succession order and unjustly took the crown to himself.

The dissension in the prophet's family has been lately brought before the law courts. Only a fortnight ago the public cherished the hope that the Ministry of Religious Affairs might reconcile the opponents.

The [Baha'i] community has property considered holy by all the adherents of this religion. In northern Acre there exists the house where the founder lived and his tomb. The house has been turned into a museum but is also being utilized as a shelter for pilgrims from overseas. This property, six-sevenths of which is registered in the name of the Baha'i family opposing the leadership of Shoghi Rabbani, forms a bone of contention which may be settled by litigation. But matters relating to spiritual values where principles of faith are involved cannot be solved or determined by human judgment. For this reason the opponents had resort to the law courts when Shoghi Rabbani ordered the demolition of a part of the said property.

When the demolition was started the opponents obtained a court's order for the stoppage of work. Consequently the head of the [Baha'i] community approached the Ministry of Religious Affairs in the matter, and a notice served by the Deputy Minister declared the property to be considered as a holy place and accordingly the dispute fell outside the jurisdiction of civil courts. Under the circumstances the opponents lodged a case in the High Court against the Deputy Minister for Religious Affairs on the basis that the declaration of the place as holy was made without their knowledge.

At this juncture when the Deputy Minister foresaw the serious developments that might arise, [he] began taking steps in order to reach a reconciliation. The main argument of the opposition was that they were not permitted access to the property, which although partially their own by right yet was wholly theirs spiritually.[9] Mediation bore fruit as Rabbani agreed to permit his

---

[9] In other words, the excommunicated members of Baha'u'llah's family were fighting not only for legal affirmation of their right to access the property in which they were part-owners, but also for recognition by the Ministry of Religious Affairs of their spiritual status as Baha'is, with full and equal rights as all

opponents both to use the house where the founder lived and to visit his tomb.

The lifting of the prohibition has reverted the dispute to its initial point and fresh developments are expected to ensue.[10]

The Baha'is are of Persian origin and do not form a large community. Their head derives his strength from his followers in the United States and Canada, from amongst whom he married a beautiful wife.[11] The Baha'i community in the United States is estimated to number one million, from whom the source of wealth emanates.[12] The Baha'is possess large estates in Haifa with big edifices and spacious gardens located in the Persian Street, besides the beautiful Baha'i Garden where improvements are being carried out in preparation for the centenary jubilee this year. It is not permitted to see the community head, not even for his entourage.[13] The affairs of the community are attended to by his Canadian wife assisted by a few Americans.

The Baha'i religion was founded 100 years ago at the birth of Baha'u'llah.[14] Tradition speaks of a precursor called "The Bab" who annunciated the impending appearance of the founder of a new religion. When Baha'u'llah grew up he began preaching the reli-

---

other Baha'is to make pilgrimage to the Shrine of Baha'u'llah. It was therefore a test case of whether the Israeli government would permit Shoghi Rabbani to prohibit some people who considered themselves Baha'is from participating in a Baha'i ritual act.

[10] Although the plaintiffs considered continuing to pursue legal action against Mr. Rabbani, perhaps in the hope that the courts might hold that he had obtained his position as head of the Baha'i community illegitimately, they decided to drop the case.

[11] Mary Sutherland Maxwell, who was given the new name and title Amatu'l-Baha Ruhiyyih Khanum by Shoghi Rabbani when she married him. *Amatu'l-Baha* means "Handmaiden of Glory."

[12] This is a huge overestimate of the number of Baha'is in the U.S. in the 1950s—and even today. But it is correct that Americans contributed a great deal of the wealth of the international Baha'i community.

[13] This may be somewhat of an exaggeration. But Shoghi Rabbani was notoriously inaccessible to the public and rarely made appearances, even among Baha'is.

[14] This is incorrect. The author presumably meant to refer to the start of Baha'u'llah's mission, not his birth.

gion of brotherhood and peace. He did not prescribe any functional rites but instructed his followers to live in light. The American community calls itself "The National Spiritual Assembly" and falls under the leadership of Shoghi Rabbani, who is in fact the third leader, the first being Baha'u'llah who died in 1892, the second Abbas Effendi who died in 1922,[15] and the third Abbas's grandson on the mother's side who violated the founder's will.

In the "brotherhood religion," brotherhood does not prevail in this jubilee year.

---

[15] 'Abdu'l-Baha actually died in 1921.

Kamar and Mousa Bahai in Lebanon.

Mousa Effendi Bahai.

34

Mousa Bahai and the Rotary Club of Haifa

Compiled from Rotary Publications

Mousa[1] Bahai (February 26, 1890 – October 9, 1950) was the youngest son of Mohammed Ali Bahai and thus the grandson of Baha'u'llah. He was the half-brother of Shua Ullah Behai and the husband of his cousin Kamar Bahai.

This chapter contains two parts: First, an article by Arie Mehulal that was written in 2002 and originally published in Hebrew in a Rotary Club periodical in Israel. Second, excerpts from an article that appeared in the March 1949 issue of *The Rotarian*, the official English-language magazine of Rotary International. The second article was written by the Board of Directors of the Rotary Club of Haifa, of which Mousa Bahai was President at the time. The section headings are the titles of each respective article.

Although excluded from the organized Baha'i community, Baha'u'llah's grandson Mousa found a way to put into practice his Baha'i faith as a respected peacemaker and bridge-builder between Arabs, Jews, and British, in the city of Haifa during the First Arab-Israeli War. This almost entirely forgotten member of the Baha'i holy family didn't wear his religion on his sleeve, but seems to have lived it in his deeds.

—The Editor

---

[1] Also spelled Musa.

Mousa Effendi Bahai, President of the Club in the Years 1947/48, 1948/49

Last week I met with Mrs. Negar Bahai Emsallem in her living room in 1 HaGefen Street in Haifa. She shared this huge and impressive living room with her father, Mr. Mousa Effendi Bahai, the one and only one in the 70 years of the Rotary Club in Haifa who served as president for two consecutive years—1947/48 and 1948/49. Please pay attention to the fact that the father of the president of the club and the grandfather of Negar was Mohammed Ali Bahai, who was the son of the founder and head of the Baha'i religion, Baha'u'llah, who is buried in Acre. Baha'u'llah had three sons: Mohammed Ali, Badi Ullah, and Abbas Effendi. Mousa Effendi Bahai was, as stated before, the third generation. He had two daughters: Negar, who was married to Mordechai Emsallem, a businessman who died two years ago. They do not have any children. The [other] daughter, Maliha [Bahai] Ansari, has three sons and one daughter, and they have been living in India for 50 years. Soon, they plan to come back and live in Haifa.

Mousa Effendi Bahai, our president and the grandson of Baha'u'llah, was born in Acre in 1890. He was educated in Jerusalem and after graduating came back to Haifa. He could have chosen to continue leading the public life of the heads of the Baha'i religion, but he preferred to build himself a private life. He started working in an agricultural bank in Acre and then continued to his permanent job in the land registry office as the head of the office, which was located in Haifa. He married and had two daughters. He worked for many years as a head under the rule of the British Mandate government and a few more months under the rule of Israel, after the establishment of the state of Israel.

In 1950 he passed away at the age of 60. A good friend of his, Dr. Mounir Mishalany, eulogized him in the club and emphasized his unusual decency, his loyalty, and the fact that he was a friend and a comrade to everyone. Dr. Mishalany told us that a week before he died, Mousa Effendi Bahai held a party to pay his respect to the Iranian ambassador in Israel, in the presence of many guests in his home at 1 HaGefen Street. Many people attended his funeral a few days later, in

Acre. His daughter Negar adds that her father was a dedicated head of the family, who loved his wife and daughters. He was also a good son to his parents, had a unique sense of humor, and was also a gifted artist.

The president Mousa Effendi Bahai held the position during the last year of the British Mandate as well as during the first year of the Israeli state. During these two years there were typically open war conditions in Israel and in Haifa. The meetings held at the garden of the Spinneys Restaurant took part in an atmosphere of battles, shootings and explosions. Many lecturers were not able to arrive at the club and in most cases the members of the club volunteered to lecture in their place. To the members' meeting of the club which took place on December 30, 1947, only eight Rotary members arrived. Instead of giving a lecture there was a conversation among the members. In the meeting of January 7, 1948, it was unanimously decided: "We will do whatever we can to keep on having the meetings on a regular basis despite the hard times." In an earlier board meeting which took place on December 10, 1947, it was decided as follows: "Personal security of the members of the club will be considered, until else stated, as a sufficient reason for not attending the club's meetings."[2]

In the appointments meeting held on April 21, 1948, it was an especially hard situation. There were many shots fired in the area of the Spinneys Restaurant. Only the president and one other member were able to arrive at the place, and of course, the meeting was cancelled. In the meeting on April 14, only eight members of the club were present and about 30 were absent. Then, the brave ones who were present sat around one big table instead of around small tables. On April 28 there were only twelve members present, and Mousa Effendi opened and said: "We are really sorry we could not overcome the horrors of the time. We are stopping our meetings today, two months before the end of the Rotary year, since the conditions are not under our control. Outside there are snipers shooting. In the future, we will remember that the Rotary wheel kept on moving, almost to the end..." The president

---

[2] The Rotary Club has long been known for its strict attendance policies, so an unusual exception such as this reflected the extremely dangerous circumstances under which the Haifa club continued to meet.

reported in a high-quality English to the international center of Rotary abroad of all those things that were going on. R[otarian] Kaiserman (Kisari[3]) went on and told as in most of the meetings a good joke or rather a juicy story.

When the days of the British Mandate came to an end, many British and Arab members started dropping out. One by one, British senior officials left their posts and went back to England. Any British senior official that left was sent a box full of oranges, as soon as his new address became known. On May 5, 1948, the club parted with his friend R[otarian] Leo, who was the last British governor of Haifa. Also most of the Arab members of the club left the country and only a few came back to Haifa.

In the meeting which took place on March 10, 1948, it was decided unanimously that due to the security situation and the special conditions in the city, it would not be wise to change the composition of the management that succeeded in keeping the club as it did, and therefore, the president Mousa Effendi was asked to serve one more year. The proposal was approved in the club meeting and Mousa Effendi agreed, but only on condition that all the members of his board would serve the club in their roles for one more year too.

In the closing lecture of the second year, the president informed the members that during the tough year there were 22 weekly meetings. In nine of them there were lecturers from outside the club, and in the remaining ones the lectures were given by the club members. In the coming year, the club moved its location to the "Zion Hotel" and then it moved to the "Windsor Hotel." There we have spent some very good years.

In one of the meetings Mr. Yehuda Araten[4] greeted the old friend

---

[3] This was presumably a moniker by which Mr. Kaiserman, a Jew, was known among his Arab friends. Having an Arab nickname signified that a particular Jewish person residing in Palestine at the time was a friend of the Arab community. Similarly, Negar Bahai's late husband Mordechai Emsallem was known to his Arab friends as "Murad."

[4] Yehuda Araten, a member of the Haifa Rotary, was one of the founders of Frutarom Industries Ltd., which today is one of the ten largest flavor and fragrance companies in the world.

M. G. Levin[5] and drinking a toast he told them: "A philosopher saw three stonemasons chiseling in stone in the middle of their work. He asked them, 'What are you doing?' The first one answered, 'I am cutting stones.' The second one answered, 'I am making money.' The third one said in a low voice, 'I am building a cathedral.' I hope," said Araten, "that when you are asked what you do in Rotary, your answer will not be 'I eat there,' or 'I listen to lectures,' but rather: 'I build human bridges.'"

Rotary Report from Haifa, Israel

Rotary in Israel has passed through difficult times. In the Haifa Club we feel that we need not to be ashamed of our efforts to uphold the ideals and aims of Rotary in a period of extreme hardships. ...

Club headquarters were situated in a border area with the approach roads frequently under fire. ... It was a regular experience to eat our Rotary luncheons to the accompaniment of the rattle of machine guns, the crack of a sniper's rifle, or the bursting of grenades.

The Rotary Club was the only place in Haifa where Arabs, Jews, and British could meet in a friendly atmosphere at that time. Of 45 members, 13 were Arab, 19 Jewish, 12 British, and one Dutch. Five principal religious denominations are represented. Our President is a Moslem,[6] our Secretary a Jew, and our Treasurer a Christian. ...

It was decided not to have elections for the new Rotary year and the Club requested the present officers to continue for another year. Our President opened the first meeting with an inspiring address, closing with the words:

---

[5] M. G. Levin, also a Rotarian, was the Chairman of the Jewish Community of Haifa.

[6] Mr. Bahai evidently chose to identify himself for public purposes as Muslim rather than Baha'i, likely because of the fact that he had been excommunicated from the Baha'i community since early childhood and he did not agree with its prevailing doctrines and leadership. However, in private he continued to affirm the faith of his grandfather Baha'u'llah, according to his daughters. Curiously, the article avoids mentioning the name of the club president, and this may reflect a desire on the part of Mr. Bahai—who either wrote or edited the piece—to avoid giving any media attention or exposure to the faith community whose name he bore, which had rejected him and his family.

Rotarians are peace-loving people and I am confident that their services were at no time more necessary than at this time.

Let us, therefore, try to forget our personal differences, if any, in the interest of the common cause, the cause of peace and humanity. Let us try this year, and try hard, to help and assist, right and left, as much as it is in our power to do so. Perchance we may be able to alleviate to a certain extent the sufferings of our fellow citizens.

In thanking the President for his opening address, Past President Kaiserman (Jewish) referred to the great services rendered to the Club by the President, whose devotion and personal courage in most dangerous days helped the Club to survive. ... Past President Spinney[7] (British) said that the Club owed much to its President, whose impartial and tactful leadership in time of conflict and fargoing [sic] differences inspired the members. ...

We believe that we have demonstrated that men of goodwill, even with opposing interests in times of strife, can still enjoy one another's friendly company.

---

[7] Arthur Rawdon Spinney (CBE) founded Spinneys, a high-end supermarket chain which has expanded throughout the Middle East.

35

Messages in *Behai Quarterly* Magazine

By Shua Ullah Behai

This chapter contains selected writings by Shua Ullah Behai from the *Behai Quarterly*, a magazine he edited and published from 1934 to 1937 with the help of Frederick A. Slack in Kenosha, Wisconsin. The periodical was distributed for free to members of the Society of Behaists and other Baha'is who were interested in or sympathetic to the Unitarian Baha'i view of the faith.

I have reproduced some of the more interesting articles by Mr. Behai which were published in the *Quarterly*, among them a piece about the spiritual meaning of life called "Life's Journey," which appeared in the Third and Fourth Quarter 1935 issue; an overview of "The Three Behai Sects" that existed at the time, which appeared in the First and Second Quarter 1937 issue (shortened to remove excerpts from the Declaration of Trust and By-Laws of the largest Baha'i organization, which are included in Chapter 32); selected Questions and Answers from the First Quarter and Third and Fourth Quarter 1935 issues; and more. The writings in this chapter are arranged in chronological order.

Archives of *Behai Quarterly* are available online at http://www.h-net.org/~bahai/docs/vol8/bq.htm.

—The Editor

Spring 1934 Foreword

The aim of this *Quarterly* is to give to the people of the world the authentic teachings of the last Sun of reality which illumined the horizon of the East, "Baha'u'llah."

The contributor in this issue of the article entitled "A Voice from the East"[1] is no less personage than Ghusn-i-Akbar, the Mightiest Branch, Mohammed Ali, my beloved father, the eldest living son of Baha'u'llah, who, as a chosen son reared in His household, received daily instructions and served Him for a period of years as inscriber of His tablets and promulgator of His teachings throughout the world.

Doubtless there is not a person living today to equal him in the knowledge of the life and teachings of Baha'u'llah, as he experienced years of personal contact with Him. He possesses numerous authentic unpublished volumes of the teachings of Baha'u'llah which he will gladly impart to the seekers after truth.[2]

I take great pleasure in calling the attention of my good readers to the fact that, in the history of this religion, this is the first publication to be directly connected with its fountainhead, and its pages are open for any discussion which is for the betterment of humanity and the elevation of the thoughts of mankind. Therefore I extend a cordial invitation to the seekers of truth to investigate while the opportunities are here.

Summer 1934 Foreword

I am grateful to my friends and kind readers of this periodical for the encouraging letters which I have received. My only object in publishing this *Quarterly* is to spread the truth, as given to us by… Baha'u'llah.

To accomplish this great work I need your cooperation to reach the thinking souls, the seekers of truth, and I will be very happy to mail a

---

[1] This article is reproduced in Chapter 13. The original heading of the article, "A Voice from the East," was the name of the author's column in *Behai Quarterly* rather than a title for the article itself.

[2] According to Negar Bahai Emsallem, these writings were eventually inherited by one of her cousins and may have been donated to a museum. This editor has not been able to determine their current location.

copy of this periodical gratis to those whom my good readers shall advise. ...

I call the attention of my kind readers to the Question and Answer page, which is an open forum for any discussion to enlighten the minds of humanity and the thoughts of mankind.

Selected Questions and Answers

Q. What is good and evil?
A. Everything in existence is good but can become evil through our actions. The power of speech is one of the faculties of man through which we know his innermost. Truth and lies both are considered speech, and its creation was good, but when misused, became evil. Fire produces heat, and it is very beneficial in our daily life, but dangerous when improperly used. Thorn is food to some animals, but may cause destruction when applied externally. Poison's nature is destruction, but also beneficial when used properly.

Q. What is heaven and hell?
A. We contain both. When in the state of perfection and clear conscience, we are in heaven, blessed with the mercy of the Creator; when in the state of imperfection and doubtful conscience, we are in hell, a condition we have produced by our acts and deeds which are contrary to the laws of God and Nature.

Q. What was the station of the "Bab"?
A. Elijah.[3] The forerunner of He Whom God Shall Manifest.
Q. What was the station of "Baha'u'llah"?
A. The fulfiller. The Manifestation [of God].
Q. Who was the founder of the Baha'i religion?
A. Baha'u'llah. Who spent forty years in revealing tablets for the enlightenment of mankind. Invited all the rulers of the world, includ-

---

[3] Judaism teaches that Elijah will return to earth to announce the coming of the Messiah. Christians believe that John the Baptist, the forerunner of Jesus Christ, was the return of Elijah (see Matthew 11:10,14). Baha'is hold a similar belief about the Bab.

ing the pope, to come to the Kingdom of the Father. Completed His mission on earth and departed in 1892.

Q. When did the news of this progressive movement reach the Occident, and by whom?

A. By travelers and historians beginning [circa] 1850. Hereunder, I record a few names:[4]

- A. H. Wright and J. Perkins, German Oriental Society, Leipzig, 1851 A.D.
- Lady [Mary Leonora Woulfe] Sheil, London, 1856 A.D.
- Robert B. M. Binning, London, 1857 A.D.
- [Bernhard Dorn,] *Bulletin de l'Académie Impériale*, St. Petersburg, 1864 A.D.
- [Arthur] Comte de Gobineau, Paris, 1865 A.D.
- Dr. Jakob Eduard Polak, Leipzig, 1865 A.D.
- John Ussher, London, 1865 A.D.
- Robert Grant Watson, London, 1866 A.D.
- Hermann[5] Vámbéry, Pest, [Hungary,] 1867 A.D.
- Baron Alfred von Kremer, Leipzig, 1868 A.D.
- Dr. Hermann Ethé, Berlin, 1872 A.D.
- M. T. Gilbert, *Journal Asiatique*, 1873 A.D.
- John Piggot, London, 1874 A.D.
- Lieut. Baron Max von Thielmann, London, 1875 A.D.
- Baron Victor Rosen,[6] St. Petersburg, 1877 A.D.
- Laurence Oliphant, Edinburgh and London, 1887 A.D.
- M. Clément Huart, Paris, 1889 A.D.
- Prof. Edward G. Browne, London, 1890 A.D.

Q. Who first brought this message to the United States?

A. The late Dr. Ibrahim G. Kheiralla, D.A.D.D., was the first to in-

---

[4] This is a shorter version of a list with detailed descriptions of books and articles written by European authors about the Babi and Baha'i faiths, which appears in Edward G. Browne's notes on *A Traveller's Narrative* (Cambridge: University Press, 1891), pp. 200-211. Available online at http://www.h-net.org/~bahai/diglib/books/A-E/B/browne/tn/tnappx.htm

[5] Born Hermann Bamberger, he later changed his name to Ármin Vámbéry.

[6] Also known as Viktor Romanovich Rozen.

troduce the teachings of Baha'u'llah, and founded the Society of Behaists in the United States of America, 1893 A.D.

Q. "Religion without clergy"—then who will be our leader?

A. Baha'u'llah commanded that His teachings are our leaders; we should study and be guided by them; also to pray individually and not in congregation. Thus He freed us from the clutches of the clergy. In the Book of *Aqdas*, He said, "If ye differ in a matter, bring it to God, so long as the Sun is shining from the Horizon of this heaven; but when He sets, bring it to what He uttered, verily it suffices the worlds."[7]

Q. Is there need of an interpreter for the utterances of Baha'u'llah?

A. No. His utterances are very clear to comprehend and He prohibited their interpretation.

In the Book of *Aqdas* He said, "He whosoever interpreteth what are descended from the heaven of revelations differently from its apparent meaning is of those who changed the Supreme Word of God, and is considered one of those who are written as losers in the Manifest Book."[8]

Q. Baha'u'llah passed unto Eternity in 1892. How many sons survived Him?

A. Four. The eldest Ghusn-i-A'zam, the Greatest Branch, Abbas ('Abdu'l-Baha); the second Ghusn-i-Akbar, the Mightiest Branch, Mohammed Ali Bahai; the third Zia Ullah, and the fourth Badi Ullah.

Q. How many of His sons are living today?

A. Two. The second son Ghusn-i-Akbar, the Mightiest Branch, Mohammed Ali Bahai, and the fourth son, Badi Ullah, both residing at Acre, Palestine.

Q. During the life of Baha'u'llah on earth, what were the duties of His sons?

A. During Baha'u'llah's exile at the fortress of Acre, his eldest son Ghusn-i-A'zam Abbas ('Abdu'l-Baha) was assigned to the entertainment of the government officials and outer circle visitors. His second

---

[7] *Kitab-i-Aqdas* ("Most Holy Book"), paragraph 53.

[8] Ibid., paragraph 105.

son Ghusn-i-Akbar Mohammed Ali Bahai was assigned to the entertainment of the inner circle, pilgrims, [and as] inscriber of Baha'u'llah's utterances and promulgator of His teachings throughout the world, especially Persia. Today he is the possessor of the seals of Baha'u'llah and His complete [written] teachings. In the latter years [of Baha'u'llah's life] His two younger sons, Zia Ullah and Badi Ullah, served as inscribers of His utterances also.

Q. In what tongue did Baha'u'llah reveal His utterances?

A. In the Persian and the Arabic languages.

Q. How many volumes of His utterances have been published, when, and where?

A. Five volumes were published in Bombay, India, 1889-1890 A.D.

Q. By whom?

A. By the commands of Baha'u'llah, His second son Ghusn-i-Akbar Mohammed Ali Bahai made a journey to Bombay, India and succeeded in publishing the same. For details please consult *Behai Quarterly*, First Quarter 1935, page fourteen.[9]

Q. What is the significance of the word "branch" applied to the sons of Baha'u'llah?

A. Baha'u'llah called himself a Tree and His sons branches of the tree.

Q. What are the stations of His sons, the branches?

A. The [verses from] the following tablets revealed by Baha'u'llah answer your question:

> The Branches who are branched from the *Sadrat* (Tree of Life) are my fingerposts amongst my creatures, and my fragrance between heaven and earth. Have ye ever seen a companion or an equal to God, your Lord? By the Lord of All the Worlds, No! Then speak not of that which God did not permit, but rather fear the Merciful and be of those who reason.

---

[9] On that page of the magazine, Mr. Behai briefly recounts the journey to India, and notes that "The world knows little of the services [Mohammed Ali Bahai] has rendered to the Baha'i cause." See Chapters 16 and 30 for descriptions of this trip from the perspectives of the elder Mr. Bahai and the younger Mr. Behai, respectively.

O people, hold after my departure to the branches who were branched from this Ancient Root. For by them the fragrance of my garment shall be diffused throughout the world, but no one can attain it, save every upright seeker.

O my brothers, we command you and your children and those who are upon earth, never to resist my branches, nor do what will grieve them. They have the supreme position and the highest rank amongst you. Fear ye God and be not of those who are unjust.

Third and Fourth Quarter 1935 Foreword

Gazing with the eyes of intellect upon this planet earth, we will observe that all in existence testifies to the greatness of the Supreme Architect, "God."

Each spark speaks of a sun, every atom contains a seed, and each green leaf represents the work of a mother plant.

The mineral kingdom produces perfect specimens through slow processes, the vegetable kingdom produces perpetually each season, and the animal kingdom is productive also.

Behold! What are the members of the human kingdom producing?

We are gifted with a great power, "mind," and through our thinking faculties we have progressed; built and ruined empires, unfortunately not for the love of humanity, but for our selfish desires.

In each cycle we had great teachers who brought us the message of truth, but the words of the wise did not appeal to the masses, and they were herded to slaughter, by some iron-handed leader who through the spirit of nationalism or religious fanaticism misguided the innocent individuals, and made them to follow him ignorantly and to take arms against their brothers in humanity.

History has repeated itself time and again and mankind has been the victim of circumstances each time.

With careful study of the life and teachings of the past Great Messengers, we will observe that each one had an object in His appearance and a message to us.

Adam spoke of the creation of the universe and its beauties. Enoch taught eternal life. Noah saved humanity from the deluge of ignorance, restoring it to the ark of knowledge. Moses saved the Israelites from Pharaoh. Buddha taught the brotherhood of man. Zaradusht[10] guided the Iranians to the light of truth. Jesus sacrificed his life for the sake of unity amongst humanity. Muhammad saved the Arabs from idolatry.

All of them bowed in reverence to the Supreme Governor of the Universe, "God," and the essences of their teachings are the same: love of our kind, better understanding of ourselves, unity and harmony of mankind.

In the last century a Great Teacher appeared on the horizon of the East, "Baha'u'llah." He brought us the same message, only more useful for today: "Truth is one though spoken in different tongues."

In the beginning of the Book of "Hidden Words" our Great Master Baha'u'llah said:

> This is that which hath descended from the Source of Majesty, through the tongue of power and strength upon the prophets of the past. We have taken its essences and clothed them with the garment of brevity, as a favor to the beloved, that they may fulfill the Covenant of God; that they may perform in themselves that which He hath entrusted to them, and attain the victory by virtue of devotion in the land of the Spirit.
>
> O Son of Spirit!
>   The first counsel is: Possess a good, pure, and enlightened heart, that thou mayest possess a Kingdom eternal, immortal, ancient, and without end.
>
> O Son of Spirit!
>   Justice is loved above all. Neglect it not, if thou desirest Me. By it thou wilt be strengthened to perceive things with thine own eyes and not by the eyes of men, to know them by thine own knowledge and not by the knowledge of any in the world. Meditate on this—how thou oughtest to be. Justice is of My bounty to

---

[10] Zoroaster.

thee and of My providence over thee; therefore, keep it ever before thy sight.[11]

The pages of this *Quarterly* are covered with His messages. Indeed they are most useful today, a day in which the peace of the entire world is threatened.

I call the attention of my good readers to a message, entitled "A Voice from the East," which is written by His eldest living son, Ghusn-i-Akbar Mohammed Ali Bahai, appearing in this issue.[12] I earnestly ask you to grant his sincere request, and pray in your own way for universal peace and better understanding amongst the children of man.

Trusting through our mutual efforts, humanity will realize that we are all members of one family regardless of race, language and habits, and [that] there is more happiness in love and unity than in discord and enmity.

Life's Journey

From time immemorial mankind has been eager for the answer to the three great questions: Whence we came, why we are here, and where we are going?

Numerous articles have been written on this subject by philosophers, scientists and theologians, explaining the line of thought they have been reared in, and each article varies considerably from another.

To the people of intellect the answer is clear, though a difficult problem to solve to the satisfaction of the individual mind.

I choose the study of the second question first, as it is more observable to our vision, why we are here?

To answer this great question, we must know ourselves, know the globe on which we reside; [and] are we created in the image of the Cre-

---

[11] The Hidden Words, Preamble and Arabic #1-2.

[12] Most of this message is reproduced in the last section of Chapter 13. The original title of the article is actually "A message to mankind," published under the heading "A Voice from the East" which was used for multiple articles by Mr. Bahai in the *Quarterly*.

ator, or evolved from the lower kingdom [i.e. animals]? What is the visible and the invisible in man, and his duties while here?

We are gifted with a great power, "mind," but unfortunately we know little of its use. Our occupation, social life, and recreations have been great barriers to our thinking faculties. In occupation we are part of the machinery, in social life often we are obliged to practice hypocrisy, and the major part of our recreation is wasted in public amusement places, gazing for hours upon the screen and absorbing fabricated events reproducing heroes, lovers, murderers, and so on.

To solve the aforesaid problem, we must first learn to think and to understand the object of our coming here.

Do we know ourselves? Nay! How can we, when we have no time to think.

Are we the image of the Creator? This is our conception, as we do not observe anything in existence better than ourselves, therefore we imagine that we are His image.

We have misinterpreted the explanation of the holy books. We should be His image in attributes, to be upright, kind, just, obedient, peaceful, loving, generous, charitable, and to follow the footsteps of the past sages, the clear and shining mirrors which the light of truth and reality reflected unto them—those who sacrificed their lives for our progress and enlightenment.

Indeed we should glory more in this, than to consider ourselves His image in body.

Did we evolve from the lower kingdom? Our body is composed from the elements of the earth; from the earth we came and to it we shall go. The law of evolution has been grossly misrepresented and misunderstood. True, we go through evolution in our life: we evolve from atom to child, from childhood to manhood, from darkness to light, from ignorance to intelligence.

Every change is evolution, each step of progress is evolution, and each new invention is the manifestation of evolution.

We direct our thoughts to man and the globe on which he resides, this human machinery composed of the elements of the earth, wonderfully erected, and vested with unlimited power which enables him to become superior to all in existence:

Mother earth under his command, cooperating with him constantly, assisting him silently, and producing for him perpetually his needs in life. With the products of the earth he secures nourishment, which supplies blood to his veins, causing him to grow to manhood. Thus, kind mother earth provides for man all his desires without complaint or expectations of gratitude, carries the burden of our weight, and accepts all we deposit in her: What a faithful Mother!

From her surface [she] provides for us livelihood, from her depths gives us treasures, and in spite of all our abusive actions, her heart is ever open, that we may dig deeper and deeper and gain more from her innermost.

Man through his great invisible power, "mind," has progressed from the stone age to the age of steel.

His marvelous discoveries shortened communications and destinations. He has harnessed the waters, producing power called electricity to gain heat, strength, light, etc. Substituted autos for horse and carriages, improved the roads for travel, and built more substantial homes for his protection and comfort. Conquered diseases, and through scientific research, learned more of the globe on which he resides.

The aforesaid progress is the production of the power of thinking; the more we think, the more we learn, the more we advance.

This powerful human machine with all his glory and might, when his time is ended on this earth and the call of the beyond reaches his ears, he must obey and leave all behind, departing in the same manner which he came, free from all earthly possessions, destitute, friendless, motionless, he has no need for home, clothing, light, heat, food, etc., and in a short duration of time he will become part of the earth, forgotten by all. If he has accumulated wealth, his offspring and relatives will share and enjoy it, or will have a long litigation over his estate usually ending with bitter memories of the dear one who has gone.

Billions of humanity have come and gone, and how many of them are mentioned on the pages of history?

Was this the object of his coming here? To grow, to toil, to accumulate and to leave to others and go? Indeed nay! Doubtless there are other motives for his coming.

To search the reason for his presence, we will turn back the pages of history and study the teachings of the past great sages and scientific writers.

Thus we will discover two branches of teachings: One that claims the existence of a soul which occupies this human form, coming from a beginning which has no beginning and remaining to the end which has no end. "Eternal life," as taught by the Great Teachers, Enoch, Zaradusht, Buddha, Jesus, Muhammad, and Baha'u'llah, who believed in God, the Supreme Governor, the Creator, the Originator, and who foretold events which came to pass. The great personages that sacrificed their lives for the progress and enlightenment of mankind.

The other branch, the materialists who believe from earth we come and to earth we go, denying the existence of a soul and contented with the theory of evolution and slow growth, as Darwin, Voltaire, etc.

Studying the two branches of teachings, we will observe that both confess to the existence of an originator and a beginner and agree to the oneness and singleness of that origin. The first atom, [on the one hand, or] the Supreme Architect of the universe, Jehovah, Everlasting Father, Supreme Governor, the Mighty "God."

Every individual is free to think as he wishes and to take the branch he desires for his salvation, but in conclusion my dear readers, I choose to follow the footsteps of the Inspired Teachers and fully believe that we are a soul and a noble one, coming to this school of learning, "the globe." To study, to learn, to go through experiences and thus to be prepared for the journey to the "Everlasting Existence," and rest in the world of harmony, love, peace and happiness, "Eternal Life."

Baha'u'llah, Glory be to Him, said:

> In answer to thy question regarding the soul and its immortality: Know thou, that it ascendeth after death until it cometh to the presence of God, clothed in a temple which the centuries and ages cannot change, neither can the events of the universe nor its modifications. It will exist eternally inasmuch as the Kingdom of God, His authority, His might and His power are eternal. Through that soul the evidences of God and His attributes shall be mani-

fested, especially His providence and His benevolence. The pen cannot name this station or describe its greatness and its sublimity. Then, the hand of Bounty will bring it (the soul) to an incomprehensible position the like of which is incomparable in the contingent world.

Blessed is the soul which leaveth the body purified from the misdeeds of the world. It shall move in the atmosphere of the Will of its Lord and enter into the highest heaven, where it shall be guided by the vanguards of the Highest Paradise visiting round. It shall associate with the prophets of God and His saints, speak with them and relate to them what had befallen it (while on earth) in the cause of God, the Lord of the Worlds. If one could realize what was ordained to him in the realms of God, at once he would burn with the fire of desire to go to that most fortified, most high, holiest and most glorious abode.

Concerning the immortality of the soul, this Oppressed One beareth witness that it is immortal. Regarding its status, this cannot be explained, and it is not meet to be mentioned save to a certain extent. The prophets and apostles came for the guidance of the people of the earth to the right path of God. Their purpose was the education and development of the people, that they may be, at the time of their ascension, holy, sanctified and abstracted, so as to be fitted for reaching the Supreme Station. By the life of God, the truth is, the glory of these souls is the cause for the development of the people and the high positions of the nations. They are the cause of the existence and the greatest motive for the manifestations [i.e. creative attainments] and sciences of the world. For them the clouds give rain and the earth brings forth its increase.

There is not a thing existing without a cause, a motive and a beginning; and the greatest cause was and shall be the consecrated souls. The difference between this world and the world to come is like unto the difference between the fetal life and this life.

After the ascension, the soul cometh to the presence of God clothed in a garment suited for eternal life and fitted for those realms. This everlasting existence of the soul is in time and is not self-subsisting existence, because it was preceded by a cause. The self-everlasting existence is not preceded by a cause; therefore, it belongs only to God, glory be to Him. Blessed are those who know.[13]

Third and Fourth Quarter 1936 Foreword

I extend my humble gratitude to the kind readers of this periodical and the beloved Baha'i friends for their generous response to my last message, entitled "Am I a Baha'i?"[14] In these days of unrest, it is indeed encouraging to receive such numerous constructive and illuminative replies and to know of the great interest which has been displayed.

We are living in a restless age, socially, economically, politically, and spiritually. Dissatisfaction prevails everywhere; hatred of race, nationality and creed is renewed; Divine teachings are laid aside, discord replaces unity, the law of balance is forgotten and Gold substituted for God.

Ambitious leaders are driving mankind to another bloody conflict and innocent masses are hoodwinked by the spirit of nationalism and religious fanaticism.

But according to all indications and in spite of the obstacles visible we are approaching a new era; a great change is coming. The day of awakening to the realization that after all we are one in humanity regardless of our differences in race, language, color, creed, and habits.

Then all this strife and discord shall cease and the great peace shall come. A peace founded on better understanding of one another, bound with the strong intellectual tie that we are children of [one] Adam and Atom and should live together as one kindred and consider mankind members of one family.

Humbly I pray that through the actions of the living example of the basic principles taught by our Great Master Baha'u'llah and the inex-

---

[13] *Lawh-i-'Abdu'l-Vahhab*. A different translation of this tablet is published in *Gleanings from the Writings of Bahá'u'lláh* (Wilmette, Ill.: US Bahá'í Publishing Trust, 1990 pocket-size edition), section LXXXI, pp. 155-158.

[14] Most of this essay was reproduced by the author in his "Address to an Occidental Gathering" (see Chapter 36)—specifically, in the last section of the speech, which this editor has given the heading "Baha'i Teachings."

haustible efforts of the diffusers of truth, humanity will become united under the glorious banner of "The Most Resplendent Glory" [i.e. *al-Abha*] and the melodious song universally be sung, "Glory is to the Father."

The Three Baha'i Sects

It grieves me even to mention the word dissension, as we aim to teach unity and love, and we should practice the same ourselves, before preaching to others to do so. But owing to the numerous past questioners regarding the present conditions among the Baha'is in the United States, the true facts must be mentioned for the enlightenment of the readers and the satisfaction of the questioners.

The Baha'is, unfortunately, are divided into three groups in America:

First: The Society of Behaists, the oldest assembly. Believing in Baha'u'llah to be the Manifestation, the beginner and the end, and the fulfiller of all the prophecies; accepting His teachings to the letter and considering them final as He declared. Obedient to all the laws revealed by Him and guided by them as He commanded. Respecting His Branches (sons) with reverence in accordance with His Will entitled *Kitab-i-'Ahdi* (the Book of My Covenant).

Second: The National Spiritual Assembly of the Baha'is of the United States and Canada. Recognizing Baha'u'llah as the Author, and His eldest son 'Abdu'l-Baha (Abbas) as Interpreter and true exemplar of the Baha'i cause; accepting the will of 'Abdu'l-Baha (Abbas) as final and incorporating the same in their organization, thus reproducing the supremacy of the Papacy by appointing infallible guardians and little popes for the next thousand years. ...

Third: The New History Society. Believing in Baha'u'llah and 'Abdu'l-Baha (Abbas), but not accepting the leadership of Shoghi Effendi in compliance with the will of 'Abdu'l-Baha.

This latter Society has done wonderful work for the advancement of the thought of mankind. The writer is well acquainted with its advocates and wishes them the best of success. We hope that someday they may see the truth through our spectacles, follow Baha'u'llah only, and consider His utterances final as He declared.

I humbly appeal to the individual Baha'is throughout the world to disregard their party affiliation and the differences in opinion and study the teachings of Baha'u'llah, as they are the only channel through which we can be united and settle our controversies.

In the Most Sacred Book (*Kitab-i-Aqdas*), He said: "If ye differ in a matter, bring it to God as long as the Sun is shining from the Horizon of This Heaven, but when He setteth, bring it to what was uttered by Him; verily it sufficeth the world."

For the enlightenment of my readers and the seekers after the truth, I hereby publish the Will of Baha'u'llah, Glory be to Him, and also the will of 'Abdu'l-Baha (Abbas), and ask you to read the two wills carefully, unbiased and unprejudiced, then form your own opinions, make your own conclusions, and pass your own judgment.[15]

May the blessings of the Almighty be with us all and guide us to understand His Will and wish.

---

[15] Both wills were published in their entirety in the pages following this article in the same issue of *Behai Quarterly*. See Chapter 6 for the Will and Testament of Baha'u'llah and Chapter 8 for selections from the Will and Testament of 'Abdu'l-Baha.

Shua Ullah Behai in his elder years.

36

Address to an Occidental Gathering

By Shua Ullah Behai

This chapter is the text of a speech delivered by Shua Ullah Behai to a Western audience at Nahariya, Palestine, on May 17, 1947. Section headings have been added. This speech provides a brief overview of the Baha'i faith, its history and principles.

—The Editor

Ladies and Gentlemen,

This is a conventional form of address, but with your permission I prefer very much to address you as Friends!

I must call your kind attention to the fact that the object of my talk this afternoon is not to teach Baha'ism, but to explain briefly some of its historical events, principles, and admonitions.

The Rise and Decline of Persian Civilization

Persia, now called Iran, was the birthplace of the Baha'i faith.

Iran is a country of ancient civilization, great empire, and a center of art and literature, which produced such philosophers and poets as Saadi, Hafez, Ferdowsi, and Omar Khayyam.

According to the [national epic] history of Iran, the *Shahnameh*, which contains over fifty thousand verses in poetry and was composed by Ferdowsi in the tenth century A.D., Iran enjoyed a great progress during many centuries; likewise the examples of ancient arts and excavations prove this progress.

Times passed as such until the Arabs conquered that empire and forced them by the sword to accept Islam. After a long period of oppression, the majority of Iranians became students of the Arabic language, devout followers of the Prophet [Muhammad] and strong believers in his book the Qur'an.

Eventually they surpassed the Arabs in their language. The first Arabic dictionary was composed by an Iranian named Fairuzabadi, which is in existence up to this day bearing his name.

The following well-known personages are a few of thousands of Iranians that served the Islamic Kingdom:

- The great Abu Hanifa, founder of the Hanafi sect of Islam.
- Estakhri, composer of the first book on geography in Arabic.
- Ibn Sina,[1] founder of the science of medicine.
- Zamakhshari, logician and grammarian.
- Razi, mathematician.
- Tusi, astronomer.

As the years went by, the Iranians progressed greatly socially and politically. Then a new idea appeared in their mind, and a decision was reached to control the government through the power of religion, hoping to regain their freedom in this way and rebuild their empire. They tried on several occasions to fulfill their desire, especially during the reign of the Abbasid caliphs, but at every attempt they failed.

While the Safavid rulers controlled the throne of Iran, during the 16th century, realizing their numerous unsuccessful attempts to predominate over the Arabian Kingdom, they encouraged the mullahs (leaders of theology) to renew the Shi'ite doctrines which originated after the reign of Ali, the fourth caliph after Muhammad, against the other Muslim sects. Thus they erected a strong wall between them, knowing that no barrier could be stronger than religious superstition, and by this means, they sowed the seeds of hatred in the hearts of the masses.

---

[1] Also known as Avicenna.

The renewal of the said doctrine shattered the peaceful minds of Iranians, drowned them in the ocean of superstition, and for over two hundred years kept them in darkness. Students of history are aware of the unbearable conditions which existed in Iran from the 16th to the 19th centuries, especially during the rule of the Qajar dynasty.

The horizon of the minds of Iranians was covered with the clouds of superstition, and reached to such a stage that all the members of the other faiths were considered filthy and untouchable. Eventually the mullahs became supreme rulers, and the government was but a tool in their hands, ruling the officials as they desired.

It is said of one of the rulers who had a distinguished long beard, that on one of his visits to the Head Mullah (high priest), during the conversation the Head Mullah struck the Shah's beard with his hand and remarked, "Is it not a pity that such a silken beard be consumed by the fire of hell." The aforesaid incident will prove the supremacy of the mullahs.

The Bab

The awakening era for liberation from religious orthodoxy began in Iran in the early 19th century.

In May 1844 A.D. there appeared in Iran a young man of twenty-four years of age, whose name was Ali Muhammad, a descendant of the Prophet. He called himself the "Bab," meaning the Gate through which to gain the knowledge of Truth.

In a short duration of time he revolutionized the thoughts of the masses. He brought them from darkness to light and from extreme religious orthodoxy to liberalism. He paved the way for the coming of the Glory of God, "Baha'u'llah."

The Bab's message spread rapidly throughout the land and thousands of theologians and learned students followed him.

The rapid spread of his message and the progress of his cause aroused the anger of the mullahs, as they feared the downfall of their leadership. They organized themselves against the Bab and his followers, calling him an impostor and a magician, and finally succeeded in sowing the seed of hatred in the hearts of the ignorant masses against this progressive movement.

The mullahs allied the governors of many provinces with themselves and caused the persecution of thousands of innocent citizens. Faithful and prominent followers of this movement were put to death without question or judgment, and many of the governors participated in these unfortunate proceedings to satisfy the desire of the mullahs.

In spite of severe persecution they [i.e. the Babis] became more energetic and enthusiastic in the spreading of the message throughout the land, so the Bab's cause became stronger as time passed.

The mullahs decided to try a new method to extinguish this great light by forcing the government to capture the Bab, and they placed him in prison, and not satisfied with this, caused his execution. The Bab was crucified in the city of Tabriz, on July 9, 1850 A.D.[2]

Three days after the execution the remains were taken away by a few faithful followers in the darkness of night and kept in a hiding place for years, and finally were brought to the Holy Land and buried on the slope of Mount Carmel, Haifa.

Baha'u'llah

Baha'u'llah was born in the city of Tehran, the present capital of Iran, on November 12, 1817, and in the same city grew to manhood.

As a young man he associated with nobilities, court officials, and the celebrities of the day. He spent some of his early days in Mazandaran in the district of Nur, the original home of his forefathers.

After the execution of the Bab, two of his [i.e. the Bab's] followers made an attempt on the life of Shah Naser al-Din. Through the influence of the mullahs, Baha'u'llah was arrested by the government, divested of all earthly possessions, and placed in an underground prison in the city of Tehran for a period of four months.

Then through the intervention of the Russian ambassador, Baha'-

---

[2] The cause of death was actually shooting by firing squad, but before this occurred, the Bab was suspended from a pole for public shaming in a manner reminiscent of crucifixion.

Chapter 36. Address to an Occidental Gathering

u'llah was released and officially vindicated of all accusations, but was requested to leave his native land, to satisfy the desires of the mullahs. By mutual agreement between Russia, Turkey, and Iran he was sent to Baghdad, Iraq, accompanied by gendarmes from the three aforesaid governments.

Baha'u'llah remained in Baghdad nearly twelve years. While there he secluded himself in the mountains of Sulaymaniyah for two years during which his whereabouts were unknown.

Through the influence of the ambassador of Iran in the Ottoman capital, engineered by the same agitating group of mullahs, Baha'u'llah was requested to come to Constantinople, now Istanbul, then the capital of Turkey. Responding to the order of the government, Baha'u'llah, accompanied by the members of his household and some of his followers, proceeded from the city of Baghdad to the other side of the river, remaining in the garden of Najib Pasha for a period of twelve days. There and then he claimed to be the one foretold by the Bab, delivering the new message to all who came to him.

During these twelve days, thousands of persons of all classes, government officials, representatives of other nations, theologians and merchants came to his presence, paying him homage and wishing him farewell. The news of his departure spread rapidly and caused such a commotion amongst the populace that Namiq Pasha, then governor of Iraq, deemed it his duty to pay him his respect also, calling on him in person, accompanied by another high official, though Baha'u'llah was his prisoner.

During the journey from Baghdad to Istanbul, which lasted about four months, he was cordially received by the people of the countryside wherever he camped, and was respected and loved by all.

From Istanbul they were removed to Adrianople, and after remaining there about five years they were banished to the fortress of Acre, arriving there August 30, 1868.

In Acre they were placed in the army barracks which form at present the Central Prison. I think that there is a sign on the door of the room which was occupied by Baha'u'llah.

After remaining there two years they were allowed to hire residences for themselves within the city wall, and after the elapse of seven years they were permitted to leave the city gate.

Inside prison walls Baha'u'llah wrote epistles to the kings and rulers of the nations, summoning them to arbitration and universal peace.

Later on, Qasr al-Mazra'a, which is now occupied by General [Angus] McNeill, was rented and Baha'u'llah used to occupy it during the summer months.

After a few years Qasr al-Bahji, now called the Baha'i House, was rented and was occupied by Baha'u'llah during his later years on earth. There he passed unto Eternity after he completed his mission to mankind, on May 29, 1892. His remains were interred in the small house located on the northwest corner of the Qasr al-Bahji.

Professor Edward G. Browne, distinguished Orientalist and lecturer in Persian, of Cambridge University, England, happened to be the only Occidental savant who visited Baha'u'llah, in 1890. He said:

> Of the culminating event of this my journey some few words at least must be said. During the morning of the day after my installation at Bahji one of Baha['u'llah]'s younger sons entered the room where I was sitting and beckoned me to follow him. I did so, and was conducted through passages and rooms at which I scarcely had time to glance to a spacious hall, paved, so far as I remember... with a mosaic of marble. Before a curtain suspended from the wall of this great ante-chamber my conductor paused for a moment while I removed my shoes. Then, with a quick movement of the hand, he withdrew, and, as I passed, replaced the curtain; and I found myself in a large apartment, along the upper end of which ran a low divan, while on the side opposite to the door were placed two or three chairs. Though I dimly suspected whither I was going and whom I was to behold... a second or two elapsed ere, with a throb of wonder and awe, I became definitely conscious that the room was not untenanted. In the corner where the divan met the wall sat a wondrous and venerable figure crowned with a felt head-dress of the kind called *taj* by dervishes... round the base of which was wound a small white turban. The face of him on whom I gazed I can never forget, though I cannot describe it. Those piercing eyes seemed to read one's very soul; power and authority sat on that

ample brow; while the deep lines on the forehead and face implied an age which the jet-black hair and beard flowing down in indistinguishable luxuriance almost to the waist seemed to belie. No need to ask in whose presence I stood, as I bowed myself before one who is the object of a devotion and love which kings might envy and emperors sigh for in vain.

A mild dignified voice bade me to be seated, and then continued:[3]

> Praise be to God that thou hast attained! ... Thou hast come to see a prisoner and an exile. ... We desire but the good of the world and the happiness of the nations; yet they deem us a stirrer up of strife and sedition worthy of bondage and banishment. ... That all nations should become one in faith and all men as brothers; that the bonds of affection and unity between the sons of men should be strengthened; that diversity of religion should cease, and difference of race be annulled—what harm is there in this? ... Yet so it shall be; these fruitless strifes, these ruinous wars shall pass away, and the "Most Great Peace" shall come. ... Do not you in Europe need this also? Is not this that which Christ foretold? ... Yet do we see your kings and rulers lavishing their treasures more freely on means for the destruction of the human race than on that which would conduce to the happiness of mankind. ... These strifes and this bloodshed and discord must cease, and all men be as one kindred and one family. ... Let not a man glory in this, that he loves his country; let him rather glory in this, that he loves his kind.[4]

The Heroine Called Tahirih

In this faith, history repeated itself, and thousands of learned men sacrificed their lives for the enlightenment of their fellow-beings.

---

[3] Ellipses original in Prof. Browne's quotation of Baha'u'llah.

[4] Edward G. Browne, *A Traveller's Narrative: Written to Illustrate the Episode of the Bab*, Volume II. English Translation and Notes (Cambridge: University Press, 1891), pp. xxxix-xl.

Amongst them was a great soul, a wonderful woman who discarded the veil and preached the new message to the masses. She was called Qurratu'l-'Ayn, meaning "Darling," and Tahirih, meaning "Pure"; a daughter of a theologian, and a well-informed student, she served the cause with great vigor and enthusiasm.

Of this noble soul an English author writes thus:

> The appearance of such a woman as Qurratu'l-'Ayn is in any country and any age a rare phenomenon, but in such a country as Persia it is a prodigy—nay, almost a miracle. Alike in virtue of her marvellous beauty... her fearless devotion, and her glorious martyrdom, she stands forth incomparable... amidst her countrywomen.[5]

Baha'i Teachings

Baha'i principles are numerous; here are a few of them:
- The oneness of mankind.
- Equality of races and sexes.
- Harmony of science and religion.
- Elimination of religious leadership.
- Association with all faiths.
- Amalgamation of races.
- Intermarriage with other faiths.
- The solution of the economic problem.[6]
- Universal religion.
- Universal language.
- Universal tribunal.
- Universal peace.

A Baha'i should study the teachings of Baha'u'llah with a broad mind, reason, care, and judgment, gaining the knowledge contained therein through diligent reading, without the assistance of an explanator.

---

[5] Ibid., p. 309.

[6] Lists of Baha'i principles have often included "elimination of the extremes of poverty and wealth," which is probably what Mr. Behai means here.

Thus one should testify to the oneness of the Supreme Ruler of the Universe.

Obey the Divine laws. Revere the past great Messengers.

Become an advocate of a universal language, universal religion, universal tribunal, and universal peace.

Believe in the oneness of mankind, equality of races and sexes. Invest himself with the garment of faithfulness, truthfulness, and trustfulness.

Respect the laws of the land in which he resides.

Adorn himself with the ornament of justice, charity, kindness, forgiveness, and serve his fellow-beings to the best of his ability.

Divest himself from religious prejudice, considering mankind leaves of one tree and drops of one sea.

Baha'u'llah said:

> Be thou a giver while thou art wealthy and grateful when thou art poor.
>
> Be thou trustworthy when thou art entrusted and face the comers with a welcome smile.
>
> Be thou a treasure to the poor, an adviser to the rich, an answerer to the seeker, a fulfiller to the promise, and faithful in every respect.
>
> Be thou silent when thou art amidst the crowd, and let thy judgment be just.
>
> Be submissive to thy fellowman and a light in the midst of darkness.
>
> Be thou a comfort to the sorrowful and a sweet sea to the thirsty. Be thou a shelter to the distressed, a help, an assistance, and a support to the oppressed.
>
> In piety let thine actions be performed, and be a home to the stranger. Be a healer to the sick, a fort to the refugee, a sight to the blind, and a path to those who are led astray.
>
> Be thou the beauty of the face of Truth, an ornament to the temple of faithfulness, a throne to the house of temperance, a spirit to the body of the world, a flag to the hosts of justice, and a map to the horizon of goodness.

Be thou a fertilizer to the good soil, a star to the heaven of bounty, a crown to the head of Wisdom, a brilliancy to the forehead of time, and a sweet fruit to the tree of obedience.[7]

---

[7] *Lawh-i-Badi'u'lláh* ("Tablet to Badi Ullah"). A different translation of this tablet is published in *Gleanings from the Writings of Bahá'u'lláh* (Wilmette, Ill.: US Bahá'í Publishing Trust, 1990 pocket-size edition), section CXXX, p. 285.

37

A Reminiscence: The Purpose, Condition and Potential of the Baha'i Faith

By Shua Ullah Behai

This chapter is the conclusion of Shua Ullah Behai's book manuscript. Section headings have been added. The first part of the original chapter has been split off and is reproduced as Chapter 4 in this book.

In this conclusion, Mr. Behai laments the lack of progress of the Baha'i cause during his lifetime, and argues that this is because Baha'is have not been living up to the progressive principles taught by the founder of their faith. Perhaps somewhat surprisingly, the grandson of Baha'u'llah "hesitate[s] to commit" himself to the Baha'i faith, because of "the existing conditions amongst us." He identifies "the defect which is causing our stagnation" as avoiding tough questions and excommunicating people who ask them, rather than practicing independent investigation of truth. He passionately urges Baha'is to hold a conference for respectful, open-minded dialogue and reconciliation between the three Baha'i sects existing at the time, also to include believers who have left all Baha'i organizations.

Although this was written about 70 years ago, much of it seems as though it could have been written today—the one big difference being that there are no longer any significant organized communities of liberal Baha'is such as the Society of Behaists and the New History Society which existed in the 1940s. No ecumenical Baha'i conference was ever held and no reconciliation occurred; instead, the liberal Baha'i sects gradually disappeared, and progressive spiritual thinkers have remained as a small and beleaguered, often invisible minority within the mainstream Baha'i community ever since.

—The Editor

The Universal Essence of Religion

It is an actual fact that the essence of all the inspired and spiritual teachings are the same. All the past prophets, Messengers and Manifestations taught the same, and their only aim was "the elevation of morals and manners of mankind, and the progress of their thoughts," and at each appearance their teachings were in harmony with the time and the people among which they appeared. To this the secular history bears witness.

Our Great Master Baha'u'llah, in the beginning of the *Hidden Words*, said:

> This is that which hath descended from the Source of Majesty, through the tongue of power and strength upon the prophets of the past. We have taken its essences and clothed them with the garment of brevity, as a favor to the beloved, that they may perform in themselves that which He hath entrusted to them, and attain the victory by virtue of devotion in the land of the Spirit.

The Challenge of the Baha'i Faith

We, the Baha'is, must search what we have: What is new and more applicable for the present civilization? The following principles are new and most exalted:

1. Association with all faiths.
2. Equality of races and sex.
3. Intermarriage with other faiths.
4. Amalgamation of races.
5. Elimination of religious leadership.
6. Harmony of science and religion.

7. True knowledge of the hereafter.
8. Recognition of all the past Manifestations.
9. Non-abolishment of the past holy books.

The above-mentioned principles are something to glory about, provided that we follow them. We, the Baha'is, should use the power of mind and ponder on this point: Are we following the teachings as we should? Can we truthfully answer this question, "Am I a true Baha'i?"

I personally hesitate to commit myself with the existing conditions amongst us, as today we observe only the differences of ideas, lack of cooperation, discord, enmity, selfishness, and hatred—while we should believe that smiles are better than frowns, kindness better than coldness, commendation better than criticism, sympathy better than deception, love better than hate, friendship better than enmity, unity better than discord, and peace better than chaos.

It is nearly half a century since these principles were introduced in the United States of America, but with all the efforts that have been made we have not progressed as we should. It is true that we have erected a magnificent temple from clay and steel in Wilmette, Illinois, and we travel around the country exhibiting the miniature of the same as a symbol of progress during the public lectures. But alas! all this propaganda did not bring the expected result. The time has come that we should arise from our slumber and pull the wool off our eyes and see the defect which is causing our stagnation. Avoiding questioners, and excommunications, are signs of weakness and anti-Baha'i principles. Independent investigation of truth should replace these flaws.

To the intellectual and unbiased observers it is evident that our lack of progress is caused by the gross violation of the commands of Baha'u'llah and the natural law that "what we sow we reap." We cannot expect wheat from tares, love from hate, unity from discord, gold from brass, oil from water, iron from wood, etc.

Now that the cause of our stagnation is evident, we may try and practice the following rules:
1. Build the Temple of God within our hearts.
2. Know ourselves.
3. Know the globe on which we reside.
4. Be faithful, truthful, and trustful.

5. Be just, honest, and sincere.
6. Discard all Baha'i party affiliations.
7. Associate with each other lovingly.
8. Meditate on the teachings of Baha'u'llah.
9. Practice the great principles we are commanded.
10. Arrange for an international Baha'i assemblage.
11. Invite all the seekers of truth to attend the same.
12. Delve into the teachings of Baha'u'llah and exchange views.
13. Unite together with complete understanding.
14. Resolve to fulfill His commands.
15. Become true disciples of Baha'u'llah.
16. Arm ourselves with His commands.
17. Guide the unfortunate to the right path.
18. Eliminate the present dissension.
19. Make the Baha'i world as we are promised, "The Paradise of Abha" (Glory).

A Plea for Reconciliation and Unity Among Baha'is

In the alleged will of 'Abdu'l-Baha the Book of *Aqdas* is sanctioned to be the last resort for the Baha'is, although the translator omitted the mention of its name [i.e. *Aqdas*] in the original language. In the photograph of the original will of 'Abdu'l-Baha, Part II, page II, the last line in the Persian language and writing appears thus: [transliterated] *Marja koll Ketab Aqdas*. A literal translation is "All must resort to *Kitab-i-Aqdas*" (the Most Sacred [or Most Holy] Book). The translation of the above-mentioned four Persian words in the published will of 'Abdu'l-Baha appears thus: "Unto the Most Holy Book every one must turn." There are over fifty volumes of the teachings of Baha'u'llah in existence and all of them are holy to us, but there is only one book entitled *Aqdas* which in the English language means "Sacred." Baha'u'llah referred to this book in numerous of his tablets, also in his will. The Occidental savant, Edward Browne, translated part of that book and mentioned its name repeatedly in his works.

A copy of the Book of *Aqdas* is in our possession in the handwriting of the well-known inscriber and calligrapher Zaynu'l-Muqarrabín, and none of the Baha'i sects could deny its authenticity, and it is ready for inspection whenever is needed.[1]

It is obvious that a great disagreement of thought exists among us regarding many vital points in our teachings and belief which could be settled, if we place as the judge the Book of *Aqdas*. Therefore it is the duty of every individual Baha'i to use his utmost effort to bring unity among us. The hour has come that the Baha'is should realize the gravity of the situation and arise with great energy and vigor, unbiased and unprejudiced, and arrange a universal Baha'i gathering in one of the large cities of the United States where it is agreeable for such an assemblage. They must forget the unwelcome titles of the past—"untouchables," "excommunicated," "polytheists," *naqizin* ("violators"), etc.[2]—and with the language of love and kindness invite the members of all the Baha'i sects, and also invite the noble souls that have kept in seclusion and severed their connections with the organizations, to attend the proposed conference.

It is evident that we differ considerably on some cardinal statutes in our faith, and this is the only channel through which we can reach the solution to our problems. The friends should come to these meetings with the intention of bringing unity and peace, and should resolve before they enter the gathering to reach an agreement, but not with the intention of contention.

---

[1] At the time when Mr. Behai was writing, a full translation of the *Kitab-i-Aqdas* had not yet been provided or authorized by the leaders of the Baha'i community in any Western languages. In fact, most Baha'is who could not read Arabic had never read the "Most Holy Book" of the Baha'i faith. 'Abdu'l-Baha and Shoghi Effendi Rabbani apparently did not consider the translation and widespread dissemination of this central Baha'i text to be a priority. The first official translation in English was published in 1992, nearly 120 years after the *Aqdas* was written. This curious delay invites speculation that leaders of the mainstream Baha'i tradition may have wished to keep this text from being studied by average Baha'is, especially Western converts, as long as possible. Leaders of the Unitarian Baha'i tradition, in contrast, emphasized the centrality of the *Aqdas* in their writings.

[2] Mainstream Baha'is considered the Unitarian Baha'is to be *naqizin*, "violators" of the Covenant or "Covenant-breakers." The Unitarian Baha'is retorted by accusing them of being "polytheists," joining partners with God instead of believing in the Manifestation of Baha'u'llah alone.

Today we do not need missionaries and propagandists, as the [Baha'i] cause is well advertised all over the world. Our true requirement is "house cleaning" and readjustment of existing conditions. The most essential need is unity: unity of faith, belief, and action. How can we guide others to become united, while we are not united? How can we expect others to practice our principles, while we are neglectful?

The Baha'i faith has a great future, provided that we give the teachings to the world as they were revealed by the Supreme Pen of Baha'u'llah, without tampering with them to suit our purpose.

The Baha'i faith is the most progressive religion the world has known so far; why pollute it with superstition?

The Baha'i faith has the capacity to bring under its banner all the different faiths in the world; why confine it to sectarianism?

The Baha'i faith is free from religious leadership; why entangle it in the cobwebs of theologians under the names of Administrators and Guardians?

The Baha'i faith teaches the Oneness and Singleness of God; why the belief in trinity [i.e. the Bab, Baha'u'llah and 'Abdu'l-Baha]?

The Baha'i faith directs us to pray individually; why the change to congregational?

The Baha'i faith is the strongest citadel for our protection; why should we seek refuge elsewhere?

The Baha'i faith is the healer of our ills; why should we apply to unskilled physicians?

The Baha'i faith is the easer of our pains; why secure other prescriptions?

The Baha'i faith is the shepherd of this flock; why go astray?

The Baha'i faith is an ocean full of pearls of wisdom; why should we sail on a muddy river of ignorance?

The Baha'i faith teaches freedom of faith; why the excommunications?

The Baha'i faith commands universal brotherhood; why the existing dissension?

Are we doubtful that the elimination of dissension is good and commanded by God? Are we uncertain that peace, unity, concord and love are His great commands? Do we not know that the association with different races and sects is our duty? Are we unaware that contention and strife are prohibited in our teachings? Have we not yet comprehended that religious dissension causes destruction? Do we not believe in the freedom of our thought and faith?

Therefore, my Baha'i friends—the members of the Society of Behaists, the members of the National Spiritual Assembly of the United States and Canada, and the members of the New History Society—I call you, at the top of my voice, to hearken to my sincere suggestions for the sake of truth. Arise for the sake of truth. Try your utmost to eliminate the existing disagreement of thoughts, and with united effort spread the real truth.

By the above suggestions I have no personal object nor private interest. My remaining days on this earth are limited, and I have no offspring that may require further consideration. My only aim is the progress of the cause, and the spread of truth.

I hereby end this reminiscence with the words of the Supreme Pen:

> O men of the House of Justice! Be ye shepherds of the sheep of God in His Kingdom and protect them from the wolves who are attired in human garments, as ye protect your own children. Thus ye are admonished by the Adviser, the Faithful.
>
> If ye differ in a matter, bring it to God, so long as the Sun is shining from the Horizon of this Heaven, but when He setteth, bring it to what was uttered by Him. Verily, it sufficeth the worlds.
>
> Verily, O people! Let not trouble take possession of you, when the Kingdom of My Appearance becometh concealed, and the waves of the Ocean of My elucidation are hushed. Verily, there is a wisdom in My appearance, and another wisdom in My occultation which none knoweth save God, the Incomparable, the All-Knowing. And We will see you from My Most Splendid Horizon, and will help him who riseth up for the helping of My Cause, with hosts from the Supreme Concourse, and a cohort of the cherubim.[3]

O Son of Him who stood by His own Entity in the Kingdom of Himself!

---

[3] *Kitab-i-Aqdas* ("Most Holy Book"), paragraphs 52-53.

Know that I have sent unto thee the fragrances of Holiness, have accomplished the Word in thee, have fulfilled the bounty through thee, and have willed for thee what I have willed for Myself. Therefore be content in Me and thankful to Me.[4]

O Son of Spirit!

The Gospel of Light I heralded to thee: Rejoice in it. And to the state of holiness I call thee: Abide in it, that thou mayest be in peace for ever and ever.[5]

---

[4] The Hidden Words, Arabic #70.
[5] Ibid., Arabic #33.

Epilogue

By Eric Stetson

"If a soul is seeking to quarrel, ask ye for reconciliation; if he blame you, praise him..."
"that we might have a name more gentle than light, and a memory more fragrant than perfume."

—Sir 'Abdu'l-Baha Abbas Effendi and
Ghusn-i-Akbar Mohammed Ali Bahai

——☼——

The Baha'i Faith: Uniquely Relevant, Tragically Flawed

When Baha'u'llah's grandson Shua Ullah Behai first wrote this book, he probably didn't foresee that it would take 70 years to get it published. The fact that the Baha'i faith has managed to last long enough for such an unexpected occurrence—yet that it remains a relatively small, obscure religion which many people would argue is not worthy of the time and effort expended to edit, annotate, and prepare this book for publication—is a testimony to the peculiar features of this faith.

Unlike any other religion I know of—and as a person with an academic degree in religious studies I have studied all the significant ones—Baha'i is the only independent world religion that combines a passionate belief in a new revelation from God with a relatively progressive set of teachings. Yes, all the major world religions were in some ways "progressive" at the time of their founding, but over the centuries, they became ossified and entrenched and often fought against further progress. And yes, there are new religious movements whose founders claim divine inspiration, but most of these movements focus on eschatology, metaphysics, or personal spiritual practice rather than social reform.

In the Baha'i tradition, we find the bizarre confluence of God-intoxicated self-confidence—a man daring to speak in the Divine voice—with genuinely modernist ideas for the advancement of civilization. Only in the writings of Baha'u'llah, for example, could we find statements such as this:

> O Queen in London! Incline thine ear unto the voice of thy Lord, the Lord of all mankind, calling from the Divine Lote-Tree: Verily, no God is there but Me, the Almighty, the All-Wise! ...
>
> We have been informed that thou hast forbidden the trading in slaves, both men and women. This, verily, is what God hath enjoined in this wondrous Revelation. God hath, truly, destined a reward for thee, because of this. ...
>
> We have also heard that thou hast entrusted the reins of counsel into the hands of the representatives of the people. Thou, indeed, hast done well ...
>
> That which the Lord hath ordained as the sovereign remedy and mightiest instrument for the healing of all the world is the union of all its peoples in one universal Cause, one common Faith. This can in no wise be achieved except through the power of a skilled, an all-powerful and inspired Physician. This, verily, is the truth, and all else naught but error.[1]

Many religious leaders of the 19th century nobly advocated for the abolition of slavery, the establishment or expansion of democracy, women's rights, universal education, respect for science, interfaith reconciliation, and other such principles as were taught by Baha'u'llah. But few claimed that these progressive principles were new commandments from God. Baha'u'llah did, and he furthermore claimed that he was the divine messenger sent into this world to command humanity's embrace of these teachings.

---

[1] Tablet to Queen Victoria. Official Baha'i translation in *The Summons of the Lord of Hosts* (Bahá'í World Centre, 2002 edition), paragraphs 171-173, 176. See Chapter 6, pp. 77-78, for a different translation.

Such a stance seems even more curious today than it must have at the time. In the postmodern era, the trend of religious innovation has moved away from bold-faced claims of divinity and prophecy and instead has tended toward the humility and relativism of those who are reluctant to issue heavenly commands. For example, it is almost inconceivable that an early 21st century spiritual leader would announce that the Supreme Being has commanded that gay people should have the right to marry, claiming prophetic authority to deliver this verdict from on high. But that is exactly the kind of thing that the founder of the Baha'i faith did in his own time, on the controversial, cutting-edge issues of his day.

Baha'u'llah claimed to be the return of Christ—a new Christ for a new age of human progress, preaching a message of social reform which for the most part would resonate with liberal-minded people today as common sense and yesterday's news. In the 1800s, his message was revolutionary. The combination of millenarian utopianism with thoughtful modernism was extraordinary. As Professor Juan Cole writes in *Modernity and the Millennium*:

> Baha'u'llah announced himself as not only the figure, "He whom God shall make manifest," prophesied by the Bab but as the messianic fulfillment of all the past major world religions. He saw himself as at once the culmination of the six-thousand-year-long Adamic cycle of prophecy and the inaugurator of a new age in world history, the major theme of which would be the gradual establishment of a global world civilization animated by his teachings. Early Baha'is believed that the advent of the end-time had turned the world upside down. Poor and humble workers were reconfigured as the backbone of the modern economy; women were reimagined as equal citizens full of manly courage and enterprise; voiceless subjects, shorn and led like sheep, were elevated to an electorate that would rule by reason in the place of emasculated monarchs; the sciences and modern philosophy were exalted over theology and the minutiae of religious law.[2]

---

[2] Juan R. I. Cole, *Modernity and the Millennium: The Genesis of the Baha'i Faith in the Nineteenth-Century Middle East* (New York: Columbia University Press, 1998), pp. 194-195.

That most of Baha'u'llah's social principles were adopted by the forward-thinking nations of the world without the Baha'i *religion* ever really catching on should be a telltale sign that something went wrong. For the most part, people decided that the principles of progressive modernity were better embraced without a divine commander—that the power of human reason is sufficient to inspire us to create a better world on our own. However, it would stand to reason that a religion whose ideals are largely in harmony with the consensus of modern times should have grown quite a bit more than the Baha'i faith has done, if for no other reason than that it would reinforce and provide confirmation of what people have already decided to believe. Many progressive people continue to believe in God, yet struggle to reconcile their modern values with the outdated teachings of the major religions that were founded many centuries ago. People like to think that God is on their side, that their values are approved by the Almighty. Yet for some reason, modern progressives by and large choose not to become Baha'i.

Lack of exposure cannot be used as an excuse; the Baha'i faith has had plenty of time to penetrate into the awareness of society. Over a hundred years ago, the wife of a United States Senator and mother of newspaper tycoon William Randolph Hearst joined the Baha'i cause.[3] The Lieutenant Governor of the State of New York, likewise, became a devotee of 'Abdu'l-Baha.[4] Many important people in those days dabbled in Baha'ism. In retrospect, in some respects, the early 1900s were the high-water mark of this faith. Its numbers have continued growing slowly, but even today, only one tenth of one percent of the world's population is Baha'i.[5] And the Baha'i faith is considerably less influential now than a century ago, when it captured the imagination of spiritual progressives and was regarded as one of the most exciting new movements of the period. Clearly, the Baha'i moment has passed.

---

[3] See Chapter 25, note 17.

[4] See the last section of Chapter 21.

[5] Adherents.com estimates that there are about 7 million Baha'is in the world (http://www.adherents.com/Religions_By_Adherents.html, accessed January 12, 2014). There are just over 7 billion people in the world in 2014.

Nevertheless, one might expect the Baha'i faith to regain some appeal—at least as something of a countercultural vehicle for spiritually inspired change—in our own era of extreme relativism and secular materialism in the West, resurgence of religious fundamentalism in the Middle East, and the retreat of progressives in many parts of the world from a full-throated advocacy of idealistic visions for society and into a defensive posture of cynicism. What better time for a faith tradition which eloquently cries out to humanity that there is a God, but not a God of hatred or division—that God has called us to build a world of peace, equality, and justice for all? Baha'u'llah's support for representative democracy, concern about the dangers of unchecked industrialization and technology, opposition to military aggression and the international arms race, and prescription for a new geopolitical order to prevent war and promote consciousness of the oneness of humanity are especially important teachings that should be at the forefront of the 21st century mind. No other religion was founded on these principles.

Although it remains uniquely relevant to modern times, the Baha'i faith has failed to live up to its potential. This persistent disconnect between potential and reality has long been a cause of frustration among Baha'is. Prophecies of "entry by troops"—the mass conversion of millions of souls, as dreamed of by members of the Baha'i community for decades—go unrealized. Baha'i evangelists wonder, perplexed and in anguish, why the people of the world are not flocking to their faith, which they believe to be God's latest revelation and so well suited to the time in which we live.

There are reasons for this failure—reasons which should not be a mystery to anyone who has studied Baha'i history and teachings with an open mind. As Shua Ullah Behai wrote 70 years ago:

> It is nearly half a century since [the Baha'i] principles were introduced in the United States of America, but with all the efforts that have been made we have not progressed as we should. ... The time has come that we should arise from our slumber and pull the wool off our eyes and see the defect which is causing our stagnation. Avoiding questioners, and excommunications, are signs of weak-

ness and anti-Baha'i principles. Independent investigation of truth should replace these flaws.[6]

For me, editing this book has been a profound exercise in independent investigation of truth. In doing so, I have read numerous other books and articles from various points of view, in order to reflect as objectively as possible on the issues at hand, properly annotate the manuscript, and write this concluding essay. I can honestly say that it has been a religious experience. I have rediscovered the faith that I rejected over ten years ago—its richness, its beauty, its worthiness to be considered—and its tragic flaws which have practically destroyed it, preventing it from achieving anything close to its truly great potential.

As Baha'u'llah's grandson points out, the main problem is that the Baha'i community stifles independent thought and purges itself of people who insist on asking difficult questions, whose conclusions don't always agree with the established dogma and historical narrative of the religion. One relatively recent example of this is the excommunication of Pauline Smith, a Baha'i from New Zealand, simply because she dared to "maintain contact and association with... some of the relatives of Shoghi Effendi" who are considered "Covenant-breakers" by the leaders of the Baha'i faith.[7] In a letter to the Baha'is of New Zealand, the Baha'i National Spiritual Assembly of that country wrote these chilling words:

> A fundamental principle of the Faith is that no believer can have any contact or association with a believer who has been deemed by the Head of the Faith to break the Covenant, whether by correspondence, telephone, or in person. Strict adherence to this rule is obligatory.[8]

---

[6] Chapter 37, p. 485.

[7] National Spiritual Assembly of the Baha'is of New Zealand, letter dated 16 December, 1996, reproduced online at http://www.fglaysher.com/bahaicensorship/shun1.htm

[8] Ibid.

It would be difficult for Baha'is to pursue an "independent investigation of truth" in order to decide what to believe about the history of their own religion if they are not allowed to associate with any of the descendants of Baha'u'llah, and thus unable to ask them questions about their unique memories and historical perspectives. For obedient members of the Baha'i community, the "fundamental principle" of shunning heretics takes precedence over an open-minded search for truth. Even the writings of excommunicated Baha'is are largely avoided by those within the fold, for fear of contaminating their minds with ideas that dissent from the party line.

The fatal flaw of the Baha'i faith is that it has created a highly questionable mythology and a culture of conformity, in an era of unprecedented access to information available to anyone with an internet connection. The advent of the Information Age has ensured that the challenges faced by previous generations of Baha'i evangelists are more challenging today, and will likely become even more so as more primary source documents become available and are discussed by people interested in discovering the truth for themselves. A thousand years ago, a new religion could carefully construct a narrative to its liking, by simply destroying documents that didn't fit the story and preventing dissenting voices from gaining a platform to be heard. The Baha'i faith is just young enough that it can't take advantage of that option. It will either have to confront the truth about itself or lose credibility among spiritual progressives—those who would otherwise be most likely to join it—not to mention the public at large.

No movement can be truly progressive if it refuses to look honestly at its history and beliefs, question its own assumptions, consider alternative points of view, tolerate differences of opinion within its ranks, and make changes when necessary. And no movement, progressive or otherwise, can ever be taken seriously by people of conscience if it claims to be one thing yet does another. The Baha'i faith has failed both of those tests, because it clings to myths of perfection and stifles much-needed reform. In the rest of this Epilogue, we'll deconstruct the Baha'i mythology on some key issues, and then consider how the Baha'i faith could reinvent itself for a positive future.

The Broken Baha'i "Covenant"

The central myth of the Baha'i faith, as it has come to be understood by its present-day adherents, is the doctrine of "the Covenant." In the broadest sense, this is the claim that there is a perfect line of divine authority, from the Bab to Baha'u'llah, to 'Abdu'l-Baha, to Shoghi Effendi, to the Universal House of Justice. Each link in the chain is believed to be solid and unquestionable.

In reality, the history of the Baha'i faith is in large part a story of shattered plans and broken promises—or to put it in Baha'i terminology, "Covenant-breaking." During the ministry of each leader and at every stage of transfer of leadership, there has been a great deal of conflict and controversy. Covenants have been broken not only by those who have traditionally been assigned the blame, but by the recognized leaders of the faith as well. With every fresh round of dissension and excommunications, there were valid arguments on both sides, but one side utterly defeated the other and demonized it to such a degree that its views are typically never considered by Baha'is or by the average person studying the Baha'i religion.

Baha'is have responded to the historical record by digging in their heels on the thoroughly refutable claim that theirs is the only religion in history which has a perfect, unbroken chain of authority passed down from one leader to the next. It does not; no major religion does. In fact, Baha'i may actually be more noteworthy among religions for its perfect record of leadership conflicts in every generation or stage of development during the first one hundred years of its existence. The Baha'i "Covenant" is broken—and always has been, from the moment Baha'u'llah declared himself to be a new Manifestation of God.

Let's start there. The Bab appointed Mirza Yahya Nuri, a younger half-brother of Baha'u'llah, as his successor. It was far from clear that another Divine Manifestation should appear anytime soon; according to Babism, the founders of religions were supposed to appear roughly every one thousand years. But because the Bab's successor was a quiet man with a reclusive personality—more interested in writing esoteric religious texts than in playing the role of a charismatic leader for the nascent Babi community—many followers of the Bab began looking for a forceful personality to provide them with the divine guidance they craved. Several prominent Babis proclaimed themselves to be "Him whom God shall make manifest," interpreting vague prophecies of the Bab in their own favor. Mirza Husayn Ali Nuri was one of these claimants, calling himself Baha'u'llah. Shortly thereafter, Mirza Yahya responded by making a similar claim, and called himself Subh-i-Azal.

It is beyond the scope of this book to investigate the conflict between these two brothers, but suffice it to say that it was ferocious. There were denunciations and counter-denunciations, and the Nuri family was split between supporters of each brother.[9] Things reached the point of assassinations and attempted assassinations. Eventually the government had to intervene and banish the two branches of the family and their respective fanatical followers to two different provinces of the Ottoman Empire: the Azalis to Cyprus, and the Baha'is to Syria (now Israel).

This was the atmosphere in which Baha'u'llah's sons grew up: a poisonous indoctrination into hatred of their own relatives who had chosen a different interpretation of the Babi religion.

I have not attempted to form a scholarly opinion about which side of the Azali-Baha'i conflict was more in the right, factually and morally speaking,[10] but I can understand why Baha'u'llah made his claim to be a new prophet rather than deferring to his younger brother: He believed—as most other Babis came to believe as well—that Mirza Yahya was a weak leader and, to the extent that he was providing leadership at all, was not leading the new religion in the right direction. In the culture of millenarian Shi'ism and Babism, the way to "get things done"

---

[9] Their half-siblings from their stepmother Kulthum Khanum mostly followed Mirza Yahya. Two other half-siblings from other stepmothers followed Mirza Husayn Ali, as did most of his full siblings. See Appendix B: Families of Baha'u'llah and the Bab.

[10] I have, however, listened to the views of both sides, as should anyone interested in Babi and Baha'i history. The Azali view is articulately presented by N. Wahid Azal, a former Baha'i and staunch opponent of the Baha'i faith, in a 2011 lecture at the University of London's School of Oriental and African Studies. The entire lecture can be viewed online, beginning at http://youtu.be/LEhLkVsXddY (Part 1 of 8).

was to claim to be a divinely guided teacher and draw fellow religious radicals under your spell. Baha'u'llah did what he felt he had to do, and his personality fit the role to a T. Within a few years, he had largely succeeded in taking over the Babi movement, which became the Baha'i faith.

So, the Baha'i faith began by one brother usurping the other brother's position as successor to the Manifestation of God in whom they both believed. Perhaps for legitimate reasons; perhaps, had Baha'u'llah not done this, Babism would have died out or fragmented into numerous insignificant sects—even if, technically, he obtained his position of leadership through an illegitimate claim.

There is also the fact that Baha'u'llah simply did not agree with some of the Bab's teachings. For example, the Bab believed in military *jihad* (holy war); his goal was the overthrow of the corrupt Persian government, and his followers rose up as political revolutionaries and fought for the triumph of their faith by the sword. Baha'u'llah strongly condemned this, and taught the Baha'is to be peaceful martyrs, obedient even to unjust governments. In an underappreciated act of intellectual courage and spiritual reformation, Baha'u'llah, who was born and raised a Muslim, did what people around the world are hoping that more Muslim leaders will do today: explicitly renounce the Islamic doctrine of holy war. In his revolutionary words, "The First Glad Tidings which is conferred in this Most Great Manifestation on all the people of the world... is the abolishing of the decree of religious warfare from the Book."[11]

Dr. Denis MacEoin, a former Baha'i who taught Arabic and Islamic studies at universities in England and Morocco, summarizes the conflict between Subh-i-Azal and Baha'u'llah as follows:

> Although later Bahá'í sources have tended to play down or distort his role, there is adequate contemporary evidence that, in the early period of the Baghdad exile, a consensus of opinion favoured the leadership of a young man widely regarded as the 'successor' (*wasi*) of the Bab—Mirza Yahya Nuri Subh-i Azal ... [B]oth he and

---

[11] *Lawh-i-Bisharat* ("Tablet of Glad-Tidings"). See Chapter 6, p. 70.

his followers emphasized a conservative, retrenched Babism centred on the doctrines of the Persian *Bayan* and other later works. Subh-i Azal seems to have remained faithful to the long-term goal of overthrowing the Qajar state by subversion ...

There are indications that Husayn 'Ali [Nuri] did not at first envisage for himself any role in the Babi community beyond that of spiritual preceptor, and, indeed, he abandoned the group at one point to embark on the life of a Sufi *darvish* at the Khalidiyya monastery in Sulaymaniyya, with every intention, it seems, of dissociating himself from the movement permanently. Persuaded to return to Baghdad in the spring of 1856, however, he began to devote himself to the reorganization of the sect... By the early 1860s, towards the end of his stay in Baghdad, he had firmly established his position within the community and begun to express his authority [and] claims in increasingly messianic terms. Numerous passages of the Persian *Bayan* refer to the future 'divine manifestation' destined to succeed the Bab as the latter had succeeded Muhammad, speaking of him eschatologically as 'he whom God shall make manifest' (*man yuzhiruhu 'llah*), and indicating that he would appear in about one to two thousand years time. ... The appeal of a new messianic impulse [i.e. the claim of Baha'u'llah] encouraged a thoroughgoing reinterpretation of the Bayanic prophecies, in order to demonstrate that the Bab had, in fact, anticipated an extremely early appearance of this saviour figure ...

Babi militancy having failed, Husayn 'Ali chose to revert to the quietist stance of orthodox Shi'ism. ... A semi-pacifist, politically acquiescent posture was consonant with and, indeed, integral to the deradicalized and increasingly universalist form of Babism being taught by Husayn 'Ali during the 1860s...[12]

The full-blown pacifism and internationalism of Baha'u'llah's later teachings were a philosophical progression that turned the Baha'i faith into something completely different from the jihadist, Iran-centric Babism from which it had sprung. The most important points to un-

---

[12] Denis MacEoin, "From Babism to Baha'ism: Problems of Militancy, Quietism, and Conflation in the Construction of a Religion." Originally published in *Religion*, vol. 13 (1983): 220-223. Available online at http://bahai-library.com/maceoin_babism_militancy

derstand are that Mirza Yahya Nuri was recognized as the Bab's successor, and that the Bab wrote that the next Manifestation of God would not come for at least one thousand years. But Mirza Husayn Ali Nuri chose to break this covenant of the Bab and declare himself Baha'u'llah, the new Manifestation, because he disagreed with the leadership style and ideas of his brother and believed that Babism should move in a different direction.

Perhaps somewhat predictably, in the next generation Baha'u'llah's sons reenacted the brother-against-brother battle of their father and uncle, concerning the future direction of the Baha'i faith. Once again, the younger brother accused the elder of making excessively grandiose claims. The issues at stake were different, of course; and in this case, it was the successor of the prophet who was more inclined to make changes to the religion rather than his competitor. But the intensity of the dispute between Abbas Effendi and Mohammed Ali Bahai, and the bitterness of the rift it created not only between themselves but in the faith community as a whole, was very similar to what had happened between Mirza Husayn Ali and Mirza Yahya. Holy war was not abolished even from their own family, despite the noble principles for humanity that Baha'u'llah had taught in his writings. Instead, impressionable young men learned from the *example* of their elders in their own lives: the authoritarian absolutism of their father, a man who claimed to be speaking for God at all times (a claim which was emulated to some degree by 'Abdu'l-Baha), and his acrimonious yet highly successful usurpation of his brother's position of religious authority (a less ambitious version of which Mr. Bahai seems to have desired to accomplish for himself).

Although the brothers Abbas and Mohammed Ali didn't fight each other with swords or pistols at dawn, perhaps brotherly fisticuffs could have helped to clear the air. But since they were brought up to be dignified religious leaders, they struck the pose of perfect gentlemen and holy men, while passive-aggressively warring against each other for decades over the future direction of the Baha'i faith. We'll discuss the causes and substance of their dispute in detail later.

For now, the important thing to understand is that Baha'u'llah wanted them both to work together, and wanted the younger brother to succeed the elder if he outlived him. Neither of these intentions of the founder of the Baha'i faith came to pass. Mohammed Ali Bahai broke his father's covenant by launching a destructive sectarian argument rather than accepting the role of second-in-command and helping to spread the Baha'i teachings to new souls, thus deviating from the spirit of Baha'u'llah's words: "O Ghusn-i-Akbar! (Mightiest Branch) Verily We have chosen thee for the help of My Cause; rise thou in a marvelous assistance."[13] 'Abdu'l-Baha also broke the covenant by refusing to reconcile with his brother when he later sought an honorable resolution to their conflict, instead condemning him in his will and appointing a different successor, thus departing from Baha'u'llah's stated plan of succession: "We have surely chosen the Mightiest (Akbar) [Mohammed Ali] after the Greatest (A'zam) [Abbas Effendi] as a command from the All-Knowing, the Omniscient."[14]

Another important point, often overlooked, is that Baha'u'llah did not teach that his sons should be the *only* source of authority in the Baha'i faith after his passing. Instead, he taught that a great deal of authority should vest in an institution he called the House of Justice, which would resolve questions and make policies not clearly specified in the scriptures. As he wrote:

> It is incumbent upon the Trustees of the House of Justice to take counsel together regarding those things which have not outwardly been revealed in the Book, and to enforce that which is agreeable to them. God will verily inspire them with whatsoever He willeth, and He, verily, is the Provider, the Omniscient.[15]

Although 'Abdu'l-Baha allowed Baha'i Houses of Justice to be established at the local level, he did not establish an international ("Universal") House of Justice, reserving all power over the Baha'i faith as a whole to himself alone. It seems unlikely that this was Baha'u'llah's in-

---

[13] "Sacred Tablet" to Ghusn-i-Akbar. See Chapter 10, p. 150.

[14] *Kitab-i-'Ahdi* ("Book of My Covenant"). See Chapter 6, p. 94.

[15] *Kalimat-i-Firdawsiyyih* ("Words of Paradise"), Eighth Leaf. Official Baha'i translation in *Tablets of Bahá'u'lláh Revealed After the Kitáb-i-Aqdas* (Wilmette, Ill.: US Bahá'í Publishing Trust, 1988 pocket-size edition), p. 68.

tention. More likely, he intended Abbas Effendi to call for the Baha'is to elect this institution during his lifetime and to serve as its chairman, and for Mohammed Ali Effendi to serve as its vice chairman.

After leading the Baha'is for almost 30 years without a Universal House of Justice, 'Abdu'l-Baha died and left the reins of authority to his grandson, Shoghi Effendi Rabbani, whom he gave the title of "Guardian." However, he made it explicitly clear in his will that Shoghi Effendi should work together with the democratically elected leadership body, at long last to be created, that Baha'u'llah had originally envisioned. As 'Abdu'l-Baha wrote:

> The sacred and youthful branch, the Guardian of the Cause of God, as well as the Universal House of Justice to be universally elected and established, are both under the care and protection of the Abhá Beauty [Baha'u'llah]... Whatsoever they decide is of God. ...
>
> [C]oncerning the House of Justice which God hath ordained as the source of all good and freed from all error, it must be elected by universal suffrage, that is, by the believers. Unto this body all things must be referred. It enacteth all ordinances and regulations that are not to be found in the explicit Holy Text. By this body all the difficult problems are to be resolved and the Guardian of the Cause of God is its sacred head and the distinguished member for life of that body.[16]

Defying his grandfather's instructions to create the Universal House of Justice and lead the Baha'i faith in conjunction with its elected members as its chairman, Shoghi Effendi chose to rule unilaterally. His ministry lasted over 35 years, and during that entire time the House of Justice was never brought into being. This was a choice he made—a choice which violated both the spirit and the letter of 'Abdu'l-Baha's will. There were plenty of eminent Baha'is from various nations who could have served capably and admirably on a Universal House of Justice, had it been created, but Shoghi Effendi evidently preferred to

---

[16] *The Will And Testament of 'Abdu'l-Bahá* (Wilmette, Ill.: US Bahá'í Publishing Trust, 1990 reprint), Part One, pp. 11, 14.

hold all power in his own hands—just as 'Abdu'l-Baha had preferred and chosen in his own ministry.

Following in the footsteps of his grandfather, Shoghi Effendi also chose to excommunicate his relatives who did not show absolute deference to his wishes and views. By the end of his life, he had excommunicated every one of the descendants of 'Abdu'l-Baha as well as all the descendants of Baha'u'llah's third wife. Thus, the entire family of Baha'u'llah—except for Shoghi Effendi himself, his wife Ruhiyyih, and 'Abdu'l-Baha's widow Munirih and sister Bahiyyih—ended up expelled from the mainstream Baha'i community and shunned.

To be fair to 'Abdu'l-Baha, the half-siblings he declared as "Covenant-breakers" were actually leaders of a competing Baha'i sect, so there is considerably more justification or at least a reasonable argument for his decision. In the case of Shoghi Effendi, he expelled his family for mostly trivial reasons, over issues of their personal relationships, based on an extremely authoritarian interpretation of his authority as the Baha'i Guardian.

One of the most disturbing examples was Shoghi Effendi's excommunication of his cousin Munib Shahid for marrying a Muslim. In the words of Hassan Jalal Shahid, the last surviving grandchild of 'Abdu'l-Baha:

> [R]egarding my brother Dr Munib Shahid of the American University of Beirut (AUB)... His wife Serene Husseini was the daughter of Jamal Husseini. He was a notable of Jerusalem, a prominent and respected Palestinian politician who had been exiled by the British to the Seychelles Islands and then to Southern Rhodesia (now Zimbabwe) to put an end to his struggle for an independent Palestine. While there, his daughter Serene wanted to get married to my brother Munib Shahid. She contacted her father, Jamal Husseini, for his consent. He did not know who Munib Shahid was and asked a fellow exile from Haifa, Mr Tanimi, about him. Mr Tamini told him to consider it an honor that the grandson of Abdul-Baha wanted to marry his daughter. On the recommendation, he consented to and blessed the marriage. ...
>
> My brother was a sincere and true Bahai and tried many times, until the last years of his life to return to the Cause [i.e. the

organized Baha'i faith]. ... Munib was no Covenant Breaker and died a disappointed man for having been deprived of something that meant so much to him and in which he sincerely believed.[17]

The marriage of one of 'Abdu'l-Baha's grandsons to the daughter of a prominent Muslim politician could have been an excellent opportunity for interfaith dialogue between the Islamic and Baha'i communities in Palestine. Instead, Shoghi Effendi saw this marriage by his cousin as disloyalty to the Baha'i faith, and expelled him for it—even though the Guardian was never given the authority to veto marriages either by members of Baha'u'llah's family or by any Baha'i.

Shoghi Effendi also excommunicated both of his sisters and another cousin for marrying relatives who were descended from Baha'u'llah through his third wife, Gawhar Khanum. Gawhar's daughter Foroughiyya Khanum and her husband Siyyid Ali Afnan sided with the Unitarian Baha'is for a while, but eventually reconciled with 'Abdu'l-Baha. Mr. and Mrs. Afnan's sons seem to have wanted to move beyond the religious conflicts of the previous generation. One of them, Nayer Afnan, is known to have been friendly with all branches of the family, including the descendants of Mohammed Ali and Badi Ullah Bahai; Negar Bahai Emsallem remembers him fondly. Shoghi Effendi apparently felt that this third branch of Baha'u'llah's family was too liberal in their attitude about "Covenant-breakers," because they didn't believe in shunning their relatives who had unorthodox ideas about the Baha'i faith. Thus, he excommunicated all of his relatives who married into that branch of the family.

Conventional wisdom among Baha'is is that Shoghi Effendi was trying to defend his family from the spread of heresy, supposedly emanating from Nayer Afnan. But as Mr. Afnan's daughter and Shoghi Effendi's niece Bahiyeh Afnan Shahid writes:

> Regarding [Foroughiyya Khanum's] second son, my father Nayer Afnan, he and my mother Rouhanguise Rabbani were married in 1928 in Haifa. The marriage took place in the Master's [i.e.

---

[17] Hassan Jalal Shahid, "Comments About Munib Shahid," http://www.abdulbahasfamily.org/writings/comments-about-munib-shahid/

'Abdu'l-Baha's] house and the Master's sister, Bahiyeh Khanum officiated at the ceremony. Present were the Master's wife Mounireh Khanum, the Master's daughters and other members of the family as well as Bahai friends. Would things have happened this way if Nayer Afnan was a covenant breaker? ...

For some strange reason my father was designated by Shoghi Effendi... as the plotter and schemer behind most of these marriages. His was the evil hand that wove this mesh of marriages, connecting generations of 'covenant breakers' with one another, serving sinister schemes that took shape seemingly nowhere but in the Guardian's mind. He simply could not see a group of cousins and relatives from a family that considered themselves Bahais in every sense of the word, but completely cut off from their roots and their natural milieu. Was it not natural that they should choose each other when they sought husbands and wives?[18]

Most likely, Nayer Afnan's liberal approach to the Baha'i faith—specifically, his refusal to shun the Unitarian Baha'is among his relatives—is what caused Shoghi Effendi to excommunicate him. Although he may have had a relatively open-minded attitude all along, it is possible that this grandson of Baha'u'llah decided to develop friendships with his Unitarian Baha'i cousins precisely because he objected to the authoritarian leadership style of Shoghi Effendi and was attracted to the relatively progressive views of the ostracized members of the family.

One more relative of Shoghi Effendi whom he excommunicated deserves special attention: his cousin Ruhi Afnan, a grandson of 'Abdu'l-Baha who was a prominent and well-respected teacher of the Baha'i faith. Ruhi Afnan was such a significant figure that the liberal Baha'i leader Ahmad Sohrab wrote a whole book about him and his case, an unauthorized biography entitled *Abdul Baha's Grandson: Story of a Twentieth Century Excommunication*, even though Mr. Afnan never supported Mr. Sohrab's denomination. Here is his summary, from that book, of Mr. Afnan's career as a Baha'i administrator and spokesperson:

---

[18] Bahiyeh Afnan Shahid, "Comments About Sayyid Ali Afnan, Forough Khanum, and Their Sons," http://www.abdulbahasfamily.org/writings/sayyid-ali-afnan-forough-khanum-and-their-sons/

Ruhi Effendi Afnan acted as confidential secretary to the Guardian of the Bahai Cause for fourteen years; and the records of the Bahai organization show that during that time, from 1922 to 1936, he was constantly in demand in a variety of capacities. In 1924, he appeared in London as Shoghi Effendi's personal representative and delivered a brilliant address on the Bahai Religion before *The Conference of Some Living Religions Within the British Empire*. In 1927, he visited the United States as traveling agent and spiritual salesman of the Guardian, championing with fervor and zeal the system of Bahai administration before *recognized* and *declared* Bahais. He was an outstanding and honored guest at the 20th Annual Bahai Convention in Chicago, where he *participated vitally in all proceedings*; was the guest speaker at Green Acre Bahai Summer School in Maine, and traveled from coast to coast, delivering Bahai speeches before churches, colleges and outside gatherings. In 1928, we find him in Geneva, Switzerland, where, as the accredited representative of the Bahai Cause, he participates in the Conference of International Peace Through the Churches. Here, we see him taking the floor, offering some constructive suggestions which, as one report says, were very much to the point, and carrying his argument. In 1935, *with the Guardian's approval* (See *Baha'i News*, page 3, October 1935), he pays his second visit to the United States; takes part in the National Bahai meeting in Chicago and, before his departure, addresses a number of local Bahai communities.[19]

Despite Ruhi Afnan's exemplary record of service to the Baha'i faith, Shoghi Effendi excommunicated him in 1941, stating three reasons: (1) that Mr. Afnan's sister married one of the sons of Foroughiyya and Ali Afnan, all of whom he considered to be Covenant-breakers; (2) that Ruhi Afnan himself married a cousin, one of the granddaughters of 'Abdu'l-Baha, of whom he apparently disapproved; and (3) that Mr. Afnan supposedly made his second trip to the United States without

---

[19] Mirza Ahmad Sohrab, *Abdul Baha's Grandson: Story of a Twentieth Century Excommunication* (New York: Universal Publishing Co., 1943), pp. 67-68. *Emphasis in original.*

Shoghi Effendi's approval.[20] On the third point, as Ahmad Sohrab mentions with documentation, the allegation is simply false. As for the first reason for Ruhi Afnan's excommunication, it seems that he refused to shun his sister after her marriage, and his continued association with her was unacceptable to Shoghi Effendi. In fact, the main reason for *most* of Shoghi Effendi's excommunications of his relatives was that they chose not to shun family members whom they loved.

Although it might have been tempting for an articulate Baha'i evangelist such as Ruhi Afnan to have joined or started a different Baha'i denomination with more respect for believers' personal freedom, instead he repeatedly sought to return to the mainstream Baha'i community—as did many other Baha'is and members of Baha'u'llah's family who had been expelled. In a long and very interesting letter Mr. Afnan wrote in 1970, he recalls, among other things, that:

> For twelve years after Shoghi Effendi cast me out of the Cause I regularly wrote a petition—at least once a year—and more often than not, took them to the House [of Shoghi Effendi] myself. Several times I saw [Shoghi's wife] Ruhiyyih Khanum who would meet me and end up by rejecting my request. I always wondered whether Shoghi Effendi read those letters or not. One day I asked [Shoghi's mother] Zia Khanum. She told me that other than myself, many people wrote such petitions, for example Rouha Khanum [Zia Khanum's sister and Ruhi's aunt]. Apparently Shoghi Effendi had a special suitcase full of such letters from members of the family, all of which he saved. Zia Khanum added that she herself, every month, sometimes every week, would write such a petition and pour out her heart, in an effort to clarify matters to her son. I don't know whether that suitcase full of letters still exists. If it does, it would tell the story of those people and the pain they bore.[21]

---

[20] These points were made by Shoghi Effendi in two cablegrams received by the leaders of the American Baha'i community on November 10, 1941 and published in the December 1941 issue of *Bahá'í News*, pp. 1-2. Archives are available online at http://bahai-news.info

[21] Letter by Ruhi Mohsen Afnan to the Baha'i Spiritual Assembly of Iran, 1970. Translation by Bahiyeh Afnan Shahid, available online at http://www.abdulbahasfamily.org/documents/Ruhi-Afnan-1970-letter.pdf, pp. 20-21.

According to Ruhi Afnan, he was even banned from visiting Baha'u'llah's tomb, and threatened by Shoghi Effendi's wife, who informed him that "orders had been given to beat me and throw me out" if he ever went to the Shrine.[22] This only changed as a result of a lawsuit by Kamar Bahai in 1952.[23]

None of Shoghi Effendi's siblings, cousins, aunts and uncles, or even his parents, were ever allowed to return to the organized Baha'i community. They were utterly and permanently shunned, by order of the Guardian and later the Universal House of Justice, which to this day teaches that the Guardian was infallible and therefore all his decisions were automatically justified.

As the facts show, the ministry of Shoghi Effendi was marked by the kind of dictatorial authoritarianism, paranoia and fanaticism that are not usually associated with great religions in the modern era. None of his relatives were even given a hearing and a chance to defend themselves before a panel of neutral judges before they were excommunicated; and once expelled from the fold, their appeals fell on deaf ears and they were either written out of history or recast as villainous characters, despite their strong belief in and service to the Baha'i faith.

Perhaps the clearest illustration of the Baha'i Guardian's attitude can be found in a polemical, triumphalistic history of the Baha'i faith he wrote called *God Passes By*. In the following passage of that book, he indulges in bone-chilling schadenfreude, recounting with relish the misfortunes, illnesses and deaths of some of the people he considered to be "Covenant-breakers" and taking comically immature potshots at their memory:

> [Mohammed Ali Bahai's] brother, Mírzá Díya'u'lláh,[24] died prematurely; Mírzá Áqá Ján [Kashani], his dupe, followed that same brother, three years later, to the grave; ... Mírzá Muhammad-'Alí's half-sister, Furúghíyyih,[25] died of cancer, whilst her husband, Siyyid 'Alí [Afnan], passed away from a heart attack before

---

[22] Ibid., pp. 28-29.
[23] See Chapter 33.
[24] Zia Ullah.
[25] Foroughiyya.

his sons could reach him, the eldest being subsequently stricken in the prime of life, by the same malady. Muhammad-Javád-i-Qazvíní,[26] a notorious Covenant-breaker, perished miserably. ... Jamál-i-Burújirdí,[27] Mírzá Muhammad-'Alí's ablest lieutenant in Persia, fell a prey to a fatal and loathsome disease; Siyyid Mihdíy-i-Dahájí,[28] who, betraying 'Abdu'l-Bahá, joined the Covenant-breakers, died in obscurity and poverty, followed by his wife and his two sons; ...

[Mohammed Ali Bahai] was stricken with paralysis which crippled half his body; lay bedridden in pain for months before he died; and was buried according to Muslim rites, in the immediate vicinity of a local Muslim shrine, his grave remaining until the present day devoid of even a tombstone—a pitiful reminder of the hollowness of the claims he had advanced, of the depths of infamy to which he had sunk, and of the severity of the retribution his acts had so richly merited.[29]

As for Shoghi Effendi himself, he and his wife found themselves unable to have children. With no heirs, and having excommunicated every living descendant of Baha'u'llah but himself, there was no one eligible to be appointed as his successor in accordance with the provisions of the Will and Testament of 'Abdu'l-Baha, so the office of the Guardianship became permanently vacant upon his passing. He died suddenly of the Asian flu, at the age of 60, while visiting London in 1957. His grave is located in that city instead of among the Baha'i shrines in Israel, because, according to Baha'i law, a body cannot be moved more than one hour's journey from the place of death.[30] He failed to leave a will, violating Baha'u'llah's command that "Unto everyone hath been enjoined the writing of a will,"[31] and thus the Baha'is

---

[26] Mohammed Jawad Gazvini.

[27] Also known as Ismu'llah Jamal.

[28] Also known as Ismu'llah Mahdi.

[29] Shoghi Effendi, *God Passes By* (US Bahá'í Publishing Trust, 1979 second printing), pp. 319-320.

[30] *Kitab-i-Aqdas* ("Most Holy Book"), paragraph 130.

[31] Ibid., paragraph 109.

had no clear guidance for how their faith should be led without a second Guardian after his passing.

The loss of the Guardianship posed a serious problem for mainstream Baha'is. They had been accustomed to having an individual leader of their faith, and in accordance with the intentions of 'Abdu'l-Baha expressed in his will, they fully expected that there would be a series of Guardians for generations to come. Shoghi Effendi had written that "In this Dispensation, divine guidance flows on to us in this world after the Prophet's ascension, through first the Master, and then the Guardians."[32] Furthermore, he wrote:

> Divorced from the institution of the Guardianship the World Order of Bahá'u'lláh would be mutilated and permanently deprived of that hereditary principle which, as 'Abdu'l-Bahá has written, has been invariably upheld by the Law of God. "In all the Divine Dispensations," He states, in a Tablet addressed to a follower of the Faith in Persia, "the eldest son hath been given extraordinary distinctions. Even the station of prophethood hath been his birthright." Without such an institution the integrity of the Faith would be imperiled, and the stability of the entire fabric would be gravely endangered. Its prestige would suffer, the means required to enable it to take a long, an uninterrupted view over a series of generations would be completely lacking, and the necessary guidance to define the sphere of the legislative action of its elected representatives would be totally withdrawn.[33]

After Shoghi Effendi's death, the inner circle of Baha'i leaders he had appointed to assist him during his ministry, called Hands of the Cause, decided to establish the Universal House of Justice. It was elected for the first time in 1963—without a Guardian as its chairman—and the Baha'is, who had been taught by Shoghi Effendi to believe in the supreme importance of a line of living Guardians, were expected to

---

[32] Shoghi Effendi, *Directives from the Guardian* (India/Hawaii, 1973 edition), section 89, p. 34.

[33] Shoghi Effendi, *The World Order of Bahá'u'lláh* (US Bahá'í Publishing Trust, 1991 first pocket-size edition), p. 148.

put this belief aside yet continue believing that "the Covenant" of their faith was being fulfilled regardless.

One distinguished Baha'i leader named Charles Mason Remey dissented and claimed that Shoghi Effendi had intended for him to become his successor, on the basis that he had appointed him as the head of an executive body called the International Baha'i Council. Mr. Remey attracted some support, because many Baha'is, quite understandably, still clung to the teaching of the absolute necessity of a Guardian to lead the faith; but the vast majority of Baha'is rejected his claim, because he was not a "branch" of Baha'u'llah's family as the Guardians were required to be according to 'Abdu'l-Baha's will, and there was no document in which Shoghi Effendi ever explicitly nominated him for the office of Guardian. Mason Remey formed a sect, the remnants of which continue to exist today as a very small Baha'i denomination called the Orthodox Baha'i Faith and three other splinter groups.

Despite all the unexpected changes, controversies, twists and turns we have described, Baha'is today believe that the succession of divine authority from the Bab, to Baha'u'llah, to 'Abdu'l-Baha, to Shoghi Effendi, to the Universal House of Justice is a perfect, unbroken Covenant—that the head of the faith at each stage was infallible and the transitions unchallengeable. As we have seen, the facts reveal that this is only a myth; that the reality is far more complex, more flawed, and indeed more interesting.

'Abdu'l-Baha and the "Covenant-Breakers"

Because the author of this book was a Unitarian Baha'i and its primary focus is the Unitarian Baha'i tradition, it is appropriate that we should delve more deeply into mainstream Baha'i mythology concerning 'Abdu'l-Baha and those whom he considered to be "Covenant-breakers." According to 'Abdu'l-Baha and the Baha'is who supported him during his lifetime—and in the view of virtually all Baha'is today—the eldest son of Baha'u'llah was completely right in everything he said and did, and his Unitarian Baha'i critics (who are not even afforded the courtesy of this name by which they called themselves) were completely wrong in every way in which they disputed with him. Moreover, the younger half-brother of 'Abdu'l-Baha, named the "Center of Sedition" in his will, is regarded as having been motivated entirely by personal jealousy or hatred, rather than any reasonable philosophical differences about the meaning of the Baha'i faith and the nature of its leaders.

This is the myth, but what was the reality? To what degree did Mohammed Ali Bahai and his supporters have legitimate concerns which prevented them from following 'Abdu'l-Baha? What were the underlying causes of the conflict between them, and why did each side take the position it did?

Mohammed Ali Effendi was excommunicated by his elder brother because he would not submit unconditionally to his leadership. Instead, he circulated pamphlets in which he expressed concern that Baha'u'llah's successor was being inappropriately idolized by Baha'is. He argued that the emphasis of the Baha'i faith should remain on Baha'u'llah and his scriptures, and that "the appointment [of a successor] is only for bringing about friendship and amity."[34] As he wrote in his autobiography:

> This delicate situation must be carefully observed: although [Baha'u'llah] has said to turn towards Ghusn-i-A'zam [Abbas Effendi], this is confined to the limitations mentioned in the holy books and is subject to the words of God and not above them. ... Yet some of the selfish people and seekers of leadership attributed an unlimited station to Ghusn-i-A'zam... They made a manifestation of him and interpreted in his favor the contents of some of the holy tablets which refer only to the appearance of the coming Manifestation [i.e. Baha'u'llah or the next Manifestation of God]. With their mischievous acts they misguided the innocent followers and held them under their control. ... The kind of leadership that they have originated is being observed by you today... Today one person is rejected, tomorrow another is expelled. ... Where is that freedom of thought which is the cause of the progress of the world...?[35]

---

[34] Will and Testament of Mohammed Ali Bahai. Chapter 17, p. 247.

[35] Autobiography of Mohammed Ali Bahai. Chapter 16, pp. 217-219.

The question of 'Abdu'l-Baha's station is indeed a delicate one, and it is the crux of the difference between the mainstream and the Unitarian Baha'i tradition. Mainstream Baha'is believe that 'Abdu'l-Baha never claimed to be a Manifestation of God, but they do believe he was divinely inspired and infallible—so much so, that he is referred to with a capital "He," like the Manifestations of God, in Baha'i publications. Baha'is today teach that 'Abdu'l-Baha, though not in essence the Divine Light, perfectly reflects and reveals it; that he is in a unique category by himself, between the Manifestations and all other human beings. Unitarian Baha'is would argue that this is a distinction without a difference, a clever way to "claim and in the same breath deny that which you claim"[36] as Shua Ullah Behai put it; that exalting 'Abdu'l-Baha to such a lofty station is still inappropriate, even if Baha'is do not technically call him a "Manifestation." As Ibrahim Kheiralla alleged—less diplomatically than Mohammed Ali Bahai—placing some of the blame on 'Abdu'l-Baha himself for the quasi-divine status he acquired:

> Abbas Effendi, in his epistles, has claimed to be a Manifestation, not always in express terms, but by hints and in obscure words and phrases. Those who preach him throughout the countries explain these obscure phrases to mean that he is God Himself; sometimes they say that the Father and the Son are one and that Abbas Effendi is a new Manifestation, and that his words are to be received as inspired texts.[37]

Mainstream Baha'is do believe that 'Abdu'l-Baha's writings are inspired texts. After all, he called many of them "tablets," like his father's purportedly divine revelations. Unitarian Baha'is, on the other hand, held that the revelation of scripture ended with Baha'u'llah until the advent of the next Manifestation of God. In their view, the authority to reveal tablets is one of the key distinctions between the Manifestations

---

[36] Open letter from Shua Ullah Behai to 'Abdu'l-Baha, 1912, reproduced in Mr. Behai's Memoirs. See Chapter 30, p. 403.

[37] Ibrahim George Kheiralla, *Facts for Behaists* (Chicago, 1901), p. 25. See Chapter 26, p. 362.

and human religious leaders; and the writings of Baha'u'llah's successors should therefore be regarded as commentaries or compositions, not divinely inspired verses. This is a difference of opinion with significant implications, since a text which is believed to be a divine "tablet" would carry more authority and its teachings would more likely be seen as permanent for the duration of the Baha'i dispensation, rather than only as temporary during the ministry of its author.

It is much more difficult to assess Dr. Kheiralla's allegation that 'Abdu'l-Baha made inappropriately lofty claims for himself in his epistles. Most of his correspondence has not been translated into English and is not widely available even in the original languages. Scholars should look into this question to the degree possible.

Based on published writings of Baha'is during 'Abdu'l-Baha's ministry, it is clear that lofty claims were made *about* him by respected believers. For example, here is what Mirza Abu'l-Fadl Gulpaygani, one of 'Abdu'l-Baha's most eminent followers and evangelists, wrote in his book *The Behai Proofs* in 1902:

> [O]ur Lord 'Abdu'l-Baha (Glorified is His Name) ... had not studied in any school, yet, from His youth, fountains of knowledge flowed in His fluent explanations. The first trace which emanated from His Holy Being in the world of knowledge was the treatise He wrote in His early youth at Baghdad. ... [W]hile it is impossible even for a scholar to show forth such great knowledge, how much more impossible would it be for a person to write such a treatise in his childhood without having studied. Therefore, such knowledge is heavenly and not earthly; it is Divine wisdom, not human, and it owes its origin to the Holy Spirit of God.[38]

Notice the use of capitalized pronouns to refer to 'Abdu'l-Baha—already customary at that time—and other language suggestive of his divinity. As these kind of statements were being circulated by distinguished 'Abdu'l-Baha loyalists, no wonder that the Unitarian Baha'is

---

[38] Mirza-Abul-Fazl, *Hujaj'ul Beheyyeh (The Behai Proofs)*, translated by Ali Kuli Khan (New York: J. W. Pratt Co., 1902), pp. 109-110.

believed the intention was to turn him into a new Manifestation of God.

Many of 'Abdu'l-Baha's American followers believed him to be the Return of Christ. Juliet Thompson, a devout Baha'i who had extensive association with Baha'u'llah's charismatic successor, described him as a Manifestation in her diary during his 1912 visit to the United States:

> The chancel was empty that night except for the Master, sitting—almost *lying*—in a semicircular chair, His head thrown back, His luminous eyes uprolled. The sleeves of His bronze-coloured 'abá[39] branched out from His shoulders like great spread wings, hiding His hands, so that I was conscious only of His head and those terribly alive eyes. There was an awful mystery about that dominance of the head. It seemed to obliterate the human form and reveal Him as the *Face of God*. The curtain behind Him might have concealed the Ark of the Covenant, which He, THE COVENANT, was guarding.
>
> Later, when He rose to speak, the Manifestation of the Glory was entirely different. He diffused a softer radiance.
>
> "Look at Him and see the Christ," whispered Lawrence White.[40]

'Abdu'l-Baha does not seem to have rebuked or distanced himself from such Baha'is who deified him. On the contrary, devotees such as Mirza Abu'l-Fadl and Juliet Thompson were embraced and held up as exemplars of the true Baha'i spirit. In light of the evidence, Mohammed Jawad Gazvini's assessment seems credible:

> [T]he more the followers of Abbas Effendi increased in the exaggeration of his praise, and described him by names and attributes proper only to the Divine Majesty, the more he magnified his gifts to them and the more graciously he treated them. So they exag-

---

[39] An *aba*, also called *abaya*, is a type of Middle Eastern robe.

[40] Juliet Thompson, *The Diary of Juliet Thompson* (Los Angeles: Kalimat Press, 1983), p. 296. *Emphasis in original.*

gerated the more, and carried matters to the point of polytheism, exceeding all limits in respect to him.[41]

An example of this can be found in the mainstream Baha'i publication *Star of the West* in 1913. A poem by Thornton Chase, one of the first American converts to the Baha'i faith, "was read in the holy presence of Abdul-Baha," who "wishes it to appear" in the periodical, according to prefaced remarks by the editors.[42] Some excerpts from that poem are as follows:

> TO THE CENTER OF THE COVENANT: *ABDUL-BAHA ABBAS.*
> *May the Souls of all Mankind be a Sacrifice to Him!*
>
> O THOU David of the Promised Kingdom of GOD!
> Thou Princely Leader of all Humanity! ...
>
> Thou Establisher of the New Jerusalem descended from the Heaven of the Will of God!
> Thou Builder of the Temple of the LORD!
> Thou Light of the City of GOD!
> Thou Brilliant Moon reflecting the Sun's full Disc of Splendor!
> Thou Enlightener of the Spirits of Men! ...
>
> Thou Ambassador of Heaven and the Manifestation of Righteousness!
> Thou King of Servitude and Defender of the Faith!
> Thou Temple of the Divine Testimony!
> Thou Witness and Aim of THE COVENANT!
> Thou Prince of Peace and Ensign of United Humanity! ...
>
> Thou Shepherd of the Sheep, and Shelter of the Birds of the Air!
> Thou Keeper of the Vineyard, and Trainer of the Children of GOD!

---

[41] Mohammed Jawad Gazvini, *An Epitome of Babi and Baha'i History to A.D. 1898*, translated by Edward G. Browne in *Materials for the Study of the Babi Religion* (Cambridge: University Press, 1918), p. 63. See Chapter 23, p. 320.

[42] *Star of the West*, Vol. IV, No. 11, p. 187.

Thou Servant of the Highest, declared by Isaiah!
Thou Right Arm of the Mighty, proclaimed by Israel!
Thou Holy One in the Hand of GOD!
Thou Lord of the Sabbath of Ages!
Thou Unique One of the Millennial Age!

Thou Lion of the Tribe of Judah!
Thou Lamb of the Sacrificial Love!
Thou Baptizer of Evanescence!
Thou Sum of Spiritual and Human Perfections!
Thou *MYSTERY OF GOD!*

Reveal Thyself to those who can bear the Knowledge![43]

Many of these epithets copiously applied by Thornton Chase to 'Abdu'l-Baha refer, as any Christian well familiar with the Bible would know, to the Messiah, Christ, or the Return of Christ. As if that were not enough praise and glorification of the Baha'i leader, Mr. Chase continues: "This grain of human dust, stirred by the Breath of the Spirit, longs for Thy Presence, for the Life-giving touch of Thy Glorious Love. ..."[44] And on and on, for three more paragraphs genuflecting before 'Abdu'l-Baha's incredibly lofty station.

A story in the same issue of *Star of the West*, immediately following the ode by the late Thornton Chase, quotes 'Abdu'l-Baha as follows: "This revered personage was the first Bahai in America. He served the Cause faithfully and his services will ever be remembered throughout ages and cycles." The article states that 'Abdu'l-Baha "told the friends to annually visit the grave of Mr. Chase" and describes his visit there with some Baha'is, scattering bouquets of flowers and uttering a long, eloquent prayer, printed in full, which effusively praises the deceased devotee of 'Abdu'l-Baha.[45]

I find it difficult to comprehend how fair-minded Baha'is could

---

[43] Thornton Chase, "Ode To the Center of the Covenant." Published in Ibid., pp. 187-188. *Emphasis in original.*

[44] Ibid., p. 188.

[45] Ibid., pp. 188-190.

persist in dismissing as baseless the concerns of Mohammed Ali Bahai and his supporters, given the fact that there is clear and convincing evidence to support their central allegation: that 'Abdu'l-Baha was idolized by his followers in terms highly suggestive of his being a new Manifestation of God. Some of the exaggerated praise of 'Abdu'l-Baha's station was even expressly approved by him, as in the case of the Thornton Chase poem. At the very least, it should be acknowledged by Baha'is that there were legitimate differences of opinion about exactly what the station of Baha'u'llah's successor should be, and that the Unitarian Baha'is represented one end of the spectrum of reasonable debate on this point—the view that 'Abdu'l-Baha was flying too close to the sun, letting himself be exalted to a level too similar to that of Baha'u'llah.

Moving on to the other aspects of the great Baha'i schism, both brothers and their followers accused each other of serious breaches of trust and heinous acts such as slander, theft, and attempted abduction or assassination. The truth of these allegations will probably never be known—little or no concrete evidence was ever presented by either side, so it mostly comes down to conflicting accounts by partisan individuals. I am inclined to the view that both sides probably did take some questionable, possibly less than honorable actions in pursuit of their religious goals, but that both sides significantly exaggerated the corruption and ill-intent of their opponents. This, admittedly, is merely an opinion, but I have formed it after having read accounts by partisans of both the mainstream and the Unitarian Baha'i traditions, as well as other Baha'is and non-Baha'i sources. Separating facts from polemical spin is a challenge; both sides seem to have been quite good at portraying their antagonists as depraved and themselves as innocent victims—too good to be fully believable. As in most such cases, the truth almost certainly lies somewhere in the middle.

A few facts, however, are known. One of them is that 'Abdu'l-Baha and Mohammed Ali Bahai were offered the opportunity by a neutral third party to photograph Baha'u'llah's will, to resolve a dispute about the contents of the original handwritten text. Mr. Bahai eagerly accepted this suggestion, but 'Abdu'l-Baha declined.[46] This suggests that

---

[46] See Chapter 24.

the Unitarian Baha'is were probably telling the truth when they alleged that part of the *Kitab-i-'Ahdi* was censored by 'Abdu'l-Baha.

It is also known that Mohammed Ali Bahai and his son Shua Ullah challenged 'Abdu'l-Baha to a public conference, to be moderated and recorded by neutral third parties, to discuss and attempt to resolve their doctrinal disagreements. The younger Mr. Behai issued this challenge through an open letter which was published in American newspapers while 'Abdu'l-Baha was on a speaking tour in the United States.[47] Although the tone and contents of the letter reflected a clear Unitarian Baha'i bias, the intention of ecumenical dialogue provided an opening for progress to be made in the long-standing dispute between the Baha'i sects. 'Abdu'l-Baha could have responded by stating his own concerns with the Unitarian Baha'is and suggesting that the views of both sides be discussed frankly and respectfully in such a conference, with the goal of finally healing the schism. He declined to take this opportunity, and no ecumenical conference between Baha'is of different opinions was ever held.

Another known fact, obviously, is that Mr. Bahai started a competing sect of the Baha'i faith during 'Abdu'l-Baha's ministry. Unity was commanded by Baha'u'llah and schism prohibited, so this has to be considered as something of a black mark against Mr. Bahai's legacy. However, to be fair, it is hard to imagine how he could have continued to teach the Baha'i faith, as Baha'is are also commanded to do, without ending up as a schismatic, given the fact that 'Abdu'l-Baha did not seem willing to compromise with him to come to any mutually acceptable resolution to their disagreement.

In all of this, I think the most important question that deserves serious consideration is *why* 'Abdu'l-Baha decided to choose the path that he did, in terms of how to interpret the leadership position conferred upon him by Baha'u'llah. Why did he feel that it was so important to magnify his station and marginalize his younger brother, whom Baha'u'llah had appointed as second-in-command? Why couldn't he have compromised, perhaps by humbly, unambiguously stating in a widely circulated epistle that he was only a man, not a divine figure, and chal-

---

[47] See Chapter 30, the section entitled "Open Letter to 'Abdu'l-Baha."

lenging Mohammed Ali Bahai to accept him as the fully legitimate Baha'i leader on those terms, disband his rival sect, and begin assisting him in a respected role as Vice President of the Baha'i community? Was it hubris that prevented 'Abdu'l-Baha from such a seemingly logical course of action, or were there deeper reasons for the unilateral charismatic authority which he unrelentingly asserted?

I believe the beginnings of an answer can be traced to Baha'u'llah's practice of polygamy and the rivalries and hurt feelings that it undoubtedly engendered among his wives and children. Baha'u'llah had three wives—a situation which was not uncommon for upper-class Persian men of that era. In the latter part of his life, the second and third wives, Mahd-i-'Ulya and Gawhar Khanum, lived with Baha'u'llah and their children in the Mansion of Bahji; but the first wife, Navvab, lived with her son 'Abdu'l-Baha, apart from her husband. The third wife was originally the first wife's maid. The second wife seems to have competed strenuously for Baha'u'llah's affections, and ultimately prevailed, relegating the first wife to another house several miles away, which Baha'u'llah infrequently visited.

Navvab died a tragic death, a fact which is almost completely unknown among Baha'is today. According to Asadu'llah Qumi, a credible mainstream Baha'i source who lived in Acre at the time, she "fell from a high elevation" and died a few days later.[48] Quite possibly this was an act of suicide. After all, Persian women in those days did not typically climb to high elevations—in fact, they never left their homes. Did she jump off the roof, perhaps reenacting the death of her beloved son Mirza Mihdi, who fell through a skylight and died as a young man? We will never know, but if she did kill herself, one can only imagine how her children would have blamed Baha'u'llah's other wives for her abandonment and depression.

In light of this possibility, it is easier to believe the following event reported by Khadimu'llah, Baha'u'llah's chief secretary:

On one occasion the wife of the Manifestation, [Mahd-i-'Ulya]... honored Abbas Effendi by paying him a visit at his house in the

---

[48] Baharieh Rouhani Ma'ani, *Leaves of the Twin Divine Trees* (Oxford, UK: George Ronald, 2008), p. 115.

city of Akka. Abbas Effendi treated her harshly. After a discussion concerning present conditions and differences of faith, Abbas Effendi... rose up and furiously attacked her with the intention of doing her bodily harm. Seeing the danger, she left his house and returned to the Palace of Bahja. This event was a source of great sorrow to his brothers and sisters. It is strange that Abbas Effendi dared to so treat the wife of his Father, the Manifestation, when he knew that Baha'u'llah commanded that she be treated with all proper respect.[49]

No, in fact it is not strange at all, considering that if 'Abdu'l-Baha was angry at his father for showing favoritism to his other wives—which may have contributed to his own mother's death—he would not have dared to blame Baha'u'llah, who was believed to be the Manifestation of God and was the source of 'Abdu'l-Baha's own position of religious leadership. Instead, he might have placed the blame entirely on those other wives, and resented their children as well. Their very presence, and their striving for position in the family and the faith, might have been a constant reminder of the unfairness of what happened to his mother.

It seems likely that 'Abdu'l-Baha despised polygamy and wanted it to be purged from the Baha'i faith. But this could not be accomplished unless he changed the laws of Baha'u'llah, who had written the following in the *Kitab-i-Aqdas*:

> God hath prescribed matrimony unto you. Beware that ye take not unto yourselves more wives than two. Whoso contenteth himself with a single partner from among the maidservants of God, both he and she shall live in tranquillity.[50]

Islam allows four wives; Baha'u'llah had three; and he recommended to his followers to limit themselves to two, or preferably only one. The text of the *Aqdas* is explicitly clear that bigamy is permitted.

---

[49] Ibrahim George Kheiralla, *Facts for Behaists* (Chicago, 1901), pp. 59-60. See Chapter 22, p. 306.

[50] *Kitab-i-Aqdas* ("Most Holy Book"), paragraph 63.

Monogamy is encouraged because, as Baha'u'llah points out, it makes it more likely that the couple will enjoy a peaceful marriage. But a man with two wives would be living within Baha'i law, according to Baha'u'llah himself.

'Abdu'l-Baha "reinterpreted" the permission to practice bigamy to mean the exact opposite: its absolute prohibition. As he wrote:

> Know thou that polygamy is not permitted under the law of God, for contentment with one wife hath been clearly stipulated. Taking a second wife is made dependent upon equity and justice being upheld between the two wives, under all conditions. However, observance of justice and equity towards two wives is utterly impossible. The fact that bigamy has been made dependent upon an impossible condition is clear proof of its absolute prohibition. Therefore it is not permissible for a man to have more than one wife.[51]

Clearly, 'Abdu'l-Baha changed Baha'i law. It may have been a good change, but a change it was—not merely an interpretation. Baha'is today are unwilling to admit this, because as they know, according to the doctrines of their own religion, only Manifestations of God may abrogate the laws of a previous Manifestation. Because they don't want to admit that 'Abdu'l-Baha claimed powers beyond that of a mere successor of Baha'u'llah, verging into the territory of a Manifestation, they must make the convoluted argument that banning bigamy was what Baha'u'llah already intended—even though Baha'u'llah's own words directly contradict this.

'Abdu'l-Baha's words also contradict this, because he contradicted himself on the subject of plural marriage. He even had the audacity to claim that his ban of bigamy, quoted above, was one of the "slanderous whisperings" of the Covenant-breakers:

> Concerning bigamy, this has been promulgated, and no one must abrogate it (*mansusast nasikhi nadarad*). 'Abdu'l Baha has not ab-

---

[51] Tablet of 'Abdu'l-Baha quoted in *The Kitáb-i-Aqdas* (Bahá'í World Centre, 1992 edition), note 89, p. 206.

rogated this law. These are false accusations and lies (spread by) the friends. ... Such false accusations (concerning 'Abdu'l Baha's prohibition of bigamy) are the slanderous whisperings (*zamzamih*) of those who wish to spread doubts (in people's hearts) and to what degree they already succeed in making matters ambiguous! (Our) purpose was to state that bigamy without justice is not lawful and that justice is very difficult (to achieve).[52]

So there is a statement, well known to Baha'is, in which 'Abdu'l-Baha claims that Baha'u'llah banned bigamy; and there is another statement, not well known to Baha'is, in which he states that bigamy "has been promulgated, and no one must abrogate it." Deflecting criticism away from himself for the confusion, he blames it on those who accused him of abrogating Baha'i law.

The fact of the matter is, Baha'u'llah's own son, Mohammed Ali Bahai, had two wives—and his bigamous marriage was arranged by Baha'u'llah himself. The modern Baha'i argument that Baha'u'llah banned bigamy is laughably untenable. 'Abdu'l-Baha banned it, and then accused the Unitarian Baha'is of falsely claiming that he banned it. Today, plural marriage is unequivocally prohibited in the Baha'i faith. Without question, this is a law of 'Abdu'l-Baha, not Baha'u'llah.

If 'Abdu'l-Baha had not excommunicated Mr. Bahai or had reconciled with him, the second successor of Baha'u'llah would have been a man who practiced bigamy. Considering how strongly 'Abdu'l-Baha felt about the subject of plural marriage—the injustice he felt was inherent in it, and his own mother's bad experience probably at the forefront of his mind—he may have decided not to compromise with his half-brother, so as to prevent him from becoming the next Baha'i leader and thus to prevent bigamy from being perpetuated as a legitimate lifestyle under Baha'i law.

'Abdu'l-Baha may also have hoped that discouraging Baha'is from associating with his half-siblings would prevent or reduce awareness

---

[52] 'Abdu'l-Baha, cited in *Amr wa Khalq* 4: 174f, translated by Sen McGlinn and quoted in a blog article, "The puzzle of the Aqdas: joining a few pieces," http://senmcglinn.wordpress.com/2008/03/29/the-puzzle-of-the-aqdas-joining-a-few-pieces/

among Western converts to the Baha'i faith that its founder had been a polygamist—a fact which would likely have been a stumbling block for Christians who were attracted to the religion's generally progressive principles. Mohammed Ali Bahai notes in his autobiography that 'Abdu'l-Baha's party "even said that there were no other offspring of Baha'u'llah except Ghusn-i-A'zam ('Abdu'l-Baha) and his sister [Bahiyyih Khanum]," i.e. the children of Baha'u'llah's first wife.[53] The children of the second and third wives were, for the most part, written out of history. The eldest among them was turned into a comic-book villain, and the others were mostly forgotten.

What must be understood is that 'Abdu'l-Baha could not have accomplished these changes—modifying a law in the *Kitab-i-Aqdas* and stripping his half-brother of the successorship identified in the *Kitab-i-'Ahdi*—unless he claimed a very exalted station. He had to make the Baha'is believe he had nearly boundless authority to make whatever changes to the faith he felt were necessary or beneficial. 'Abdu'l-Baha is known to have been very interested in spreading Baha'ism to Europe and America, but the lands of Christendom would not have been as receptive to the Islamic-oriented faith of his father had he not tried to Westernize it in some ways. For the same reason, he did not share the *Aqdas* with Western believers or seekers, as the "Most Holy Book" of Baha'u'llah contained several teachings that would have seemed peculiar or backward to non-Muslims. If Abbas Effendi had contented himself with the more humble type of leadership role that Mohammed Ali Effendi believed was appropriate for Baha'u'llah's successors, and passed the torch to him with his two wives and his focus on Baha'u'llah's writings, it is quite possible that Baha'ism would have had limited appeal in the West, gaining adherents primarily in the Muslim world.

Thus, the legacy of 'Abdu'l-Baha is that he used the power of a charismatic, autocratic leadership style to begin the process of making the Baha'i faith a more universal world religion, casting aside some of the outdated baggage of Persian Islamic culture; but in the process of doing so, he treated some of his close relatives as the baggage. The legacy of Mohammed Ali Bahai is that he advocated for freedom of thought in

---

[53] Chapter 16, p. 213.

the Baha'i faith and limitations on the authority of its leaders; but in doing so, he started a contentious schism rather than using his considerable talents to assist the ministry of the legitimate successor of Baha'u'llah. Both, in some ways, can be said to have "broken the Covenant." In hindsight, perhaps they both needed to, for the long-term benefit of the faith.

Infallibility, Progressive Revelation, and the Future of the Baha'i Faith

In the religion of Islam, Shi'ites believe that the Prophet Muhammad was succeeded by a series of divinely-guided Imams; but Sunnis believe spiritual authority was vested in the body of believers, not any single charismatic leader after the Prophet. Most Shi'ite Muslims believe the Imams are sinless and infallible (*ma'súm*)—especially the First Imam, Muhammad's son-in-law Ali, who is called "the perfect man" (*al-insan al-kamil*). Sunni Muslims reject this doctrine.

The mainstream Baha'i faith holds a similar position regarding the station of 'Abdu'l-Baha, and as with the Shi'ite Imamate, extends some degree of infallibility to the Baha'i Guardianship. The Unitarian Baha'is, like Sunni Muslims, rejected these ideas. The conflict between the supporters of 'Abdu'l-Baha and Mohammed Ali Bahai was therefore a struggle between Baha'is who felt that their religion should be more like Shi'ism and those who favored a more Sunni approach to their faith.

The key issue was infallibility. The Unitarian Baha'is were willing to accept 'Abdu'l-Baha as the Baha'i leader, but not as an infallible commander like Baha'u'llah, or like the Shi'ite conception of Imam Ali. Alluding to the Sunni vision of successorship, in which the successors do not share in the perfection of the Messenger of God, Mr. Bahai wrote:

> In the Qur'an [God] says: "Obey God, obey the Messengers, and the people in command amongst you." With all their lofty station, no one considered them (i.e. the people in command) to be a partner of God and His Messengers. It is evident that the object was to

create unity between the governors and the governed in performing their service to the cause.⁵⁴

This is how Mohammed Ali Bahai saw 'Abdu'l-Baha and his appropriate role in the Baha'i community. But Shoghi Effendi saw him very differently:

> He is... the stainless Mirror of [Baha'u'llah's] light, the perfect Exemplar of His teachings, the unerring Interpreter of His Word, the embodiment of every Bahá'í ideal, the incarnation of every Bahá'í virtue, the Most Mighty Branch sprung from the Ancient Root, the Limb of the Law of God, the Being "round Whom all names revolve,"... the Moon of the Central Orb of this most holy Dispensation... [I]n the person of 'Abdu'l-Bahá the incompatible characteristics of a human nature and superhuman knowledge and perfection have been blended and are completely harmonized.⁵⁵

It is unclear whether 'Abdu'l-Baha himself claimed to be infallible. On the one hand, he is reported to have said: "Any opinion expressed by the Center of the Covenant is correct, and there is no reason for disobedience by anyone."⁵⁶ On the other hand, he is also reported to have said: "I do not make a claim of infallibility (*ma'sumiyyat*). I am the first of sinners (*avval-i gunahkar*)."⁵⁷

Just as on the issue of bigamy, 'Abdu'l-Baha seems to have wanted to have it both ways. Perhaps he claimed infallibility when it was useful to his cause, and denied it when he felt that his audience would not accept it. In any case, Baha'is today definitely believe 'Abdu'l-Baha was

---

⁵⁴ Will and Testament of Mohammed Ali Bahai. Chapter 17, p. 243.

⁵⁵ Shoghi Effendi, *The World Order of Bahá'u'lláh* (US Bahá'í Publishing Trust, 1991 first pocket-size edition), p. 134.

⁵⁶ 'Abdu'l-Baha, talk at home of Mrs. Corinne True, Chicago, Illinois, November 1, 1912. Published in *The Promulgation of Universal Peace* (US Bahá'í Publishing Trust, 1982 second edition), p. 386.

⁵⁷ 'Abdu'l-Baha, quoted by Yunis Afrukhtih in *Khatirat-i Nuh Salih* (Los Angeles: Kalimat Press, 1983), p. 521. Quotation translated by Juan Cole with commentary at http://www-personal.umich.edu/~jrcole/abinfall.htm

perfect and infallible, based on the teachings of Shoghi Effendi, who is also regarded as infallible (to a lesser extent) by Baha'is.

Dr. William Garlington, a former Baha'i and professor of history and religious studies, writes in his book *The Baha'i Faith in America*:

> To a considerable degree, the authoritarian aspects of Baha'i leadership can be seen to stem from the religion's Shi'ite cultural roots, where the concept of divinely guided *imāms* is given great reverence. As a self-proclaimed Manifestation of God, Baha'u'llah is believed to have been infallible, and his legitimate heirs to authority, 'Abdu'l-Baha, Shoghi Effendi, and the Universal House of Justice, are, to varying degrees, also seen in this light. What adds emphasis to the Baha'i belief in the unquestionable nature of ultimate authority are the challenges and resulting schisms that have occurred at each stage of leadership change. These events have resulted in an overriding fear of disunity and created widespread suspicion that any disagreement with authority harbors a challenge to community identity. Those who have been the sources of rupture have been labeled as covenant-breakers and given a demonic image.[58]

The Unitarian Baha'is, who were demonized more than any other Baha'i splinter group, challenged the underlying assumption that the Shi'ite concept of infallible successors to God's Messenger was something worthy of being reproduced in the Baha'i faith. As Shua Ullah Behai wrote:

> While the Safavid rulers controlled the throne of Iran during the 16th century... they encouraged the mullahs (leaders of theology) to renew the Shi'ite doctrine... By this means, they sowed the seeds of hatred in the hearts of the masses. ...
>
> The Shi'ites believe that the true spiritual leaders after the Prophet were his descendants, and they are called Imams. The Imam is the divinely ordained successor of the Prophet, one endowed with all perfections and spiritual gifts, one whom all the

---

[58] William Garlington, *The Baha'i Faith in America* (Westport, Conn.: Praeger Publishers, 2005), p. 185.

faithful must obey, whose decision is absolute and final, whose wisdom is superhuman, and whose words are authoritative. ...

The renewal of the Shi'ite doctrine shattered the peaceful minds of Iranians, drowned them in the ocean of superstition and for two hundred years kept them in darkness. ... [Unnumbered people endured] extreme agonies for the freedom of their thoughts, and thousands of noble souls sacrificed their lives to free their fellow beings from the clutches of religious leaders and their superstitions.[59]

Mr. Behai goes on to describe the emergence of the Babi and Baha'i faith as an antidote to Shi'ism, the desperately needed new vision of a faith of freedom for which these noble souls suffered and died. Mohammed Ali Bahai similarly emphasized the importance of rejecting authoritarian interpretations of religion and embracing individual freedom of thought and conscience. Alluding to otherwise intelligent and progressive Baha'is who had submitted to the restrictive concept of an infallible successorship in their faith, he wrote:

[I]n this age of fast progress with such advance in human development, it is pitiful to observe that the so-called intellectual people belittle their true station, that divinely endowed individuals lack confidence and self-understanding. Free souls, yet remaining enslaved, allowing themselves and others to be caught in the meshes of religious superstition, to be ruled over by a small group of hand-picked leaders. O friends and brothers ... Arise with great energy and vigor and fly in the vast and unlimited space of freedom.[60]

Kamar Bahai even went so far as to present the Manifestations of God as perhaps more human than perfectly infallible and divine: "The founders of the great religions in the world are but inspired people carrying holy messages to different corners of the world at different inter-

---

[59] Chapter 2, pp. 14, 16.
[60] Mohammed Ali Bahai, article in *Behai Quarterly*, First Quarter 1935, p. 13. See Chapter 14, p. 177.

vals of time."[61] This is the view of most members of the Unitarian Universalist church today, and millions upon millions of people who call themselves "spiritual but not religious." The Unitarian Baha'is were developing a version of the Baha'i faith that was moving away from rigid notions of "infallibility," thus opening the door for Baha'ism to attract and retain genuine free thinkers and spiritual humanists to swell the ranks of its cause.

Such a broad-minded conception of the Baha'i cause is impossible today, because Baha'is have utterly rejected the ideas of the more liberal members of Baha'u'llah's family—so-called Covenant-breakers whose views are not worth considering—and instead doubled-down on belief in the infallibility of Baha'u'llah, 'Abdu'l-Baha, and Shoghi Effendi. One of the reasons more people don't join or identify with the Baha'i faith is because the infallibility doctrine is untenable.

Baha'u'llah may have been inspired by God, but he didn't always get everything right. For example, in his "Tablet of Wisdom" he wrote that "Empedocles, who distinguished himself in philosophy, was a contemporary of David, while Pythagoras lived in the days of Solomon, son of David."[62] In fact, the Greek philosopher Empedocles lived about 500 years after the Israelite King David, and Pythagoras lived about 400 years after Solomon. Even the order in which the two philosophers lived was reversed by Baha'u'llah. If he was a Manifestation of God, he was also a mere human, and the limitations and errors of his human mind sometimes interfered with the transmission of divine knowledge by the Manifestation.

'Abdu'l-Baha made mistakes of his own. On the subject of race, he wrote that "[T]he people of Persia... have always excelled all other peoples in endowments conferred by birth."[63] And he stereotyped "the savages of central Africa, who are scarcely higher than the beast in mental

---

[61] Circular letter by Kamar Bahai, entitled "Baha U'llah," January 1953. See Chapter 1, p. 4.

[62] *Lawh-i-Hikmat* ("Tablet of Wisdom"). Official Baha'i translation in *Tablets of Bahá'u'lláh Revealed After the Kitáb-i-Aqdas* (Wilmette, Ill.: US Bahá'í Publishing Trust, 1988 pocket-size edition), p. 145.

[63] 'Abdu'l-Baha, *The Secret of Divine Civilization* (US Bahá'í Publishing Trust, 1990 pocket-size edition), p. 9.

development."⁶⁴ Regarding Buddhism, he erroneously claimed that Buddha "established the Oneness of God" and that the religion had degenerated into "the worship of statues and images."⁶⁵ These kind of remarks reflect the limited knowledge and typical biases of the time and culture in which he lived, and undercut the doctrine that 'Abdu'l-Baha was infallible. Most of the time, on most issues, he was indeed ahead of his time, but sometimes his views were unenlightened or simply incorrect.

'Abdu'l-Baha also made false prophecies. For example, he predicted "the unity of nations—a unity which in this century [i.e. the 20th century] will be securely established, causing all the peoples of the world to regard themselves as citizens of one common fatherland."⁶⁶ He said that peace "will be universal in the twentieth century. ... By international agreement [the nations] will lay down their arms and the great era of peace will be ushered in."⁶⁷ World War II proved him wrong, as well as the many other wars that have broken out since then.

Two issues that have increasingly become a problem for the Baha'i faith are gender equality and homosexuality. In both cases, the doctrine of infallibility prevents changes from being made which would help to bring the practices and policies of the Baha'i community into the 21st century. Baha'is believe that Shoghi Effendi, the Guardian, was infallible in all his interpretations of the writings and teachings of Baha'u'llah and 'Abdu'l-Baha—and that his interpretations can never be changed. Because he interpreted some of their statements in a way that is incom-

---

⁶⁴ 'Abdu'l-Baha, talk at home of Mr. and Mrs. William Sutherland Maxwell, Montreal, Canada, September 2, 1912. Published in *The Promulgation of Universal Peace* (US Bahá'í Publishing Trust, 1982 second edition), p. 311. To be fair, 'Abdu'l-Baha did say in the same talk that these "savages" could be raised to a higher condition through education, i.e. they were not inherently inferior.

⁶⁵ 'Abdu'l-Baha, *Some Answered Questions* (US Bahá'í Publishing Trust, 1990 reprint of pocket-size edition), p. 165.

⁶⁶ Tablet of 'Abdu'l-Baha quoted by Shoghi Effendi in *The World Order of Bahá'u'lláh* (US Bahá'í Publishing Trust, 1991 first pocket-size edition), p. 39.

⁶⁷ 'Abdu'l-Baha, quoted in "'Abdu'l-Bahá in Canada" (Thornhill: Bahá'í Canada Publications, 1987), pp. 34-35. Reproduced in *Peace*, compiled by the Research Department of the Universal House of Justice (Bahá'í World Centre, August 1985), section 42, p. 17.

patible with modern progressive sensibilities concerning women's rights and sexual orientation, few people in the developed world who are culturally liberal would feel comfortable anymore becoming a Baha'i.

The "equality of women and men" is one of the core principles of the Baha'i faith, yet women are prohibited from being elected to the highest Baha'i leadership institution, the Universal House of Justice. This glaring hypocrisy is undoubtedly a source of considerable embarrassment to Baha'is, but they don't believe they can do anything to change it. 'Abdu'l-Baha wrote: "The House of Justice... according to the explicit text of the Law of God, is confined to men; this for a wisdom of the Lord God's, which will erelong be made manifest as clearly as the sun at high noon."[68] The "explicit text" that he was referring to is Baha'u'llah's references in the *Kitab-i-Aqdas* to the "men [*rijál*] of the House of Justice."[69]

It certainly would have been possible—even quite logical—for 'Abdu'l-Baha to have interpreted the Arabic word *rijál* to include people of both genders, had he wished to do so. Baha'u'llah himself said that "Today, the maidservants of God are accounted as men"; that "A goodly number of women are today mentioned by God as men"; and that "Verily, in the eyes of Baha women are the same as men."[70] The reason 'Abdu'l-Baha decided not to allow women to serve on the House of Justice is because, according to his own words, he did not approve of women's participation in politics:

> Now the world of women should be a spiritual world, not a political one, so that it will be radiant. The women of other nations are

---

[68] *Selections From the Writings of 'Abdu'l-Bahá* (Bahá'í World Centre, 1982 lightweight edition), section 38, p. 80.

[69] For example, Baha'u'llah says "O ye Men of Justice!" in paragraph 52 of the *Aqdas*, and "men of the House of Justice" in the supplementary Questions and Answers, #101.

[70] Previously untranslated tablets by Baha'u'llah, quoted by Juan R. I. Cole in *Modernity and the Millennium: The Genesis of the Baha'i Faith in the Nineteenth-Century Middle East* (New York: Columbia University Press, 1998), p. 176.

all immersed in political matters. Of what benefit is this, and what fruit doth it yield? ... In America, the cradle of women's liberation, women are still debarred from political institutions because they squabble. They are yet to have a member in the House of Representatives. Also Bahá'u'lláh hath proclaimed: "O ye men of the House of Justice."[71]

Initially, 'Abdu'l-Baha did not allow women to serve on *any level* of the House of Justice, even Local Spiritual Assemblies, but he eventually liberalized his position. As Juan Cole points out, there is no logical reason to believe that 'Abdu'l-Baha's intention was to permit women to serve on Local and National Houses of Justice (now called "Spiritual Assemblies") but not the international level of that institution, which didn't even exist yet during 'Abdu'l-Baha's ministry:

> By 1912, during his visit to the United States, he had been convinced by the Baha'i suffragists to allow women to serve on local administrative bodies. Reversing himself on the issue, he decreed that women should be allowed to stand for election to the Chicago house of justice. ... Later Baha'i tradition has held that he meant only to put women on local and national houses of justice and that they remain forever ineligible to serve on the Universal House of Justice (first elected in 1963), but the texts and their historical context regarding the issue remain unclear. (As a simple logical issue, if the reason for which women were excluded from houses of justice was, per the 1902 letter [in which he had restricted the institution to men only], that Baha'u'llah addressed their members as "men," or rijál, then this form of address cannot be employed to explain why they could serve on local bodies but not on the Universal House of Justice.) ... It may be that this was an issue 'Abdu'l-Baha left to future generations to settle.[72]

---

[71] Tablet of 'Abdu'l-Baha translated from the Persian in *A Compilation on Women*, compiled by the Research Department of the Universal House of Justice (Bahá'í World Centre, January 1986), section 11, p. 7.

[72] Juan R. I. Cole, *Modernity and the Millennium: The Genesis of the Baha'i Faith in the Nineteenth-Century Middle East* (New York: Columbia University Press, 1998), pp. 183-184.

The source of the "later Baha'i tradition" to which Dr. Cole refers is none other than Shoghi Effendi, regarded by Baha'is as the infallible interpreter of the teachings of the Baha'i faith. As he wrote:

> As regards your question concerning the membership of the Universal House of Justice: there is a Tablet from 'Abdul-Bahá in which He definitely states that the membership of the Universal House is confined to men, and that the wisdom of it will be fully revealed and appreciated in the future. In the local as well as the national Houses of Justice, however, women have the full right of membership. It is, therefore, only to the International House that they cannot be elected.[73]

Baha'is today are stuck with this inconsistent and exclusionary policy, which is incompatible with the fundamental Baha'i principle of equality of women and men, because they believe Shoghi Effendi was infallible. Even if he might have interpreted 'Abdu'l-Baha's intentions incorrectly, Baha'is do not believe this is open to further research, discussion, and potential revision. And if he did interpret 'Abdu'l-Baha's intentions correctly, then Baha'is are stuck with an all-male Universal House of Justice anyway, because they believe 'Abdu'l-Baha was infallible. Either way, the Baha'i faith cannot move forward and fully implement the principle of gender equality in its own religious institutions. This sad situation is entirely because of the doctrine of infallibility, an authoritarian religious concept which the Unitarian Baha'is warned against over a hundred years ago.

A similar situation exists regarding the issue of homosexuality. In the *Kitab-i-Aqdas*, Baha'u'llah mentioned in passing: "We shrink, for very shame, from treating of the subject of boys."[74] A literal interpretation of this statement would mean the prohibition of pedophilia or pederasty—and this is consistent with the cultural phenomenon called

---

[73] Letter to an individual believer written on behalf of Shoghi Effendi, July 28, 1936, quoted in *A Compilation on Women*, compiled by the Research Department of the Universal House of Justice (Bahá'í World Centre, January 1986), section 27, p. 13.

[74] *Kitab-i-Aqdas* ("Most Holy Book"), paragraph 107.

bacha bazi, not uncommon in the time of Baha'u'llah, in which wealthy Persian men took boys as concubines.[75] However, Shoghi Effendi interpreted this verse in the *Aqdas* to imply a broad prohibition of all homosexual relationships, gay and lesbian, even between consenting adults:

> No matter how devoted and fine the love may be between people of the same sex, to let it find expression in sexual acts is wrong. To say that it is ideal is no excuse. Immorality of every sort is really forbidden by Bahá'u'lláh, and homosexual relationships He looks upon as such, besides being against nature. To be afflicted this way is a great burden to a conscientious soul. But through the advice and help of doctors, through a strong and determined effort, and through prayer, a soul can overcome this handicap.[76]

Because these words are regarded by Baha'is as infallible, acceptance of intimate gay and lesbian relationships as within the spectrum of normal human behavior, rather than as a moral failing or a disease, is impossible in the Baha'i faith. Same-sex marriage, which is rapidly becoming acceptable and legal in Western societies—and even is practiced in various liberal religious denominations—is off-limits to Baha'is, and not even open to discussion. Once again, this problem is entirely because of the doctrine of infallibility.

One of the most basic Baha'i teachings is "progressive revelation"— the idea that God periodically reveals new truths to humanity, and inspires societies to change their laws and culture, when people are ready for it. This can come through major Manifestations of God, who found new religions, or lesser prophets who bring new insights and interpretations and reform them. In the Baha'i faith, it could come about if the infallibility doctrine were abandoned and the Universal House of Justice began making new policies and recommendations without neces-

---

[75] An eye-opening article on this subject, "Baha'u'llah & 'The Subject of Boys'" can be found on the *Baha'i Rants* blog at http://bahairants.com/bahaullah-the-subject-of-boys-123.html

[76] Letter written on behalf of Shoghi Effendi, quoted in *The Kitáb-i-Aqdas* (Bahá'í World Centre, 1992 edition), note 134, p. 223.

sarily feeling constrained by what 'Abdu'l-Baha and Shoghi Effendi said or decided.

'Abdu'l-Baha's vision of the Guardianship was probably intended as an institutional means for the Baha'i faith to have a series of charismatic leaders, one in every generation, who would be regarded by the Baha'is as possessing divine authority to initiate and advocate for reforms of the faith as necessary. I very much doubt that his intention was for his own interpretations and policies, or those of the First Guardian Shoghi Effendi, to remain set in stone; instead, future Guardians, working with the House of Justice, could have updated things according to the needs of the time.

The Unitarian Baha'is, had their denomination continued to exist, would have been happy to see that the Guardianship came to an end, because they correctly foresaw that such an institution could lead to authoritarianism, as was demonstrated in the ministry of Shoghi Effendi. Tragically, however, the end of the Guardianship has been interpreted by Baha'is not as an opportunity for freedom from the questionable or outdated interpretations and decisions of past Baha'i leaders, but instead as the endless perpetuation of their decrees. Baha'is today believe that the words of 'Abdu'l-Baha and Shoghi Effendi must remain as definitive guidance for the rest of the life of the religion. The Universal House of Justice has decided not to dare to put aside any of their teachings, because, as a result of their authoritarian leadership style, nearly all Baha'is who rejected the doctrine of infallibility in favor of a more liberal interpretation of Baha'ism were driven out of the Baha'i community during their ministries. Thus, the faith has become frozen in the mindset, ideas and assumptions of the early to mid 1900s, when 'Abdu'l-Baha and Shoghi Effendi were leading it. The result is that fewer and fewer people see this religion as relevant and as a cause of further progress for humanity.

Baha'u'llah wrote in the *Kitab-i-Iqan* that religious leaders are often to blame for preventing people from finding and adhering to the true path of God:

> Leaders of religion, in every age, have hindered their people from attaining the shores of eternal salvation, inasmuch as they held

the reins of authority in their mighty grasp. Some for the lust of leadership, others through want of knowledge and understanding, have been the cause of the deprivation of the people. ... For this reason, in all sacred books mention hath been made of the divines of every age. Thus He [i.e. God] saith: ... "O people of the Book! Why clothe ye the truth with falsehood? Why wittingly hide the truth?"[77] Again, He saith: "Say, O people of the Book! Why repel believers from the way of God?"[78] It is evident that by the "people of the Book," who have repelled their fellow-men from the straight path of God, is meant none other than the divines of that age, whose names and character have been revealed in the sacred books, and alluded to in the verses and traditions recorded therein, were you to observe with the eye of God.[79]

It is no different in the Baha'i faith, as the evidence shows. The biggest mistake the "Baha'i divines," as we might call them, have made is their insistence on trying to conceal the shadow side of their religion and present a phony façade of perfection. This has been done by 'Abdu'l-Baha, Shoghi Effendi, the Hands of the Cause, and the Universal House of Justice alike. Beginning with 'Abdu'l-Baha's decision to shun the Unitarian Baha'is rather than attempting the challenging process of ecumenical dialogue, compromise and reconciliation; followed by Shoghi Effendi's expulsion of all remaining members of his family for dubious reasons, and his creation and dissemination of one-sided, triumphalist narratives as official Baha'i history; then the Hands of the Cause who pretended that nothing significant had changed with the loss of the Guardianship, rather than entertaining the possibility that God had become displeased with the direction of the religion under its autocratic leaders; and the Universal House of Justice which has fostered a culture of conformity and stagnation and purged the Baha'i community of nearly all remaining liberals, free-thinkers, creative intellectuals and genuinely truth-seeking scholars, thus ensuring that most discussion of the Baha'i faith remains within the narrow strictures

---

[77] Qur'an 3:71.

[78] Qur'an 3:99.

[79] *Kitab-i-Iqan* ("Book of Certitude"), paragraph 15.

it wishes to permit. Where Baha'ism goes from here, only time will tell, but I doubt it will grow—or even avoid dwindling in the coming decades—unless it is willing to confront the difficult truths about itself and change.

Baha'u'llah instructed his followers, the Baha'is, to avoid the Shi'ite Islamic practice of *taqlid* (blind imitation or conformity to religious leaders). Warning against such fundamentalism and advocating instead for freedom of thought and conscience, he wrote:

> Say: O people, act not as did the people of the Qur'an, and never surrender the reins of your insight into the hands of anyone else. Seize upon the grace proffered you in these days, and see with your own eyes.[80]

On the same theme, Baha'u'llah also wrote that seekers of truth should "turn away from imitation [*taqlid*], which is following the traces of their forefathers and sires."[81] If Baha'is today wish to create a positive future for their faith, they should follow this advice and form their own new ideas and opinions about their religion, its history, and the direction it should evolve in their own time, rather than blindly accepting the assumptions and interpretations of those whose time has passed.

In doing so, it is also important that Baha'is come to appreciate the contributions to their faith—or the faith that Baha'i could be—of those who believed in Baha'u'llah but who, to varying degrees, questioned the doctrines of infallibility and blind obedience to religious leaders. This includes almost all the descendants of Baha'u'llah, beginning with the Unitarian Baha'is and later the followers of 'Abdu'l-Baha who were excommunicated by Shoghi Effendi. Their writings offer alternative visions for the Baha'i faith which, if rediscovered and considered by Baha'is today, could provide much inspiration for a better way forward. Baha'is should think for themselves, take the best from all sides and

---

[80] *Suratu'dh-Dhibh* ("Surah of the Sacrifice"). Translation by Juan Cole at http://bahai-library.com/bahaullah_surih_dhibh

[81] *Haft-Vadi* ("Seven Valleys"). Official Baha'i translation in *The Seven Valleys and the Four Valleys* (US Bahá'í Publishing Trust, 1991 pocket-size edition), p. 5.

leave the rest behind. In the words of Baha'u'llah's great-grandson Ruhi Afnan:

> Obedience [to] the 'mirrors that speak of Him' [i.e. Baha'u'llah's successors] is conditional upon their words conforming with the words of the Sun of Reality. Otherwise it would be wrong. And whoever places obedience before belief is wrong and that obedience is no longer mandatory. ...
>
> Blind obedience turns a human being into an instrument devoid of conscience or will, depriving his speech and actions of any moral content. Here action becomes worthless. In this world knowledge, insight and freedom of choice are the supreme sources of justice. Without them God's will could not be realised.[82]

It is very much an open question whether religion as we know it will continue to play a major part in the future development of world civilization. Atheism and unstructured spirituality are on the rise; organized religion, in the more developed parts of the world, is on the decline—and if anything, the trend seems to be accelerating. Baha'i is hardly alone among religions, in the 21st century, in its struggle to make converts and retain members. But I would venture to guess that religion will continue to exist, maybe even flourish, for a long time to come, because religion is "high drama." It is the most sublime form of theater in the human experience.

In the Information Age, when facts can no longer be hidden from the masses, the religions that are rich with authenticity, complex characters and dramatic controversies, and which can accept and embrace the questions and imperfections in their history, may actually have the advantage in terms of survival and perhaps even growth. Many people may be attracted precisely to such traditions—if they choose to participate in religion at all—in the same way that culturally sophisticated people appreciate great literature, the plays of Shakespeare, historical drama films and documentaries, and so forth. All "great" world reli-

---

[82] Letter by Ruhi Mohsen Afnan to the Baha'i Spiritual Assembly of Iran, 1970. Translation by Bahiyeh Afnan Shahid, available online at http://www.abdulbahasfamily.org/documents/Ruhi-Afnan-1970-letter.pdf, p. 26.

gions have the disturbing, shadowy aspects of their history which can shock us into learning and growth of conscience; whereas the temporary religions that eventually die out (i.e. "cults") tend to be the ones that desperately try to manufacture and cling to a cleaned-up narrative that is too convenient to be real and therefore becomes absurd and meaningless—or which never had any real richness, complexity, and disturbing aspects to begin with.

Indeed, the worst flaw a religion can have nowadays is to pretend, in the face of available evidence, that it has no flaws at all. All the great religions have had their share of madmen, scoundrels in high places, competing sects and traditions, epic battles between rivals on issues large and small, mistakes that are corrected, reforms that are rationalized, and real-life plotlines that nevertheless seem so perfectly contrived as to make one believe that only the hand of God could have brought them to pass. The Baha'i faith is filled with karmic subplots and ironic twists of fate. Whether or not the hand of God is present in this religion, the hand of Irony surely has been.

The presence of darkness, the shadow side of religion, may in fact be necessary to bring the light into sharper relief. The Baha'i faith is sufficiently filled with both darkness and light that, if its adherents allow it, it just might become a major source of illumination to the world. It is my sincere hope that this book will be of assistance to that end—which can only begin if the Baha'is themselves have the courage to read it, "unbiased and unprejudiced," as its author requested, and then to talk about it together without fear, saying, "All things are of God."[83]

---

[83] Baha'u'llah, *Kitab-i-'Ahdi* ("Book of My Covenant").

Appendix A:
List of Writings of Baha'u'llah

By Shua Ullah Behai

This list was compiled by Shua Ullah Behai and appears in his book manuscript. The collection of Baha'u'llah's writings listed here is presumably the "library" that Mohammed Ali Bahai refers to in the conclusion of Chapter 3, which he held in his possession during his lifetime and invited the Baha'is to study.

The present-day whereabouts of this collection of original manuscripts and first-edition printed books by Baha'u'llah is uncertain. Mr. Bahai's granddaughter, Negar Bahai Emsallem, believes they were passed down to one of her cousins, who she thinks may have donated them to a museum. Locating these documents should be a high priority for scholars of the Baha'i faith, because this collection apparently contained thousands of pages of Baha'u'llah's tablets—most of which have never been published or made available by the Baha'i organization, and some of which might not even be held in the archives at the Baha'i World Centre in Haifa, Israel.

—The Editor

The following list of the manuscripts is the most complete collection of the teachings of Baha'u'llah in existence. They are as they were revealed in the original language, Arabic and Persian.

They comprise fifty volumes, containing over twelve thousand pages.

Indeed, every volume is an ocean full of pearls of wisdom from which to gain knowledge, and a universe full of shining stars from which to be enlightened.

VOL.	NAME OF BOOK	PAGES	CALLIGRAPHER
1	Book of *Aqdas*	311	Zaynu'l-Muqarrabín
2	Book of *Haykal*	520	Zaynu'l-Muqarrabín
3	Epistle of Badi	277	Aqa Sayyid [Ismu'llah] Mahdi
4	Holy Tablets	205	[blank]
5	Holy Tablets	355	Mirza Abdullah Bahhaj
6	Holy Tablets	226	Ghusn-i-Akbar
7	Holy Tablets	200	Ghusn-i-Akbar
8[1]	Holy Tablets	321	Ghusn-i-Akbar
9	Holy Tablets	381	Ghusn-i-Akbar
10	Holy Tablets	522	[blank]
11	Holy Tablets	319	Mirza Amin Ullah[2]
12	Holy Tablets	319	Mirza Moussa [Kalim]
13	Holy Tablets	287	Mirza Moussa [Kalim]
14	Holy Tablets	60	Mirza Moussa [Kalim]
15	Holy Tablets	221	Haji Muhammad Yazdi
16	Holy Tablets	232	Haji Muhammad Yazdi
17	Holy Tablets	568	[blank]
18	Holy Tablets	226	Mirza Jamil
19	Holy Tablets	302	Ghusn-i-Akbar
20	Holy Tablets	318	Ghusn-i-Akbar
21	Holy Tablets	299	Mirza Kamal
22	Holy Tablets	347	Mirza Amin Ullah
23	Epistle of Shaykh[3]	193	Ghusn-i-Akbar
24	Holy Tablets	158	Ghusn-i-Akbar
25	Holy Tablets	265	Mirza Majdeddin
26	Holy Tablets	357	Mirza Moussa [Kalim]

---

[1] Note by Shua Ullah Behai: "Large pages, small writing, equal to five volumes."

[2] Presumably not Baha'u'llah's grandson by that name, who was only a boy when Baha'u'llah was alive.

[3] The *Lawh-i-Shaykh*, also known as the *Lawh-i-Ibn-i-Dhib* ("Epistle to the Son of the Wolf").

27	Hidden Words	46	Ghusn-i-Akbar
28	Holy Tablets	264	Zaynu'l-Muqarrabín
29	Holy Tablets	289	Haydar Ali Usku'i
30	Holy Tablets	366	Ghusn-i-Akbar
31	Holy Tablets	277	Ghusn-i-Akbar
32	Holy Tablets	157	Ghusn-i-Akbar
33	Holy Tablet	158	Ghusn-i-Akbar
34	Holy Tablets	259	Ghusn-i-Akbar
35	Book of *Iqan*	214	Printed in Bombay, 1891 A.D.
36	Book of *Ishraqat*	295	Printed in Bombay, 1891 A.D.
37	Seven Valleys/Four Valleys	55	Printed in Bombay, 1895 A.D.
38	Supplications	235	Printed in Bombay, 1891 A.D.
39	Supplications	80	Printed in Bombay, 1891 A.D.
40	Correspondence	318	Mirza Amin Ullah
41	Correspondence	277	Mirza Moussa [Kalim]
42	Correspondence	231	Mohammed Jawad Gazvini
43	Correspondence	319	Mirza Abdullah Bahhaj
44	Correspondence	297	Mirza Abdullah Bahhaj
45	Correspondence	286	Ghusn-i-Akbar
46	Correspondence	385	Mohammed Jawad Gazvini

Appendix B:
Families of Baha'u'llah and the Bab

This appendix contains two genealogical lists, one of the descendants of Baha'u'llah's father, and one of the descendants of the Bab's great-grandfather. The information included here has been compiled from a family tree provided by Negar Bahai Emsallem as well as from various publicly available sources.

There was a great deal of intermarriage between these two families, as well as between cousins within the families, as indicated in these charts. Many of the people who appear in this book can be found listed here. The Babi and Baha'i movements were in large part a family affair—a complex web of relatives working together or against each other in religious dramas, undoubtedly intertwined with their intimate relationships.

In most cases I have omitted offspring who died in childhood. In many cases I have not named the descendants of branches of the families who did not play a significant role in the history of the Baha'i faith. I have only included descendants of the founding patriarchs of these families through the fifth generation (i.e. great-great-grandchildren), although in some cases I know of, or am acquainted with, members of younger generations.

Individuals are numbered from top to bottom in the lists for ease of reference. Multiple wives of one husband are indicated with letters (A, B, C, etc.). The "official" Baha'i spellings of names are given in parentheses, after the spellings used by the persons themselves or their families.

—The Editor

Descendants of Baha'u'llah's Father, Mirza Buzurg

(1) Mirza Buzurg ("The Great") Abbas Nuri.
[A.] Married Khan-Nanih. Offspring:
- (2) Mirza Aqa. No issue.
- (3) Mirza Muhammad-Hasan. Married. Offspring. Supporter of (5) Baha'u'llah.

[B.] Married Khadijah (Khadíjih) Khanum Jani. Offspring:
- (4) Sárih Khanum. Married. Offspring. Supporter of Baha'u'llah.
- (5) Mirza Husayn Ali Nuri, Baha'u'llah.
  [A.] Married Ásíyih Khanum, Navváb. Offspring:
  o (6) Abbas Effendi, Ghusn-i-A'zam, 'Abdu'l-Baha. Married Fatimah Nahri, a.k.a. Muníri h Khanum. Offspring:
    - (7) Zia('iyya) (Diyá'iyyih) Khanum. Married (66) Mirza Hadi Shirazi Afnan. Offspring:
      - (8) Shoghi Effendi Rabbani. Married Mary Sutherland Maxwell, a.k.a. Rúhíyyih Khanum. No issue.
      - (9) Ruhanguise (Ruhangiz). Married (45) Nayer Afnan. Offspring listed under him.
      - (10) Mehranguise (Mehrangiz). Married (49) Hassan Afnan.
      - (11) Hussein (Husayn) Rabbani. Married. Offspring.
      - (12) Riaz (Riyád) Rabbani. Did not marry. No issue.
    - (13) Touba (Túbá) Khanum. Married (75) Mirza Muhsin Afnan. Offspring:
      - (14) Ruhi Afnan. Married (21) Zahra Shahid. Offspring.
      - (15) Soraya (Thurayya). Married (48) Dr. Fayzi Afnan.
      - (16) Soheil (Suhayl) Afnan.

Appendix B: Families of Baha'u'llah and the Bab

- (17) Fuad (Fu'ád) Afnan.
- (18) Ruha Khanum. Married Mirza Jalal Shahid.[1] Offspring:
  - (19) Maryam.
  - (20) Dr. Munib Shahid. Married Serene Husseini.[2] Offspring.
  - (21) Zahra. Married (14) Ruhi Afnan. Offspring.
  - (22) Hassan Jalal Shahid. Married (46) Bahiyeh Afnan. Offspring.
- (23) Munavvar Khanum. Married Mirza Ahmad Yazdi. No issue.
- (24) Bahiyyih Khanum. Did not marry. No issue.
- (25) Mirza Mihdi. Died in young adulthood. Did not marry. No issue.

[B.] Married "Bibi" Fatimah (Fátimih) Khanum, Mahd-i-'Ulya. Offspring:

- (26) Mohammed Ali Bahai (Mirza Muhammad 'Alí), Ghusn-i-Akbar:

  [A.] Married Ma'suma Khanum. Offspring:
  - (27) Shua Ullah Behai. Married. No issue.
  - (28) Amin Ullah Bahai. Did not marry. No issue.

  [B.] Married (52) Laqa'iyya Khanum. Offspring:
  - (29) Mousa (Músá) Bahai. Married (38) Kamar. Offspring:
    - (30) Maliha Bahai Ansari. Married. Offspring.

---

[1] Mirza Jalal Shahid was the son of Sayyid Hasan, who was known as *Sultánu'sh-Shuhadá* ("King of Martyrs"). See "The Martyrdom of Sayyid Hasan and Sayyid Husayn" in Chapter 5.

[2] Serene Husseini Shahid was the daughter of Jamal al-Husayni, a Palestinian politician. The Husaynis were one of the most influential families of Jerusalem at the time, including various political and religious leaders. Mrs. Shahid was an author and humanitarian activist for Palestinian refugees. See http://en.wikipedia.org/wiki/Serene_Husseini_Shahid

- (31) Negar Bahai Emsallem (Nigar Bahai Amsalem). Married Mordechai Emsallem. No issue.
  - (32) Samadiyya Khanum. Married (51) Majdeddin bin Moussa Irani. Offspring:
    - (33) Maryam
    - (34) Zaranguise (Zarangiz)
  - (35) Zia Ullah Effendi. Married Soraya (Thurayya) Khanum Samandari. No issue.
  - (36) Badi Ullah Bahai. Married Alia Khanum. Offspring:
    - (37) Salah Bahai. No issue.
    - (38) Kamar (Qamar). Married (29) Mousa Bahai. Offspring listed under him.
    - (39) Sazij. Married. Offspring.
    - (40) Ismat. Married (59) Jalal Azal.
    - (41) Iffat.

[C.] Married Gawhar Khanum. Offspring:
  - (42) Forough(iyya) (Furúghiyyih) Khanum. Married (74) Sayyid Ali Afnan. Offspring:
    - (43) Hussein (Husayn) Afnan. Married Badí'ah. Offspring:
      - (44) Furugh. Married Cecil Fadlo Hourani.[3] Offspring.
    - (45) Nayer (Nayyir) Afnan. Married (9) Ruhanguise Rabbani. Offspring:
      - (46) Bahiyeh. Married (22) Hassan Jalal Shahid. Offspring.
      - (47) Maliha.
    - (48) Dr. Fayzi (Faydi) Afnan. Married (15) Soraya Afnan.
    - (49) Hassan Afnan. Married (10) Mehranguise Rabbani.

---

[3] Cecil Fadlo Hourani was a Lebanese author and advisor to Habib Bourguiba, the first president of the Republic of Tunisia.

- (50) Mirza Moussa (Músá) (Áqáy-i-)Kalím. Married. Offspring:
  - (51) Majdeddin bin Moussa Irani (Mirza Majdi'd-Dín): Married (32) Samadiyya Khanum. Offspring listed under her.
  - (52) Laqa'iyya Khanum: Married (26) Mohammed Ali Bahai. Offspring listed under him.
  - (53) Ali Reza. Married. Offspring.
  - (54) Jamil. Married. Offspring.
- (55) Nisá' Khanum. Married Mirza Majid-i-Ahi.

[C.] Married Kulthum Khanum. Offspring followed the Azali Babism of (57) Subh-i-Azal or remained Muslim:
- (56) Mirza Ridá-Qulí. Married Maryam, a.k.a. *Waraqatu'l-Hamrá'* ("Crimson Leaf"), who followed Baha'u'llah. Offspring.
- Other descendants.

[D.] Took a concubine, Kuchik Khanum. Offspring:
- (57) Mirza Yahya Nuri, Subh-i-Azal.
  [A.] Married Badr-i-Jahan. Offspring.
  [B.] Married Ruqiyya. Offspring.
  [C.] Married Maryam, a.k.a. Qanita. Offspring.
  [D.] Married Mulk-i-Jahan. Offspring:
    - (58) Abdul-Ali Azal. Married Ismat Isfahani. Offspring:
      - (59) Jalal Azal. Married (40) Ismat Bahai. No issue.
      - Other descendants.
    - Other descendants.
  [E.] Married Fatimah. Offspring.

[E.] Took a concubine, Nabat Khanum. Offspring.

[F.] Took a concubine, Turkamaniyyih. Offspring:
- (60) Mirza Muhammad-Quli. Married. Offspring. Supporter of Baha'u'llah.

[G.] Married Shah Bigum. No issue.

Descendants of the Bab's Great-Grandfather, Mirza 'Ábid

(61) Mirza 'Ábid, a.k.a. Mirza Zaynu'l-'Abidín. Married. Offspring:

- (62) Haji Mirza Siyyid 'Ali. Married. Offspring:
    - (63) Haji Mirza Abu'l-Qásim. Married. Offspring:
        - (64) Maryam-Sultán-Bagum. Married (77) Aqa Mirza Aqa. Offspring.
        - (65) Siyyid Muhammad-Husayn. Married. Offspring:
            - (66) Mirza Hadi Shirazi Afnan. Married (7) Zia Khanum. Offspring listed under her.
            - Other descendants.
        - (67) Mirza Ibrahim Afnan
        - (68) Sárá-Sultán Bagum. Married (72) Haji Siyyid Mirza Afnan. Offspring.
        - Other descendants.
    - (69) Khadijih Bagum. Married (80) 'Ali Muhammad Shirazi, the Bab. Offspring:
        - (70) Ahmad. Died at birth.
    - (71) Haji Mirza Siyyid Hasan, a.k.a. Afnan Kabir ("The Great"). Married Bíbí-Ján-Ján Bagum. Offspring:
        - (72) Haji Siyyid Mirza Afnan. Married (68) Sárá-Sultán Bagum. Offspring.
        - (73) Haji Siyyid Muhammad Afnan. Married Khanum Haya. Offspring.
        - (74) Haji Siyyid 'Ali Afnan. Married (42) Forough Khanum. Offspring listed under her.
        - (75) Mirza Muhsin Afnan. Married (13) Touba Khanum. Offspring listed under her.
        - Other descendants.
    - (76) Zahrá-Bagum. Married. Offspring:
        - (77) Aqa Mirza Aqa, a.k.a. Núri'd-Dín. Married (64) Maryam-Sultán-Bagum. Offspring.
- (78) Mirza Muhammad-Husayn. Married. Offspring:
    - (79) Fátimih-Bagum. Married. Offspring:
        - (80) 'Ali Muhammad Shirazi, the Bab. Married (69) Khadijih Bagum.
    - Other descendants.

www.ingramcontent.com/pod-product-compliance
Lightning Source LLC
Chambersburg PA
CBHW031357290426
44110CB00011B/196